# NFT™

## Not For Tourists Guide to
# CHICAGO

Get more on
**notfortourists.com**

Keep connected with:
**Twitter:**
twitter/notfortourists

**Facebook:**
facebook/notfortourists

**iPhone App:**
nftiphone.com

**Not For Tourists, Inc**

**Skyhorse Publishing**

designed by:
**Not For Tourists, Inc**
**NFT$_{TM}$—Not For Tourists$_{TM}$ Guide to Chicago**
www.notfortourists.com

**Publisher**
Skyhorse Publishing

**Creative Direction &
Information Design**
Jane Pirone

**Director**
Stuart Farr

**Managing Editor**
Scott Sendrow

**Production Manager**
Aaron Schielke

**Writing and Editing**
Benjamin Kelner
Anne Kasdorf
Scott Sendrow

**Research**
Jess Bender

**Graphic Design and
Production**
Aaron Schielke
Sarah Smith

**Information Systems
Manager**
Juan Molinari

Printed in China
ISBN# 978-1-62636-050-1 $21.95
ISSN 2162-724X
Copyright © 2014 by Not For Tourists, Inc.
12th Edition

Every effort has been made to ensure that the information in this book is as up-to-date as possible at press time. However, many details are liable to change—as we have learned. Not For Tourists cannot accept responsibility for any consequences arising from the use of this book.

Not For Tourists does not solicit individuals, organizations, or businesses for listings inclusion in our guides, nor do we accept payment for inclusion into the editorial portion of our book; the advertising sections, however, are exempt from this policy. We always welcome communications from anyone regarding ANYTHING having to do with our books; please visit us on our website at www.notfortourists.com for appropriate contact information.

Skyhorse Publishing books may be purchased in bulk at special discounts for sales promotion, corporate gifts, fund-raising, or educational purposes. Special editions can also be created to specifications. For details, contact the Special Sales Department, Skyhorse Publishing, 307 West 36th Street, 11th Floor, New York, NY 10018 or specialsales@skyhorsepublishing.com.

All Rights Reserved. No part of this book may be reproduced in any manner without the express written consent of the publisher, except in the case of brief excerpts in critical reviews or articles. All inquiries should be addressed to Skyhorse Publishing, 307 West 36th Street, 11th Floor, New York, NY 10018.

Skyhorse® and Skyhorse Publishing® are registered trademarks of Skyhorse Publishing, Inc.®, a Delaware corporation.

www.skyhorsepublishing.com

10 9 8 7 6 5 4 3 2 1

Dear NFT User,

There are certain things Chicagoans know: the best stories happen on the Red Line late at night; the Cubbies are going to win the World Series (…next year); the swear jar in Rahm's office is overflowing with coins; your out-of-town relatives are going to ask you about Al Capone; there's a 50/50 chance your alderman is going to be indicted this year; the winters make you stronger and the summers make you lazier; and every New Yorker you know will tell you how shocked they are that there aren't cows and corn filling up your downtown ("Wow, this actually is an amazing city!").

But you don't need us to tell you that Chicago is much more than this. As possessive and proud Chicagoans are of their city, they're even more so of their neighborhoods, each one offering its own unique experience. Travelling from one to the next is like a different vacation onto itself, and that's where we come in. Consider us your insider to the best of your own city. You're the ultimate urban adventurer and we can't wait to be your companion on the journey.

But print publishing has its shortcomings—it can only reflect what was happening in the city at the time of publication, and things are always changing. That's where the website (www.NotForTourists.com/Chicago) and mobile apps come in. And while you can't scribble notes on a computer screen or iPhone app, we think they nicely complement what you now hold in front of you.

Thank you for picking up the Not For Tourist's Guide to Chicago. As the only guidebook of the city written by fellow Chicagoans that includes detailed map-by-map descriptions of every neighborhood in Chicago (as well as Evanston, Oak Park, and Skokie), we hope to worm our way into your heart as your indispensable right-hand tool for navigating this dynamic and energetic city that we love.

—Jane, Scott, Ben, Anne, et al.

## Chicago Neighborhoods

### The Greater Loop

Map 1 • River North / Fulton Market District. . . . . 6
Map 2 • Near North / River North. . . . . . . . . . . 8
Map 3 • Streeterville / Mag Mile . . . . . . . . . . 14
Map 4 • West Loop Gate / Greek Town . . . . . . . 16
Map 5 • The Loop. . . . . . . . . . . . . . . . . . . . 20
Map 6 • The Loop / Grant Park . . . . . . . . . . . 24
Map 7 • South Loop / River City. . . . . . . . . . . 26
Map 8 • South Loop / Printers Row /
          Dearborn Park . . . . . . . . . . . . . . . . 28
Map 9 • South Loop / South Michigan Ave. . . . . 30
Map 10 • East Pilsen / Chinatown . . . . . . . . . . 32
Map 11 • South Loop / McCormick Place. . . . . . . 34

### The South Side

Map 12 • Bridgeport (West) . . . . . . . . . . . . . 36
Map 13 • Bridgeport (East). . . . . . . . . . . . . . 38
Map 14 • Prairie Shores / Lake Meadows . . . . . . 42
Map 15 • Canaryville / Fuller Park . . . . . . . . . . 44
Map 16 • Bronzeville. . . . . . . . . . . . . . . . . . 46
Map 17 • Kenwood. . . . . . . . . . . . . . . . . . . 48
Map 18 • Washington Park. . . . . . . . . . . . . . 50
Map 19 • Hyde Park . . . . . . . . . . . . . . . . . . 52
Map 20 • East Hyde Park / Jackson Park. . . . . . . 56

### The Near West Side

Map 21 • Wicker Park / Ukrainian Village . . . . . . 58
Map 22 • Noble Square / Goose Island . . . . . . . 64
Map 23 • West Town / Near West Side. . . . . . . . 68
Map 24 • River West / West Town . . . . . . . . . . 72
Map 25 • Illinois Medical District . . . . . . . . . . . 76
Map 26 • University Village / Little Italy / Pilsen. . 78

### The Near North Side

Map 27 • Logan Square. . . . . . . . . . . . . . . . . 82
Map 28 • Bucktown . . . . . . . . . . . . . . . . . . . 86
Map 29 • DePaul / Wrightwood / Sheffield. . . . . 90
Map 30 • Lincoln Park. . . . . . . . . . . . . . . . . . 94
Map 31 • Old Town / Near North . . . . . . . . . . 100
Map 32 • Gold Coast / Mag Mile . . . . . . . . . . 104

## The North Side

Map 33 • Rogers Park / West Ridge. . . . . . . . . . .110
Map 34 • East Rogers Park . . . . . . . . . . . . . . .114
Map 35 • Arcadia Terrace / Peterson Park. . . . .118
Map 36 • Bryn Mawr / Bowmanville . . . . . . . . .120
Map 37 • Edgewater / Andersonville . . . . . . . . .122
Map 38 • Ravenswood / Albany Park . . . . . . . . .126
Map 39 • Ravenswood / North Center. . . . . . . .130
Map 40 • Uptown . . . . . . . . . . . . . . . . . . . . .136
Map 41 • Avondale / Old Irving. . . . . . . . . . . . .140
Map 42 • North Center / Roscoe Village /
          West Lakeview . . . . . . . . . . . . . . . .142
Map 43 • Wrigleyville / East Lakeview. . . . . . . .146
Map 44 • East Lakeview. . . . . . . . . . . . . . . . . .152

## Greater Chicago

Northwest. . . . . . . . . . . . . . . . . . . . . . . . . .156
Map 45 . . . . . . . . . . . . . . . . . . . . . . . . . . . .158
Map 46 . . . . . . . . . . . . . . . . . . . . . . . . . . . .159
Map 47 . . . . . . . . . . . . . . . . . . . . . . . . . . . .160
Map 48 . . . . . . . . . . . . . . . . . . . . . . . . . . . .161
West. . . . . . . . . . . . . . . . . . . . . . . . . . . . . .162
Map 49 . . . . . . . . . . . . . . . . . . . . . . . . . . . .164
Map 50 . . . . . . . . . . . . . . . . . . . . . . . . . . . .165
Map 51 . . . . . . . . . . . . . . . . . . . . . . . . . . . .166
Map 52 . . . . . . . . . . . . . . . . . . . . . . . . . . . .167
Southwest. . . . . . . . . . . . . . . . . . . . . . . . . .168
Map 53 . . . . . . . . . . . . . . . . . . . . . . . . . . . .170
Map 54 . . . . . . . . . . . . . . . . . . . . . . . . . . . .171
Map 55 . . . . . . . . . . . . . . . . . . . . . . . . . . . .172
Map 56 . . . . . . . . . . . . . . . . . . . . . . . . . . . .173
South . . . . . . . . . . . . . . . . . . . . . . . . . . . . .174
Map 57 . . . . . . . . . . . . . . . . . . . . . . . . . . . .176
Map 58 . . . . . . . . . . . . . . . . . . . . . . . . . . . .177
Map 59 . . . . . . . . . . . . . . . . . . . . . . . . . . . .178
Map 60 . . . . . . . . . . . . . . . . . . . . . . . . . . . .179

## Parks & Places

Beverly / Morgan Park . . . . . . . . . . . . . . . . .180
Brookfield Zoo . . . . . . . . . . . . . . . . . . . . . .182
Chicago Botanic Garden . . . . . . . . . . . . . . . .184
Chicago Cultural Center . . . . . . . . . . . . . . . .186
Harold Washington Library Center . . . . . . . . .187
Evanston . . . . . . . . . . . . . . . . . . . . . . . . . .188
Garfield Park . . . . . . . . . . . . . . . . . . . . . . .192
Grant Park . . . . . . . . . . . . . . . . . . . . . . . . .194
Historic Pullman . . . . . . . . . . . . . . . . . . . . .196
Jackson Park . . . . . . . . . . . . . . . . . . . . . . . .198
Lincoln Park. . . . . . . . . . . . . . . . . . . . . . . .200
McCormick Place. . . . . . . . . . . . . . . . . . . . .202
Millennium Park . . . . . . . . . . . . . . . . . . . . .204
Museum Campus . . . . . . . . . . . . . . . . . . . . .206
Navy Pier. . . . . . . . . . . . . . . . . . . . . . . . . .208
Oak Park . . . . . . . . . . . . . . . . . . . . . . . . . .210
Six Flags Great America . . . . . . . . . . . . . . . .212
Skokie. . . . . . . . . . . . . . . . . . . . . . . . . . . .214

## Colleges & Universities

Columbia College Chicago . . . . . . . . . . . . . . 216
DePaul University . . . . . . . . . . . . . . . . . . . .218
Illinois Institute of Technology . . . . . . . . . . . .220
Loyola University (Lake Shore Campus) . . . . . . .222
Northwestern University (Evanston Campus). . . .224
University of Chicago. . . . . . . . . . . . . . . . . .226
University of Illinois at Chicago. . . . . . . . . . . .228
Continuing Education . . . . . . . . . . . . . . . . . .230

## Sports

Biking. . . . . . . . . . . . . . . . . . . . . . . . . . . .232
Billiards and Bowling . . . . . . . . . . . . . . . . . .233
Golf . . . . . . . . . . . . . . . . . . . . . . . . . . . . .234
Recreational Paths. . . . . . . . . . . . . . . . . . . .235
Skating . . . . . . . . . . . . . . . . . . . . . . . . . . .237
Swimming. . . . . . . . . . . . . . . . . . . . . . . . .238
Tennis Courts . . . . . . . . . . . . . . . . . . . . . . .239
Soldier Field . . . . . . . . . . . . . . . . . . . . . . . .240
US Cellular. . . . . . . . . . . . . . . . . . . . . . . . .241
United Center. . . . . . . . . . . . . . . . . . . . . . .242
Wrigley Field . . . . . . . . . . . . . . . . . . . . . . .243
Sports Leagues and Clubs . . . . . . . . . . . . . . .244

## Transit

O'Hare Airport . . . . . . . . . . . . . . . . . . . . . 245
Midway Airport. . . . . . . . . . . . . . . . . . . . . .248
CTA Overview / Fares . . . . . . . . . . . . . . . . . .250
CTA Fares / Buses. . . . . . . . . . . . . . . . . . . . .251
The L . . . . . . . . . . . . . . . . . . . . . . . . . . . .252
Other Buses . . . . . . . . . . . . . . . . . . . . . . . .254
Metra Train Lines. . . . . . . . . . . . . . . . . . . . .256
South Shore Train Lines . . . . . . . . . . . . . . . .258
Amtrak . . . . . . . . . . . . . . . . . . . . . . . . . . .259
Train Stations . . . . . . . . . . . . . . . . . . . . . . .260
Driving . . . . . . . . . . . . . . . . . . . . . . . . . . .262
Parking . . . . . . . . . . . . . . . . . . . . . . . . . . .263
Pedway. . . . . . . . . . . . . . . . . . . . . . . . . . .264

## General Information

Practical Information . . . . . . . . . . . . . . . . . .265
Chicago Media . . . . . . . . . . . . . . . . . . . . . .266
Calendar of Events. . . . . . . . . . . . . . . . . . . .268
Police . . . . . . . . . . . . . . . . . . . . . . . . . . . .270
Hospitals. . . . . . . . . . . . . . . . . . . . . . . . . .271
Post Offices . . . . . . . . . . . . . . . . . . . . . . . .272
Zip Codes . . . . . . . . . . . . . . . . . . . . . . . . .273
Libraries . . . . . . . . . . . . . . . . . . . . . . . . . .274
Hotels. . . . . . . . . . . . . . . . . . . . . . . . . . . .275
For the Kids . . . . . . . . . . . . . . . . . . . . . . . .276
Dog Parks, Runs, and Beaches . . . . . . . . . . . .284
Internet and Wi-Fi . . . . . . . . . . . . . . . . . . . .285

## Arts & Entertainment

Restaurants . . . . . . . . . . . . . . . . . . . . . . . .286
Nightlife . . . . . . . . . . . . . . . . . . . . . . . . . .289
Shopping . . . . . . . . . . . . . . . . . . . . . . . . . .291
Art Institute of Chicago. . . . . . . . . . . . . . . . .293
Bookstores. . . . . . . . . . . . . . . . . . . . . . . . .295
Museums . . . . . . . . . . . . . . . . . . . . . . . . . .299
Movie Theaters . . . . . . . . . . . . . . . . . . . . . .301

## Street Index . . . . . . . . . . . . . . . . . . . .307

## Essential Phone Numbers . . . . . . . . . . . .333

Highway Map. . . . . . . . . . . . . . . foldout in back

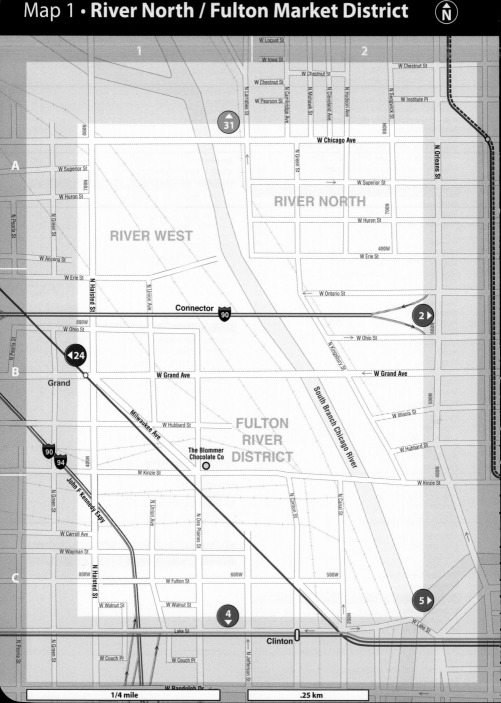

# Map 1 • River North / Fulton Market District

Criss-crossed by rail tracks, I-90/94 and the Chicago River, this section of the Windy City is quickly turning from industrial warehousing district to indie-hipster home. Cheaper rent lures artsy types and suits alike to the west where **The Blommer Chocolate Company** pumps sweet, chocolate-coated air into the streets all day. Diabetics, beware.

## ○ Landmarks
- **Blommer Chocolate Co.** • 600 W Kinzie St
312-226-7700
Opened in 1939. Eventually became the largest commercial chocolate manufacturer in the US.

## ▼ Nightlife
- **Bub City** • 435 N Clark St
312-610-4200
Honky tonk for the River North scene.
- **Emmit's Irish Pub** • 495 N Milwaukee Ave
312-563-9631
An old-school Chicago establishment.
- **Funky Buddha Lounge** • 728 W Grand Ave
312-666-1695
See and be seen at this trendy live music lounge.
- **The Grid** • 351 W Hubbard St
312-321-1351
Swanky sports bar.
- **Lumen** • 839 W Fulton St
312-733-2222
Cool, expensive decor and cool, expensive drinks.
- **The Motel Bar** • 600 W Chicago Ave
312-822-2900
Hotel bar without the hourly rates!
- **Rednofive** • 440 N Halsted St
312-733-6699
Two levels of existence: downstairs=dancing, upstairs=posing.
- **Richard's Bar** • 491 N Milwaukee Ave
312-733-2251
Old man bar good for starter drinks.

## 🍴 Restaurants
- **Baume & Brix** • 351 W Hubbard St
312-321-0351 • $$$
Globally-inspired small plates.
- **Carnivale** • 702 W Fulton St
312-850-5005 • $$$
Authentic, soulful Latin fusion cuisine.
- **Iguana Café** • 517 N Halsted St
312-432-0663 • $
Internet cafe with bagels and such.
- **Japonais** • 600 W Chicago Ave
312-822-9600 • $$$
Elegant, way-upscale Asian.
- **La Scarola** • 721 W Grand Ave
312-243-1740 • $$
Authentic Italian in a super-close atmosphere.
- **Piccolo Sogno** • 464 N Halsted St
312-421-0077 • $$$$
You wish your mama in the old country cooked this good.
- **Publican** • 837 W Fulton Market
312-733-9555 • $$$
Much buzzed new Kahan joint is meat and beer lover's nirvana.
- **Reza's** • 432 W Ontario St
312-664-4500 • $$$
Huge portions of Persian fare.
- **Robust Coffee Lounge** • 416 W Ontario St
312-526-3420 • $
Second location for the South Side coffeehouse.
- **Scoozi!** • 410 W Huron St
312-943-5900 • $$
Once-trendy Italian has had its day.

## 🛍 Shopping
- **Doolin's** • 511 N Halsted St
312-243-9424
Party decorations galore, closed Sundays.
- **Isaacson & Stein Fish Company** •
800 W Fulton Market
312-421-2444
Fish gutters! Quick and fresh!
- **Trunk Club** •
High-end menswear loft with attentive stylists.
- **Veruca Salt** • 520 N Kingsbury St
773-276-3888
Flirty ladies fashions.

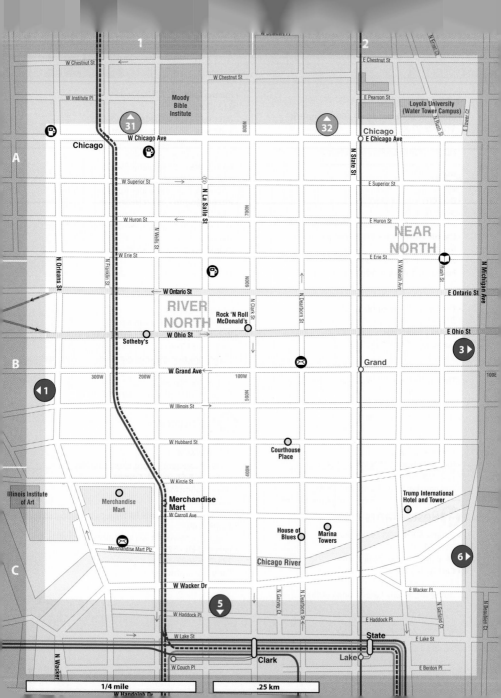

On the west side, monolithic **Merchandise Mart** (seriously—it has its own zip code) casts its shadow over River North, helping the area maintain its old industrial edge. On the east side, the **Trump International Hotel and Tower** rounds that edge into the pinnacle of luxury living. In between, **Rock N Roll McDonald's** turns up the volume on America's favorite pastime: grease.

## ○ Landmarks

- **Courthouse Place** • 54 W Hubbard St
  This Romanesque-style former courthouse has witnessed many legendary trials.
- **House of Blues** • 329 N Dearborn St
  312-923-2000
  Branch location of well-known chain o' blues clubs; music is far better than the crap-filled interior suggests.
- **Marina Towers** • 300 N State St
  Bertrand Goldberg's riverside masterwork. Love the parking.
- **Merchandise Mart** • 222 Merchandise Mart Plz
  312-527-4141
  Houses furniture showrooms and a small mall.
- **Rock N Roll McDonald's** • 600 N Clark St
  312-867-0455
  Glitzy take on fast food fodder.
- **Sotheby's** • 188 E Walton St
  312-475-7900
  Renowned auction house. We bid $5.
- **Trump International Hotel and Tower** •
  401 N Wabash Ave
  312-588-8000
  Shiny happy 92-story skyscraper.

## ▼ Nightlife

- **Andy's Jazz Club** • 11 E Hubbard St
  312-642-6805
  Old-school jazz—a Chicago legend.
- **Bin 36** • 339 N Dearborn St
  312-755-9463
  Wineology 101.
- **Blue Frog Bar & Grill** • 676 N La Salle Dr
  312-943-8900
  Chutes and Ladders, Howdy Doody, and Karaoke.
- **The Boss Bar** • 420 N Clark St
  312-527-1203
  Give tomorrow's hangover extra fuel at this 4 AM dive.
- **Brehon Pub** • 731 N Wells St
  312-642-1071
  Irish pub, lots of TVs for Masterpiece Theater, er, sports.
- **Bull & Bear** • 431 N Wells St
  312-527-5973
  Got cash? Reserve a table with its own beer tap.
- **Celtic Crossings** • 751 N Clark St
  312-337-1005
  No food, all alcohol—a true Irish pub.

Map

| 25 | 26 |
| 10 | 11 |

Whether you're hoping to enjoy craft beers with your dog (seriously, they're invited, too) at **Clark Street Ale House** or impress a date with your fluent French at **Bistro Voltaire**, this 'hood welcomes two-legged and four-legged types. For can't-afford-to-miss Latin flavors that you probably can't afford, head to **Topolobampo** for gourmet Mexican cooking. Hint: go for lunch for less of a dent in your bank account.

- **Central Standard** • 169 W Kinzie St
  312-527-9409
  Booze with your ten o'clock news.
- **Clark Street Ale House** • 742 N Clark St
  312-642-9253
  No pretense, just beer—and lots of it.
- **Enclave** • 220 W Chicago Ave
  312-654-0234
  So big they have a floorplan on the website.
- **English** • 444 N La Salle St
  312-222-6200
  Pimm's Cups and Earl Grey Mint Martinis.
  Adequately priced.
- **Gilt Bar** • 230 W Kinzie St
  312-464-9544
  Old-time cocktails meet the spirit of new-school
  alcohol artistry.
- **The Green Door Tavern** • 678 N Orleans St
  312-664-5496
  A Chicago landmark; old-school classic.
- **Havana** • 412 N Clark St
  312-644-1900
  Cuban cocktail creations with a live Latin
  soundtrack.
- **Howl at the Moon** • 26 W Hubbard St
  312-863-7427
  Late-night dinner and pianists who encourage
  patrons to sing.
- **Martini Ranch** • 311 W Chicago Ave
  312-335-9500
  Martinis and after-work mingling.
- **Municipal Bar** • 216 W Ohio St
  312-951-2125
  Slick sports bar paying homage to the city's
  architectural roots.
- **Ontourage** • 157 W Ontario St
  312-573-1470
  Fat chance getting near any of the celebrities who
  come here.

- **Pippin's Tavern** • 806 N Rush St
  312-787-5435
  Old union haunt = lots of beer.
- **Pops for Champagne** • 601 N State St
  312-266-7677
  Jazz and champers.
- **The Redhead Piano Bar** • 16 W Ontario St
  312-640-1000
  Snug piano bar favorite of the area.
- **Rossi's Liquors** • 412 N State St
  312-644-5775
  A dive in the best sense of the word.
- **Snicker's** • 448 N State St
  312-527-0437
  Eastern European female bartenders imported for
  beauty at this dive.
- **Social Twenty-Five** • 25 W Hubbard St
  312-670-2200
  High-class sports bar with live music on the
  weekends.
- **Sound Bar** • 226 W Ontario St
  312-787-4480
  High-end bells and whistles dance club with tough
  door.
- **Spy Bar** • 646 N Franklin St
  312-337-2191
  Basement club, house music, fashionable crowd,
  pricey drinks.
- **Stay Lounge** • 111 W Erie St
  312-475-0816
  Exclusive after-hours bar, if you can find it.
- **Streeters** • 50 E Chicago Ave
  312-944-5206
  Ritzy dive bar for students and tourists.
- **Untitled** • 111 W Kinzie St
  312-880-1511
  Can't find this modern "speakeasy?" Just look for
  the CVS.
- **Watershed** • 601 N State St
  312-266-4932
  Drinking is easier without windows in this
  basement bar.

# Restaurants

- **American Junkie** • 15 W Illinois St
312-239-0995 • $$
A dose of patriotism with your upscale bar food.
- **Bel 50** • 738 N Clark St
312-496-3948 • $
Trade your usual turkey on wheat for, well,
anything on waffles.
- **Bistro Voltaire** • 226 W Chicago Ave
312-265-0911 • $$$
These servers even speak with French accents. Oui.
- **Boarding House** • 720 N Wells St
312-280-0720 • $$$
Mammoth of a restaurant from local celebrated
sommelier Alpana Singh.
- **Brett's Kitchen** • 233 W Superior St
312-664-6354 • $
Charming breakfast and sandwich stop.
- **Brewstone** • 414 N Orleans St
312-464-9456 • $$
Expanding gastropub chain.
- **Brindille** • 534 N Clark St
312-595-1616 • $$$$$
Luxe Parisian cuisine.
- **Brunch** • 644 N Orleans St
312-265-1411 • $$
Lunch meets breakfast meets locally sustainable
ingredients.
- **Café Iberico** • 737 N La Salle St
312-573-1510 • $
Shoulder-to-shoulder tapas joint.
- **Chicago Chop House** • 60 W Ontario St
312-787-7100 • $$$$$
Old-school steaks meet old-school politicos and
similar characters.
- **Chick-fil-A** • 30 E Chicago Ave
312-266-8888 • $
Fast-food. 5-star service. For real.
- **Club Lago** • 331 W Superior St
312-951-2849 • $$
Generous servings of basic Italian.

- **Coco Pazzo** • 300 W Hubbard St
312-836-0900 • $$$$$
Hearty, high-end Italian.
- **David Burke's Primehouse** • 616 N Rush St
312-660-6000 • $$$$$
Aged steaks by former Smith & Wollensky VP.
- **Dragon Ranch Moonshine & BBQ** • 441 N Clark St
312-955-1900 • $$
Rockit Ranch brand unites Asian flavors and
American BBQ.
- **English** • 444 N La Salle St
312-222-6200 • $$
Crab burgers and other above-average pub food.
- **Farmhouse** • 228 W Chicago Ave
312-280-4960 • $$
Barn vibe meets craft brewhouse.
- **Firecakes Donuts** • 68 W Hubbard St
312-329-6500 • $
Old standbys (chocolate iced) and new favorites
(lemon verbena meringue).
- **Frontera Grill** • 445 N Clark St
312-661-1434 • $$
Rick Bayless's famous cantina—expect to wait
awhile.
- **Fulton's on the River** • 315 N La Salle St
312-822-0100 • $$$$
Best. Oysters. In. Chicago.
- **Gene & Georgetti** • 500 N Franklin St
312-527-3718 • $$$$$
Big steaks.
- **Gilt Bar** • 230 W Kinzie St
312-464-9544 • $$$
Chandelier-lit dining room upstairs, speakeasy
cellar lounge below.
- **Gino's East** • 633 N Wells St
312-943-1124 • $$
Legendary deep dish pizza since 1966.
- **Ginza** • 19 E Ohio St
312-222-0600 • $$
Unhip and unsung sushi.
- **Graham Elliot** • 217 W Huron St
312-624-9975 • $$$$
Over the top food gimmickry puts the irk in quirky.

Map

| 25 | 26 |
| 10 | 11 |

- **GT Fish & Oyster** • 531 N Wells St
312-929-3501 • $$$
Proof that oysters are aphrodisiacs.
- **Havana** • 412 N Clark St
312-644-1900 •
Soak up happy hour with a range of Southwestern flavors.
- **Karyn's Cooked** • 738 N Wells St
312-587-1050 • $$
Hot vegetarian by the queen of raw food.
- **Keefer's** • 20 W Kinzie St
312-467-9525 • $$$
French-influenced steakhouse.
- **The Kerryman** • 661 N Clark St
312-335-8121 • $$
Standard Irish pub, plus the bonus of an outdoor patio.
- **Kinzie Chophouse** • 400 N Wells St
312-822-0191 • $$$
Neighborhood steak house.
- **Lawry's The Prime Rib** • 100 E Ontario St
312-787-5000 • $$$
Carnivore's delight.
- **Lou Malnati's Pizzeria** • 439 N Wells St
312-828-9800 • $
Famous in a city famous for pizza.
- **Maggiano's Little Italy** • 516 N Clark St
312-644-7700 • $$
Gut-busting family-style Italian.
- **Meli Cafe & Juice Bar** • 540 N Wells St
312-527-1850 • $$
Fresh, inviting; favors healthy selections and early risers.
- **The Melting Pot** • 609 N Dearborn St
312-573-0011 • $$$$$
Cheesy indeed.
- **Mr. Beef** • 666 N Orleans St
312-337-8500 • $
Get your Italian beef fix at this tried-and-true Chicago classic.
- **Nacional 27** • 325 W Huron St
312-664-2727 • $$$
Pan-Latin supper club with dance floor. Babaloo!

- **Naha** • 500 N Clark St
312-321-6242 • $$$$
Mediterranean-inspired luxury.
- **Osteria Via Stato** • 620 N State St
312-642-8450 • $$$$
Menu-oriented Italian. Fancy, but reasonably priced.
- **Pizzeria Uno** • 29 E Ohio St
312-321-1000 • $
Legendary Chicago pizza.
- **Portillo's** • 100 W Ontario St
312-587-8910 • $
Classic Chicago-style dogs.
- **Quartino** • 626 N State St
312-698-5000 • $$$
Trendy Italian small plates and house-cured salami.
- **RL Restaurant** • 115 E Chicago Ave
312-475-1100 • $$$$$
Somehow they even got the Polo logo on the sole.
- **Rosebud on Rush** • 720 N Rush St
312-266-6444 • $$
A branch of Chicago's legendary, old-school Italian.
- **Roy's** • 720 N State St
312-787-7599 • $$$
Pretty Hawaiian contemporary cuisine.
- **Ruth's Chris Steak House** • 431 N Dearborn St
312-321-2725 • $$$$
Consistent steak chain.
- **Shanghai Terrace** • 108 E Superior St
312-573-6744 • $$$$
The city's most extravagant Chinese restaurant.
- **Shaw's Crab House** • 21 E Hubbard St
312-527-2722 • $$$$
A seafood destination.
- **Siena Tavern** • 51 W Kinzie St
312-595-1322 • $$$
Housemade pastas from "Top Chef" celeb Fabio Viviani.
- **Sixteen** • 401 N Wabash Ave
312-588-8030 • $$$$
Drinks and dinner with a view from the Donald.
- **Slurping Turtle** • 116 W Hubbard St
312-464-0466 • $$
Celebrity chef Takashi Yagihashi's ramen, libations and other treats.

- **Smith & Wollensky** • 318 N State St
312-670-9900 • $$$$
Chicago branch of New York steak emporium.
- **Soupbox** • 50 E Chicago Ave
312-951-5900 • $
12 fresh soups every day!
- **Sullivan's Steakhouse** • 415 N Dearborn St
312-527-3510 • $$$$
Another upscale steakhouse.
- **Sumi Robata Bar** • 702 N Wells St
312-988-7864 • $$
Traditional Japanese cuisine cooked over a
charcoal grill.
- **Sunda** • 110 W Illinois St
312-644-0500 • $$$$
Pretentious "New Asian" for folks with more
attitude than taste.
- **Sushi Naniwa** • 607 N Wells St
312-255-8555 • $$
Quality sushi. Great outdoor.
- **Taco Burrito King** • 114 W Chicago Ave
312-526-3258 • $
The royalty of late-night Mexican grub at peasant
prices.
- **Topolobampo** • 445 N Clark St
312-661-1434 • $$$$
Standard bearer for upscale Mexican.
- **Vermillion** • 10 W Hubbard St
312-527-4060 • $$$
Indian-Latin fusion—what next?
- **Wildfire** • 159 W Erie St
312-787-9000 • $$
Fun, trendy American.
- **XOCO** • 449 N Clark St
312-334-3688 • $$
Mexican food guru Rick Bayless's most affordable
cantina.
- **Yolk** • 747 N Wells St
312-787-2277 • $$
Sunny egg-focused breakfast and brunch.
- **Zocalo** • 358 W Ontario St
312-302-9977 • $$
Fresh guacamole flights, flaming cheese, and tons
of tequila.

# Shopping

- **Jazz Record Mart** • 27 E Illinois St
312-222-1467
Jazz lover's emporium.
- **Jonathan Adler** • 676 N Wabash Ave
312-274-9920
Hip and happy home furnishings.
- **Lightology** • 215 W Chicago Ave
312-944-1000
Lights, camera, chandeliers!
- **Montauk Sofa** • 401 N Wells St
312-951-5688
The most comfortable sofas.
- **Orange Skin** • 223 W Erie St
312-335-1033
Contemporary Italian furniture.
- **P.O.S.H.** • 613 N State St
312-280-1602
An Aladdin's cave featuring old hotel silverware
and other finds.
- **Paper Source** • 232 W Chicago Ave
312-337-0798
Great paper and invitations.
- **Pinkberry** • 635 N State St
312-475-0641
West Hollywood froyo innovators.

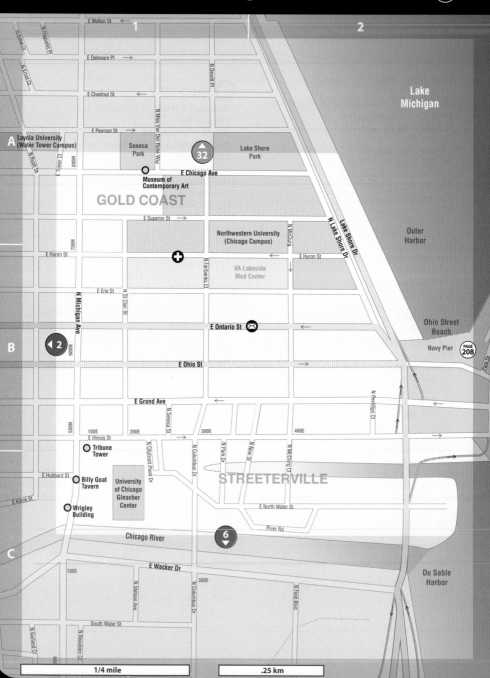

# Map 3 · **Streeterville / Mag Mile**

N

E Walton St

1

2

Lake
Michigan

E Delaware Pl

N Dewitt Pl

E Chestnut St

N Mies Van Der Rohe Way

E Pearson St

Loyola University
(Water Tower Campus)

N Rush St

N Tower Ct

800N

Seneca
Park

32

Lake Shore
Park

N Ernst Ct

N Hughsort Pl

N Ernst Ct

A

Museum of
Contemporary Art

E Chicago Ave

**GOLD COAST**

E Superior St

Outer
Harbor

700N

N McClurg

N Lake Shore Dr

Lake Shore Dr

E Huron St

Northwestern University
(Chicago Campus)

E Huron St

N Fairbanks Ct

+

VA Lakeside
Med Center

E Erie St

N St Clair St

N Michigan Ave

E Ontario St

✉

Ohio Street
Beach

B

2

600N

E Ohio St

Navy Pier

PAGE
208

N Peshtigo Ct

N Park Dr

E Grand Ave

500N

100E

200E

N Seneca St

300E

400E

E Illinois St

Tribune
Tower

N Columbus Dr

N New St

N McClurg

University
of Chicago
Gleacher
Center

N Clyfford Plaza Dr

**STREETERVILLE**

Billy Goat
Tavern

E Hubbard St

Wrigley
Building

E Kinzie St

E North Water St

River Rd

Chicago River

6

C

E Wacker Dr

Du Sable
Harbor

100E

300E

N Stetson Ave

N Columbus Dr

N Field Blvd

South Water St

N Garland Ct

N Beaubien Ct

1/4 mile

.25 km

As out-of-towners aiming to spend cash crash into each other, locals spend their time in lavish high-rises. Whether you're looking to rent a bike, take a Segway tour or see Lake Michigan via old-fashioned foot, the lakefront trail offers an escape from the epicenter of retail therapy.

## ○ Landmarks

- **Billy Goat Tavern** • 430 N Michigan Ave
  312-222-1525
  Cheezborger! Cheezborger!
- **Museum of Contemporary Art** • 220 E Chicago Ave
  312-280-2660
  Party down on First Fridays.
- **Tribune Tower** • 435 N Michigan Ave
  312-222-9100
  Check out the stones from famous buildings around the world including a real-life rock from the moon!
- **Wrigley Building** • 401 N Michigan Ave
  Monument to chewing gum.

## ▼ Nightlife

- **Billy Goat Tavern** • 430 N Michigan Ave
  312-222-1525
  Cheezboiga; no fries, chips; pepsi, no coke.
- **Timothy O'Toole's Pub** • 622 N Fairbanks Ct
  312-642-0700
  Irish sports bar with tons of TV space.

## 🍴 Restaurants

- **Bandera** • 535 N Michigan Ave
  312-644-3524 • $$
  Lunch above Mag Mile.
- **Billy Goat Tavern** • 430 N Michigan Ave
  312-222-1525 • $
  Cheezboiga; no fries, chips; pepsi, no coke.
- **The Capital Grille** • 633 N St Clair St
  312-337-9400 • $$$$
  Macho steak and zin.
- **D4 Irish Pub & Cafe** • 345 E Ohio St
  312-624-8385 • $$$
  Upscale Irish pub with a copy of the Book of Kells.
- **Emilio's Tapas Sol Y Nieve** • 215 E Ohio St
  312-467-7177 • $$$
  One of the nicest branches of the local tapas chain.
- **Fox & Obel Café** • 401 E Illinois St
  312-379-0112 • $$
  Creative café grub with gourmet ingredients from next-door market.
- **Grand Lux Cafe** • 600 N Michigan Ave
  312-276-2500 • $$$
  A Mag Mile vittle and view indulgence. Go ahead, be a tourist!
- **Heaven on Seven** • 600 N Michigan Ave
  312-280-7774 • $$
  Cajun grub and cocktails.

- **Howells & Hood** • 435 N Michigan Ave
  312-262-5310 • $$$
  Eclectic dining and craft beer in the iconic Tribune Tower.
- **Indian Garden** • 247 E Ontario St
  312-280-4910 • $$
  Good veggie options.
- **Les Nomades** • 222 E Ontario St
  312-649-9010 • $$$$$
  Deluxe haute cuisine.
- **The Market Bistro** • 401 E Illinois St
  312-379-0132 • $$
  River views for the wine and cheese crowd.
- **NoMI Kitchen** • 800 N Michigan Ave
  312-239-4030 • $$$$$
  Deluxe French fusion.
- **Sayat Nova** • 157 E Ohio St
  312-644-9159 • $$
  Armenian fare in a romantic setting.
- **TRU** • 676 N St Clair St
  312-202-0001 • $$$$$
  Dazzling contemporary cuisine.
- **Volare** • 201 E Grand Ave
  312-410-9900 • $$$
  Killer bolognese sauce; lick the plate clean.

## 🛍 Shopping

- **Apple Store** • 679 N Michigan Ave
  312-529-9500
  All of their newest, shiniest offerings plus classes and seminars.
- **Disney Store** • 717 N Michigan Ave
  312-654-9208
  M-i-c-k-e-Why?
- **Garrett Popcorn** • 625 N Michigan Ave
  884-476-7267
  Chicago popcorn legend. Cheese caramel blend not-to-be-missed.
- **Henri Bendel** • 845 N Michigan Ave
  312-951-1928
  Branch of venerable NYC department store.
- **Neiman Marcus** • 737 N Michigan Ave
  312-642-5900
  Affectionately known as "Needless Mark-up" by those who can afford it anyway.
- **Niketown** • 669 N Michigan Ave
  312-642-6363
  Nike label sports clothing.
- **Ralph Lauren** • 750 N Michigan Ave
  312-280-1655
  If you love those little polo horses...
- **Tiffany & Co.** • 730 N Michigan Ave
  312-944-7500
  Lack's appropriate breakfast options.

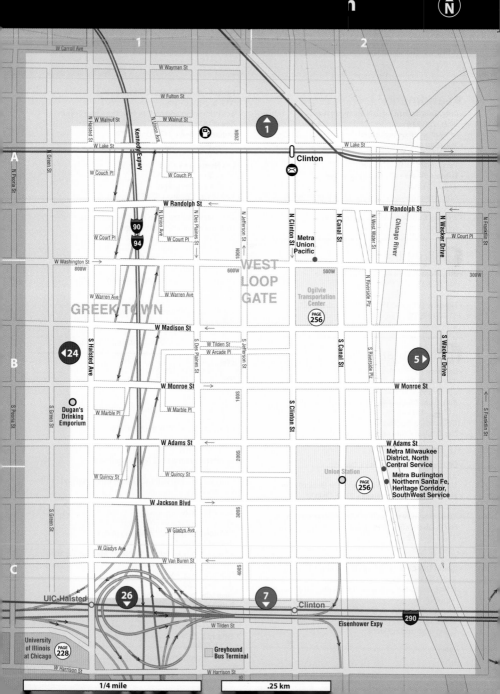

Trains, buses and gyros define this 'hood. From suburban 9 to 5-ers arriving on the Metra at **Union Station** to Megabus passengers traveling on a mega-budget, this is commuter central. While plenty of lofts have risen to jump start residential growth, there are an equal number of gritty pockets here, too. Not surprising when you consider that some passengers buy their bus tickets for $1, is it?

| 25 | 26 | | |
| --- | --- | --- | --- |
| | | 10 | 11 |

Map

## ○ Landmarks

- **Dugan's on Halsted** • 128 S Halsted St
  312-421-7191
  Sports bar in Greektown. Fantastic beer garden and favorite cop hangout.
- **Union Station** • 210 S Canal St
  312-322-4269
  Built in 1925, the architecture is not to be missed!

## Nightlife

- **Dugan's on Halsted** • 128 S Halsted St
  312-421-7191
  Lively Irish pub. Free popcorn to help soak up the booze.
- **Dylan's Tavern & Grill** • 118 S Clinton St
  312-876-2008
  Unpretentious West Looper with grub.
- **Haymarket Pub and Brewery** •
  737 W Randolph St
  312-638-0700
  Lesser-known member of Chicago's beer scene with late-night eats.
- **Nara** • 623 W Randolph St
  312-887-9999
  Hip and laid-back Korean bar.
- **Snuggery** • 222 S Riverside Plaza
  312-441-9334
  Commuter bar inside Union Station.
- **Spectrum Bar & Grill** • 233 S Halsted St
  312-715-0770
  Sports bar with Mediterranean flair.

## Restaurants

- **Athena** • 212 S Halsted St
  312-655-0000 • $$$
  Goddess Athena-inspired outdoor and indoor.
- **Au Cheval** • 800 W Randolph St
  312-929-4580 • $$
  5-star flavor pairings in a more affordable diner vibe.
- **Avec** • 615 W Randolph St
  312-377-2002 • $$
  Small plates, big flavors, chefs' hangout—nuff said.
- **Blackbird** • 619 W Randolph St
  312-715-0708 • $$$$
  Chic les plus ultra.
- **Bombacigno's J & C Inn** • 558 W Van Buren St
  312-663-4114 • $
  Traditional Italian subs.
- **De Cero** • 814 W Randolph St
  312-455-8114 • $$$
  Made-to-order tacos, fresh fruit cocktail, Mexican heaven.
- **Dine** • 733 W Madison St
  312-602-2100 • $$$
  Martinis and comfort food at the Crowne Plaza.
- **Gold Coast Dogs** • 225 S Canal St
  312-258-8585 • $
  Gotta have the dogs.
- **Grace** • 652 W Randolph St
  312-234-9494 • $$$$$
  Ultra fine dining on Restaurant Row.
- **Greek Islands** • 200 S Halsted St
  312-782-9855 • $$$
  Noisy, fun crowd-pleasing spectacle.

Map 2

| 25 | 26 | 7 | 8 | 9 |
| | | 10 | 11 | |

This marks the beginning of foodie central in Chicago. Randolph Street includes some of the best upscale eats, from Girl and the Goat-related **Little Goat** to the date-friendly **Avec**. On a budget? Head to **Mr. Greek Gyros**. Wash it all down with a craft beer at **Haymarket Brewing**.

- **Jubilee Juice** • 140 N Halsted St
  312-491-8500 • $$
  A Better Smoothie.
- **Little Goat** • 820 W Randolph St
  312-888-3455 • $$
  Comfy little sib to famed Girl and the Goat.
- **Lou Mitchell's** • 565 W Jackson Blvd
  312-939-3111 • $
  Rub shoulders with local pols at this legendary grill.
- **Meli** • 301 S Halsted St
  312-454-0748 • $
  Brunch spot makes us wanna challah.
- **Mr. Greek Gyros** • 234 S Halsted St
  312-906-8731 • $
  The best late night gyro spot in the city, hands down.
- **N9NE Steakhouse** • 440 W Randolph St
  312-575-9900 • $$$
  Toast marshmallows at the table at this ultra-trendy contemporary spot.
- **Nine Muses** • 315 S Halsted St
  312-902-9922 • $$$
  Brick bars and backgammon.
- **The Parthenon** • 314 S Halsted St
  312-726-2407 • $$$
  Creators of flaming saganaki!
- **Pegasus Restaurant and Taverna** •
  130 S Halsted St
  312-226-3377 • $$$
  Rooftop garden—Chicago secret!

- **Perez** • 853 W Randolph St
  312-421-2488 • $$
  Standard Mexican fare, outstanding pico de gallo.
- **Province** • 161 N Jefferson St
  312-669-9900 • $$
  Ambitious organic fare strikes hits and misses.
- **Robinson's No. 1 Ribs** • 225 S Canal St
  312-258-8477 • $
  Dress down and dig in.
- **Rodity's** • 222 S Halsted St
  312-454-0800 • $$$
  Greek lamb since 1972.
- **Santorini** • 800 W Adams St
  312-829-8820 • $$$
  Fish, shellfish, and roasted chicken. Yum.
- **Sepia** • 123 N Jefferson St
  312-441-1920 • $$$$
  Contemp. American with flare.
- **Takumi** • 555 W Madison St
  312-669-1999 • $$
  Tiny sushi spot with excellent lunch specials.
- **Vivo** • 838 W Randolph St
  312-733-3379 • $$$$
  Restaurants Row's first residence of Italian dining.

# 🛍 Shopping

- **Athenian Candle Co.** • 300 S Halsted St
  312-332-6988
  Candles, curse-breakers, Greek trinkets, and much more.
- **Greektown Music** • 304 S Halsted St
  312-263-6342
  Music, T-shirts, hats—everything Greek!
- **Northwestern Cutlery** • 810 W Lake St
  312-421-3666
  The self-described "candy store for cooks."
- **Pan Hellenic Pastry Shop** • 322 S Halsted St
  312-454-1886
  Greek sweets in Greektown.

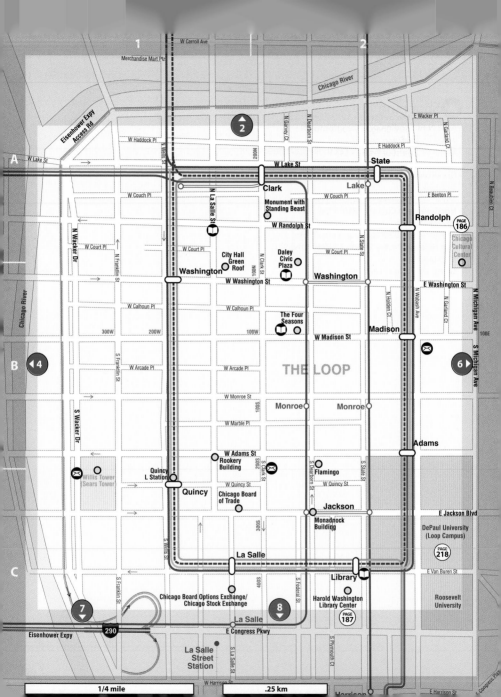

The Loop derives its moniker from the L tracks that lasso the city's heart. This here is the bustling financial and business district, where banks are plentiful and parking is pricey. The intersection of State and Madison is literally ground zero (0 east, 0 west, 0 north, 0 south) for Chicago's easy-to-follow street numbering grid. Watching over it all is North America's tallest building the Sears Tower—no wait, the **Willis Tower**, but don't ever call it that in public.

## ⊙ Landmarks

- **Chagall's Four Seasons** • 10 S Dearborn St
Mosaic by Marc Chagall—you know, the one who did all those flying people.
- **Chicago Board of Trade** • 141 W Jackson Blvd
312-435-3590
The goddess Ceres tops this deco monolith.
- **Chicago Board Options Exchange** •
400 S La Salle St
312-786-5600
The world's largest options market.
- **Chicago Cultural Center** • 78 E Washington St
312-744-6630
The spot for free lectures, exhibits, concerts, and movies.
- **Chicago Mercantile Exchange** • 20 S Wacker Dr
312-930-1000
Economics at work in polyester jackets.
- **Chicago Stock Exchange** • 440 S La Salle St
312-663-2222
The second-largest stock exchange in the country.
- **City Hall Green Roof** • 121 N La Salle St
First green roof on a municipal building. Cool.
- **Daley Plaza** • 50 W Washington St
Home of a Picasso sculpture, a Christmas tree ceremony, and many alfresco lunches.
- **Flamingo** • 230 S Dearborn St
Alexander Calder's fabulous red flamingo.
- **Harold Washington Library Center** •
400 S State St
312-747-4300
The world's largest public library building; nearly 100 works of art on every floor.
- **James R. Thompson Center** • 100 W Randolph St
312-814-3089
Lots of glass combined with the colors red, silver and blue. Ghastly!
- **Macy's** • 111 N State St
312-781-4483
Folks are still mourning the passing of Marshall Fields. Luckily the clock and Tiffany dome remain.
- **Miro's Chicago** • 69 W Washington St
Part of the Loop's outdoor public artwork program.
- **Monadnock Building** • 53 W Jackson Blvd
312-922-1890
Claim to fame: world's largest office building when completed in 1893.

- **Monument with Standing Beast** •
100 W Randolph St
Jean DuBuffet sculpture. Looks like melted snow.
- **Quincy L Station** • 220 S Wells St
Restored to its original glory.
- **The Rookery** • 209 S La Salle St
312-553-6100
Take a peek inside at Frank Lloyd Wright's spectacular remodelled interior.
- **Willis Tower (Sears Tower)** • 233 S Wacker Dr
312-875-9696
Currently the tallest building in the US, with a cool skydeck.

## 🍸 Nightlife

- **Brando's Speakeasy** • 343 S Dearborn St
773-216-3213
Karaoke to "Free Bird" drunk on fancy martinis or cheap beer.
- **Ceres Cafe** • 141 W Jackson Blvd
312-427-3443
The epitome of a stiff drink.
- **Close Up 2** • 416 S Clark St
312-385-1111
Sophisticated smooth jazz in the heart of the financial district.
- **Exchequer** • 226 S Wabash Ave
312-939-5633
Loop location for the working class.
- **Miller's Pub** • 134 S Wabash Ave
312-263-4988
A Loop tradition.
- **Monk's Pub** • 205 W Lake St
312-357-6665
Wall of books. And beer.
- **Petterino's** • 150 N Dearborn St
312-422-0150
Go to church on Sunday, then cabaret here on Monday.
- **Potter's Lounge** • 17 E Monroe St
312-917-4933
Posh cocktails in the Palmer House Hilton.
- **Roof on The Wit** • 201 N State St
312-239-9501
A rooftop playground for those who want to be seen.

Map

25 26

10 11

The post-work crowd hangs here just long enough to forget that they have to return to the office the next morning. From stomping on a floor covered in peanut shells at **Monk's Pub** to sipping martinis at **South Branch**, drinking environments range from dive to high-dollar. If you're here past happy hour, head to "Broadway in Chicago" for proof that, yes, you are cultured. Make your mom proud and your wallet happy with a free history lesson at the **Chicago Cultural Center**.

- **South Branch Tavern & Grille** • 100 S Wacker Dr
  312-546-6177
  Sip martinis on the patio.
- **Stocks and Blondes** • 40 N Wells St
  312-372-3725
  Happy hour dive stocked with blond (and brunette) waitresses.

 Restaurants

- **Atwood Café** • 1 W Washington St
  312-368-1900 • $$$
  High tea with contemporary flair.
- **Billy Goat Tavern** • 330 S Wells St
  312-554-0297 • $
  Grubby cheezboiga joint made famous by John Belushi.
- **Caffe Rom** • 71 S Wacker Dr
  312-379-0291 • $$
  A slice of modern Milan in the Loop.
- **Crumbs** • 303 W Madison St
  312-263-6500 • $
  Cupcakes bigger than your head.
- **Everest** • 440 S La Salle St
  312-663-8920 • $$$$$
  Classic fine dining experience with a knock-out view.
- **Frontera Fresco** • 111 N State St
  $$
  Popular Mexican joint.
- **Gold Coast Dogs** • 159 N Wabash Ave
  312-917-1677 • $
  Classic dog joint.
- **Goodwin's** • 175 N Franklin St
  312-634-1134 • $
  Great West Loop sandwiches and wraps.
- **Hannah's Bretzel** • 180 W Washington St
  312-621-1111 • $
  Homemade pretzels and organic lunch fare.
- **Heaven on Seven** • 111 N Wabash Ave
  312-263-6443 • $$
  Cajun Chicago classic. Closed for dinner.

- **Jaffa Bakery** • 186 W Van Buren St
  312-322-9007 • $
  Best fresh turkey you will ever taste.
- **La Cantina Enoteca** • 71 W Monroe St
  312-332-7005 • $$
  Casual Italian with seafood specialty.
- **La Cocina** • 45 N Wells St
  312-346-1638 • $
  Cinco de Mayo. All year long.
- **Oasis Café** • 21 N Wabash Ave
  312-443-9534 • $$
  Middle Eastern hideout inside of a jewelry store.
- **Plymouth Restaurant** • 327 S Plymouth Ct
  312-362-1212 • $
  24-hour diner with bar and grill.
- **Protein Bar** • 235 S Franklin St
  312-346-7300 • $
  On-the-go meals for eaters avoiding grease.
- **Russian Tea Time** • 77 E Adams St
  312-360-0000 • $$$
  Rich food. Richer interior. Copious amounts of vodka.
- **Toni Patisserie & Cafe** • 65 E Washington St
  312-726-2020 • $
  Fin-de-siecle ambiance, French pastries, and light fare.
- **Trattoria No. 10** • 10 N Dearborn St
  312-984-1718 • $$$
  Popular pre-theater food.
- **The Village** • 71 W Monroe St
  312-332-7005 • $$
  Quaint, casual Italian looks like a village.
- **Vivere** • 71 W Monroe St
  312-332-4040 • $$$
  Dated Italian luxury.
- **Westminster Hot Dog** • 11 N Wells St
  312-445-9514 • $
  Total sausage fest.
- **Wow Bao** • 175 W Jackson Blvd
  312-334-6395 • $
  Nice buns.

# Shopping

- **A New Leaf** • 312 S Dearborn St
  312-427-9097
  Florists of paradise. Minus the price.
- **After School Matters Retail Store** • 66 E
  Randolph St
  312-744-7274
  Speciality gifts, many made by local student artists.
- **Arts & Artisans** • 35 E Wacker Dr
  312-578-0126
  Art Gallery.
- **Ashley Stewart** • 7 W Madison St
  312-920-0646
  Clothes for your curves.
- **Blick Art Materials** • 42 S State St
  312-920-0300
  Get creative here.
- **Block 37** • 108 N State St
  312-261-4700
  All the mall greatest hits right here in the Loop.
- **Central Camera Company** • 230 S Wabash Ave
  312-427-5580
  Family owned camera shop.
- **Florodora** • 330 S Dearborn St
  312-212-8860
  Vintage-inspired, wildly-priced.

- **Garrett Popcorn** • 26 W Randolph St
  312-201-0511
  The caramel cheddar mix is their signature.
- **Kramer's Health Food Center** • 230 S Wabash Ave
  312-922-0077
  Healthy hippie haven.
- **Lush Cosmetics** • 111 N State St
  312-795-0863
  Handmade soaps and natural cosmetics—too bad they aren't edible!
- **Macy's** • 111 N State St
  312-781-1000
  The former home of Chicago establishment Marshall Field's.
- **Pastoral** • 53 E Lake St
  312-658-1250
  One of Chicago's favorite cheese shops. Start your picnic here.
- **Reckless Records** • 26 E Madison St
  312-795-0878
  Instant satisfaction for the vinyl-hungry masses.
- **Sears** • 2 N State St
  312-373-6000
  Blue-collar stalwart.
- **Ulta** • 114 S State St
  312-279-5081
  Four story beauty emporium.
- **Urban Outfitters** • 20 S State St
  312-269-9919
  Retro-fun clothing, nifty gifts, and silly t-shirts.

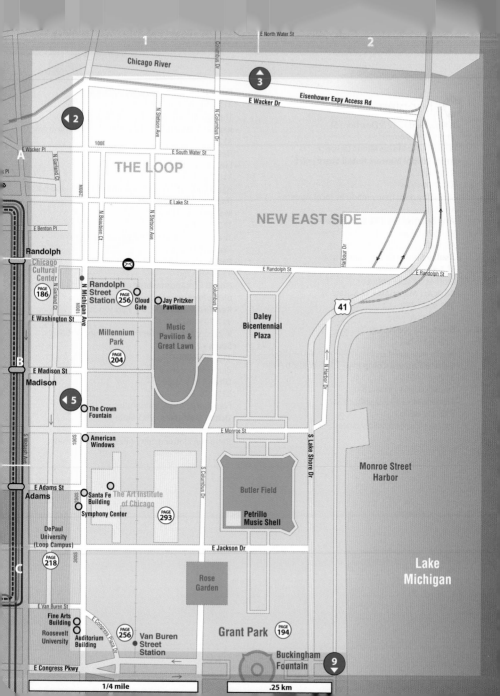

1

2

E North Water St

Chicago River

N Columbus Dr

Columbus Dr

▲
3

Eisenhower Expy Access Rd

E Wacker Dr

◄ 2

E Wacker Pl

100E

N Stetson Ave

E South Water St

A

N Garland Ct

E Benton Pl

THE LOOP

N Beaubien Ct

E Lake St

N Stetson Ave

NEW EAST SIDE

Harbour Dr

Randolph

E Randolph St

E Randolph St

Chicago
Cultural
Center

PAGE
186

N Garland Ct

✉

Randolph
Street
Station

PAGE
256

Cloud
Gate

Jay Pritzker
Pavilion

Columbus Dr

Daley
Bicentennial
Plaza

41

E Washington St

N Michigan Ave

Millennium
Park

PAGE
204

Music
Pavilion &
Great Lawn

N Harbor Dr

B

E Madison St

Madison

◄ 5

The Crown
Fountain

E Monroe St

S Lake Shore Dr

American
Windows

E Adams St

Adams

S Wabash Ave

Santa Fe
Building

Symphony Center

The Art Institute
of Chicago

S Columbus Dr

Butler Field

Monroe Street
Harbor

PAGE
293

Petrillo
Music Shell

DePaul
University
(Loop Campus)

C

PAGE
218

E Jackson Dr

Lake
Michigan

E Van Buren St

Rose
Garden

Fine Arts
Building

E Congress Plaza Dr

Roosevelt
University

Auditorium
Building

PAGE
256

Van Buren
Street
Station

Grant Park

PAGE
194

E Congress Pkwy

Buckingham
Fountain

9
▼

1/4 mile

.25 km

A giant silver bean and 50-foot-tall animated faces...yes, really! **Millennium Park** is definitely the Chicago show-stopper, with its unique blend of artwork and landscaping. Farther down Michigan Avenue, the more traditional **Grant Park** brings highbrow and lowbrow culture side by side. Tasteful music or Taste of Chicago, there's something for everyone.

## ○ Landmarks

- **America Windows** • 111 S Michigan Ave
  312-443-3600
  Spectacular stained glass by Marc Chagall.
- **Art Institute of Chicago** • 111 S Michigan Ave
  312-443-3600
  World-class art museum.
- **Auditorium Building** • 430 S Michigan Ave
  Designed by Louis Sullivan; on National Register of Historic Places.
- **Chicago Symphony Orchestra** •
  220 S Michigan Ave
  312-294-3000
  Classical music headquarters.
- **Cloud Gate** • 201 E Randolph St
  312-742-5000
  Much-photographed sculpture, affectionately known as "the bean."
- **Crown Fountain** • 201 E Randolph St
  Captivating modern take on traditional fountain, swarming with kids.
- **Fine Arts Building** • 410 S Michigan Ave
  312-566-9800
  The country's first artists' colony, converted from a Studebaker carriage plant in 1898.
- **Grant Park** • 331 E Randolph St
  312-742-7648
  Where Marathon, Music and Taste all begin and end.
- **Jay Pritzker Pavilion** • 201 E Randolph St
  Frank Gehry signature steel structure, offering free outdoor concerts.
- **Millennium Park** • 201 E Randolph St
  312-742-1168
  One of the best public spaces on the planet.
- **One Prudential Plaza** • 130 E Randolph St
  Classic—50s skyscraper.
- **Santa Fe Building** • 224 S Michigan Ave
  Home to the world-renowned Chicago Architecture Foundation.

---

##  Nightlife

- **Houlihan's** • 111 E Wacker Dr
  312-616-3663
  Trendy, semi-obnoxious sports bar.

## 🍴 Restaurants

- **American Craft Kitchen & Bar** •
  151 E Upper Wacker Dr
  312-565-1234 • $$
  Lunch with your wi-fi.
- **Aria** • 200 N Columbus Dr
  312-444-9494 • $$$$
  Artistic, creative pan-global grub.
- **Artists Café** • 412 S Michigan Ave
  312-583-9940 • $$
  Sit at the counter. They've got the chattiest waiters in town.
- **Eggy's Diner** • 333 E Benton Pl
  773-234-3449 • $
  Varied menu at this airy diner.
- **Friendship Chinese Restaurant** •
  200 N Lake Front Dr
  312-228-5080 • $$
  Non-Navy Pier lakefront dining.
- **The Gage** • 24 S Michigan Ave
  312-372-4243 • $$
  Classy brews, burgers and meat.
- **Grahamwich** • 615 N State St
  312-265-0434 • $$
  Affordable gourmet sandwiches from a MasterChef judge.
- **The Green at Grant Park** • 352 E Monroe St
  312-540-9013 • $$
  Did you make a birdie? Celebrate with a cocktail on the patio.
- **Park Grill** • 11 N Michigan Ave
  312-521-7275 • $$$
  Contemporary American cooking in Millenium Park.

## 🛍 Shopping

- **Chicago Architecture Foundation** •
  224 S Michigan Ave
  312-922-3432
  All things architectural: tours, exhibits, shopping.
- **Mariano's** • 333 E Benton Pl
  312-228-1349
  Full-service gourmet grocery, butcher and deli.
- **Museum Shop of the Art Institute** •
  111 S Michigan Ave
  800-518-4214
  Art Institute gift shop.
- **Poster Plus** • 30 E Adams St
  312-461-9277
  Vintage posters and custom framing.
- **Precious Possessions** • 28 N Michigan Ave
  312-726-8118
  Mineral shop.

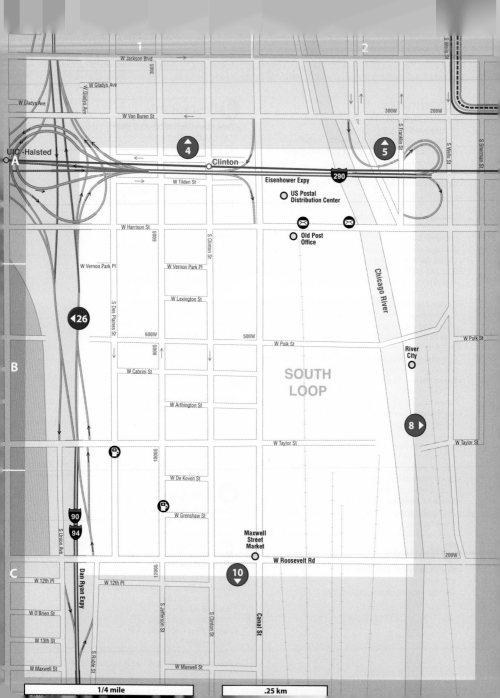

Map 7

This longtime industrial deadzone is emerging as a bustling business district—including a swanky new **Whole Foods**—to serve the rampant residential growth in all of the adjacent 'hoods. River City residents have never had it so good. Seriously, they haven't.

## ○ Landmarks

- **Maxwell Street Market** •
  W Roosevelt Rd & S Des Plaines St
  Outdoor bazaar where you can shop for dish soap or bicycle parts while grazing at authentic taco stands.
- **Old Post Office** • 404 W Harrison St
  This massive, vacant edifice straddling I-90/94 and I-290 is a benchmark for traffic reports.
- **US Postal Distribution Center** • 433 W Harrison St
  312-447-0979
  The city's main mail routing center, employing over 6,000 people and operating 24 hours a day.

## Restaurants

- **Manny's** • 1141 S Jefferson St
  312-939-2855 • $
  Famous deli—popular with politicians.
- **White Palace Grill** • 1159 S Canal St
  312-939-7167 • $
  An ode to grease, and some fine omelettes to boot.

## Shopping

- **Fishman's Fabrics** • 1101 S Des Plaines St
  312-922-7250
  Huge fabric wholesaler.
- **Lee's Foreign Car Service** • 727 S Jefferson St
  312-633-0823
  Import parts and service.
- **Morris & Sons** • 557 W Polk St
  312-243-5635
  Mostly men, off-price Italian designers.
- **Vogue Fabrics** • 623 W Roosevelt Rd
  312-829-2505
  An iconic craft store in East Pilsen for over 60 years.
- **Whole Foods Market** • 1101 S Canal St
  312-435-4600
  Perhaps not quite Bertrand Goldberg's vision, but works for us.

Map 8 • **South Loop / Printers Row / Dearborn Park**

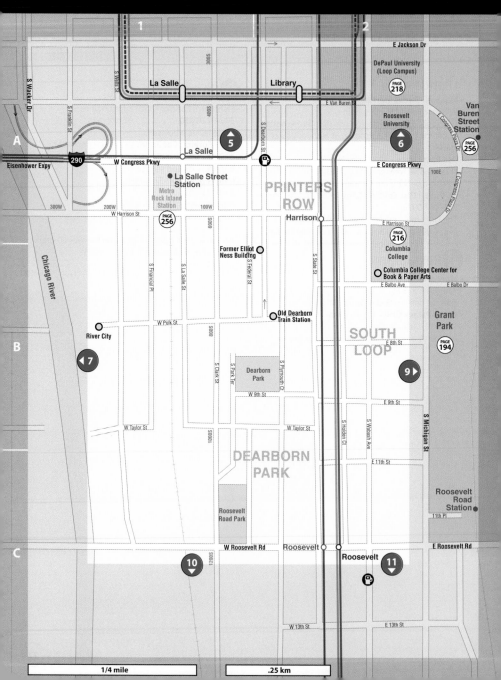

1

2

E Jackson Dr

DePaul University
(Loop Campus)
PAGE
218

La Salle

Library

Roosevelt
University

E Van Buren St

Van
Buren
Street
Station
PAGE
256

S Wacker Dr

S Franklin St

S Wells St

3900S

4000S

S Dearborn St

E Congress Plaza Dr

A

5

La Salle

6

Eisenhower Expy

290

W Congress Pkwy

E Congress Pkwy

100E

La Salle Street
Station

PRINTERS
ROW

300W

200W

100W

Metra
Rock Island
Station

PAGE
256

W Harrison St

6000S

Harrison

E Harrison St

PAGE
216

Chicago River

Former Elliot
Ness Building

S State St

Columbia
College

Columbia College Center for
Book & Paper Arts

S Financial Pl

S La Salle St

S Federal St

E Balbo Ave

E Balbo Dr

Old Dearborn
Train Station

B

River City

7

W Polk St

7000S

SOUTH
LOOP

E 8th St

Grant
Park
PAGE
194

Dearborn
Park

9

S Clark St

S Park Ter

S Plymouth Ct

W 9th St

E 9th St

W Taylor St

8000S

W Taylor St

S Holden Ct

S Wabash Ave

S Michigan St

DEARBORN
PARK

E 11th St

Roosevelt
Road
Station

Roosevelt
Road Park

11th Pl

C

W Roosevelt Rd

12000S

Roosevelt

Roosevelt

E Roosevelt Rd

10

11

W 13th St

E 13th St

1/4 mile

.25 km

With all the student-friendly dining near the Columbia College campus, the upscale **Mercat a la Planxa** is a welcome addition, offering elegant tapas and lovely wines. Meanwhile, **Epic Burger** offers trendy organic burgers for about double the price of Micky D's but exactly none of whatever else goes into a Big Mac. As to be expected in a 'hood with such a dense student population, undergrads, grads, and profs alike frequent local watering holes **George's**, **Kasey's** and the **South Loop Club**.

Map

## ⊙ Landmarks

- **Columbia College Center for Book & Paper Arts** •
  1104 S Wabash Ave
  312-369-6632
  Two galleries feature changing exhibits of handmade books, paper, letterpress, and other related objects.
- **Former Elliot Ness Building** • 600 S Dearborn St
  If he sends one of yours to the hospital, you send one of his to the morgue…
- **Old Dearborn Train Station** • 47 W Polk St
  312-554-8100
  Turn-of-the-century train station with a lighted clocktower visible for several blocks. Al Capone took a train to prison from here.
- **River City** • 800 S Wells St
  A fluid cement design experiment built by architect Bertrand Goldberg in the—80s; considered a flop, but actually brilliant.

## Nightlife

- **Buddy Guy's Legends** • 700 S Wabash Ave
  312-427-1190
  One of the oldest blues clubs in Chicago, and the hardest to get a drink in.
- **George's Cocktail Lounge** • 646 S Wabash Ave
  312-427-3964
  Columbia students and faculty quaff in this dive between classes.
- **Kasey's Tavern** • 701 S Dearborn St
  312-427-7992
  108-year-old neighborhood oasis.
- **South Loop Club** • 701 S State St
  312-427-2787
  There's something creepy about this place.
- **Tantrum** • 1023 S State St
  312-939-9160
  Tucked-away, nicely appointed bar that attracts a lively South Loop following.

## 🍴Restaurants

- **Amarit** • 600 S Dearborn St
  312-939-1179 • $$
  Pretty good Thai.
- **Blackie's** • 755 S Clark St
  312-786-1161 • $
  A famous burger, lesser-known best breakfast in South Loop on Fri, Sat, Sun.

- **Bongo Room** • 1152 S Wabash Ave
  312-291-0100 • $$
  Best brunch in the South Loop. Warning, though: no booze.
- **Eleven City Diner** • 1112 S Wabash Ave
  312-212-1112 • $$
  Traditional Jewish deli.
- **Epic Burger** • 517 S State St
  312-913-1373 • $$
  Organic fast food burger joint featuring grass-fed beef. Eye roll.
- **Hackney's** • 733 S Dearborn St
  312-461-1116 • $$
  A specialty burger and onion loaf; a north shore legend since 1939.
- **Mercat a La Planxa** • 638 S Michigan Ave
  312-765-0524 • $$$$
  Precious Catalan tapas or a whole suckling pig (with 48 hour notice).
- **South Loop Club** • 701 S State St
  312-427-2787 • $
  Very casual bar/restaurant with surprisingly good kitchen.
- **SRO** • 610 S Dearborn St
  312-360-1776 • $$
  Boasting Chicago's #1 Turkey Burger.
- **Tamarind** • 614 S Wabash Ave
  312-379-0970 • $$
  Sushi and Pan-Asian; sake-based "fruitinis."
- **Trattoria Caterina** • 616 S Dearborn St
  312-939-7606 • $$
  A little touch of Italy, and a great value for Italian cuisine.

## 👜Shopping

- **Arts & Artisans** • 720 S Michigan Ave
  312-786-6224
  Art Gallery
- **Loopy Yarns** • 47 W Polk St
  312-583-9276
  For all your knitting needs. Classes, too.
- **Sandmeyer's Bookstore** • 714 S Dearborn St
  312-922-2104
  Dream come true if you love books and atmosphere.

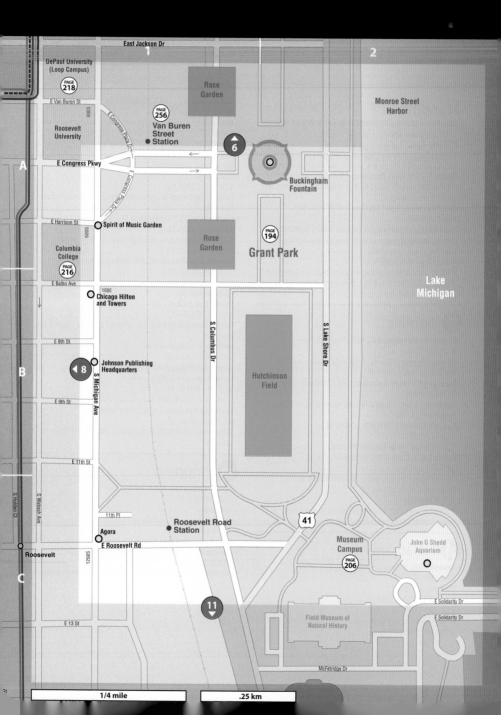

Built atop the rubble of the Great Chicago Fire of 1871, **Grant Park** is now affectionately known as Chicago's front yard. Ring the doorbell for a spectacular view, no matter where you turn: the skyline to the north, Lake Michigan to the east, Museum Campus to the south or the gardens of the park itself.

## ○ Landmarks

- **Agora** • S Michigan Ave & E Roosevelt Rd
  If you've ever wanted to see 106 headless metal people, here's where you can.
- **Buckingham Fountain** • 500 S Columbus Dr
  312-742-7529
  Built of pink marble; inspired by Versailles.
- **Hilton Chicago** • 720 S Michigan Ave
  312-922-4400
  Check out the frescoes in the lobby; sneak a kiss in the palatial ballroom.
- **Johnson Publishing Headquarters** •
  820 S Michigan Ave
  312-322-9200
  Largest African-American-owned publishing company, home of Ebony and Jet magazines.
- **Shedd Aquarium** • 1200 S Lake Shore Dr
  312-692-2723
  Marine and freshwater creatures from around the world are on view in this 1929 Classical Greek-inspired Beaux Arts structure.
- **Spirit of Music Garden** • 601 S Michigan Ave
  Where the city struts during Chicago SummerDance.

## Restaurants

- **Oysy** • 888 S Michigan Ave
  312-922-1127 • $$$
  Chic, industrial sushi setting.
- **Yolk** • 1120 S Michigan Ave
  312-789-9655 • $$
  Bright, clean brunch spot with eggs o'plenty.

## Shopping

- **The Spertus Shop** • 610 S Michigan Ave
  312-322-1740
  Unique Hanukkah gifts include yiddishwear and the Moses action figure.

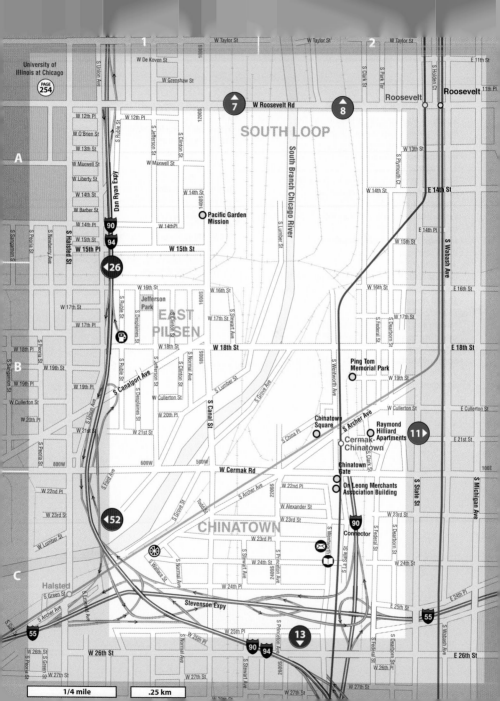

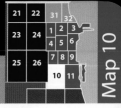

Map 10

Nestled between the University of Illinois at Chicago campus and the official South Side, East Pilsen gives artists, families and hipsters all a place to call home. The neighborhood's up and coming qualities haven't quite up and came, making rent more affordable than most of its northern counterparts. Celebrate the Chinese New Year just across the river with street sales reminiscent of Shanghai.

## ○ Landmarks

- **Chinatown Gate** •
  S Wentworth Ave & W Cermak Rd
  Built in 1976. The characters on the gate read "The world belongs to the people."
- **Hilliard Apartments** • 2111 S Clark St
  312-225-3715
  Another Bertrand Golberg gem going from subsidized senior housing to mixed-income residential.
- **On Leong Merchants Association Building** •
  2216 S Wentworth Ave
  312-328-1188
  1926 building inspired by architecture of the Kwangtung district of China. Now the home of the Pui Tak Center.
- **Pacific Garden Mission** • 1458 S Canal St
  312-492-9410
  America's oldest continuously-operating rescue mission with free showings of long running radio drama Unshackled!
- **Ping Tom Park** • 300 W 19th St
  Park with Chinese landscape elements.

## 🍴 Restaurants

- **Ahjoomah's Apron** • 218 W Cermak Rd
  312-326-2800 • $$
  Lone taste of Korea amidst dim sum and duck sauce.
- **Chi Cafe** • 2160 S Archer Ave
  312-842-9993 • $
  Crowd-pleasing Pan-Asian.
- **Double Li** • 228 W Cermak Rd
  312-842-7818 • $$
  Authenic Schezuan in nondescript space.
- **Emperor's Choice** • 2238 S Wentworth Ave
  312-225-8800 • $
  Start with seafood; finish with tea.
- **Evergreen** • 2411 S Wentworth Ave
  312-225-8898 • $$
  More upscale than most Chinatown grub.
- **Joy Yee's Noodles** • 2159 South China Place
  312-842-8928 • $$
  Huge portions of Korean and Chinese, plus bubble tea.

- **Lao Sze Chuan** • 2172 S Archer Ave
  312-326-5040 • $
  Authentic Chinese dishes plus great evening karaoke.
- **Phoenix** • 2131 S Archer Ave
  312-328-0848 • $
  The best Chinese breakfast in town.
- **Saint's Alp Teahouse** • 2131 S Archer Ave
  312-842-1886 • $
  Hong Kong chain bears bubble tea.
- **Three Happiness** • 209 W Cermak Rd
  312-842-1964 • $
  Long waits for dim sum.
- **Won Kow** • 2237 S Wentworth Ave
  312-842-7500 • $
  Cheap, tasty dim sum.

## 🛍 Shopping

- **Chinatown Bazaar** • 2221 S Wentworth Ave
  312-225-1088
  Part clothing store, part knick-knack shop.
- **Feida Bakery** • 2228 S Wentworth Ave
  312-808-1113
  Tasty Chinese baked goods.
- **Giftland** • 2212 S Wentworth Ave
  312-225-0088
  With a premium on Hello Kitty and other sorts of "Asian adorableness."
- **Pacific Furniture** • 2200 S Wentworth Ave
  312-808-0456
  Mostly home furnishings.
- **Sun Sun Tong Co.** • 2260 S Wentworth Ave
  312-842-6398
  Stock up on Chinese herbs and teas.
- **Ten Ren Tea** • 2247 S Wentworth Ave
  312-842-1171
  The only place to buy ginseng.
- **Woks 'n' Things** • 2234 S Wentworth Ave
  312-842-0701
  Stir-fry utensils and cookware.

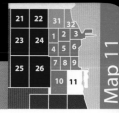

Map 11

In the summer, joggers and bicyclists crowd the lakefront trail and soak in the sun in Burnham Park. Once temperatures reach a friendly sub-zero reading in December, Bears fans turn parking lots into 6:30 a.m. Sunday Funday spots. Throughout the year, **McCormick Place** looms over the neighborhood to welcome meetings, trade shows and business gatherings of all kinds.

## ○ Landmarks

- **Adler Planetarium** • 1300 S Lake Shore Dr
  312-922-7827
  Depression era wonder that thrilled millions at 1933 Century of Progress Exposition.
- **America's Courtyard** • 1300 S Lake Shore Dr
  A spiral of stones that echoes both the Milky Way and ancient structures. Designed by Denise Milan and Ary R. Perez.
- **Chicago Women's Park and Gardens** • 1800 S Prairie Ave
  312-328-0821
  A garden from a former first lady.
- **Clarke House Museum** • 1827 S Indiana Ave
  312-326-1480
  Built in 1836 by an unknown architect, this Greek Revival-style home has been relocated twice and is now an official Chicago landmark.
- **The Field Museum** • 1400 S Lake Shore Dr
  312-922-9410
  Go to see Sue, world's largest known T. Rex; stay for the jam-packed halls of vaguely macabre taxidermy.
- **Hyatt Regency McCormick Place** • 2233 S King Dr
  312-567-1234
  The only hotel attached to the city's main convention center.
- **McCormick Place** • 2301 S Lake Shore Dr
  312-791-7000
  Hard to miss.
- **National Veterans Art Museum** • 1801 S Indiana Ave
  312-326-0270
  Features art about the war created by Vietnam veterans from all sides of the conflict.
- **Northerly Island Park** • 1400 S Linn White Dr
  312-745-2910
  Greenspace now encompassing former site of Meigs Field airport.
- **Quinn Chapel African Methodist Episcopal Church** • 2401 S Wabash Ave
  312-791-1846
  Built in 1892, this Victorian Gothic-style church houses Chicago's oldest African-American congregation.
- **Second Presbyterian Church** • 1936 S Michigan Ave
  312-225-4951
  Reconstructed in 1900 by Howard Van Doren Shaw, this ponderous Gothic Revival-style church has stained glass by Tiffany.
- **Soldier Field** • 1410 Museum Campus Dr
  312-235-7000
  Once on the National Register of Historic places, this renovated monster is home to Da Bears.
- **The Wheeler Mansion** • 2020 S Calumet Ave
  312-945-2020
  This Second Empire-style mansion now houses a boutique hotel for high-end travelers.
- **Willie Dixon's Blues Heaven Foundation** •
  2120 S Michigan Ave
  312-808-1286
  Former Chess Records studio. Tours, exhibits, workshops, and performances.

## 🍸 Nightlife

- **M Lounge** • 1520 S Wabash Ave
  312-447-0201
  Chic lounge with live jazz.
- **Reggie's** • 2105 S State St
  312-949-0120
  Record store, all-age live music venue, and sports bar & grill all in one place.
- **Square 1** • 1400 S Michigan Ave
  847-414-3699
  Craft brews, cocktails and…wait for it…self-service wine dispensers.
- **Wabash Tap** • 1233 S Wabash Ave
  312-360-9488
  South Loop, no ties, relax-after-work joint.

## 🍴 Restaurants

- **Chef Luciano** • 49 E Cermak Rd
  312-326-0062 • $
  Walk-in restaurant with eclectic entrees; Italian/African/Cajun influences.
- **Chicago Firehouse Restaurant** • 1401 S Michigan Ave
  312-786-1401 • $$$$
  Transformed Chicago firehouse complete with pole and fine dining.
- **Gioco** • 1312 S Wabash Ave
  312-939-3870 • $$$
  Great Italian dining.
- **Kroll's** • 1736 S Michigan Ave
  312-235-1400 • $$
  Chicago outpost of Green Bay grill. Packers Backers better watch their backs.
- **La Cantina Grill** • 1911 S Michigan Ave
  312-842-1911 • $$
  Comfy Mexican with no surprises.
- **Nepal House** • 1301 S Michigan Ave
  312-922-0601 • $$
  Nepalese and Himalayan cuisine.
- **Tapas Valencia** • 1530 S State St
  312-842-4444 • $$
  Par for the course tapas for the South Loop.
- **Triad Sushi Lounge** • 1933 S Indiana Ave
  312-225-8833 • $$$
  Guess what? Another sleek sushi lounge.
- **Waffles** • 1400 S Michigan Ave
  312-854-8572 • $$
  Your morning made better with syrup.
- **Zapatista** • 1307 S Wabash Ave
  312-435-1307 • $$
  Fancified Mexican food in big, loud environment.

## 🛍 Shopping

- **Blue Star Auto Stores** • 2001 S State St
  312-225-7174
  All your auto needs.
- **Cycle Bike Shop** • 1465 S Michigan Ave
  312-987-1080
  Bike shop, obviously.
- **Waterware** • 1829 S State St
  312-225-4549

# Map 12 · **Bridgeport (West)**

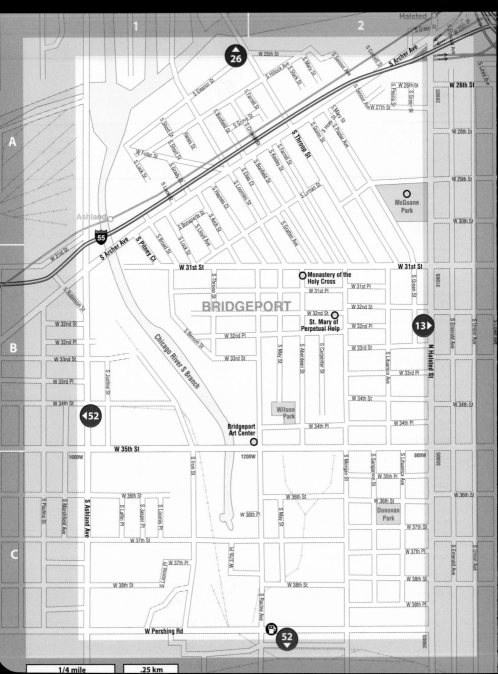

Nestled just north of the old stockyards, this working-class neighborhood's plentiful land and warehouses ripe for conversions have spurred a recent wave of development and given rise to a bustling arts district. Most notable is tony Bridgeport Village, set smack-dab on a stretch of the Chicago River known as Bubbly Creek, so-named for its gaseous stew made from the animal carcasses dumped in it by the former stockyards. Its banks now boast pricey homes, but the bubbles still linger.

## ○ Landmarks

- **McGuane Park** • 2901 S Poplar Ave
  312-747-6497
  A park for playing.
- **Monastery of the Holy Cross** •
  3111 S Aberdeen St
  773-927-7424
  Have your breakfast served by monks in this bed and breakfast monastery.
- **St Mary of Perpetual Help** • 1039 W 32nd St
  773-927-6646
  Built in the 1880s, this was the first Polish Roman Catholic Church in the US to be consecrated.

## Nightlife

- **Maria's Packaged Goods & Community Bar** •
  960 W 31st St
  773-890-0588
  Liquor store and bar with artisanal beers and craft cocktails.

## Restaurants

- **Ed's Potsticker House** • 3139 S Halsted St
  312-326-6898 • $$
  Authentic Northern Chinese cuisine in the heart of Bridgeport.
- **Pleasant House Bakery** • 964 W 31st St
  773-523-7437 • $$
  Handmade meat/vegetables pies, pasties and other British classics.
- **Polo Cafe and Catering** • 3322 S Morgan St
  773-927-7656 • $$$
  Frequented by Bridgeport locals, and famous for their 'Bloody Mary Brunch.'

## Shopping

- **Bridgeport Antique Mall** • 2963 S Archer Ave
  773-927-9070
  Old stuff.
- **Unique Thrift Store** • 3000 S Halsted St
  312-842-0942
  Half-off Mondays and Early-Bird Thursdays!

Bridgeport exemplifies how the "City That Works" actually works. The stomping grounds of the Daley family and de facto political center of the city, Bridgeport is also the quintessential Chicago neighborhood with its close-knit residents, legions of patronage workers, and distinctive "dese, dem, and dose" vernacular.

| 15 | 16 | 17 | |
|----|----|----|----|
| 54 | 57 | 18 | 19 | 20 |

Map

## ◦ Landmarks

- **Illinois Institute of Technology** •
  31st to 35th St, b/w Dan Ryan Expy & Michigan Ave
  312-567-3000
  Mies van der Rohe designed campus. Jewel in the crown? Crown Hall of course.
- **Old Neighborhood Italian American Club** •
  3031 S Shields Ave
  312-326-6420
  Founded by Angelo LaPietra, a former high-ranking Chicago mobster, after his release from Leavenworth.
- **Richard J Daley House** • 3536 S Lowe Ave
  Childhood home of Mayor Richard J. Daley.
- **Richard J. Daley Library Fountain** •
  3400 S Halsted St
  Pretty water.

## Nightlife

- **Bernice's Tavern** • 3238 S Halsted St
  312-907-1580
  60+ year-old dive bar with live music and open mics.
- **Ethyl's Party** • 2600 S Wentworth Ave
  312-326-3811
  Funeral home turned neighborhood bar-with free snacks on weekends.
- **Schaller's Pump** • 3714 S Halsted St
  773-376-6332
  Neighborhood Sox bar with grub.

Map

15 16 17
54  57 18 19 20

The South Side proves that you don't have to be glitzy to get the job done. Ditto for the much-maligned US Cellular Field, where pure baseball and terrific sight lines trump drunken revelry at crosstown Wrigley. Aside from ballpark fare, **Schaller's Pump** serves the best steak sandwich and hash browns in town.

##  Restaurants

- **All Star Stand** • 333 W 35th St
  312-559-1212 •
  Multifarious food offerings between innings.
- **Carbon** • 300 W 26th St
  312-225-3200 • $
  So what if they use gas? The food is still delicious.
- **Franco's Ristorante** • 300 W 31st St
  312-225-9566 • $$
  Family-style Italian near Sox park.
- **Freddie's** • 701 W 31st St
  312-808-0147 • $
  Italian ice, beef sandwiches, and appropriate attitude.
- **Gemellato Ristorante** • 260 W 26th St
  312-706-8081 • $$$
  Slightly more upscale Italian fare with huge menu and equally big portions.
- **Gio's** • 2724 S Lowe Ave
  312-225-6368 • $
  BYOB Italian deli with groceries.
- **Golden Horse Carriage** • 2826 S Wentworth Ave
  312-949-9222 • $
  Great egg custard tarts and daily lunch specials at this Chinese bakery.
- **Grand Palace** • 225 W 26th St
  312-225-3888 • $
  Cheap eats and authentic homestyle Chinese food at this hole-in-the-wall.
- **Han 202** • 605 W 31st St
  312-949-1314 • $$$
  Trendy BYOB featuring an eclectic Asian/Fusion menu.

- **Kevin's Hamburger Heaven** • 554 W Pershing Rd
  773-924-5771 • $
  Hamburgers and milkshakes.
- **Maxwell Street Depot** • 411 W 31st St
  312-326-3514 • $
  Counter-service only joint serving signature pork chop sandwiches 24 hours a day.
- **Nana** • 3267 S Halsted St
  312-929-2486 • $$$
  Organic, sustainable, locally sourced restaurant famous for their brunches.
- **New Furama Restaurant** • 2828 S Wentworth Ave
  312-225-6888 • $$
  Great dim sum; far easier to find parking than in Chinatown.
- **Pancho Pistolas** • 700 W 31st St
  312-225-8808 • $$$
  Two words: Eggs and beans.
- **Phil's Pizza** • 1102 W 35th St
  773-523-0947 • $
  Pizza-rific.
- **Schaller's Pump** • 3714 S Halsted St
  773-376-6332 • $
  Try the steak sandwiches and hash browns.
- **Scoops** • 608 W 31st St
  312-842-3300 • $
  Family-owned ice cream parlor serving up old-fashioned shakes and other desserts.
- **Stages** • 657 W 31st St
  312-225-0396 • $
  Fuel up at this diner attached to a gas station.
- **Wing Yip Chop Suey** • 537 W 26th St
  312-326-2822 • $
  Nader bumper sticker on window.

## 🛍 Shopping

- **Ace Bakery** • 3241 S Halsted St
  312-225-4973
  Excellent breads and pastries.
- **Augustine's Eternal Gifts & Spiritual Goods** •
  3327 S Halsted St
  773-843-1933
  Mystical and religious knick-knacks.
- **Biscotti's Galore and More** • 3160 S Wells St
  312-842-7670
  Italian cookies by the tray.
- **Health King Enterprise & Balanceuticals Group** • 238 W 31st St
  312-567-9978
  Natural remedies.
- **Henry's Sports & Bait Shop** • 3130 S Canal St
  312-225-8538
  Fishing mecca.
- **Let's Boogie Records & Tapes** • 3321 S Halsted St
  773-254-0139
  Pick up some vintage vinyl here.
- **Monster Island Toys** • 3335 S Halsted St
  773-247-5733
  Self-proclaimed Godzilla superstore with great selection of imported Japanese figurines.

# Map 14 • Prairie Shores / Lake Meadows

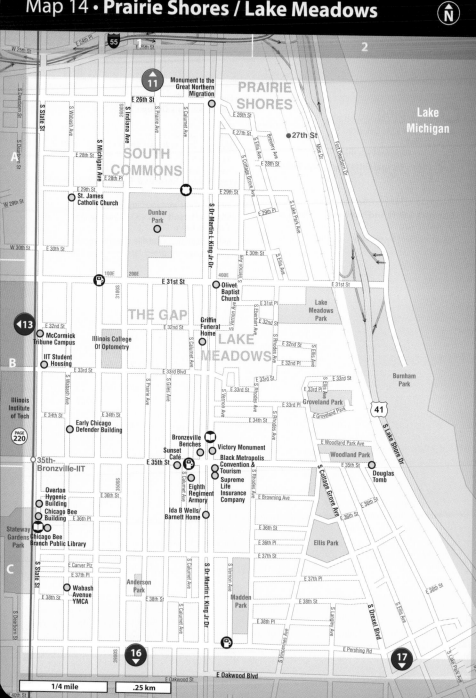

Named after two rather imposing urban apartment complexes, this area has experienced a recent rebirth with the expansion of the nearby Illinois Institute of Technology campus. An influx of student residents, plenty of green space, and its proximity to the Loop and lakefront have made this area one of the fastest growing new residential communities in Chicago.

## ○ Landmarks

- **Black Metropolis Convention & Tourism Council** •
3501 S King Dr
773-373-2865
Information central for questions on everything Bronzeville.
- **Bronzeville 1st Bed & Breakfast** • 3911 S King Dr
773-373-8081
Fine lodging in the old Goldblatt mansion.
- **Bronzeville Benches** •
S King Jr Dr b/w E 33rd St & E 35th St
13 artists created these 24 unique bench sculptures. Sit on them.
- **Chicago Bee Building** • 3647 S State St
Formerly the HQ of the *Chicago Bee* Newspaper; now offices.
- **Chicago Bee Public Library** • 3647 S State St
312-747-6872
Originally home of black newspaper, *Chicago Bee*.
- **Douglas Tomb** • 636 E 35th St
312-225-2620
Resting place of Lincoln's nemesis, overlooking tracks of Illinois Central railroad and the subdivision he founded. The entrance is on the east side of Lake.
- **Dunbar Park** • 300 E 31st St
312-747-6287
Dunbar High's girl's softball team plays here.
- **Early Chicago Defender Building** •
3435 S Indiana Ave
Originally an 1899 synagogue, was home of *Chicago Defender* from 1920-1940.
- **Eighth Regiment Armory** • 3533 S Giles Ave
First armory built in US for black regiment, 1914-1918, now a Chicago public high school.
- **Griffin Funeral Home** • 3232 S King Dr
312-842-3232
Site of Civil War era Camp Douglas, with Civil War museum, founder forefather drilled there.
- **Ida B Wells-Barnett Home** • 3624 S King Dr
Former home of the journalism and civil rights pioneer.
- **McCormick Tribune Campus Center** •
3201 S State St
Student center wrapped around the L. Wow!
- **Monument to the Great Northern Migration** •
S King Dr & E 26th St
Statue by Alison Sarr depicts a man with a briefcase atop a pile of old shoes. Represents the journey of African Americans from the south.
- **Olivet Baptist Church** • 3101 S King Dr
312-538-0124
Church with a longstanding tradition of civil rights organizing ranging from abolitionist and feminist mass meetings to Black Panther Party programs.

- **Overton Hygenic Building** • 3619 S State St
Former headquarters of foremost producer of black cosmestics.
- **St James Catholic Church** • 2942 S Wabash Ave
312-842-1919
Traditional community caretaking that included caring for Confederate POWs at Camp Douglas
- **State Street Village (IIT Student Housing)** • 3303 S State St
312-808-9771
Supercool housing for this iconic institute.
- **Sunset Café** • 315 E 35th St
One of Chicago's earliest and most legendary jazz venues.
- **Supreme Life Insurance Company Head Office** •
3501 S King Dr
Built in 1921 and remodeled in 1950, this former major black insurance company enoys new life as a mixed commercial structure.
- **Victory Monument** • S King Dr & E 35th St
Early postwar tribute to WWI's black Eighth Regiment of the Illinois National Guard that served as part of the US 370th Infantry in France.
- **Wabash Avenue YMCA** • 3763 S Wabash Ave
Since 1913 provided housing and job training for new black arrivals from the South, where the Association for the Study of Negro Life and History, the first group devoted to black studies, was founded in 1915.

## Restaurants

- **Hong Kong Delight** • 327 E 35th St
312-842-2929 • $$
Not quite like being there, but close enough.
- **Mississippi's Ricks** • 3351 S King Dr
312-791-0090 • $$
Unassuming BBQ joint tucked away in a strip mall.
- **Pearl's Place** • 3901 S Michigan Ave
773-285-1700 • $
Mama's soul food at a snail's pace.

## Shopping

- **Ashley Stewart** •
3455 S Dr Martin Luther King Jr Dr
312-567-0405
Clothes for your curves.

# Map 15 • Cana

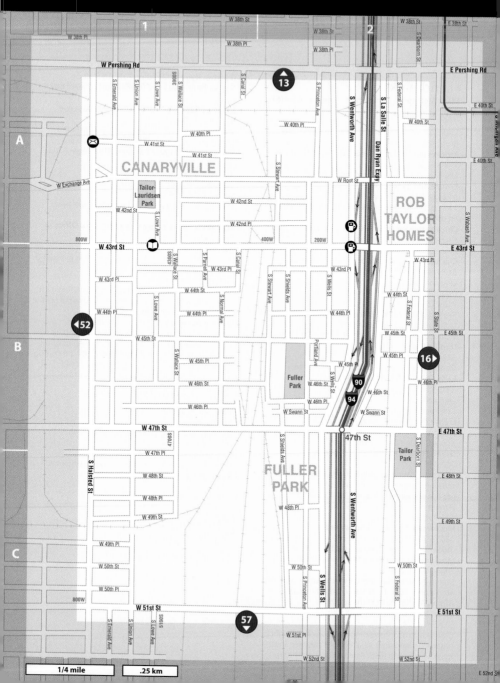

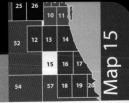

Christmas 1865 was a bad day for livestock, as the sprawling Union Stock Yards opened, all beasts on the lookout. All that's left now is the imposing limestone gate (moment of silence). While cattle around the country breathed a collective sigh when the Yards closed, this area headed south afterward and is still in recovery.

# Nightlife

• **Kelley's Tavern** • 4403 S Wallace St
773-924-0796
A neighborhood place.

# Restaurants

• **Amelia's Mestizo Grill** • 4559 S Halsted St
773-538-8200 • $$
Accomplished menu as surprising as their unlikely locale.

Map 15

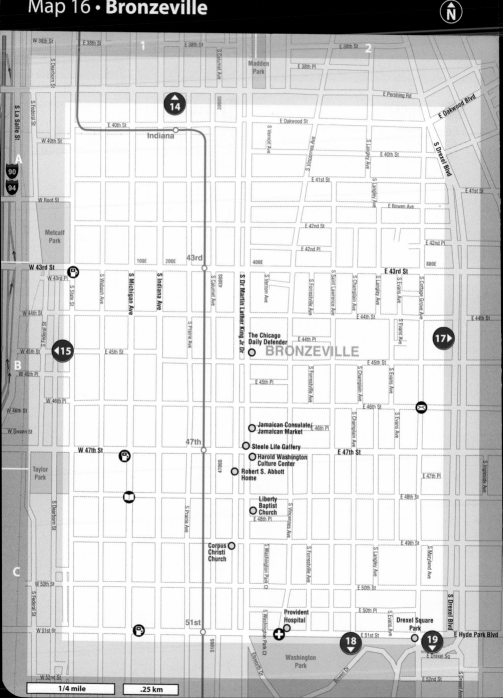

# Map 16 · **Bronzeville**

N

1

2

W 38th St
E 38th St
E 38th St
S Calumet Ave
Madden Park
E 38th Pl
E Pershing Rd
E Oakwood Blvd
S Dearborn St
S La Salle St
E 40th St
Indiana
14
S Vernon Ave
S Saint Lawrence Ave
E Oakwood St
S Langley Ave
E 40th St
S Drexel Blvd
90
94
A
W 40th St
E 41st St
E 41st St
W Root St
E Bowen Ave
E 42nd St
Metcalf Park
E 42nd Pl
E 42nd St
E 42nd Pl
100E
200E
400E
800E
43rd
W 43rd St
E 43rd St
W 43rd Pl
S State St
S Wabash Ave
S Michigan Ave
S Indiana Ave
S Calumet Ave
S Prairie Ave
S Dr Martin Luther King Jr Dr
S Vernon Ave
S Forrestville Ave
S Saint Lawrence Ave
S Champlain Ave
S Langley Ave
S Evans Ave
S Cottage Grove Ave
W 44th St
E 44th St
S Evans Ave
15
The Chicago Daily Defender
E 44th Pl
17
E 44th Pl
W 45th St
E 45th St
BRONZEVILLE
S Forrestville Ave
S Champlain Ave
S Evans Ave
E 44th St
W 45th Pl
E 45th St
E 45th Pl
W 46th Pl
W 46th St
E 46th Pl
W Swann St
Jamaican Consulate/ Jamaican Market
E 46th Pl
S Evans Ave
Steele Life Gallery
E 47th St
S Ingleside Ave
W 47th St
Harold Washington Culture Center
47th
S Prairie Ave
S 47th St
Robert S. Abbott Home
E 47th Pl
Taylor Park
Liberty Baptist Church
E 48th St
S Dearborn St
S Vincennes Ave
E 48th Pl
E 49th St
S Langley Ave
S Maryland Ave
S Drexel Blvd
Corpus Christi Church
E 49th St
C
W 50th St
W 50th St
S Federal St
51st
S Washington Park Ct
S Forrestville Ave
E 50th Pl
E 50th Pl
Drexel Square Park
W 51st St
Provident Hospital
S Evans Ave
E 51st St
18
19
E Hyde Park Blvd
S Drexel Blvd
W 52nd St
S Washington Park Ct
Bowen Dr
Washington Park
Elsworth Dr
E Drexel Sq
E 52nd St
S Drexel Blvd

1/4 mile  .25 km

Once the glorious heart of Chicago's African-American community, Bronzeville is in the midst of an impressive 21st century urban renewal. Decades of poverty, crime, empty lots and dilapidated housing projects have given way to yuppie transplants, restored greystones, and glitzy condos.

## Landmarks

- **The Chicago Daily Defender** • 4445 S King Dr
  312-225-2400
  Founded in 1905, it was the country's most influential black newspaper through the '50s. Still in operation, but much-diminished.
- **Corpus Christi Church** • 4900 S King Dr
  773-285-7720
  Built in 1921 for a predominately Irish parish that rapidly evolved into a predominately black parish.
- **Drexel Square Park** • 5101 S Cottage Grove Ave
  Victorian gem boasting city's oldest surviving fountain donated by prominent banking family.
- **Harold Washington Cultural Center** •
  4701 S King Dr
  773-373-1900
  Beautiful homage to the late mayor; it's a jaw-dropping technology & arts center.
- **Jamaican Consulate/Jamaican Market Place** •
  4655 S King Dr
  773-373-8988
  A bit of Kingston on the Old South Side.
- **Liberty Baptist Church** • 4849 S King Dr
  773-268-6757
  An afrocentric 1958 Go-Go styled temple considered King's original Chicago workshop.
- **Provident Hospital** • 500 E 51st St
  312-527-2000
  Now county controlled, this century old hospital was the first to train black doctors and nurses and the site of the first successful open heart surgery.
- **Robert S Abbott Home** • 4742 S King Dr
  Former home of *Chicago Defender* founder.
- **Steele Life Gallery** • 4655 S King Dr
  773-538-4773
  House of art that inspires the people.

## Nightlife

- **Jokes and Notes** •
  4641 S Martin Luther King Dr
  773-373-3390
  Upscale comedy/jazz club on fire, with stainless steel bar.

## Restaurants

- **Abundance Bakery** • 105 E 47th St
  773-373-1971 • $$
  Neighborhood bakery famous for cobblers and caramel upside-down cakes.
- **Ain't She Sweet** • 526 E 43rd St
  773-373-3530 • $
  Fresh, hearty sandwiches, yummy treats and uncompromised service.
- **Chicago's Home of Chicken & Waffles** •
  3947 S King Dr
  773-536-3300 • $$$
  Authentic Southern classics, including their famous fried chicken and waffles.
- **Harold's Chicken Shack** • 108 E 47th St
  773-285-8362 • $
  It may say #7 but it is #1 around here.
- **Le Fleur de Lis** • 301 E 43rd St
  773-268-8770 • $$$
  An authentic taste of New Orleans and Southern cooking.

## Shopping

- **Ibiza Couture** • 233 E 47th St
  773-924-5199
  High-fashion hip-hop rock star gear & denim.
- **Issues Barber & Beauty Salon** •
  3958 S Cottage Grove Ave
  773-924-4247
  Beauty salon.
- **Jordan's Closets** • 106 E 51st St
  773-624-4104
  Adorable resale shop for sassy little girls and fashionista mommies.
- **Sensual Steps** • 4518 S Cottage Grove Ave
  773-548-3338
  A sanctuary for fancy kicks, handbags, camisoles, jewelry, and shawls by black designers.

Many a 19th-century suburb prided itself on wide lawns and tranquil settings, and Kenwood was no exception. Though it was annexed to Chicago over a century ago, the suburban feeling lingers. These days, the architecturally-enriched neighborhood contains everything from the residence of Louis Farrakhan to the oldest Jewish congregation in the city, KAM Isaiah Israel.

| 15 | 16 | 17 | |
|----|----|----|----|
| 54 | 57 | 18 | 19 | 20 |

## ○ Landmarks

- **Barack Obama's Chicago Residence** •
  5046 S Greenwood Ave
  Chicago home of the 44th President.
- **George Blossom House** • 4858 S Kenwood Ave
  Frank Lloyd Wright's early work—note the Roman influences.
- **Hyde Park Art Center** • 5020 S Cornell Ave
  773-324-5520
  Has plenty of visual arts activities for the shorties and grown folk. Check out the Cocktails & Clay night!
- **KAM Isaiah Israel** • 1100 E Hyde Park Blvd
  Oldest Jewish congregation in the city.
- **Louis Farrakhan Home** • 4855 S Woodlawn Ave
  Well-guarded home of the leader of the Nation of Islam.
- **Rainbow/PUSH Coalition Headquarters** •
  930 E 50th St
  773-373-3366
  Originally the 1924 home of KAM Isaiah Israel, Chicago's oldest Jewish congreation, with late 1940s addition.
- **Warren McArthur House** • 4852 S Kenwood Ave
  More work by Frank Lloyd Wright, still tethered to Louis Sullivan.

## 🍴 Restaurants

- **Fung's Chop Suey** • 1400 E 47th St
  773-924-2328 • $
  When you're thinking delivery.
- **Lake Shore Café** • 4900 S Lake Shore Dr
  773-288-5800 • $$
  Basic hotel food.

## 🛍 Shopping

- **Fort Smith** • 1007 E 43rd St
  773-268-8200
  Stylish boutique featuring apparel, jewelry, and accessories designed in-house.
- **Gamestop** • 1400 E 47th St
  773-285-3215
  Teen boys' hang-out.
- **Goree Shop** • 1122 E 47th St
  773-285-1895
  Fabric and crafts boutique featuring Senegalese and other imported items.
- **Max & Co. Hair Designs** • 1453 E Hyde Park Blvd
  773-288-2255
  The place to go if you need to straighten every kink on your nappy little head.

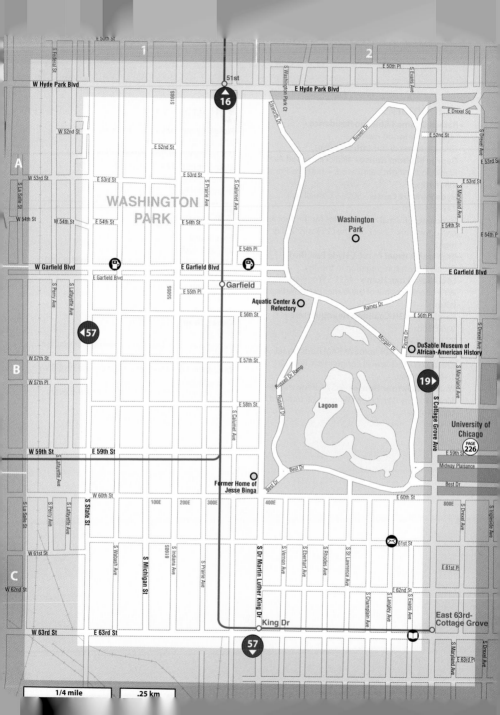

Map 18

Anchored by its namesake park and the **DuSable Museum**, one of the nation's most important institutions dedicated to African American history and culture, this area has seen a bit of urban renewal lately. **Washington Park** itself is a registered historic district and features Lorado Taft's 127-foot-long concrete sculpture, Fountain of Time, at its eastern gate, as well as a pond, track and swimming pool.

## ○ Landmarks

- **Aquatic Center & Refectory** • 5531 S King Dr
  773-256-1248
  Designed by Daniel Burnham's firm, the Refectory now holds locker rooms for the Aquatic Center and its 36-foot waterslide.
- **DuSable Museum of African American History** •
  740 E 56th Pl
  773-947-0600
  Founded in 1961 and dedicated to preserving and honoring African-American culture. The oldest non-profit institution of its kind.
- **Former Home of Jesse Binga** • 5922 S King Dr
  Home of nation's first African-American banker.
- **Washington Park** •
  5531 S Dr Martin Luther King Jr Dr
  773-256-1248
  A sprawling 367-acre park with beautiful lagoons and fields. Check out the "Fountain of Time" sculpture in the southeast corner of the park.

## Nightlife

- **Odyssey II** • 211 E Garfield Blvd
  773-947-0956
  So laid back, they don't even have set hours.

## Restaurants

- **Miss Lee's Good Food** • 203 E Garfield Blvd
  773-752-5253 • $
  Soul food carry-out by ex-Gladys' Luncheonette.
- **Ms. Biscuit** • 5431 S Wabash Ave
  773-268-8088 • $
  Popular neighborhood brunch spot known for homemade hot biscuits.

## Shopping

- **The Cat's Meow** • 6107 S Martin Luther King Dr
  773-684-3220
  Sexy lingerie, games, toys, and other classy smut to keep his attention.

# Map 19 · **Hyde Park**

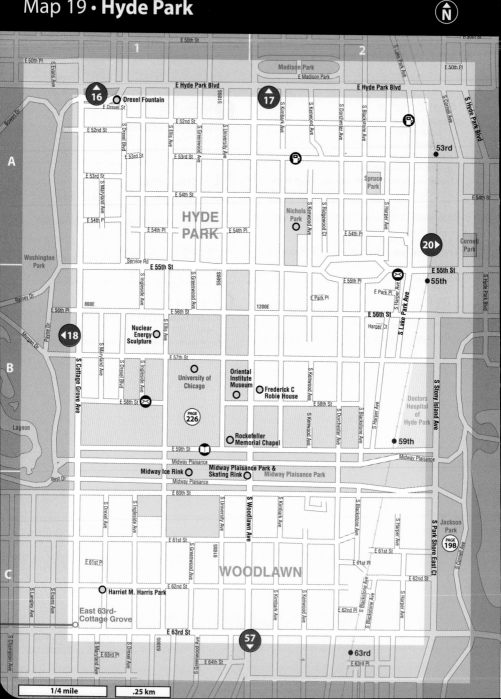

Madison Park
E Madison Park
E Hyde Park Blvd
E Hyde Park Blvd

**16** Drexel Fountain
**17**

E Drexel St
E 52nd St
E 53rd St
E 53rd St
E 54th St
E 54th St
E 54th Pl

Spruce Park

53rd

**HYDE PARK**

Nichols Park

E 54th Pl
E 54th Pl
E 54th St

**20**

Cornell Park

Washington Park

E 55th St
E 55th St
E 55th Pl
E Park Pl

E 55th St
55th

Rainey Dr

E 56th Pl
800E
1200E
E Park Pl
E 56th St
Harper Ct

**18**

Nuclear Energy Sculpture

E 57th St

University of Chicago

Oriental Institute Museum

Frederick C Robie House

E 58th St

Doctors Hospital of Hyde Park

Lagoon

**PAGE 226**

Rockefeller Memorial Chapel

59th

E 59th St

Midway Plaisance

Midway Ice Rink

Midway Plaisance Park & Skating Rink

Midway Plaisance Park

Midway Plaisance

E 60th St

**WOODLAWN**

E 61st St
E 61st St
E 62nd St
E 62nd St

**PAGE 198**

Jackson Park

Harriet M. Harris Park

East 63rd-Cottage Grove

E 63rd St

**57**

63rd

E 63rd St
E 63rd Pl
E 64th St
E 63rd Pl

1/4 mile
.25 km

Map

| 15 | 16 | 17 |
| 54 | 57 | 18 | 19 | 20 |

A university's best attempt to summon up images of Oxford collides with its misguided efforts toward urban renewal in this neighborhood, where the student and middle classes drink in the same bars as the academics and politicians governing their lives. In one of Chicago's most racially integrated neighborhoods, ethnic dining abounds, as does artistic graffiti. Don't miss the bookstores along 57th Street; replicas of Borges's libraries?

## ○ Landmarks

- **Drexel Fountain** • 5100 S Drexel Ave
  The city's oldest remaining fountain.
- **Frederick C Robie House** • 5757 S Woodlawn Ave
  Designed by Frank Lloyd Wright; renovations proceeding, stay tuned.
- **Harriet M. Harris Park** • 6200 S Drexel Ave
  312-747-2706
  Historic Park building with Mural of Woodlawn Heroes, swimming & arts.
- **Midway Ice Rink** • Midway Plaisance
  312-745-2470
  Professors' kids collide while the speakers blare Motown and the Beatles.
- **Midway Plaisance Park & Skating Rink** •
  1130 Midway Plaisance
  312-745-2470
  Olympic-sized outdoor skating rink.
- **Nichols Park** • 1355 E 53rd St
  312-747-2703
  Home of the Parrots of Hyde Park.
- **Nuclear Energy Sculpture** • 5600 S Ellis Ave
  Birthplace of the Atomic Age.
- **The Oriental Institute** • 1155 E 58th St
  773-702-9514
  Educate yourself.
- **Rockefeller Memorial Chapel** •
  5850 S Woodlawn Ave
  773-702-2100
  Built in 1928, this English Gothic styled cathedral contains one of the world's largest carillons.
- **University of Chicago** •
  S University Ave & E 57th St
  773-702-1234
  A pretty spot for wandering on the south side.

## ▼ Nightlife

- **Checkerboard Lounge** • 5201 S Harper Ave
  773-684-1472
  This legendary blues and jazz club is back!
- **Falcon Inn** • 1601 E 53rd St
  Cheap dive of regulars where you can hide out.
- **The Pub** • 1212 E 59th St
  773-702-9737
  A basement student bar redeemed by the people-watching and wood panels.
- **Seven Ten Lanes** • 1055 E 55th St
  773-347-2695
  1920s décor in Hyde Park haven.
- **Woodlawn Tap** • 1172 E 55th St
  773-643-5516
  U of Chicago legend.

**Map**

| 15 | 16 | 17 |
| 54 | 57 | 18 | 19 | 20 |

Hyde Park boasts plentiful entertainment and dining options, including many of President Obama's favorites, such as **Valois** and **57th Street Books**. Blues and jazz fans flock to hear live music daily at the **Checkerboard Lounge**. For more upscale dining, savor the cuisine at **La Petite Folie**. The University of Chicago's Logan Arts Center built on a vibrant arts and entertainment scene.

# Restaurants

- **Bonjour Café Bakery** • 1550 E 55th St
  773-241-5300 • $
  Have a pastry and be seen.
- **Boston Market** • 1424 E 53rd St
  773-288-2600 • $
  Hyde Park outpost of the ubiquitous rotisserie chicken chain.
- **C'est Si Bon** • 643 E 47th St
  773-536-2600 • $$
  Go for Sunday Brunch.
- **Cedars Mediterranean Kitchen** • 1206 E 53rd St
  773-324-6227 • $$
  Great food, horrible service.
- **Chant** • 1509 E 53rd St
  773-324-1999 • $$$
  Upscale Asian for Hyde Parkers.
- **Daley's Restaurant** • 809 E 63rd St
  773-643-6670 • $$
  Century old restaurant serving comfort food.
- **Harold's Chicken** • 1208 E 53rd St
  773-752-9260 • $
  Buckets and buckets of crispy, crumbling chicken. Best in the 'hood.
- **Hyde Park Gyros** • 1368 E 53rd St
  773-947-8229 • $
  Gyros and Fried Mushrooms–yum!
- **Kikuya** • 1601 E 55th St
  773-667-3727 • $$
  Best sushi in the neighborhood.
- **La Petite Folie** • 1504 E 55th St
  773-493-1394 • $$$$
  The only haute cuisine in the neighborhood. Expensive and worth it.
- **Maravillas Restaurant** • 5506 S Lake Park Ave
  773-643-3155 • $
  Cheap, good Mexican. Stinging salsa. Open real late.

- **Medici on 57th** • 1327 E 57th St
  773-667-7394 • $
  The essence of life at U of C.
- **Mellow Yellow** • 1508 E 53rd St
  773-667-2000 • $
  Comfort food for morning and night.
- **Nathan's Chicago Style** • 1372 E 53rd St
  773-288-5353 • $
  A Taste of Jamaica.
- **Park 52** • 5201 S Harper Ave
  773-241-5200 • $$$
  Classic American supper club comfort food in bold, Jerry Kleiner setting.
- **Pepe's Mexican Restaurant** • 1310 E 53rd St
  773-752-9300 • $
  Damn fine guacamole. You might want it when you're high.
- **Rajun Cajun** • 1459 E 53rd St
  773-955-1145 • $
  Neon lights oversee the marriage of chicken tikka masala and cornbread.
- **Ribs 'N Bibs** • 5300 S Dorchester Ave
  773-493-0400 • $
  Finger lickin'. Wear the bib.
- **Salonica** • 1440 E 57th St
  773-752-3899 • $
  Where to go the morning after.
- **Sammy's Touch** • 5659 S Cottage Grove Ave
  773-288-2645 • $
  Gyros like you once had from a street stall in New York.
- **The Sit Down Cafe & Sushi Bar** • 1312 E 53rd St
  773-324-3700 • $$
  Sake with your caprese salad? Must be fusion.
- **Valois** • 1518 E 53rd St
  773-667-0647 • $
  See Your Food.

# Shopping

- **57th Street Books** • 1301 E 57th St
  773-684-1300
  Brainy, independent bookstore.
- **Freehling Pot & Pan** • 1365 E 53rd St
  773-643-8080
  All sorts of kitchen gadgets, plus bulk coffee and tea.
- **Futons N More** • 1370 E 53rd St
  773-324-7083
  Futons 'n' more.
- **House of Africa** • 1510 E 63rd St
  773-324-6858
  Afrocentric everything.
- **Hyde Park Produce Market** • 1226 E 53rd St
  773-324-7100
  A grocery store full of cheap produce and ethnic ingredients.

- **Hyde Park Records** • 1377 E 53rd St
  773-288-6588
  Buy/sell vintage LPs.
- **O'Gara & Wilson** • 1448 E 57th St
  773-363-0993
  Rare and out-of-print books.
- **Powell's Bookstore** • 1501 E 57th St
  773-955-7780
  Famous bookstore.
- **Toys Et Cetera** • 1502 E 55th St
  773-324-6039
  Just for fun.
- **Wesley's Shoe Corral** • 1506 E 55th St
  773-667-7463
  Quality shoes from around the world.
- **What the Traveler Saw** • 1508 E 55th St
  773-955-5055
  Gifts and accessories from over fifty cultures.

## ○Landmarks

- **Museum of Science and Industry** •
  5700 S Lake Shore Dr
  773-684-1414
  Get your geek on.
- **Osaka Garden/Wooded Island** •
  Just south of the Museum of Science and Industry,
  between the West and East Lagoons
  A Japanese garden in the middle of Jackson Park—
  why not?
- **Promontory Point Park** • 5491 S Shore Dr
  312-747-6620
  Picnic with a view.

## ●Nightlife

- **Bar Louie** • 5500 S South Shore Dr
  773-363-5300
  Corporate chain martini bar.
- **The Cove Lounge** • 1750 E 55th St
  773-684-1013
  Down-and-outers meet life-of-the-minders.

## ●Restaurants

- **Morry's Deli** • 5500 S Cornell Ave
  773-363-3800 • $
  Good on the go.
- **The Nile** • 1611 E 55th St
  773-324-9499 • $
  Varied Middle Eastern.
- **Piccolo Mondo** • 1642 E 56th St
  773-643-1106 • $$
  Best Italian in the area.
- **Siam Restaurant** • 1639 E 55th St
  773-324-9296 • $
  More Thai in Hyde Park.
- **The Snail Thai Cuisine** • 1649 E 55th St
  773-667-5423 • $
  Great Hyde Park Thai.
- **Thai 55 Restaurant** • 1607 E 55th St
  773-363-7119 • $
  Good Americanized Thai.

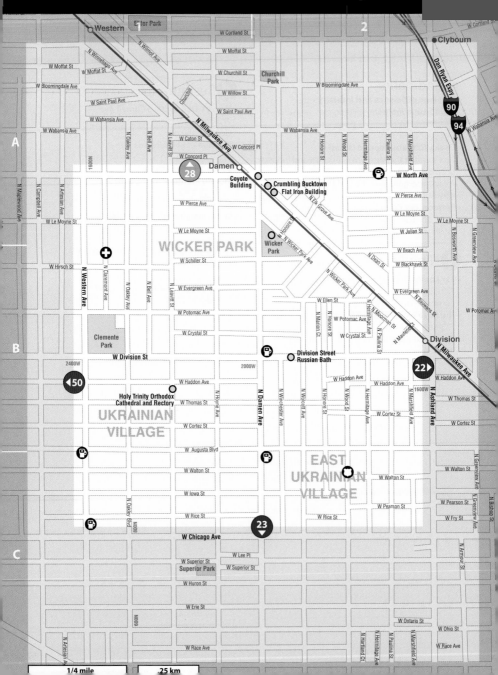

●Western
Etter Park
1

W Cortland St

2

●Clybourn

W Cortland St

N Winnebago Ave
N Wilmot Ave

W Moffat St

W Moffat St
W Moffat St

W Churchill St

Churchill
Park

W Bloomingdale Ave

Dan Ryan Expy

W Bloomingdale Ave

W Willow St

90

W Saint Paul Ave

Churchill

W Saint Paul Ave

94

N Milwaukee Ave

W Wabansia Ave

W Wabansia Ave

W Wabansia Ave

N Honore St

N Wood St

N Hermitage Ave

N Paulina St

N Marshfield Ave

W Wabansia Ave

N Oakley Ave

N Bell Ave

N Leavitt St

N Maplewood Ave

N Campbell Ave

N Artesian Ave

N0061

**A**

W Caton St

W Concord Pl

W North Ave

**28**

W Concord Pl

Damen○

W Pierce Ave

Coyote
Building

Crumbling Bucktown
Flat Iron Building

W Le Moyne St

W Le Moyne St

N Bosworth Ave

N Greenview Ave

W Pierce Ave

W Le Moyne St

W Le Moyne St

N Honore St

N Elk Grove Ave

W Julian St

W Hirsch St

N Western Ave

N Claremont Ave

N Oakley Ave

N Bell Ave

N Leavitt St

✚

W Le Moyne St

**WICKER PARK**

Wicker
Park

N Wicker Park Ave

W Beach Ave

W Blackhawk St

N Dean St

W Schiller St

W Evergreen Ave

N Wicker Park Ave

W Evergreen Ave

N Stevens St

W Evergreen Ave

N Moorman St

N Mandell St

W Potomac Ave

W Potomac Ave

W Ellen St

N Marion Ct

N Honore St

N Paulina St

N Hermitage Ave

W Potomac Ave

W Potomac Ave

W Crystal St

W Crystal St

W Crystal St

Division

**B**

Clemente
Park

W Division St

2000W

Division Street
Russian Bath

N Milwaukee Ave

2400W

**◀50**

W Haddon Ave

W Haddon Ave

W Haddon Ave

**22▶**

W Haddon Ave

Holy Trinity Orthodox
Cathedral and Rectory

N Hoyne Ave

N Damen Ave

W Thomas St

N Winchester Ave

N Wood St

N Honore St

N Wood St

N Hermitage Ave

W Cortez Ave

N Marshfield Ave

N Ashland Ave

1600W

W Thomas St

W Thomas St

**UKRAINIAN
VILLAGE**

W Thomas St

W Cortez St

W Cortez St

W Augusta Blvd

N Oakley Blvd

W Walton St

**EAST
UKRAINIAN
VILLAGE**

W Walton St

W Walton St

N Greenview Ave

W Pearson St

N Greenview Ave

N Bishop St

W Iowa St

W Pearson St

N0091

W Rice St

W Rice St

W Fry St

**23**

W Chicago Ave

**C**

N Artesian Ave

W Superior St

Superior Park

W Lee Pl

W Superior St

W Superior St

W Huron St

W Erie St

W Ontario St

N Hermitage Ct

N Paulina St

N Marshfield Ave

N Armour St

W Ohio St

W Race Ave

W Race Ave

1/4 mile

.25 km

Wicker Park/Ukrainian Village play host to a brewing battle between shiny gentrified district and gritty arts enclave. Mammoth Victorian homes and angular new constructions line the leafy and historic streets. Stroller-wielders and tattooed-cyclists share Milwaukee Avenue: each equally comfortable sipping Metropolis Coffee next to the full-size replica of a Delorean time machine at **Wormhole**. Who will ultimately claim the territory as their own? Just ask Bucktown.

## ○ Landmarks

- **Coyote Building** • 1600 N Milwaukee Ave
  This 12-story Art Deco building was constructed in 1929 and is currently a shrine to actor Peter Coyote.
- **Crumbling Bucktown** • 1579 N Milwaukee Ave
  Structural icon visible from miles away; nucleus of Around the Coyote Arts Festival.
- **Division Street Russian Bath** • 1914 W Division St
  773-384-8150
  Treat yourself to an old-school day at the spa, complete with Swedish massages and a granite heating room.

- **Flat Iron Arts Building** • 1579 N Milwaukee Ave
  This distinct triangular-shaped building is a part of the Chicago Coalition of Community Cultural Centers and houses artist studios.
- **Holy Trinity Orthodox Cathedral and Rectory** •
  1121 N Leavitt St
  773-486-6064
  Designed by Louis Sullivan to look like a Russian cathedral.
- **Wicker Park** • W Schiller St & N Damen Ave
  The homes in this district reflect the style of Old Chicago.

**Map**

| 25 | 26 | 7 | 8 | 9 |
| | | 10 | 11 | |
| 52 | 12 | 13 | 14 | |

The neighborhood's cozy artist community warily eyes the yuppies inching their way westward, and local businesses are beginning to reflect these migratory patterns. Upscale chain retailers and slick sports bars wedge themselves between indie shops and cafés. Find the two populations intermingling over gourmet tacos and tequila on **Big Star**'s summer patio. As always, Indie bands and avant-garde jazz wail through the night from **Empty Bottle**.

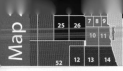 Nightlife

- **Beachwood Inn** • 1415 N Wood St
773-486-9806
Atari, potato chips, and basement-price beers.
- **Between Peruvian Cafe & Lounge** •
1324 N Milwaukee Ave
773-292-0585
Home of the beer martini.
- **The Blind Robin** • 853 N Western Ave
773-395-3002
Neighborhood dwellers flock for cheap beer and board games.
- **Club Foot** • 1824 W Augusta Blvd
773-489-0379
Cool rock bar, cheap drinks, and DJs every night.
- **Davenport's Piano Bar** • 1383 N Milwaukee Ave
773-278-1830
Once legendary skanker bar, now yuppy fern bar. Whattya gonna do?
- **Debonair Social Club** • 1575 N Milwaukee Ave
773-227-7990
Friendly and glam go hand in hand in this hipster club.
- **Double Door** • 1572 N Milwaukee Ave
773-489-3160
Top local and national alt-rock acts.
- **Empire Liquors** • 1566 N Milwaukee Ave
773-278-1600
Eclectic DJs and overflow crowds.
- **Emporium Arcade Bar** • 1366 N Milwaukee Ave
773-697-7922
Number of retro arcade games>extensive beer list.
- **Empty Bottle** • 1035 N Western Ave
773-276-3600
Avant-garde jazz and indie rock. Smells like cat.
- **Estelle's Café & Lounge** • 2013 W North Ave
773-782-0450
Last time we were here a girl puked on my shoes and no one cared.
- **The Flat Iron** • 1565 N Milwaukee Ave
773-365-9000
Average and open late.
- **Gold Star Bar** • 1755 W Division St
773-227-8700
Hear the Cars and Cash in under an hour.

- **Happy Village** • 1059 N Wolcott Ave
773-486-1512
Ping pong inside, lush beer garden outside—a divey gem.
- **High Noon Saloon** • 1560 N Milwaukee Ave
773-227-9339
Old West meets high definition.
- **Inner Town Pub** • 1935 W Thomas St
773-235-9795
Wicker Park art dorks.
- **Innjoy** • 2051 W Division St
773-394-2066
WP Scene-ster place for drinking and local acts.
- **Mana Food Bar** • 1742 W Division St
773-342-1742
Gourmet vegetarian with a global influence.
- **Ola's Liquor** • 947 N Damen Ave
773-384-7250
Polish-Ukrainian liquor store-bar (Old Style, literally and figuratively).
- **Phyllis' Musical Inn** • 1800 W Division St
773-486-9862
Divey hot-spot for local music acts.
- **Piece** • 1927 W North Ave
773-772-4422
Beer. Pizza.
- **Rainbo Club** • 1150 N Damen Ave
773-489-5999
Cool-kid mecca and favorite hang of local celeb John Cusack. Enough said.
- **Rodan** • 1530 N Milwaukee Ave
773-276-7036
Ultra modern lounge—video mirrors in the bathrooms.
- **Small Bar** • 2049 W Division St
773-772-2727
Small is the new big at this hipster-cool, cozy hang.
- **Standard Bar and Grill** • 1332 N Milwaukee Ave
773-904-8615
The name says it all at this newbie sports bar.
- **Subterranean** • 2011 W North Ave
773-278-6600
Semi-cool music spot.
- **The Violet Hour** • 1520 N Damen Ave
773-252-1500
Speakeasy that makes perfect drinks. Get there early.

# 🍴Restaurants

- **Antique Taco** • 1360 N Milwaukee Ave
  $$
  Shabby-chic taqueria.
- **Bangers & Lace** • 1670 W Division St
  773-252-6499 • $$
  Brit pub meets Wisconsin lodge.
- **Big Star** • 1531 N Damen Ave
  773-235-4039 • $$
  Pretty long wait, pretty good tacos, pretty pretty people.
- **Birchwood Kitchen** • 2211 W North Ave
  773-276-2100 • $
  Sophisticated sandwiches for grown-ups.
- **Bite Cafe** • 1039 N Western Ave
  773-395-2483 • $
  Comfy cafe, go in and get warm. Next to Empty Bottle. Eat, stay, rock.
- **Blue Fin Sushi Bar** • 1952 W North Ave
  773-394-7373 • $$$
  Upscale, trendy sushi bar.
- **Blue Line Lounge & Grill** • 1548 N Damen Ave
  773-395-3700 • $$
  Mix a diner with a Martini club and here you go.
- **Bob San** • 1805 W Division St
  773-235-8888 • $$$$
  Youthful sushi joint.
- **Briciola** • 937 N Damen Ave
  773-772-0889 • $$
  Charming al fresco dining.
- **Cumin** • 1414 N Milwaukee Ave
  773-342-1414 • $$
  Modern take on Nepalese and Indian cuisines.
- **Feast** • 1616 N Damen Ave
  773-772-7100 • $$$
  Popular for Sunday brunch.
- **The Fifty/50** • 2047 W Division St
  773-489-5050 • $
  Great inexpensive food.
- **Flash Taco** • 1570 N Damen Ave
  773-772-1997 • $
  Cheap late-night tacos.
- **Glazed & Infused** • 1553 N Damen Ave
  312-226-5556 • $
  Doughnuts are the new cupcakes.
- **Handlebar** • 2311 W North Ave
  773-384-9546 • $$
  Bicycle-themed (largely) vegetarian restaurants decorated with off-duty messengers.
- **Hash** • 1357 N Western Ave
  773-661-2964 • $
  Beyond traditional corned beef at this 70s-inspired brunch spot.
- **Jam** • 3057 W Logan Blvd
  773-292-6011 • $$
  Open for breakfast and lunch.
- **Jerry's Wicker Park** • 1938 W Division St
  773-235-1006 • $$
  Jerry's knows good sandwiches, and isn't afraid to…make them.
- **Las Palmas** • 1835 W North Ave
  773-289-4991 • $
  Great al fresco Mexican goes beyond the norm.
- **Letizia's Natural Bakery** • 2144 W Division St
  773-342-1011 • $
  Addictive sweets and savory fare that holds its own
- **Mana Food Bar** • 1742 W Division St
  773-342-1742 • $$
  Gourmet vegetarian with a global influence.
- **Milk & Honey** • 1920 W Division St
  773-395-9434 • $
  Heaven for breakfast.
- **Mirai** • 2020 W Division St
  773-862-8500 • $$
  Chic dining and good sushi.
- **The Monarch** • 1745 W North Ave
  773-252-6053 • $$
  Try the dill pickle chicken wings.
- **Native Foods Cafe** • 1484 N Milwaukee Ave
  773-489-8480 • $$
  Vegan selections made daily with a West Coast vibe.
- **Oiistar** • 1358 N Milwaukee Ave
  773-360-8791 • $$
  Pan-Asian ramen that meanders through France and Italy.
- **Picante Taqueria** • 2016 W Division St
  773-328-8800 • $
  Very very very very very small taqueria.

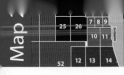

- **Piece** • 1927 W North Ave
  773-772-4422 • $$
  Beer. Pizza.
- **Red Square** • 1914 W Division St
  773-227-2284 • $$
  Russian café and spa within the historic
  bathhouse.
- **Santullo's** • 1943 W North Ave
  773-227-7960 • $
  New York-style thin crust pizza in a deep dish
  town.
- **Smoke Daddy** • 1804 W Division St
  773-772-6656 • $
  Barbecue and blues.
- **The Southern** • 1840 W North Ave
  773-342-1840 • $$
  Comfort food served up with locally sourced
  ingredients.
- **Sultan's Market** • 2057 W North Ave
  773-235-3072 • $
  Cheap Middle Eastern, groceries.
- **Takito** • 2013 W Division St
  773-687-9620 • $
  Contemporary taqueria.
- **Taxim** • 1558 N Milwaukee Ave
  773-252-1558 • $$
  Fancy, contemporary greek. Duck gyros, anyone?
- **Thai Lagoon** • 2322 W North Ave
  773-489-5747 • $$
  Great Thai, funky atmosphere.
- **Thai Village** • 2053 W Division St
  773-384-5352 • $
  Cheap, tasty, and great outdoor seating.
- **Trenchermen** • 2039 W North Ave
  773-661-1540 • $$$
  Dash of whimsy with your pickle tots and candied
  quinoa.

# 🛍 Shopping

- **Akira** • 1814 W North Ave
  773-489-0818
  High fashion for wanna-be Eurotrash.
- **Art + Science Salon** • 1552 N Milwaukee Ave
  773-227-4247
  Beakers bring you back to science class. Student
  discounts available.
- **Artemio's Bakery** • 1443 N Milwaukee Ave
  773-342-0757
  Mexican sweetstuffs.
- **Asrai Garden** • 1935 W North Ave
  773-782-0680
  Unique home accents and garden doodads.
- **Beadniks** • 1937 W Division St
  773-276-2323
  DIY activity of the 00s.
- **Broken Cherry** • 1734 W North Ave
  773-278-4000
  Rockin' boutique with custom apparel options.
- **Brooklyn Industries** • 1426 N Milwaukee Ave
  773-360-8182
  Industrial yet sustainable designs.
- **Brooklyn Industries** • 1426 N Milwaukee Ave
  773-360-8182
  All your bags are belong to us.
- **Cattails** • 1935 W Division St
  773-486-1621
  A unique flower market.
- **City Soles** • 1566 N Damen Ave
  773-489-2001
  You could wear your paycheck, one on each foot.
  But beautifully handcrafted European soles.

- **DeciBel Audio** • 1429 N Milwaukee Ave
773-862-6700
New and used stereo equipment.
- **Dr. Martens** • 1561 N Milwaukee Ave
773-489-5499
Yep, they're back.
- **FoundRe** • 2151 W Division St
773-235-3600
Custom frames and furnishings created from
salvaged wood.
- **G-Star Raw** • 1525 N Milwaukee Ave
773-342-2623
More denim than your little heart could desire.
- **Greenheart** • 1911 W Division St
312-264-1625
Fair-trade items galore!
- **iCream** • 1537 N Milwaukee Ave
773-342-2834
Techno ice cream: hydrogen robo-machine
operated.
- **John Fluevog** • 1539 N Milwaukee Ave
773-772-1983
Funky, eco-friendly shoes.
- **Lomography** • 1422 N Milwaukee Ave
872-206-2253
Analog photography makes a comeback.
- **Moon Voyage** • 2010 W Pierce Ave
773-203-8757
Luxe boho clothing, accessories and home goods.
- **Myopic Books** • 1564 N Milwaukee Ave
773-862-4882
A Wicker Park brainy-hipster institution.

- **Paper Doll** • 2027 W Division St
773-227-6950
Paper, cards, and great gifts.
- **Penelope's** • 1913 W Division St
773-395-2351
Pad your wardrobe with adorable at remarkably
reasonable prices.
- **Quimby's** • 1854 W North Ave
773-342-0910
Books and music.
- **Reckless Records** • 1532 N Milwaukee Ave
773-235-3727
Instant satisfaction for the vinyl-hungry masses.
- **Ruby Room** • 1743 W Division St
773-235-2323
A "spa for the spirit" of the chic.
- **Saint Alfred** • 1531 N Milwaukee Ave
773-486-7159
Who knew Alfred was the patron saint of super
cool sneakers?
- **Silver Moon** • 1721 W North Ave
773-235-5797
Amazing vintage.
- **The Silver Room** • 1442 N Milwaukee Ave
773-278-7130
Clothing and accessories.
- **Una Mae's** • 1528 N Milwaukee Ave
773-276-7002
A Wicker Park staple—vintage and new clothing.

# Map 22 · **Noble Square / Goose Island**

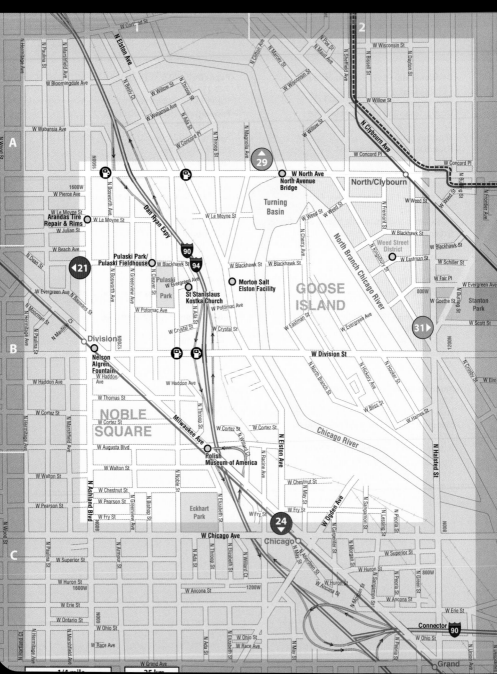

Turning Basin

GOOSE ISLAND

NOBLE SQUARE

North Avenue Bridge

North/Clybourn

Weed Street District

Stanton Park

Arandas Tire Repair & Rims

Pulaski Park/ Pulaski Fieldhouse

Pulaski Park

St Stanislaus Kostka Church

Morton Salt Elston Facility

Nelson Algren Fountain

Division

Polish Museum of America

Eckhart Park

Chicago

Connector

Grand

Gritty Goose Island industry crosses paths with arty fringes of East Ukrainian Village. Lovely historical churches exist, often buried under sca?olding. Expressway access abounds, and there's a cab stand by the **Nelson Algren Fountain** on Milwaukee. Elston is a popular route to crisscross the city. Wave to the **Morton Salt Girl** as you pass by.

## ○ Landmarks

- **Arandas Tires & Rims** • 1511 N Ashland Ave
  773-252-6292
  Glowing, plastic palm trees, metal flames on the gate, and rows of tricked-out hubcaps in the second-floor, neon-lit windows above the tire bays.
- **Morton Salt Elston Facility** • 1357 N Elston Ave
  773-235-1010
  Has a painting of the famous salt girl, and, hey: acres of salt!
- **Nelson Algren Fountain** •
  Ashland Ave & Division St
  Has a recent controversial addition.
- **North Avenue Bridge** • 1200 W North Ave
  Wretched traffic jams; river view.
- **Polish Museum of America** •
  984 N Milwaukee Ave
  773-384-3352
  Right-to-life painting on the side.
- **Pulaski Park Fieldhouse** • 1419 W Blackhawk St
  312-742-7559
  Has an outdoor swimming pool.
- **St. Stanislaus Kostka Parish** •
  1351 W Evergreen Ave
  773-278-2470
  One of the oldest in Chicago.
- **Weed Street District** • W Weed St
  Several bars and clubs in one area. Party on.

## ▼ Nightlife

- **The Chipp Inn** • 832 N Greenview Ave
  312-421-9052
  Swig a Schlitz with hipsters at this vintage storefront tavern.
- **Chris's Northland Tavern** • 1610 W North Ave
  773-342-8181
  No-frills dive full of characters.
- **Exit** • 1315 W North Ave
  773-395-2700
  Ooohhh. Dark and scary. Eighties punk/goth throwback.
- **Joe's Bar** • 940 W Weed St
  312-337-3486
  Huge sports bar and music venue for national bands and drunk people.

25 26
10 11
52 12 13 14

# Restaurants

- **The Bedford** • 1612 W Division St
  773-235-8800 • $$
  Housed in a former bank-see and be seen in the vault.
- **Blue Star Bistro and Wine Bar** • 1209 N Noble St
  773-278-2233 • $$$
  New American-style small plates and global wines.
- **El Barco** • 1035 N Ashland Blvd
  773-486-6850 • $$
  Outdoor seating, terrific ceviche.
- **Hollywood Grill** • 1601 W North Ave
  773-395-1818 • $
  1950s style dining 27/7.
- **La Pasadita** • 1141 N Ashland Ave
  773-278-0384 • $
  Yummy, no-frills take-out. Order the carne asada burrito.
- **La Pasadita** • 1132 N Ashland Ave
  773-384-6537 • $
  Muy deliciosa, muy casual. Prime after-hours hot-spot.
- **Luc Thang Noodle** • 1524 N Ashland Blvd
  773-395-3907 • $
  Thai with Chinese and Vietnamese touches.

- **Mariscos El Veneno** • 1024 N Ashland Ave
  773-252-7200 • $
  Escape grimy Ashland for this tiny Mexican playa-style seafood shack.
- **Marrakech Cuisine** • 1413 N Ashland Ave
  773-227-6451 • $$
  Moroccan BYOB.
- **NYC Bagel Deli** • 1001 W North Ave
  312-274-1278 • $
  NY-style deli, best egg salad in the city.
- **Podhalanka** • 1549 W Division St
  773-486-6655 • $
  Authentic Polish hole-in-the-wall with potato pancakes, buttery pierogies, and more.
- **Schwa** • 1466 N Ashland Ave
  773-252-1466 • $$$$
  Innovative fine dining with a hipster vibe.
- **Tocco** • 1266 N Milwaukee Ave
  773-687-8895 • $$
  Come for the wood-fired pizzas. Skip everything else.
- **Usagi Ya** • 1178 N Milwaukee Ave
  773-292-5885 • $$
  Affordable sushi.

## 🛍 Shopping

- **Blick Art Materials** • 1574 N Kingsbury St
  312-573-0110
  Get creative here.
- **Circa Modern** • 1114 N Ashland Ave
  773-697-9239
  Thoughtfully edited collection of refurbished mid-century modern furniture pieces.
- **Design Within Reach** • 1574 N Kingsbury St
  312-482-8661
  North side outpost for the hip modern design studio.
- **Dusty Groove Records** • 1120 N Ashland Ave
  773-342-5800
  Vinyl and CDs. Specializes in funk, soul, rare groove, now sound, and world music.
- **Nina** • 1655 W Division St
  773-486-8996
  Yarn shop includes delicate, frayed thread from old saris.
- **Restoration Hardware** • 938 W North Ave
  312-475-9116
  Fancy housewares.
- **Roots & Culture** • 1034 N Milwaukee Ave
  773-580-0102
  Find contemporary art and a community-minded spirit at this non-profit art center.
- **Vintage Pine** • 904 W Blackhawk St
  312-943-9303
  Custom-made furniture from the English and French countryside.

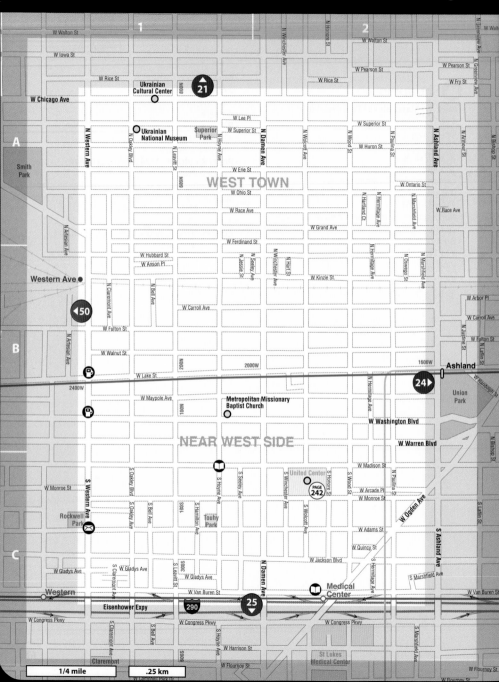

# Map 23 • **West Town / Near West Side**

N

1

2

W Walton St
W Iowa St
W Rice St

**Ukrainian Cultural Center**

21
8008

W Walton St
W Pearson St
W Rice St
W Pearson St
W Fry St

W Chicago Ave

N Western Ave
N Oakley Blvd
N Leavitt St
9006
N Hoyne Ave
N Damen Ave
N Winchester Ave
N Honore Ave

**Ukrainian National Museum**

Superior Park
W Lee Pl
W Superior St
W Superior St

N Wolcott Ave
N Wood St
N Paulina Ave
N Ashland Ave
N Armour St
N Bishop St
N Greenview Ave

A

Smith Park

W Huron St
W Erie St

**WEST TOWN**

W Ontario St

N Hartland Ct
N Hermitage Ave
N Marshfield Ave
N Race Ave

W Ohio St
W Race Ave
W Grand Ave

N Artesian Ave

W Ferdinand St
W Hubbard St
W Anson Pl

W Kinzie St

N Jessie St
N Seeley Ave
N Winchester Ave
N Hart St
N Hermitage Ave
N Oswego St
N Marshfield Ave

W Arbor Pl
W Carroll Ave

Western Ave.

N Claremont Ave
N Bell Ave

W Carroll Ave

N Justine St
W Fulton St

50

W Fulton St
W Walnut St

B

N Artesian Ave

2000W
9000

1600W

**Ashland**

24

Union Park

2400W
W Lake St
W Maypole Ave

N Hermitage Ave
W Randolph St

**Metropolitan Missionary Baptist Church**

**NEAR WEST SIDE**

W Washington Blvd
W Warren Blvd

S Western Ave
S Oakley Blvd
S Bell Ave
S Hoyne Ave
S Seeley Ave
S Winchester Ave
S Honore Ave
S Wood St
N Paulina Ave

W Madison St

**United Center**
PAGE 242

W Arcade Pl
W Monroe St

W Ogden Ave
S Bishop St

W Monroe St

Rockwell Park

Touhy Park

W Adams St
W Quincy St

S Oakley Blvd
S Hamilton Ave
S Leavitt St
3005

W Jackson Blvd

S Hermitage Ave
S Ashland Ave
S Marshfield Ave

C

W Gladys Ave
W Gladys Ave
S Gladys Ave

N Damen Ave

**Medical Center**

W Van Buren St
W Van Buren St

Western
Claremont

S Claremont Ave
S Bell Ave

W Van Buren St

**Eisenhower Expy**
I-290
290

W Congress Pkwy

25

S Hoyne Ave
9005

W Congress Pkwy

S Hermitage Ave
S Marshfield Ave

W Congress Pkwy
W Harrison St
W Flournoy St

St Lukes Medical Center

W Flournoy St

| 1/4 mile | .25 km |

This neighborhood was once the heart of the city's produce and meat markets. **United Center**, a.k.a. The House That Mike Built, infused energy into the area. A few food supplier warehouses still exist, mixing in with new loft conversions. Today it's a great place to spend your money, lots of your money, on locally made and grown necessaries.

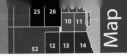

## ○ Landmarks

- **Metropolitan Missionary Baptist Church •**
  2151 W Washington Blvd
  312-738-0053
  An attempt to find an appropriate design for the then-new Christian Science religion. Sold to Baptists in 1947.
- **Ukrainian Cultural Center** • 2247 W Chicago Ave
  773-384-6400
  A gathering place to share and celebrate Ukrainian culture. Yeah!
- **Ukrainian National Museum** • 2249 W Superior St
  312-421-8020
  Museum, library, and archives detail the heritage, culture, and people of Ukraine.
- **United Center** • 1901 W Madison St
  312-455-4500
  Statue of His Airness still draws tourists.

## 🍸 Nightlife

- **Bar Deville** • 701 N Damen Ave
  312-929-2349
  A local scene for those who love a proper drink and a respectable atmosphere.
- **Cleo's** • 1935 W Chicago Ave
  312-243-5600
  Hooray for Wing Night Mondays.
- **High Dive** • 1938 W Chicago Ave
  773-235-3483
  Beating the pants off everyday bar food. Make this your reliable favorite.
- **Tuman's Tap & Grill** • 2159 W Chicago Ave
  773-782-1400
  Ukranian Village cozy bar. Respectable weekend dancefloor.

Between the architectural haven **Salvage One**, cowboy costumer **Alcala**'s, retro fashion treasure trove **Very Best Vintage** and gardening boutique **Sprout Home**, the shopping is anything but ordinary in this neck of the woods. Get your coffee with a side of hipster at **Atomix**. If you've got the leggings for it, head over to **Tuman**'s for cheap drinks and priceless people-watching.

 Restaurants

- **A Tavola** • 2148 W Chicago Ave
  773-276-7567 • $$$
  Upscale Italian charm in an intimate setting.
- **Chickpea** • 2018 W Chicago Ave
  773-384-9930 • $
  It's mama's specials that keep 'em comingback at the Palestinian fave.
- **Old Lviv** • 2228 W Chicago Ave
  773-772-7250 • $
  Eastern European buffet.

- **Sunrise Café** • 2012 W Chicago Ave
  773-276-8290 • $
  Good coffee, good breakfast puts a smile on the face.
- **Takie Outit** • 2132 W Chicago Ave
  773-252-1880 • $
  Dim sum in the tum tum.
- **Tecalitlan Restaurant** • 1814 W Chicago Ave
  773-384-4285 • $
  Popular family-style, Mexican restaurant.

# Shopping

- **Alcala's Western Wear** • 1733 W Chicago Ave
  312-226-0152
  Western-wear emporium sells boots, jeans, and cowboy hats.
- **Martyn George** •
  Vintage kitchen and housewares.
- **Modern Times** • 2100 W Grand Ave
  312-243-5706
  Vintage mid-century modern funishings.
- **Permanent Records** • 1914 W Chicago Ave
  773-278-1744
  The place to head for vinyl.
- **Rotofugi** • 2780 N Lincoln Ave
  773-868-3308
  Really cool toy store with urban vinyl figures.
- **Salvage One** • 1840 W Hubbard St
  312-733-0098
  Warehouse of antique, vintage, and salvaged architectural pieces for home/loft restoration.

- **Second Chance Thrift** • 1674 W Ogden Ave
  312-997-2222
  Tuesdays are half off at this clean, organized resale shop.
- **Sprout Home** • 745 N Damen Ave
  312-226-5950
  Plants and gardening supplies meet modernism.
- **Study Hall** • 2016 W Chicago Ave
  312-733-4255
  Indie boutique schools its clientele in stationery, clothing and housewares.
- **Tomato Tattoo** • 1855 W Chicago Ave
  312-226-6660
  Every hip strip needs a tattoo parlor.
- **Unison** • 2000 W Fulton St
  877-492-7960
  Modern home design studio offering locally-manufactured textiles.
- **Very Best Vintage** • 1919 W Chicago Ave
  312-226-5530
  Huge selection of vintage threads, shoes, and accessories.

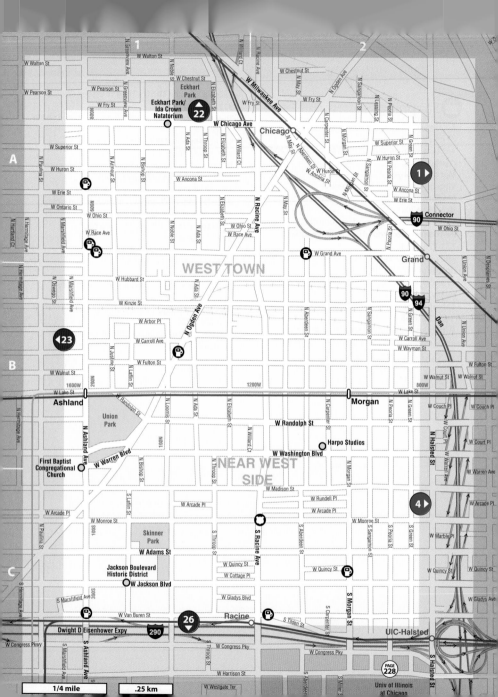

Food distribution centers and wholesalers, warehouses, and loading docks rub shoulders with an alternative gallery scene, trendy restaurants, and hot clubs in the transitional 'hood. Once a transit abyss, a shiny new el station just opened up smack dab in the middle of both scenes. Loft-style warehouses-turned event (read: weddings $$$) spaces abound.

Map

## ○ Landmarks

- **First Baptist Congregational Church** •
1613 W Washington Blvd
312-243-8047
Can seat 2000 people and houses one the largest totally enclosed organs in the country. There's a joke here somewhere.
- **Harpo Studios** • 1058 W Washington Blvd
312-591-9222
Home of the Oprah Winfrey Show.
- **Ida Crown Natatorium** • 1330 W Chicago Ave
312-746-5490
One of two swimming pools in the area.
- **Jackson Boulevard Historic District** •
W Jackson Blvd & S Laflin St
Amazingly, this cluster of preserved late-nineteenth century mansions survives in this declining area.

## ▼ Nightlife

- **694 Wine & Spirits** • 694 N Milwaukee Ave
312-492-6620
Find rare wines, meats and cheeses at this wine bar.
- **The Aviary** • 955 W Fulton Market
312-226-0868
Reservations by email only at this upscale cocktail creation destination.
- **Clutch** • 459 W Ogden Ave
312-526-3450
Gas station-turned bar offering craft cocktails and brews.
- **Cobra Lounge** • 235 N Ashland Ave
312-226-6300
Live bands, dj, and no TVs.
- **Five Star Bar** • 1424 W Chicago Ave
312-850-2555
Thirty bourbons, upscale bar menu, pool, and a stripper pole.
- **J Patricks** • 1367 W Erie St
312-243-0990
Irish flags, beers, and accents.
- **Jak's Tap** • 901 W Jackson Blvd
312-666-1700
From the good folks who brought us the Village Tap.
- **Mahoney's Pub & Grille** • 551 N Ogden Ave
312-733-2121
Hard-core sports bar.
- **The Matchbox** • 770 N Milwaukee Ave
312-666-9292
Chicago's smallest bar…bar none.
- **Park Tavern** • 1645 W Jackson Blvd
312-243-4276
Pre-Bulls/Hawks game stop for craft beers.
- **The Tasting Room** • 1415 W Randolph St
312-942-1313
Swank, low-key wine bar.
- **Twisted Spoke** • 501 N Ogden Ave
312-666-1500
$2 Jim Beams served by Suicide Girls and free porn on Saturday nights.
- **Victor Hotel** • 311 N Sangamon St
312-730-3900
Vintage lounge with dramatic decor.

River West restaurants continue to build celebrity status. Foodies fight for coveted tickets to **NEXT**, recent winner of the prestigious James Beard award for Best New Restaurant. Meanwhile, Top Chef fans ogle as **Girl and the Goat** owner Stephanie Izard expedites food. Down the road, Union Park annually hosts Lolla's more chill, indie counterpart, Pitchfork Music Festival.

# Restaurants

- **Bella Notte** • 1374 W Grand Ave
  312-733-5136 • $$$$
  Romantic, Italian, and schmoozy.
- **Belly Q** • 1400 W Randolph St
  312-563-1010 • $$$
  New, yet beloved, Asian BBQ.
- **Billy Goat Tavern** • 1535 W Madison St
  312-733-9132 • $
  Cheezeboiga chain.
- **Bombon Café** • 36 S Ashland Ave
  312-733-8717 • $
  Upscale tortas in a bright sunny setting!
- **The Breakfast Club & Grill** • 1381 W Hubbard St
  312-666-2372 • $$
  Brunch and then some.
- **Burger Baron** • 1381 W Grand Ave
  312-733-3285 • $
  Burgers and beer for the Everyman.
- **Butterfly Sushi Bar and Thai Cuisine** •
  1156 W Grand Ave
  312-563-5555 • $$
  Cute BYOB sushi storefront in the East Village.
- **Café Central** • 1437 W Chicago Ave
  312-243-6776 • $$
  Tasty Puerto Rican cuisine, diner décor, and
  vintage neighborhood photos.
- **Carmichael's Chicago Steak House** •
  1052 W Monroe St
  312-433-0025 • $$$$
  Great steaks in a vintage style dining room.
- **Coalfire** • 1321 W Grand Ave
  312-226-2625 • $$
  Chicago's first coal-fired pizza.
- **Flo** • 1434 W Chicago Ave
  312-243-0477 • $$
  Mexican-influenced breakfast in a relaxed
  atmosphere.
- **Girl and the Goat** • 809 W Randolph St
  312-492-6262 • $$$
  Ultra popular gastropub from "Top Chef" favorite
  Stephanie Izard.
- **Green Zebra** • 1460 W Chicago Ave
  312-243-7100 • $$$$
  Innovative and mostly vegetarian, by Spring's
  Shawn McClain.

- **Habana Libre** • 1440 W Chicago Ave
  312-243-3303 • $$
  BYOB plantain paradise.
- **Ina's** • 1235 W Randolph St
  312-226-8227 • $$$
  Special occasion breakfasts. Try the scrapple—it's
  better than it sounds.
- **La Sardine** • 111 N Carpenter St
  312-421-2800 • $$
  Tuesdays fixed price for $20!
- **Mexique** • 1529 W Chicago Ave
  312-850-0288 • $$$
  French/Mexican pairing seems odd? Trust us, they
  pull it off.
- **Moto** • 945 W Fulton Market
  312-491-0058 • $$$$
  Conceptual laboratory food creations.
- **Next** • 953 W Fulton Market
  312-226-0858 • $$$$
  Advance tix required for this trendy tour of world
  cuisine.
- **Oggi Trattoria** • 1378 W Grand Ave
  312-733-0442 • $$
  One of the godfathers of the neighborhood.
- **Palace Grill** • 1408 W Madison St
  312-226-9529 • $
  Stop in for classic diner fare pre-Hawks game.
- **Salerno's Pizza and Pasta** • 1201 W Grand Ave
  312-666-3444 • $$
  Tony Soprano would be proud, and full.
- **The Silver Palm** • 768 N Milwaukee Ave
  312-666-9322 • $$$
  Dine in a 1940s train car on upscale American
  food.
- **Sushi X** • 1136 W Chicago Ave
  312-491-9232 • $$
  Speakeasy sushi bar with fish so fresh they swim to
  your plate. BYOB.
- **Swim Café** • 1357 W Chicago Ave
  312-492-8600 • $
  Fresh, homemade breakfast and lunch fair with
  aquatic theme.
- **Twisted Spoke** • 501 N Ogden Ave
  312-666-1500 • $
  Famous for serving smut movies and eggs
  simultaneously.
- **TWO** • 1132 W Grand Ave
  312-624-8363 • $$
  One word about TWO: local.

- **Vera** • 1023 W Lake St
  312-243-9770 • $$
  Delectable small plates and an extensive wine list.
- **Vinnie's Sub Shop** • 1204 W Grand Ave
  312-738-2985 • $
  No frills, handy for construction workers.
- **West Town Tavern** • 1329 W Chicago Ave
  312-666-6175 • $$$
  Upscale comfort food.
- **Windy City Café** • 1062 W Chicago Ave
  312-492-8010 • $
  Small town diner feel and menu, grab a booth.
- **Wishbone** • 1001 W Washington Blvd
  312-850-2663 • $$
  Comfort food, comfort folks.

# 🛍 Shopping

- **65Grand** • 1369 W Grand Ave
  312-719-4325
  Contemporary art comes at an affordable price by local and national artists.
- **Brody's Balloons** • 1101 W Randolph St
  312-666-9520
  Piñatas and balloons!
- **Casati Gallery** • 949 W Fulton St
  312-421-9905
  Mid-century Italian furniture and accessories.
- **Chicago Antique Market** • 1340 W Randolph St
  312-666-1200
  Leases space to a variety of vendors.
- **Chicago Avenue Discount** • 1637 W Chicago Ave
  312-226-0004
  Shoes for $1.93!
- **Décollage** • 1219 W Madison St
  312-226-8087
  Vintage and couture resale boutique.
- **Design Inc.** • 1847 W Grand Ave
  312-243-4333
  Architecturally centered home design.
- **Douglas Dawson Gallery** • 400 N Morgan St
  312-226-7975
  Fancy artifacts from around the world.
- **Dovetail** • 1452 W Chicago Ave
  312-508-3398
  Accessories, clothing and cabinetry. Vintage.

- **Green Grocer** • 1402 W Grand Ave
  312-624-9508
  Give the planet a high-five. Local, organic, awesome groceries.
- **Halo** •
  312-526-3260
  Hip men's haircare.
- **Hoosier Mama Pie Company** •
  1618 W Chicago Ave
  312-243-4846
  "Keep your fork, there's pie!"
- **J.P. Graziano Grocery Co.** • 901 W Randolph St
  312-666-4587
  Spices, pasta, and dried beans in bulk.
- **Jan's Antiques** • 225 N Racine Ave
  312-563-0275
  Mind-boggling antique emporium.
- **Lush Wine and Spirits** • 1412 W Chicago Ave
  312-666-6900
  Wine, microbrews, and booze!
- **Pet Care Plus** • 1328 W Lake St
  312-397-9077
  For the pet-obsessed.
- **Roots Hair Salon** • 1140 W Grand Ave
  312-666-6466
  Trendy hair salon.
- **RR #1 Chicago** • 814 N Ashland Ave
  312-421-9079
  Idiosyncratic gift shop in a 1930s pharmacy.
- **Seek Vintage** • 1432 W Chicago Ave
  312-526-3164
  Retro clothing and housewares for the "Mad Men" era.
- **Snap Hair** • 470 N Ogden Ave
  773-255-9228
  Hair and nail salon.
- **Terry's Toffee** • 1117 W Grand Ave
  312-733-2700
  Gourmet, house-made toffee, ice creams, and biscotti.
- **Tonya's Hush** • 34 S Ashland Ave
  312-738-1090
  Unique upscale retail for women.
- **Upgrade Cycle Works** • 1130 W Chicago Ave
  312-226-8650
  Bikes, accessories, and servicing.

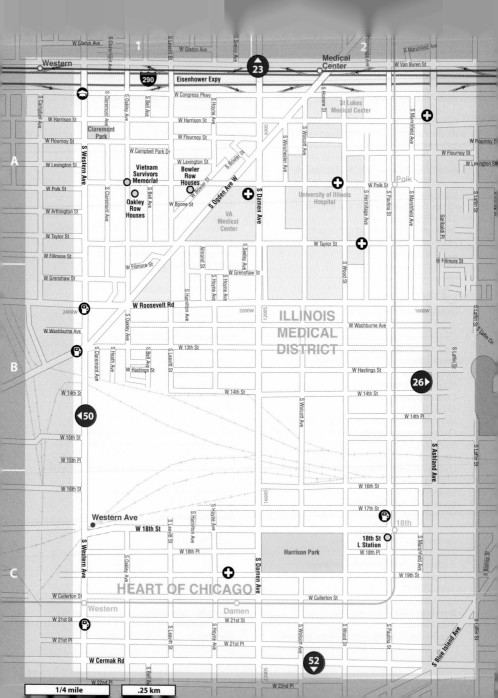

The conglomerated facilities making up the Illinois Medical District comprise the second largest such quarter in the nation. Rush University recently opened the doors to its architecturally complex but simply named Tower building, a butterfly-shaped, hard-to-miss facility at the eastern end of the medical campus. A townhouse colony of new constructions in the area house green MDs.

## ⊙ Landmarks

- **18th St L Station** • W 18th St & S Paulina St
  Gateway to Pilsen features colorful murals celebrating Mexican culture.
- **Bowler Row Houses** • 2148 W Bowler St
  Historical row houses that have survived the wrecking ball.
- **Oakley Row Houses** • 801 S Oakley Ave
  Italianate row houses that date back to 1870's.
- **Vietnam Survivors Memorial** • 815 S Oakley Ave
  Privately funded memorial was erected by Vets.

## 🍸 Nightlife

- **Water Hole Lounge** • 1400 S Western Ave
  312-243-7988
  Neighborhood hangout hosting occasional live blues shows.

## 🍴 Restaurants

- **Carnitas Uruapan Restaurant** • 1725 W 18th St
  312-226-2654 • $
  Carnitas muy necesitas.
- **Damenzo's** • 2324 W Taylor St
  312-421-1142 • $
  Pizza, pizza puffs, small bar.
- **Lulu's Hot Dogs** • 1000 S Leavitt St
  312-243-3444 • $
  Dog's popular with local med students.
- **Original Ferrara Bakery** • 2210 W Taylor St
  312-666-2200 • $
  Serving Italian pastries since 1908.
- **Taqueria Los Alamos** • 2157 S Damen Ave
  773-254-8095 • $
  Great Taqueria
- **TJ's Family Restaurant** • 1928 W Cermak Rd
  773-927-3349 • $
  Neighborhood diner.

## 🛍 Shopping

- **Textile Discount Outlet** • 2121 W 21st St
  773-847-0572
  City block-wide fabric mecca.

# Map 26 • University Village/Little Italy/Pilsen

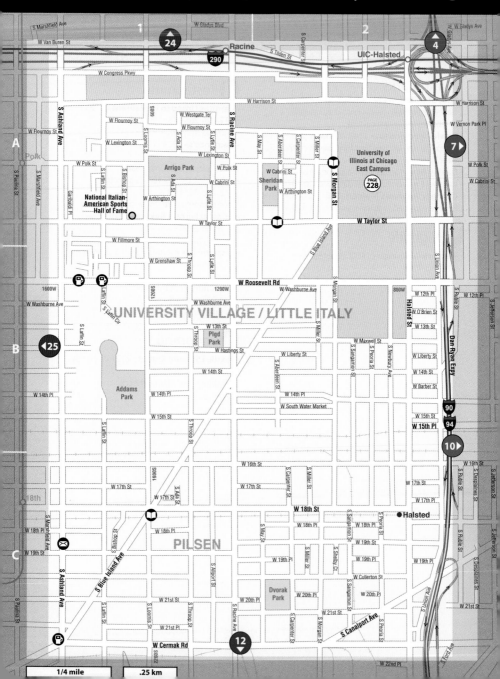

1/4 mile     .25 km

Jane Addams wouldn't recognize her old 'hood today, but it retains her feisty spirit. From the nearby **National Museum of Mexican Art** (just across the border in Map 25) to the **National Italian American Sports Hall of Fame**, institutions pay homage to diverse native groups. UIC definitely holds sway around here; the area bustles with the textbook-toting set from sunup to sundown. Farther south, a proud Mexican community rubs shoulders with working creatives around the 18th and Halsted artistic epicenter of Pilsen.

## ○ Landmarks

• **National Italian American Sports Hall of Fame** •
1431 W Taylor St
312-226-5566
How many Italian American sports stars do you know? DiMaggio is right out front.

## 🍸 Nightlife

• **BeviAmo Wine Bar** • 1358 W Taylor St
312-455-8255
Good selection, if a bit pricey.
• **The Drum and Monkey** • 1435 W Taylor St
312-563-1874
Irish pub-style student hangout.
• **Hawkeye's Bar & Grill** • 1458 W Taylor St
312-226-3951
Quality bar food (including the healthy side).
• **Simone's** • 960 W 18th St
312-666-8601
Hipster bar made from funky recycled materials.
• **Skylark** • 2149 S Halsted St
312-948-5275
Hip hangout for Pilsen arty crowd.

Map 2

Sprawling over the city's Near West Side is the University of Illinois at Chicago. On your next trip to Little Italy, skip the marked up vino with your pasta. **Davanti Enoteca** sells bottles at retail cost with a nominal corkage fee alongside their rustic cuisine. Kill the wait time at adjacent **BeviAmo.** In Pilsen, local artists frequent the **Skylark**, and people travel from far and wide for the authentic Mexican food on 18th Street.

## Restaurants

- **Al's Beef** • 1079 W Taylor St
  312-226-4017 • $
  Where's the beef? Right here.
- **Birreria Reyes de Ocotlan** • 1322 W 18th St
  312-733-2613 • $$
  Local no-frills Mexican favored by Rick Bayless.
- **Carm's Beef and Italian Ice** • 1057 W Polk St
  312-738-1046 • $
  Italian subs and sausages.
- **Chez Joel** • 1119 W Taylor St
  312-226-6479 • $$$
  Delicious French cuisine in Little Italy.
- **China Dragon Restaurant** • 1343 W 18th St
  312-666-3766 • $$
  Dependably fantastic Chinese.
- **Couscous** • 1445 W Taylor St
  312-226-2408 • $$
  Middle Eastern and Maghrebin Cuisine. Unique falafel.
- **Davanti Enoteca** • 1359 W Taylor St
  312-226-5550 • $$
  Wine bar and simple Italian from the Mia Francesca brand.
- **De Pasada** • 1517 W Taylor St
  312-243-6441 • $
  Inexpensive, good quality Mexican—friendly staff.
- **Decolores** • 1626 S Halsted St
  312-226-9886 • $$
  Pilsen's burgeoning arts scene and Latino culinary traditions unite.
- **Demitasse Coffee** • 1066 W Taylor St
  312-226-7666 • $
  Delightful breakfast spot.
- **Don Pedro Carnitas** • 1113 W 18th St
  312-829-4757 • $
  Mexican fast food muy authentico.
- **Express Grill** • 1260 S Union Ave
  312-738-2112 • $
  A 24/7 greasy spoon with noteworthy hot dogs.
- **Francesca's** • 1400 W Taylor St
  312-829-2828 • $$
  Loud, bustling dining room.
- **Golden Thai** • 1509 W Taylor St
  312-733-0760 • $
  Always busy, but there's better Thai out there.
- **Hashbrowns** • 731 W Maxwell St
  312-226-8000 • $$
  Sweet potato hashbrowns—enough said.
- **Joy Yee's Noodles** • 1335 S Halsted St
  312-997-2128 • $$
  Good Asian food, better bubble tea.
- **Kohan** • 730 W Maxwell St
  312-421-6254 • $$
  Sushi for UIC students.

- **La Cebollita Grill** • 1807 S Ashland Ave
  312-492-8443 • $
  Gorditas, sopas, to dine-in or carry out.
- **May Street Café** • 1146 W Cermak Rd
  312-421-4442 • $
  Inexpensive, super casual pan-Latin.
- **Mundial Cocina Mestiza** • 1640 W 18th St
  312-491-9908 • $$
  Lovingly-prepared, family-owned Mexican.
- **Nuevo Leon** • 1515 W 18th St
  312-421-1517 • $
  Real-deal Mexican grub in Pilsen.
- **The Rosebud** • 1500 W Taylor St
  312-942-1117 • $
  Popular with the United Center crowd.
- **Steak 'n Egger** • 1174 W Cermak Rd
  312-226-5444 • $
  24-hour comfort food.
- **Sweet Maple Cafe** • 1339 W Taylor St
  312-243-8908 • $
  Super-homey breakfast, homemade biscuits.
- **Taj Mahal** • 1512 W Taylor St
  312-226-6546 • $$
  Affordable Indian.
- **Taqueria Los Comales** • 1544 W 18th St
  312-666-2251 • $
  Mexican fast food in cheerful environment.
- **Tuscany** • 1014 W Taylor St
  312-829-1990 • $$
  Elegant Taylor Street Italian.

## Shopping

- **Conte Di Savoia** • 1438 W Taylor St
  312-666-3471
  European and Italian specialties.
- **Lush Wine and Spirits** • 1257 S Halsted St
  312-738-1900
  Wine, microbrews, and booze.
- **Mario's Italian Lemonade** • 1068 W Taylor St
  312-829-0672
  The best summer treat in the city. Prepare to wait.
- **Modern Cooperative** • 818 W 18th St
  312-226-8525
  Home furnishings old and new.

Map 27 · **Logan Square**

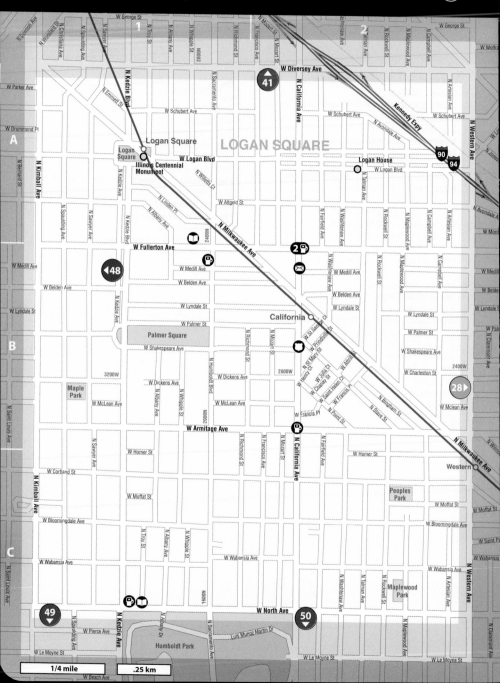

The natural redoubt for creative professionals fleeing higher rent and stroller gridlock in Wicker Park, Logan Square's leafy boulevards seem to sprout new bars and restaurants every month. Milwaukee forms the spread-out strip of commercial activity, where artsy bars mingle with auto shops and tasty 24-hour taquerias.

y

## ○ Landmarks

- **Illinois Centennial Monument** •
  3100 W Logan Blvd
  Every city needs an obelisk or two…
- **Logan House** • 2656 W Logan Blvd
  Renowned for over-the-top holiday décor.

## ○ Nightlife

- **Billy Sunday** • 3143 W Logan Blvd
  773-661-2485
  Cocktail-focused bar named after the infamous 1920s prohibitionist.
- **Fireside Bowl** • 2648 W Fullerton Ave
  773-486-2700
  No longer a punk rock venue, it's just bowling now.
- **Longman & Eagle** • 2657 N Kedzie Ave
  773-276-7110
  Bourbon like nobody's business; also a restaurant and six-room inn.
- **The Rocking Horse** • 2535 N Milwaukee Ave
  773-486-0011
  Generically hip bar and brunch spot to bookend your debauchery.
- **Scofflaw** • 3201 W Armitage Ave
  773-252-9700
  Neighborhood spot with meticulously crafted gin cocktails.
- **Suite 25** • 2529 N Milwaukee Ave
  773-360-7478
  Peruvian sports bar perched amidst the neighborhood's artsy hot spots.
- **Two Way Lounge** • 2928 W Fullerton Ave
  773-227-5676
  This downright rugged bar offers cheap Old Style.
- **Ultra Lounge** • 2169 N Milwaukee Ave
  773-269-2900
  Velvet ropes in this stretch of Milwaukee? Give me a break.
- **Whirlaway Lounge** • 3224 W Fullerton Ave
  773-276-6809
  Old Style, old couches, and a truly eclectic jukebox.
- **The Whistler** • 2421 N Milwaukee Ave
  773-227-3530
  Classic cocktails, live music, and art gallery all in one!

Map

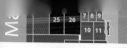

# Restaurants

- **Anong Thai** • 2532 N California Ave
  773-292-5007 • $
  Much closer than Charley Thai, if you live near it.
- **Azucar** • 2647 N Kedzie Ave
  773-486-6464 • $$
  Clubby tapas spot.
- **Bang Bang Pie Shop** • 2051 N California Ave
  773-276-8888 • $
  Pie, pie, and more homemade pie.
- **Blue Sprout** • 2171 N Milwaukee Ave
  773-772-0988 • $
  Neighborhood Thai BYOB.
- **Borinquen Restaurant** • 1720 N California Ave
  773-227-6038 • $
  Order a jibarito—a steak sandwich between two plantain slices.
- **Buona Terra Ristorante** • 2535 N California Ave
  773-289-3800 • $$
  Logan Square shmoozy Italian.
- **Chilapan** • 2459 W Armitage Ave
  773-697-4597 • $$
  Authentic and traditional Mexican cuisine.
- **Choi's Chinese Restaurant** •
  2638 N Milwaukee Ave
  773-486-8496 • $$
  Good, fresh Chinese food.
- **Cozy Corner Diner & Pancake House** •
  2294 N Milwaukee Ave
  773-276-2215 • $
  Perfect if your brunch doesn't need salmon or capers.
- **Dunlay's on the Square** • 3137 W Logan Blvd
  773-227-2400 • $$
  American food and sports viewing.
- **El Charro** • 2410 N Milwaukee Ave
  773-278-2514 • $
  24/7 taqueria. Conveniently adjacent to Two Way Lounge.
- **El Nandu** • 2731 N Fullerton Ave
  773-278-0900 • $$
  Argentinian delicacies mixed with music.
- **Fat Rice** • 2957 W Diversey Pkwy
  773-661-9170 • $$$$
  Fans line up early at this Portuguese-Macanese fusion spot.
- **Gaslight Coffee Roasters** • 2385 N Milwaukee Ave
  • $
  Coffee fluent in the neighborhood dialect: house roasted, locally sourced.
- **Hachi's Kitchen** • 2521 N California Ave
  773-276-8080 • $$
  Locals rave over this Logan Square sushi spot.
- **Johnny's Grill** • 2545 N Kedzie Blvd
  773-278-2215 • $
  Diner food for the grunge crowd.
- **Longman & Eagle** • 2657 N Kedzie Ave
  773-276-7110 • $$
  Bourbon like nobody's business; also a restaurant and six-room inn.
- **Lula** • 2537 N Kedzie Blvd
  773-489-9554 • $$
  Pan-ethnic nouveau for hipsters.
- **Philly's Best** • 2436 N Milwaukee Ave
  773-276-1900 • $
  Gigantic steak sandwiches, et al.
- **Real Tenochtitlan** • 2451 N Milwaukee Ave
  773-227-1050 • $$$$
  Come for Chef Geno Bahena's amazing moles. BYOB.
- **Reno** • 2607 N Milwaukee Ave
  773-697-4234 • $$
  Wood-fired bagels by day, artisanal pizzas by night
- **Taqueria Moran** • 2226 N California Ave
  773-235-2663 • $
  Stand apart marinated pork tacos.
- **Telegraph** • 2601 N Milwaukee Ave
  773-292-9463 • $$$
  Wine bar with a flair of gastropub.

# 🛍Shopping

- **Boulevard Bikes** • 2535 N Kedzie Blvd
  773-235-9109
  Friendly neighborhood bike shop.
- **City Lit Books** • 2523 N Kedzie Blvd
  773-235-2523
  Indie bookstore with extensive children's and
  Spanish sections.
- **Dill Pickle Food Co-op** • 3039 W Fullerton Ave
  773-252-2667
  Tiny as an organic kumquat, but with a dense food
  selection.
- **Disco City Records No. 6** • 2630 N Milwaukee Ave
  773-486-1495
  Latin music emporium.

- **Fleur** • 3149 W Logan Blvd
  773-395-2770
  Not your mother's floral arrangements, plus
  handmade goods from locals.
- **Provenance Food and Wine** •
  2528 N California Ave
  773-384-0699
  Reasonably priced wines and unreasonably priced
  groceries.
- **Threads, Etc.** • 2327 N Milwaukee Ave
  773-276-6411
  Resale clothes and furniture.
- **Village Discount Outlet** • 2032 N Milwaukee Ave
  866-545-3836
  Tons of clothes and weekly specials.
- **Wolfbait & B-Girls** • 3131 W Logan Blvd
  312-698-8685
  Two young designers showcase funky wares by
  dozens of locals.

W George St

1

2

W George St

N Maplewood Ave
N Campbell Ave

W Wolfram St

N Oakley Ave

W Wolfram St

W Wolfram St

N Damen Ave

W Diversey Ave

N Paulina St

N Marshfield Ave

N Ashland Ave

N Bosworth Ave

N Greenview Ave

▲ 42

W Schubert Ave

N Artesian Ave

A

N Western Ave

N Elston Ave

W Logan Blvd

N Leavitt St

N Hoyne Ave

W Rex Ave

W Wrightwood Ave

N Clybourn Ave

W Terra Cotta Pl

W Altgeld St

Trebes Park

N Bosworth Ave

N Lill Ave

W Logan Blvd

Kennedy Expy

N Jones St

N Leavitt St

N Avondale Ave

W Montana Ave

N Wolcott Ave

W Fullerton Pkwy

N Montana Ave

N Wolcott Ave

N Racine Ave

2 ▣ W Fullerton Ave

N Maplewood Ave

N Campbell Ave

N Artesian Ave

▣

W Medill Ave

N Oakley Ave

W Belden Ave

N Avondale Ave

N Hamilton Ave

N Seeley Ave

N Winchester Ave

N Lister Ave

N Wolcott Ave

N Wood St

W Medill Ave

Chicago River

N Honore St

N Honore St

B

W Lyndale St

W Lyndale St

W Lyndale St

Holstein Park

W Palmer St

N Claremont Ave

W Palmer St

N Oakley Ave

N Oakley Ave

N Bell Ave

W Palmer St

W Webster Ave

W Shakespeare Ave

W Shakespeare Ave

N Avondale Ave

1600W

◀ 27

W Charleston St

N Claremont Ave

W Charleston St

W Dickens Ave

W Dickens Ave

N Wood St

29 ▶

N Dominick St

W Shakespeare Ave

W Mclean Ave

BUCKTOWN

W Dickens Ave

W Mclean Ave

N Winchester Ave

N Wolcott Ave

N Avondale Ave

90

94

N Hobson Ave

N Holt Ave

N Marcey St

W Armitage Ave

W Homer St

▣

2400W

Margie's Candies

N Milwaukee Ave

W Mclean Ave

2000W

W Armitage Ave

N Hermitage Ave

Clybourn

W Homer St

W Homer St

Ehler Park

N Hoyne Ave

W Cortland St

N Honore St

N Wood St

W Cortland St

N Paulina St

N Marshfield Ave

W Western

N Wilmot Ave

W Moffat St

W Moffat St

N Winnebago Ave

W Churchill St

Churchill Park

N Bloomingdale Ave

C

W Bloomingdale Ave

▣

W Saint Paul Ave

N Churchill St

N Wilmot Ave

W Willow St

W Saint Paul Ave

W Bloomingdale Ave

W Wabansia Ave

N Western Ave

W Wabansia Ave

W Wabansia Ave

N Maplewood Ave

W Homer St

N Artesian Ave

N Oakley Ave

N Claremont Ave

N Bell Ave

W Caton St

W Concord Pl

W Concord Pl

1600W

21 ▼

W North Ave

Damen

W Pierce Ave

N Elk Grove Ave

W Pierce Ave

N Bosworth Ave

W Le Moyne St

W Le Moyne St

W Le Moyne St

1/4 mile

.25 km

Map

## ○ Landmarks

- **Margie's Candies** • 1960 N Western Ave
  773-384-1035
  The Beatles ate here.

---

## Nightlife

- **The Bluebird** • 1749 N Damen Ave
  773-486-2473
  American tapas and wine bar.
- **The Charleston** • 2076 N Hoyne Ave
  773-489-4757
  Yuppie dive.
- **Cortland's Garage** • 1645 W Cortland St
  773-862-7877
  Garage-themed bar for wanna-be grease monkeys.
- **Danny's** • 1951 W Dickens Ave
  773-489-6457
  Hipster house bar with candlelit alcoves.
- **Ed and Jean's** • 2032 W Armitage Ave
  773-489-6509
  Your dive bar home away from home.
- **Gallery Cabaret** • 2020 N Oakley Ave
  773-489-5471
  Hip dive bar with local acts, attracts plenty of wannabe barflies.

- **Green Eye Lounge** • 2403 W Homer St
  773-227-8851
  Microbrews within crawling distance of the Blue Line Western stop.
- **Lemming's** • 1850 N Damen Ave
  773-862-1688
  Lite Brite works of art.
- **Liar's Club** • 1665 W Fullerton Ave
  773-665-1110
  Only sometimes overly hipster, otherwise rad music and good times.
- **Map Room** • 1949 N Hoyne Ave
  773-252-7636
  Global theme mixed with the occasional free buffet.
- **The Mutiny** • 2428 N Western Ave
  773-486-7774
  All bands start somewhere…unfortunately it's here.
- **Northside Bar & Grill** • 1635 N Damen Ave
  773-384-3555
  Popular Wicker Park pick-up bar.
- **Quenchers Saloon** • 2401 N Western Ave
  773-276-9730
  Crowded on the weekends, but ultra comfy couches and free popcorn.
- **WhirlyBall** • 1880 W Fullerton Ave
  773-486-7777
  Drinking while driving bumper cars. Safety is nothing to me.

 Restaurants

- **The Art of Chicken** • 2041 N Western Ave
  773-697-9266 • $
  Simple poultry. Express yourself with a choice of two marinades.
- **Arturo's Tacos** • 2001 N Western Ave
  773-772-4944 • $
  24-hour taqueria boasts cheap eats and a boisterous crowd
- **Belly Shack** • 1912 N Western Ave
  773-252-1414 • $$
  Latin/Asian/Incredible. BYOB and please don't skip dessert.
- **The Bento Box** • 2246 W Armitage Ave
  773-278-3932 • $$
  Asian BYOB no bigger than an actual bento box.
- **The Bluebird** • 1749 N Damen Ave
  773-486-2473 • $$
  American tapas and wine bar.
- **The Bristol** • 2152 N Damen Ave
  773-862-5555 • $$$
  Charcuterie lover's dream with Mediterranean roots.
- **Café Laguardia** • 2111 W Armitage Ave
  773-862-5996 • $$
  Cuban food like you wouldn't believe.
- **Club Lucky** • 1824 W Wabansia Ave
  773-227-2300 • $$
  Italian retro-styled joint.
- **Coast Sushi Bar** • 2045 N Damen Ave
  773-235-5775 • $$
  BYOB sushi.
- **Fat Willy's Rib Shack** • 2416 W Schubert Ave
  773-782-1800 • $$
  Finger-lickin' ribs and brisket.
- **Grassfed** • 1721 N Damen Ave
  773-342-6000 •
  Grass fed sirloin, green salad and fries for $25.

- **Honey 1 BBQ** • 2241 N Western Ave
  773-227-5130 • $$
  BBQ cooked in a big ole smoker. Yum.
- **Irazu** • 1865 N Milwaukee Ave
  773-252-5687 • $
  Hipsters and bikers gather 'round for Central American staples.
- **Jane's** • 1655 W Cortland St
  773-862-5263 • $$$
  Good-for-you gourmet.
- **Le Bouchon** • 1958 N Damen Ave
  773-862-6600 • $$
  Affordable, crowded French.
- **Margie's Candies** • 1960 N Western Ave
  773-384-1035 • $
  Immense ice cream concoctions.
- **Mindy's Hot Chocolate** • 1747 N Damen Ave
  773-489-1747 • $$
  Much more than just hot chocolate.
- **Owen and Engine** • 2700 N Western Ave
  773-235-2930 • $$
  Rustic British meals served with artisan crafted ales.
- **Red Door** • 2118 N Damen Ave
  773-697-7221 • $$
  Globally-inspired gastropub.
- **Rio's D'Sudamerica** • 2010 W Armitage Ave
  773-276-0170 • $$$$
  Swanky South American for date nights.
- **Ripasso** • 1619 N Damen Ave
  773-342-8799 • $$
  Homemade pastas and carefully crafted Italian-inspired favorites.
- **Riverside Café** • 1656 W Cortland St
  773-278-3354 • $$
  Great deli, with awesome Sunday brunch.
- **Silver Cloud** • 1700 N Damen Ave
  773-489-6212 • $$
  A mac&cheese and meat-loaf kind of place.
- **Takashi** • 1952 N Damen Ave
  773-772-6170 • $$$
  Japanese fusion by James Beard Award winning chef.

# Shopping

- **Alan Design Studio** • 2134 N Damen Ave
773-278-2345
House and home goodies.
- **Cynthia Rowley** • 1653 N Damen Ave
773-276-9209
Cute feminine designs that flatter the body.
- **G Boutique** • 2131 N Damen Ave
773-235-1234
Lingerie and bedroom accessories.
- **The Goddess and Grocer** • 1646 N Damen Ave
773-342-3200
Gourmet groceries and take-out.
- **Halo** •
773-342-4256
Hip men's haircare.
- **Intermix** • 1633 N Damen Ave
773-292-0894
The NYC shopper's mecca.
- **Lululemon** • 1627 N Damen Ave
773-227-1869
Canadian-based yoga wear brand brings soft-as-cashmere soy clothes and sleek attire.
- **p.45** • 1643 N Damen Ave
773-862-4523
Edgy women's boutique.
- **Pagoda Red** • 1714 N Damen Ave
773-235-1188
Fine Asian antiques.
- **Pavilion** • 2055 N Damen Ave
773-645-0924
Antique furniture.

- **Pinch Spice Market** • 1913 N Milwaukee Ave
773-360-8708
Spice store dedicated to organic, fair trade seasonings.
- **Psycho Baby** • 1630 N Damen Ave
773-772-2815
Hip gear for the urban baby.
- **The Red Balloon** • 1940 N Damen Ave
773-489-9800
A unique store for children—toys, clothes and furniture.
- **Robin Richman** • 2108 N Damen Ave
773-278-6150
Arty, indie boutique.
- **Scoop NYC** • 1702 N Milwaukee Ave
773-227-9930
On top of the trends.
- **Soutache** • 2130 N Damen Ave
773-292-9110
A treasure trove of ribbons, buttons and trim.
- **T-Shirt Deli** • 1739 N Damen Ave
773-276-6266
Pricey—but quality—custom-made t-shirts.
- **Tangerine** • 1719 N Damen Ave
773-772-0505
Feminine women's boutique.
- **Vienna Beef Factory Store** • 2501 N Damen Ave
773-278-7800
Here's the beef.
- **Vive La Femme** • 2048 N Damen Ave
773-772-7429
Style beyond size.

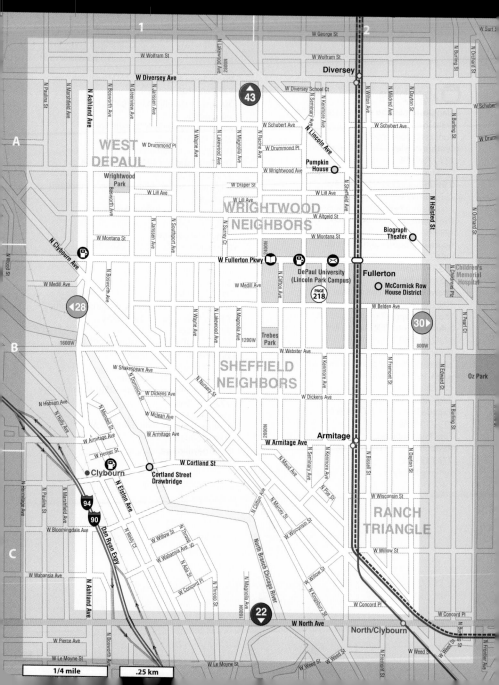

# Map 29 • **DePa**

College students rule the scene with DePaul University's central location, filling the neighborhood with fun-filled late nights and early morning walks-of-shame, while still maintaining a vibrant academic environment for both students and residents (consider the free **DePaul Art Museum**). Less raucous areas have an upscale collection of restaurants and boutiques for those who can afford to live on the charming tree-lined residential streets.

## ○ Landmarks

- **Cortland Street Drawbridge** •
  1440 W Cortland St
  Built in 1902 by John Ernst Erickson, this innovative leaf-lift bridge changed the way the world built bridges, and vice versa.
- **McCormick Row House District** •
  830 W Chalmers Pl
  Quaint example of late 19th-century urban planning and architecture.
- **Pumpkin House** • 1052 W Wrightwood Ave
  A Halloween spectacle of lighted pumpkins.
- **Victory Gardens Biograph Theater** •
  2433 N Lincoln Ave
  773-871-3000
  Site of gangster John Dillinger's infamous death in 1934; currently closed for renovation.

## Nightlife

- **Bird's Nest** • 2500 N Southport Ave
  773-472-1502
  Cheap wings, live music, and plenty of bros.
- **Cagney's** • 2142 N Clybourn Ave
  773-857-1111
  Old-timey meets high-tech at this sports bar.
- **Delilah's** • 2771 N Lincoln Ave
  773-472-2771
  Punk rock dive specializing in whisky.
- **Faith & Whiskey** • 1365 W Fullerton Ave
  773-248-9119
  Rockin' Lincoln Park with over 100 whiskeys.
- **Gaslight Bar & Grille** • 2426 N Racine Ave
  773-929-7759
  Like you never left OSU.
- **The Hideout** • 1354 W Wabansia Ave
  773-227-4433
  Haven for alt-country and other quirky live tune-age.
- **Irish Eyes** • 2519 N Lincoln Ave
  773-348-9548
  …are often crying.
- **Kincade's** • 950 W Armitage Ave
  773-348-0010
  Happy-hour sports bar.
- **Lincoln Hall** • 2424 N Lincoln Ave
  773-525-2501
  Rock concert venue serving food and drink.
- **Local Option** • 1102 W Webster Ave
  773-348-2008
  Neighborhood hole-in-the-wall and proud of it.
- **Rose's Lounge** • 2656 N Lincoln Ave
  773-327-4000
  DePaul dive chock full of tchotchkes and cheap beer.
- **Tripoli Tap** • 1147 W Armitage Ave
  773-477-4400
  Quality bar food.
- **Webster's Wine Bar** • 1480 W Webster Ave
  773-868-0608
  Perfect place for "getting to know you" while enjoying flights and pairings.
- **Wrightwood Tap** • 1059 W Wrightwood Ave
  773-549-4949
  Neighborhood feel-good spot.

Map 29

# DePaul / Wrightwood / Sheffield

**Facets** runs a slate of obscure art-house films and rents DVDs as well. For music, **The Hideout** draws Bloodshot Records fans with its basement rec-room ambience and **Lincoln Hall** brings musical acts into the heart of the neighborhood. Aging punk rockers tipple a vast array of spirits at **Delilah's**. Armitage Avenue boasts a variety of boutiques.

## Restaurants

- **Ambrosia Café** • 1963 N Sheffield Ave
  773-404-4450 • $
  Smoothies and hookahs? Huh.
- **Butcher & the Burger** • 1021 W Armitage Ave
  773-697-3735 • $$
  DIY gourmet burger joint.
- **Derby** • 1224 W Webster Ave
  773-248-0900 • $$
  Horse racing-themed bar and grill for every bourbon need.
- **Goose Island** • 1800 N Clybourn Ave
  312-915-0071 • $
  Pub grub at its best.
- **Homeslice** • 938 W Webster Ave
  312-789-4900 • $$
  Pizza from the Pacific Northwest? Yep, it's a thing.
- **Ja' Grill** • 1008 W Armitage Ave
  773-929-5375 • $$
  Fun, authentic Jamaican in Lincoln park? Go figure.
- **Jam 'n Honey** • 958 W Webster Ave
  773-327-5266 • $$
  Creative, classic breakfast restaurant also serving lunch and dinner.

- **John's Place** • 1200 W Webster Ave
  773-525-6670 • $$
  Healthy comfort food.
- **Ringo** • 2507 N Lincoln Ave
  773-248-5788 • $
  All-u-can-eat & BYOB. Nice.
- **Sai Café** • 2010 N Sheffield Ave
  773-472-8080 • $$$
  Traditional sushi place.
- **The Squared Circle** • 2418 N Ashland Ave
  773-904-8170 • $$
  How many pizzerias boast a female pro-wrestler as owner?
- **State** • 935 W Webster Ave
  773-975-8030 • $$$
  Flashy service-oriented spot with concierge service.
- **Sweet Mandy B's** • 1208 W Webster Ave
  773-244-1174 • $
  Picture-perfect sweet shoppe.
- **Taco & Burrito House** • 1548 W Fullerton Ave
  773-665-8389 • $
  Super-cheap burrito shack, open very late.
- **The Twisted Lizard** • 1964 N Sheffield Ave
  773-929-1414 • $$
  Yuppie Mexican.

## 🛍 Shopping

- **Art Effect** • 934 W Armitage Ave
773-929-3600
"A modern day general store" for everything fabulous.
- **Balance Health + Wellness** •
1901 N Clybourn Ave
773-472-0560
Striving to help clients return to a state of balance.
- **Crate & Barrel Outlet** • 1864 N Clybourn Ave
312-787-4775
What you wish you could furnish your home with.
- **Dirk's Fish** • 2070 N Clybourn Ave
773-404-3475
Carry out fresh fish and seafood spot.
- **Intermix** • 841 W Armitage Ave
773-404-8766
The NYC shopper's mecca.
- **Jayson Home** • 1885 N Clybourn Ave
773-248-8180
Dedicated to making sure you live beautifully.
- **Kaveri** • 1211 W Webster Ave
773-296-2141
Boutique lines by designers like Trovata and Ulla Johnson.
- **Langford Market** • 851 W Armitage Ave
773-327-9815
Affordable, feminine clothing and accessories.
- **The Left Bank** • 1155 W Webster Ave
773-929-7422
Jewelry and home décor.
- **Lush Cosmetics** • 859 W Armitage Ave
773-281-5874
Handmade soaps and natural cosmetics—too bad they aren't edible!
- **Tabula Tua** • 1015 W Armitage Ave
773-525-3500
Housewares.
- **Wine Discount Center** • 1826 N Elston Ave
773-489-3454
Wine warehouse—free tastings every Saturday.

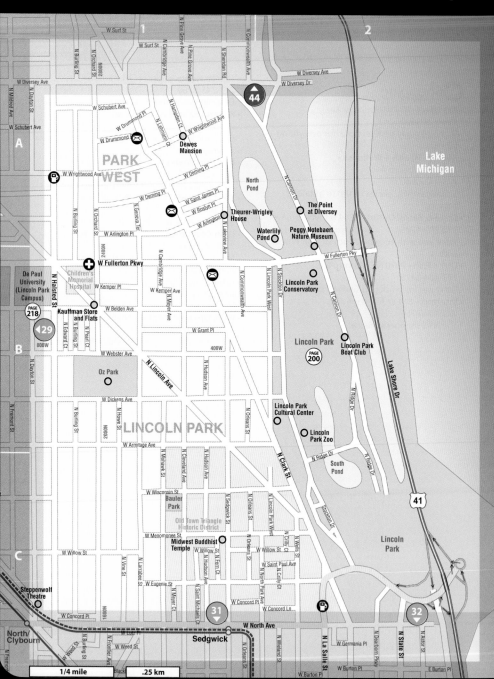

# Map 30 · **Lincoln Park**

N

W Surf St
W Surf St
W Diversey Ave
W Diversey Dr
W Diversey Ave
W Diversey Dr

1
2

N Mildred Ave
N Dayton St
N Burling St
N Orchard St
2800 N
N Cambridge Ave
N Fremont Ave
N Pine Grove Ave
N Sheridan Rd
N Commonwealth Ave

44

W Schubert Ave
W Schubert Ave
W Drummond Pl
W Drummond
W Drummond

**PARK WEST**

Dewes Mansion

N Hampden Ct
N Lehmann Ct
N Wrightwood Ave
W Wrightwood Ave
N Clifton Dr

North Pond

**Lake Michigan**

A

W Wrightwood Ave
W Deming Pl
W Deming Pl
W Saint James Pl
W Roslyn Pl
W Arlington
W Arlington Pl
N Burling St
N Orchard St
2000 N
N Geneva Ter
N Lakeview Ave

Theurer-Wrigley House

Waterlily Pond

The Point at Diversey

Peggy Notebaert Nature Museum

N Clifton Dr

W Fullerton Pkwy

De Paul University (Lincoln Park Campus)

**PAGE 218**

◀ **29**
800 W

Children's Memorial Hospital

W Fullerton Pkwy

Kaufman Store and Flats

N Halsted St
N Edward Ct
N Burling St
N Pearl Ct
N Cambridge Ave
W Kemper Pl
W Kemper Ave
W Belden Ave
N Mildred Ave
N Commonwealth Ave
W Grant Pl
400 W

Lincoln Park Conservatory

N Stockton Dr
N Lincoln Park West
N Cannon Dr

B

N Dayton St
N Fremont St
W Webster Ave
N Burling St
N Howe St
2000 N
N Lincoln Ave
W Dickens Ave
N Hudson Ave

Oz Park

W Grant Pl
400 W

**LINCOLN PARK**

**PAGE 200**

Lincoln Park Boat Club

N Ridge Dr
N Ridge Dr

**Lake Shore Dr**

W Armitage Ave
N Mohawk St
N Cleveland Ave
N Hudson Ave
N Orleans St
N Clark St
Lincoln Park Cultural Center
Lincoln Park Zoo
N Ridge Dr
South Pond
Stockton Dr

W Wisconsin St
Bauler Park
Old Town Triangle Historic District
W Menomonee St

Midwest Buddhist Temple

**41**

**Lincoln Park**

C

Steppenwolf Theatre

W Willow St
N Vine St
N Larrabee St
W Eugenie St
N Fern Ct
N Hudson Ave
W Willow St
N Orleans St
W Willow St
N Cleveland Ave
W Saint Paul Ave
N Wells St
N North Park Ave

W Concord Pl
N Meyer Ct
N Saint Michaels Ct
W Concord Pl
W Concord Ln

**31**

W North Ave

**32**

North/Clybourn

Sedgwick

N Weed St
N Fremont St
N Burling St
N Frontier Ave
N Weed St
Black
N Orleans St
N La Salle St
N Wieland St
N Wells St
W Germania Pl
W Burton Pl
N Dearborn Pkwy
N State St
N Astor St
E Burton Pl

1/4 mile
.25 km

Lincoln Park's yuppie vibe may strike fear into the heart of the city's hipsters, but with cultural institutions like the famed **Steppenwolf Theatre** and cultural institutions like the **Chicago History Museum**, the **Peggy Notebaert Nature Museum** and **Lincoln Park Zoo's** Nature Boardwalk just for starters, the neighborhood is one of the tops in popularity for a reason. High rent and real estate prices make most want to just pay a visit.

## ○ Landmarks

- **Dewes Mansion** • 503 N Wrightwood Ave
  773-477-3075
  Ornate historic home done in the German Baroque style and built in 1896.
- **Kauffman Store and Flats** • 2312 N Lincoln Ave
  One of the oldest existing buildings designed by Adler and Sullivan. It's amazing that its characteristic features have survived.
- **Lincoln Park Boat Club** • 2341 N Cannon Dr
  312-715-7220
  Paddling, rowing, and sculling since 1910.
- **Lincoln Park Conservatory** • 2391 N Stockton Dr
  312-742-7736
  The place to warm up in those brutal Chicago winters.
- **Lincoln Park Cultural Center** •
  2045 N Lincoln Park W
  312-742-7726
  Programming in visual arts for all ages.
- **Lincoln Park Zoo** • 2001 N Clark St
  312-742-2000
  Oldest free zoo in the U.S.

- **Midwest Buddhist Temple** • 435 W Menomonee St
  312-943-7801
  Enter their annual haiku contest.
- **Oz Park** • 2021 N Burling St
  312-742-7898
  You're not in Kansas anymore.
- **The Peggy Notebaert Nature Museum** •
  2430 N Cannon Dr
  773-755-5100
  An oasis for adults and kids to reconnect with nature by playing with wildflowers and butterflies.
- **The Point at Diversey** •
  Lakefront at Diversey Harbor
  One of the best views of the skyline. Ever.
- **Steppenwolf Theatre Company** •
  1650 N Halsted St
  312-335-1650
  The one John Malkovich, Gary Sinise, and co. started.
- **Theurer-Wrigley House** • 2466 N Lakeview Ave
  Early Richard E. Schmidt (and maybe Hugh H.G. Garden) based on late-Italian Renaissance architecture.
- **Waterlily Pond** • W Fullerton Pkwy & N Cannon Dr
  You might forget you're in a city.

While **Alinea** may get the most attention as the nation's most renowned restaurant, less expensive fare at spots like **Frances' Deli** (Lincoln Park's oldest) keep people coming to eat. Halsted Street's designer boutiques might be too much for some, but the bricks-and-mortar location of online consigner **eDrop-Off** saves the day for today's recessionista fashionistas.

# 🍸 Nightlife

- **B.L.U.E.S.** • 2519 N Halsted St
773-528-1012
Smaller but notorious blues bar with an older African-American crowd.
- **The Burwood Tap** • 724 W Wrightwood Ave
773-525-2593
Chug-a-lug.
- **Crossroads Public House** • 2630 N Clark St
773-248-3900
Cavernous "Irish" bar without the Irish flair.
- **D.O.C. Wine Bar** • 2602 N Clark St
773-883-5101
Unwind with a glass of Pinot by the fireplace. (Choose from Noir or Gregio!)
- **Duke's** • 2616 N Clark St
773-248-0250
If a bar were a log cabin with tasty burgers.
- **Gamekeepers** • 345 W Armitage Ave
773-549-0400
Where young singles mingle.
- **Glascott's** • 2158 N Halsted St
773-281-1205
Wannabe Irish joint with frat-boy written all over it.
- **Hidden Shamrock** • 2723 N Halsted St
773-883-0304
We played darts with Joe Walsh here one night. Righteous.

- **Kingston Mines** • 2548 N Halsted St
773-477-4646
Chicago blues bar in a neighborhood safe for tourists.
- **Lincoln Station** • 2432 N Lincoln Ave
773-472-8100
Back room is good for events.
- **Lion Head Pub** • 2251 N Lincoln Ave
773-348-5100
DePaul nightspot.
- **Neo** • 2350 N Clark St
773-528-2622
Popular eighties retro night. Gag me with a spoon.
- **Park West** • 322 W Armitage Ave
773-929-1322
Costs extra to reserve a table.
- **The Second City** • 1616 N Wells St
312-337-3992
Drama and food in front of you.
- **Trinity** • 2721 N Halsted St
773-880-9293
Perfect sports bar featuring great food and tons of TVs.
- **Wise Fools Pub** • 2270 N Lincoln Ave
773-525-5401
Vibes are high for live local legends and jam sessions.

# 🍽 Restaurants

- **Alinea** • 1723 N Halsted St
  312-867-0110 • $$$$$
  Conceptual experiments in fine dining.
- **Aloha Eats** • 2534 N Clark St
  773-935-6828 • $
  Tropical treats made with aloha (and Spam).
- **Austrian Bakery & Deli** • 2523 N Clark St
  773-244-9922 • $
  Low-carb diets are so over. Celebrate here.
- **Balena** • 1633 N Halsted St
  312-867-3888 • $$$
  Rustic Italian for the carb-loader.
- **Boka** • 1729 N Halsted St
  312-337-6070 • $$$
  Ambitious menu, swank décor.
- **Bricks** • 1909 N Lincoln Ave
  312-255-0851 • $$
  Thin-crust pizza and Trappist ales hold sway here.
- **Café Ba-Ba-Reeba!** • 2024 N Halsted St
  773-935-5000 • $$$
  Noisy, bustling tapas joint.
- **Duke's** • 2616 N Clark St
  773-248-0250 • $$
  If a bar were a log cabin with tasty burgers.

- **Dunlay's On Clark** • 2600 N Clark St
  773-883-6000 • $$$
  Casual traditional american dinner spot.
- **Edzo's Burger Shop** • 2218 N Lincoln Ave
  773-697-9909 • $
  Burgermeister Eddie Lakin expands his wildly
  successful Evanston emporium.
- **Frances' Deli** • 2552 N Clark St
  773-248-4580 • $
  Inventive deli.
- **Geja's Café** • 340 W Armitage Ave
  773-281-9101 • $$$
  Romantic fondue with live flamenco.
- **Hema's Kitchen** • 2411 N Clark St
  773-529-1705 • $$
  Almost as good as original on Devon.
- **Karyn's Fresh Corner** • 1901 N Halsted Ave
  312-255-1590 • $$
  The queen of raw food.
- **L20** • 2300 N Lincoln Park W
  773-868-0002 • $$$$
  Spendy seafood joint specializing in strange name
  pronunciations and tasty sea creatures.
- **Lito's Empanadas** • 2566 N Clark St
  773-857-1337 • $
  He don't make no burritos.

- **Mon Ami Gabi** • 2300 N Lincoln Park W
  773-348-8886 • $$$
  French bistro.
- **Nookies** • 1746 N Wells St
  312-337-2454 • $
  Inventive omelettes with some strong coffee.
- **Nookies Too** • 2114 N Halsted St
  773-327-1400 • $
  Inventive omelettes with some strong coffee.
- **North Pond** • 2610 N Cannon Dr
  773-477-5845 • $$$$
  Earthy contemporary American.
- **Original Pancake House** • 2020 N Lincoln Park W
  773-929-8130 • $$
  Breakfast-y grill.
- **P.S. Bangkok 2** • 2521 N Halsted St
  773-348-0072 • $
  Popular Thai with delivery.
- **The Pasta Bowl** • 2434 N Clark St
  773-525-2695 • $$
  Mangia huge portions of pasta in an intimate
  neighborhood joint.
- **Perennial Virant** • 1800 N Lincoln Ave
  312-981-7070 • $$$$
  Instant gratification for foodies across from the
  Green City Market.
- **R.J. Grunts** • 2056 N Lincoln Park W
  773-929-5363 • $$
  Comfy, psychedelic salad bar and burger joint.
- **Riccardo Trattoria** • 2119 N Clark St
  773-549-0038 • $$$
  Authentic Italian cuisine.
- **Rickshaw Republic** • 2312 N Lincoln Ave
  773-697-4750 • $
  Southeast Asian street food.
- **Robinson's No 1 Ribs** • 655 W Armitage Ave
  312-337-1399 • $
  Down home ribs in Lincoln Park.

- **Salvatore's Ristorante** • 525 W Arlington Pl
  773-528-1200 • $$$
  Cute neighborhood Italian.
- **Sedgwick's Bar & Grill** • 1935 N Sedgwick St
  312-337-7900 • $
  Home-style breakfast buffet.
- **Sushi O Sushi** • 346 W Armitage Ave
  773-871-4777 • $$
  Newly remodeled fresh seafood.
- **Sushi Para II** • 2256 N Clark St
  773-477-3219 • $$
  A.Y.C.E. sushi that's good. No, really.
- **Swirlz Cupcakes** • 705 W Belden Ave
  773-404-2253 • $
  Gourmet cupcakes, including gluten-free options.
- **Tandoor Char House** • 2652 N Halsted St
  773-327-2652 • $$
  Traditional Indian and Pakistani faire.
- **Toro Sushi** • 2546 N Clark St
  773-348-4877 • $$
  Worth the wait for raw fish lovers
- **Trinity** • 2721 N Halsted St
  773-880-9293 • $
  Perfect sports bar featuring great food and tons
  of TVs.
- **Twin Anchors** • 1655 N Sedgwick St
  312-266-1616 • $$
  Sinatra came for the ribs and stayed for the drinks
  and atmosphere.
- **Vinci** • 1732 N Halsted St
  312-266-1199 • $$$
  Homemade pasta raises the bar.
- **Wells on Wells** • 1617 N Wells St
  312-944-1617 • $$
  Two words: pretzel buns.
- **Wiener's Circle** • 2622 N Clark St
  773-477-7444 • $
  Classic dogs served with a generous helping of
  sass.

# Shopping

- **A New Leaf** • 1818 N Wells St
312-642-8553
Perhaps the most elegantly designed flower shop in Chicago.
- **Art + Science Salon** • 1971 N Halsted St
312-787-4247
Beakers bring you back to science class. Student discounts available.
- **BCBGMAXAZRIA** • 2140 N Halsted St
773-281-2224
Upscale chic women's fashion.
- **Buy Popular Demand** • 2629 N Halsted St
773-868-0404
Consignment shop offering affordable fashions.
- **Crossroads Trading Co.** • 2711 N Clark St
773-296-1000
Hip styles, thrift store prices.
- **Dave's Records** • 2604 N Clark St
773-929-6325
All LPs, from Janacek to Jay-Z.
- **Drop-Off** • 2117 N Halsted St
773-525-7467
Designer consignment storefront for e-bay store and reality TV subject.
- **Francesca's Collections** • 2012 N Halsted St
773-244-4075
Forever 21 in terms of price, something stylish in terms of style.

- **Lori's—The Sole of Chicago** • 824 W Armitage Ave
773-281-5655
Designer shoes.
- **Lululemon** • 2104 N Halsted St
773-883-8860
Canadian-based yoga wear brand brings soft-as-cashmere soy clothes and sleek attire.
- **McShane's** • 815 W Armitage Ave
773-525-0282
Designer resale. Head on upstairs for some serious markdowns.
- **Molly's Cupcakes** • 2536 N Clark St
773-883-7220
Featuring 'build-your-own-cupcakes.'
- **Nest Furniture** • 2707 N Clark St
773-525-0530
Modern and antique furniture at all price levels.
- **Old Town Triangle** • 1763 N North Park Ave
312-337-1938
Don't miss their openings.
- **Quiltology** • 1221 W Diversey Pkwy
773-549-6628
Make quilt, keep self warm.
- **Smart Optical** • 2730 N Clark St
773-868-9189
As if eyewear wasn't cool enough.
- **Urban Outfitters** • 2352 N Clark St
773-549-1711
Retro fun clothing, nifty gifts, and silly t-shirts.

# Map 31 • **Old Town / Near North**

With its narrow, cobblestoned streets lined with Queen Anne-style homes and rehabbed cottages, Old Town's appropriate moniker perfectly encapsulates its nineteenth century charms. Only a few blocks to the south, the vast land where the Cabrini Green housing project stood waits for development.

# 🍸 Nightlife

- **Burton Place** • 1447 N Wells St
  312-664-4699
  Great late night; good bar food.
- **McGinny's Tap** • 313 W North Ave
  312-943-5228
  Laid-back crowd.
- **Old Town Ale House** • 219 W North Ave
  312-944-7020
  Crusty old-timers meet performing arts crowd.
- **UP Comedy Club** • 230 W North Ave
  312-662-4562
  Stand-up and improv seven nights a week.
- **Weeds** • 1555 N Dayton St
  312-943-7815
  Pinball, bras, shoes, poetry, and tequila.
- **Zanies Comedy Club** • 1548 N Wells St
  312-337-4027
  After a few drinks, everything is funny. Well, almost.

Wells Street provides the neighborhood's main drag with an array of new and old restaurants, shops and stores. **The Spice House**, **The Fudge Pot** and **Up Down Cigar** have been providing Old Town with their specialty items for over half a century, while new entries like **Old Town Social** keep the vibe fresh. Second City's **UP Comedy Club** breathes new life into the city's historic comedy scene.

 Restaurants

- **Big & Little's** • 860 N Orleans St
312-943-0000 • $
Fish-and-chips shack run by Hell's Kitchen contestant.
- **Bistrot Margot** • 1437 N Wells St
312-587-3660 • $$$$
Great date place.
- **Dining Room at Kendall College** •
900 N North Branch St
312-752-2328 • $$
When students cook: Gourmet food, layman price!
- **Dinotto Ristorante** • 215 W North Ave
312-202-0302 • $$
Everyone's a regular at this neighborhood Italian joint.
- **The Fireplace Inn** • 1448 N Wells St
312-664-5264 • $$$
Popular spot to watch sports.
- **Garlic and Chili** • 1232 N La Salle Dr
312-255-1717 • $
Off the beaten track and located next to the transient motel, it's a hidden gem.
- **The Goddess and Grocer** • 901 N Larrabee St
312-988-9870 • $
Newest installment of the gourmet to-go food shop.
- **Kamehachi** • 1531 N Wells St
312-664-3663 • $$$
Sushi favorite with upstairs lounge.
- **Kiki's Bistro** • 900 N Franklin St
312-335-5454 • $$$$
Stylish French.
- **Kilwins** • 1405 N Wells St
312-654-1692 • $
Handmade fudge and ice cream for both tourists and natives.

- **Mangia Roma** • 1623 N Halsted St
312-475-9801 • $$
Casual Roman spot with pizza.
- **Mizu** • 315 W North Ave
312-951-8880 • $$
Sushi and skewered meats with dipping sauces.
- **MK** • 868 N Franklin St
312-482-9179 • $$$$
Very stylish.
- **O'Brien's** • 1528 N Wells St
312-787-3131 • $$$
Best outdoor in Old Town.
- **Old Jerusalem** • 1411 N Wells St
312-944-0459 • $$
Cheap, good food.
- **Old Town Pour House** • 1419 N Wells St
312-477-2800 • $$
A beer lover's dream come true.
- **Old Town Social** • 455 W North Ave
312-266-2277 • $$
Large selection of specialty beers, meats, and cheeses.
- **Salpicon** • 1252 N Wells St
312-988-7811 • $$
Colorful Mexican with tequila tastings.
- **Sammy's Red Hots** • 238 W Division St
312-266-7290 • $
The seediness only makes it better.
- **Topo Gigio** • 1516 N Wells St
312-266-9355 • $$$
Crowded reliable Italian. Big outdoor.
- **The Twisted Baker** • 1543 N Wells St
312-932-1128 • $
Fresh and authentic classic desserts and pastries.

Map 31

## 🛍 Shopping

- **Cityblue** • 1444 N Wells St
312-664-2222
High-end denim and apparel.
- **The Fudge Pot** • 1532 N Wells St
312-943-1777
A chocolate institution.
- **Nicole Miller** • 1419 N Wells St
312-664-3532
High-end lingerie, bridal, and formal attire for ladies who can afford to look this good.
- **Old Town Gardens** • 1555 N Wells St
312-266-6300
Beautiful plants and flowers.

- **REI** • 1466 N Halsted St
312-951-6020
This co-op gets Chicago outdoors.
- **The Spice House** • 1512 N Wells St
312-274-0378
Spice up your cooking.
- **The Twisted Baker** • 1543 N Wells St
312-932-1128
And you thought they just served pleasing melodies. Try ice box cookies!
- **Up Down Cigar** • 1550 N Wells St
312-337-8025
One stop shopping for the cigar enthusiast.
- **Village Cycle Center** • 1337 N Wells St
312-751-2488
Good urban cycling store.

# Map 32 · **Gold Coast / Mag Mile**

Between the sticky bars on Division Street and the Viagra Triangle pick-up joints on Rush, it's easy for locals to find fun. But the Gold Coast/Mag Mile (actually only eight-tenths of a mile, but who's counting?) is also home to some of Chicago's most impressive architecture, libraries (including **The Newberry**), and beautiful beaches. The **Museum of Contemporary Art** and the **Lookingglass Theatre** add to the cultural cache.

## ○ Landmarks

- **Charnley-Persky House** • 1365 N Astor St
  312-915-0105
  Louis Sullivan and Frank Lloyd Wright designed this national historic landmark. Go look before it becomes a CVS.
- **John Hancock Observatory** • 875 N Michigan Ave
  888-875-8439
  Zone out the tourists, and focus in on the prettiest view of the city.

- **Lake Shore Drive Apartments** •
  860 Lake Shore Dr
  Less is more—by Mies van der Rohe.
- **The Newberry** • 60 W Walton St
  312-943-9090
  There's plenty on offer at this humanities library.
- **Old Playboy Mansion** • 1340 N State Pkwy
  You have no idea what happened here.
- **Water Tower Place** • 835 N Michigan Ave
  312-440-3166
  Huge shopping—6 floors—Marshall Field's, Macy's.

Map

50  23  24  1  2  3
         4  5  6
25  26   7  8  9
         10 11

**Gucci**, **Chanel**, **Barney's**, **Prada**; they don't call it the Gold Coast for nothing. But with **Urban Outfitters** and **H&M**, there's plenty for us regular folk as well. Splurge on creative Italian at **Spiaggia** (the Obamas' favorite Chicago date place), or grab a quick corned beef sandwich as **Ashkenaz Deli**. And admit it: You've dodged admission to the **Hancock Observatory** by getting a $14 martini at **The Signature Room** at the 96th two floors above.

# Nightlife

- **The Back Room** • 937 N Rush St
  312-751-2433
  Old jazz club w/ lots of baby boomers.
- **Butch McGuire's** • 20 W Division St
  312-787-4318
  Wet T-shirt contests anyone?
- **Coq d'Or** • 140 E Walton St
  312-932-4623
  A sophisticate's lodge: red leather, dark wood, torch singers, and pub food.
- **The Drawing Room** • 937 N Rush St
  312-266-2694
  Swank cocktails and sit-down dining.
- **Dublin's** • 1050 N State St
  312-266-6340
  Gold Coast pub.

- **The Hangge Uppe** • 14 W Elm St
  312-337-0561
  No-frills, all fun, dancing. Hip hop upstairs, '80s classics downstairs.
- **The Leg Room** • 7 W Division St
  312-337-2583
  Huge singles scene.
- **Shenanigan's** • 16 W Division St
  312-642-2344
  Another Rush vicinity hellhole.
- **The Signature Room** • 875 N Michigan Ave
  312-787-9596
  It's the view, not the food. Proposal hot spot.
- **Underground Wonder Bar** • 710 N Clark St
  312-266-7761
  Mostly jazz.
- **Zebra Lounge** • 1220 N State Pkwy
  312-642-5140
  Garish, cramped piano bar—in other words, it's a hit.

# 🍴Restaurants

- **Ashkenaz Deli** • 12 E Cedar St
312-944-5006 • $
Chicago's true Jewish deli.
- **Balsan** • 11 E Walton St
312-646-1400 • $$$
The high-end Elysian Hotel's "casual" option.
- **Bar Toma** • 110 E Pearson St
312-266-3110 • $$
Chef Tony Mantuano's (Spiaggia) take on the
classic Italian pizzeria.
- **Bistrot Zinc** • 1131 N State St
312-337-1131 • $$
Quiet elegance.
- **Cafe des Architectes** • 20 E Chestnut St
312-324-4063 • $$$
French Mediterranean with late kitchen.
- **Cape Cod** • 140 E Walton Pl
312-656-9562 • $$$$
Over-the-top nautical décor.
- **Carmine's** • 1043 N Rush St
312-988-7676 • $$$
Crowded and pricey Italian.
- **Del Frisco** • 58 E Oak St
312-888-2489 • $$
Sleek modern steakhouse.
- **The Drawing Room** • 937 N Rush St
312-266-2694 • $$
Swank cocktails and sit-down dining.
- **Fornetto Mei** • 107 E Delaware Pl
312-573-6301 • $$$
Authentic pizza. Deep dish lovers stay away.
- **Freshii** • 835 N Michigan Ave
312-202-9009 • $
Tasty wraps, hold the guilt.
- **Gaylord** • 100 E Walton St
312-664-1700 • $
Improbably named Indian spot.
- **Gibson's Steakhouse** • 1028 N Rush St
312-266-8999 • $$$$$
If you love steak, get a reservation.
- **The Goddess and Grocer** • 25 E Delaware Pl
312-896-2600 • $
Specialty groceries and ready-made gourmet
sandwiches.
- **Hugo's Frog Bar & Fish House** • 1024 N Rush St
312-640-0999 • $$$
Hearty seafood.

Map
50 23 24 1 2 3 / 4 5 6 / 25 26 7 8 9 / 10 11

- **Le Colonial** • 937 N Rush St
  312-255-0088 • $$$
  Indochine comes to the Second City. Very nice.
- **Le Petit Paris** • 260 E Chestnut St
  312-787-8260 • $$$$
  Shhh! Don't tell anyone about this Gallic hideaway!
- **Mario's Gold Coast Ristorante** • 21 W Goethe St
  312-944-0199 • $$$
  Classic Italian neighborhood gem.
- **McCormick & Schmick's** • 41 E Chestnut St
  312-397-9500 • $$$$
  Seafood chain that outdoes itself on portions and taste.
- **Merlo on Maple** • 16 W Maple St
  312-335-8200 • $$$
  Fine dining Italian in a classic, quaint romantic setting.
- **Morton's the Steakhouse** • 1050 N State St
  312-266-4820 • $$$$$
  The steakhouse standard.
- **Mr. J's Dawg & Burger** • 822 N State St
  312-943-4679 • $
  Mom & pop burger joint.
- **Original Pancake House** • 22 E Bellevue Pl
  312-642-7917 • $$
  The apple waffle/pancake is right!
- **Pump Room** • 1301 N State Pkwy
  312-787-3700 • $$$$$
  Chicago old-school tradition. Dress code.
- **RA Sushi** • 1139 N State St
  312-274-0011 • $$$
  Rock-n-roll sushi bar.
- **Spiaggia** • 980 N Michigan Ave
  312-280-2750 • $$$$$
  One of Chicago's best—gorgeous lake view and Italian cuisine.
- **Sprinkles Cupcakes** • 50 E Walton St
  312-573-1600 • $
  Gourmet cupcakes for the Gold Coast crowd.
- **Table Fifty-Two** • 52 W Elm St
  312-573-4000 • $$$
  Oprah-sanctioned New American.
- **Tavern on Rush** • 1031 N Rush St
  312-664-9600 • $$$$
  Summer mainstay, American menu.
- **Tempo Cafe** • 6 E Chestnut St
  312-943-4373 • $$
  24/7 patio seating and huge menu.

# Shopping

- **900 North Michigan Shops** • 900 N Michigan Ave
  312-915-3916
  High-end mall stores.
- **Agent Provocateur** • 47 E Oak St
  312-335-0229
  A British lingerie invasion in the Gold Coast.
- **Barney's New York** • 15 E Oak St
  312-587-1700
  Upscale boutique, clothing and accessories.
- **BCBGMAXAZRIA** • 113 E Oak St
  312-475-0053
  Upscale chic women's fashion.
- **Branca** • 17 E Pearson St
  312-787-1017
  Celebrated interior designer Alessandra Branca's atelier.
- **Bravco** • 43 E Oak St
  312-943-4305
  For those who like to be pampered.
- **Calypso Christiane Celle** • 50 E Oak St
  312-649-9934
  From finger puppets and feminine dresses to candles.
- **Chanel** • 935 N Michigan Ave
  312-787-5500
  Classic, expensive clothing, accessories, and fragrances.
- **Club Monaco** • 900 N Michigan Ave
  312-787-8757
  Fashion-forward clothing that doesn't try too hard.
- **Flight 001** • 1133 N State St
  312-944-1001
  Modern retro-style travel gear.
- **Gucci** • 900 N Michigan Ave
  312-664-5504
  Tom Ford's alluring and provocative clothes and accessories.
- **H&M** • 840 N Michigan Ave
  855-466-7467
  European department store taking Chicago by storm.
- **Hendrickx Belgian Bread Crafter** •
  100 E Walton St
  312-649-6717
  Artisanal breads, croissants, and coffee with a European flair.

- **Hermes** • 25 E Oak St
312-787-8175
Fancy scarves and more.
- **Hershey's Chocolate World** • 822 N Michigan Ave
312-337-7711
Dumb and fun chocoholic tourist trap.
- **The Hutch** • 1550 W Olive St
773-506-0406
Recreate your grandmother's kitchen (delicious baked goods not included).
- **Ikram** • 15 E Huron St
312-587-1000
The First Lady's favorite boutique.
- **Independence** • 47 E Oak St
312-675-2105
Menswear and shoes made in the Land of Liberty.
- **Intermix** • 40 E Delaware Pl
312-640-2922
The NYC shoppers' mecca.
- **Judy Maxwell Home** • 1151 N State St
312-787-9999
Joan Cusack's funhouse of hyperbolic gifts, art and, ahem, more.
- **Lululemon** • 930 N Rush St
312-915-0627
Canadian-based yoga wear brand brings soft-as-cashmere soy clothes and sleek attire.
- **More Cupcakes** • 1 E Delaware Pl
312-951-0001
The BLT cupcake is exactly what it sounds like.

- **Prada** • 30 E Oak St
312-951-1113
Expensive, but delightful, clothing and accessories.
- **Pratesi** • 67 E Oak St
312-943-8422
Linens.
- **Sofia** • 100 E Walton St
312-640-0878
Trendy boutique featuring emerging designer pieces and occasional celeb sightings.
- **Tod's** • 121 E Oak St
312-943-0070
Italian luxury leather goods.
- **Topshop** • 830 N Michigan Ave
312-280-6834
Hip, trendy UK retailer of women's togs and accessories.
- **Ultimate Bride** • 106 E Oak St
312-337-6300
Bridal gear.
- **Urban Outfitters** • 935 N Rush St
312-640-1919
Retro clothing, nifty gifts, and cool accessories.
- **Water Tower Place** • 835 N Michigan Ave
312-440-3166
Marshall Fields, er, Macy's.
- **Y-3** • 50 E Oak St
312-573-3310
High-end collaboration between Japanese designer Yohji Yamamoto and Adidas.

Map 35 • **Roge**

Dobson St

W Howard St
W Jerome St
W Birchwood Ave
W Fargo Ave
W Jarvis Ave
W Sherwin Ave
W Chase Ave

N Kedzie Ave
N Albany Ave
N Sacramento Ave
N Francisco Ave
N California Ave
N Fairfield Ave
N Talman Ave
N Maplewood Ave
N Campbell Ave
N Artesian Ave
N Claremont Ave
N Oakley Ave
N Bell Ave
N Ridge Blvd
N Hamilton Ave
N Hoyne Ave

**A**

W Birchwood Ave
W Fargo Ave
W Jarvis Ave
W Chase Ave

Rogers Park

W Jarlath St

Bernard
Horwich JCC

High Ridge
YMCA

W Touhy Ave
W Touhy Ave

**B**

W Fitch Ave

ROGERS PARK AND WEST RIDGE

W Estes Ave
W Greenleaf Ave

◀46

W Estes Ave
W Greenleaf Ave

W Lunt Ave
2800W
2400W
W Coyle Ave

Indian Boundary
Park

Lerner
Park

34▶

W Morse Ave

N Washtenaw Ave
N Rockwell St
N Maplewood Ave
N Oakley Ave
N Bell Ave
N Hamilton Ave

W Morse Ave

W Farwell Ave

W Pratt Ave
W Pratt Ave

Chippewa
Park

W North Shore Ave

N Richmond St
N Francisco Ave
N Mozart St
N Maplewood Ave

Warren Park

N Western Ave
N Bell Ave
N Bridge Blvd

**C**

W Albion Ave

W Arthur Ave

N Troy St
N Albany Ave
N Whipple St
N Sacramento Ave
N California Ave
N Fairfield Ave
N Washtenaw Ave
N Maplewood Ave
N Campbell Ave
N Artesian Ave
N Claremont Ave
N Oakley Ave
N Bell Ave
N Leavitt St
N Hamilton Ave
N Hoyne Ave

N Kedzie Ave

Thillen's
Stadium

Croatian
Cultural Center

India
Town

W Devon Ave
W Devon Ave

35
▼

36
▼

W Highland Ave

W Rosemont Ave

1/4 mile          .25 km

As far north as you can go and still be in Chicago, Rogers Park and West Ridge have an intimate, residential feel drawing many families and retirees. Edged by Evanston, the neighborhoods are dotted with gardens, parks, sledding hills, baseball diamonds, tennis courts and jogging paths. Thanks in part to the spill-over population from East Rogers Park and Loyola University, Rogers Park has a tendency to attract academics and students.

Map

## ○ Landmarks

- **Bernard Horwich JCC** • 3003 W Touhy Ave
773-761-9100
Community center with programming for kids/adults, pool/fitness center, senior center, and sports leagues.
- **Croatian Cultural Center** • 2845 W Devon Ave
773-338-3839
A place where families can relax, socialize and congregate. Intended to benefit the Croatian community in Chicago (duh).
- **High Ridge YMCA** • 2424 W Touhy Ave
773-262-8300
Community center with programming for kids/adults, summer activities, child care programs, sport teams, and a pool.
- **India Town** • W Devon Ave & N Washtenaw Ave
Features Indian and Pakistani shops, grocery stores, restaurants, and more.
- **Indian Boundary Park** • 2500 W Lunt Ave
773-262-8658
Petting zoo, tennis courts, chess tables, ice rink, skate park, batting cages, spray pool, with seasonal community center classes.
- **Thillens Stadium** • 6404 N Kedzie Ave
312-742-4870
Chicago landmark. 16 softball fields. Features little league baseball and various other games and benefits.
- **Warren Park** • 6601 N Western Ave
773-262-6314
Seasonal free entertainment, pony rides, ethnic food festivals, amusement park rides, arts and crafts, winter sledding hill, baseball diamond, picnic pavilions, and dog play areas.

## Nightlife

- **Cary's Lounge** • 2251 W Devon Ave
773-743-5737
Locals' place to go for a nightcap.
- **McKellin's** • 2800 W Touhy Ave
773-973-2428
Cozy neighborhood Irish bar.
- **Mullen's** • 7301 N Western Ave
773-465-2113
Food until 1 am (10 pm on Sundays).

Map 48

41 42 43 44
27 28 29 30

Most of the action in West Rogers Park occurs on Devon Avenue. Thanks to the culture clash of its residents, the international marketplace is supported by dozens of inexpensive Indian and Pakistani restaurants, Bollywood video rentals, the best saris you'll find in the States and a slew of Islamic, Russian and Jewish bookstores and bakeries.

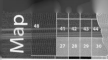# Restaurants

- **Annapurna** • 2608 W Devon Ave
  773-764-1858 • $
  Vegetarian fast food.
- **Arya Bhavan** • 2508 W Devon Ave
  773-274-5800 • $$
  Northern Indian all-vegetarian.
- **Candlelite** • 7452 N Western Ave
  773-465-0087 • $
  Rogers Park pizza institution, with cocktails.
- **Chopal Kabab & Steak** • 2240 W Devon Ave
  773-338-4080 • $
  When you need a kebob—late.
- **Hema's Kitchen** • 2439 W Devon Ave
  773-338-1627 • $$
  Like naan other.
- **Indian Garden** • 2546 W Devon Ave
  773-338-2929 • $$
  Get your tandoori here.
- **Mysore Woodlands** • 2548 W Devon Ave
  773-338-8160 • $$
  One of the better Indian spots in this strip.

- **Sabri Nihari** • 2502 W Devon Ave
  773-465-3272 • $$
  No booze here but super way delicious Pakistani food. Let's go!
- **Siam Pasta** • 7416 N Western Ave
  773-274-0579 • $
  Bangkok home cookin'.
- **Sukhadia Sweets and Snacks** •
  2559 W Devon Ave
  773-338-5400 • $
  Indian sweet maker and caterer.
- **Tiffin** • 2536 W Devon Ave
  773-338-2143 • $$
  Most upscale Indian restaurant on Devon, yet moderately priced.
- **Uru-Swati** • 2629 W Devon Ave
  773-381-1010 • $
  Vegetarian fast food and snacks.
- **Viceroy of India** • 2520 W Devon Ave
  773-743-4100 • $$
  Popular Indian restaurant, vegetarian options.

# Shopping

- **Al Mansoor Video** • 2600 W Devon Ave
773-764-7576
All-in-one Bollywood music and DVD.
- **Argo Georgian Bakery** • 2812 W Devon Ave
773-764-6322
Some Russian baked goods for your trouble?
- **AutoZone** • 2555 W Touhy Ave
773-764-5277
Stuff for your car.
- **JR Dessert Bakery** • 2841 W Howard St
773-465-6733
Over 20 flavors of cheesecakes.
- **Levinson's Bakery** • 2856 W Devon Ave
773-761-3174
Always fresh!

- **Office Mart** • 2801 W Touhy Ave
773-262-3924
Combination office supply store and and Internet coffee shop.
- **Raj Jewels** • 2652 W Devon Ave
773-465-5755
For all your Indian wedding needs.
- **Resham's** • 2540 W Devon Ave
773-764-9692
Saris and fabric fill the store.
- **Taj Sari Palace** • 2553 W Devon Ave
773-338-0177
Beautiful Indian clothing and accessories.
- **Tel-Aviv Kosher Bakery** • 2944 W Devon Ave
773-764-8877
Under the supervision of Rabbi Chaim Goldzweig!

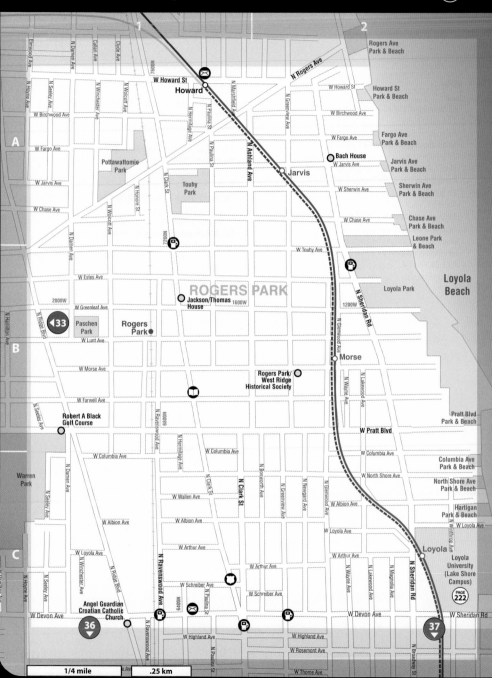

# Map 34 • **East Rogers Park**

N

1

2

Rogers Ave
Park & Beach

N Rogers Ave

W Howard St
**Howard**

W Howard St

Howard St
Park & Beach

N 1800W

N Marshfield Ave

N Paulina St

N Hermitage Ave

N Ashland Ave

N Greenview Ave

W Birchwood Ave

W Birchwood Ave

**A**

W Fargo Ave

Fargo Ave
Park & Beach

W Fargo Ave

Pottawattomie
Park

N Clark St

N Honore St

Touhy
Park

**Bach House**

W Jarvis Ave

**Jarvis**

Jarvis Ave
Park & Beach

W Jarvis Ave

N Wolcott Ave

N Damen Ave

N Seeley Ave

N Winchester Ave

W Chase Ave

W Sherwin Ave

Sherwin Ave
Park & Beach

W Chase Ave

Chase Ave
Park & Beach

N 1700W

W Touhy Ave

Leone Park
& Beach

W Estes Ave

2000W

**ROGERS PARK**

1600W

**Jackson/Thomas
House**

Loyola Park

N Sheridan Rd

**Loyola
Beach**

◀**33**

W Greenleaf Ave

Paschen
Park

**Rogers
Park**

N Hamilton Blvd

N Seeley Ave

1200W

**B**

W Lunt Ave

N Glenwood Ave

**Morse**

W Morse Ave

Rogers Park/
West Ridge
Historical Society

N Wayne Ave

N Lakewood Ave

W Farwell Ave

**Robert A Black
Golf Course**

N Ravenswood Ave

N 1600W

Pratt Blvd
Park & Beach

W Pratt Blvd

W Columbia Ave

W Columbia Ave

N Hermitage Ave

W Columbia Ave

Columbia Ave
Park & Beach

Warren
Park

N Damen Ave

N Clark St

N Bosworth Ave

N Greenview Ave

N Newgard Ave

N Glenwood Ave

W North Shore Ave

North Shore Ave
Park & Beach

W Wallen Ave

W Albion Ave

W Albion Ave

N Albion Ave

Hartigan
Park & Beach

N Seeley Ave

W Albion Ave

W Arthur Ave

W Loyola Ave

N Winthrop Ave

W Loyola Ave

**C**

W Loyola Ave

N Winchester Ave

N Ridge Blvd

W Arthur Ave

N Wayne Ave

N Lakewood Ave

N Magnolia Ave

N Sheridan Rd

W Arthur Ave

**Loyola**

Loyola
University
(Lake Shore
Campus)

N Hoyne Ave

**Angel Guardian
Croatian Catholic
Church**

N Ravenswood Ave

N 600W

N Paulina St

W Schreiber Ave

W Schreiber Ave

W Devon Ave

W Devon Ave

**PAGE
222**

**36**
▼

W Devon Ave

W Highland Ave

W Highland Ave

W Sheridan Rd

N Broadway St

**37**
▼

W Rosemont Ave

W Thome Ave

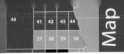

East Rogers Park is stitched together with Loyola students, civic-minded young professionals, new immigrants, old hippies and blue-collared middle-class denizens. While densely populated and lively, the neighborhood's seams sometimes show as crime and gang activity continues to be a problem. The draw of easy access to public transportation, lakefront accessibility, cultural diversity and Loyola's campus makes East Rogers Park an inexpensive, colorful neighborhood to reside in.

## Landmarks

- **Angel Guardian Croatian Catholic Church** •
  6346 N Ridge Ave
  773-262-0535
  1905 red-brick Romanesque church. Turn-of-the-century German stained glass windows by Franz Mayer and F. X. Zettler.
- **Bach House** • 7415 N Sheridan Rd
  One of Frank Lloyd Wright's final "small" houses, c. 1915.
- **Jackson/Thomas House** • 7053 N Ridge Ave
  Lovely Italianate home dates back to 1874.
- **Robert A. Black Golf Course** • 2045 W Pratt Blvd
  312-742-7931
  The newest Chicago Park District course. 2,300-yard, par 33 layout for all skill levels.
- **Rogers Park/West Ridge Historical Society** •
  1447 W Morse Ave
  773-764-4078
  Photos/memorabilia/historical documents of the community's history detailing its ethnic diversity.

## Nightlife

- **Hop Haus** • 7545 N Clark St
  773-262-3783
  Burgers 'n' beer.
- **Jackhammer** • 6406 N Clark St
  773-743-5772
  Gay bar with a welcoming neighborhood vibe.
- **Mayne Stage** • 1328 W Morse Ave
  773-381-4551
  Catch a comedy show and more.
- **Red Line Tap** • 7006 N Glenwood Ave
  773-274-5463
  Brews and bands on the Red Line.
- **Touche** • 6412 N Clark St
  773-465-7400
  Drunken gay leather bar.

115

Cheap eats abound if you know where to look in East Rogers Park (hint: follow the students). Health-nuts will feel at home in the **Heartland Café** which features a gift shop, open mic nights and live music. Head to Clark Street where Mexican eateries offering authentic food at low prices dot the area, while Howard Street's **Caribbean American Bakery** and **Tickie's** give you a sweet taste of Afro-Caribbean culture. The **Jackhammer** complex of gay bars offers something for everyone—a sports bar, a fern bar and a leather bar, all in one. Weekend nights, catch a comedy show at the **Mayne Stage** and have dinner next door at gastropub **Act One Pub**.

# Restaurants

- **A&T Grill** • 7036 N Clark St
773-274-0036 • $
Classic diner-grill.
- **Act One Pub** • 1330 W Morse Ave
773-381-4550 • $$$
Round out a show at the Mayne Stage with dinner.
- **Buffalo Joe's** • 1841 W Howard St
773-764-7300 • $
Wings and fast food carryout spot, with a soul food flava.
- **Capt'n Nemos** • 7367 N Clark St
773-973-0570 • $
Free soup sample while you wait at this always jovial local sandwich chain.
- **Caribbean American Bakery** • 1539 W Howard St
773-761-0700 • $
Jamaican bakery featuring meat pies, pastries, and jerk chicken for carryout.
- **Ciao Bella Café** • 6800 N Sheridan Rd
773-942-6613 • $$
Pop in for coffee or stay for brunch.
- **Deluxe Diner** • 6349 N Clark St
773-743-8244 • $
Retro-styled greasy spoon.
- **El Famous Burrito** • 7047 N Clark St
773-465-0377 • $
Best greasy burrito in Chicago.
- **Ethiopian Diamond** • 7537 N Clark St
773-764-2200 • $$
Roger's Park outpost of beloved Uptown Ethiopian.
- **Ghareeb Nawaz** • 2032 W Devon Ave
773-761-5300 • $
Indo-Pakistani lunch counter on the east side of the strip.
- **Good to Go Jamaican Jerk and Juice Bar** • 1947 W Howard St
773-381-7777 • $$
Jamaican cuisine.

- **Grande Noodles and Sushi Bar** • 6632 N Clark St
773-761-6666 • $$
Damn fine pot stickers.
- **Heartland Cafe** • 7000 N Glenwood Ave
773-465-8005 • $$
Brown rice, socialist newspapers, and vegetarian tidbits reign here.
- **Jamaica Jerk** • 1631 W Howard St
773-764-1546 • $
Jamaican comfort food best for carry-out.
- **Masouleh** • 6653 N Clark St
773-262-2227 • $
Within this unassuming storefront lies the best Iranian food in the city.
- **Noon Hour Grill** • 6930 N Glenwood Ave
773-338-9494 • $
Korean diner and grill is neighborhood favorite.
- **Sahara Kabob** • 6649 N Clark St
773-262-2000 • $
Local fave for fresh & tasty Middle eastern.
- **Sauce and Bread Kitchen** • 6338 N Clark St
773-942-6384 • $
Sandwiches starring the cafés housemade hot sauces and baked goods.
- **Tamales Lo Mejor de Guerrero** • 7024 N Clark St
773-338-6450 • $
Carry out tamales so good, that may ruin "the tamale guy" for you.
- **Taste of Peru** • 6545 N Clark St
773-381-4540 • $
Barebones spot for cheap, authentic Peruvian food.
- **Thai Spice** • 1320 W Devon Ave
773-973-0504 • $
Look beyond the grim exterior for freshly prepared Thai.
- **Tickie's Belizean Cuisine** • 7605 N Paulina St
773-973-3919 • $
Authentic Caribbean food in cheerful storefront across from the Howard L.

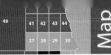

# Shopping

- **The Armadillo's Pillow** • 6753 N Sheridan Rd
  773-761-2558
  Score some paperbacks for cheap.
- **Flatts & Sharpe Music Company** • 6749 N
  Sheridan Rd
  773-465-5233
  Cheap guitars ($150), offering lessons and music
  accessories.

- **Marjen Furniture** • 1536 W Devon Ave
  773-338-6636
  Cheap futons, dorm furniture.
- **Newleaf Natural Grocery** • 1261 W Loyola Ave
  773-743-0400
  Adorable, horribly expensive organic grocery, as
  per usual.
- **Romanian Kosher Sausage Co.** • 7200 N Clark St
  773-761-4141
  Kosher meat and poultry.

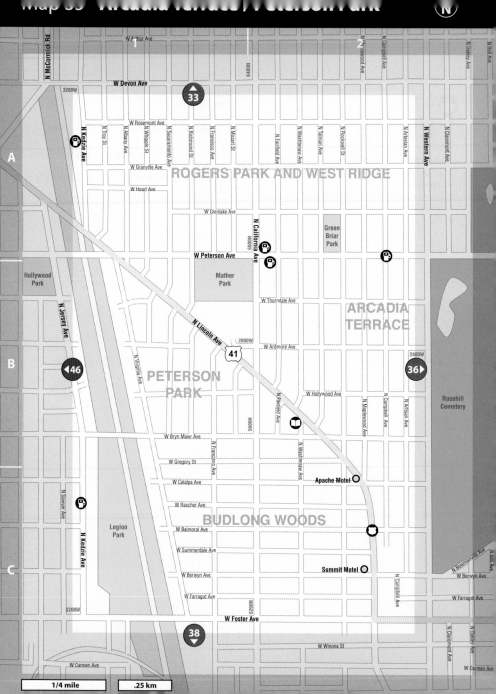

Map 35  Arcadia Terrace / Peterson Park

N

1/4 mile

.25 km

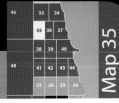

Map 35

This quiet enclave snuggled between the Chicago River and Rosehill Cemetery is home to many Koreans, Middle Easterners, and Eastern Europeans. Touted by real estate agents as an "up and comer" as the seedy motels on Lincoln Avenue, once reputable, are torn down one-by-one due to their decrepit conditions and increasingly bad reputations and new condos dot the skyline. Arcadian Terrace and Peterson Park are becoming increasingly desirable for young families priced out of Ravenswood and Andersonville.

## ○ Landmarks

- **Apache Motel** • 5535 N Lincoln Ave
  773-728-9400
  Another sleazy motel on Lincoln with cool vintage signs.
- **Summit Motel** • 5308 N Lincoln Ave

## ▼ Nightlife

- **Emerald Isle** • 2537 W Peterson Ave
  773-775-2848
  Ahh, the Emerald Isle!
- **Hidden Cove** • 5338 N Lincoln Ave
  773-275-6711
  Sports bar with trivia, darts, and karaoke.
- **Karaoke Restaurant** • 6248 N California Ave
  773-274-1166
  Korean food and private karaoke rooms.
- **Lincoln Karaoke** • 5526 N Lincoln Ave
  773-895-2299
  Korean karaoke parlor with bar and private party rooms.

## 🍴 Restaurants

- **Aztecas Mexican Taqueria** • 5421 N Lincoln Ave
  773-506-2052 • $
  Standard Mexican fare.
- **Charcoal Delights** • 3139 W Foster Ave
  773-583-0056 • $
  Great gyros to go.
- **Da Rae Jung** • 5220 N Lincoln Ave
  773-907-9155 • $$
  Mom and Pop Seoul food storefront.
- **Fondue Stube** • 2717 W Peterson Ave
  773-784-2200 • $$
  Fun fondue!
- **Hae Woon Dae** • 6240 N California Ave
  773-764-8018 • $$
  Fish heads and pork shoulders above competing late-night Korean bbq joints.
- **IHOP** • 5929 N Lincoln Ave
  773-769-1550 • $
  It's an IHOP for Pete's sake. What else do you need to know?
- **Katsu** • 2651 W Peterson Ave
  773-784-3383 • $$$
  Familiar, family sushi place.
- **Pueblito Viejo** • 5429 N Lincoln Ave
  773-784-9135 • $$
  Adorable Columbian village-theme with live music on weekends.
- **Solga** • 5828 N Lincoln Ave
  773-728-0802 • $$$
  Korean BBQ with charcoal grill.
- **Sweet Collective** • 5333 N Lincoln Ave
  773-293-0888 • $
  It's the homemade ice cream, stupid.
- **Wolfy's Hot Dogs** • 2734 W Peterson Ave
  773-743-0207 • $
  Dine in and carry out dogs, burgers, and such.
- **Woo Chon** • 5744 N California Ave
  773-728-8001 • $
  Authentic Korean BBQ. Brusque but oddly fun service.

# Map 36 • Bryn Mawr / Bowmanville

ROGERS PARK
AND WEST RIDGE

Green
Briar
Park

Rosehill
Cemetery

BOWMANVILLE

Winnemac
Park

1/4 mile          .25 km

Old fashioned iron lamp posts line Bryn Mawr's charming historic district while young families push strollers, walk dogs, and have brunch. Bryn Mawr/Bowmanville also boasts **Rosehill Cemetery**, a 350-acre Chicago landmark that is the final resting place for luminaries like Montgomery Ward, Richard Sears, Oscar Mayer, several Chicago mayors and one Vice President (Charles Gates Dawes).

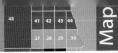
## ○ Landmarks

- **Rosehill Cemetery** • 5800 N Ravenswood Ave
  773-561-5940
  Chicago's historical glitterati entombed among unsurpassed sculpture and architecture.

## 🍸 Nightlife

- **Big Joe's** • 1818 W Foster Ave
  773-784-8755
  Corner bar endorsed by the Windy City Darters.
- **Bobbie's Runaway** • 5305 N Damen Ave
  773-271-6488
  Mr. Winkie holds court here.
- **Claddagh Ring** • 2306 W Foster Ave
  773-271-4794
  Traditional Irish-American bar.
- **Fireside Restaurant & Lounge** •
  5739 N Ravenswood Ave
  773-561-7433
  Good late-night bar with above average grub.
- **K's Dugout** • 1930 W Foster Ave
  773-561-2227
  Drink and watch sports, drink and watch sports, drink and…
- **Leadway Bar** • 5233 N Damen Ave
  773-728-2663
  Artsy bar with free picture-painting and pool-playing.
- **Sherry's Bar** • 5652 N Western Ave
  773-784-2143
  The perfect local spot for the aging hipsters who've been moving into this 'hood.

## 🍴 Restaurants

- **Blue Nile** • 6118 N Ravenswood Ave
  773-465-6710 • $
  Hefty portions of Ethiopian stews to be sopped up with inerja.
- **Fireside Restaurant & Lounge** •
  5739 N Ravenswood Ave
  773-561-7433 • $$
  Cajun-tinged barfood and late kitchen.
- **Greenhouse Inn** • 6300 N Ridge Ave
  773-273-4182 • $
  Church and bridge groups meet for homemade soups.
- **Max's Italian Beef** • 5754 N Western Ave
  773-989-8200 • $$
  Chicago institution; home of the pepper-and-egg sandwich.
- **Pauline's** • 1754 W Balmoral Ave
  773-561-8573 • $
  Weekend breakfast hotspot; try the famous five-egg omelet, if you must.
- **San Soo Gab San** • 5247 N Western Ave
  773-334-1589 • $$
  Do-it-yourself Korean barbeque at 4 am.
- **Yes Thai** • 5211 N Damen Ave
  773-878-3487 • $
  Noodles and curries in a cozy atmosphere.

## 🛍 Shopping

- **Target** • 2112 W Peterson Ave
  773-761-3001
  All you need, under one roof.

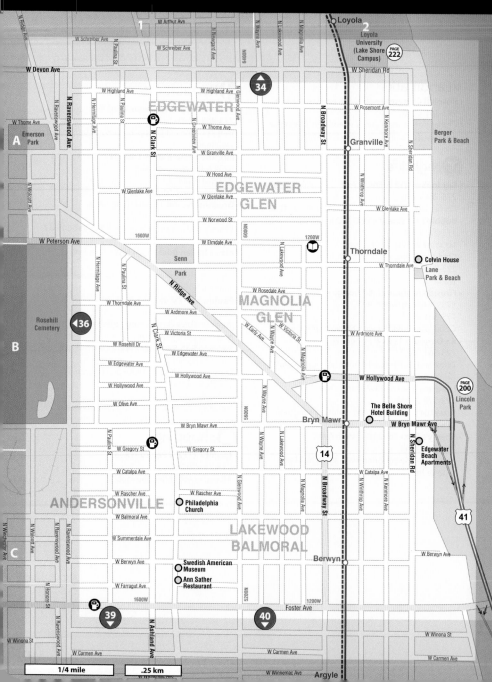

Map 37 • **Edge**

A century ago, Chicago had a robust Swedish population whose epicenter was Andersonville. The Swedish influence remains, dotting the stroll-friendly commercial areas with Swedish businesses and restaurants, but gentrification is slowly creeping in with swelling property taxes and encroaching big chains. Lakefront community Edgewater is a liberal, pretty paradise and features Chicago's gay beach at Hollywood.

| | | | | |
|---|---|---|---|---|
| 48 | 41 | 42 | 43 | 44 |
| | 27 | 28 | 29 | 30 |

## ○ Landmarks

- **Ann Sather Restaurant** • 5207 N Clark St
773-271-6677
More than a restaurant; a cultural field trip.
- **Belle Shore Apartment Hotel** •
1062 W Bryn Mawr Ave
Former homes of roaring 1920s nightlife, now historic landmarks restored to their former glory as apartments.
- **Colvin House** • 5940 N Sheridan Rd
Designed by George Maher and built in 1909.
- **Edgewater Beach Apartments** •
5555 N Sheridan Rd
The big pink building symbolizing the end of the lakeshore bike path.
- **Philadelphia Church** • 5437 N Clark St
Complete with can't-miss neon sign.
- **Swedish American Museum** • 5211 N Clark St
773-728-8111
Everything you want to know about Swedish culture, which is more than you thought.

## 🍸 Nightlife

- **@tmosphere** • 5355 N Clark St
773-784-1100
Trendy gay bar with dance floor and DJs.
- **Edgewater Lounge** • 5600 N Ashland Ave
773-878-3343
Alehouse with open-mike on Tuesdays for singers.
- **Farraguts** • 5240 N Clark St
773-728-4903
Neighborhood dive, less yuppie than Simon's.
- **Granville Anvil** • 1137 W Granville Ave
773-973-0006
Gay old-timers drink here.
- **Joie de Vine** • 1744 W Balmoral Ave
773-989-6846
Casual wine bar popular with local lesbians.
- **Marty's Martini Bar** • 1511 W Balmoral Ave
773-454-0161
Compact and classy.
- **Moody's Pub** • 5910 N Broadway St
773-275-2696
Best beer garden in the city. Long wait times.
- **Ollie's Lounge** • 1064 W Berwyn Ave
773-784-5712
A rare quiet neighborhood joint.
- **The Pumping Company** • 6157 N Broadway St
773-465-9500
Cozy neighborhood dive with a fireplace and beergarden.
- **Simon's Tavern** • 5210 N Clark St
773-878-0894
Thrift-store-attired hipsters and Swedish nautical theme.
- **Sovereign Liquors** • 6202 N Broadway St
773-274-0057
Cheap, laidback neighborhood joint frozen in time.
- **St. Andrew's Inn** • 5938 N Broadway St
773-784-5540
Food and spirits…of the haunted sort.

Map
48
41 42 43 44
27 28 29 30

No other neighborhood rewards a weekend afternoon ramble like Andersonville. Brunchers gorge on five-egg omelets at **Pauline's** and sip the dizzying selection of artisan beers served up at the **Hopleaf**. Follow an indulgent meal with a stroll down Clark Street, populated with independently owned shops with international wares including **Pars Persian Store** and the **Swedish Bakery**.

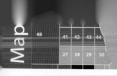 Restaurants

- **Andies** • 5253 N Clark St
  773-784-8616 • $$
  Fresh Middle Eastern in airy atmosphere.
- **Ann Sather Restaurant** • 5207 N Clark St
  773-271-6677 • $
  Heavenly cinnamon rolls and swedish meatballs.
- **Anteprima** • 5316 N Clark St
  773-506-9990 • $$$
  This cozy A-Ville Italian just feels right.
- **Antica Pizzeria** • 5663 N Clark St
  773-944-1492 • $
  Brick oven goodness.
- **Big Jones** • 5347 N Clark St
  773-275-5725 • $$$
  High falutin' southern chow.
- **Edgewater Beach Cafe** • 5545 N Sheridan Rd
  773-275-4141 • $$$
  Neighborhood Frenchie in the pink building.
- **Ethiopian Diamond** • 6120 N Broadway St
  773-338-6100 • $$$
  Visit for jazz on Fridays.
- **Francesca's Bryn Mawr** • 1039 W Bryn Mawr Ave
  773-506-9261 • $$
  Dined in an SRO before?
- **George's Ice Cream and Sweets** • 5306 N Clark St
  773-271-7600 • $
  Ice cream of every flavor. Fat Elvis tastes the best.
- **Hamburger Mary's** • 5400 N Clark St
  773-784-6969 • $$
  Flamboyant burger joint popular with families and The Gays.
- **Huey's Hot Dogs** • 1507 W Balmoral Ave
  773-293-4800 • $
  Fast, friendly dogs and burgers.
- **Icosium Kafe** • 5200 N Clark St
  773-271-5233 • $
  It's crepe-tastic!
- **Indie Café** • 5951 N Broadway St
  773-561-5577 • $$
  Thai and sushi. Yummy and cheap.

- **Jin Ju** • 5203 N Clark St
  773-334-6377 • $$$
  Upscale Korean.
- **Kitchen Sink Cafe** • 1107 W Berwyn Ave
  773-944-0592 • $
  Serves savory specialty mochas. Has a nice skylight.
- **La Fonda Latino Grill** • 5350 N Broadway St
  773-271-3935 • $$
  Real tasty pan-Latin.
- **Loving Hut** • 5812 N Broadway St
  773-275-8797 • $
  Vegan diner with new owners. Bright decor, cheap, and crunchy.
- **M. Henry** • 5707 N Clark St
  773-561-1600 • $$
  Stylish brunch option in Andersonville.
- **Moody's Pub** • 5910 N Broadway St
  773-275-2696 • $
  Burgers only, but the best.
- **Piatto Pronto** • 5624 N Clark St
  773-334-5688 • $
  Tasty sandwiches for not a lot of dough.
- **Ras Dashen** • 5846 N Broadway St
  773-506-9601 • $$
  Traditional Ethiopian comfort food; vegan-friendly.
- **Reza's** • 5255 N Clark St
  773-561-1898 • $$
  Many Persian options, leftovers for lunch the next day.
- **Sunshine Cafe** • 5449 N Clark St
  773-334-6214 •
  Wait on wkends for excellent & cheap Japanese noodles.
- **Svea** • 5236 N Clark St
  773-275-7738 • $
  Adorable, tiny Swedish diner.
- **Tanoshii** • 5547 N Clark St
  773-878-6886 • $$
  Order from the chef for innovative sushi.
- **Taste of Lebanon** • 1509 W Foster Ave
  773-334-1600 • $
  Dongy room, rock-bottom prices, above-average Mid-east fare.

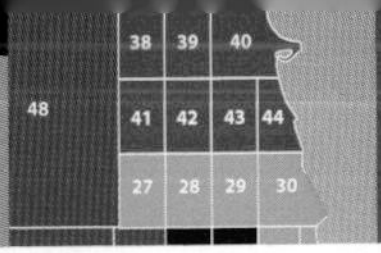

Map 3

# Shopping

- **Alamo Shoes** • 5321 N Clark St
773-784-8936
Large selection for the soles from local retailer.
- **Andersonville Galleria** • 5247 N Clark St
773-878-8570
Indie mall with over 90 vendors.
- **Brimfield** • 5219 N Clark St
773-271-3501
Eclectic design sensibility favoring plaid.
- **Broadway Antique Market** • 6130 N Broadway St
773-743-5444
BAM! Calling all mallrats and antique freaks—one
of America's most reviewed antique stores.
- **The Brown Elephant** • 5404 N Clark St
773-271-9382
Resale shop benefits local HIV clinic.
- **Brownstone Antiques** • 5234 N Clark St
773-878-9800
Cluttered estate sale finds.
- **Cassona** • 5241 N Clark St
773-506-7882
Gorgeous home furnishings.
- **Early to Bed** • 5232 N Sheridan Rd
773-271-1219
Woman-oriented grown-up toys. Boy friendly.
- **Edgewater Antique Mall** • 6314 N Broadway St
773-262-2525
20th century antiques and vintage.
- **Elda de la Rosa** • 5555 N Sheridan Rd
773-769-3128
Custom gowns and dresses.
- **Gethsemane Garden Center** • 5739 N Clark St
773-878-5915
Like mini-trip to a botanical garden; but you can
take it home.
- **Johnny Sprockets** • 1052 W Bryn Mawr Ave
773-293-1697
Caters to all your bicycle needs.

- **Middle East Bakery & Grocery** •
1512 W Foster Ave
773-561-2224
So good, so cheap.
- **Mr. & Mrs. Digz** • 5668 N Clark St
773-447-8527
Funky used clothes boutique.
- **Pars Persian Store** • 5260 N Clark St
773-769-6635
$1/lb for curry powder. Enough curry for Chicago's
winterpocalypse.
- **Presence** • 5216 N Clark St
773-989-4420
Cool boutique for young women.
- **The Red Balloon Company** • 5407 N Clark St
773-989-8500
A unique store for children—toys, clothes and
furniture.
- **Room Service** • 5438 N Clark St
773-878-5438
Mid-Century design.
- **Roost** • 5634 N Clark St
773-506-0406
Cute furniture for your cute home.
- **Scout** • 5221 N Clark St
773-275-5700
Beautiful urban antiques.
- **Toys Et Cetera** • 5311 N Clark St
773-769-5311
Educational toys and quality books for kids.
- **True Nature Foods** • 6034 N Broadway St
773-465-6400
Pick up your weekly CSA box of fruits and veggies
from your local farmers.
- **Tulip Toy Gallery** • 1480 W Berwyn Ave
773-275-6110
Woman-owned, inviting sex paraphenalia shop.
- **White Attic** • 5225 N Clark St
773-907-9800
Clean home furnishings and art work.
- **Women & Children First** • 5233 N Clark St
773-769-9299
World's biggest feminist bookstore.

Once home to Charlie Chaplin, and hallowed jogging ground of infamously incarcerated Governor Rod "Blago" Blagojevich, a Ravenswood local, the quarter-mile section of Ravenswood known as The Manor has been a charming riverside haven for generations of Chicago's elite. Farther west, Albany Park boasts the distinction of being one of the nation's most culturally diverse 'hoods, a diversity reflected in local shops where you'll find the kim chee shelved between taramasalata and queso quesadillas.

## ○ Landmarks

- **Charlie Chaplin House** • 4637 N Manor Ave
  Charlie Chaplin's home during his Essanay studio stint.
- **Paradise Sauna** • 2916 W Montrose Ave
  773-588-3304
  It's a sushi restaurant. It's a beauty shop. It's a sauna ($12, unlimited time). It's Paradise. Of course, it's a neighborhood landmark.
- **Ravenswood Manor Park** • 4626 N Manor Ave
  It's just a tiny triangle wedged between the non-elevated L and several streets, but it's ground zero for garden sales, neighborhood associations, dogs, kids, and community activity.
- **River Park** • 5100 N Francisco Ave
  312-742-7516
  More than 30 acres of park, including one of the few city canoe launches.
- **Ronan Park Nature Trail** • 3000 W Argyle St
  These boots are made for…walking!

## Nightlife

- **Brown Rice** • 4432 N Kedzie Ave
  312-543-7027
  Tiny venue for tiny jazz acts.
- **Lincoln Square Lanes** • 4874 N Lincoln Ave
  773-561-8191
  Brews and bowling above a hardware store. Cheap date.
- **Montrose Saloon** • 2933 W Montrose Ave
  773-463-7663
  Classic Chicago "Old Style." No cell phones, please.
- **The Peek Inn** • 2825 W Irving Park Rd
  773-267-5197
  Cool little dive worth a peek.

Map
48
41 42 43 44
27 28 29 30
21 22 31 32

If you're in the mood for halal meat or in the market to purchase a hookah, North Kedzie around Lawrence Avenue is a magnificent Middle Eastern mélange of grocery stores and restaurants. If, on the other hand, you're in the mood for a wild night, be prepared to hail a cab. There isn't much of a nightlight in this charming but sleepy neighborhood.

# Restaurants

- **Arun's** • 4156 N Kedzie Ave
  773-539-1909 • $$$$$
  Worldwide rep for four-star prix fixe Thai.
- **Brasa Roja** • 3125 W Montrose Ave
  773-866-2252 • $$
  Friendly Columbian place specializing in flame-roasted chicken.
- **Dawali** • 4911 N Kedzie Ave
  773-267-4200 •
  Try the "classic felafel" sandwich with potato and cauliflower.
- **Dharma Garden** • 3109 W Irving Park Rd
  773-588-9140 • $
  Thai vegetarian and seafood dishes. Karaoke some evenings.
- **Golden Crust Pizzeria** • 4620 N Kedzie Ave
  773-539-5385 • $
  Honkin' portions of the Italian-American comfort food of yore.
- **Goosefoot** • 2656 W Lawrence Ave
  773-942-7547 • $$$$$
  Upscale Contemporary American cuisine nestled in Chicago's North Side.
- **Lutz Café & Pastry Shop** • 2458 W Montrose Ave
  773-478-7785 • $$
  If Grandma was German, she would serve these pastries.
- **Mi Ciudad** • 3041 W Irving Park Rd
  773-866-2066 • $$
  Simple Ecuadorean: corn cakes, empanadas, fruit shakes.
- **Nhu Lan's Bakery** • 2612 W Lawrence Ave
  773-878-9898 • $
  Vietnamese sandwich shop.
- **Noon O Kabab** • 4661 N Kedzie Ave
  773-279-9309 • $
  Bring a doggie bag for day-after lunch.
- **Paradise Sauna** • 2916 W Montrose Ave
  773-588-3304 • $$
  Competent sushi connected to a Korean spa.
- **Rockwell's Neighborhood Grill** •
  4632 N Rockwell St
  773-509-1871 • $
  Familiar bar food and brunchtime favorites in a friendly atmosphere.
- **Salam** • 4634 N Kedzie Ave
  773-583-0776 • $
  Home of the 19-cent falafel.
- **Semiramis** • 4639 N Kedzie Ave
  773-279-8900 • $$
  Lebanese with great value to quality ratio. Try the sumac fries.
- **Thai Valley** • 4600 N Kedzie Ave
  773-588-2020 • $
  BYOB Thai restaurant with lunch specials.

Map 3

# 🛍Shopping

- **Lincoln Antique Mall** • 3115 W Irving Park Rd
773-604-4700
Mid-sized antique mall.

- **The Music Store** • 3121 W Irving Park Rd
773-478-7400
Guitars and other musical instruments.

- **Village Discount Outlet** • 4027 N Kedzie Ave
866-545-3836
Tons of clothes and weekly specials.

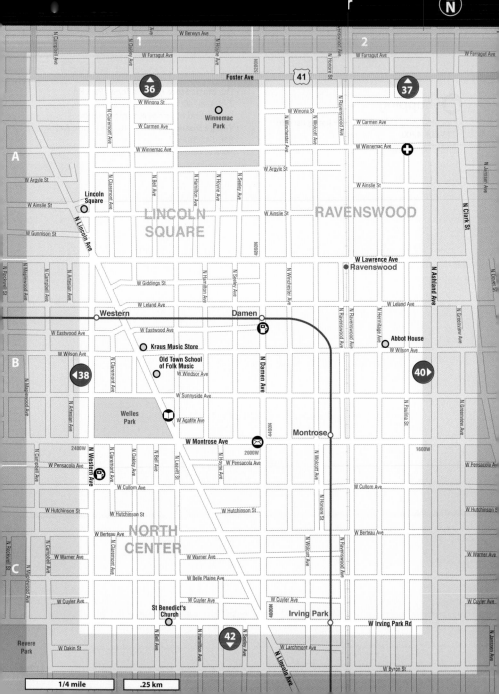

Ravenswood and North Center are by and large the hip place to be seen pushing an expensive stroller. Lincoln Square is its epicenter, featuring plenty of wine stores and bars with stroller parking. It's not all yuppie though. An old German immigrant presence still exists in restaurants like the **Chicago Brauhaus** (featuring live Oompah bands on the weekends) and annual German festivals (Mayfest and Christkindl) directly off the Western L.

## ⊙ Landmarks

- **Abbott House** • 4605 N Hermitage Ave
  Comely Queen Anne painted-lady built in 1891 for Abbott labs founder.
- **Krause Music Store** • 4611 N Lincoln Ave
  It's easy to overlook this Louis Sullivan beauty on a bustling commercial strip.
- **Lincoln Square** • 4800 N Lincoln Ave
  773-728-3890
  A virtual tour through a European-style neighborhood.
- **Old Town School of Folk Music** •
  4544 N Lincoln Ave
  773-728-6000
  Northern expansion of beloved Chicago institution. Classes and concert venue.
- **St. Benedict Parish & School** •
  2215 W Irving Park Rd
  773-588-6484
  The namesake of the St. Ben's neighborhood.
- **Winnemac Park** • 5001 N Leavitt St
  312-742-5101
  Cute neighborhood park, replete with families and children playing.

## 🍸 Nightlife

- **Celtic Crown Public House** • 4301 N Western Ave
  773-588-1110
  Great specials without over-Irishing it!
- **Chicago Brauhaus** • 4732 N Lincoln Ave
  773-784-4444
  More German than Germany…even in Oktober.
- **Daily Bar & Grill** • 4560 N Lincoln Ave
  773-561-6198
  Bar food in retro ambiance.
- **The Globe Pub** • 1934 W Irving Park Rd
  773-871-3757
  Great music venue gone sportsbar.
- **The Grafton** • 4530 N Lincoln Ave
  773-271-9000
  Outstanding bar food and friendly atmosphere.

- **Horseshoe** • 4115 N Lincoln Ave
  773-549-9292
  They have both kinds of music here: country and western.
- **Huettenbar** • 4721 N Lincoln Ave
  773-561-2507
  German-town favorite with great beer selection.
- **Katerina's** • 1920 W Irving Park Rd
  773-348-7592
  Live jazz, gypsy music, and local rock at this European lounge.
- **Laschet's Inn** • 2119 W Irving Park Rd
  773-478-7915
  Pull on the Lederhosen!
- **The Lincoln Lodge** • 4008 N Lincoln Ave
  773-251-1539
  A funny night on the town.
- **O'Donovan's** • 2100 W Irving Park Rd
  773-478-2100
  It's a neighborhood bar. You can watch sports.
- **O'Lanagan's** • 2335 W Montrose Ave
  773-583-2252
  Not an Irishman in sight!
- **Oakwood 83** • 1959 W Montrose Ave
  773-327-2785
  Glorified version of your uncle Frank's basement.
- **The Rail** • 4709 N Damen Ave
  773-878-9400
  One-time dive, the rail rocks in Ravenswood.
- **Resi's Bierstube** • 2034 W Irving Park Rd
  773-472-1749
  Wear your leiderhosen.
- **Tiny Lounge** • 4352 N Leavitt St
  773-463-0396
  Tiny name, but big on flavorful cocktails.
- **Wild Goose** • 4265 N Lincoln Ave
  773-281-7112
  Guy's bar. Cheap eats, TVs and games.
- **Windy City Inn** • 2257 W Irving Park Rd
  773-588-7088
  Nice family feel…if you're from Kentucky.

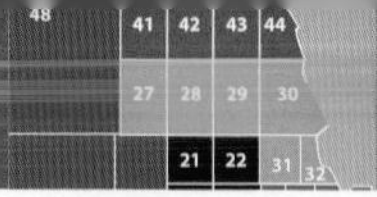

Map 48  41 42 43 44  27 28 29 30  21 22 31 32

By day, local yuppies shop at places like the **Book Cellar**, a cute bookshop cum wine café, and browse-friendly **Merz Apothecary**. By night, a stretch of Lincoln Avenue becomes restaurant row featuring mouth-watering international fare including **Opart Thai**, **Chicago Brauhaus**, and **Spacca Napoli**. The **Davis Theater** sates cinephiles with their no-frills, low-priced flicks.

# 🍴 Restaurants

- **Bad Dog Tavern** • 4535 N Lincoln Ave
  773-334-4040 • $$
  Food, fireplace, and folk music.
- **Bistro Campagne** • 4518 N Lincoln Ave
  773-271-6100 • $$
  Organic French fare in a cozy room.
- **Browntrout** • 4111 N Lincoln Ave
  773-472-4111 • $$
  Sustainable hoodie with a fish proclivity.
- **Budacki's Drive-In** • 4739 N Damen Ave
  773-561-1322 • $
  Artery clogging late-night eats.
- **Café Selmarie** • 4729 N Lincoln Ave
  773-989-5595 • $$
  Bright clean, bakery/cafe with wine and beer.
- **Chalkboard** • 4343 N Lincoln Ave
  773-477-7144 • $$$
  Inventive spin on comfort classics.
- **Chicago Brauhaus** • 4732 N Lincoln Ave
  773-784-4444 • $$
  Live German music in beerhouse atmosphere.
- **Diner Grill** • 1635 W Irving Pk Rd
  773-248-2030 • $
  Home to the infamous "Slinger." Motto: Eat it here, leave it somewhere else.

- **Eat N Drink** • 4649 N Damen Ave
  773-506-8689 • $
  Cheap Chinese food and fresh smoothies.
- **Elizabeth** • 4835 N Western Ave
  773-681-0651 • $$$$$
  Communal dining at its finest.
- **Essence of India** • 4601 N Lincoln Ave
  773-506-0002 • $$
  Traditional northern Indian food, fancier than Devon St.
- **First Slice** • 4401 N Ravenswood Ave
  773-506-7380 • $$
  Upscale café benefiting the hungry in more ways than one.
- **Glenn's Diner** • 1820 W Montrose Ave
  773-506-1720 • $$
  Fish-focused American fare.
- **Glunz Bavarian Haus** • 4128 N Lincoln Ave
  773-472-4287 • $$
  Weiner schnitzel and beer.
- **Golden Angel Restaurant** • 4340 N Lincoln Ave
  773-583-6969 • $
  24-hour diner.
- **Horseshoe** • 4115 N Lincoln Ave
  773-549-9292 • $
  They have both kinds of music here: country and western.

- **House of Wah Sun** • 4319 N Lincoln Ave
773-477-0800 • $
Chinese/Cantonese/Mandarin eatery.
- **La Amistad** • 1914 W Montrose Ave
773-878-5800 • $
No fusion here, just reliable Mexican.
- **La Boca della Verita** • 4618 N Lincoln Ave
773-784-6222 • $$
Cozy Italian café.
- **Lincoln Restaurant** • 4008 N Lincoln Ave
773-248-1820 • $$
Old-school family joint. Been there forever.
- **Los Nopales** • 4544 N Western Ave
773-334-3149 • $$
Creative, cheap Mexican BYOB.
- **Margie's Candies** • 1813 W Montrose Ave
773-348-0400 • $
Ridiculously decadent sundaes and homemade
confections.
- **Opart Thai House** • 4658 N Western Ave
773-989-8517 • $
Local favorite for fresh Thai. BYOB.
- **Orange Garden** • 1942 W Irving Park Rd
773-525-7479 • $$
Over seventy years of Cantonese cooking.

- **Over Easy Café** • 4943 N Damen Ave
773-506-2605 • $
Bright breakfast spot.
- **Pannenkoeken Cafe** • 4757 N Western Ave
773-769-8800 • $
It's like having dessert for breakfast!
- **Roong Petch** • 1828 W Montrose Ave
773-989-0818 • $
Vegetarians get their own special menu.
- **Smokin' Woody's** • 4160 N Lincoln Ave
773-880-1100 • $$
Ribs 'n' wings 'n' other sticky eats.
- **Snappy's Shrimp House** • 1901 W Irving Park Rd
773-244-1008 • $
Frozen or friend shrimp to go.
- **Spacca Napoli** • 1769 W Sunnyside Ave
773-878-2420 • $$
Neapolitan styles pizza in Ravenswood.
- **Sticky Rice** • 4018 N Western Ave
773-588-0133 • $
No frills storefront serves amazing Thai for cheap!
- **Tank Sushi** • 4514 N Lincoln Ave
773-769-2600 • $$
Fresh sushi with Latin flair.

Map

| 48 | | | | |
|---|---|---|---|---|
| | 41 | 42 | 43 | 44 |
| | 27 | 28 | 29 | 30 |
| | 21 | 22 | 31 | 32 |

# 🛍 Shopping

- **Alapash Home** • 1944 W Montrose Ave
773-769-8825
Terrariums and other home goods.
- **Angel Food Bakery** • 1636 W Montrose Ave
773-728-1512
Whimsical bakery with interesting sandwiches to
go.
- **Architectural Artifacts** • 4325 N Ravenswood Ave
773-348-0622
Renovator's dream.
- **Book Cellar** • 4736 N Lincoln Ave
773-293-2665
Book store/coffee shop/wine bar. Also has
sandwiches.
- **Chicago Soccer** • 4839 N Western Ave
773-271-2255
All things soccer store.
- **The Chopping Block** • 4747 N Lincoln Ave
773-472-6700
Gourmet cooking utensils and cooking classes.

- **Dark Tower Comics & Collectibles** •
4835 N Western Ave
773-654-1490
Comics with extra awesome service.
- **East Meets West** • 2118 W Lawrence Ave
773-275-1976
Handpicked fair-trade global wares; totally boring.
- **Eclecticity** • 4718 N Lincoln Ave
773-275-3080
You'll never know what cool stuff you'll find here.
- **Fleet Feet Sports** • 4762 N Lincoln Ave
773-271-3338
Runner's mecca.
- **Gallimaufry Gallery** • 4712 N Lincoln Ave
773-728-3600
Artisan crafts including instruments, incense,
stone fountains.
- **The Glass Art & Decorative Studio** •
4507 N Lincoln Ave
773-561-9008
Stained glass and gifts.

Map 3

- **Griffins & Gargoyles** • 2140 W Lawrence Ave
  773-769-1255
  Pine furniture from Europe.
- **Hazel** • 1902 W Montrose Ave
  773-769-2227
  Stylish gifts and jewelry, plus an extensive
  stationery section.
- **Laurie's Planet of Sound** • 4639 N Lincoln Ave
  773-271-3569
  Funky CD shop with unpretentious service.
- **Margie's Candies** • 1813 W Montrose Ave
  773-348-0400
  Second generation of a Chicago classic.
- **Merz Apothecary** • 4716 N Lincoln Ave
  773-989-0900
  German and other imported toiletries, herbal
  supplements, etc. The original.
- **Nadeau** • 4433 N Ravenswood Ave
  773-728-3497
  This furniture warehouse may change your life.

- **Old Town School Music Store** •
  4544 N Lincoln Ave
  773-751-3398
  Guitars and such.
- **Provenance Food and Wine** • 2312 W Leland Ave
  773-784-2314
  Select offerings of wine, cheese, olives & other
  gourmet fare.
- **Quake Collectibles** • 4628 N Lincoln Ave
  773-878-4288
  Vintage toys and fun!
- **Rock N Roll Vintage** • 4740 N Lincoln Ave
  773-878-8616
  Guitars galore.
- **Salamander** • 4740 N Lincoln Ave
  773-784-7463
  European shoes for men, women, and children.
- **Timeless Toys** • 4749 N Lincoln Ave
  773-334-4445
  Old-fashioned toys.

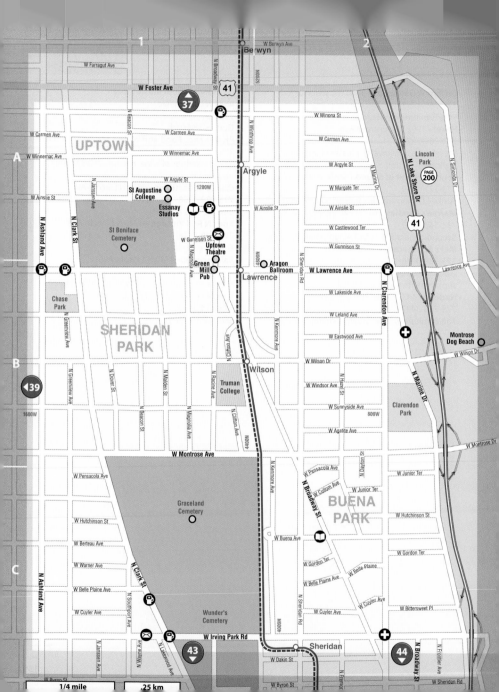

An uneasy truce exists in Uptown amongst Starbucks-hopping yuppies and the perpetually displaced poor. Gentrification is slowly creeping into Uptown as condos and super chains like Target pop up, but be wary of where you are, block to block. Uptown boasts several milestones of Chicago history including still operational **Green Mill** and the **Uptown Theatre**, currently in renovation. **Graceland Cemetery** is a pretty walk for those who don't mind the morbid. The landmark is full of elaborate mausoleums, the final resting place of the men and women who built the Second City.

## ○ Landmarks

- **Aragon Ballroom** • 1106 W Lawrence Ave
  773-561-9500
  One of the better smaller music venues in the city.
- **Essanay Studios** • 1333 W Argyle St
  Former movie studio. Charlie Chaplin and Gloria Swanson made movies here.
- **Graceland Cemetery** • 4001 N Clark St
  773-525-1105
  Chicago's famous buried in a masterpiece of landscape architecture.
- **Green Mill** • 4802 N Broadway St
  773-878-5552
  Live jazz seven nights a week. Capone drank here.
- **Montrose Dog Beach** •
  W Wilson Ave & N Simonds Dr
  Fun and frolic with your pup.
- **St. Augustine College** • 1333 W Argyle St
  773-878-8756
  Episcopalian bilingual training school occupying original headquarters of Essanay Studios, where Chaplin, Broco Billy, and Swanson made films before moving to Southern CA.
- **St. Boniface Cemetery** • 4901 N Clark St
  773-561-2790
  Historic gravestones in a scenic cemetery.
- **Uptown Theatre** • 4816 N Broadway
  An acre of seats in a magic city.

## ▼ Nightlife

- **The Bar on Buena** • 910 W Buena Ave
  773-525-8665
  Microbrews and tasty burgers in this plush neighborhood café.
- **Big Chicks** • 5024 N Sheridan Rd
  773-728-5511
  Friendly gay bar with fabulous art collection.
- **Carol's Pub** • 4659 N Clark St
  773-334-2402
  Hillbillies gone yuppie…thanks to a little press.
- **Crew Bar** • 4804 N Broadway St
  773-784-2739
  Gay sports bar with 50 beers and several televisions, or vice versa.
- **Green Mill** • 4802 N Broadway St
  773-878-5552
  Chicago legend… And birthplace of the poetry slam.
- **Hopleaf** • 5148 N Clark St
  773-334-9851
  Tons of imports if you can get a seat.
- **Konak** • 5150 N Clark St
  773-271-6688
  Overflow option for when Hopleaf is too packed, which means always.
- **The Long Room** • 1612 W Irving Park Rd
  773-665-4500
  Yes, it's long, but not as long as you might think.
- **Max's Place** • 4621 N Clark St
  773-784-3864
  At $1.25 per draft, who wouldn't pass out?
- **Nick's Uptown** • 4015 N Sheridan Rd
  773-975-1155
  Open late with a great beer selection.
- **The Sofo Tap** • 4923 N Clark St
  773-784-7636
  Friendly boy's bar by owner of T's.
- **T's** • 5025 N Clark St
  773-784-6000
  Popular with local gays and lesbians.
- **Uptown Lounge** • 1136 W Lawrence Ave
  773-878-1136
  Former dump becomes trendy lounge in up-and-coming neighborhood.

Uptown's nightlife is lively, chock full of shiny new bars as well as reliable old standbys. **Green Mill** (famous for live jazz, Big Band Thursdays and Sunday night poetry slams) and **Big Chicks** (a favored, gay neighborhood bar with great art) have long drawn folks to Uptown. **Bar on Buena** is justifiably renowned for their beer menus and flights, and **T's** draws a friendly mix of local LGBTs with their great outdoor patio and budget-friendly drink and menu specials.

#  Restaurants

- **Agami** • 4712 N Broadway St
  773-506-1845 • $$$
  Swanky sushi.
- **Anna Maria Pasteria** • 4400 N Clark St
  773-506-2662 • $$
  Cute, neighborhood Italian, casual date spot.
- **Carmela's Taqueria** • 1206 W Lawrence Ave
  773-275-5321 • $
  Above average al pastor (for the northside).
- **City Farms Market and Grill** •
  1467 W Irving Park Rd
  773-883-2767 • $
  Farm-to-table gem with a menu emphasizing
  comfort food.
- **Deleece** • 3747 N Southport Ave
  773-325-1710 • $$
  Ambitious global fare in cute storefront.
- **Demera** • 4801 N Broadway St
  773-334-8787 • $$
  Neighborhood Ethiopian.
- **Furama** • 4936 N Broadway St
  773-271-1161 • $$
  Dim sum with karaoke.
- **Hai Yen** • 1055 W Argyle St
  773-561-4077 • $$
  Chinese and veggie pho.
- **Inspiration Kitchens** • 4715 N Sheridan Rd
  773-275-0626 • $
  Uptown café provides job training for the
  homeless.
- **Iyanze** • 4623 N Broadway St
  773-944-1417 • $$
  Spacious pan-African from folks who brought us
  Lakeview's Bolat.
- **Joy Yee's Noodles** • 1465 W Irving Park
  773 281-2318 • $
  Huge pan-Asian menu and the best Thai iced teas
  around.
- **Le's Pho** • 4925 N Broadway St
  773-784-8723 • $
  Vietnamese soup for beginners and veterans alike.

- **Magnolia Café** • 1224 W Wilson Ave
  773-728-8785 • $$
  American bistro.
- **Mixteco Grill** • 1601 W Montrose Ave
  773-868-1601 • $$
  BYOB at this tasty, stand out Mexican Grill by a
  Frontera alum.
- **Palace Gate** • 4548 N Magnolia Ave
  773-769-1793 • $$
  True blue Ghanaian grub.
- **Pho 777** • 1065 W Argyle St
  773-561-9909 • $
  Try the tripe.
- **Real Kitchen** • 1433 W Montrose Ave
  773-281-2888 • $
  Mini café featuring gourmet food made with love,
  from scratch.
- **Siam Noodle & Rice** • 4654 N Sheridan Rd
  773-769-6694 • $
  Damn fine Thai food.
- **Silver Seafood** • 4829 N Broadway St
  773-784-0668 • $$
  Asian delights from the sea.
- **Sun Wah BBQ** • 5039 N Broadway St
  773-769-1254 • $$
  Notable for the barbequed ducks hanging in the
  window.
- **Tac Quick** • 3930 N Sheridan Rd
  773-327-5253 • $$
  Cheap and delicious. Thai-language menu
  available for the adventurous.
- **Taqueria Caminos de Michoacan** •
  3948 N Sheridan Rd
  773-296-9709 • $
  No ambiance, bad Mexican soap operas, incredibly
  delicious regional Mexican food.
- **Thai Pastry** • 4925 N Broadway St
  773-784-5399 • $
  Free pastry with every order!
- **Tiztal Cafe** • 4631 N Clark St
  773-271-4631 • $
  Chilaquiles and oatmeal shakes.
- **Tweet** • 5020 N Sheridan Rd
  773-728-5576 • $$
  Gourmet food without pretension.

## 🛍 Shopping

- **Baan Home** • 5053 N Clark St
773-905-1228
Thai home decor and art.
- **Baker and Nosh** • 1303 Wilson Ave
773-989-7393
Bread made by hand fresh daily and coffee.
- **Eagle Leathers** • 5015 N Clark St
773-728-7228
Come to daddy.
- **Foursided** • 5061 N Clark St
773-506-8300
Framing and more at this funky shop.
- **La Patisserie P** • 1052 W Argyle St
773-878-3226
The EuroAsian bakery of your dreams.
- **Milk Handmade** • 5137 N Clark St
773-234-7053
Fashion forward, handmade AND affordable? A first time for everything.
- **Salvation Army Thrift Store** • 4315 N Broadway St
773-348-1401
Good 'ol fashioned thrifting.

- **Shake Rattle and Read Book Box** •
4812 N Broadway St
773-334-5311
Funky used bookstore, great finds, but cluttered.
- **Tai Nam Market** • 4925 N Broadway St
773-275-5666
Vietnamese. Very good.
- **Tattoo Factory** • 4441 N Broadway St
773-989-4077
High-profile place to get inked.
- **Transistor** • 3819 N Clark St
773-642-9539
Electronic music CDs & equipment, art books, sleek and shiny.
- **Unique Thrift Store** • 4445 N Sheridan Rd
773-275-8623
Half-price Mondays.
- **Uptown Bikes** • 4653 N Broadway St
773-728-5212
Cool, grungy bike shop.
- **Village Discount Outlet** • 4898 N Clark St
866-545-3836
Tons of clothes and weekly specials.
- **The Wooden Spoon** • 5047 N Clark St
773-293-3190
Heaven for foodies.

# Map 41 · **Avondale / Old Irving**

That screeching sound you hear is Avondale development, which, like much of Chicago's westward expansion, has been riding the breaks since the recession fueled decline. Even real estate speculators are hard pressed to gild the dandelion of frame two-flats in foreclosure in this "park poor," mostly concrete area. The results: bleary-eyed hipsters wandering around in confusion, wondering how the hell they ended up here.

## ○ Landmarks

- **ComEd Plant** • N California Ave & W Roscoe St
  What's that humming sound in Avondale? Must be this ginormous electrical plant.

## Nightlife

- **Chief O'Neill's** • 3471 N Elston Ave
  773-583-3066
  Celtic music and top-of-the-line pub food.
- **Kuma's Corner** • 2900 W Belmont Ave
  773-604-8769
  Heavy metal bar with great microbrew selection and kobe beef sliders.
- **Ã** • 2977 N Elston Ave
  773-866-9898
  Argentine flair with electro grooves.
- **Nelly's Saloon** • 3256 N Elston Ave
  773-588-4494
  Romanian hangout with occasional live music.
- **Small Bar** • 2956 N Albany Ave
  773-509-9888
  This Logan Square watering hole offers great domestic and imported booze and a chill vibe.
- **Square Bar & Grill** • 2849 W Belmont Ave
  773-267-0123
  A burger showdown in Avondale.

## Restaurants

- **Burrito House** • 3145 W Addison St
  773-279-9111 • $
  At least they're open late.
- **Chief O'Neill's** • 3471 N Elston Ave
  773-583-3066 • $
  Excellent traditional pub fare.
- **Dragon Lady Lounge** • 3188 N Elston Ave
  773-267-1970 • $
  Korean dive bar with GREAT vegan buffet.
- **Hot Doug's** • 3324 N California Ave
  773-279-9550 • $
  Super popular gourmet hot dogs and duck fat fries.
- **Kuma's Corner** • 2900 W Belmont Ave
  773-604-8769 • $$
  Heavy metal bar and grill with famous burgers and lots of ink.
- **Mr. Pollo** • 3000 W Belmont Ave
  773-509-1208 • $
  South American chicken joint. Get a guanabana shake.
- **Taqueria Traspasada** • 3144 N California Ave
  773-539-4533 • $
  Tasty, cheap tacos and salsas—no atmosphere.
- **Urban Belly** • 3053 N California Ave
  773-583-0500 • $$
  Incredibly good dumplings and noodle bowls, quick turn around BYOB.
- **Zacatecas** • 2934 W Diversey Ave
  773-278-4828 • $
  Taqueria. Typical.

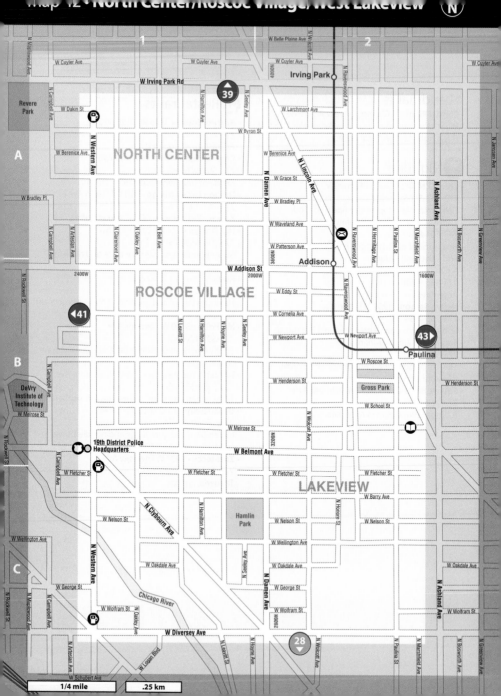

The tan, fit, stroller-pushing set rule in Roscoe Village and West Lakeview. The north side jewel is populated with gray- and brownstones, lush, tiny green lawns, funky boutiques, expensive grocery stores and cozy neighborhood restaurants. The nightlife here is mostly subdued with Saturday nights consisting of dive bar crawls.

## Landmarks

- **19th District** • 3600 S Halsted St
  312-744-8320
  Going to "Western & Belmont" is synonymous for being in deep sh#*.

## Nightlife

- **Beat Kitchen** • 2100 W Belmont Ave
  773-281-4444
  Hip music spot in a not so hip hood.
- **Black Rock** • 3614 N Damen Ave
  773-348-4044
  Not sure what this place is.
- **Brownstone Tavern and Grill** •
  3937 N Lincoln Ave
  773-528-3700
- **Cody's Public House** • 1658 W Barry Ave
  773-528-4050
  Named after the owner's dog.
- **Constellation** • 3111 N Western Ave
  773-528-4050
  Links Hall-Mike Reed partnership in former Viaduct Theatre.
- **Four Moon Tavern** • 1847 W Roscoe St
  773-929-6666
  Neighborhood tavern. Cozy back room. Thespian crowd.
- **The Four Treys** • 3333 N Damen Ave
  773-549-8845
  One of 5,000 drinking options in this area.

- **G&L Fire Escape** • 2157 W Grace St
  773-472-1138
  Attention ladies! It's a fireman's hangout!
- **Goldie's Bar** • 3839 N Lincoln Ave
  773 404-5322
  Cozy dive with daily $1 PBR and battered board games.
- **Hungry Brain** • 2319 W Belmont Ave
  773-709-1401
  Mellow, friendly artist hangout. Experimental jazz on Sundays.
- **Martyrs'** • 3855 N Lincoln Ave
  773-404-9494
  Great stage for live acts.
- **Mulligan's Public House** • 2000 W Roscoe St
  773-549-4225
  Villagers do not go thirsty.
- **Riverview Tavern** • 1958 W Roscoe St
  773-248-9523
  Another Roscoe Village watering hole.
- **Roscoe Village Pub** • 2159 W Addison St
  773-472-6160
  Karaoke in a dive bar…doesn't get much better than that.
- **Underbar** • 3243 N Western Ave
  773-404-9363
  There are more depressing 4 am bars.
- **Village Tap** • 2055 W Roscoe St
  773-883-0817
  Neighborhood icon with a touch of class.
- **Waterhouse** • 3407 N Paulina Ave
  773-871-1200
  Local lounge aiming for a classy feel.

## Map 42

# North Center/Roscoe Village/West Lakeview

By daylight, browse the hand-picked selection at "High Fidelity" lookalike **Hard Boiled Records and Video**. Come night time, catch a show at **Beat Kitchen**, try the crispy egg rolls at **Hot Woks Cool Sushi** and enjoy the generous portions at **Piazza Bella Trattoria**. Unwind with a late night pint at local favorites **The Village Tap** and rugby bar **Black Rock**.

## Restaurants

- **90 Miles Cuban Cafe** • 3101 N Clybourn Ave
773-248-2822 • $
Casual Cuban, counter-seating only.
- **Brownstone Tavern and Grill** •
3937 N Lincoln Ave
773-528-3700 • $
Charming sports bar with a lovely summer patio.
- **Café Orchid** • 1746 W Addison St
773-327-3808 • $$
Authentic Turkish food served in a romantic hideaway.
- **Delicious Cafe** • 3827 N Lincoln Ave
773-697-4857 •
Vegan cafe fare.
- **El Tinajon** • 2054 W Roscoe St
773-525-8455 • $$
Good, cheap Guatemalan. Great mango margaritas.
- **Frasca** • 3358 N Paulina St
773-248-5222 • $$
European-style pizza with a cozy wine bar and outdoor seating.
- **Hot Woks Cool Sushi** • 2032 W Roscoe St
773-880-9800 • $$$
Try the crispy egg rolls.
- **Kitsch'n on Roscoe** • 2005 W Roscoe St
773-248-7372 • $$
Clever retro food and tiki bar. Friendly staff.

- **Murphy & Sons Irish Bistro** • 3905 N Lincoln Ave
773-248-3905 • $$$
Fancy Irish food: An oxymoron, or reality? Decide for yourself here.
- **Namo Thai** • 3900 N Lincoln Ave
773-327-8818 • $$
Traditional Thai in a slick, big city setting.
- **Piazza Bella Trattoria & Osteria** •
2116 W Roscoe St
773-477-7330 • $$$
Neighborhood Italian.
- **Scooter's Frozen Custard** • 1658 W Belmont Ave
773-244-6415 • $
The tastiest custard this side of St. Louis.
- **Sola** • 3868 N Lincoln Ave
773-327-3868 • $$$
Contemporary American with Polynesian flair.
- **Thai Linda Café** • 2022 W Roscoe St
773-868-0075 • $$
Standard-issue neighborhood Thai.
- **Turquoise Restaurant** • 2147 W Roscoe St
773-549-3523 • $$
Fresh and creative Middle-Eastern fare.
- **Victory's Banner** • 2100 W Roscoe St
773-665-0227 • $
Vegetarian brunch served by toga-clad Sri Chimnoy followers.
- **Volo Restaurant Wine Bar** • 2008 W Roscoe St
773-348-4600 • $$$
New American small plates with swirl.

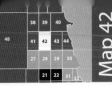
## Shopping

- **Andy's Music** • 2300 W Belmont Ave
  773-868-1234
  Knock yourself out browsing all the exotic musical instruments sold here.
- **Antique Resources** • 1741 W Belmont Ave
  773-871-4242
  Large inventory of antique furniture.
- **Bazar Apparel** • 3350 N Paulina St
  773-388-9851
  Women's young contemporary apparel.
- **Be By Baby** • 1654 W Roscoe St
  773-404-2229
  Unique maternity wear and eco-friendly toys, clothes, and accessories for moms.
- **Caravan Beads** • 3339 N Lincoln Ave
  773-248-9555
  Loads of beads for all your beady needs.
- **Community Home Supply** • 3924 N Lincoln Ave
  773-281-7010
  One of the best (and priciest) kitchen and bath boutiques.
- **Father Time Antiques** • 2108 W Belmont Ave
  773-880-5599
  A plethora of timepieces.
- **Glam to Go** • 2002 W Roscoe St
  773-525-7004
  Girly-girls get pampered.
- **Good Old Days** • 2138 W Belmont Ave
  773-472-8837
  Antiques and treasures.
- **Hubba Hubba** • 2040 W Roscoe St
  773-477-1414
  Boutique clothing and jewelry at moderate prices.
- **Jazze Junque** • 3419 N Lincoln Ave
  773-472-6450
  An entire store devoted to cookie jars.
- **Lulu's at the Belle Kay** • 3862 N Lincoln Ave
  773-404-5858
  Vintage clothing and jewelry.
- **Lush Wine and Spirits** • 2232 W Roscoe St
  773-281-8888
  Wine, microbrews, and booze.
- **Lynn's Hallmark** • 3353 N Lincoln Ave
  773-281-8108
  Cards, stationery, and gift wrap.
- **The Needle Shop** • 3738 N Lincoln Ave
  Fabric store that offers classes.
- **The Pleasure Chest** • 3436 N Lincoln Ave
  773-525-7151
  Sextastic adult store.
- **Shangri-La Vintage** • 1952 W Roscoe St
  773-348-5090
  Funky pleather jackets, plenty o' accessories, nylon shirts galore.
- **Skyscraper Heels** • 2202 W Belmont Ave
  773-477-8495
  Sky-high heels up to size 17.
- **Surplus of Options** • 3664 N Lincoln Ave
  773-827-1330
  Everything you wanted that grandma gave up.

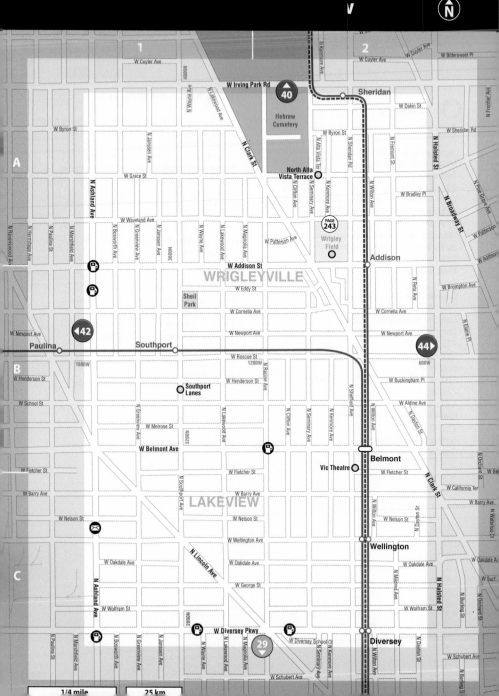

The population of Wrigleyville/East Lakeview swells during beautiful summer afternoons and evening while the Cubs are at home (making the parking impossible and towing imminent). To avoid the crowds, walk the pleasant, pretty streets during away games. Try Clark Street for rows and rows of sports bars and airy patio dining and Southport Avenue for quieter date- and family-friendly establishments.

## ○ Landmarks

**• North Alta Vista Terrace •**
3809 W Alta Vista Terrace
London-style row houses with Edwardian elegance.

**• Southport Lanes & Billiards •**
3325 N Southport Ave
773-472-6600
Four hand-set lanes. Eat a Honeymooner while you wait.

**• The Vic •** 3145 N Sheffield Ave
773-472-0449
Drink, watch films, and take in an occasional band at this old theatre.

**• Wrigley Field •** 1060 W Addison St
773-404-2827
Charm-filled and crumbling ballpark that remains indifferent to wins or losses on the field.

Map
48 41 42 43 44
27 28 29 30
21 22 31

Since the Friendly Confines dominate the neighborhood, it's no surprise that most local bars and restaurants cater to sports fans. Jocks will feel at home in the 3-floor sports bar mecca **Slugger's** featuring dueling pianos, batting cages, and, during the winter, the basketball/trampoline hybrid Hi-Ball. Non-sports fans have plenty to do on the weekends too: head to the **Metro** for live rock or the gorgeous, historic **Music Box Theatre** for art films and trashy/fun midnight movies.

# Nightlife

- **The Bar Celona** • 3474 N Clark St
  773-244-8000
  Two bars, one in the basement, DJ spins upstairs.
- **Berlin** • 954 W Belmont Ave
  773-348-4975
  Tiny classic "pansexual" dance club.
- **Bernie's** • 3664 N Clark St
  773-525-1898
  Favored Wrigleyville spot.
- **Blokes and Birds** • 3343 N Clark St
  773-472-5252
- **Cooper's** • 1232 W Belmont Ave
  773-929-2667
  Beer and stylish/casual bar food.
- **The Cubby Bear** • 1059 W Addison St
  773-327-1662
  Drunk cubs fans and bar bands.
- **Elbo Room** • 2871 N Lincoln Ave
  773-549-5549
  Didn't RATT play here?
- **Fizz Bar and Grill** • 3220 N Lincoln Ave
  773-348-6000
  Good specialty drinks. Tiki nights and more.
- **The Full Shilling** • 3724 N Clark St
  773-248-3330
  Best Wrigleyville bar.
- **The Gingerman Tavern** • 3740 N Clark St
  773-549-2050
  Plays classical music to ward off Cubs fans.

- **Guthrie's Tavern** • 1300 W Addison St
  773-477-2900
  Comfortable atmosphere, good drinks, a range of board games to play with.
- **Higgins' Tavern** • 3259 N Racine Ave
  773-281-7637
  Yuppies and drunks.
- **Houndstooth Saloon** • 3369 N Clark St
  773-244-1166
  Southern hospitality and Crimson Tide alumni and fans.
- **iO** • 3541 N Clark St
  773-880-0199
  Get laughs and get drunk.
- **The Irish Oak** • 3511 N Clark St
  773-935-6669
  Seriously authentic Irish pub.
- **Justin's** • 3358 N Southport Ave
  773-929-4844
  Great bar for Sunday football.
- **Kirkwood** • 2934 N Sheffield Ave
  773-770-0700
  Drink like a fish or out of a fish bowl.
- **L&L Tavern** • 3207 N Clark St
  773-528-1303
  Overfriendly dive bar with decent jukebox.
- **Lange's Lounge** • 3500 N Southport Ave
  773-472-6030
  Total dive, but not disgusting.
- **Lincoln Tap Room** • 3010 N Lincoln Ave
  773-868-0060
  Great mix of people, comfortable couches.

- **Merkle's Bar & Grill** • 3516 N Clark St
  773-244-1025
  Cubs + Iowa Hawkeyes = sports year-round.
- **Metro** • 3730 N Clark St
  773-549-4140
  Internationally renowned venue for top local and touring rock music.
- **Murphy's Bleachers** • 3655 N Sheffield Ave
  773-281-5356
  Outdoor Cubbie haven with drunks galore.
- **Newport Bar & Grill** • 1344 W Newport Ave
  773-325-9111
  For an ass-whooping in Pictionary, meet us here tomorrow night.
- **Raw Bar** • 3720 N Clark St
  773-348-7291
  Post-Metro rock star hangout.
- **Red Ivy** • 3525 N Clark St
  773-472-0900
  Part sports bar, part pizzeria, part speakeasy.
- **Risque Cafe** • 3419 N Clark St
  773-525-7711
  Tangy BBQ and over 300 craft beers
- **Rockit Burger Bar** • 3700 N Clark St
  773-645-4400
  River North hotspot's new location now sporting drunken Cubs fans.
- **Schubas** • 3159 N Southport Ave
  773-525-2508
  Top live music staple with attached restaurant.

- **Sheffield's** • 3258 N Sheffield Ave
  773-281-4989
  Outdoor area attracts afternoon revelers. Great beer selection.
- **Slugger's** • 3540 N Clark St
  773-248-0055
  Batting cages—some people's heaven, others' hell.
- **Smart Bar** • 3730 N Clark St
  773-549-4140
  Club kids unite!
- **Stretch Bar & Grill** • 3485 N Clark St
  773-755-3980
  Wrigleyville's upscale choice for watching sports and eating good grub.
- **Tai's Til 4** • 3611 N Ashland Ave
  773-348-8923
  Well, they're open till 4am, so you can probably guess what it's like. Hookup central.
- **Ten Cat Tavern** • 3931 N Ashland Ave
  773-935-5377
  Artsy type relaxing spot.
- **Toons Bar & Grill** • 3857 N Southport Ave
  773-935-1919
  Buncha characters in that joint (groan).
- **Uncommon Ground** • 3800 N Clark St
  773-929-3680
  Local acts play while sipping a latte.
- **Underground Lounge** • 952 W Newport Ave
  773-327-2739
  Cool music spot tucked away below the street.
- **Yak-Zies Wrigleyville** • 3710 N Clark St
  773-525-9200
  Loud post-Cubs hangout.

Map

48
41 42 43 44
27 28 29 30
21 22 31

# 🍴 Restaurants

- **Ann Sather** • 909 W Belmont Ave
  773-348-2378 • $
  Warm, family friendly ambience, Swedish comfort food.
- **Blokes and Birds** • 3343 N Clark St
  773-472-5252 • $$$
  Yummy traditional English fare. Devils on horseback are served here.
- **Blue Bayou** • 3734 N Southport Ave
  773-871-3300 • $$
  New Orleans-themed, in case you couldn't guess.
- **Bolat** • 3346 N Clark St
  773-665-1100 • $$
  West African cuisine—try the okra with rice.
- **Capt'n Nemos** • 3650 N Ashland Ave
  773-929-7687 • $
  Great sandwiches and yummy soup.
- **Chen's** • 3506 N Clark St
  773-549-9100 • $$
  Sleek Chinese food oasis in the heart of Wrigleyville's madness.
- **Coobah** • 3423 N Southport Ave
  773-528-2220 • $$
  Trendy Latin spot near Music Box.
- **Cozy Noodles n' Rice** • 3456 N Sheffield Ave
  773-327-0100 • $$
  Yep, it's cozy.
- **Crepe Town** • 3915 N Sheridan Rd
  773-248-8844 • $$
  Asian/French fusion serving up sweet and savory crepes.
- **Dimo's Pizza** • 3463 N Clark St
  773-525-4580 •
  Late night pizza (sometimes topped with mac and cheese).
- **Fish Bar** • 2956 N Sheffield Ave
  773-687-8177 • $$
  DMK Burger Bar's cousin serves seafood and refreshing "sea sippers."
- **Golden Apple** • 2971 N Lincoln Ave
  773-528-1413 • $
  24-hour greasy hangover food. Once featured on This American Life.
- **Indie Burger** • 1034 W Belmont Ave
  773-857-7777 • $$
  Organic burger bar serving milkshakes made from local dairy.

- **Lucky's Sandwich Company** • 3472 N Clark St
  773-549-0665 • $
  They put fries IN the sandwich. Genius.
- **Lulu Belle's Pancake House** •
  3819 N Southport Ave
  773-975-5858 • $$
  Family friendly brunch hub.
- **Mia Francesca** • 3311 N Clark St
  773-281-3310 • $$
  Contemporary Italian date place.
- **Mystic Celt** • 3443 N Southport Ave
  773-529-8550 • $$
  Irish pub-style restaurant. Awesome Irish eggrolls.
- **Panes** • 3002 N Sheffield Ave
  773-665-0972 • $
  Homemade sandwiches, muffins, cookies, and brownies.
- **Penny's Noodle Shop** • 3400 N Sheffield Ave
  773-281-8222 • $$
  Pad thai, pad see ew, popular place for a lite lunch.
- **PS Bangkok** • 3345 N Clark St
  773-871-7777 • $
  Popular neighborhood Thai that delivers.
- **Rise** • 3401 N Southport Ave
  773-525-3535 • $$
  Sushi nightspot.
- **Risque Cafe** • 3419 N Clark St
  773-525-7711 • $$$
  Tangy barbecue and over 300 craft beers.
- **S&G** • 3000 N Lincoln Ave
  773-935-4025 • $
  Cop hangout with chintzy decorating and fake plants. In other words, we love it.
- **Salt & Pepper Diner** • 3537 N Clark St
  773-883-9800 • $
  "Old-school" styled diner.
- **Socca** • 3301 N Clark St
  773-248-1155 • $$
  Tasty, satisfying Mediterannean.
- **Tango Sur** • 3763 N Southport Ave
  773-477-5466 • $$
  Vegetarian's vision of hell: big juicy Argentine steaks.
- **Wrigleyville Dogs** • 3737 N Clark St
  773-296-1500 • $
  Post Metro stop for chili-cheese fries.

# 🛍Shopping

- **The Alley** • 3228 N Clark St
  773-348-5000
  Skulls, tattoos, big boots.
- **Belmont Army** • 855 W Belmont Ave
  773-549-1038
  Mostly fashion; little bit of military.
- **Bittersweet Pastry Shop and Cafe** •
  1114 W Belmont Ave
  773-929-1100
  Cookies as big as your head.
- **Bookworks** • 3444 N Clark St
  773-871-5318
  Friendly, well-organized used books.
- **Fashion Tomato** • 937 W Belmont Ave
  773-281-2921
  Cheap, trendy clothes for girls who go to clubs and
  like to "party."
- **Heritage Bicycles** • 2959 N Lincoln Ave
  773-245-3005
  Gourmet coffee and treats with your handcrafted
  bike.
- **J. Toguri Mercantile Co.** • 851 W Belmont Ave
  773-929-3500
  Find Japanese books, paper, and foodstuffs here.
- **Krista K** • 3458 N Southport Ave
  773-248-1967
  Snobby clothes for snobby women but good
  selection of jeans.
- **Leahey & Ladue Consignment** •
  3753 N Southport Ave
  773-929-4865
  Classy resale shop, mostly expensive, but good
  buys on the sale rack.
- **Midwest Pro Sound and Lighting** •
  1613 W Belmont Ave
  773-975-4250
  DJ equipment, fog machines, strobe lights.
- **Never Mind** • 3240 N Clark St
  773-472-4922
  Trendy accessories and clothes for trixie girls.
- **Play It Again Sports** • 3939 N Ashland Ave
  773-305-9900
  Sporting goods.
- **Powell's Books** • 2850 N Lincoln Ave
  773-248-1444
  Remainders and off-price books. Mostly scholarly.
  Famous bookstore.
- **Saturday Audio Exchange** • 1021 W Belmont Ave
  773-935-4434
  Great bargains on name brand audio.
- **Strange Cargo** • 3448 N Clark St
  773-327-8090
  Hip affordable threads for the 20-somethings.
- **Thousand Waves Spa** • 1212 W Belmont Ave
  773-549-0700
  Get away from it all at this female-only spa.
- **Uncle Dan's Great Outdoor Store** •
  3551 N Southport Ave
  773-348-5800
  Camping gear with a granola, Grateful Dead kind
  of feel.
- **Uncle Fun** • 1338 W Belmont Ave
  773-477-8223
  Cramped and crazy retro toys and novelties.

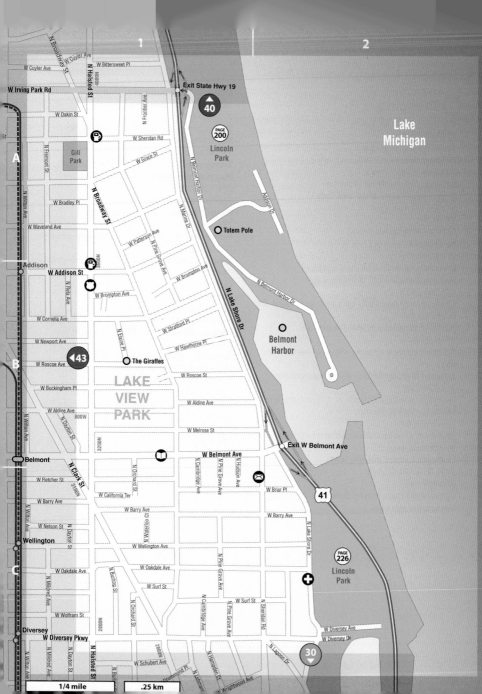

A.K.A. Boystown thanks to its highly visible gay community, East Lakview is brimming with great shopping and dining. The Chicago summer festival season piques in Boystown with the annual Pride Parade and the equally flamboyant Halsted Street Market Days. The neighborhood quiets down a bit in the beautiful gray- and brownstone-lined blocks south of Belmont.

## Landmarks

- **Belmont Harbor** • 3600 Recreation Dr
  312-742-7673
  Home to the Chicago Yacht Club sailing school.
- **The Giraffes** • W Roscoe Ave & N Elaine Pl
  Iconic public art.
- **Totem Pole** • 3600 N Lake Shore Dr
  Where did it come from? Why is it there? Nobody knows.

## Nightlife

- **Bridget McNeill's** • 420 W Belmont Ave
  773-248-6654
  A fun hangout and godsend for those living along the lake.
- **Charlie's Chicago** • 3726 N Broadway St
  773-871-8887
  Gay country and western bar. That's right.
- **The Closet** • 3325 N Broadway St
  773-477-8533
  Boy-friendly lesbian bar, 4 am license.
- **Duke of Perth** • 2913 N Clark St
  773-477-1741
  Shades of Edinburgh, along with requisite whiskies and haddock.
- **F. O'Mahony's** • 3701 N Broadway St
  773-549-0226
  Food when you need it (late!) and a seasonal menu.
- **Friar Tuck** • 3010 N Broadway St
  773-327-5101
  Enter through a barrel. Yup, a barrel.

- **Hydrate** • 3458 N Halsted St
  773-975-9244
  Just what Boystown needs—a gay-friendly fern bar!
- **Kit Kat Lounge** • 3700 N Halsted St
  773-525-1111
  Live drag queen shows.
- **Little Jim's** • 3501 N Halsted St
  773-871-6116
  Halsted Street Gay Dive.
- **minibar** • 3339 N Halsted St
  773-871-6227
  Fancy cocktails in a smoke-free lounge.
- **Monsignor Murphy's** • 3019 N Broadway St
  773-348-7285
  Irish Pub with plenty of board games.
- **Rocks Lakeview** • 3463 N Broadway St
  773-472-0493
  Microbrews, good whisky list, and excellent bar food.
- **Roscoe's** • 3356 N Halsted St
  773-281-3355
  Cavernous mingling for the gay sweater set.
- **Sidetrack** • 3349 N Halsted St
  773-477-9189
  Popular showtune sing-a-longs!
- **Spin** • 800 W Belmont Ave
  773-327-7711
  Lots of theme days throughout the week.
- **Town Hall Pub** • 3340 N Halsted St
  773-472-4405
  Unassuming, mixed clientele, live music.
- **Wilde** • 3130 N Broadway St
  773-244-0404
  Classy bar for bookish set.

Map

48
41 42 43 44
27 28 29 30
21 22 31

East Lakeview's nightlife is unquestionably the most fun you'll have in the city. Dining options run the gauntlet from ultra chic to comfortably casual. The neighborhood is stacked with gay nightclubs and bars like **Roscoe's** and **Sidetrack**. No Saturday night visit to Boystown is complete without a drag show. You'll go (Lady) Gaga for the queens at the **Kit Kat Lounge & Supper Club**. Parking is rough in this busy borough, but it's a cinch to hail a cab at any hour.

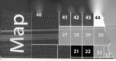

# Restaurants

- **Angelina Ristorante** • 3561 N Broadway St
  773-935-5933 • $$$
  Casual, romantic Italian.
- **Ann Sather Broadway Cafe** • 3411 N Broadway St
  773-305-0024 • $
  Airy branch of local comfort food chain.
- **The Bagel** • 3107 N Broadway St
  773-477-0300 • $
  Great deli fare.
- **Baladoche** • 2905 N Clark St
  773-880-5090 • $
  Don't call them waffles.
- **Bobtail Soda Fountain** • 2951 N Broadway St
  773-880-7372 • $
  Norman Rockwell would be proud.
- **Bow Truss Coffee** • 2934 N Broadway St
  773-857-1361 • $
  In-house roasting.
- **The Chicago Diner** • 3411 N Halsted St
  773-935-6696 • $$
  A vegetarian institution.
- **Chilam Balam** • 3023 N Broadway St
  773-296-6901 •
  Yummy organic, small plate Mexican.
- **Clark Street Dog** • 3040 N Clark St
  773-281-6690 • $
  24-hour hot dogs and cheese fries.
- **Falafill** • 3202 N Broadway
  773-525-0052 • $
  Streamlined veggie-friendly falafel stand.
- **Flub A Dub Chub's** • 3021 N Broadway St
  773-857-6500 • $
  Hot dogs Chicago-style. No ketchup.
- **Half Shell** • 676 W Diversey Pkwy
  773-549-1773 • $$$
  Casual raw bar.
- **HB** • 3404 N Halsted St
  773-661-0299 • $$$
  Nice date spot for upscale comfort food.
- **Hiro's Café** • 2936 N Broadway St
  773-477-8510 • $$
  Enjoy a side of Beyonce with your sushi.
- **Jack's on Halsted** • 3201 N Halsted St
  773-244-9191 • $$$$
  Great wine list.

- **Joy's Noodles & Rice** • 3257 N Broadway St
  773-327-8330 • $$
  Standard noodles, soup, or fried rice; impressively simple.
- **Kuma's Too** • 666 W Diversey Pkwy
  773-472-2666 • $$
  A second outpost for Chicago's most sought after burgers.
- **La Creperie** • 2845 N Clark St
  773-528-9050 • $$
  Live French music. Shabby, but cute.
- **Mark's Chop Suey** • 3343 N Halsted St
  773-281-9090 • $
  The BEST eggrolls.
- **New Tokyo** • 3139 N Broadway St
  773-248-1193 • $$
  Reasonably priced sushi and BYOB at this cozy Japanese spot.
- **Nookies Tree** • 3334 N Halsted St
  773-248-9888 • $
  24-hour diner.
- **Paciugo** • 3241 N Broadway
  773-248-8433 • $
  What's better than creamy gelato handcrafted daily? Nothing.
- **Ping Pong** • 3322 N Broadway St
  773-281-7575 • $$$
  Always busy BYO, hit or miss Asian fusion.
- **Sandwich Me In** • 3037 N Clark St
  773-348-3037 • $
  Eco-conscious sandwich shop.
- **Senza** • 2873 N Broadway St
  773-770-3527 • $$$$$
  Gluten-free gourmet.
- **Stella's Diner** • 3042 N Broadway St
  773-472-9040 • $
  Can you say diner?
- **Tapas Gitana** • 3445 N Halsted St
  773-296-6046 • $$$
  Intimate tapas; great sangria.
- **Wakamono** • 3317 N Broadway St
  773-296-6800 • $$
  Sushi and Japanese small plates.
- **Yoshi's Café** • 3257 N Halsted St
  773-248-6160 • $$$
  Franco-Japanese fusion.

# 🛍 Shopping

- **Akira** • 643 W Diversey Pkwy
773-649-9257
High fashion for wanna-be Eurotrash.
- **Andrea Vangna** • 3341 N Broadway St
773-525-6199
Custom-tailored menswear.
- **Bookman's Corner** • 2959 N Clark St
773-929-8298
Chicago's most surprising bookstore, last of a dying breed.
- **Borderline Music** • 3333 N Broadway St
773-975-9533
Dance music store named after Madonna song.
- **Century Shopping Centre** • 2828 N Clark St
773-929-8100
Most notable occupants include the cinema and Bally's Fitness.
- **GayMart** • 3457 N Halsted St
773-929-4272
Gay Barbie and other homo kitsch and gifts.
- **Gramaphone Records** • 2843 N Clark St
773-472-3683
DJ's shop here for the latest wax.
- **Halo** •
773-248-4256
Hip men's haircare.
- **He Who Eats Mud** • 3247 N Broadway St
773-525-0616
no air-conditioning, cards with a campy appeal.
- **Hollywood Mirror** • 812 W Belmont Ave
773-404-2044
Vintage clothes and kitschy doo-dads.
- **Johnny Sprockets** • 3001 N Broadway
773-244-1079
Catering to all your bicycle needs.

- **Milk & More** • 702 W Diversey Pkwy
773-281-6455
Small yet mighty grocer, amazing quality; also good for browsing.
- **Pastoral Artisan Cheese, Bread & Wine** • 2945 N Broadway St
773-472-4781
One of Chicago's favorite cheese shops. Start your picnic here.
- **Ragstock** • 812 W Belmont Ave
773-868-9263
Vintage resale and trendy off-price clothes.
- **Rainbow Flowers** • 2917 N Broadway St
773-248-7272
Fresh flowers: necessary to get through a Chicago winter.
- **Reckless Records** • 3126 N Broadway St
773-404-5080
Oldies and new releases on vinyl.
- **Spare Parts** • 2947 N Broadway St
773-525-4242
Cool bags, purses, and man purses.
- **Threadless** • 3011 N Broadway St
773-525-8640
Get your snarky t-shirt on.
- **Tulip Toy Gallery** • 3459 N Halsted St
773-975-1515
Woman-owned, inviting sex paraphenalia shop.
- **Unabridged Bookstore** • 3251 N Broadway St
773-883-9119
Helpful bookstore with great travel, kids and gay sections.
- **Windy City Sweets** • 3308 N Broadway St
773-477-6100
Old-fashioned candy shop with homemade fudge.

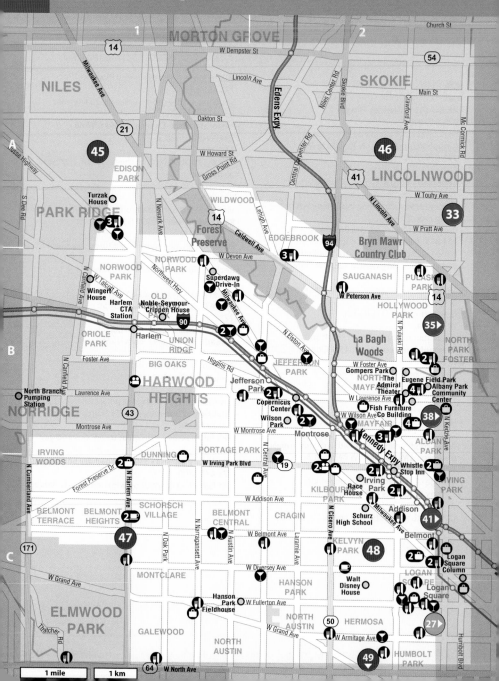

1

2

MORTON GROVE

Church St

14

W Dempster St

SKOKIE

54

Lincoln Ave

Main St

NILES

Oakton St

21

Mc Cormick Rd

Crawford Ave

A

W Howard St

46

Jesse Highway

EDISON PARK

Gross Point Rd

41

LINCOLNWOOD

W Touhy Ave

Turzak House

WILDWOOD

33

PARK RIDGE

3

W Pratt Ave

14

Forest Preserve

Caldwell Ave

Lehigh Ave

EDGEBROOK

94

Bryn Mawr Country Club

S Dee Rd

N Newark Ave

W Devon Ave

3

NORWOOD PARK

Northwest Hwy

SAUGANASH

PULASKI PARK

N Talcott Ave

Superdawg Drive-In

W Peterson Ave

14

Wingert House

NORWOOD PARK

OLD Noble-Seymour-Crippen House

Milwaukee Ave

HOLLYWOOD PARK

35

N Pulaski Rd

N Garfield Ave

Harlem CTA Station

90

N Elston Ave

La Bagh Woods

NORTH PARK FOSTER

B

ORIOLE PARK

Harlem

UNION RIDGE

Higgins Rd

JEFFERSON PARK

W Foster Ave
Gompers Park

NORTH MAYFAIR

The Admiral Theater

Eugene Field Park

2

Foster Ave

BIG OAKS

HARWOOD HEIGHTS

Jefferson Park

2

Albany Park Community Center

N Carfield Ave

Lawrence Ave

Copernicus Center

W Lawrence Ave

4

38

North Branch Pumping Station

NORRIDGE

43

Wilson Park

Fish Furniture Co Building

ALBAN PARK

Montrose Ave

W Wilson Ave

MAYFAIR

4

Montrose

3

N Ketzie Ave

IRVING WOODS

Forest Preserve Dr

DUNNING

PORTAGE PARK

N Central Ave

Kennedy Expy

Whistle Stop Inn

2

IRVING PARK

W Irving Park Blvd

19

2

Irving Park

2

N Cumberland Ave

N Harlem Ave

W Addison Ave

KILBOURN PARK

Race House

2

Addison

BELMONT TERRACE

BELMONT HEIGHTS

SCHORSCH VILLAGE

2

BELMONT CENTRAL

Schurz High School

Milwaukee Ave

41

171

47

N Oak Park Ave

N Naragansett Ave

N Austin Ave

W Belmont Ave

CRAGIN

Belmont

C

MONTCLARE

W Diversey Ave

KELVYN PARK

48

Logan Square Column

2

ELMWOOD PARK

Hanson Park Fieldhouse

HANSON PARK

Walt Disney House

LOGAN SQUARE

Logan Square

27

Thatcher Rd

W Fullerton Ave

NORTH AUSTIN

50

HERMOSA

GALEWOOD

NORTH AUSTIN

W Grand Ave

W Armitage Ave

49

HUMBOLT PARK

Humbolt Blvd

64

W North Ave

1 mile

1 km

## Essentials

If there's one thing you can count on in Northwest Chicago, it's that you can count on just about everything. Compared to other sections of the city, the Northwest is a bastion of stability. Most of the people and businesses have been around forever, and even typically transitory ethnic enclaves—in this case Eastern European, Middle Eastern, North African, Korean, and Italian—are fairly entrenched. That said, the slow but steady growth of the northwest side communities of Jefferson Park, Mayfair, and Edison Park is notable, as more young families discover the affordable housing and excellent school districts offered here. Additionally, Northwest Chicago is blessed with an abundance of small parks and field houses, as well as a large hunk of forest preserve, giving much of the area a bucolic, suburban feel.

### ○ Landmarks
- **The Admiral Theater** • 3940 W Lawrence Ave
- **Albany Park Community Center** • 3401 W Ainslie St
- **Copernicus Center** • 5216 W Lawrence Ave
- **Eugene Field Park** • 5100 N Ridgeway Ave
- **Gompers Park** • 4222 W Foster Ave
- **Fish Furniture Co Building** • 3322 W Lawrence Ave
- **Hanson Park Fieldhouse** • 5501 W Fullerton Ave
- **Harlem CTA Station** • 5550 N Harlem Ave
- **Logan Square Column** • 3100 W Logan Blvd

- **Noble-Seymour-Crippen House** • 5624 N Newark Ave
- **North Branch Pumping Station** • W Lawrence Ave & NE River Rd
- **Schurz High School** • 3601 Milwaukee Ave
- **Superdawg Drive-In** • 6363 N Milwaukee Ave
- **Turzak House** • 7059 N Olcott Ave
- **Walt Disney House** • 2156 N Tripp Ave
- **Whistle Stop Inn** • 4200 W Irving Park Rd
- **Wilson Park** • 4630 Milwaukee Ave
- **Wingert House** • 6231 N Canfield Ave

## Sundries / Entertainment

Northwest Chicago wears its blue-collar ethnic proclivities on its sleeve. Local shops and restaurants don't go out of their way to attract clientele outside their own, and even the staff at the area's abundant Korean and Eastern European businesses make little effort to communicate in English. Adventuresome diners and cooks rise to the challenge-some of the city's best restaurants and ethnic grocers can be found here, including Thai vegan spot Amitabul and Korean Joong Boo Market. American Science and Surplus has you covered for telescopes, army gear, UV spy pens and (to say the least!) more. Further south, Logan Square's young contingent is sprawling out along a quiet stretch of Armitage at Kedzie thanks to a new crop of bars and restaurants.

### Movie Theaters
- **AMC Loews Norridge 10** • 4520 N Harlem Ave
- **LaSalle Bank Cinema** • 4901 W Irving Park Rd

### Nightlife
- **5th Province Pub** • Irish-American Heritage Ctr • 4626 N Knox Ave
- **Abbey Pub** • 3420 W Grace St
- **Babe's** • 4416 N Milwaukee Ave
- **The Burlington** • 3425 W Fullerton Ave
- **Edison Park Inn** • 6715 W Olmstead Ave
- **Emerald Isle** • 6686 N Northwest Hwy
- **Fantasy Lounge** • 4400 N Elston
- **Fischman Liquors** • 4780 N Milwaukee Ave
- **Flo's Algiers Lounge** • 5436 W Montrose Ave
- **Ham Tree** • 5333 N Milwaukee Ave
- **Hollywood Lounge** • 3303 W Bryn Mawr Ave
- **Jimmy Mack** • 5581 N Northwest Hwy
- **Moretti's** • 6727 N Olmsted Ave
- **New Polonia Club** • 6101 W Belmont Ave
- **Original Dugan's** • 6051 N Milwaukee Ave
- **Rabbits** • 4945 W Foster Ave
- **Rosa's Lounge** • 3420 W Armitage Ave
- **Three Counties** • 5856 N Milwaukee Ave
- **Vaughan's Pub** • 5485 N Northwest Hwy
- **Weegee's Lounge** • 3659 W Armitage Ave

### Restaurants
- **Al Primo Canto** • 5414 W Devon Ave
- **Amarind's** • 6822 W North Ave
- **Amitabul** • 6207 N Milwaukee Ave
- **Big Pho** • 3737 W Lawrence Ave
- **Blue Angel** • 5310 N Milwaukee Ave
- **Brown Sack** • 3706 W Armitage Ave
- **Café con Leche** • 2714 N Milwaukee Ave
- **Carthage Café** • 3446 W Foster Ave
- **Chai's Asian Bistro** • 4748 W Peterson Ave
- **Chiyo** • 3800 W Lawrence Ave
- **Chocolate Shoppe Ice Cream** • 5337 W Devon Ave
- **Don Juan** • 6730 N Northwest Hwy

- **Eat First Chinese Restaurant** • 3337 W Belmont Ave
- **Edgebrook Coffee Shop** • 6322 N Central Ave
- **El Cubanito** • 2555 N Pulaski Rd
- **El Huarachin Huarachon** • 3320 W Lawrence Ave
- **Elliott's Seafood Grille & Chop House** • 6690 N Northwest Hwy
- **Friendship Chinese Restaurant** • 2830 N Milwaukee Ave
- **Gale Street Inn** • 4914 N Milwaukee Ave
- **Gloria's Café** • 3300 W Fullerton Ave
- **Gorditas Aguascaliente** • 2106 N Cicero Ave
- **Great Sea Chinese Restaurants** • 3254 W Lawrence Ave
- **Grota Smorgasborg** • 3112 N Central Ave
- **Halina's Polish Delights** • 5914 W Lawrence Ave
- **Hiromi's** • 3609 W Lawrence Ave
- **La Villa Restaurant** • 3638 N Pulaski Ave
- **Lawrence Fish Market** • 3914 W Lawrence Ave
- **Manee Thai** • 3558 N Pulaski Rd
- **Mayan Sol** • 3830 W Lawrence Ave
- **Mic Duck's Drive In** • 3401 W Belmont Ave
- **Mirabell** • 3454 W Addison St
- **Montasero's Ristorante** • 3935 W Devon Ave
- **Paul Zakopane's Harnas Restaurant** • 2943 N Milwaukee Ave
- **Pollo Campero** • 2730 N Narragansett Ave
- **Pupuseria Las Delicias** • 3300 W Montrose Ave
- **Red Apple** • 3121 N Milwaukee Ave
- **Ristorante Agostino** • 2817 N Harlem Ave
- **Russell's Barbecue** • 1621 N Thatcher Ave
- **Sabatino's** • 4441 W Irving Park Rd
- **Seo Hae** • 3534 W Lawrence Ave
- **Shiraz** • 4425 W Montrose
- **Shokran** • 4027 W Irving Park Rd
- **Smak-Talk** • 5961 N Elston Ave
- **Smoque** • 3800 N Pulaski Rd
- **So Gong Dong Tofu House** • 3307 W Bryn Mawr Ave
- **Sol de Mexico** • 3018 N Cicero Ave
- **Super Pollo** • 3640 W Wrightwood Ave
- **Tassili Café** • 4342 N Elston Ave
- **Teresa II Polish Restaurant & Lounge** • 4751 N Milwaukee Ave

- **Trattoria Pasta D'Arte** • 6311 N Milwaukee Ave
- **Tre Kronor** • 3258 W Foster Ave
- **Via Veneto** • 6340 N Lincoln Ave
- **Zebda** • 4344 N Elston Ave
- **Zia's Trattoria** • 6699 N Northwest Hwy

### Shopping
- **Albany Office Supply** • 3419 W Lawrence Ave
- **American Science & Surplus** • 5316 N Milwaukee Ave
- **Chicago Data Recovery** • 3525 W Peterson Ave
- **Discovery Clothing** • 3348 W Belmont Ave
- **Dom Itp** • 6840 W Belmont Ave
- **Fantasy Costumes** • 4065 N Milwaukee Ave
- **Fishguy** • 4423 N Elston Ave
- **Galos Caves** • 6501 W Irving Park Rd
- **H & B True Value Hardware** • 5329 Milwaukee Ave
- **Harlem Irving Plaza** • Irving Park Rd & W Forest Preserve Ave
- **Hats Plus** • 4706 W Irving Park Rd
- **Heavenly Gelato and Ice Cream** • 2654 N Sawyer Ave
- **Joong Boo Market** • 3333 N Kimball Ave
- **Kurowski Sausage Shop & Rich's Bakery** • 2976 N Milwaukee Ave
- **Old Town Tatu** • 3313 W Irving Park Rd
- **Perfume Outlet** • 3608 W Lawrence Ave
- **Rave Sports** • 3346 W Lawrence Ave
- **Rolling Stone Records** • 7300 W Devon Ave
- **Salvation Army Thrift Store** • 3837 W Fullerton Ave
- **Srpska Tradicija** • 3615 W Lawrence Ave
- **Sweden Shop** • 3304 W Foster Ave
- **Sunrise Fresh Market** • 2722 Milwaukee Ave
- **Unique Thrift Store** • 6560 W Fullerton Ave
- **Village Discount Outlet** • 4635 N Elston Ave
- **Village Discount Outlet** • 3301 W Lawrence Ave
- **Whole Foods** • 6020 N Cicero Ave
- **WIG** • 4621 N Lawndale

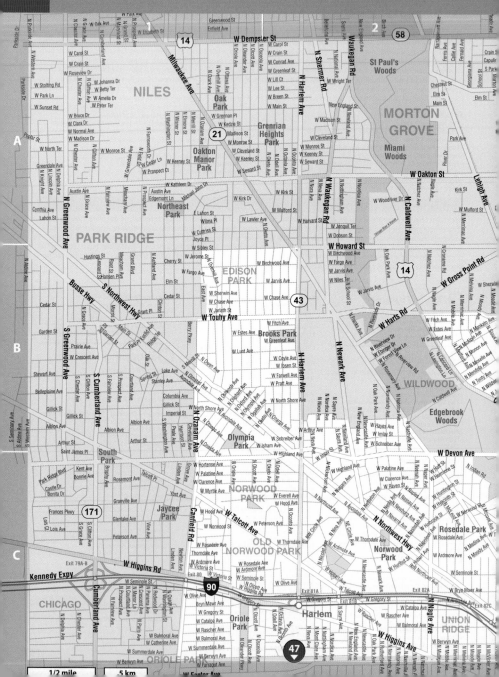

**NILES**

**Oak Park**

**Grenrian Heights Park**

**Oakton Manor Park**

**MORTON GROVE**

**Miami Woods**

**St Paul's Woods**

**Northeast Park**

**PARK RIDGE**

**Edison Park**

**Brooks Park**

**WILDWOOD**

**Edgebrook Woods**

**Olympia Park**

**South Park**

**Jaycee Park**

**NORWOOD PARK**

**Norwood Park**

**Rosedale Park**

**CHICAGO**

**OLD NORWOOD PARK**

**Harlem**

**Oriole Park**

**UNION RIDGE**

**ORIOLE PARK**

1/2 mile  5 km

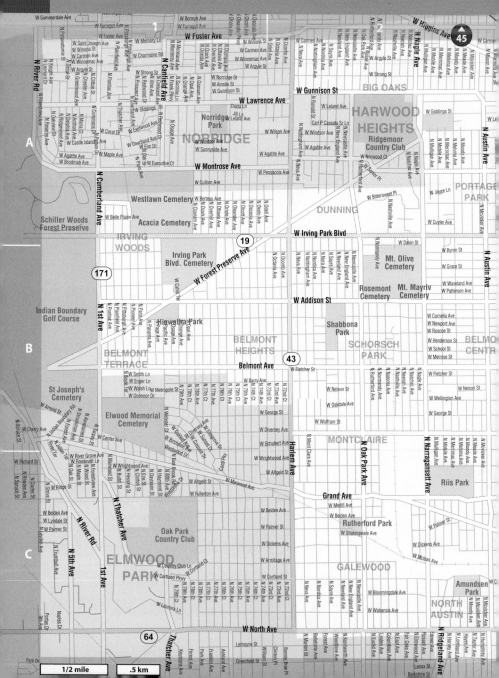

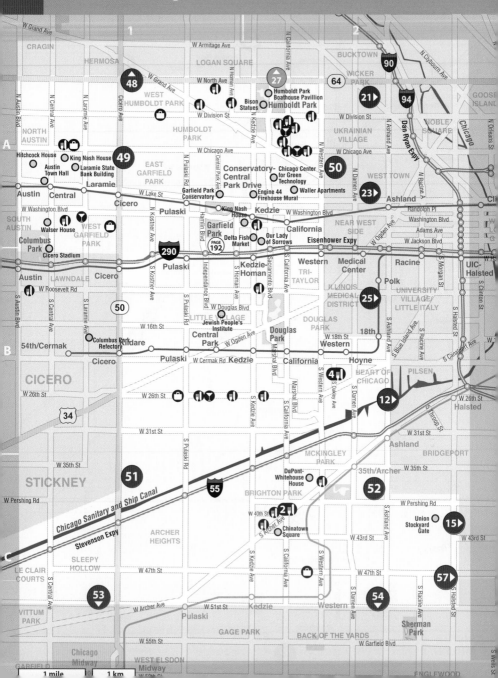

1 mile

1 km

## Essentials

Despite the turf between Humboldt and Columbus Park's lush greens, idyllic lagoons and historic buildings being some of Chicago's roughest, the city's west side is home to spirited folk. 26th Street is the commercial artery of Little Village's thriving Mexican population, and Puerto Rican pride prevails along Division Street and North Avenue through vibrant public art and a jubilant annual parade. Garfield Park Conservatory is a popular spot to tie the knot. Brighton Park and Archer Heights epitomize the classic Chicago blue collar-ethic, where labor unions rule and the Old Style flows freely.

## ○ Landmarks

- **Austin Town Hall** · 5610 W Lake St
- **Bison Statues at Humboldt Park** · 1400 N Sacramento Ave
- **Chicago Center for Green Technology** ·
  445 N Sacramento Blvd
- **Chinatown Square** · S Archer Ave
- **Columbus Park Refectory** · Columbus Park, 500 S Central Ave
- **Delta Fish Market** · 228 S Kedzie Ave
- **DuPont-Whitehouse House** · 3558 S Artesian Ave
- **Engine 44 Firehouse Mural** · 412 N Kedzie Ave
- **Garfield Park Conservatory** · 300 N Central Park Ave
- **Hitchcock House** · 5704 W Ohio St
- **Humboldt Park Boathouse Pavillion** · 1301 N Humboldt Dr
- **Jewish People's Institute** · 3500 W Douglas Blvd
- **King Nash House** · 3234 W Washington Blvd
- **Laramie State Bank Building** · 5200 W Chicago Ave
- **Our Lady of Sorrows** · 3121 W Jackson Blvd
- **Union Stock Yard Gate** · Exchange Ave & Peoria St
- **Waller Apartments** · 2840 W Walnut St
- **Walser House** · 42 N Central Ave

## Sundries / Entertainment

Try Flying Saucer for healthy, hearty breakfasts tailored to vegans and meat eaters alike. Vinyl collectors scour Out of the Past Records' mountainous collection of blues, soul, jazz, and gospel recordings. Down in McKinley Park, La Palapa's thatched umbrellas and mariscos will transport you to Mexico. (Just turn your chair away from Damen Avenue.)

## 🍸 Nightlife

- **Archie's** · 2600 W Iowa St
- **Black Beetle** · 2532 W Chicago Ave
- **California Clipper** · 1002 N California Ave ·
- **Division Street Bar & Grill** · 2525W Division St
- **Illinois Bar & Grill on 47th** · 4135 W 47th St
- **La Justicia** · 3901 W 26th St
- **Linda's Lounge** · 1044 W 51st St
- **Rooster's Place** · 4501 W Madison St
- **Rootstock Wine & Beer Bar** · 954 N California Ave

## 🍴 Restaurants

- **Amarind's** · 6822 W North Ave
- **Bacchanalia Ristorante** · 2413 S Oakley Ave
- **Birria Huentitan** · 4019 W North Ave
- **Birrieria Zaragoza** · 4852 S Pulaski Rd
- **Bruna's** · 2424 S Oakley Ave
- **Cemitas Puebla** · 3619 W North Ave
- **CJ's Eatery** · 3839 W Grand Ave
- **Coco** · 2723 W Division St
- **Coleman's Hickory House** · 5754 W Chicago Ave
- **Depot** · 5840 W Roosevelt Rd
- **Edna's** · 3175 W Madison St
- **El Salvador Restaurante** · 4125 S Archer Ave
- **Falco's Pizza** · 2806 W 40th St
- **Feed** · 2803 W Chicago Ave
- **Flying Saucer** · 1123 N California Ave

- **I. C. Y. Vegetarian Restaurant & Juice Bar** ·
  3141 W Roosevelt Rd
- **Ignotz** · 2421 S Oakley Ave
- **La Cebollita** · 4343 W 47th St
- **La Palma** · 1340 N Homan Ave
- **Lalo's** · 3515 W 26th St
- **Lindy's and Gertie's** · 3685 S Archer Ave
- **MacArthur's** · 5412 W Madison Ave
- **Maiz** · 1041 N California Ave
- **New Life Health Foods & Restaurant** ·
  3141 W Roosevelt Rd
- **Submarine Piers** · 4048 S Archer Ave
- **Taqueria Atotonilco** · 3916 W 26th St
- **Taqueria Los Comales** · 3141 W 26th St
- **Taqueria Los Gallos 2** · 4252 S Archer Ave
- **TipsyCake** · 1043 N California Ave
- **Tommy's Rock-n-Roll Café** · 2548 W Chicago Ave

## 🛍 Shopping

- **Ashland Swap-o-Rama** · 4100 S Ashland Ave
- **Ashley Stewart** · 800 N Kedzie Ave
- **Buyer's Flea Market** · 4545 W Division St
- **Dulcelandia** · 3300 W 26th St
- **Family Dollar** · 5410 W Chicago Ave
- **Family Dollar** · 1360 N Pulaski Rd
- **Unique Thrift Store** · 3542 S Archer Ave
- **Village Discount Outlet** · 2514 W 47th St
- **Village Discount Outlet** · 4020 W 26th St
- **Watra Church Goods** · 4201 S Archer Ave

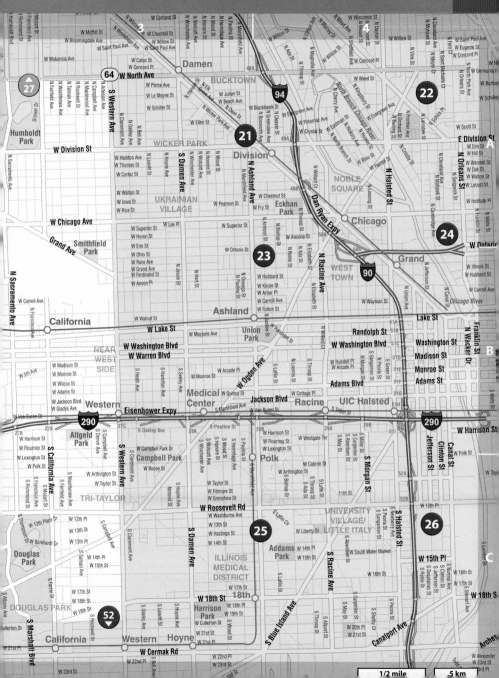

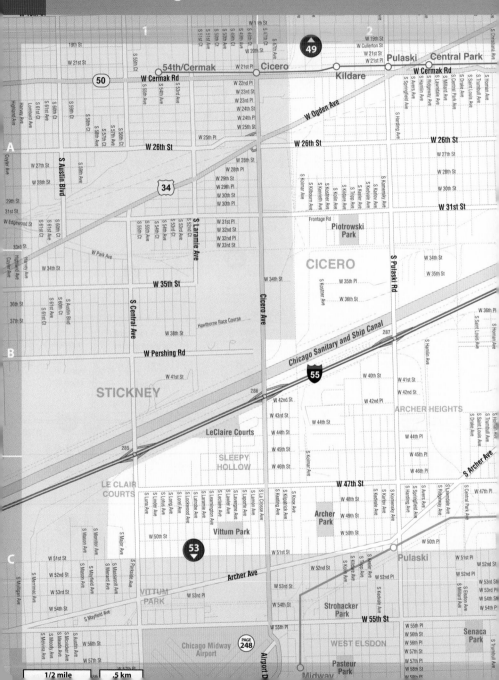

S York St

1

S 19th St
W Cullerton St
W 21st St
W 21st St

2

Pulaski    Central Park

49

54th/Cermak    Cicero    Kildare

W Cermak Rd

50

W Cermak Rd

W 22nd Pl
W 23rd St
W 23rd Pl
W 24th St
W 24th Pl
W 25th St

W Ogden Ave

W 25th Pl

A

W 26th St    W 26th St    W 26th St
W 27th St

W 28th St
W 28th Pl
W 29th St
W 29th Pl
W 30th St
W 30th Pl

34

W 28th St
W 30th St

W 31st St

29th St
31st St

W Edgewood Ave

W 31st Pl
W 32nd St
W 32nd Pl
W 33rd St

Frontage Rd

Piotrowski
Park

33rd St

W Park Ave

W 34th St    W 34th St
W 35th St

CICERO

W 34th St    W 35th St
W 36th St

W 35th St

Hawthorne Race Course

W 36th St

287

B

W Pershing Rd

Chicago Sanitary and Ship Canal

55

W 40th St    W 41st St
W 42nd St

W 41st St

STICKNEY

286

W 42nd St
W 43rd St
W 44th St

W 44th Pl

ARCHER HEIGHTS

LeClaire Courts

285

SLEEPY
HOLLOW

W 45th St
W 46th St

W 45th Pl
W 46th St

W 47th St    W 47th St

LE CLAIR
COURTS

W 48th St
Archer
Park

W 49th St

S Archer Ave

C

W 50th St

Vittum Park

53

W 51st St    W 51st St
W 52nd St
W 52nd Pl

Pulaski

W 51st St
W 52nd St
W 53rd St
W 53rd Pl
W 54th St
W 54th St

W 52nd St
W 53rd St

Archer Ave

W 53rd Pl

VITTUM
PARK

Strohacker
Park

W 55th St

W 55th Pl
W 56th St
W 56th Pl
W 57th St
W 57th Pl
W 58th St
W 58th Pl

Senaca
Park

WEST ELSDON

Chicago Midway
Airport

PAGE
248

Pasteur
Park

Midway

1/2 mile    .5 km

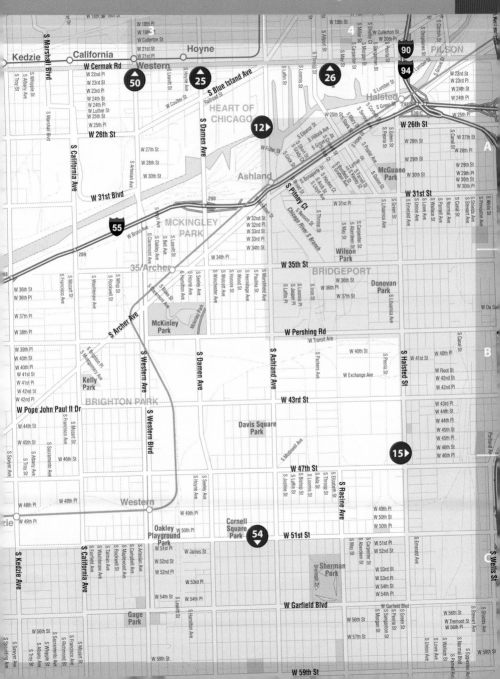

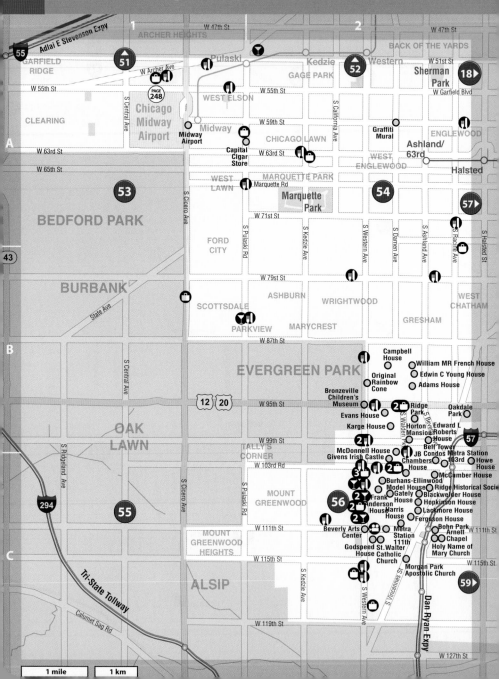

Adlai E Stevenson Expy

**1**

W 47th St

ARCHER HEIGHTS

**2**

W 47th St

BACK OF THE YARDS

55

GARFIELD RIDGE

51

W Archer Ave

Pulaski

Kedzie

52

Western

W 51st St

Sherman Park

18

W 55th St

GAGE PARK

PAGE 248

WEST ELSON

W 55th St

W 51st St

W Garfield Blvd

CLEARING

S Central Ave

Chicago Midway Airport

W 59th St

Western

ENGLEWOOD

Midway Airport

Midway

W 59th St

CHICAGO LAWN

Graffiti Mural

Ashland/ 63rd

**A**

W 63rd St

Capital Cigar Store

W 63rd St

WEST ENGLEWOOD

Halsted

W 65th St

MARQUETTE PARK

43

WEST LAWN

Marquette Rd

54

57

**53**

BEDFORD PARK

Marquette Park

S Kedzie Ave

S Western Ave

S Damen Ave

S Ashland Ave

S Racine Ave

S Halsted St

FORD CITY

W 71st St

S Pulaski Rd

S Cicero Ave

W 79st St

WEST CHATHAM

BURBANK

ASHBURN

WRIGHTWOOD

GRESHAM

State Ave

SCOTTSDALE

PARKVIEW

MARYCREST

W 87th St

**B**

S Central Ave

EVERGREEN PARK

Campbell House

William MR French House

12  20

W 95th St

Original Rainbow Cone

Edwin C Young House

Adams House

Bronzeville Children's Museum

Ridge Park

Oakdale Park

OAK LAWN

Evans House

S Walden Pkwy

Horton Mansion

Edward L Roberts House

294

55

S Ridgeland Ave

W 99th St

Karge House

S Beverly Ave

Bell Tower

W 103rd Rd

McDonnell House

JB Condos Metra Station

TALLY'S CORNER

Givens Irish Castle

Chambers House

103rd

Howe House

S Pulaski Rd

S Cicero Ave

McCumber House

MOUNT GREENWOOD

Burhans-Ellinwood Model House

**56**

Frank Anderson House

Gately House

Ridge Historical Society

Blackwelder House

Hopkinson House

Harris House

Lackmore House

Ferguson House

W 111th St

Beverly Arts Center

Bohn Park Arnett

W 111th St

MOUNT GREENWOOD HEIGHTS

Metra Station 111th

Chapel

Holy Name of Mary Church

Godspeed St. Walter House

Catholic Church

**C**

Tri-State Tollway

ALSIP

S Kedzie Ave

W 115th St

Morgan Park Apostolic Church

W 115th St

**59**

Calumet Sag Rd

W 119th St

S Western Ave

S Vincennes St

Dan Ryan Expy

W 127th St

1 mile       1 km

## Essentials

The Southwest side comprises several communities steeped in Chicago's ethnic blue collar history, including a large Lithuanian population, Italians, Arab-Americans, African-Americans and the Irish. This cultural diversity has not arisen without conflict—Marquette Park was once a gathering spot for white-supremacy groups. Today, the park is better known for its fishing pond, golf course, and occasional outbursts of gang violence. Southernmost in the southwest side, the Beverly and Morgan Park areas are chock-a-block with historic homes and civic pride.

## ○ Landmarks

- **Adams House** • 9326 S Longwood Dr
- **Arnett Chapel, African Methodist Episcopal Church** • 11218 S Bishop St
- **Bell Tower Condos** • 10321 S Longwood Dr
- **Blackwelder Summerlin House** • 10910 S Prospect Ave
- **Bohn Park** • 1966 111th St
- **Bronzeville Children's Museum** • 9600 S Western Ave
- **Burhans-Ellinwood Model House** • 10410 S Hoyne Ave
- **Campbell House** • 9250 S Damen Ave
- **Capital Cigar Store** • 6258 S Pulaski Rd
- **Edward L Roberts House** • 10134 S Longwood Dr
- **Edwin C Young House** • 9215 S Pleasant Ave
- **Evans House** • 9914 S Longwood Dr
- **Ferguson House** • 10954 S Prospect Ave
- **Frank Anderson House** • 10400 S Longwood Dr
- **Gately House** • 10655 S Hoyne Ave
- **Givens Irish Castle** • 10244 S Longwood Dr
- **Goodspeed House** • 11216 S Oakley Ave
- **Graffiti Mural** • W 59th St & S Damen Ave
- **Harris House** • 10856 S Longwood Dr
- **Holy Name of Mary Church** • 11159 S Loomis St
- **Hopkinson House** • 10820 S Drew St
- **Horton Mansion** • 10200 S Longwood Dr
- **Howe House** • 10208 S Wood St
- **JB Chambers House** • 10330 S Seeley Ave
- **Karge House** • 2035 W 99th St
- **Lackore House** • 10956 S Prospect Ave
- **McCumber House** • 10305 S Seeley Ave
- **Metra 103rd/Washington Heights Rock Island District Branch Line Station** • 103rd St & Vincennes Ave
- **Metra Rock Island Main Line 111th St/Monterey Ave Station** • 111th St & Monterey Ave
- **Midway Airport** • 5700 S Cicero Ave
- **Morgan Park Apostolic Penecostal Church** • 11401 S Vincennes Ave
- **Morgan Park United Methodist Church** • 11030 S Longwood Dr
- **Oakdale Park** • 956 W 95th St
- **Original Rainbow Cone** • 9233 S Western Ave
- **Ridge Historical Society** • 10621 S Seeley Ave
- **Ridge Park** • 9625 S Longwood Dr
- **St Walter Catholic Church** • 11722 S Oakley Ave
- **William MR French House** • 9203 S Pleasant Ave

## Sundries/Entertainment

We're still lamenting the reform of the nation's largest, sloppiest St. Paddy's Day parade into a more wholesome day of family fun. If you're still looking to be reckless in this neck of the woods, you still have Engelwood's Fat Johnnie's hot dog stand, where you can enjoy a southside institution: a tamale in a hot dog bun covered with chili and cheese. And the collection of neighborhood pubs dotting Western Avenue won't turn you away either.

## 👥 Movie Theaters

- **AMC Ford City 14** • 7601 S Cicero Ave

## 🍸 Nightlife

- **Cookie's Cocktail Lounge** • 1024 W 79th St
- **Cork & Kerry** • 10614 S Western Ave
- **Groucho's** • 8355 S Pulaski Rd
- **Halina's Bar** • 7023 W Archer Ave
- **Jeremy Lanigan's Irish Pub** • 3119 W 111th St
- **Keegan's Pub** • 10618 S Western Ave
- **Mrs O'Leary's Dubliner** • 10910 S Western Ave
- **O'Rourke's Office** • 11064 S Western
- **Patrick's** • 6296 S Archer Ave
- **Sean's Rhino Bar** • 10330 S Western Ave
- **Tom's Tap** • 6707 W Archer Ave

## 🍴 Restaurants

- **Beverly Woods Restaurant** • 11532 S Western Ave
- **Birrieria de la Torre** • 6724 S Pulaski Rd
- **Bobak's Sausage Company** • 5275 S Archer Ave
- **Café 103** • 1909 W 103rd St
- **Fat Johnnie's** • 7232 S Western Ave
- **Fox's Beverly Restaurant and Pizza** • 9956 S Western Ave
- **Franconello's Italian Restaurant** • 10222 S Western Ave
- **Harold's Chicken Shack** • 7274 S Racine Ave
- **Janson's Drive-In / Snyder's Red Hots** • 9900 S Western Ave
- **Koda** • 10352 S Western Ave
- **Lagniappe** • 1525 W 79th St
- **Lume's** • 11601 S Western Ave
- **New China Tea** • 4020 W 55th St
- **Nile Restaurant** • 3259 W 63rd St
- **The Original Vito and Nick's Pizzeria** • 8433 S Pulaski Rd
- **Szalas** • 5214 S Archer Ave
- **Tatra Inn** • 6040 S Pulaski Rd
- **Top Notch Beefburger** • 2116 W 95th St
- **Uncle Joe's Jerk** • 10210 S Vincennes Ave

## 🛍 Shopping

- **The Beverly Cigar Company** • 10513 S Western Ave
- **Beverly & Novelty Costume Shop** • 11626 S Western Ave
- **Beverly Rare Records** • 11612 S Western Ave
- **Bobak's Sausage Company** • 5275 S Archer Ave
- **Calabria Imports** • 1905 W 103rd St
- **County Fair** • 10800 S Western Ave
- **Evergreen Plaza Shopping Center** • 9730 S Western Ave
- **Ford City Shopping Center** • 7601 S Cicero Ave
- **Markskis CD** • 5106 S Archer Ave
- **Mr Peabody Records** • 11832 S Western Ave
- **Ms Priss** • 9915 S Walden Pkwy
- **Optimo Fine Hats** • 10215 S Western Ave
- **Southwest Ace Hardware** • 6908 W Archer Ave
- **Southwest Book & Video** • 7733 S Cicero Ave
- **Village Discount Outlet** • 6419 S Kedzie Ave
- **Village Discount Outlet** • 7443 S Racine Ave
- **World Music Company** • 1808 W 103rd St

44th St
45th St
46th St
W 44th Pl
W 45th St
W 45th Pl
W 46th St

**55**

Adlai E Stevenson Expy

W 47th St
W 48th St
W 49th St
W 50th St

Archer Park

Vittum Park

**ARCHER HEIGHTS**
Pulaski

**51**

W 51st St
W 51st Pl
W 52nd St
W 53rd St
W 54th St

W Archer Ave
W 53rd Pl

W 52nd St
W 52nd Pl

Park Number 468

**A**

**GARFIELD RIDGE**

W 55th St

**WEST ELSON**

S Pulaski Rd

W 55th St
W 56th St
W 57th St

W Archer Ave

W 56th St
W 57th St
W 58th St
W 59th St
W 60th Pl
W 61st St
W 62nd St

Wentworth Kinzie Park

Minuteman Park

Chicago Midway Airport

Airport Dr

**Midway**

Pasteur Park

Valley Forge Park

**43**

Nathan Hale Park

**PAGE 248**

**50**

W 59th St

**B**

W 63rd St

W 63rd St

**WEST LAWN**

W 63rd Pl
W 64th St
W 64th Pl
W 65th St
W 66th St

Lawler Park

W 64th St
W 65th Pl
W 66th St
W 66th Pl

West Lawn Park

W 66th Pl

W 67th St
W 68th St

W 67th St

S Cicero Ave

W 68th St
W 69th Pl
W 70th Pl
W 70th St

W 68th St

W 69th St

**BEDFORD PARK**

S Belt Circle Dr

W 70th Pl

W 71st St

W 71st St
W 72nd St
W 72nd Pl
W 73rd St
W 73rd Pl
W 74th St
W 74th Pl
W 75th St

W 73rd St

W 72nd St

S Cicero Ave

S Pulaski Rd

W 75th St
W Hayford St

Briartree Ln

W 76th St
W 76th Pl
W 77th St
W 77th Pl
W 78th St
W 78th St

W 76th St

W 77th St
W 77th Pl

Rainey Hancock Park

**C**

W 79th Pl
W 80th Pl
W 80th Pl
W 81st St

79th St

79th St

**SCOTTSDALE**

Bogan Park

W 79th St

S Crestline Ave
W 81st St
W 82nd St
W 82nd Pl
W 83rd St
W 83rd Pl
W 84th St
W 84th Pl
W 85th St
W 85th Pl

W 81st Pl

**BURBANK**

Scottsdale Park

W 82nd St
W 82nd Pl
W 83rd St

Durkin Center Park

W 86th St

**55**

W 87th St
W 87th Pl
W 88th St

W 87th St

Harlem Ave

1/2 mile   .5 km

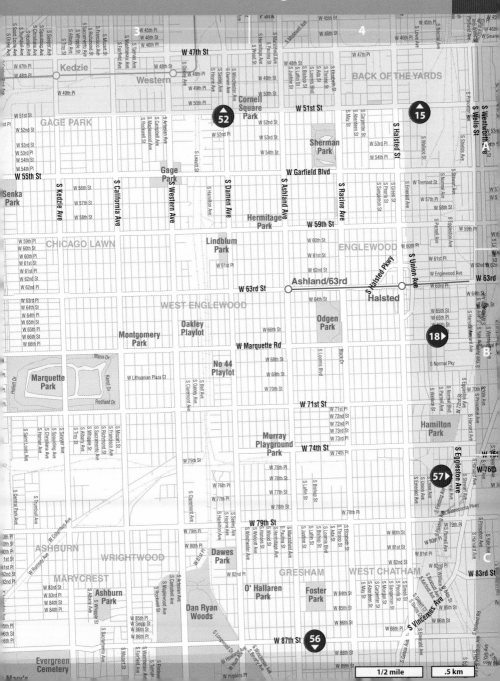

S Saint Louis Ave
S Drake Ave
S Sawyer Ave
S Christiana Ave
S Spaulding Ave
S Sacramento Ave
S Francisco Ave
S Troy St
S Albany Ave
S Fairfield Ave

W 45th Pl
W 45th St
W 46th St
W 46th Pl
W 47th St
W 48th St
W 48th Pl
W 49th Pl
W 49th Pl
W 50th St

**3**

**4**

Kedzie

Western

Cornell
Square
Park

S Marshfield Ave
S Paulina St
S Hermitage Ave
S Wood St

W 45th St
W 46th St
W 47th St

S McDowell Ave
W 45th St
W 46th St

S Portland Ave
W 45th St
W 45th St
W 45th Sw

S Lowe Ave
S Normal Ave

**BACK OF THE YARDS**

S Wells St
S Wentworth Ave

**A**

**52**

**15**

GAGE PARK

Gage
Park

S Kedzie Ave
S California Ave
S Western Ave
S Artesian Ave
S Campbell Ave
S Rockwell St

S Damen Ave
S Hamilton Ave
S Seeley Ave
S Winchester Ave
S Hoyne Ave
S Damen Ave

W 51st St
W 52nd St
W 53rd St
W 54th St
W 55th St
W 56th St
W 57th St
W 58th St

W 51st St
W 52nd Pl
W 53rd St
W 54th St

W Garfield Blvd

Sherman
Park

S Ashland Ave
S Loomis Blvd
S Bishop St
S Laflin St
S Justine St
S Elizabeth St
S Throop St
S Ada St
S Racine Ave
S Carpenter St
S Aberdeen St
S May St
S Peoria St
S Sangamon St
S Morgan St

S Halsted St
S Wallace St
S Emerald Ave

S Green St
S Normal Ave
S Stewart Ave
S Tremont St
S Eggleston Ave
S Parnell Ave

W 53rd St
W 54th St
W 57th St
W 58th St

Senka
Park

W 55th St

Hermitage
Park

W 59th St

Lindblum
Park

W 59th St
W 60th St
W 60th St
W 61st St
W 61st St
W 62nd St
W 62nd St

CHICAGO LAWN

W 60th St
W 61st St
W 62nd St
W 61st Pl

**ENGLEWOOD**

S Halsted Pkwy
S Union Ave

W 60th St
W 61st Pl
W Englewood Ave
W 63rd St

Ashland/63rd

Halsted

W 63rd St

W 63rd St
W 64th St
W 65th St
W 66th St
W 66th St

WEST ENGLEWOOD

Oakley
Playlot

Montgomery
Park

No 44
Playlot

Odgen
Park

W 63rd St
W 64th St
W 65th St
W 66th St
W Marquette Rd
W 67th St
W 68th St
W 69th St
W 70th St

S Bell Ave
S Oakley Ave
S Claremont Ave

S Loomis Blvd
Black Dr

**18**

S Harvard Ave
S Yale Ave
S Princeton Ave

**B**

S Normal Pkwy
S Parnell Ave
S Wallace St
S Eggleston Ave

Marquette
Park

Mano Dr
Kean Dr
Redfield Dr

S Saint Louis Ave
S Homan Ave
S Sawyer Ave
S Spaulding Ave
S Christiana Ave
S Mozart St
S Francisco Ave
S Richmond St
S Sacramento Ave
S Whipple St
S Albany Ave
S Troy St

W 71st St
W 71st St
W 72nd St
W 72nd St
W 73rd St
W 73rd St

Murray
Playground
Park

S Hermitage Ave
S Wolcott Ave
S Bell St
S Bishop St
S Loomis Blvd
S Ada St
S Laflin St
S Justine St
S Throop St

Hamilton
Park

S Eggleston Ave
S Parnell Ave
S Wallace St
S Harvard Ave

W 71st St
W 74th St
W 75th Pl
W 76th St
W 77th St
W 78th Pl

W 74th St
W 74th St

W 75th St
W 76th St
W 77th St
W 78th St

W 79th St
W 79th St

W 79th St

**57**

W 76th St

S Eggleston Ave
S Union Ave
S Emerald Ave
S Stewart Ave

ASHBURN

WRIGHTWOOD

MARYCREST

Ashburn
Park

Dawes
Park

GRESHAM

WEST CHATHAM

S Central Park Ave
S Trumbull Ave
W Columbus Ave
S Homan Ave
S Ramon Ave
S Spaulding Ave
S Artesian Ave
S Campbell Ave
S Maplewood Ave
S Rockwell Ave
S Whipple St
S Albany Ave
S Sacramento Ave

S Marshfield Ave
S Hermitage Ave
S Wood St
S Paulina St
S Ashland Ave
S Marshfield Ave

S Emerald Ave
S Green St
S Peoria St
S Sangamon St
S Morgan St
S Carpenter St
S Aberdeen St
S May St

S Wallace St
S Green St
S Halsted St

W 80th St
W 80th St
W 81st St
W 81st St
W 82nd St

W 83rd St
W 83rd Pl
W 84th St
W 84th St

W 79th St
W 80th St
W 81st St
W 81st St

Dan Ryan
Woods

O' Hallaren
Park

Foster
Park

**C**

W 79th St
W 82nd St
W 83rd St

S Vincennes Ave

W 83rd St

Evergreen
Cemetery

S Central Park Ave
S Homan Ave
S Trumbull Ave
S Whipple St
S Albany Ave

S Artesian Ave
S Maplewood Ave
S Rockwell Ave

W 85th Pl
W 85th St
W 86th Pl
W 86th St

W 87th St

**56**

W 87th St
W 88th St
W 89th St

1/2 mile

.5 km

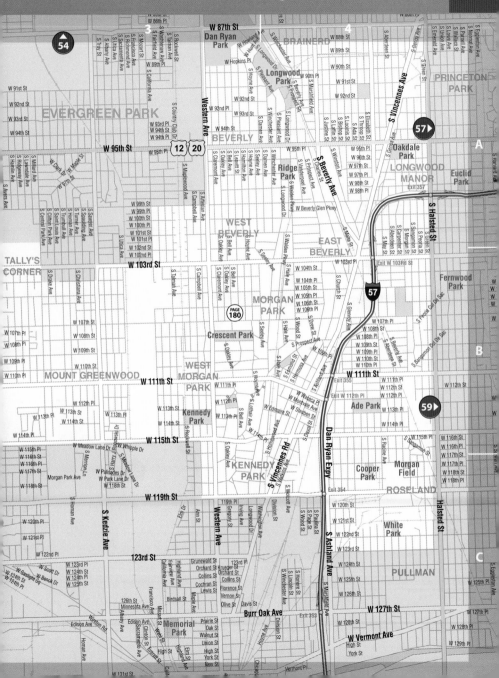

Lake Michigan

**INDIANA**
**ILLINOIS**

E 51st St
51st
Garfield
Garfield Blvd
Garfield
Hyde Park Blvd
Jackson
Park
Washington
Park
W 55th St
E 59th St
East 63rd/
Cottage
Grove
Ban Ryan Expy
63rd
**18**
**19**
**20**
E Hayes Dr
Halsted
E 63rd St
Halsted
WEST
WOODLAWN
E Marquette Rd
69th
E 67th St
Oak Woods
Cemetery
Kenna
Apartments
South Shore
Cultural Center
WOODLAWN
SOUTH
SHORE
S Jeffery Blvd
PARK
MANOR
E 71st St
GRAND
CROSSING
Miller House
**58**
**3**
E 74th St
E 75th St
E 75th St
E 76th St
CHATHAM
79th
E 79th St
**2**
MARYNOOK
E 79th St
SOUTH CHICAGO
New Regal
Theatre
**41**
S Stony Island Ave
**57**
STONY
ISLAND
PARK
S Chicago Ave
**2**
E 83rd St
E 87th St
87th
BURNSIDE
Chicago
Skyway
CALUMET
HEIGHTS
Peoples Gas
South Chicago
S Commercial Ave
S Mackinaw Ave
Calumet River
**54**
S Vincennes Ave
S State St
S Lafayette Ave
S Cottage Grove Ave
WEST
CHESTERFIELD
PILL
HILL
**90**
**94**
Carter G Wooden
Regional
Library
E 95th St
95th/Dan Ryan
PRINCETON
PARK
Trinity United
Church of Christ
Chicago State
University
Robert S.
Abbott Park
COTTAGE GROVE
HEIGHTS
**12** **20**
JEFFERY
MANOR
E 95th St
S Ewing Ave
S Exchange Ave
**57**
LONGWOOD
MANOR
ROSEMOOR
W 103rd St
Stony Island Ave
E 100th St
E 103rd St
SOUTH
DEERING
S Colfax Ave
WASHINGTON
HEIGHTS
Lilydale Progressive
Missionary Baptist
FERNWOOD
S King Dr
**59**
Pullman
Clock Tower
Hyde Park
E 106th St
**60**
Eggers
Woods
S Torrence Ave
S Avenue O
S Ewing Ave
Chicago Skyway
ROSELAND
E 111th St
E 113th St
Market
Hall
Palmer
Park
Lilydale First
Baptist Church
E 115th St
Lake Calumet
Calumet River
**41**
Indianapolis Blvd
Calumet Ave
**56**
West Pullman
Elementary
School
Foster
House &
Stable
PULLMAN
S State St
Wolf Lake
Park
Wolf Lake
WEST PULLMAN
West Pullman Park
S Burnham Ave
Cedar Park Cemetery
& Funeral Home
W 127th St
E 127th St
W Vermont Ave
GOLDEN
GATE
S Indiana Ave
Ford Freeway
E 130th St
ALTGELD
GARDENS
Forest
Preserve
Little Calumet River
S Saginaw Ave
S Brainard Ave
HEGEWISCH
**ILLINOIS**
**INDIANA**
**912**

RIVERDALE

1 mile
1 km

## Essentials

Former lifeblood of the southside economy, US Steel Company left behind expansive, desolate acreage decades ago. But despite squashed Olympic development hopes, transit artery Lake Shore Drive is currently being extended south, and solid plans for housing and infrastructure may become reality over the next few years. Still, life goes on in the southside; one of the most crime-riddled areas in the city between Garfield Blvd. and Englewood, as well as the comfortable middle-class enclaves of South Shore to Chatham to Burnside, a bungalow belt that defies the area's rough-and-tumble reputation.

### ⊙ Landmarks

- **Bronzeville Children's Museum** • 9301 S Stony Island Ave
- **Cedar Park Cemetary & Funeral Home** • 12540 S Halsted St
- **Chicago Skyway** • 8801 S Anthony St
- **Chicago State University** • 9501 S King Dr
- **Foster House & Stable** • 12147 S Harvard Ave
- **Kenna Apartments** • 2214 E 69th St
- **Lilydale First Baptist Church** • 649 W 113th St
- **Lilydale Progressive Missionary Baptist Church** • 10706 S Michigan Ave
- **Market Hall** • E 112th St & Champlain Ave
- **Miller House** • 7121 S Paxton Ave
- **Mosque Maryam and the Nation of Islam National Center** • 7351 S Stony Island Ave
- **New Regal Theatre** • 1641 E 79th St
- **Oak Woods Cemetery** • 1035 E 67th St
- **Palmer Park** • 201 E 111th St
- **Peoples Gas South Chicago** • 8935 S Commercial Ave
- **Pullman Clock Tower** • 11141 S Cottage Grove Ave
- **Robert S Abbott Park** • 49 E 95th St
- **South Shore Cultural Center** • 7059 South Shore Dr
- **Trinity United Church of Christ** • 400 W 95th St
- **West Pullman Elementary** • 11941 S Parnell Ave
- **West Pullman Park** • 401 W 123rd St
- **Woodson Regional Public Library** • 3525 S Halsted St

## Sundries/Entertainment

75th St is a hub of southside action: legendary Army & Lou's has served soul food to every civil rights leader you can imagine. Lee's Unleaded Blues offers a truer Chicago blues experience than anything downtown or on the northside. South Shore's Jeffrey Pub offers a friendly haven for the southside's GLBTQ folks. South Deering received its 15 minutes of fame when the smoked fish offerings of Calumet Fisheries were featured on Anthony Bourdain's No Reservations.

### 🎥 Movie Theaters

- **ICE Chatham 14** • 210 87th St

### 🍸 Nightlife

- **Jeffrey Pub** • 7041 S Jeffery Blvd
- **Lee's Unleaded Blues** • 7401 S South Chicago Ave
- **Reds** • 6926 S Stony Island Ave

### 🍴 Restaurants

- **5 Loaves Eatery** • 405 E 75th St
- **Army & Lou's** • 422 E 75th St
- **Barbara Ann's BBQ** • 7617 S Cottage Grove Ave
- **BJ's Market & Bakery** • 8734 S Stony Island Ave
- **Café Trinidad** • 557 E 75th St
- **Cal Harbor Restaurant** • 546 E 115th St
- **Calumet Fisheries** • 3259 E 95th St
- **Capri Pizza** • 8820 S Commercial Ave
- **Captain's Hard Time** • 436 E 79th St
- **Daddy O Jerkpit** • 7518 S Cottage Grove Ave
- **Dat Old Fashioned Donut** • 8251 S Cottage Grove Ave
- **Desde Puerto Rico** • 8810 S Commercial Ave
- **Hand-Burgers** • 11322 S Halsted St
- **Heinie's Shrimp House** • 10359 S Torrence Ave
- **Helen's Restaurant** • 1732 E 79th St
- **Izola's** • 522 E 79th St
- **Jamaican Jerk Spice** • 6500 S Cottage Grove Ave
- **Lem's** • 311 E 75th St
- **Leon's Bar-B-Que** • 8249 S Cottage Grove Ave
- **Old Fashioned Donuts** • 11248 S Michigan Ave
- **The Parrot Cage** • 7059 S South Shore Dr
- **Phil's Kastle** • 3532 E 95th St
- **Pupuseria El Salvador** • 3557 E 106th St
- **Seven Seas Submarine** • 11216 S Michigan Ave
- **Soul Queen** • 9031 S Stony Island Ave
- **Soul Vegetarian East** • 205 E 75th St
- **Sunugal** • 2051 E 79th St
- **That's-A-Burger** • 2134 E 71st St
- **Three J's** • 1713 E 75th St
- **Uncle Joe's** • 8211 S Cottage Grove Ave
- **Uncle John's BBQ** • 339 E 69th St
- **Wings Around the World** • 510 E 75th St
- **Yassa African Restaurant** • 716 E 79th St

### 🛍 Shopping

- **A&G Fresh Market** • 5630 W Belmont Ave
- **African Hedonist** • 8501 S Cottage Grove Ave
- **Hagen's Fish Market** • 5635 W Montrose Ave
- **Halsted Indoor Mall** • 11444 S Halsted St
- **Hyman's Ace Hardware** • 8614 S Commercial Ave
- **Jordan's Beauty Supply** • 1911 E 79th St
- **K & G Fashion Superstore** • 7540 S Stony Island Ave
- **Underground Afrocentric Bookstore** • 1727 E 87th St

1 mile

1 km

3

4

A

*Lake Michigan*

B

C

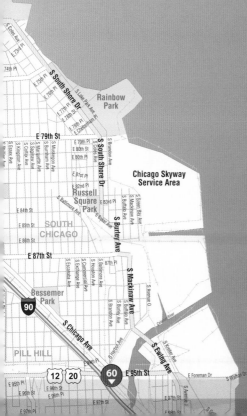

S Coles Ave

E 73rd Pl

74th Pl

S 75th Pl

**S South Shore Dr**

E 76th Pl

S Lake Park Ave

E 77th Pl

S 78th St

Rainbow
Park

E 78th Pl

E Chatanham Pl

S Brandon Ave

**E 79th St**

S Muskegon Ave

E 79th Pl

S Burnham Ave

E 80th St

S Marquette Ave

S Colfax Ave

S Saginaw Ave

S Essex Ave

S Kingston Ave

E 80th Pl

**S South Shore Dr**

S Phillips Ave

E 81st St

E 82nd Pl

**Chicago Skyway
Service Area**

E 83rd St

S Green Bay Ave

S Mackinaw Ave

S Buffalo Ave

**S Burley Ave**

S Baltimore Ave

S Baker Ave

**Russell
Square
Park**

E 84th St

E 85th St

**SOUTH
CHICAGO**

E 86th St

**E 87th St**

87th Pl

S Houston Ave

S Baltimore Ave

S Commercial Ave

S Exchange Ave

S Escanaba Ave

**S Mackinaw Ave**

S Buffalo Ave

S Burley Ave

S Brandon Ave

S Avenue O

**Bessemer
Park**

**90**

**S Chicago Ave**

S Kreiter Ave

**PILL HILL**

**12** **20**

**60**

S 91st St

**E 95th St**

**S Ewing Ave**

E Foreman Dr

S Walton Dr

E 95th St

E 96th St

E 96th Pl

E 97th St

S Avenue J

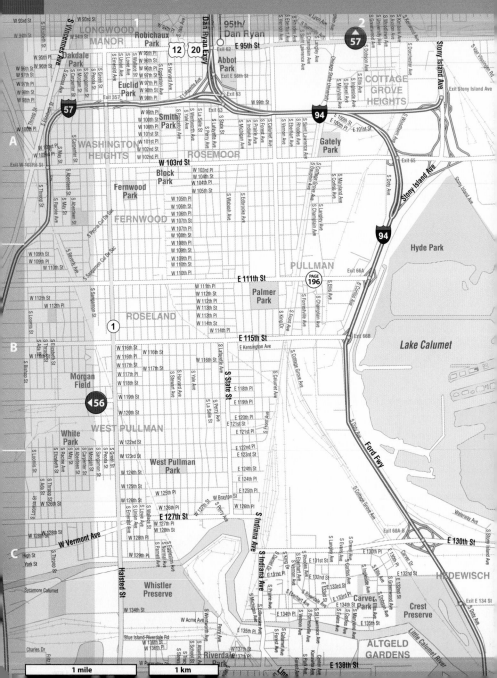

E 94th St
E Foreman Dr
S Whipple Dr
**4**

E 95th St
12  20  3
**58**
E 96th St
Calumet
Park
E 97th St
E 98th St

S Hoxie Ave
S Crandon Ave
S Oglesby Ave
S Bennett Ave
S 96th Cr
S 95th Pl
E 95th Pl
E 95th St
E 96th St
E 97th St
E 97th Pl

S Commercial Ave
S Baltimore Ave
S Houston Ave
S Exchange Ave
S Marquette Ave
S Manistee Ave
S Escanaba Ave
S Muskegon Ave

Veterans
Memorial
Park
E 99th St
E 100th St

Lake Michigan

S Calhoun Ave
S Yates Ave
S Oglesby Ave
S Crandon Ave
S Bennett Ave
S Paxton Ave
S Merrill Ave
S Clyde Ave
S Van Vlissingen Rd

E 100th St
E 101st St
E 102nd St

S Ewing Ave
S Avenue M
S Avenue L
S Avenue H
S Avenue G
S Avenue F
S Avenue E
S Avenue D
S Avenue C

S Avenue G
S Avenue H
S Grnty Dr

**A**

S Colfax Ave
E 103rd St
Trumbull
Park
E 104th St
E 105th St
S Minister Ave
E 103rd St
S Green Bay Ave
S Avenue N
South Ave N
E 104th St
E 105th St
**41**
Hwy 12

E 106th St
E 106th St
JEFFERY
MANOR
E 107th St
E 108th St
E 109th St
Wolfe Plg
Park
S Avenue O
E 107th St
E 108th St
E 109th St
S Ewing Ave
S Avenue J
S Avenue H
S Avenue G
S Avenue F
S Avenue E

S Indianapolis Ave

S Torrence Ave
E 110th St
SOUTH
DEERING
E 111th St
E 112th St
E 113th St
E 114th St
S Green Bay Ave
S Mackinaw Ave
S Buffalo Ave
S Burley Ave
S Paxton Ave
S Merrill Ave
S Clyde Ave
S Chapel Ave
E 110th St
E 114th St

Calumet River

Rowen
Park
S Greenbay Ave
Eggers
Woods
E 115th St
E 116th St
E 117th St
E 118th St

Brown St
Warwick St
Pool St
Amy Ave
Ohio St
Myrtle Ave
Howe Ave
Bensley Ave
Oliver Ave
Sheridan Ave
Center St
Front Ave

**B**

E 116th St
E 117th St
E 119th St
E 120th St
E 121st St
E 120th Pl
S Oglesby Ave
S Luella Ave
S Paxton Ave
S Merrill Ave
S Clyde Ave

Stewart St
Burton Ct
Roosevelt St
Superior Ave
West Park Ave
Lincoln Ave
Lake Ave
Stanton Ave
Davis Ave
Central St
Atchison Ave
119th Ave
Fischrupp Ave
John St
Fred St

E 121st St
E 122nd St
E 123rd St
E 124th St
E 125th St
E 126th St
S Wolf Lake Blvd
Wolf Lake
Park
E 122nd St
124th St
College St
125th St

Calumet Ave

Wolf Lake
126th St
127th St
**41**
White Oak Ave
Birch Ave
New York Ave
Elder Ave
Eggers Ave

E 127th St
E 128th St
E 129th St
S Carondelet Ave
S Escanaba Ave
S Muskegon Ave
S Brandon Ave
S Burley Ave
S Avenue O
129th St
Shefield St

ILLINOIS
INDIANA

E 130th St
E 130th St
Mann
Park
S Brainard Ave
E 131st St
E 132nd St
E 133rd St
S Paxton Ave
S Manistee Ave
S Marquette Ave
S Carondelet Ave
S Baltimore Ave
S Houston Ave
S Burley Ave
S Mackinaw Ave
S Green Bay Ave
S Avenue O
133rd St
Baltimore Ave
Torrence Ave
Henry St
Johnson St
**912**
**C**

S Saginaw Ave
E 134th St
E 135th St
E 136th St
E 137th St
HEGEWISCH
S Luella Ave
S Paxton Ave
S Merrill Ave
S Clyde Ave
E 134th St
E 135th St
S Green Bay Ave
S Buffalo Ave
S Baltimore Ave
S Brandon Ave
S Mackinaw Ave
S Avenue O
S Avenue N
S Avenue M
S Avenue K
S Avenue F

Burnham
Woods
Pulaski
Park
137th St
138th St
Victoria St
Holman Ave
Henry St
Thorne St

1 mile        1 km

## Overview

Beverly Hills, best known simply as Beverly, is the stronghold of Chicago's heralded "South Side Irish" community. An authentic medieval castle, baronial mansions, rolling hills, and plenty of pubs compose Chicago's Emerald Isle of 39,000 residents.

Once populated by Illinois and Potawatomi Indian tribes, Beverly became home to clans of Irish-American families after the Great Chicago Fire. Famous residents include Andrew Greeley, Brian Piccolo, George Wendt, the Schwinn Bicycle family, and decades of loyal Chicago civil servants.

Proud and protective of their turf, these close-knit South Siders call Beverly and its sister community, Morgan Park, "the Ridge." The integrated neighborhood occupies the highest ground in Chicago, 30 to 60 feet above the rest of the city atop Blue Island Ridge.

Although the Ridge is just 15 miles from the Loop, most North Siders only trek there for the South Side Irish Parade, which attracts hundreds of thousands of people each year around St. Patrick's Day. The parade was cancelled for a few years (thanks to the immense crowds and rowdy celebrations), but returned in 2012 promising to bring the event back to its "family friendly" roots.

But there is more than a 6-pack of reasons to visit Beverly. The Ridge Historic District is one of the country's largest urban areas on the National Register of Historic Places. Surprised, huh?

## Architecture

Sadly, many Chicagoans are unaware of the rich architectural legacy on the city's far South Side. Beverly and Morgan Park encompass four landmark districts including the Ridge Historic District, three Chicago Landmark Districts, and over 30 Prairie-style structures.

Within approximately a nine-mile radius, from 87th Street to 115th Street and Prospect Avenue to Hoyne Avenue, one can view a vast collection of homes and public buildings representing American architectural styles developed between 1844 and World War II.

The 109th block of Prospect Avenue, every inch of Longwood Drive, and the Victorian train stations at 91st Street, 95th Street, 99th Street, 107th Street, 111th Street, and 115th Street are all great Chicago landmarks. Walter Burley Griffin Place on W 104th Street has Chicago's largest concentration of Prairie School houses built between 1909 and 1913 by Griffin, a student of Frank Lloyd Wright and designer of the city of Canberra in Australia.

Beverly Area Planning Association (BAPA) (11107 S Longwood Drive, 773-233-3100; www.bapa.org) provides a good architectural site map, plus events and shopping information for the district. History buffs might want to visit the Ridge Historical Society, open Tuesdays, Thursdays, and Sundays from 2 pm to 5 pm (10621 S Seeley Ave, 773-881-1675; www.ridgehistoricalsociety.org).

## Culture & Events

The Beverly Arts Center is the epicenter of Ridge culture. The $8 million facility provides visual and performance art classes for all ages and hosts Chicago's only contemporary Irish film festival during the first week of March (2407 W 111th St, 773-445-3838; www.beverlyartcenter.org).

Historic Ridge homes open their doors to the public on the third Sunday of May for the annual Home Tour, Chicago's oldest such tour. Sites are chosen for their diverse architectural styles and historical significance. Tickets can be purchased through BAPA or the Beverly Arts Center for $25 in advance or $30 the day of the event. All tours depart from the Beverly Arts Center between the hours of 11 am and 5 pm; the last tour leaves at 3 pm, and homes close promptly at 5 pm. Guided trolley tours are also offered for an additional $4, departing every half hour between 11 am and 3pm. Contact BAPA at 773-233-3100 or www.bapa.org for more details.

## Where to Eat

- **Janson's Drive-In**, 9900 S Western Ave, 773-238-3612. No indoor seating at this classic drive-thru.
- **Rainbow Cone**, 9233 S Western Ave, 773-238-7075. Ice cream. On summer nights more than 50 folks line up for sweet treats at this 76-year-old soda fountain.
- **Top Notch Beefburger**, 2116 W 95th St, 773-445-7218. Burgers really are top notch at this '50s-style grill.

## Where to Drink

- **Lanigan's Irish Pub**, 3119 W 111th St, 773-233-4004. Anyone know where you can find a pint in Beverly? I've got quite a mean thirst.
- **Mrs. O'Leary's Dubliner**, 10910 S Western Ave, 773-238-0784. Affectionately known as the Dubliner, this is one of the many Irish pubs lining Western Avenue.

## Where to Shop

- **Bev Art Brewer and Winemaker Supply**, 10033 S Western Ave, 773-233-7579. Everything Ridge you need to brew and bottle it yourself.
- **Calabria Imports**, 1905 W 103rd St, 773-396-5800. Imported Italian gourmet foodstuffs.
- **Optimo Hat Co**, 10215 S Western Ave, 773-238-2999. Custom made men's hats.
- **World Folk Music Company**, 1808 W 103rd St, 773-779-7059. Instruments, sheet music, and lessons for budding Guthries and Baezs.

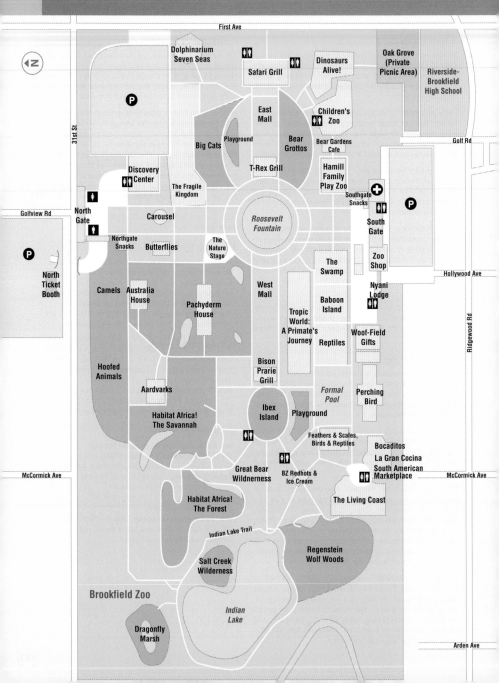

First Ave

31st St

Golfview Rd

McCormick Ave

N

Dolphinarium Seven Seas

Safari Grill

Dinosaurs Alive!

Oak Grove (Private Picnic Area)

Riverside-Brookfield High School

P

East Mall

Children's Zoo

Big Cats

Playground

Bear Grottos

Bear Gardens Cafe

Golf Rd

Discovery Center

T-Rex Grill

Hamill Family Play Zoo

The Fragile Kingdom

Southgate Snacks

P

North Gate

Carousel

Roosevelt Fountain

South Gate

Golfview Rd

Northgate Snacks

Butterflies

The Nature Stage

Zoo Shop

North Ticket Booth

P

Camels

Australia House

West Mall

The Swamp

Hollywood Ave

Pachyderm House

Baboon Island

Nyani Lodge

Tropic World: A Primate's Journey

Woof-Field Gifts

Hoofed Animals

Reptiles

Ridgewood Rd

Aardvarks

Bison Prarie Grill

Formal Pool

Perching Bird

Habitat Africa! The Savannah

Ibex Island

Playground

Feathers & Scales, Birds & Reptiles

Bocaditos

La Gran Cocina South American Marketplace

Great Bear Wildnerness

BZ Redhots & Ice Cream

McCormick Ave

The Living Coast

Habitat Africa! The Forest

Indian Lake Trail

Brookfield Zoo

Salt Creek Wilderness

Regenstein Wolf Woods

Indian Lake

Dragonfly Marsh

Arden Ave

## General Information

Address:      31st St & First Ave
                    Brookfield, IL 60513
Phone:        708-688-8000
Website:      www.brookfieldzoo.org
Hours:        Open daily from 10 am-5 pm, and until 6 pm daily and 7:30 on Sundays from Memorial Day to Labor Day.
Admission:  $15.00 adults, $10.50 children 3-11, seniors over 65, free for children two and under

## Overview

While Lincoln Park Zoo is free, Brookfield offers a far more comprehensive wild animal experience with a strong emphasis on conservation education. 216 acres of creepy critters make for a memorable day trip. We'll skip the analogy with the Joliet Riverboat Casino.

## Hamill Family Play Zoo

This interactive play area is part of a program to create a huge new wing of the zoo dedicated solely to kids. Great—just what a zoo needs: more kids. Children get to interact in a variety of ways, including donning costumes to play "zoo keeper" or "ring-tailed lemur," creating and frolicking in their own simulated habitats, planting seeds in the greenhouse, or spotting creepy insects in the outdoor bug path. Think a grownup would look silly dressed like a lemur? We want to play! Admission $3.50 adults, $2.50 children 3-11, seniors over 65, free for children two and under.

## Regenstein Wolf Woods

The zoo's impressive wolf exhibit allows visitors to follow the progress of a small pack of endangered male wolves as they do the wolfy things wolves do. One-way glass allows spectators to get up close and personal with the wolves without freaking them out. So far, the mirrors have been 100% unsuccessful in detecting any wolf shoplifting.

## Other Exhibits

Of course the zoo is full of exhibits, some more fascinating than others. Among them are the seasonal butterfly exhibit and the dragonfly marsh. Here are some other worthwhile sights:

- **Habitat Africa**: This is broken up into two sections: The Rainforest, with its zebras and African millipedes (heebie-jeebies), and The Savannah, with our favorite, the giraffes.
- **Tropic World**: Visit Kamba, the baby gorilla born in front of a captivated, slightly disgusted crowd of zoo visitors (mother Koola now knows how Marie Antoinette felt when she shared the delivery of her offspring with the French peasantry) and Bakari, the newest addition to the Gorilla family, who was born to mother Binto in May '05.

- **Stingray Bay:** 50 cownose rays swim in a 16,000 saltwater tank, ready for slimy cuddles! Get up close and personal with the creatures as they glide underneath your fingertips. Admission is $4 for adults, $2 for seniors 65 and over and children 3 to 11.
- **Feathers and Scales: Birds and Reptiles:** We're pretty sure there are bats in there, but we've blocked the traumatic memory from our unstable minds. Enter at your own risk.
- **Big Cats:** Visit lions, tigers, and snow leopards and they prance, purr, and prowl. Part of The Fragile Kingdom exhibit, the Big Cats are impressive and beautiful in their natural habitat.
- **Great Bear Wilderness:** Brand new at the Brookfield Zoo, the Great Bear Wildness features two iconic North American animals: Polar bears and Grizzly Bears.

## Eating at the Zoo

- **La Gran Cocina**: At the South American Marketplace. Walk-up stir-fry, chicken, pizza, and fruit.
- **Safari Grill**: Near the Seven Seas Exhibit. Burgers, pizza, sandwiches, salads, and ice cream.
- **Bison Prairie Grill**: Large restaurant on the West Mall. Grilled meat sandwiches, snacks, and sweets, plus margaritas and beer. Indoor and outdoor seating available.
- **North Gate Snack Shop and South Gate Snack Shop**: Hot dogs, subs, and ice cream located at the north and south gates.
- **Elephant Snacks**: Hot dog stand near the Pachyderm House.
- **Bear Gardens Café**: Watch bears watch you eat at this sandwich and pizza shop.
- **Nyani Lodge**: If watching monkeys throw feces at each other is your idea of a good dinnertime show, definitely check this place out.

## How to Get There

**By Car:** From the Eisenhower or Stevens Expressway, exit at First Avenue. From there, signs will direct you the short distance to the zoo. Lot parking is $8.

**By Train:** From downtown Chicago, take the Burlington Northern Metra line to Zoo Stop/Hollywood Station.

**By Bus:** Pace buses 304 and 331 stop right at the zoo's gates.

If you're coming in from out of town, consider staying at a Holiday Inn, Doubletree Hotel, Country Inn & Suites, or Best Western all of which offer Brookfield Zoo packages, which include admission to Brookfield Zoo, admission to the Dolphin Show, admission to the Children's Zoo, 1 parking pass, and coupons for restaurants and gift shops. Details and booking information can be found on Brookfield Zoo's website, www.brookfieldzoo.org.

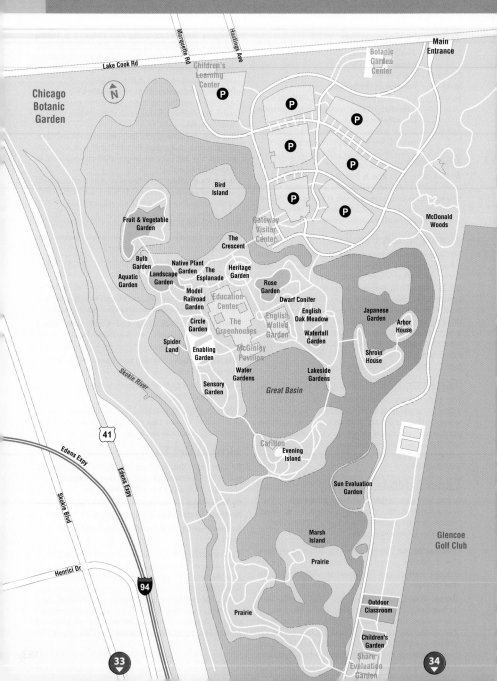

Main
Entrance

Botanic
Garden
Center

Lake Cook Rd

Children's
Learning
Center

Chicago
Botanic
Garden

N

Bird
Island

McDonald
Woods

Fruit & Vegetable
Garden

Gateway
Visitor
Center

The
Crescent

Bulb
Garden

Native Plant
Garden

Heritage
Garden

Aquatic
Garden

Landscape
Garden

The
Esplanade

Rose
Garden

Model
Railroad
Garden

Dwarf Conifer

Japanese
Garden

Education
Center

English
Oak Meadow

Arbor
House

Circle
Garden

The
Greenhouses

English
Walled
Garden

Waterfall
Garden

Spider
Land

Enabling
Garden

McGinley
Pavilion

Shroin
House

Skokie River

Water
Gardens

Lakeside
Gardens

Sensory
Garden

Great Basin

41

Edens Expy

Carillon

Evening
Island

Edens Expy

Sun Evaluation
Garden

Skokie Blvd

Marsh
Island

Glencoe
Golf Club

Prairie

Henrici Dr

94

Prairie

Outdoor
Classroom

Children's
Garden

Share
Evaluation
Garden

## General Information

| | |
|---|---|
| Address: | 1000 Lake Cook Rd, Glencoe, IL 60022 |
| Phone: | 847-835-5440 |
| Website: | www.chicagobotanic.org |
| Hours: | Open 364 days, 8 am to sunset; closed Dec. 25 |
| Admission: | Free |

## Overview

Occupying 385 acres, the serene and lovely Chicago Botanic Garden has been the backdrop for many a chi-chi wedding since they opened the gates in 1972. Both the Ikebana Society and Macy's sponsor flower shows throughout the year; check the events schedule at www.chicagobotanic.org to see what's going on when you're visiting. The Chicago Botanic Garden also offers lifestyle/wellness classes, including yoga and tai chi. Availability and times vary, so check the website or call for more information.

## Nature

Twenty-three gardens and three prairie habitats make up the Botanic Garden. Among them are a specialized Japanese garden, a rose garden, a bulb garden, a greenhouse full of tropical vegetation, a waterfall garden, and several beds solely dedicated to indigenous plants and flowers.

## Where to Eat

• **Garden Café:** Serves breakfast and café fare—salads, sandwiches, beer, and wine. Wifi enabled. Open 8 am–5 pm weekdays, 8 am–5:30 pm weekends, and open to 7 pm on Carillion Concert Mondays.

• **Garden Grille:** Grill being the operative word, serves burgers, dogs, and the like. Open from June to early September, 11am–3pm and 5pm–8 pm, featuring a barbeque buffet and beer garden.

• **Rose Terrace Café:** Enjoy a beverage overlooking the roses. Open from June to early September, 11am–5pm.

Note: Picnicking allowed in designated areas only.

## How to Get There

**By Car:** Take I-90/94 W (The Kennedy) to I-94 (The Edens) and US 41. Exit on Lake Cook Road, then go a half-mile east to the garden. Parking costs $20 per car, $7 for seniors on Tuesdays.

**By Train:** Take the Union Pacific North Line to Braeside Metra station in Highland Park. Walk west about one mile along Lake Cook Road (aka County Line Road). If you ride the train to the Glencoe station, you can take a trolley directly to the garden. Round-trip tickets cost $2, free for children five and under.

**By Bus:** The Pace bus 213 connects at Davis Street in Evanston, and the Park Avenue Glencoe and Central Street Highland Park Metra stops. Buses don't run on Sundays and holidays.

**By Bicycle:** The Chicago Bikeway System winds through the forest preserves all the way up to the garden. Join it near the Billy Caldwell Golf Club at 6200 N Caldwell. A bicycle map is available on the Botanic Garden website.

## Where to Stay

You can make an excursion of your visit to Ravinia and/or the Botanic Garden by booking a room at:

**Renaissance Chicago North Shore** (933 Skokie Blvd, Northbrook, 847-498-6500); **Residence Inn Chicago** (530 Lake Cook Rd, Deerfield, 847-940-4644); **Hyatt Deerfield** (1750 Lake Cook Rd, 847-945-3400); **Highland Park Courtyard** (1505 Lake Cook Rd, 847-831-3338).

## Ravinia Festival

| | |
|---|---|
| Address: | 200 Ravinia Park Rd, Highland Park, IL 60035 |
| Phone: | 847-266-5100 |
| Website: | www.ravinia.org |
| Hours: | June through mid-September, gates open three hours before concert time |

## Overview

Not to be outdone, the adjoining Ravinia Festival, the nation's oldest outdoor concert venue, has been hosting classical music concerts since 1904. The summer home of the CSO, Ravinia eventually added pop and jazz to their bill, including such notables as Janis Joplin, Aretha Franklin (a Ravinia regular), k.d. lang, Tony Bennett (also a regular), as well as top names from opera and world music.

**The Pavilion**—Those who are serious about the music experience pay a premium for one of the 3,200 seats in this covered, open-air pavilion, affording them a view of the stage and better acoustics.

**The Lawn**—Although you can't see the stage, great outdoor acoustics bring the concert to you on the lawn, where blanket rights come cheap—typically $10 a pop. Just add picnic.

**The Martin Theatre**—The only remaining building original to the Festival, the 1904 Martin Theatre now hosts Martinis at the Martin, a cabaret series celebrating the Great American Songbook.

## Eating at Ravinia

Ravinia is well known for lawn picnickers who compete to outdo each other with elaborate spreads, including roll-up tables, table linens, candelabras, champagne, and caviar. For those less ambitious, Ravinia offers take-out sandwiches and picnic fare at The Gatehouse, ice cream and other sweet treats at Carousel Ice Cream Shop, or you can make reservations to eat in at their fine-dining restaurant, Mirabelle. Ravinia Market offers eclectic food, from grilled skewers to brick-oven pizzas. The Park View and Mirabelle restaurants offer full-service dining options before the show. Wine, beer, and soft drinks are also available at concession stands throughout the park.

## How to Get There

**By Car:** I-94 and I-294 have marked exits for Ravinia. Skip traffic back-ups on Lake Cook Road by exiting at Deerfield, Central, or Clavey Roads, and following directions to Park and Ride lots, which offer free parking and shuttle buses to Ravinia. The West Lot, Ravinia's closest parking spot, costs $15–$25 for parking and fills up early for the most popular concerts.

**By Train:** During festival season, the Union Pacific North Line offers the "Ravinia Special." For $7 round-trip, the train departs Madison and Canal at 5:50 pm, with stops at Clybourn, Ravenswood, Rogers Park, and Evanston, arriving at the Ravinia gates at 6:30 pm, and departing for the city 15 minutes after the concert's end.

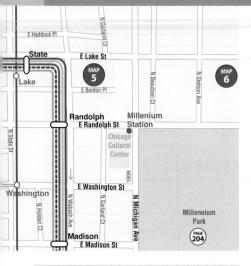

## General Information

| | |
|---|---|
| NFT Maps: | 5, 6 |
| Address: | 78 E Washington St |
| | Chicago, IL 60602 |
| Phone: | 312-744-6630 |
| Website: | www.chicagoculturalcenter.org |
| Hours: | Mon–Thurs 8 am–7 pm, Fri 8 am–6 pm, |
| | Sat 9 am–6 pm, Sun 10 am–6 pm, |
| | and closed on holidays |

## Overview

The Chicago Cultural Center is the Loop's public arts center. Free—that's right, we said FREE—concerts, theatrical performances, films, lectures, and exhibits are offered daily. Admission to the Cultural Center and its art galleries are all free, too. Call 312-FINE ART (312-346-3278) for weekly event updates.

The building itself, constructed in 1897, is a neoclassical landmark featuring intricate glass and marble mosaics on its walls and grand stairways. Once the city's central public library, the Cultural Center boasts the world's largest Tiffany dome in Preston Bradley Hall. Free (there's that lovely word again) 45-minute architectural tours are held on Wednesdays, Fridays, and Saturdays at 1:15 pm. If you're interested in a guided group tour highlighting the building's history, call 312-744-6630 for more information. The building is also home to the Chicago Greeter Program, which allows visitors the opportunity to take a 2–4 hour walking tour with a chatty and knowledgeable guide around one of any number of neighborhoods throughout the city. Interested parties must book in advance at www.chicago-greeter.com. Surprise, surprise: it's free, as well.

## Performances

The Chicago Cultural Center offers a number of concerts around the year in the genres of classical, jazz and world music.

## Art Galleries

A permanent exhibit in the Landmark Gallery, Chicago Landmarks Before the Lens is a stunning black-and-white photographic survey of Chicago architecture. Five additional galleries regularly rotate exhibits, showcasing work in many media by renowned and local artists. Tours of current exhibits are ongoing.

## How to Get There

**By Car:** Travel down Michigan Avenue to Randolph Street. From Lake Shore Drive, exit at Randolph Street. For parking garages in the area, see Map 6.

**By Train:** From the Richard B. Ogilvie Transportation Center, travel east to Michigan Avenue on CTA buses 20, 56, 127, and 157. From Union Station, take CTA buses 60, 151, and 157 ($2.25, $2 with Chicago Card). From the Randolph Street station below Millennium Park, walk west across Michigan Avenue. For schedules contact the RTA Information Center (312-836-7000; www.rtachicago.com).

**By L:** Take the Green, Brown, Orange, Purple, or Pink Line to the Randolph stop ($2.25, $1.75 with Chicago Card/Ventra Card). Walk east one block.

**By Bus:** CTA buses : 3, 145, 147, 151 stop on Michigan Avenue in front of the Cultural Center ($2.25, $2 with Chicago Card/Ventra Card).

## General Information

NFT Map:       5
Address:       400 S State St
               Chicago, IL 60605
Phone:         312-747-4300
Website:       www.chipublib.org

## Overview

Harold Washington Library Center is the world's largest public library. Named after Chicago's first African-American mayor, the 756,640-square-foot neoclassical architectural monstrosity has over 70 miles of shelves storing more than 9 million books, microforms, serials, and government documents. Notable works of sculpture, painting, and mosaics liven up the building's ample wall space and open areas.

Harold Washington's popular library, containing current general titles and bestsellers, is easy to find on the ground floor. The library's audio-visual collection (including an impressive collection of books on tape as well as videos, DVDs, and popular music CDs) is also housed here. The second floor is home to the children's library, and the general reference library begins on the third floor where the circulation desks are located. Among the notable features of the library is the eighth floor Music Information Center housing sheet music and printed scores, 150,000 recordings, the Chicago Blues Archives, eight individual piano practice rooms, and a chamber music rehearsal room. The ninth fl oor Winter Garden, with its olive trees and soaring 100-foot high ceilings is a popular site for special events. If you have your sights set on getting hitched here, leave your priest or rabbi at home—the library's status as a civic building precludes religious services on its premises.

Frequent free public programs are held in the lower level's 385-seat auditorium, video theater, exhibit hall, and meeting rooms. Call 312-747-4649 for information on scheduled events. Additionally, the website houses a bbs (bulletin board system) for those participating in Chicago's "One City, One Book" reading club who want to discuss the latest selection.

Operating hours are Monday through Thursday 9 am–9 pm, Friday and Saturday 9 am–5 pm, and Sunday 1 pm–5 pm.

## Research Services

To check the availability or location of an item, call Catalog Information at 312-747-4340 or search the library's Online Catalog on www.chipublib.org. Their Email Reference Service responds to information requests within two days. For faster answers to common research questions, check out the website's handy Virtual Library Service under Selected Internet Resources, then click on "Reference Shelf."

## Computer Services

The Chicago Public Library's High Speed Wireless Internet System provides free access; all you need is a wireless enabled laptop computer, tablet PC, or PDA. The Library's network is open to all visitors free of charge and without filters. No special encryption settings, user names, or passwords are required.

The library's 96 computers with Internet access and 37 more with word processing, desktop publishing, graphic presentation, and spreadsheet applications are located on the third floor in the Computer Commons. Computer use is free and available on a first-come-first-served basis. You can reserve computers online and for up to one hour per day based on walk-in availability. For downloads, bring your own formatted disk or purchase one at the library for $2. Laser printing is also provided for 15 cents a page. Operating hours are Monday through Thursday 9 am–8:30 pm, Friday and Saturday 9 am–4:30 pm, and Sunday 1 pm–4:30 pm.

## Thomas Hughes Children's Library

The 18,000-square-foot Thomas Hughes Children's Library on the second floor serves children through age 14. A British citizen and member of Parliament, Thomas Hughes was so taken by news of the tragic Chicago Fire that he started a book collection for Chicago. His collection resulted in the 8,000 titles that composed the first Chicago Public Library. In addition to more than 120,000 children's books representing 40 foreign languages, there is a reference collection on children's literature for adults. Twenty free computers, twelve with Internet connections, are also available. Children's programs are hosted weekly (312-747-4200).

## Special Collections

The library's Special Collections & Preservation Division's highlights include: Harold Washington Collection, Civil War & American History Research Collection, Chicago Authors & Publishing Collection, Chicago Blues Archives, Chicago Theater Collection, World's Columbian Exposition Collection, and Neighborhood History Research Collection. The collections' reading room is closed Sunday.

## How to Get There

**By Car:** The library is at the intersection of State Street and Congress Parkway in South Loop. Take I-290 E into the Loop. See Map 5 for area parking garages.

**By L:** The Brown, Purple, Orange, and Pink Lines stop at the Library Station. Exit the Red Line and O'Hare Airport Blue Line at Van Buren Station; walk one block south. Change from the Harlem/Lake Street Green Line to the northbound Orange Line at Roosevelt Road station; get off at Library Station ($2.25, $2.00 with Chicago Card/Ventra Card).

**By Bus:** CTA buses that stop on State Street in front of the library are the 2, 6, 29, 36, 62, 151, 145, 146, and 147.

# Parks & Places • Evanston

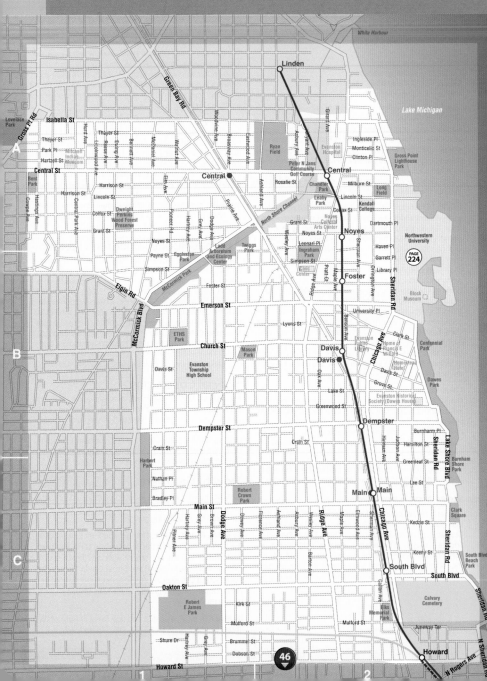

## Overview

Bordering the city to the north and surrounded by beautiful lakeshore scenery and affluent suburbs, Evanston may seem a world away. Truth be told, this town is only 12 miles from Chicago's bustling Loop. Spacious Victorian and Prairie Style homes with mini-vans and Mercedes parked on tree-lined streets overlook Lake Michigan and surround the quaint college town's downtown. Unlike other development-minded and sub-divided suburbs, Evanston still maintains a Chicago-esque feel and remains one of its most attractive bordering neighbors. Of course, Evanston residents still walk with their noses in the air and even charge their city neighbors to visit their beaches. We wonder what their tax base would look like without the city.

Once home to Potawatami Indians, Evanston was actually founded after the establishment of the town's most well-known landmark, Northwestern University. Plans for the school began in 1851, and after the university opened for business four years later, its founder John Evans (along with a bunch of other Methodist dudes) proposed the establishment of the city, and so the town was incorporated as the village of Evanston in 1863. Today, residents are as devoted to cultural and intellectual pursuits as the morally minded patriarchs were to enforcing prohibition.

The sophisticated, racially diverse suburb of over 74,000 packs a lot of business and entertainment into its 8.5 square miles. Superb museums, many national historic landmarks, parks, artistic events, eclectic shops, and theaters make up for the poor sports performances by Northwestern University's Wildcats in recent Big Ten football and basketball seasons.

## Culture

Evanston has several museums and some interesting festivals that warrant investigation. Besides Northwestern's Block Museum of Art, the impressive Mitchell Museum of the American Indian showcases life of the Midwest's Native Americans (3001 Central St, 847-475-1030). The 1865 home of Frances E. Willard, founder of the Women's Christian Temperance Union and a women's suffrage leader, is located at 1730 Chicago Avenue (847-328-7500). Tours of the historic home are offered on the afternoons of every first and third Sunday of each month. Admission costs $10 for adults and $5 for children 12 and under.

## Festivals & Events

- **April**: Evanston goes Baroque during Bach Week, 847-293-6686, www.bachweek.org.

- **June:** Fountain Square Arts Festival, 773-868-3010, and free Starlight Concerts hosted in many of the city's 80 parks through August, 847-448-8058

- **July**: Ethnic Arts Festival, 847-448-8260

- **September**: Town architectural walking tour, 312-922-3432, www.architecture.org.

## Nature

Evanston is blessed with six public beaches open June 10th through Labor Day. Non-residents should remember their wallets to pay for beach passes. For hours, fees, and boating information, contact the City of Evanston's Recreation Division (847-448-4311; www.cityofevanston.org). The town's most popular parks (and there are nearly 90 of them) encircle its beaches: Grosse Point Lighthouse Park, Centennial Park, Burnham Shores Park, Dawes Park, and South Boulevard Beach Park. All are connected by a bike path and fitness trail. On clear days, Chicago's skyline is visible from Northwestern's campus. West of downtown, McCormick, Twiggs, and Herbert Parks flank the North Shore Channel. Bicycle trails thread along the shore from Green Bay Road south to Main Street. North of Green Bay Road is Peter N. Jans Community Golf Course, a short 18-hole, par 60 public links at 1031 Central Street (847-864-5181) and the Ladd Memorial Arboretum and Ecology Center, located at 2024 McCormick Boulevard (847-448-8256).

## How to Get There

**By Car:** Lake Shore Drive to Sheridan Road is the most direct and scenic route from Chicago to Evanston. Drive north on LSD, which ends at Hollywood; then drive west to Sheridan and continue north. Near downtown, Sheridan becomes Burnham Place briefly, then Forest Avenue. Go north on Forest, which turns into Sheridan again by lakefront Centennial Park.

**Parking:** Watch how and where you park. The rules and regulations are strict and fiercely enforced. Remember…Evanston police do not have much to do.

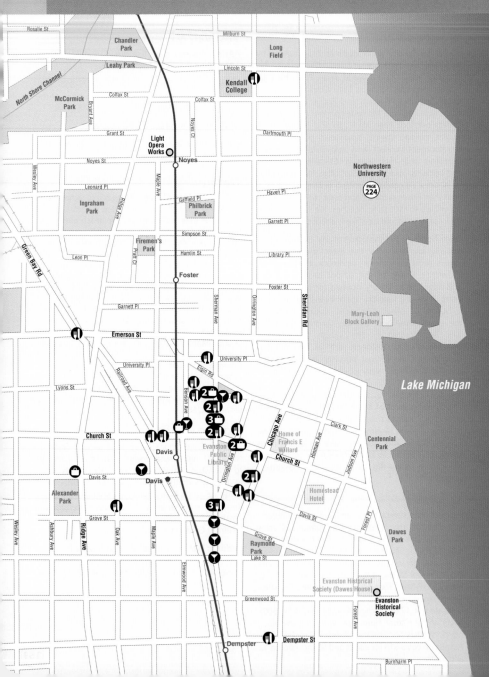

**By Train:** Metra's Union Pacific North Line departing from the Richard B. Ogilvie Transportation Center in West Loop stops at the downtown Davis Street CTA Center station, 25 minutes from the Loop ($3.05 one-way). This station is the town transportation hub, where Metra and L trains and buses interconnect. For all Metra, L, and CTA bus schedules, call 312-836-7000; www.rtachicago.com.

**By L:** The CTA Purple Line Express L train travels direct to and from the Loop during rush hours ($2.25, $2.00 with Chicago Card/Ventra Card). Other hours, ride the Howard-Dan Ryan Red Line to Howard Street, and transfer to the Purple Line for free.

**By Bus:** From Chicago's Howard Street Station, CTA and Pace Suburban buses service Evanston ($2.25 via CTA, $1.75 via Pace).

## Additional Information
**Chicago's North Shore Convention & Visitors Bureau** 866-369-0011; www.visitchicagonorthshore.com

**Evanston Public Library**, 1703 Orrington Ave, 847-448-8600; www.epl.org

## Landmarks
- **Evanston Historical Society** · 225 Greenwood St
- **Light Opera Works** · 516 4th Street; Wilmette

## Nightlife
- **1800 Club** · 1800 Sherman Ave
- **Keg of Evanston** · 810 Grove St
- **Prairie Moon** · 1502 Sherman Ave
- **The Stained Glass Wine Bar** · 1735 Benson Ave
- **Tommy Nevin's Pub** · 1450 Sherman Ave

## Restaurants
- **Blind Faith Café** · 525 Dempster St
- **Buffalo Joe's** · 812 Clark St
- **Café Mozart** · 600 Davis St
- **Clarke's** · 720 Clark St
- **Dave's Italian Kitchen** · 1635 Chicago Ave
- **Dixie Kitchen and Bait Shop** · 825 Church St
- **Dozika** · 601 Dempster St
- **Hecky's Barbeque** · 1902 Green Bay Rd
- **Joy Yee's Noodle Shop** · 521 Davis St
- **Kafein Café** · 1621 Chicago Ave
- **Kansaku** · 1514 Sherman Ave
- **Las Palmas** · 817 University Pl
- **Lulu's Dim Sum and Then Sum** · 804 Davis St
- **Mt Everest** · 630 Church St
- **Noodles & Company** · 930 Church St
- **Olive Mountain** · 610 Davis St
- **Pete Miller's Original Steakhouse** · 1557 Sherman Ave
- **Tapas Barcelona** · 1615 Chicago Ave
- **Trattoria Demi** · 1571 Sherman Ave
- **Unicorn Café** · 1723 Sherman Ave
- **Va Pensiero** · Margarita Inn· 1566 Oak Ave

## Shopping
- **Art + Science Hair Salon** · 811 Church St
- **Asinamali Women's Boutique** · 1722 Sherman Ave
- **Campus Gear** · 1717 Sherman Ave
- **Coucou** · 1716 Sherman Ave
- **Uncle Dan's Great Outdoors** · 901 W Church St
- **William's Shoes** · 710 Church St

## Overview

For a century now, the historic West Side has been home to an equally historic botanical gem—Garfield Park Conservatory. The mid 1990s saw major restoration efforts, along with the creation of The Garfield Park Conservatory Alliance, an organization that has raised money for various programs involving the Conservatory. The rest of the vast 185-acre park boasts fishing lagoons, a swimming pool, an ice rink, baseball diamonds, and basketball and tennis courts. Garfield Park's landmark Gold Dome Building houses a fitness center, a basketball court, and the Peace Museum.

Garfield and its sister parks—Humboldt Park (1400 N Sacramento Ave, 312-742-7549) and Douglas Park (1401 S Sacramento Ave, 773-762-2842)—constitute a grand system of sprawling green spaces linked by broad boulevards designed in 1869 by William Le Baron Jenney (better known as the "father of the skyscraper"). However, Jenney's plan didn't bear fruit until almost 40 years later (after the uprooting of corrupt park officials), when Danish immigrant and former park laborer Jens Jensen became chief landscape architect. In 1908, Jensen completed the parks and consolidated their three small conservatories under the 1.8-acre Garfield Park Conservatory's curvaceous glass dome, designed to resemble a "great Midwestern haystack."

## Garfield Park Conservatory

| | |
|---|---|
| Address: | 300 N Central Park Ave |
| | Chicago, IL 60624 |
| Phone: | 312-746-5100 |
| Website: | www.garfield-conservatory.org |
| Hours: | 9 am–5 pm daily; Wed: 9 am–8 pm |
| Admission: | FREE |

One of the nation's largest conservatories, Garfield Park has six thematic plant houses with 1,000 species and more than 10,000 individual plants from around the world. Plants Alive!, a 5,000-square-foot children's garden, has touchable plants, a soil pool for digging, a Jurassic Park–sized bumble bee, and a two-story, twisting flower stem that doubles as a slide. School groups often book the garden for field trips, so call first to determine public access hours. Annual Conservatory events include the Spring Flower Show, Azalea/Camellia Show, Chocolate Festival, Summer Tropical Show, Chrysanthemum (Chicago's city flower) Show, and Holiday Garden Show. Call for program scheduling. Every weekend, seasonally, visitors can browse the open air Garfield Market featuring crafts, plants, and produce. There is a farmer's market at the park on Saturday mornings from June through October.

## Fishing

Garfield Park's two lagoons at Washington Boulevard and Central Park Avenue and those at Douglas and Humboldt Parks are favorite West Side fishing holes. Seasonally, they are stocked with bluegill, crappie, channel catfish, and largemouth bass, along with an occasional unfortunate gang member. The fish here are perfect for those who need a little pollution with their protein. Kids can take free fishing classes at the park lagoons during the summer through the Chicago Park District (312-747-PLAY). Groups of ten kids or more fish every day of the week at a new location. You'll have to call in advance, as groups are organized by appointment only. The program runs June 20–August 12, Mon–Fri, between 10 am and 4 pm.

## Nature

The Chicago Park District leads free nature walks and has created marked trails with information plaques at the city's bigger parks, Garfield, Douglas, and Humboldt Parks included. Seasonally, visitors can view as many as 100 species of colorful butterflies at the formal gardens of the three parks. The parks' lagoons are officially designated Chicago "birding parks," so take binoculars. Picnics for 50 people or more, or tent set-up, require party-throwers to obtain permits issued by the Chicago Park District.

## How to Get There

**By Car:** Garfield Park is ten minutes from the Loop. Take I-290 W; exit on Independence Boulevard and drive north. Turn east on Washington Boulevard to Central Park Avenue. Go north on Central Park Avenue two blocks past the Golden Dome field house and Lake Street to the Conservatory. A free parking lot is on the building's south side, just after Lake Street. Street parking is available on Central Park Avenue, Madison Street, and Washington Boulevard.

**By L:** From the Loop, take the Green Line west ($2.25, $2.00 with Chicago Card/Ventra Card) to the Conservatory-Central Park Drive stop, a renovated Victorian train station at Lake Street and Central Park Avenue.

**By Bus:** From the Loop, board CTA 20 Madison Street bus westbound ($2.25, $2 with Chicago Card/Ventra Card). Get off at Madison Street and Central Park Avenue. Walk four blocks north to the Conservatory.

## Additional Information

**Chicago Park District**, 312-742-PLAY;
www.chicagoparkdistrict.com

**Nature Chicago Program—City of Chicago and Department of the Environment**, 312-744-7606;
www.cityofchicago.org

**Chicago Ornithological Society**, 312-409-9678;
www.chicagobirder.org

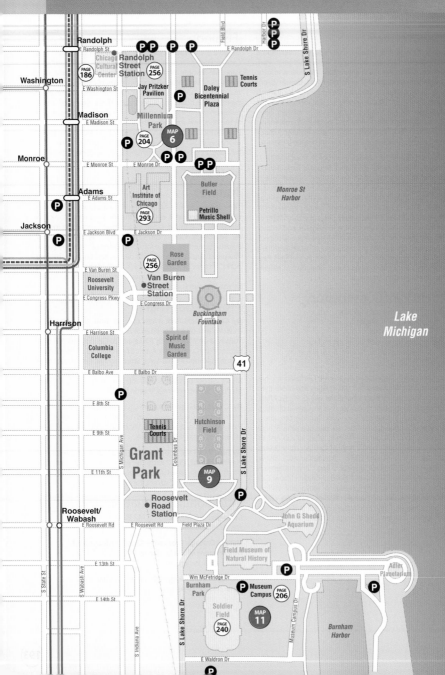

Washington

Randolph
E Randolph St
Chicago
Cultural
Center
PAGE
186
Randolph
Street
Station
PAGE
256

E Washington St

Jay Pritzker
Pavilion

Field Blvd
Harbor Dr

E Randolph Dr

Tennis
Courts

S Lake Shore Dr

Daley
Bicentennial
Plaza

Madison
E Madison St

Millennium
Park

PAGE
204

MAP
6

Monroe
E Monroe St

E Monroe Dr

Butler
Field

Monroe St
Harbor

Adams
E Adams St

Art
Institute of
Chicago
PAGE
293

Petrillo
Music Shell

Jackson
E Jackson Blvd

E Jackson Dr

E Van Buren St

PAGE
256

Rose
Garden

Roosevelt
University

Van Buren
Street
Station

E Congress Pkwy

E Congress Dr

Buckingham
Fountain

Harrison

E Harrison St

Columbia
College

Spirit of
Music
Garden

E Balbo Ave

E Balbo Dr

41

Lake
Michigan

E 8th St

E 9th St

Tennis
Courts

Hutchinson
Field

S Michigan Ave

S Lake Shore Dr

E 11th St

Grant
Park

Columbus Dr

MAP
9

Roosevelt/
Wabash

Roosevelt
Road
Station

E Roosevelt Rd

E Roosevelt Rd

Field Plaza Dr

John G Shedd
Aquarium

E 13th St

Field Museum of
Natural History

Adler
Planetarium

S State St

S Wabash Ave

E 14th St

Wm McFetridge Dr

Burnham
Park

Museum
Campus
PAGE
206

S Lake Shore Dr

Soldier
Field
PAGE
240

MAP
11

Museum Campus Dr

Burnham
Harbor

S Indiana Ave

E Waldron Dr

## Overview

Grant Park, where grass meets glass, is Chicago's venerable "front lawn." Spanning the Lake Michigan shoreline from N Randolph Street to S Roosevelt Road and west to Michigan Avenue, it's safe to say there's not a more trafficked park this side of New York City's Central Park. Grant Park is a study in contrasts: on the one side featuring massive summer festivals (such as the annual homage to obesity known as Taste of Chicago) that turn the park into Chicago's dirty doormat; but during the rest of the year, a quiet place to relax, play, and count the number of panhandlers who ask if you can "help them out with a dollar."

The park's history can be traced back to 1835 when concerned citizens lobbied to prevent development along their pristine waterfront. Little did they know that when the State of Illinois ruled to preserve the land as "public ground forever to remain vacant of buildings" this meant for everyone, including the wealthy elite who were literally perched on the lofty balconies of the tawny palaces that lined the downtown shores of Lake Michigan. Be careful what you wish for, yes? Architect and city planner Daniel Burnham laid the groundwork for the park and made plans to erect museums, civic buildings, and general park attractions along the waterfront. This plan got somewhat sidetracked by the Great Chicago Fire of 1871. Interestingly enough, remaining debris from the fire was pushed into the lake and now forms part of the foundation for much of Grant Park and Chicago's famous shoreline. Chicagoans can thank local land-lover and legendary mail-order magnate Aaron Montgomery Ward for pressuring the State of Illinois in 1911 to preserve the land as an undeveloped open space.

## Nature

Grant Park's lawns, gardens, lakefront, and bench-lined paths attract a mixed crowd of lunching office workers, exercise fanatics, readers, gawking tourists, homeless and not-so-homeless vagabonds, and just your run-of-the-mill idiots. South and north of famous Buckingham Fountain are the formal Spirit of Music Garden and Rose Garden, respectively. There are also a multitude of sculptures, ranging in form and style, strewn with abandon throughout the park, so expect to see art appreciators and imitators alike milling about as well.

## Sports

Much of the sports areas in Grant Park are on the south end of the park. Baseball diamonds and tennis courts are available on a first-come basis unless they are reserved for league play. There is also a skate park, volleyball courts and a field house.

## Maggie Daley Park

In October 2012 construction began on Chicago's new centerpiece, Maggie Daley Park—named in honor and memory of Chicago's beloved former first lady. The park will cover 20 acres in Grant Park's northeast corner. Currently it is just a giant construction site, but if projections are correct, it will be complete in winter 2014/spring 2015. Among other features, the park will contain a rock climbing area, an ice skating ribbon, a playground and gardens. To see the full plan and follow construction updates, visit www.maggie-daleyparkconstruction.org.

## Buckingham Fountain

Buckingham Fountain is Grant Park's spouting centerpiece at the intersection of Congress Parkway and Columbus Drive, and was the original starting point of Route 66. Designed by Edward Bennett, the fountain is an homage to Lake Michigan and houses four statues that represent the Lake's four surrounding states (Illinois, Indiana, Michigan, and Wisconsin, ya big idiot). It has been showering onlookers with wind-blown spray since 1927 and, unfortunately, is notable for its role in the opening sequence of the sitcom *Married…with Children*. Today the water flows April through October from 8 am to 11 pm daily. For 20 minutes each hour the center basin jettisons water 150 feet into the air. Lights and music accompany the skyrocketing water display during evening hours. Food concessions and restrooms can be found nearby.

## Festivals & Events

Chicagoans used to gather at the Petrillo Music Shell for free Grant Park Orchestra and Chorus concerts during the summer months. Now they go to the Jay Pritzker Pavilion in Millennium Park, located between Michigan and Columbus Avenues that, in and of itself, is worth a visit. Concerts take place June through August (312-742-7638; www.grantparkmusicfestival.com). You can't always pass up a free headliner concert at Grant Park's monstrous summer festivals. If at all possible, avoid the gut-to-gut feeding frenzy that is the Taste of Chicago. But if you must go, hit it on a weekday afternoon. We'll accept your "thank you" now; if you go on the weekend, you'll understand why. In June, get your groove on at the Chicago Blues Fest or chill out at the Chicago Jazz Fest in September. If you're really a diehard fan, spend a full paycheck for a three-day pass to Lollapalooza in August. Extra deodorant required. For a complete event schedule, contact the Chicago Department of Cultural Affairs and Special Events at 312-744-3316 or on its department homepage at www.cityofchicago.org/dcase.

## How to Get There

**By Car:** Exits off Lake Shore Drive west to Grant Park are Randolph Street, Monroe Drive, Jackson Drive, Balbo Drive, and Roosevelt Road. Also, enter the park from Michigan Avenue heading east on the same streets. The underground East Monroe Garage is off Monroe Drive. Columbus Drive runs through Grant Park's center and has metered parking.

**By Train:** From the Richard B. Ogilvie Transportation Center, travel east to Michigan Avenue and Grant Park on CTA buses 14, 20, and 56 ($2.25, $2 with Chicago Card). From Union Station, board CTA buses 60, 123, 151, and 157.

Metra trains coming from the south stop at the Roosevelt Road station on the south end of Grant Park before terminating at the underground Millennium Station at Randolph Street.

**By L:** Get off at any L stop in the Loop between Randolph Street and Van Buren Street ($2.25, $2.00 with Chicago Card/Ventra Card). Walk two blocks east to Grant Park.

**By Bus:** CTA buses 13, 10 (weekends and daily in summer),145, 146, 147, 151 stop along Michigan Avenue in front of Grant Park ($2.25, $2 with Chicago Card/Ventra Card).

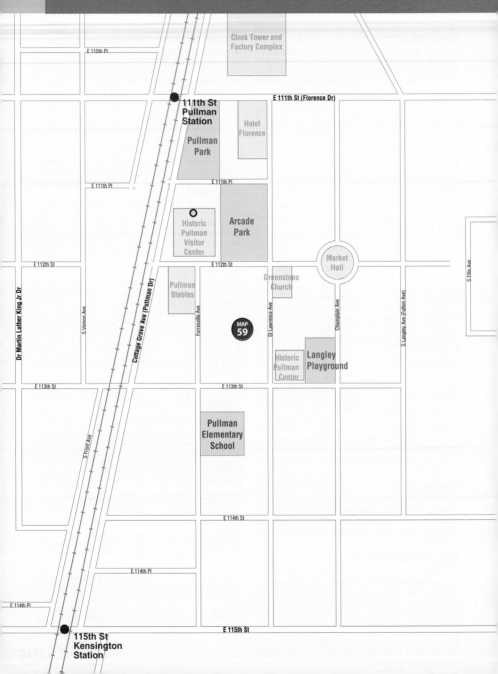

Clock Tower and
Factory Complex

E 110th Pl

E 111th St (Florence Dr)

111th St
Pullman
Station

Hotel
Florence

Pullman
Park

E 111th Pl

E 111th Pl

Historic
Pullman
Visitor
Center

Arcade
Park

E 112th St

Market
Hall

E 112th St

Greenstone
Church

Pullman
Stables

MAP
59

Historic
Pullman
Center

Langley
Playground

E 113th St

E 113th St

Pullman
Elementary
School

E 114th St

E 114th St

E 114th Pl

E 114th Pl

115th St
Kensington
Station

E 115th St

Dr Martin Luther King Jr Dr

S Vernon Ave

Cottage Grove Ave (Pullman Dr)

S Front Ave

Forrestville Ave

St Lawrence Ave

Champlain Ave

S Langley Ave (Fulton Ave)

S Ellis Ave

## Overview

Although railroad magnate George Pullman's utopian community went belly-up, the Town of Pullman he founded 14 miles south of the Loop survives as a National Landmark Historic District. Built between 1880 and 1885, Pullman is one of America's first planned model industrial communities.

The "workers' paradise" earned Pullman humanitarian hoorahs, as well as a 6% return on his investment. Pullman believed that if laborers and their families lived in comfortable housing with gas, plumbing, and ventilation—in other words, livable conditions—their productivity would increase, as would his profits. Pullman was voted "the world's most perfect town" at the Prague International Hygienic and Pharmaceutical Exposition of 1896.

All was perfect in Pullman until a depression incited workers to strike in 1894, and the idealistic industrialist refused to negotiate with his ungrateful workers. While George Pullman's dream of a model community of indentured servitude died with him in 1897, hatred for him lived on. Pullman's tomb at Graceland Cemetery is more like a bomb shelter. To protect his corpse from irate labor leaders, Pullman was buried under a forest of railroad ties and concrete.

The grounds and buildings that make up Pullman went through most of the twentieth century stayed intact until 1998, when a man who heard voices in his head torched several of the site's primary buildings. Fortunately, die-hard Pullmanites have banded together to maintain the remaining structures, and for anyone interested in labor history or town planning, the city is worth a train or bus ride down from the Loop.

## Architecture & Events

Architect Solon Beman and landscape architect Nathan Barrett based Pullman's design on French urban plans. Way back when, Pullman was made up of mostly brick rowhouses (95% still in use), several parks, shops, schools, churches, and a library, as well as various health, recreational, and cultural facilities.

Today, the compact community's borders are 111th Street (Florence Drive), 115th Street, Cottage Grove Avenue (Pullman Drive), and S Langley Avenue (Fulton Avenue). If you're interested in sightseeing within the historic district, we suggest you start at the Pullman Visitor Center (11141 S Cottage Grove Ave, 773-785-8901; www.pullmanil.org). There you can pick up free, self-guided walking tour brochures and watch an informative 20-minute film on the town's history. Call the center for additional specialty tour information and lecture details.

Along with self-guided tours, the Visitor Center offers 90 minute guided tours on the first Sunday of the month from May to October. Tours start at 1:30 and cost $7 for adults, $5 for seniors and $4 for students.

The annual House Tour on the second weekend in October is a popular Pullman event where several private residences open their doors to the public from 11 am to 5 pm on Saturday and Sunday ($17 in advance, $20 on day of event). May through October, the center also offers a ninety-minute Guided Walking Tour every first Sunday of the month at 1:30 pm ($5). Key tour sites include Hotel Florence, Greenstone Church (interior), Market Square, the stables, and the fire station.

## Where to Eat

- **Seven Seas Submarine**, 11216 S Michigan Ave, 773-785-0550. Dine in or take out at this tiny sandwich shop.
- **Cal Harbor Restaurant**, 546 E 115th St, 773-264-5435. Omelettes, burgers, etc. at this family grill.

## How to Get There

**By Car:** Take I-94 S to the 111th Street exit. Go west to Cottage Grove Avenue and turn south, driving one block to 112th Street to the Visitor Center surrounded by a large, free parking lot.

**By Train:** Metra's Electric Main Line departs from Millennium Station (underground) at Michigan Avenue between S Water Street and Randolph Street. Ride 30 minutes to Pullman Station at 111th Street ($3.35 one-way). Walk east to Cottage Grove Avenue, and head south one block to 112th and the Visitor Center.

**By L:** From the Loop, take the Red Line to the 95th Street station. Board CTA 111 Pullman bus going south ($2.25, $2.00 with Chicago Card/Ventra Card).

**By Bus:** CTA 4 bus from the Randolph Street Station travels south to the 95th Street and Cottage Grove stop. Transfer to 111 Pullman bus heading south ($2.50 with transfer).

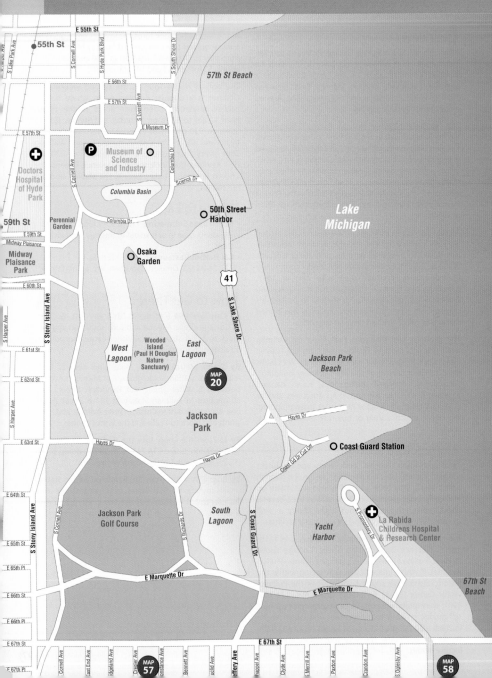

## Overview

Historic Jackson Park, named for Mary Jackson, original owner of the land and cousin to president Andrew Jackson, borders Lake Michigan, Hyde Park, and Woodlawn, and was, for a long time, an unused tract of fallow land. The 500-acre parcel was eventually transformed into a real city park in the 1870s thanks to Frederick Law Olmsted of Central Park fame. The Midway Plaisance connects Jackson to Washington Park.

Jackson Park experienced its 15 minutes of worldwide fame in 1893 when it played host to the World's Fair Columbian Exposition. Today, the Museum of Science and Industry and La Rabida Children's Hospital and Research Center occupy two of the former fair structures.

Until recently Jackson Park had gone to seed, but thanks to Mayor Daley's green thumb, the government has been pumping money into park rehabilitation projects and Jackson Park is reaping the benefits. Major improvements to the area's lakefront, bike path, athletic centers, and beaches have Jackson Park shimmering again.

## Museum of Science and Industry

Address:      57th St & Lake Shore Dr
              Chicago, IL 60637
Phone:        773-684-1414
Website:      www.msichicago.org
Hours:        9:30 am–5 pm daily. Visit website for select
              dates with extended hours.
Admission:    $18 for adults, ($15 for Chicagoans); $11 for
              children 3-11, ($10 for Chicagoans); $17 for
              seniors, ($14 for Chicagoans)
(Note: The Museum offers free admission to Illinois residents on what seem to be arbitrary days, and hours vary month to month, so check the website regularly.)

The 1893 World's Fair Arts Palace is now home to the Museum of Science and Industry. The mammoth 350,000-square-foot bastion is one of the largest science museums in the world. Generations of Chicagoans and visitors have been wowed by a vast array of exhibits, including hatching baby chicks, *U-505* (the only World War II German submarine captured), and the Walk-Through Heart. The model railroad, another favorite exhibit, has been expanded to the now 3,500-square-foot *Great Train Journey*, which depicts the route from Chicago to Seattle. Other popular attractions include the coal mine, the Fairy Castle, and the Omnimax theatre showcasing scientific adventures in a five-story, domed, wrap-around theatre.

## Nature

Two lagoons surround Wooded Island, a.k.a. Paul H. Douglas Nature Sanctuary. Osaka Garden, a serene Japanese garden with an authentic tea house and entrance gate, sits at the island's northern tip. The ceremonial garden, like the golden replica of Statue of the Republic on Hayes Avenue, recalls the park's 1893 Exposition origins. The Chicago Audubon Society (773-539-6793; www.chicagoaudubon.org) conducts bird walks in the park. These sites and the Perennial Garden at 59th Street and Cornell Drive are also butterfly havens.

## Sports

Back in the very beginning of the 20th century, the Jackson Park Golf Course was the only public course in the Midwest. Today, the historic 18-hole course is certified by the Audubon Cooperative Sanctuary and has beautiful wilderness habitats. (Or are those scruffy fairways?) Greens fees are $23 during the week and $26 on weekends (all rates are discounted for residents). A driving range is adjacent to the course (773-667-0524).

In the past six years, the city has spent over $10 million to improve fitness facilities in its parks, and the Jackson Park field house was the happy recipient of a much-needed facelift. The swanky new weight room and gymnasium are open to adults weekdays from 9 am to 9:30 pm, and weekends from 9 am to 4:15 pm. The facilities are open to teens from 2 pm to 6 pm. Adult membership passes cost $55 for ten weeks, $25 for seniors, and teens work out for free. From Hayes Drive north along Cornell Avenue are outdoor tennis courts, baseball diamonds, and a running track. Tennis courts are on the west side of Lakeshore Drive at 63rd Street. Jackson Park's beaches are at 57th Street and 63rd Street (water playground, too). Inner and Outer Harbors allow shore fishing (6401 S Stony Island Ave, 773-256-0903). Fitness center hours are Monday-Friday 9 am-9:30 pm, Saturday 11 am-4:30 pm, Sunday 12 pm-5 pm.

## Neighboring Parks

North of Jackson Park at 55th Street and Lake Shore Drive is Promontory Point, a scenic lakeside picnic spot. Harold Washington Park, 51st Street and Lake Shore Drive, has a model yacht basin and eight tennis courts on 53rd Street.

To the west, 460-acre Washington Park (5531 S Martin Luther King Dr, 773-256-1248) has an outdoor swimming pool, playing fields, and nature areas. It's also worth stopping by to see Lorado Taft's 1922 Fountain of Time sculpture and the DuSable Museum of African-American History (740 E 56th Pl, 773-947-0600; www.dusablemuseum.org).

At 71st Street and South Shore Drive are South Shore Beach, with a harbor, bird sanctuary, and South Shore Cultural Center (7059 South Shore Dr, 773-256-0149). South Shore Golf Course is a nine-hole public course. Greens fees are $14.75 weekdays and $16 on weekends (773-256-0986).

## How to Get There

**By Car:** From the Loop, drive south on Lake Shore Drive, exit west on 57th Street. From the south, take I-94 W. Exit on Stony Island Avenue heading north to 57th Drive. The museum's parking garage entrance is on 57th Drive. The Music Court lot is behind the museum. A free parking lot is on Hayes Drive.

**By Bus:** From the Loop, CTA buses 6 and 10 (weekends and daily in summer) stop by the museum ($2.25, $2 with Chicago Card/Ventra Card).

**By L:** (the quickest way to get to Jackson Park): Take the Green Line to the Garfield Boulevard (55th Street) stop ($2.25, $2.00 with Chicago Card/Ventra Card); transfer to the eastbound 55 bus.

**By Train:** Sporadic service. From the Loop's Millennium Station at Randolph Street and Van Buren Street stations, take Metra Electric service ($2.35 one-way). Trains stop at the 55th, 56th, and 57th Street Station platform (may be under construction). Walk two blocks east. From the Richard B. Ogilvie Transportation Center, walk two blocks south to Union Station on Canal Street and catch CTA bus 1.

## Overview

The largest of Chicago's 552 parks, Lincoln Park stretches 1,208 acres along the lakefront from the breeder cruising scene at the North Avenue Beach to the gay cruising scene at Hollywood Beach. The park boasts one of the world's longest bike trails, but thanks to an ever-increasing abundance of stroller-pushers, leashless dogs, and earbud-wearing rollerbladers, the path proves treacherous for cyclists and pedestrians alike. Nonetheless, sporty types and summertime dawdlers still find satisfaction indoors and out at Lincoln Park. Take a break from winter inside the Lincoln Park Conservatory, a tropical paradise full o' lush green plants no matter what the thermometer reads. Public buildings, including animal houses at the Lincoln Park Zoo, Café Brauer, Peggy Notebaert Nature Museum, and vintage beach bath houses, make the park as architecturally attractive as it is naturally beautiful.

Much of southern Lincoln Park is open green space populated by football, soccer, dog play, and barbeques. Paths shaded by mature trees lead to stoic statues. Until the 1860s, Lincoln Park was nothing more than a municipal cemetery filled with the shallow graves of cholera and smallpox victims, and it was concern about a public health threat that instigated the creation of the park. Although the city attempted to relocate all the bodies in the cemetery-to-park conversion of 1869, digging doggies may unearth more than picnickers' chicken bones.

## Nature

In spring, bird watchers flock to Lincoln Park's ponds and nature trails. Addison Bird Sanctuary Viewing Platform north of Belmont Harbor overlooks five fenced-in acres of wetlands and woods. Birding programs around North Pond are run by the Lincoln Park Conservancy (www.lincolnparkconservancy.org) and the Chicago Ornithological Society (312-409-9678; www.chicago-birder.org). More than 160 species of birds have been identified at the 10-acre pond. Free guided walks are held on Wednesdays starting at 7:30 am. Bring binoculars and a canteen of coffee. The Fort Dearborn Chapter of the Illinois Audubon Society hosts free park and zoo bird walks (847-675-3622; www.illinoisaudubon. org). Migratory birds gather around the revamped 1889 Alfred Caldwell Lily Pool at Fullerton Parkway and North Cannon Drive. Next to the Conservatory, Grandmother's Garden and the more formal French-style garden across the street are favorites for both wedding party photos and the homeless during the warmer months.

## Sports

Baseball diamonds on the park's south end are bordered by La Salle Drive and Lake Shore Drive, next to the newly renovated field house and NorthStar Eatery. Upgrades planned for the area include a running track, soccer field, and basketball and volleyball courts. Bicyclists and runners race along Lincoln Park Lagoon to the footbridge over Lake Shore Drive to North Avenue Beach, Chicago's volleyball mecca. To reserve courts and rent equipment, go to the south end of the landmark, boat-shaped bath house (312-742-3224). Just north of the bath house is a seasonal rollerblade rink and fitness club. North of Montrose Harbor on the North Wilson Drive lakefront is a free skateboard park.

The 9-hole Sydney R. Marovitz Public Golf Course (3600 Recreation Dr, 312-742-7930) hosts hackers year-round. Snail-slow play allows plenty of time to enjoy skyline views from this lakefront cow pasture, which is always crowded. You'll never see a golf cart on this course. Greens fees are $20.50 weekdays, $23.50 on weekends, and you can rent clubs for $10. Reserve tee times by calling 312-245-0909, or show up at sunrise. The starter sits in the northeast corner of the clock tower field house. For those who want to take it even more leisurely, check out the Diversey Miniature Golf Course (312-742-7929), which offers an 18-hole course complete with waterfalls and footbridges. Diversey mini-golf rates are $7 adults, $5.50 juniors/seniors. Also nearby is the Diversey Golf Range (141 W Diversey Ave, 312-742-7929), open year-round (large bucket $13.00, small bucket $9.00).

Four clay tennis courts, the last ones left in Chicago, are open 7 am–8 pm and cost $16 per hour (the 7 am–9 am early bird special costs $24); tennis shoes are required. For reservations and further information, call 312-742-7821. Tennis courts—the free courts are on Recreation Drive at Waveland. They are free, first come, first served.

An archery range on the north end of Belmont Harbor is where the Lincoln Park Archery Club (www.lincolnparkarcheryclub.org) meets. They offer a number of clinics throughout the summer for newcomers to the sport.

Members of the Lincoln Park Boat Club row in Lincoln Park Lagoon. Rowing classes for the public are offered May through September (www.lpbc.net).

The newly renovated Nature Boardwalk surrounds the South Pond at the Lincoln Park Zoo. Take a walk or jog through the urban oasis which acts as a natural haven for native birds, frogs, fish, and turtles. The Patio at Café Brauer (2021 North Stockton) is sunny spot to take in the view and sip on a specially brewed Boardwalk Blue blueberry-infused golden ale from Goose Island.

## Green City Market

| | |
|---|---|
| Address: | 2430 N Cannon Drive |
| | Chicago, IL 60614 |
| Phone: | 733-880-1266 |
| Website: | www.chicagogreencitymarket.org |
| Hours: | Wednesdays and Saturdays, mid-October through |
| | mid-April: indoors 8:30 am–1 pm; |
| | mid-April through mid-October: 7 am–1 pm |

No Lincoln Park experience would be complete without visiting a quintessential yuppie hotspot—the farmer's market. What began in an alley next to the Chicago Theatre in 1998 has since become Chicago's only year round sustainable market, showcasing local farmers selling everything from organic produce and cheese to elk meat and microgreens (whatever those are). Free chef demonstrations take place every Saturday at 10:30 am and from June to September, a different fruit or vegetable is featured every month according to what's in season.

## Lincoln Park Zoo

| | |
|---|---|
| Address: | 2200 N Cannon Dr |
| | Chicago, IL 60614 |
| Phone: | 312-742-2000 |
| Website: | www.lpzoo.com |
| Hours: | April-May 10 am-5 pm; Memorial Day-Labor |
| | Day 10 am-5 pm on weekdays, 10 am-6:30 pm |
| | on weekends; September-October 10 am-5 pm; |
| | November-March 10 am-4:30 pm. |
| Admission: | FREE |

Lions and tigers and bears and kids, oh my! We're not sure which scares us most. Established in 1868, Lincoln Park Zoo is the country's oldest free zoo, and while questions were raised in regards to nine animal deaths between 2005 and 2006, it still is a leader in wildlife conservation. National TV shows *Zoo Parade* and Ray Rayner's show *Ark in the Park* were filmed here. Look for some family (or, at least, in-law) resemblance at the cushy Regenstein Center for African Apes which opened in 2004, cost $26 million to build, and covers 29,000 square feet of living space. (Don't worry, it's supported by corporate sponsorships and private funds, not your tax dollars.) Come early and hear the white-cheek gibbons, the smallest of the ape family, mimic car alarms in their morning song to mark their territory. You may even catch one peeing off his tree before a captivated audience. Flanking the zoo's northwest side is the free Lincoln Park Conservatory, a fantastic source of oxygen renewal recommended for hangover sufferers. The new Pritzker Family Children's Zoo simulates a North American woods.

## Peggy Notebaert Nature Museum

| | |
|---|---|
| Address: | 2430 N Cannon Dr |
| | Chicago, IL 60614 |
| Phone: | 773-755-5100 |
| Website: | www.naturemuseum.org |
| Hours: | Mon–Fri 9 am–5 pm, Sat–Sun 10 am–5 pm |
| Admission: | $9 adults, $7 seniors & students, |
| | $6 children ages 3–12; Thursdays free for Illinois |
| | residents |

The Peggy Notebaert Nature Museum succeeds in making Illinois' level landscape interesting. The contemporary version of the 1857 Chicago Academy of Sciences, this hands-on museum depicts the close connection between urban and natural environments and represents global environmental issues through a local lens. A flowing water lab and flitting butterfly haven invite return visits. A must-see for anyone with a passion for taxidermy and/or *Silence of the Lambs*. You can also discover how pollutive you are in your everyday life—and how to change it—in their Extreme Greenhouse exhibit. Get back to nature with a full class and summer camp schedule.

## Chicago History Museum

| | |
|---|---|
| Address: | 1601 N. Clark St & North Ave |
| | Chicago, IL 60614 |
| Phone: | 312-642-4600 |
| Website: | www.chicagohistory.org |
| Hours: | Mon–Fri 9:30 am–4:30 pm, Sun 12 noon–5 pm |
| Admission: | $14 adults, $12 seniors & students, |
| | children under 12 free; Free days for Illinois |
| | residents vary, visit website for full schedule |

The Chicago History Museum holds over 20 million primary documents relating to the history of the Chicago area. Exhibits about the city's pioneer roots, architecture, music, fashion, neighborhoods, windy politics, and oral histories breathe life into an otherwise dry museum. Locals can access the excellent research center (open Tuesday through Saturday, $5/day, $15/year; students through grade 12 are free) for genealogical information and housing history. North & Clark Café explores Chicago's love of food.

## Performances

Lincoln Park Cultural Center (2045 N Lincoln Park W, 312-742-7994) stages plays, theater workshops, and family-friendly performances year-round. Theater on the Lake (Fullerton Ave & Lake Shore Dr, 312-742-7529) performs nine weeks of alternative drama in summer. The newly renovated theater now hosts events throughout the calendar year, thanks to much-needed climate control improvements. Lincoln Park Zoo hosts outdoor summer concerts as well. Call the events hotline at 312-742-2283.

## How to Get There

**By Car:** Lake Shore Drive exits to Lincoln Park are Bryn Mawr Avenue, Foster Avenue, Lawrence Avenue, Wilson Drive, Montrose Drive, Irving Park Parkway, Belmont Avenue, Fullerton Avenue, and North Avenue.

Free parking lots are at Recreational Drive near Belmont Harbor and Simonds Drive near Montrose Harbor. Paid lots are at North Avenue Beach, Chicago Historical Society, Lincoln Park Zoo, and Grant Hospital Garage. Stockton Drive and Cannon Drive have free street parking. A metered lot is on Diversey Parkway, next to the golf range.

**By Bus:** TA buses 151, 156, 77, 146, and 147 travel through Lincoln Park ($2.25, $2 with Chicago Card/Ventra Card). For schedules and fares, contact the RTA Information Center (312-836-7000; www.rtachicago.com).

**By L:** Get off the Red Line at any stop between Fullerton and Bryn Mawr avenues ($2.25, $1.75 with Chicago Card/Ventra Card), then head one mile east. On the Brown Line, all stops between Sedgwick and Belmont are about a mile east of the park as well.

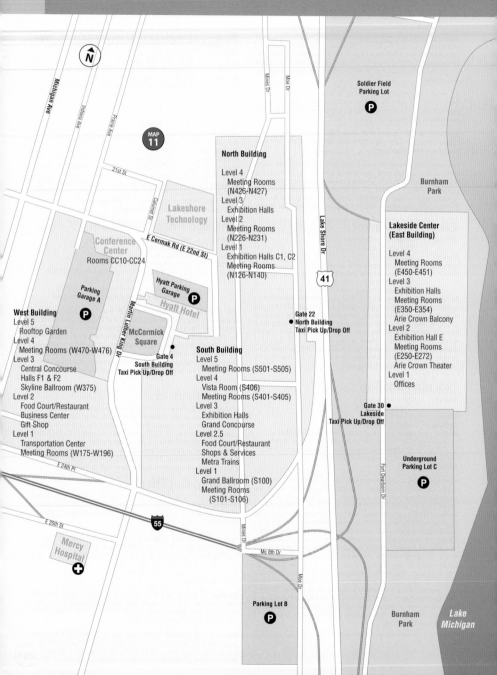

N

MAP
11

Michigan Ave

Indiana Ave

Prairie Ave

Calumet St

21st St

E Cermak Rd (E 22nd St)

Lakeshore
Technology

Conference
Center
Rooms CC10-CC24

Parking
Garage A
P

Hyatt Parking
Garage
P

Hyatt Hotel

Martin Luther King Dr

**West Building**
Level 5
  Rooftop Garden
Level 4
  Meeting Rooms (W470-W476)
Level 3
  Central Concourse
  Halls F1 & F2
  Skyline Ballroom (W375)
Level 2
  Food Court/Restaurant
  Business Center
  Gift Shop
Level 1
  Transportation Center
  Meeting Rooms (W175-W196)

McCormick
Square

Gate 4
**South Building**
Taxi Pick Up/Drop Off

E 24th Pl

E 25th St

55

Mercy
Hospital

**North Building**

Level 4
  Meeting Rooms
  (N426-N427)
Level 3
  Exhibition Halls
Level 2
  Meeting Rooms
  (N226-N231)
Level 1
  Exhibition Halls C1, C2
  Meeting Rooms
  (N126-N140)

Nines Dr

Moe Dr

Lake Shore Dr

41

Gate 22
North Building
Taxi Pick Up/Drop Off

**South Building**
Level 5
  Meeting Rooms (S501-S505)
Level 4
  Vista Room (S406)
  Meeting Rooms (S401-S405)
Level 3
  Exhibition Halls
  Grand Concourse
Level 2.5
  Food Court/Restaurant
  Shops & Services
  Metra Trains
Level 1
  Grand Ballroom (S100)
  Meeting Rooms
  (S101-S106)

Nines Dr

Mc 8th Dr

Moe Dr

Soldier Field
Parking Lot
P

Burnham
Park

**Lakeside Center
(East Building)**

Level 4
  Meeting Rooms
  (E450-E451)
Level 3
  Exhibition Halls
  Meeting Rooms
  (E350-E354)
  Arie Crown Balcony
Level 2
  Exhibition Hall E
  Meeting Rooms
  (E250-E272)
  Arie Crown Theater
Level 1
  Offices

Gate 30
Lakeside
Taxi Pick Up/Drop Off

Fort Dearborn Dr

**Underground
Parking Lot C**
P

Parking Lot B
P

Burnham
Park

**Lake
Michigan**

## General Information

| | |
|---|---|
| NFT Map: | 11 |
| Mailing Address: | 2301 S Lake Shore Dr |
| | Chicago, IL 60616 |
| Phone: | 312-791-7000 |
| Website: | www.mccormickplace.com |
| South Building: | Exhibit Hall A; charter bus stop |
| North Building: | Exhibit Halls B and C; |
| | Metra train station |
| Lakeside Center: | Exhibit Halls D and E; 4,249-seat |
| | Arie Crown Theater (Level 2); |
| | underground parking garage |

## Overview

When it comes to the convention business, size matters. With 2.2 million square feet of exhibit space spread among three buildings, McCormick Place is the largest convention center in the country and the third largest in the world. The center hosts more than three million visitors every year for trade shows and public exhibitions in the South Building, North Building, and Lakeside Center (East Building), including the Chicago Auto Show. McCormick Place also includes the Arie Crown Theatre, second largest theatre in Chicago according to seating capacity, which holds a variety of plays, concerts, and seminars. The city's colossal cash cow has gotten bigger with the addition of a new $850 million West Building. A City of Chicago project ahead of time and on budget? Surely another sign that the apocalypse will be occurring soon. End times notwithstanding, the expansion added 460,000 square feet of exhibit space and 250,000 square feet of meeting rooms to the already gargantuan center.

McCormick Place's growth continues to bolster the rapid gentrification of South Loop, and with each expansion the complex's overall aesthetic appeal steadily improves. But despite major renovations, Chicagoans still refer to the complex as "the mistake on the lake." Mayor Daley called the black boxy behemoth the "Berlin Wall" that separates Chicagoans from their beloved lakefront.

## Finding Your Way Around

Getting to McCormick Place is the easy part. Then you have to navigate the inside. The main entrance is off Martin Luther King Drive, next to the Hyatt Hotel. Here's how to crack the code names for meeting rooms and exhibit halls:

All meeting room locations start with E (Lakeside Center/East Building), N (North Building), or S (South Building). The first numeral represents the floor level, and the last two digits specify which room. Room numbers are never duplicated among the complex's three buildings.

Exhibit halls are named by consecutive letters starting with the South Building where Hall A (Level 3) is located. North Building houses Halls B (Level 3) and C (Level 1). Exhibit Halls D (Level 3) and E (Level 2) are in Lakeside Center.

Got all that?

## Restaurants & Services

Connie's Pizza and McDonald's Express are in the North Building (Level 2). The Fine Print Restaurant has a full-service dining option. The new West Building expansion has a large food court on the second floor, as well as the full-service option 270 Degree. The Plate Room Food Court is in the Grand Concourse (Level 2.5 and 3), where Starbucks, shops, a shoe shine, and massage services are also located. (Aren't convention centers just *great?*) Business centers and ATMs are in the Grand Concourse (Level 2.5), North Building (Level 2), and Lakeside Center (Level 2). The new West Building expansion will have a large food court on the second floor. If you're totally lost, there are Visitor Information Centers in each building. Good luck finding them.

## How to Get There

**By Car:** From the Loop, take Lake Shore Drive south; from the southeast, travel north on Lake Shore Drive. Signage to McCormick Place on Lake Shore Drive is frequent and clear. Parking garages are in Lakeside Center and the Hyatt. Lots are at 31st Street and Lake Shore Drive and at Martin Luther King Drive across from the South Building. Additional lots are north of McCormick Place at Burnham Harbor and Soldier Field.

**By Bus:** From the Loop, CTA buses 3 and 4 stop in front of the South Building. From Richard B. Ogilvie Transportation Center, take buses 124, 125, or 157 to Michigan Avenue; transfer to a southbound 3 or 4 ($2.25, $2 with Chicago Card/Ventra Card). From Union Station, board eastbound bus 1 to Michigan Avenue; transfer to a southbound 3 or 4.

During major shows, countless charter buses circle downtown hotels, transporting conventioneers to McCormick Place for free. With the new express busway, charter buses travel from Randolph Street to the South Building in less than ten minutes. For schedules, check with the hotels and at McCormick Place information desks.

**By Train:** A Metra train ride from the Loop's Millennium Station at Randolph Street and Van Buren Street stations to the McCormick Place Station takes nine minutes ($2.15 one-way). Escalators to the train platform are on the west side of the Grand Concourse (Level 2.5).

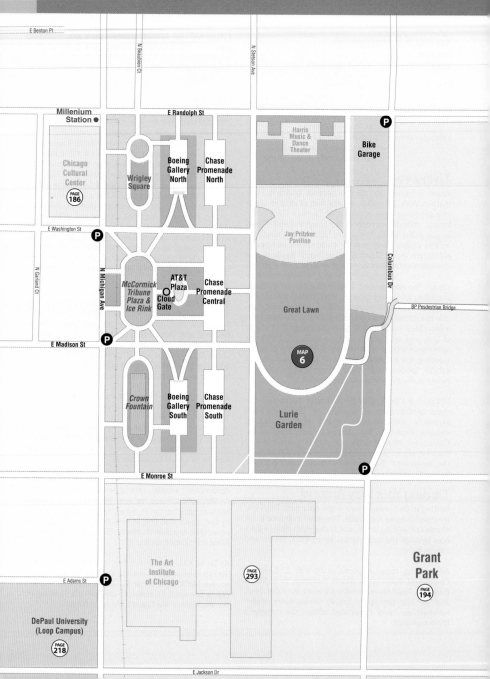

## Overview

Only four years behind schedule (who's counting?) and hundreds of millions of dollars over budget (okay, this we counted), Millennium Park finally launched itself in July 2004 as the cultural epicenter Mayor Daley promised us it would be back in 1997. Even if it did take myriad stopgap funding measures resembling yesteryear Al Capone strong-arm tactics to eternally endow us with the AT&T Plaza, McCormick Tribune Plaza & Ice Rink, and the Chase Promenade, locals and tourists alike agree it was well worth it. Even, staunch, longtime local naysayers have come to acknowledge that, when all is said and done, the end result really is an amazing addition to Grant Park's northpoint and is, without a doubt, one of downtown Chicago's crowning jewels. The last piece of the puzzle in this vision is the Art Institute's Modern Wing, designed by architect Renzo Piano. Only a couple of years behind schedule (what, you're shocked?), the wing opened with great fanfare in May 2009.

## Jay Pritzker Pavilion

The cornerstone of Millennium Park, without question, is the Pritzker Pavilion. It seems the whole park may have very well been conceived to give Frank Gehry's architectural masterpiece an appropriate setting. Spectacularly innovative, the pavilion's façade features immense stainless steel ribbons unfurling 40 feet into the sky. The pavilion's stage area is as big as Orchestra Hall across the street and can accommodate a 120-person orchestra and a 150-person choir. Seating for the free concert events includes a 4,000-seat terrace and an additional 95,000-square-foot lawn area that can accommodate 7,000 picnickers. A one-of-a-kind integrated sound system offers outdoor acoustics that rival the best in the world.

## Harris Theater for Music & Dance

Several dance and theatrical troupes share the 1,500-seat underground space behind Gehry's behemoth bandshell, including Hubbard Street Dance Chicago (not to be missed, but good luck getting tickets!), the Chicago Children's Choir, and the Jazz Institute of Chicago. Two underground parking garages flank the theater, and as with all parking in this area, it's first come/first served and a bit of a mess on the weekends.

Tickets and schedule available at www.harristheaterchicago.org

## Nature & Sculpture

The park has several different defined spaces: Wrigley Square, with its neoclassical epistyle; the Chase Promenade, gearing up to house art fairs and ethnic festivals; and the AT&T Plaza (between the skating rink and promenade), which is home to Anish Kapoor's 100-ton stainless steel jelly-bean sculpture, *Cloud Gate* (be sure to take a picture of yourself staring into it—a dead tourist giveaway, but an awesome picture). Flanking the skating rink to the south is the modernist Crown Fountain, which features two glass brick towers, 50 feet in height, with projected video images of the faces of actual Chicago residents. The Lurie Garden, a ridiculously conceptual assemblage of seasonal foliage, offers a beautiful public gathering space as well as more contemplative environments. The BP Bridge, a 925-foot-long winding bridge—Frank Gehry's fi rst—connects Millennium Park to Daley Bicentennial Plaza just east of the park. Clad in brushed stainless steel panels, the BP Bridge complements the Pritzker Pavilion in function as well as design by creating an acoustic barrier for traffic noise. It's well worth the walk.

## Sports

The 15,910-square-foot McCormick Tribune ice skating rink opens annually in November. On Saturdays in the summer, take part in free fitness classes on the Great Lawn. The options range from tai chi to yoga, with some more danceable aerobics as well. The park also houses a state-of-the-art, heated bicycle garage, which provides parking for 300 bikes, showers, a repair facility, and a café.

## Dining

The 300-seat Park Grill (voted "Top 5 Best Burger in Chicago") overlooking the skating rink offers burgers, steaks, and salads year round. In the summer, carry-away grub is available from a variety of kiosks throughout the park.

## How to Get There

No matter your mode of travel, approach the area around Millennium Park with patience and allow extra time. For train, L, and bus transportation recommendations, see our Grant Park or Art Institute sections. Metra's Randolph Street train station, servicing only south-bound trains, is located under Millennium Park.

If you choose to drive, underground parking is available in several areas. Access the Grant Park North Garage from Michigan Avenue. Enter Millennium Park Garage from the lower levels of Randolph Street and mid-level of Columbus Drive.

Grant Park

PAGE 194

41

Water Taxi Dock

E Roosevelt Rd

Ped Underpass

Main Entrance
Handicap Entrance

Shedd Aquarium

Group Entrance

North Main Entrance

North Entrance

Adler Planetarium

Handicap Entrance

The Field Museum

Solidarity Dr
Solidarity Dr

Planetarium Lot

P

Group & Handicap Entrance

S Columbus Dr

South Main Entrance

McFetridge Dr

P

North Garage

P

Lynne White Dr

12th St Beach

Burnham Harbor

St

Soldier Field

PAGE 240

Museum Campus Dr

Northerly Island Park

Waldron Dr

MAP 11

S Prairie Ave

S Lake Shore Dr

Waldron Garage

P

Burnham Park

Merrill C Meigs Field

18th St Station

Main Museum Visitor Entrance

E 18th St

S Calumet Ave

South Lot

P

E Cullerton St

Lake Michigan

E 21st St

S Calumet Ave

200E
E Cermak Rd

300E

S Dr Martin L King Jr Dr

S Dr Martin L King Jr Dr

S Prairie Ave

E 23rd St

400E

E 23rd Dr

Arie Crown Theater

S Calumet Ave

23rd St McCormick Place Station

S Cottage Grove Ave

Burnham Park

McCormick Place

PAGE 202

E 24th St

E 24th St

S Prairie Ave

E 24th Pl

Stevenson Expy

E 24th Pl

55

## Overview

Museum Campus is the ultimate destination for educational field trips. South of Grant Park at the intersection of Roosevelt Road and Lake Shore Drive, Museum Campus's 57 acres of uninterrupted lakefront parkland connect three world-renowned Chicago institutions: The Field Museum, Shedd Aquarium, and Adler Planetarium & Astronomy Museum. You've got Mayor Daley to thank for all of this beautiful space; it was the bossman himself who championed the rerouting of Lake Shore Drive to create the Museum Campus, which opened in 1998. Chicagoans, take note: although none of the museums that make up the museum campus are shouting from rooftops about it, all three offer reduced admission rates to locals. Be sure to ask for it.

## The Field Museum

| | |
|---|---|
| Address: | 1400 S Lake Shore Dr |
| | Chicago, IL 60605 |
| Phone: | 312-922-9410 |
| Website: | www.fieldmuseum.org |
| Hours: | Open daily 9 am–5 pm, except Christmas |
| Admission: | Basic admission is $15 Adults, $12 students & seniors, $10 children ages 3–11. Additional admission fees apply for full museum experience. Free days for Illinois residents vary, visit website for full schedule. |

The massive, Greek Revival-style museum constructed in 1921 houses over 20 million artifacts. From dinosaurs, diamonds, and earthworms to man-eating lions, totem poles, and mummies, there is just too much to savor in a single visit. In 2006, the museum introduced a new permanent exhibit called The Evolving Planet, featuring an interactive stroll through 4 billion years of evolution, from single-celled organisms through dinosaurs, hominids, and finally to human beings. Science: 1, Intelligent Design: 0. Another noteworthy permanent exhibit is Sue, the largest, most complete, and best preserved Tyrannosaurus Rex discovered to date. Complete with a half-smoked pack of Marlboros, since we now know that's what killed the dinosaurs. As with most museums, some temporary exhibits cost additional bucks on top of normal museum fees. Free museum tours are held weekdays at 11 am and 2 pm.

## John G. Shedd Aquarium

| | |
|---|---|
| Address: | 1200 S Lake Shore Dr |
| | Chicago, IL 60605 |
| Phone: | 312-939-2438 |
| Website: | www.shedd.org |
| Hours: | Memorial Day–Labor Day: Daily, 9 am–6 pm (Jun–Aug open 'til 10 pm on Thurs) Labor Day–Memorial Day: Mon–Fri: 9 am–5 pm; Sat–Sun: 9 am–6 pm. Closed Christmas |
| Admission: | Basic admission is $8 adults, $6 children ages 3–11. Additional admission fees apply for full museum experience. Free days for Illinois residents vary, visit website for full schedule. |

Opened in 1929, the Beaux Arts-style aquarium's six wings radiate from a giant, circular coral reef tank. The museum features revolving exhibits with a special focus on marine ecology and preservation. Popular favorites include Wild Reef, where you can get up close and personal with the sharks. On Thursday evenings from mid-June through August, the Shedd hosts "Jazzin at the Shedd" from 5 to 10 pm, featuring live jazz, a light sit-down dinner with cocktails overlooking the downtown skyline, and full access to the aquarium until 10 pm. The Oceanarium reopened in 2009 after a complete renovation.

## Burnham Park

Burnham Park, the site of the 1933 Century of Progress exhibition, encompasses McCormick Place, Burnham Harbor, the former Merrill C. Meigs Airport (closed in a political coup by Mayor Daley in 2003), and Soldier Field. A free skateboard park is located at Lake Shore Drive and 31st Street. The 12th Street Beach, especially popular with swimmers and divers because of the deep water east of the beach, is on Northerly Island. Other beaches are at 31st Street and 49th Street. Outdoor basketball courts are east of Lake Shore Drive around 35th Street and 47th Street. Fishing is welcome along Solidarity Drive and Burnham Harbor shore,. The wilderness Nature Area at 47th Street attracts butterflies and birds.

## Adler Planetarium

| | |
|---|---|
| Address: | 1300 S Lake Shore Dr |
| | Chicago, IL 60605 |
| Phone: | 312-922-7827 |
| Website: | www.adlerplanetarium.org |
| Hours: | Mon–Fri 9:30 am–4 pm; Sat–Sun 9:30 am–4:30pm; Third Thursdays (21+ Adler After Dark) 6:30 pm– 10:30 pm; check website for special extended summer hours |
| Admission: | Basic admission is $12 adults, $8 children. Additional admission fees apply for full museum experience. Free days for Illinois residents vary, visit website for full schedule. |

The Adler Planetarium & Astronomy Museum offers interactive exhibits explaining space phenomena and intergalactic events; its 2,000 historic astronomical and navigational instruments form the western hemisphere's largest collection. On the first Friday of every month, weather permitting, amateur astronomers young and old are invited to bring their own telescopes to the Planetarium lawns. Roving scientists offer tips and instructions on telescope usage and observational features. Come summer, the 21+ Alder After Dark events are great, nerdy date nights featuring both kinds of cosmos. Chicago skyline views from the planetarium grounds are out of this world any day of the week, and are always worth the trip.

## How to Get There

**By Car:** From the Loop, take Columbus Drive south; turn east on McFetridge Drive. From the south, take Lake Shore Drive to McFetridge Drive. Area parking lots are near Soldier Field, Field Museum, Adler Planetarium, and McCormick Place. All parking $19 in the lot adjacent to the Adler and $19 in the Soldier Field lot. Fees are higher on days when there's Park District-sponsored special events. Metered parking is available on Solidarity Drive.

**By Bus:** CTA buses 2, 6, 10, 12, 14, 127, 130, and 146 serve the area ($2.25 one-way, $2 with Chicago Card/Ventra Card). For schedules and fares, contact the RTA Information Center at 312-913-3110; www.rtachicago.com

**By L:** Ride the Orange, Red, or Green Lines to the Roosevelt Road stop ($2.25 one-way, $2.00 with Chicago Card/Ventra Card). Walk east through the pedestrian underpass at Roosevelt Road.

**By Train:** From Richard B. Ogilvie Transportation Center, travel east on CTA bus 20 to State Street; transfer to the 146 ($2.25 one-way, $2 with Chicago Card/Ventra Card). From Union Station take CTA bus 1, 126, or 151; transfer at State Street to the 10 or 146. From La Salle Street station, take the 146 ($2.25 one-way, $2 with Chicago Card). South Shore and Metra trains stop at the Roosevelt Road station.

**On Foot:** Walk south through Grant Park past bobbing boats and the gushing Buckingham Fountain to the Museum Campus.

**Water Taxis:** Seasonally, water taxis operate between Navy Pier and Museum Campus (312-222-9328; www.shorelinesightseeing.com).

207

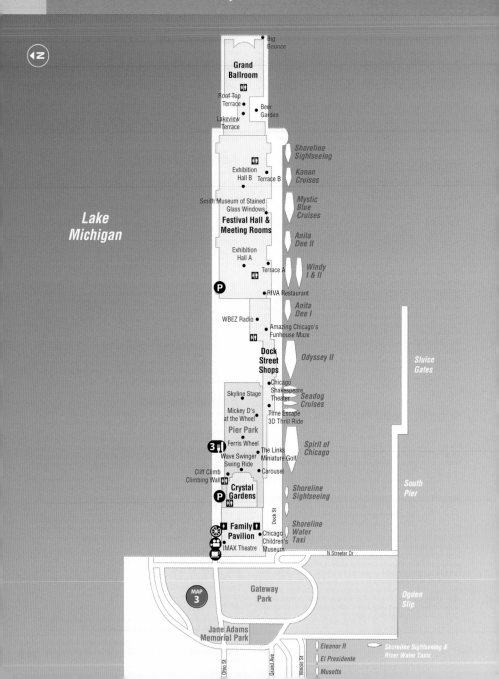

Big Bounce

**Grand Ballroom**

Roof Top Terrace

Beer Garden

Lakeview Terrace

*Lake Michigan*

*Shoreline Sightseeing*

*Kanan Cruises*

Exhibition Hall B

Terrace B

*Mystic Blue Cruises*

Smith Museum of Stained Glass Windows

**Festival Hall & Meeting Rooms**

*Anita Dee II*

Exhibition Hall A

Terrace A

*Windy I & II*

P

RIVA Restaurant

*Anita Dee I*

WBEZ Radio

Amazing Chicago's Funhouse Maze

**Dock Street Shops**

*Odyssey II*

*Sluice Gates*

Chicago Shakespeare Theater

Skyline Stage

*Seadog Cruises*

Mickey D's at the Wheel

Time Escape 3D Thrill Ride

**Pier Park**

Ferris Wheel

3

Wave Swinger Swing Ride

The Links Miniature Golf

*Spirit of Chicago*

Cliff Climb Climbing Wall

Carousel

**Crystal Gardens**

*Shoreline Sightseeing*

*South Pier*

P

Family Pavilion

*Shoreline Water Taxi*

Chicago Children's Museum

IMAX Theatre

Dock St

N Streeter Dr

MAP 3

**Gateway Park**

*Ogden Slip*

Jane Adams Memorial Park

Ohio St

Grand Ave

Illinois St

Eleanor R

El Presidente

Musetts

*Shoreline Sightseeing & River Water Taxis*

## General Information

| | |
|---|---|
| NFT Map: | 3 |
| Address: | 600 E Grand Ave<br>Chicago, IL 60611 |
| Phone: | 312-595-7437 |
| Website: | www.navypier.com |
| Pier Hours: | Opens 10 am daily. Closing times of restaurants, shops, and attractions vary by season, holiday, and public exhibitions/ events. |
| Skyline Stage: | 1,500-seat outdoor performance pavilion in Pier Park, performances are May through September; 312-595-5022 |
| IMAX Theatre: | 312-595-5629 |
| Free Fireworks: | Memorial Day to Labor Day, Wednesdays (9:30 pm) & Saturdays (10:15 pm). Free to the public. |
| WBEZ Radio: | National Public Radio's local station, 312-948-4600; www.wbez.org. |
| Exhibit Space: | Festival Hall, Lakeview Terrace, Ballroom Lobby, Grand Ballroom; 36 meeting rooms |

## Overview

A quintessential tourist trap, Navy Pier (a.k.a. the mall on the lake) is often avoided by real Chicagoans, who scoff at its self-consciously inoffensive blandness. Save for an occasional Skyline Stage concert, speed-boat ride, or high-end nosh at Riva, a trek to the pier is best reserved for those times when you have Grandma and a bevy of nieces and nephews in town, not to mention plenty of spending cash.

Opened to the public in 1916 as a municipal wharf, the pier has also done time as a) the University of Illinois at Chicago's campus, b) a hospital, c) a military training facility, d) a concert venue, and e) a white elephant. In 1989, the Metropolitan Pier and Exposition Authority invested $150 million to transform the crumbling pier into a peninsular entertainment-exhibition complex that attracts 8 million uninspired people a year. In addition to convention space, Navy Pier also houses two museums, the Shakespeare Theater, the Crystal Gardens, an outdoor concert pavilion, a vintage grand ballroom, a 15-story Ferris wheel, an IMAX Theatre, and, just for the hell of it, a radio station.

## Chicago Shakespeare Theater

The Chicago Shakespeare Theater has a 510-seat, court-yard-style theater and a 180-seat studio theater that are Chicago's sole venues dedicated to performing wordsmith Willy's works. In addition to the season's plays, the theater produces Shakespeare "shorts" for younger patrons. A bookstore and teacher resource center are also on-site (312-595-5600; www.chicagoshakes.com).

## Chicago Children's Museum

The Chicago Children's Museum features daily activities, a creative crafts studio, and 15 interactive exhibits ranging from dinosaur digs and waterworks to a toddler tree house, safety town, and construction zone. The museum is open daily from 10 am to 5 pm, and Thursday until 8 pm. Admission is $14 for adults and children, $13 for seniors, and Target First Free Sundays allow children 15 and under in free the first Monday of every month. Thursdays 5 pm to 8 pm are Kraft Free Family Nights, which means free admission for all. Dates vary. (312-527-1000; www.chicagochildrens-museum.org).

## Smith Museum of Stained Glass Windows

Smith Museum is the first stained-glass-only museum in the country. The 150 windows installed in the lower level of Festival Hall are mainly from Chicago-area buildings and the city's renowned stained glass studios. Windows representing over a century of artistic styles include works by Louis Comfort Tiffany, Frank Lloyd Wright, Louis Sullivan, and John LaFarge. The free museum is open during Pier hours (312-595-5024).

## Getting There

**By Car:** From the north, exit Lake Shore Drive at Grand Avenue; proceed east. From the southeast, exit Lake Shore Drive at Illinois Street; go east. Three garages are on the Pier's north side, and plenty of parking lots are just west of Lake Shore Drive in Streeterville (Map 3).

**By Bus:** CTA buses 29, 65, 66, 120, 121, and 124 serve Navy Pier.

**By L:** Take the Green or Red Line to Grand Avenue ($2.25, $2.00 with Chicago Card/Ventra Card). Board eastbound CTA Bus 29, or take the free trolley.

**By Train:** From Richard B. Ogilvie Transportation Center, take CTA buses 56 or 124. From Union Station, board bus 121.

**By Trolley:** Free, daily trolleys that typically run every 20 minutes travel between Navy Pier and State Street along Grand Avenue and Illinois Street from Memorial Day to Labor Day. Pick-up points are indicated by "Navy Pier Trolley Stop" signs along the route.

**By Boat:** Seasonal water shuttles (one-way $3–13 adults, $3–6 kids) travel between Navy Pier and the Museum Campus and along the Chicago River to the Sears Tower (312-222-9328; www.shorelinesightseeing.com).

## Pizza

- **Connie's Pizza** • 600 E Grand Ave

## Coffee

- **Starbucks** • 600 E Grand Ave

## Movie Theaters

- **Navy Pier IMAX Theatre** • 600 E Grand Ave

## Restaurants

- **Capi's Italian Kitchen** • 700 E Grand Ave
- **Riva** • 700 E Grand Ave

## General Information

Oak Park Visitors Bureau:  708-524-7800;
www.visitoakpark.com
Oak Park Tourist:  www.oprf.com

## Overview

You can thank Oak Park for Prairie Style architecture, *A Moveable Feast*, McDonald's, and, yes, *Tarzan*. The creators of each called this charming suburb their home: Frank Lloyd Wright, Ernest Hemingway, Ray Kroc, and Edgar Rice Burroughs, respectively.

Best known for its architectural gems and strong public schools, Oak Park (pop. 52,500) is a happy hunting ground for homebuyers seeking upscale, integrated living 10 miles from the Loop. Less impressed than most with his picture-perfect hometown, Hemingway famously described Oak Park as "a village of wide lawns and narrow minds."

Village trustees must still be smarting from Hemingway's crack because they publicize an official policy on maintaining diversity. The "diversity statement" sounds like some sort of disclaimer or a zealot's vision for heaven on Earth: "Ours is a community that encourages contributions of all citizens regardless of race, gender, ethnicity, sexual orientation, disability, religion ..." —and indeed, Oak Park has quite a reputation as the place all the hip GLBT kids go when it's time to become hip GLBT parents.

## Architecture

Oak Park harbors the nation's largest concentration of Frank Lloyd Wright buildings, 25 in the village and another 6 in neighboring River Forest. The village's must-see sites are located in a compact area bordered by Division Street, Lake Street, Forest Avenue, and Ridgeland Avenue. Designs by Wright, William Drummond, George W. Maher, John Van Bergen, and E. E. Roberts are represented throughout.

You can ground yourself in Prairie Style architectural principles at the brilliant Frank Lloyd Wright Home and Studio. Maintained by the Frank Lloyd Wright Preservation Trust, guided tours of the designer's personal space are offered weekdays at 11 am, 1 pm, and 3 pm and every twenty minutes on weekends between 11 am and 3:30 pm (951 Chicago Ave, 708-848-1976; www.gowright.org). Only 15 people are allowed per tour, and tickets can be purchased on the foundation's website or on-site (early arrival recommended) at a cost of $15 for adults, $12 for youth 14–17 and seniors, and free for children 3 and under. Worthwhile walking tours of the surrounding streets are also offered, and a combination tour, which includes a self-guided audio tour of the neighborhood costs $25 for adults, $20 for youth 4-17 and seniors, and free for children under 3. Worth every penny. A personal photography pass is available for $5.

Completed in 1908, Unity Temple (875 Lake St, 708-383-8873; www.unitytemple-utrf.org) was Wright's first commissioned public building; today it houses Oak Park's Unitarian-Universalist congregation. Unity Temple is open daily for self-directed tours and on weekends for guided visits ($15). Designed by George W. Maher, historic Pleasant Home (217 S Home Ave, 708-383-2654; www.pleasanthome.org) aptly illustrates the architectural evolution from Victorian design to early Prairie Style with tours held Thursday through Sunday at 12:30 pm, 1:30 pm, and 2:30 pm ($10 adults, $8 for students and seniors, $5 children; Fridays "pay what you can").

The Oak Park Visitors Center offers maps and a PDA walking tour of the Ridgeland Historic District highlighting 15 of the area's Victorian "Painted Ladies" ($10 for adults, $5 for students and seniors) 10 am–3:30 pm daily. Call 708-524-7800, or visit www.visitoakpark.com for more information.

## Culture & Events

Once a year in May, the public gets to snoop inside Wright-designed private residences during the popular Wright Plus Housewalk ($100). His home-studio and Robie House in Hyde Park (shuttle provided) are also included in the tour (708-848-3559; www.gowright.org).

Get your fill of he-man author Hemingway at the Ernest Hemingway Museum (200 N Oak Park Ave, 708-848-2222; www.hemingway.org), open Sunday through Friday 1 pm–5 pm, and Saturday 10 am–5 pm ($10 adults, $8 students and seniors). His birthplace, also included with the price of admission, is located just up the street at 339 N Oak Park Avenue. For a one-stop confab with both of Oak Park's favorite sons, stroll three blocks north and two west to the 600 block of N. Kenilworth Ave, where Wright's Balch House (611) stands across the street from the Prairie Style home (600) to which Hemingway's family moved when he was 5 years old.

Summer evenings, catch Shakespeare's works performed outdoors in Austin Gardens by the Oak Park Festival Theatre company (708-445-4440; www.oakparkfestival.com). The lush Oak Park Conservatory, originally built in 1929 to provide a place for all of the exotic plants Oak Park residents collected on their travels abroad, is located at 615 Garfield Street (708-386-4700; www.oprf.com/conservatory; suggested $2 donation) and definitely worth a visit.

## ○ Landmarks

- **Frank Lloyd Wright Home and Studio** • 951 Chicago Ave

## ○ Nightlife

- **Avenue Ale House** • 825 S Oak Park Ave

## ○ Restaurants

- **Buzz Café** • 905 S Lombard Ave
- **Cucina Paradiso** • 814 North Blvd
- **Jerusalem Café** • 1030 Lake St
- **Khyber Pass** • 1031 Lake St
- **Mama Thai** • 1112 W Madison St
- **Marion Street Grill** • 189 N Marion St
- **New Rebozo** • 1116 Madison St
- **Pete's Red Hots** • 6346 W Roosevelt Rd
- **Petersen Ice Cream** • 1100 Chicago Ave
- **Poor Phil's Shell Bar** • 139 S Marion St

## ○ Shopping

- **Magic Tree Bookstore** • 141 N Oak Park Ave
- **Pumpkin Moon** • 1028 North Blvd

## General Information

Address:    542 N Rte 21
            Gurnee, IL 60031
Phone:      847-249-4636
Website:    www.sixflags.com/parks/greatamerica
Hours:      Open May to October. Hours are generally
            10 am–10 pm, but vary by season.
            See website for specific hours and dates.
Entry:      $61.99 adult fare, $41.99 for kids under 54", includes
            admission to both Six Flags and Hurricane Harbor.

## Overview

Long lines, crappy food, hokey entertainment, and sun poisoning…if that isn't the stuff dreams are made of, then baby, we don't know what is.

## Tickets

Reduced rates are available for advanced purchase through the website and via promotions throughout the season—look for discounted deals at Dominick's as well as on specially marked Coke cans. "The Flash" passes are available for impatient riders, offering cuts in line for $39.99. If you want to come back for a second day, "twickets" are available at the park; the fee varies, but it's usually around $10 or $15. For die-hard thrill seekers, season passes offer the best deal at $79.99. Individual tickets and season passes can be purchased online at www.sixflagsticketing.com.

## For the Kiddies

Camp Cartoon Network and Bugs Bunny National Park offer easy-going rides and playgrounds for tykes 54 inches and under, while Bugs, Yosemite Sam, and the rest amble around for photo ops. The double-decker classic kiddie ride Columbia Carousel, located just past the park's main entrance, may be too tame for young 'uns hopped up on funnel cake and Tweety-pops. New in 2007 is Wiggles World, inspired by Australian band The Wiggles. Characters Dorothy the Dinosaur, Captain Feathersword, Wags the Dog, and Henry the Octopus are available daily for photoops, meet-n-greets, and other humiliating activities you'll be forced to engage in for the sake of your children's fragile psyches. If your kids are a little older and more badass (but still too chickenshit to experience the real deal), take them on the Whizzer, mini-coaster and quintessential training wheels for every 'tween. Other rides the height-challenged set can get on include the Orbit, the Whirligig, the Ragin' Cajun, and the good old-fashioned Tilt-a-Whirl, spinning fun guaranteed to make your kids laugh and your stomach retch.

## Thrill Rides

Every few years, Six Flags tries to outdo itself with a new, even more death-defying and harrowing ride. Most recently, this magnificent feat was accomplished with the opening of the Superman-Ultimate Flight ride. Passengers soar through the air head-first as though they were flying, nearly brushing the ground below them on the giant loop-de-loop. Other thrills include the Raging Bull "hyper-twister," where you drop at incredible degrees and speeds into subterranean depths. Batman The Ride allows your feet to dangle free, while riders remain standing, supported by a bicycle seat between the legs (men who desire children, be wary). Also try the equally frightening Vertical Velocity, V2 for short, which propels riders backward and forward up a corkscrew at 70 mph in less than 4 seconds, suspended by the same paltry harness that barely staves off fatality. Meanwhile, the classic wooden American Eagle coaster offers vintage, but no-less-worrisome, rickety thrills. The Viper, newer and sexier cousin to the geriatric American Eagle, provides a similar timber ride, but with a 100% less chance of death than the Eagle. Shock Wave, also known as concussion-central, is no longer around, but try The Demon in its place if you're interested in forgetting your

name and address. If you're feeling nostalgic, try Splashwater Falls, a blink-and-it's-over water ride in which a boat goes up a hill, around a curve, and down a big drop, soaking riders and bystanders on the overhead bridge/ride exit in the process. New in 2009 was Buccaneer Battle, a pirate-themed raft ride that allows you to soak other people with super-powered soak guns. Cool.

## Hurricane Harbor Water Park

Opened in 2005, Great America's adjoining Hurricane Harbor water park introduced attractions such as "Skull Island," which press materials dub the thrill-evoking "world's largest interactive water play structure." How's that for screaming "fun?" There are also miles of water rides, including Hurricane Mountain, Vortex, and Typhoon (tube and bowl slides), and a splashing park for wee tots ("Mommy, why is the water yellow?"). The new and popular Tornado, a combination tube and bowl slide, allows four riders to experience spinning in the 60-foot-wide tunnel together. An adventure river, Castaway Creek, offers both exciting adventures complete with geysers, as well as leisurely relaxation under waterfalls and mists. The park also features a 1,000+ gallon water drop that dumps itself upon unsuspecting visitors every ten minutes. Leave the Prada at home.

## Fright Fest

Avoid the heat and long lines of the summer season and creep into the park during the month of October (mostly on weekends) among the Halloween-themed décor (last year, the Viper was dressed up as "Snakes on a Train," based on Samuel Jackson's recent "hit" movie) and scary music playing over the P.A. This is, by far, our favorite time to go and worth the price of a season pass for the convenience of just dropping by for a few thrills whenever the hell you feel like it (the park is open until midnight on most Saturday nights during Fright Fest). Water rides in the park are usually less crowded now, so take advantage of Splashwater Falls, Logger's Run, and Roaring Rapids (complete with blood-red water) to get the pasty white complexion and blue-tinged lip effect that will help you fit in since costumes aren't allowed.

## Make a Night of It

Where to stay in Gurnee:
- **La Quinta Inn**, 5688 Northridge Dr, 847-662-7600
- **Country Inn & Suites**, 5420 Grand Ave, 847-625-9700
- **Fairfield Inn**, 6090 Gurnee Mills Cir, 847-855-8868
- **Grand Hotel & Suites**, 5520 Grand Ave, 847-249-7777
- **Hampton Inn**, 5550 Grand Ave, 847-662-1100
- **KeyLime Cove Indoor Waterpark Resort**, 1700 Nations Dr, Gurnee, 877-360-0403

## How to Get There

**By Car:** Take I-94 or I-294 west, exit at Grand Avenue. Be aware that traffic is very congested in July and August! Arrive extra early or extra late to beat the crowds.

**By Train & Bus:** Take the Metra Union Pacific North Line to Waukegan, where you can catch the Pace bus 565 to Great America. Note: Public transportation to Great America from the Ogilvie Transportation Center and Madison and Canal takes just over two hours each way.

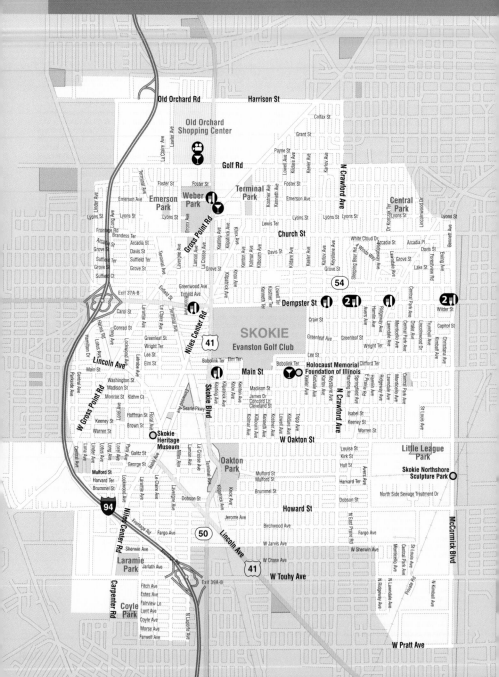

## General Information

www.skokie.org

## Overview

When Skokie was first incorporated under the moniker Niles Centre in 1888, it was considered to be the rowdy neighbor of temperate Evanston due to the large number of taverns within its borders. By 1940, residents were clamoring for a name change and a PR face-lift. In November of that year, the village was renamed Skokie after the nearby Skokie River and canals, which themselves were named after an old Native American word for "swampland." Personally, we'd be more attracted to a party town, but nonetheless, the facelift was a success. With the completion of the Edens Expressway in the 1950s, residential development in Skokie was booming.

A chunk of the growth comprised Eastern European refugees from World War II, many of whom were Jewish. It is estimated that between 1945 and 1955, 3,000 Jewish families resettled in Skokie. Synagogues and Jewish services followed, and the village soon developed a self-perpetuating reputation as a thriving Jewish enclave.

Skokie made international headlines in 1977–78 when it contested plans by the National Socialist Party of America, a branch of the American Nazi Party, to march on the village square. The NSPA was defended by the ACLU in a divisive case that brought the contest between free expression and freedom against hate speech into the international fore. As far as the NSPA was concerned, the decision to march in Skokie was an act of political nomination. Chicago had denied the Nazis' right to march in SW Chicago's Marquette Park, which was the NSPA's home turf. The group then threatened to re-locate their planned assembly to Skokie. When the Village of Skokie lost their bid to ban the march, Chicago finally conceded, allowing the Nazis to gather at Marquette Park in June 1978. A handful of Nazis showed up, countered by thousands of anti-Nazi protestors.

As if being the head of a neo-Nazi movement and threatening to march on the front lawns of concentration camp survivors doesn't already make you the world's biggest jackass/creep, NSPA leader Frank Collin secured the title in 1979 when he was arrested and in-carcerated on child molestation charges.

## Culture & Events

In 1988, an urban renewal project to restore the North Shore's de-crepit Chicago River waterfront resulted in the two-mile Sculpture Park, an outdoor recreation area with walking paths, picnic areas, and featuring more than 72 sculptures by artists of local, national, and international renown (although, rubes that we are, we confess we haven't heard of any of 'em). The park, sandwiched between McCormick Blvd and the north branch of the Chicago River, runs the two miles from Touhy to Dempster.

Time travel through history at the Skokie Heritage Museum—an assemblage of historical photos, papers, and artifacts painstakingly gathered by the Skokie Historical Society. The museum, housed in a restored 1887 firehouse, also features the history of Skokie's fire-fighters. Behind the museum, an authentic 1840s log cabin relocat-ed to this location allows kids a glimpse into the town's pioneer past.

Skokie is now home to the Illinois Holocaust Museum & Education Center (9603 Woods Dr, 847-967-4800), which opened in 2009. www.ilholocaustmuseum.org It's open to the public weekdays 10 am – 5 pm and Thursday evening until 8 pm. Saturday and Sunday from 11 am- 4pm. Admission is $12 for adults, $8 for seniors and students aged 12-22, $5 for children 5-12. Active military and their families receive 50% off general admission.

Skokie Park District has many fairs up their sleeves, including a late-summer night's dream for kids. In the sticky heat of late-August, carnies set up for the Back-to-School Carnival. Backpack toting tots mingle with tweenies for a farewell-to-freedom bash (while parents openly celebrate with their "can't wait" grins). Running just one weekend, the summer ends with "a veritable smorgasbord" of rickety rides, corn dogs and the sickly sweet smell of elephant ears.

Every year in mid-May, the Skokie Festival of Cultures draws clog dancers, falafel hawkers, and accordion players from around the state for a weekend festival celebrating Skokie's diverse cultural heritage. The sulky loitering high-schoolers and fat ladies in track suits, on the other hand, are 100% local.

## North Shore Center for the Performing Arts

Home to the Skokie Valley Symphony Orchestra, the Centre East Theater, and, most notably, the highly acclaimed Northlight Theater, the North Shore Center for the Performing Arts (9510 Skokie Blvd, 847-673-6300; www.northshorecenter.org) is a state-of-the-art performance venue. Touring artists perform here, world class theater (sometimes featuring ensemble members from Steppenwolf) is mounted here, and it's also a North Shore venue for exhibits and trade shows. Designed by architect Graham Gund in 1996, The North Shore Center for the Performing Arts has given Northeast Illinois culture seekers a reason to come to Skokie besides bagels and lox.

## Where to Drink

Despite its alcohol-fueled history, Skokie is not really known as a place to imbibe socially. Young residents head to youthful water-ing holes in the vicinity of the Northwestern campus in formerly tee-totaling Evanston (will the ironies never end?). Meanwhile, local drunks hang out at anonymous corner taverns just like any-where else. Retail workers, middle managers, and the secretarial set mingle and mate at the food and booze joints adjacent to Old Orchard.

## Where to Eat

Old Orchard Shopping Center is filled with family-friendly chain options. Happily, Skokie still houses enough locally owned, inde-pendent restaurants to add interest and diversity to their dining scene. Folks travel from all over Chicagoland for local delis and kosher fare ever debating the superiority of Kaufman's v. New York Bagel and Bialy as THE place for a bagel and shmear.

## How to Get There

**By L:** The Skokie Swift Yellow Line runs non-stop between the Howard Street Red Line terminus and the Skokie Dempster station at 5001 Dempster St. Trains run approximately every 10-15 minutes between 5 am and 10 pm.

**By Car:** Take the Edens Expressway (I-94), and exit at Dempster.

## Movie Theaters

- **AMC Loews Gardens 1/6** • 4999 Old Orchard Shopping Center

## Nightlife

- **Champps** • 134 Old Orchard Ctr
- **Principal's Pub** • 4249 Main St

## Restaurants

- **El Tipico** • 3341 Dempster St
- **Grecian Kitchen Delights** • 3938 Dempster St
- **Hub's Gyros** • 3727 Dempster St
- **Hy Life Bistro** • 4120 Dempster St
- **Kabul House** • 3320 Dempster St
- **Kaufman's Bagel & Delicatessen** • 4905 Dempster St
- **Pita Inn** • 3910 Dempster
- **Ruby of Siam** • 9420 Skokie Blvd
- **Shallots Bistro** • 7016 Carpenter Road

# Columbia College Chicago

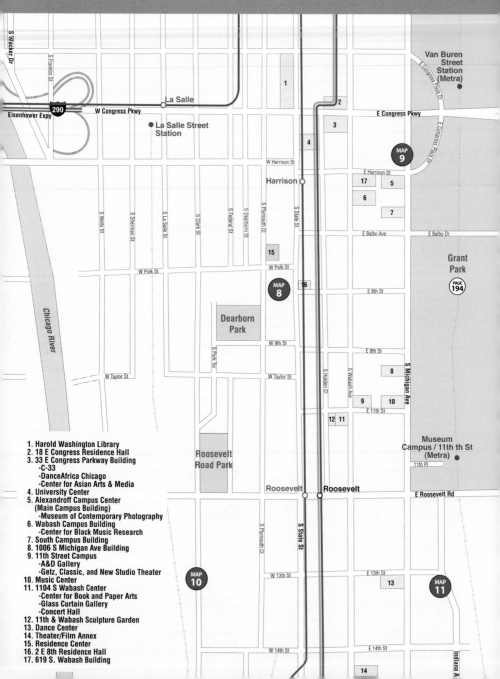

1. Harold Washington Library
2. 18 E Congress Residence Hall
3. 33 E Congress Parkway Building
   -C-33
   -DanceAfrica Chicago
   -Center for Asian Arts & Media
4. University Center
5. Alexandroff Campus Center
   (Main Campus Building)
   -Museum of Contemporary Photography
6. Wabash Campus Building
   -Center for Black Music Research
7. South Campus Building
8. 1006 S Michigan Ave Building
9. 11th Street Campus
   -A&D Gallery
   -Getz, Classic, and New Studio Theater
10. Music Center
11. 1104 S Wabash Center
    -Center for Book and Paper Arts
    -Glass Curtain Gallery
    -Concert Hall
12. 11th & Wabash Sculpture Garden
13. Dance Center
14. Theater/Film Annex
15. Residence Center
16. 2 E 8th Residence Hall
17. 619 S. Wabash Building

## General Information

NFT Maps:          8, 9, 11
Address:           600 S Michigan Ave
                   Chicago, IL 60605
Phone:             312-663-1600
Website:           www.colum.edu
Event Information: www.colum.edu/calendar

## Overview

Named in honor of the World's Columbian Exposition, Columbia College Chicago first opened in 1890 as a women's speech academy. Over time, it has become one of America's most diverse private arts and media schools. It is best known for its film, television, and fiction departments, which turn out prominent professionals. Columbia alumni played key writing and production roles in *Barbershop*, *Real Women Have Curves*, *Analyze This*, *Schindler's List,* and *Leaving Las Vegas*. They win Emmy Awards (for art direction on *Alias*, special effects on *Star Trek: Enterprise*, animation on *Samurai Jack*, and cinematography on *Carnivale*). And they write acclaimed books (in addition to NFT); celebrated scribblers Joe Meno, Don DeGrazia, and Sam Weller all returned to Columbia's fi ction writing department as faculty. Other programs include photography, dance, theater, music, art and design, journalism, fashion design, poetry, education, and management for the arts, entertainment, and media. Columbia's campus is the bustling South Loop, and its colorful student body immerse themselves in the city.

## Tuition

Tuition for full-time undergrads is around $20,000. There's fees, books, art supplies, CTA passes, and obligatory museum visits, too. And have you heard about the Superdorm? There, you can live in the middle of the Loop with 1,680 of your closest friends. Hey, college is a perpetual slumber party.

## Culture

Columbia College is one of Chicago's most esteemed cultural arts presenters; more than 300,000 visitors attend Columbia events each year. The college brings the DanceAfrica Chicago Festival to the city every fall and hosts a regular slate of innovative dance performances throughout the year. The Museum of Contemporary Photography is one of two fully accredited photography museums in the United States. The Chicago Jazz Ensemble, directed by ethnomusicologist and esteemed session musician Dana Hall, also makes its home at Columbia. The Story Week Festival of Writers, held in the spring, is among Chicago's top literary draws. The college brings in authors, editors, agents, and publishers for a week of readings, panels, and special events, such as "Read-Like-a-Rockstar" night at the Metro. Spring also brings Fashion Columbia and the Manifest Urban Arts Festival, celebrating graduate achievements. The college's galleries and theaters feature the work of students alongside notable outside artists. The school's new Media Production Center (MPC), located at 1327 S Wabash, opened in early 2010. Designed by local architects Studio Gang, it's a 35,000 sq. ft. state-of-the-art facility—containing studios, labs and classrooms—which allows for cross-disciplinary collaboration unlike anywhere else in the U.S. at the college/university level.

- **Center for Book and Paper Arts**
  1104 S Wabash Ave, 2nd Fl
  312-369-6630
  www.colum.edu/book_and_paper

- **Museum of Contemporary Photography**
  600 S Michigan Ave
  312-663-5554
  www.mocp.org

- **A&D Gallery**
  619 S. Wabash Ave
  312-344-8687
  www.colum.edu/adgallery

- **Glass Curtain Gallery**
  1104 S Wabash Ave, 1st Fl
  312-369-6643

- **C33**
  33 E Congress Pkwy
  312-369-6856

- **Dance Center**
  1306 S Michigan Ave
  312-369-8300
  www.colum.edu/dance_center

- **Getz, Classic, and New Studio Theaters**
  72 E 11th St
  312-369-6126
  www.colum.edu/theater_center

- **Concert Hall**
  1014 S Michigan Ave
  312-369-6179

- **Center for Black Music Research**
  618 S Michigan Ave, 6th Fl
  312-369-7559
  www.colum.edu/cbmr

- **Media Production Center (MPC)**
  1327 S Wabash, 60605
  312-369-3314

## Department Contact Information

Undergraduate Admissions.....................................312-369-7130
Graduate Admissions..............................................312-369-7260
School of Fine and Performing Arts.....................312-369-8404
School of Media Arts..............................................312-369-8837
School of Liberal Arts and Sciences....................312-369-8211

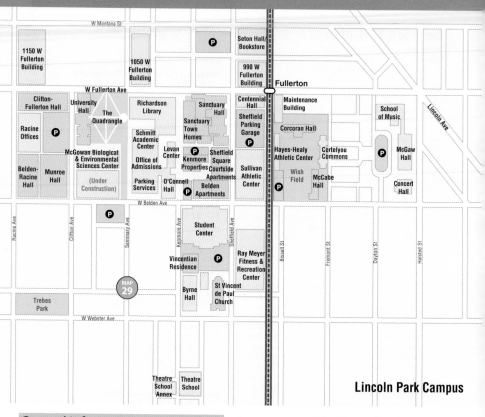

**Lincoln Park Campus**

## General Information

Lincoln Park Campus: Schmitt Academic Center
2320 N Kenmore Ave
Chicago, IL 60614-3298
Phone: 773-325-7000 x5700

Loop Campus: 1 E Jackson Blvd
Chicago, IL 60604
Phone: 312-362-8000

Website: www.depaul.edu

Suburban Campuses: University Center of Lake County
(Grayslake) 847-665-4000
Naperville: 312-476-4500/630-548-9378
Oak Forest: 312-476-3000/708-633-9091
O'Hare: 312-476-3600/847-296-5348

## Overview

Established in 1898 by the Vincentian Fathers as a school for immigrants, DePaul has become the country's largest Catholic university (with over 23,000 students) and the biggest private educational institution in Chicago, offering 150 undergraduate and graduate programs of study. According to The Princeton Review's recent survey of college students nationwide, DePaul students rated as some of the happiest college students in the country; it must be all the bars near campus on Halsted Street and Lincoln Avenue.

Of the university's seven campuses in the Chicago area, the Lincoln Park and Loop campuses serve as the core locations. The highly acclaimed Theatre School, College of Liberal Arts and Sciences, School of Music, and School of Education hold down the 36-acre Lincoln Park campus amidst renovated historic homes on tree-lined streets. Changes to the surrounding area at DePaul's northside location include: the venerable Red Lion Pub is now closed, and longtime neighbor to the east Children's Memorial Hospital moved much of its operation two miles south in Spring 2012.

DePaul's Loop Campus at Jackson Boulevard and State Street is where you'll find the College of Commerce, College of Law, and School of Computer Science, Telecommunications, and Information Systems. Nationally respected Kellstadt Graduate School of Business and DePaul's thriving continuing education program, the "School of New Learning," can also be found on the Loop Campus. The heart of the Loop campus is DePaul Center, located in the old Goldblatt Brothers Department Store, now grounded by a university-sanctioned Barnes and Noble. Most students in the Loop campus are adults, so popular hangouts include the Brown Line L, Red Line L, and Metra stations while they're all waiting for the train home. Prominent DePaul alumni include Chicago father-son mayors Richard M. Daley and his dad, the late Richard J. Daley; McDonald's Corporation's former CEO Jack Greenberg; Pulitzer Prize-winning composer George Perle; and actors Gillian Anderson and John C. Reilly.

## Tuition

Full-time undergraduates paid between $33,390 (the School of Education and the Colleges of Business, Communication, Computing and Digital Media, Science and Health, and Liberal Arts and Social Sciences) and $34,400 (the Theatre School and the School of Music) for tuition in the 2013-2014 school year. Graduate tuition varies by department, too, but really what counts is your bar tab when you're attending school with as many bars per capita as there are in this part of town. Your beer will cost more than your books come June.

## Sports

The DePaul Blue Demons might be named a bit oddly as the athletic ambassadors of the largest Catholic university in the United States, but their teams are strong despite any identity confusion. In basketball, the Blue Demons beat Kansas in a landmark battle. They made it to the National Invitation Tournament that year, but ultimately lost to Air Force in the last bracket. Lately, a few standout players have been tapped for the NBA.

For tickets, contact Ticketmaster (ticketmaster.com, 800-745-3000) or visit the ticket depot (depaulbluedemons.com, 773-325-7526, 2323 N Sheffield Ave). Look out for the twofer Tuesday deal. The Blue Demons play at McGrath Arena (women's basketball and volleyball, 2323 N Sheffield Ave), Allstate Arena (men's basketball, 6920 N Mannheim Rd, Rosemont, IL, 847-635-6601; allstatearena.com), and Wish Field and Cacciatore Stadium (men's and women's soccer and softball, respectively, both on the 900 block of Belden Ave).

DePaul's teams include men's and women's basketball, cross-country, soccer, tennis, and track and field, men's golf, and women's softball and volleyball.

## Culture on Campus

DePaul's vibrant Theatre School is the oldest of its kind in the Midwest. Founded in 1925 as the Goodman School of Drama, the school stages over 200 performances during its Showcase, Chicago Playworks, New Directors Series, and School Workshop seasons. The Theatre School Showcase performs contemporary and classic plays at its 1,325-seat Merle Reskin Theatre, a French Renaissance–style theater built in 1910 and located at 60 E Balbo Drive in the South Loop. The Chicago Playworks for Families and Young Audiences and the School of Music's annual opera are also performed at the Merle Reskin Theatre. For tickets ($8–$12), directions, and parking garage locations, call 312-922-1999 or go to theatreschool.depaul.edu. Take the Red Line to the Harrison Street or Jackson Street stops just southwest of the theater. CTA buses 29, 36, 151, and 146 also stop nearby. Check the Theatre School website for New Directors Series and School Workshop productions, theater locations, and ticket prices.

Loop Campus

DePaul's new and expanded Art Museum (DPAM), located at 935 W Fullerton, is open everyday and offers free admission to all visitors. Permanent collections of sculpture and oil paintings from local and international artists adorn the galleries. A pay parking lot is located one block east of the library on N Sheffield Avenue. DePaul's John T. Richardson Library and Loop campus library in DePaul Center are open to the public year-round. Take plenty of change for the copy machines as check-out privileges are reserved for students and faculty.

## Department Contact Information

Lincoln Park Campus Admissions Office...........773-325-7500
Loop Campus Admissions Office..........................312-362-8300
College of Commerce ............................................... 312-362-6783
College of Law.........................................................312-325-8701
Undergraduate College of Arts & Sciences ...... 773-325-7310
Graduate College of Arts & Sciences ...................773-325-7315
John T Richardson Library ................................... 773-325-7862
Kellstadt Graduate School of Business ..............312-362-8000
Loop Campus Library ...........................................312-362-8433
School for New Learning ....................................... 312-362-8001
School of Computer Science, Telecommunications
  and Information Systems ................................... 312-362-8381
School of Music...................................................773-325-7260
Theatre School..................................................773-325-7917

# Illinois Institute of Technology

## General Information

| | |
|---|---|
| NFT Map: | 13, 14 |
| Main Campus: | 3300 S Federal St |
| | Chicago, IL 60616 |
| Phone: | 312-567-3000 |
| Website: | www.iit.edu |

## Overview

In the 19th century, when higher education was reserved for society's upper crust, meat magnate Philip Danforth Armour put his money to good use and funded an institution dedicated to students who wished to learn a variety of industrial arts. The Armour Institute carried his name until a merger with the engineering school Lewis Institute in 1940 changed the name to Illinois Institute of Technology. Over the next 40 years, the college continued to merge with other small technical colleges, resulting in the IIT we know today. The school is notable for its Mies Van Der Rohe–designed campus (although it is arguably not his best work) as for its groundbreaking work in aeronautics research. The new student center, designed by Dutch architect Rem Koolhaas, includes a space-aged metallic tube through which the local L train travels.

Chicago-Kent College of Law, Stuart School Graduate School of Business, and the Institute of Design are based in the Loop. The Rice campus, in west suburban Wheaton, offers undergraduate continuing education and degree programs to working professionals. The National Center for Food Safety and Technology, located in the southwest suburbs, and the IIT Research Institute, housed in IIT's tallest building on its main campus in Bronzeville, are just two of the many research organizations IIT has incorporated since 1936 to serve various needs of private industry and government. IIT grants PhDs and other professional degrees in a vast array of areas including science, mathematics, engineering, architecture, psychology, design, business, and law. The interprofessional, technology-focused curriculum is designed to prepare the 8,000 students to become groundbreakers in an increasingly complex global workplace. IIT was recently named a "College of Distinction" by a new college guide honoring some of America's top educational institutions.

In June 2004, IIT's Research Institute Life Sciences Group was awarded $28 million in research funding. The prestigious award is among the largest ever received by IITRI for drug development.

## Tuition

Undergrads pay around $39,000 per academic year plus room and board, $1,000 to $1,500 for books, and $1,600 for fees including a CTA pass. Graduate, law and business school tuition varies by program.

## Sports

IIT's Scarlet Hawks compete in the NAIA Division I Chicagoland Collegiate Athletic Conference. Sports may be a bit drab here, as IIT aborted both men's and women's basketball in 2009, but its men's and women's soccer, swimming and diving, cross-country, men's baseball, and women's volleyball are safe for now.

## Developments on Campus

The State Street Village student residence, completed in 2003, continues to be a popular home base for IIT denizens. Located at State and 33rd Streets, the hall was designed by well-known Chicago-based architect Helmut Jahn. The German-born designer was named one of the Ten Most Influential Living American Architects by the American Institute of Architects (AIA) in 1991. Jahn, a graduate of IIT himself, created the six-building complex across the street from Van Der Rohe's historical landmark, the S.R. Crown Hall. Jahn's new building brings student housing to a new level with poured-in-place concrete and glass-clad and corrugated stainless steel panels that reduce noise and vibrations from passing trains while simultaneously exhibiting a cutting-edge aesthetic. More recently, IIT's $50 million University Technology Park development initiative opened its 33,000 sq. ft. Incubator—featuring wet and dry labs, conference/office space, as well as other amenities—within its larger Technology Business Center building to start-up and established tech research companies and firms alike.

## Department Contact Information

| | |
|---|---|
| Undergraduate Admissions | 312-567-3025 |
| Graduate Admissions | 312-567-3020 |
| Alumni Office | 312-567-5040 |
| Armour College of Engineering | 312-567-3009 |
| Center for Law and Financial Markets | 312-906-6576 |
| Center for Professional Development | 630-682-6040 |
| Chicago-Kent College of Law | 312-906-5000 |
| College of Architecture | 312-567-3263 |
| College of Science & Letters | 312-567-3800 |
| Keating Sports Center | 312-567-3000 |
| Institute of Business and Interprofessional Studies | 312-567-3947 |
| Institute of Design | 312-595-4900 |
| Institute of Psychology | 312-567-3500 |
| Stuart Graduate School of Business | 312-906-6500 |
| University Technology Park | 312-567-3900 |

# Loyola University (Lake Shore Campus)

## General Information

| | |
|---|---|
| Lake Shore: | 6525 N Sheridan Rd |
| | Chicago, IL 60626 |
| Phone: | 773-274-3000 |
| Water Tower/Lewis | 820 N Michigan Ave |
| Towers Campus: | Chicago 60611 |
| Phone: | 312-915-6000 |
| Medical Center: | 2160 S First Ave |
| | Maywood, IL 60153 |
| Phone: | 708-216-9000 |
| Website: | www.luc.edu |

## Overview

Loyola University, one of the largest Jesuit universities in the United States, is known throughout the Midwest for its first-rate schools of business and law, as well as for its Medical Center (a well-respected research institution). It was originally established in 1870 as St. Ignatius College and was re-named in 1909. Approximately 15,000 students attend the university.

Lake Shore Campus, the largest campus of Loyola's four campuses, is on the lake in Rogers Park and houses the College of Arts & Sciences, the Graduate School, Niehoff School of Nursing, Mundelein College Adult Education Program, and Cudahy Library. The university's Water Tower campus downtown on Michigan Avenue is home to the Schools of Business, Education, Law, and Social Work and some College of Arts & Sciences courses. Loyola operates the Stritch School of Medicine and the Master's degree programs through the Niehoff School of Nursing at its suburban Maywood campus. The university also has a campus in Rome, one of the largest American campuses in Western Europe. Notable graduates include Sho Yano, who ranks first in the world with the highest known I.Q. Other notable grads include pro sports team (Chicago Bears) owner George S. Halas Jr., actor/comedian Bob Newhart, and celebrated authors Sandra Cisneros and Stuart Dybek.

Loyola now participates in study abroad opportunities in China at the Beijing Center located on the campus of Beijing University (semester, year and summer programs are available to qualified undergraduates).

## Tuition

In the 2013–2014 academic year, undergraduate tuition cost $35,500 (give or take a couple hundred dollars depending on the program of study), including most added fees. First-year room and board prices in 2012–2013 ranged from $11,700 to $16,170 with an on-campus residence requirement for all freshmen. Sophomore, upperclass and graduate students' tuition, housing, fees and expenses vary by college and living arrangement. It can be a slap in the bank account, but both the Jesuits and U.S. News & World Report seem to like it, for what that's worth.

## Sports

Represented by their mascot the LU Wolf, the Loyola Ramblers compete in the Horizon League of the NCAA Division I. Their league's title may allude to their faded glory, as the Ramblers haven't made it any championships since, uh, the 1980s. The stalwart who feel secure in the Ramblers chances this millennium should catch them at the Joseph J. Gentile Center on the Lake Shore Campus. For tickets, visit the box office, call 773-508-WOLF or visit loyolaramblers.com.

Loyola rambles in many varsity sports: men's and women's basketball, cross-country, golf, soccer, track and field, and volleyball and women's softball.

## Culture on Campus

Since its opening in 2005, the Loyola University Museum of Art (LUMA) continues to showcase the famous Martin D'Arcy collection of Medieval, Renaissance and Baroque art. Paintings by masters Tintoretto, Guercino, Bassano, and Stomer, plus sculpture, furniture, jewelry, decorative arts, and liturgical vessels, are part of the over 500-piece collection dating from 1150 to 1750. The museum, located at 820 N Michigan Avenue, is free on Tuesdays. Suggested general admission is $8, $6 for seniors and $2 for non-Loyola students under age 25. Hours: Tues: 11 am–8 pm; Wed–Sun: 11 am–6 pm. For more information, call 312-915-7600.

The university's Cudahy Library, Lewis Library at the Water Tower Campus, Science Library, Health Sciences Library, and Graduate Business School Library are all open to the public. Checkout privileges, however, are reserved for the university's students and faculty.

The Loyola University Theatre performs four classic dramas per year at the Kathleen Mullady Theatre (1125 W Loyola Ave, 773-508-3847) in the Centennial Forum/Mertz Hall building on the Lake Shore campus. A second studio stage is active with student productions during the fall and spring term, and a number of Loyola arts alumni events take place every year on campus.

The Loyola Campus also offers a variety of media options for its students. Inside Loyola, Loyola Magazine and The Phoenix are available for readers, while WLUW exists for those students overwhelmed by textbooks, NFT Guides, or the newest issue of Jesuit Life International.

## Department Contact Information

| | |
|---|---|
| Undergraduate Admissions | 773-915-6500 |
| School of Continuing and Professional Studies | 312-915-6501 |
| College of Arts & Sciences | 773-508-3500 |
| School of Business Administration | 312-915-6112 |
| School of Education | 312-916-6800 |
| School of Law | 312-915-7120 |
| Stritch School of Medicine | 708-216-3229 |
| Niehoff School of Nursing | 773-508-3249 |
| Rome Center of Liberal Arts | 800-344-7662 |
| School of Social Work | 312-915-7005 |
| Graduate School of Business | 312-915-6124 |
| The Graduate School | 773-508-3396 |
| University Libraries | 773-508-2658 |

# Northwestern University (Evanston Campus)

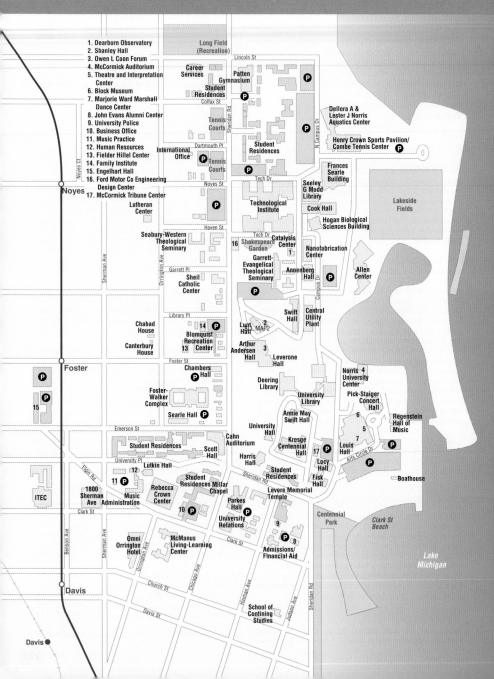

1. Dearborn Observatory
2. Shanley Hall
3. Owen L Coon Forum
4. McCormick Auditorium
5. Theatre and Interpretation Center
6. Block Museum
7. Marjorie Ward Marshall Dance Center
8. John Evans Alumni Center
9. University Police
10. Business Office
11. Music Practice
12. Human Resources
13. Fielder Hillel Center
14. Family Institute
15. Engelhart Hall
16. Ford Motor Co Engineering Design Center
17. McCormick Tribune Center

Long Field (Recreation)
Lincoln St
Career Services
Patten Gymnasium
Student Residences
Colfax St
Dellora A & Lester J Norris Aquatics Center
Tennis Courts
Sheridan Rd
N Campus Dr
Henry Crown Sports Pavilion/ Combe Tennis Center
Dartmouth Pl
International Office
Tennis Courts
Student Residences
Noyes Ct
Noyes
Noyes St
Tech Dr
Frances Searle Building
Seeley G Mudd Library
Lakeside Fields
Lutheran Center
Technological Institute
Cook Hall
Hogan Biological Sciences Building
Haven St
Tech Dr
Catalysis Center
Nanofabrication Center
Sherman Ave
Seabury-Western Theological Seminary
Shakespeare Garden
Garrett-Evangelical Theological Seminary
Annenberg Hall
Allen Center
Orrington Ave
Garrett Pl
Sheil Catholic Center
Swift Hall
Central Utility Plant
Library Pl
Chabad House
Blomquist Recreation Center
Lunt Hall
MAP2
Canterbury House
Arthur Andersen Hall
Leverone Hall
Foster St
Chambers Hall
Deering Library
Norris University Center
Foster
Foster-Walker Complex
University Library
Pick-Staiger Concert Hall
Regenstein Hall of Music
Emerson St
Searle Hall
University Hall
Annie May Swift Hall
Louis Hall
Cahn Auditorium
Student Residences
Scott Hall
Kresge Centennial Hall
Locy Hall
Boathouse
University Pl
Lutkin Hall
Harris Hall
Fisk Hall
Elgin Rd
Music Administration
Student Residences
Millar Chapel
Student Residences
Levere Memorial Temple
1800 Sherman Ave
Rebecca Crown Center
Parkes Hall
ITEC
Clark St
University Relations
Centennial Park
Clark St Beach
Omni Orrington Hotel
McManus Living-Learning Center
Admissions/ Financial Aid
Lake Michigan
Benson Ave
Church St
Chicago Ave
Clark St
Human Ave
Judson Ave
Sheridan Rd
Davis
Davis St
School of Continuing Studies
Davis

## General Information

Evanston Campus:   633 Clark St
                   Evanston, IL 60208
                   Phone: 847-491-3741
Chicago Campus:    Abbot Hall
                   710 N Lake Shore Dr
                   Chicago, IL 60611
                   Phone: 312-503-8649
Website:           www.northwestern.edu

## Overview

Northwestern University, along with the University of Chicago, likes to think of itself as part of the "Ivy League of the Midwest." While this might seem a lofty moniker, the University is certainly the cream of the crop in the Big Ten Conference. Almost 20,000 full- and part-time students attend Northwestern's 11 schools, located in Evanston and downtown Chicago, a far cry from the 2 original faculty members and 10 students in attendance when the school opened in 1855. NU's newest campus—located in Doha, Qatar—mainly offers communication, media and journalism courses, but is quickly growing to encompass other liberal arts majors. The University's name was derived from its founders' desire to service the citizens of the former Northwest Territory.

Founded in 1851, Northwestern University was established in Evanston by many of the same Methodist founding fathers of the town itself, including the founder of Chicago's Board of Trade. The 240-acre lakefront campus is bordered roughly by Lincoln Street to the north and extends south to Clark Street and west to Sheridan Road. The Evanston campus houses the Weinberg College of Arts and Sciences; McCormick School of Engineering and Applied Science; the Schools of Music, Communication, Education and Social Policy; the Graduate School; Medill School of Journalism; and J.L. Kellogg School of Management.

The university did a bit of branching out when it purchased land for the Chicago campus in 1920. Located on a 25-acre lot between the lake and Michigan Avenue in the Streeterville neighborhood, the Chicago campus houses the Schools of Law, Medicine, and Continuing Studies. Graduate school and Kellogg courses are also offered at the Chicago campus. Several excellent hospitals and medical research institutions affiliated with the university dominate the northern edge of Streeterville. The Robert H. Lurie Medical Research Center at Fairbanks Court and Superior Street, completed in 2004, has expanded the university's research abilities with nine floors of laboratory space. The Prentice Women's Hospital, completed in 2007, continues to offer comprehensive and innovative treatments bolstering women's and infants' health.

## Tuition

The university charges around $45,000 for undergrad tuition only. Room and board rates hover around $15,000 for an undergraduate student living in a double room and on a 14-meal-per-week plan. (Approximately half of Northwestern's undergraduate students live in University residence halls.) (Approximately 4,000 of Northwestern's 8,100 undergraduate students live in University residence halls.) Graduate school tuition and fees vary by college.

## Sports

The only private school in the Big Ten conference, Northwestern trains eight men's and eleven women's intercollegiate teams along with a host of club teams. The women's lacrosse team won the NCAA national championship for each of the five years ending in 2009, a year when it also went undefeated. The Wildcats' football fortune is slowly looking up, as the purple-clad boys broke a 33-year losing streak in 2004.

The Wildcats' home is Ryan Field at 1501 Central Avenue, about three blocks west of the Central stop on the elevated Purple Line of the CTA. Basketball games are held at the Welsh-Ryan Arena behind the stadium. For tickets, call 847-491-2287. All sporting events are listed at www.nusports.com, where you can also purchase tickets online. Northwestern students can also obtain free tickets to any home game with the presentation of their Wildcard ID.

Northwestern also has men's wrestling and baseball teams, plus men's basketball and women's basketball, golf, soccer, tennis, and swimming and diving teams. Wildcat women also complete in cross-country, fencing, softball, field hockey, and volleyball.

## Culture on Campus

The Mary and Leigh Block Museum of Art on the Evanston campus (40 Arts Circle Dr; 847-491-4000; www.blockmuseum. northwestern.edu) has 4,000 items in its permanent collection, including Old Masters' prints, architectural drawings, contemporary photographic images, and modern sculpture. The Block is also home to the state-of-the-art Pick-Laudati Auditorium that hosts film festivals and contemporary classics, as well as different cinema series' and lectures throughout the year. Hours: Tues: 10 am to 5 pm; Wed–Fri: 10 am to 8 pm; weekends: 10 am to 5 pm. Admission is always free. A $5 suggested donation is appreciated.

The Pick-Staiger Concert Hall (50 Arts Circle Dr, 847-491-5441; www.pickstaiger.com), is not only the main stage for the university's musical performances, but it is also home to several professional performance organizations such as the Chicago Chamber Musicians, Symphony of the Shores, Chicago String Ensemble, Performing Arts Chicago, and others. Each year, Pick-Staiger Concert Hall also hosts the Segovia Classical Guitar Series and the Keyboard Conversations Series. Call 847-467-4000 to purchase tickets.

A & O Productions (a student-led and –funded group) continue their longstanding tradition of bringing popular comedy and music acts (Lupe Fiasco, Tracy Morgan) as well as award-winning films ('The Artist') to campus. Also, Northwestern recently hosted TEDx events on the topics of Identity (2010) and Fertility (2012). More information on these symposia can be found at http://www.tedx.northwestern.edu.

For the upper echelon student interested in art or vandalism, one can visit the famed "Rock" that students began defacing in the 1940s. "Go Cats!," "Rich Kids Can Tag As Well!" and "I'm wasting my parent's money!" have all made brief appearances.

Northwestern University also runs a student newspaper, The Daily Northwestern, and a student radio station, WNUR.

## Department Contact Information

| | |
|---|---|
| Undergraduate Admissions | 847-491-7271 |
| Graduate School (Evanston) | 847-491-5279 |
| Graduate School (Chicago) | 312-503-8900 |
| Weinberg College of Arts and Sciences | 847-491-7561 |
| Feinberg School of Medicine | 312-503-8649 |
| Kellogg School of Management | 847-491-3300 |
| Medill School of Journalism | 847-467-1882 |
| School of Communication | 847-491-7023 |
| School of Continuing Studies (Evanston) | 847-491-5611 |
| School of Education and Social Policy | 847-491-8193 |
| McCormick School of Engineering and Applied Science | 847-491-5220 |
| School of Law | 312-503-3100 |
| School of Music | 847-491-7575 |

1. Laboratory for Astrophysics and Space Research
2. Astronomy and Astrophysics Center
3. Research Institutes
4. Biopsychological Research Center
5. Disciples Divinity House
6. Kovler Viral Oncology Laboratories
7. Ingleside Hall
8. Searle Chemical Laboratory
9. Jones Laboratory
10. Zoology
11. Hutchinson Commons
12. Reynolds Club
13. Statistics and Mathematics
14. Development Office- 5733 S University
15. Calvert House
16. Student Counseling and Resource Service
17. Human Development
18. Development Office- 5736 S Woodlawn
19. Nursery School- 5740 S Woodlawn
20. Nursery School- 5750 S Woodlawn
21. Abbott Memorial Hall
22. Goldblatt Pavillion
23. Armour Clincial Research
24. Goldblatt Memorial Building
25. McElwee Building
26. Gates-Blake Hall
27. Goodspeed Hall
28. Wieboldt Hall
29. Harper Memorial Library
30. Beecher Hall
31. Green Hall
32. Kelly Hall
33. Foster Hall
34. University High School
35. Orthogenic School
36. D'Angelo Law Library
37. Kane Center for Clinical Legal Education

MAP 19

## General Information

| | |
|---|---|
| NFT Map: | 19 |
| Mailing Address: | University of Chicago |
| | Administration Building |
| | 5801 S Ellis Ave |
| | Chicago, IL 60637 |
| Phone: | 773-702-1234 |
| Website: | www.uchicago.edu |
| Visitor's Center: | Ida Noyes Hall, 1st Fl |
| | 1212 E 59th St |
| Phone: | 773-702-8650 |
| Guest Parking: | Lot located off Woodlawn Ave |
| | b/w 58th St and 59th St Metered |
| | parking is available north of Ida Noyes Hall. |

## Overview

Located amidst the pleasant tree-lined streets of Hyde Park just seven miles south of downtown Chicago, the 16,000 student University of Chicago is a world-renowned research institution with a winning tradition in Nobel prizes. Eighty-seven Nobel laureates have been associated with the university as faculty, students or researchers. The university prides itself on its rigorous academic standards and top-ranked programs, while its students thrive in an environment that encourages creative exploring, taking risks, intellectual rigor, and determining the direction and focus of one's own education.

While its business, law, and medical schools are renowned for cranking out brainy gurus with assembly line efficiency, the university also has a long alumni list filled with artists, writers, politicians, film directors, and actors. To name a few: Studs Terkel, Sara Paretsky, Carol Moseley-Braun, Kurt Vonnegut, Susan Sontag, David Auburn, Ed Asner, Saul Bellow, Katharine Graham, Philip Glass, Saul Alinsky, Paul Goodman, Mike Nichols, and Second City improv theater founders Bernard Sahlins and Paul Sills.

Established in 1890, the University of Chicago was founded and funded by John D. Rockefeller. Built on 200 acres donated by Marshall Field and designed by architect Henry Ives Cobb, the university's English Gothic buildings of ivy-clad limestone ooze old money and intellectual achievements. Rockefeller described the university as "the best investment I ever made." We just hope parents footing the bill for their kids' education feel the same

## Tuition

The University of Chicago operates on a trimester schedule rather than the more common two-semester academic year. An undergraduate student pays about $43,500 for tuition fees with an additional 13,137 for room and board. So if you add up all the books costs, lab fees, personal expenses…carry the one…that comes to around fifty-five grand a year. Costs for graduate students vary based on the school. Chicago has about 15,000 students, 5,000 of which are undergraduates. About 2,000 of the graduate students attend classes at the downtown riverfront campus Gleacher Center (450 N City/Front Plaza Dr, 312-464-8787; www.gleachercenter.com), where the popular Graham School of General Studies holds most of its continuing education classes.

## Sports

A long time ago, the famous nickname "Monsters of The Midway" belonged to The University of Chicago's football team (not 'da Bears'), and the institution garnered football trophies right along with Nobel Prizes. The Maroons racked up seven Big Ten Football championships between 1899 and 1924, but the gridiron glory of yore faded and losing teams became the norm. The bleachers at Stagg field, where fans once flocked to witness athletic triumphs, earned more fame as the site where Enrico Fermi and university scientists split the atom on Dec. 2, 1942. Four years later, President Robert Maynard Hutchins put in the university's walking papers from the Big Ten and abolished the football team. Perhaps this was a step towards prioritizing scholarly pursuits over athletic achievement, however the catastrophic results of the "controlled release of nuclear energy" might be to blame.
But the school hasn't totally abandoned sports. Varsity football,

reinstated in 1969, is back, albeit in a different form. UChicago is a member of the NCAA Division III UAA (University Athletic Association) and hosts 19 varsity athletic sports in a conference comprised of some of the nation's leading research institutions, and since 1990 has won team championships in men's basketball, women's cross country, football, men's and women's soccer, softball, men's indoor track & field, and wrestling. The campus also boasts over 45 club sports and hundreds of intramural teams.

## Culture on Campus

The Reva and David Logan Center for the Arts is a new multidisciplinary arts center at the University of Chicago opened in 2012. The 184,000 square foot building integrates a dynamic mix of spaces to create a rich environment for arts and scholarship for the university, the South Side and greater Chicago. Visit logan.uchicago.edu for the calendar of events.

Located at 5757 S. Woodlawn Avenue is Frank Lloyd Wright's residential ode to all things horizontal and structurally organic: The Robie House 708-848-1976; www.gowright.org). This Prairie Style masterpiece is considered one of the most important buildings in the history of American architecture and with the exterior restoration phase recently completed on the $8-million dollar renovation, it once again appears fresh off the proverbial drafting board. Adult tickets cost $15, students (4-17) and seniors pay $12. If you want to adopt an art glass cabinet for restoration, its $20,000.

Two must-see but often overlooked free museums on campus are the Oriental Institute Museum (1155 E. 58th St., 773-702-9514; www.oi.uchicago.edu) and the Smart Museum of Art 5550 S. Greenwood Ave., 773-702-0200; www.smartmuseum.uchicago.edu. Showcasing ancient treasures from university digs since the 1900s (and yes, Indiana Jones did his undergraduate studies at U of C), the Oriental Institute houses permanent galleries devoted to ancient Egypt, Nubia, Persia, Mesopotamia, Syria, Anatolia, the ancient site of Megiddo, along with a rotation of special exhibits. The Smart Museum boasts a permanent collection of 10,000 fine art objects spanning five millennia of both Western and Eastern civilizations—so yes, it'll be enough to look at for that afternoon you have to kill.

To satisfy your inner cineaste, take in a picture show at Doc Films (Max Palevsky Cinema 1212 E 59th St., 773-702-8575; www.docfilms.uchicago.edu), the largest continuously running student film society in the nation. The screenings at their state-of-the-art theater range from foreign art house fare to documentaries to Hollywood classics, and feature companion lectures and Q&A with professors, actors, directors, and producers. If you're jonesing for a music fix, University of Chicago Presents is one of the city's landmark classical music presenters and features a variety of performers in the elegant, Victorian-style Mandel Hall.

The university's Equity playhouse Court Theater continues its national reputation of staging critically-acclaimed contemporary and classical productions by renowned playwrights (5535 S Ellis Ave, 773-753-4472); www.courttheatre.org).

## Department Contact Information

Log on to www.uchicago.edu/uchi/directories for a university directory and links to division and department web pages.

| | |
|---|---|
| Undergraduate Student Admissions | 773-702-8650 |
| Biological Sciences | 773-702-9000 |
| Humanities | 773-702-8512 |
| Physical Sciences | 773-702-7950 |
| Social Sciences | 773-702-8799 |
| Divinity School | 773-702-8200 |
| Graduate School of Business | 773-702-7743 |
| Graduate Affairs | 773-702-7813 |
| Graham School of General Studies | 773-702-1722 |
| Harris Graduate School of Public Policy Studies | 773-702-8401 |
| Law School | 773-702-9494 |
| Pritzker School of Medicine | 773-702-1939 |
| School of Social Service Administration | 773-702-1250 |

# University of Illinois at Chicago

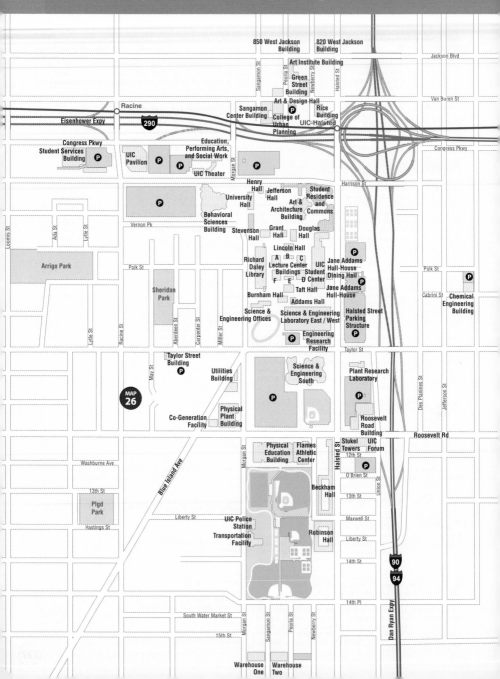

## General Information

| | |
|---|---|
| NFT Map: | 26 |
| Address: | 1200 W Harrison St |
| | Chicago, IL 60680 |
| Phone: | 312-996-7000 |
| Website: | www.uic.edu |

## Overview

With over 27,000 students, the University of Illinois at Chicago (UIC) is the largest university in the city. Located on the Near West Side, UIC is ethnically diverse and urban to the core. It is a leading public research university and home to the nation's largest medical school.

Its legacy as a builder in Chicago, however, is a bit spotty. In the mid-1960s, the school leveled most of what was left of a vibrant Italian-American neighborhood to build its campus next to the Eisenhower Expressway. Today, UIC continues to consume city blocks south of Roosevelt Road in further developing the South Campus. The expansions have all but erased the colorful, landmark Maxwell Street flea market area (this bustling mess of market now takes place only on Sundays along nearby S Canal Street). Of course, not eveyone is crying over the loss of the eyesore market or the decrepit, crumbling buildings and homes that comprised the area, although we question whether a community of pricey cookie-cutter townhomes really constitutes much of an improvement. One thing that everyone seems to agree on is that many of the campus's original, ugly cement slab structures are kissing the wrecking ball as well. Even with the multi-million-dollar improvements, the campus is still fairly average; unless you're going to class or the doctor, a lone trip to UIC to see the Jane Addams Hull-House Museum is sufficient.

## Tuition

An Illinois resident undergraduate student's total tuition and fees ranged from approximately $14,000 for nursing to $11,000 (for most other programs; room and board for a shared dorm ranged from $12,600 to $14,200 depending on the meal plan. These fi gures do not include books, supplies, lab fees, or personal expenses. Primarily a commuter institution, UIC has about 17,000 undergraduates; graduate and professional enrollment varies by department.

## Sports

The UIC Flames are hot these days. The men's basketball team competed in the NCAA tournament in 2004, 2002 and 1998. Additionally, the Flames women's gymnastics, tennis squad, and softball teams have all advanced to NCAA Tournament play in recent years. Other Flames men's and women's teams include swimming & diving and cross-country/track & field. UIC also has men's tennis, gymnastics, baseball, and soccer, as well as women's basketball and volleyball. Basketball games and women's volleyball matches are played at the recently renovated UIC Pavilion at the corner of S Racine Avenue and Harrison Street. For tickets, call 312-413-8421, or visit www.uicflames.com.

Too bad the NCAA doesn't have a bowling tournament because UIC would be a strong contender. The campus has its own alley located at 750 S Halsted Street (312-413-5170) where the public is welcome to sling balls and swig beers with students.

## Culture on Campus

Jane Addams Hull-House (800 S Halsted St, 312-413-5353; www.uic.edu/jaddams/hull), America's first settlement house, opened in 1889. The free museum documents the pioneering organization's social welfare programs that supported the community's destitute immigrant workers. Jane Addams was cool. Way cool. Museum hours are 10 am to 4 pm Tuesday through Friday and noon to 4 pm on Sunday, closed on Mondays and Saturdays.

## Department Contact Information

*All area codes are 312 unless otherwise noted.*

| | |
|---|---|
| Admissions and Records | 996-4350 |
| Graduate College | 413-2550 |
| College of Architecture & the Arts | 996-5611 |
| College of Applied Health Sciences | 996-6695 |
| College of Dentistry | 996-1020 |
| College of Business Administration | 996-2700 |
| College of Education | 996-5641 |
| College of Engineering | 996-2400 |
| College of Liberal Arts and Sciences | 413-2500 |
| College of Medicine | 996-3500 |
| College of Nursing | 996-7800 |
| College of Pharmacy | 996-7240 |
| School of Public Health | 996-6620 |
| College of Social Work | 996-7096 |
| College of Urban Planning and Public Affairs | 413-8088 |
| Office of Continuing Education | 996-8025 |
| University of Illinois Medical Center | 800-842-1002 |

## Continuing Education in Chicago

Whether you want to change careers or just your waistline, learn a foreign language or learn more about the one you already know, Chicago is a great city to channel your inner student.

Get to the point of the matter with fencing classes from Midwest Fencing Academy. Turn off the Food Network, and learn to do it yourself at Kendall College, The French Pastry School, or The Chopping Block. Learn to put your foot down with style at the Flamenco Arts Center. Find out why laughter truly is the best medicine at The Second City Training Center or Comedy Sportz. Run away and join the circus after trapeze classes from Trapeze School Chicago. And discover that you really can teach an old dog new tricks at AnimalSense.

## Continuing Education And Professional Development

**Adler School of Professional Psychology**, www.adler.edu, 312-662-4000, 17 N Dearborn St, 60602

**City Colleges of Chicago** (various locations), www.ccc.edu, 773-263-5343

**Cortiva Institute** (massage therapy), www.cortiva.com, 312-253-3313, 17 N State, Ste 500, 60602

**The French Pastry School**, www.frenchpastryschool.com, 312-726-2419, 226 W Jackson Blvd, 60606

**John Marshall Law School**, www.jmls.edu, 312-427-2737, 317 S Plymouth Ct, 60604

**Kendall College**, www.kendall.edu, 866-667-3344, 900 N Branch St, 60622

**Pacific College of Oriental Medicine**, www.pacificcollege.edu, 888-729-4811, 65 E Wacker Pl, 21st Flr, 60601

**Roosevelt University**, www.roosevelt.edu, 312-341-3500, 430 S Michigan Ave, 60605

**School of the Art Institute of Chicago**, www.saic.edu, 312-629-6100, 37 S Wabash, 7th Fl, 60603

**School of Continuing Studies at Northwestern University**, www.scs.northwestern.edu, 312-503-6950, 399 E Chicago Ave, 60611

**Spertus College** (Jewish culture), www.spertus.edu, 312-322-1700, 610 S Michigan Ave, 60605

**Tribeca Flashpoint Media Arts Academy**, www.tfa.edu, 312-332-0707, 28 N Clark St, Ste 500, 60602

## A Little Bit Of Everything

**AnimalSense**, www.animalsense.com, 312-564-4570, various locations.

**The Discovery Center**, www.discoverycenter.cc, 773-348-8120, 2855 N Lincoln Ave, 60657

**The Feltre School** (English grammar, writing , public speaking), www.feltre.org, 312-255-1133, 22 W Erie St, 60610

**Kayak Chicago**, www.kayakchicago.com, 312-852-9258, 1220 W LeMoyne Ave, 60622

**Motorcycle Riding School**, www.motorcyclelearning.com, 773-968-7433, 1400 N Halsted St, 60622

**Ride Chicago Motorcycle School**, www.ride-chicago.com, 773-878-7433, 5215 N Ravenswood Ave, 60640

**StoryStudio Chicago**, www.storystudiochicago.com, 773-477-7710, 4043 N Ravenswood, Ste 222, 60613

**Writers The Loft**, www.thewritersloft.com, 773-348-4116, 1450 W Waveland Ave, 60613

## Arts And Lifestyle

**Act One Studios, www.actone.com**, 312-787-9384, 640 N LaSalle St, Ste 535, 60610

**Annoyance Theatre** (comedy improv classes), www.annoyanceproductions.com, 773-561-4664, 4830 N Broadway, 60640

**Chicago Dramatists**, www.chicagodramatists.org, 312-633-0630, 1105 W Chicago Ave, 60642

**Comedy Sportz**, www.comedysportzchicago.com, 773-549-8080, 929 W Belmont Ave, 60657

**Fire Arts Center of Chicago**, www.firearts.org, 773-544-9908, 1800 W Cornelia Ave, 60657

**Lillstreet Art Center**, www.lillstreet.com, 773-769-4226, 4401 N Ravenswood Ave, 60640

**Old Town School of Folk Music**, www.oldtownschool.org, 773-728-6000, 4544 N Lincoln Ave, 60625

**Palette & Chisel Academy of Fine Art**, www.paletteandchisel.org, 312-642-4400, 1012 N Dearborn, 60610

**The Second City Training Center**, www.secondcity.com, 312-664-3959, 1608 N Wells St, 60614

**WoodSmyth's** (woodworking classes), www.woodsmythschicago.com, 773-477-6482, 1835 W School St, 60657

## Athletics And Dance

**8 Count Boxing Gym**, www.8countboxinggym.com, 312-226-5800, 410 N Oakley Blvd, 2nd Flr, 60612

**All About Dance**, www.allaboutdance.org, 773-572-8701, 501 W North Ave, 60610

**Chicago Sailing Club**, www.chicagosailing.com, 773-871-7245, 2712 N Campbell Ave, 60647

**Degerberg Academy Martial Arts**, www.degerbergacademy.com, 773-728-5300, 4717 N Lincoln Ave, 60625

**Flamenco Arts Center**, www.flamencoartscenter.com, 773-868-4130, 3755 N Western Ave, 60618

**The Flying Gaonas**, www.flyinggaonastrapeze.com, 773-398-9881.

**Latin Street Dancing**, www.laboriqua.com, 312-427-2572, 1335 W Lake St, Ste 103, 60607

**Midwest Fencing Academy**, www.midwestfencingacademy.com, 773-895-0055, 6100 N Cicero Ave, 60646

**The School of Ballet Chicago**, www.balletchicago.org, 312-251-8838, 17 N State St, 19th Flr, 60602

**Thousand Waves** (martial arts), www.thousandwaves.org, 773-472-7663, 1220 W Belmont, 60657

**Together We Tri** (triathalon training), www.togetherwetri.com, 866-889-3874

**Trapeze School Chicago**, www.chicago.trapezeschool.com, 773-484-8861, various locations

## Food And Wine

**BIN 36**, www.bin36.com, 312-755-9463, 339 N Dearborn, 60610

**Calphalon Culinary Center**, www.calphalonculinarycenter.com, 312-529-0100, 1000 W Washington St, 60607

**City Winery**, www.citywinery.com/chicago, 312-733-9463, 1200 W Randolph St, 60607

**Chicago Wine School**, www.wineschool.com, 773-565-4363, 911 W 31st St, 60608

**The Chopping Block**, www.thechoppingblock.net, 773-472-6700, 4747 N Lincoln Ave; 312-644-6360, The Merchandise Mart Plaza, Ste 107, 60654.

**The Wooden Spoon**, www.woodenspoonchicago.com, 773-293-3190, 5047 N Clark, 60640

## Foreign Languages

**Alliance Francaise de Chicago**, www.af-chicago.org, 312-337-1070, 810 N Deaborn St, 60610

**Chicago Mandarin Chinese Center**, www.chicagomcc.com, 312-316-6038, 19 N State St, Ste 1700, 60602

**Goethe Institut**, www.goethe.de/ins/us/chi/enindex.htm, 312-263-0472, 150 N Michigan Ave, Ste 200, 60601

**Instituto Cervantes Chicago**, www.chicago.cervantes.es, 312-335-1996, 31 W Ohio St, 60610

**Italian Cultural Institute of Chicago**, www.iicchicago.esteri.it/iic_chicago, 312-822-9545, 500 N Michigan Ave, Ste 1450, 60611

# Sports • Biking

## General Information

| | |
|---|---|
| Active Transportation Alliance: | 9 W Hubbard St, Ste 402, www.activetrans.org; 312-427-3325 |
| Chicago Park District: | www.chicagoparkdistrict.com; 312-742-PLAY |
| Chicago Cycling Club: | www.chicagocyclingclub.org; 773-509-8093 |
| | (Organized weekend rides April through October) |
| Chicago Transit Authority: | www.transitchicago.com |
| DOT Bikes Website: | www.chicagobikes.org |
| The Chainlink Social Network: | www.thechainlink.org |

## Overview

In its own words, the Emanuel administration has set forth a comprehensive strategy to make Chicago the best big city for bicycling. By 2020, the city plans for a 645-mile network of biking facilities in order to provide a bicycle accommodation within a half-mile of every Chicagoan. In addition, their plan calls for more bikeways where more people live and to build more infrastructure where ridership is high, while establishing a strong backbone of infrastructure where ridership is currently lower.

Well, that's all well and fine for 2020, but what does that mean for today? All in all, the situation is not bad, but not great either—although the good news is it's getting better all the time. Bike riders still need to carefully navigate the city streets and trails as residents learn to adjust to the city's bicycle initiatives. Currently, Chicago has more than 170 miles of on-street protected, buffered and shared bike lanes; many miles of off-street paths (including the 18.5 mile Lakefront Trail); more than 13,000 bike racks; and sheltered, high-capacity bike parking areas at many CTA rail stations. One of the city's most recent initiatives was to make a two-way, protected bike lane on Dearborn Street through the Loop.

Perhaps the best new initiative is the city's bike share system, which debuted in the spring of 2013. By the time the full system is in place by Spring 2014, the system—called Divvy—will provide 4,000 bikes at 400 locations available for sharing. Divvy bikes are available 24 hours a day, 7 days a week, 365 days a year for short point-to-point trips. Users pick up a bike from a self-service docking station and return it to any other station nearest their destination. Yearly membership is $75 and day passes are $7, allowing for unlimited trips of up to 30 minutes each. Users can learn more and enroll at www.divvybikes.com.

If you are a cyclist in Chicago, bear in mind that bicycles, like other vehicles of the roads, are subject to the same laws and rights as drivers. You might feel like you're the only biker in the city who comes to a full stop at a sign, but fastidiously sticking to the laws is a good way to make a case for drivers to accept bikers. This includes the right to take a lane and the obligation to hand signal for turns. It goes without saying that you should always ride defensively (but don't bike on sidewalks: you can be ticketed). Helmets are still optional, but you'd have to have a pretty thick head to tempt fate without one. The many white "ghost bikes" set up throughout the city serve as vigils for fallen bikers, and remind riders of the need to buy and wear a helmet. Besides, one of the many perks of cycling is that no matter how goofy you may feel in your gear, there is always someone who looks much, much stupider beside you. The same goes for an adequate assortment of chains and u-locks, as bike thievery is rampant in every neighborhood in the city. The police department now offers a bike registration service, so you'll have legal recourse if you stumble upon your stolen bike on eBay.

## Bikes Onboard Mass Transit

Bicycles are permitted (free) on all L trains at all times except 7 am–9 am and 4 pm–6 pm on weekdays. Use the accessible turnstile or ask an attendant to open an access gate. Don't try to take your bike through the tall steel gates—it will get stuck! Only two bikes per carriage are allowed, so check for other bikes before you get on. The CTA has equipped all of its buses with front exterior bike racks, which are much less intimidating to use than they appear. If your bike is the first to be loaded, lower the rack and place it in position with the front wheel facing the curb. If there is already a bike on the rack, place your bike's rear wheel toward the curb. If two bikes are already loaded, wait for the next bus (whenever that may be). Bus-traveling bicyclists be warned, horror stories abound about bikes falling off racks, and there are even hit-by-bus-while-trying-to-remove-bike rumors. Always tell the driver that you are going to be loading or removing your bike, and ask for help if you need it—not all bus drivers are as gruff as they appear. On Metra commuter trains, bikes are allowed to travel free of charge in off-peak hours. There is a maximum number of bikes allowed per rail car (it varies by line—check the Metra website for your planned route), so follow the conductor's instructions if he or she asks you to board a different car.

| Bike Shops | Address | Phone | Map |
|---|---|---|---|
| Bike and Roll Chicago - Riverwalk | 316 N. Wabash Avenue | 312-729-1000 | 02 |
| Bike and Roll Chicago- Navy Pier | 600 E Grand Ave | 312-729-1000 | 03 |
| Bike and Roll Chicago- Ohio St Beach | 400 N Lake Shore Dr | 312-729-1000 | 03 |
| Bike and Roll Chicago | 239 E Randolph St | 312-729-1000 | 06 |
| Bike and Roll Chicago - 53rd Street Bike Center | 1558 E. 53rd Street | 312-729-1000 | 20 |
| Cycle Bike Shop | 1465 S Michigan Ave | 312-987-1080 | 11 |
| Blue City Cycles | 3201 S Halsted St | 312-225-3780 | 13 |
| Bike and Roll Chicago- DuSable Museum | 740 E 56th Pl | 312-729-1000 | 18 |
| Blackstone Bicycle Works | 6100 S Blackstone Ave | 773-241-5458 | 19 |
| DJ's Bike Doctor | 1500 E 55th St | 773-955-4400 | 19 |
| Bike and Roll Chicago- 53rd Street Bike Center | 1558 E 53rd St | 312-729-1000 | 20 |
| Rapid Transit Cycle Shop | 1900 W North Ave | 773-227-2288 | 21 |
| Quick Release Bike Shop | 1527 N Ashland Ave | 773-871-3110 | 22 |
| Upgrade Cycle Works | 1130 W Chicago Ave | 312-226-8650 | 24 |
| Boulevard Bikes | 2535 N Kedzie Blvd | 773-235-9109 | 27 |
| Smart Bike Parts | 3031 W Armitage Ave | 773-384-3010 | 27 |
| Bike and Roll Chicago- Foster Beach | 5200 N Lake Shore Dr | 312-729-1000 | 30 |
| Cycle Smithy | 2468 N Clark St | 773-281-0444 | 30 |
| Village Cycle Center | 1337 N Wells St | 312-751-2488 | 31 |
| Bike and Roll Chicago- North Ave Beach | 1603 N Lake Shore Dr | 312-729-1000 | 32 |
| Gary's Cycle Shop | 6317 N Clark St | 773-743-4201 | 37 |
| Iron Cycles | 3136 W Montrose Ave | 773-539-4766 | 38 |
| Roscoe Village Bikes | 2016 W. Roscoe | 773-477-7550 | 42 |
| Kozy's Cyclery | 3712 N Halsted St | 773-281-2263 | 44 |

# Billiards

The city's affluent "nesters" may be more interested in big-screen TVs than pool tables these days. But you'd rather mix your pleasure with strategy, a convivial game of billiards is still a fine way of turning strangers into friends… not to mention learning the angles above the angles above the angles. Many bars, from the seedy to the swanky, have a table or four. Chicago is also home to a good number of establishments that cater specifically to pool sharks. Have a good one, and don't get hustled.

The game's popularity goes in cycles. It spiked in the '80s thanks largely to *The Color of Money*, a pool-themed film starring Paul Newman and Tom Cruise, part of which was shot at **Chris's Billiard (Map 48)**. With two-dozen tables, no booze and no nonsense, this Jefferson Park institution remains the most credible spot among Chicago's seasoned players, although it sometimes intimidates newcomers. (We wouldn't call it "sleazy," but we wouldn't eat off the floor, either.) **Uno Billiards (Map 38)** is an oasis of seediness in the otherwise upscale Albany Park area. The equipment's not in tip-top shape, but cut this place and it bleeds character. **Chicago Billiards (Map 35)** is also a hike from downtown, but it's a more family-oriented room with a full food menu. If you're looking for snooker, a billiards variation wildly popular in Britain, they've got the hook-up here.

Somewhat hipper environs can be found at **City Pool Hall Food & Spirits (Map 1)**, a well-kept room also noted for its delectable burgers, and **Pressure Billiards & Café (Map 37)**, which boasts regulation tournament tables and, on weekends, one of the city's least hack-prone standup comedy nights. If racking the balls ever gets seriously trendy again, you can bet that the folks at **G Cue Billiards (Map 24)** will be the first to know. Professional player Tom Karabatsos runs this two-level lounge, which accommodates more hangers-out than pool purists.

For an even more gloriously inauthentic pool adventure, you can usually find a table at one of Chicago's bowling alleys. **Diversey-River Bowl (Map 42)** may be better known for its blacklights and throbbing pop soundtrack, but for those who can't shoot straight sober, it's got a game room with a full-service bar. It's open 'til 3 am on weekends. **Waveland Bowl (Map 42)** has tables all night, every night, though there's often a wait, and it's hard to focus when high school and college kids keep distracting us with their air hockey and their Dance Dance Revolution. **Southport Lanes (Map 43)** is a mite classier, with lovely Brunswick tables in a welcoming back area. Table rates at all of Chicago's pool halls vary by time of day and number of players. To save money, show up early—many halls offer discounts for pre-5 pm players.

A few major music venues also have tables, where musicians can be found relieving their road-warrior angst between sound checks. Show up early at the **Double Door** or the **Empty Bottle** (See Nightlife Map 21), and you might get to hustle the people who wrote your favorite song. South Loop blues joint **Buddy Guy's** also offers pool, and although the cover may be a bit intimidating, there is nothing quite like shooting stick while some of Chicago's saddest songsters wail next door.

| Billiards | Address | Phone | Fee | Map |
|---|---|---|---|---|
| City Pool Hall | 640 W Hubbard St | 312-491-9690 | $12 per hour | 01 |
| G Cue Billiards | 157 N Morgan St | 312-850-3170 | $14 per hour | 24 |
| Seven Ten Lounge | 2747 N Lincoln Ave | 773-549-2695 | $12 per hour | 29 |
| Pressure Billiards & Cafe | 6318 N Clark St | 773-743-7665 | $7.50-10 per hour | 37 |
| Uno Billiards | 3112 W Lawrence Ave | 773-267-8166 | $10 per hour | 38 |
| Waveland Bowl | 3700 N Western Ave | 773-472-5900 | $8-15 per hour | 42 |
| Southport Lanes | 3325 N Southport Ave | 773-472-6600 | $15-20 per hour | 43 |

# Bowling

Bowling is supposed to be the most blue-collar of all sports, so in the City of Big Shoulders, you'd expect comb-overs, beer frames, unfashionable wrist guards, and visible plumber's cracks to abound. In the '90s, several local alleys jazzed it up for the teenagers with rock music and late-night fog-and-light shows, and we can live with that. Lately, however, the trend is toward atmosphere-conscious boutique spots that treat strikes and spares as an afterthought. These are nice places to take a date, but we're a little scared when so-called bowling alleys advertise "small plates."

But if you're intrigued by the idea of high-end lounges that mash-up retro kitsch with modern glam, head to **10 Pin-Strike Bar Bowl & Grille (Map 2)**, where you can sip a trend-'tini on a cushy couch with an urban professional crowd. And the upscale, Hollywood-themed chain, **Lucky Strike Lanes (Map 3)**, is a good place to kill time if you're waiting to catch a movie at the adjacent AMC River East.

If you prefer not to define your bowling experience as "sophisticated" or "cutting edge," we recommend the newly-renovated Lincoln Square Lanes (Map 38), the city's only second-floor alley, which has been open since 1918. Climb a flight of stairs above Matty K's Hardware store and find twelve lanes with old-school wood floors, live blues and rockabilly music on weekends, and a balcony from which to watch the action. Other good choices for an authentic Chicago bowling adventure include **Diversey-River Bowl (Map 42)**, where there's an eclectic mix of league fanatics and hipster rockers ordering bottles of Bud shaped like bowling pins, or the only-slightly-grungy **Waveland Bowl (Map 42)**, which has been open 24 hours a day, seven days a week since 1969.

For a place that successfully maintains a vibe of "real deal" authenticity while welcoming newcomers, head to the **Timber Lanes (Map 39)**, where hand scoring still reigns amidst wood-paneled walls, a pinball machine, and a well-stocked bar. Owner Bob is a ubiquitous presence during league play, bowling left-handed to maintain the pretense of fairness. Since opening 1945, they've had leagues for men, women, mixed, gay and lesbian, and the blind. They've also hosted full-contact, Mexican wrestling-style bowling and nude nights—though shoes were still required. The cost to crush pins at each of these destinations varies based on time of day and whether you'll be bringing your own stylish shoes. Our advice: call ahead to make sure lanes are available and inquire about fees.

| Bowling | Address | Phone | Map |
|---|---|---|---|
| 10 Pin Bowling Lounge | 330 N State St | 312-644-0300 | 02 |
| Lucky Strike Lanes | 322 E Illinois St | 312-245-8331 | 03 |
| Seven Ten Lanes | 1055 E 55th St | 773-347-2695 | 19 |
| Fireside Bowl | 2648 W Fullerton Ave | 773-486-2700 | 27 |
| Seven Ten Lounge | 2747 N Lincoln Ave | 773-549-2695 | 29 |
| Lincoln Square Lanes | 4874 N Lincoln Ave | 773-561-8191 | 38 |
| Timber Lanes | 1851 W Irving Park Rd | 773-549-9770 | 39 |
| Diversey River Bowl | 2211 W Diversey Pkwy | 773-227-5800 | 42 |
| Waveland Bowl | 3700 N Western Ave | 773-472-5900 | 42 |
| Southport Lanes | 3325 N Southport Ave | 773-472-6600 | 43 |

Weather permitting, golfers can tee up all year round in Chicago. The Chicago Park District offers six public courses open daily, dawn to dusk. At **Jackson Park's (South)** premier 18-hole facility, the scenery alone will make you forget the bustle of the city. The nine-hole **Sydney R. Marovitz (Waveland) Golf Course (43)** is usually busy, but it has great views of the lake. And **Robert A. Black's (Map 34)** nine-hole, 2,339-yard, par-33 layout was designed by the renowned Dick Nugent. In addition, the park district operates three driving ranges and three learning centers, including one for juniors at **Douglas Park**.

The Forest Preserve District of Cook County offers 11 public courses in and around the city. **Indian Boundary's (Northwest)** huge fairways and fast-moving greens make for fun play and golfers often catch glimpses of visiting deer. At **Edgebrook (Northwest)**, bordered by mature trees along the Chicago River, the signature fifth hole—a 93-yard par three with an elevated green—offers a serious test of skill. Just 10 minutes from downtown, **Billy Caldwell's (Northwest)** sharply undulating greens make it a great place to play a quick nine. Many of the city's courses offer twilight specials, so bring your glow-in-the-dark balls if you're looking to save some cash.

And, for a real urban golf experience, the privately owned **Harborside International**, host to some Illinois PGA events, offers two tricky 18-hole, Scottish-links courses open to the public in season. Private courses in the city include the **Beverly**, **Ridge**, and **Ridgemoor** country clubs and **Riverside Golf Club**. However, if you want to see Tiger Woods play, you'll have to head out to the suburbs; the PGA tour visits clubs like Cog Hill in southwest Lemont and the members-only Medinah Country Club in the western 'burbs.

If you prefer your golf a little smaller, in-the-know mini-golfers head to the Park Districts' exceptionally cheap miniature golf course on Diversey, or head down south to the ultimate in windmill-dodging action, supernatural-themed Haunted Trails Amusement Park. Navy Pier also has a course, but the throngs of tourists with multi-colored balls makes it hard to recommend for the putt-putt purist.

## Golf Courses

| | Address | Phone | Map | Weekdays | Weekends |
|---|---|---|---|---|---|
| The Green at Grant Park | 352 E Monroe St | 312-540-9013 | 6 | | |
| Robert A Black Golf Course | 2045 W Pratt Blvd | 312-742-7931 | 34 | $20 | $22 |
| Sydney R Marovitz Golf Course | 3600 N Recreation Dr | 312-742-7930 | 44 | $24 | $27 |
| Edgebrook Golf Course | 6100 N Central Ave | 773-763-8320 | NW | $25 | $29 |
| Indian Boundary Golf Course | 8600 W Forest Preserve Ave | 773-625-9630 | NW | $29 | $31 |
| Columbus Park Golf Course | 5701 W Jackson Blvd | 312-746-5573 | W | $18 | $20 |
| Marquette Park Golf Course | 6700 S Kedzie Ave | 312-747-2761 | SW | $18 | $20 |
| South Shore Country Club | 7059 S South Shore Dr | 773-256-0986 | S | $18 | $20 |
| Harborside International Golf Center | 11001 S Doty Ave | 312-782-7837 | S | $82 | $95 |
| Jackson Park Golf Course | 6401 S Richards Dr | 773-667-0524 | S | $26 | $29 |

## Driving Ranges

| | Address | Phone | Map | Fees |
|---|---|---|---|---|
| Diversey Driving Range | 141 W Diversey Dr | 312-742-7929 | 3 | Small bucket $10 Large bucket $15 $2 clubs |
| Marquette Park Golf Course | 6700 S Kedzie Ave | 312-747-2761 | SW | $9/60 balls |
| Harborside International Golf Center | 11001 S Doty Ave | 312-782-7837 | S | $10/100 balls |
| Jackson Park Golf Course | 6401 S Richards Dr | 773-667-0524 | S | Small bucket $8.50, large bucket $12.50 (no fee for clubs) |

## Mini Golf Courses

| | Address | Phone | Map | Fees |
|---|---|---|---|---|
| Diversey Miniature Golf | 141 W. Diversey Parkway | 312.742.7929 | | Adults $9.00, Juniors/ Seniors $7 |
| Douglas Park | 1401 S. Sacramento | 312.747.7670 | | FREE |
| Haunted Trails Amusement Park | 7759 S. Harlem Ave. | 708-598-8580 | | Adults $6, 12& under $4.50 |
| Navy Pier Mini Golf | 600 East Grand Avenue | 800-595-PIER | | $15 |

## General Information

| | |
|---|---|
| Chicago Park District: | www.chicagoparkdistrict.com |
| | 312-742-PLAY (7528) |
| Active Transportation | www.activetrans.org |
| Alliance: | 312-427-3325 |
| Chicago Area Runner's | www.cararuns.org |
| Association: | 312-666-9836 |

## Overview

Greater Chicago offers more than 250 recreational off-road paths that allow bikers, skaters, walkers, and joggers to exercise without worrying about vehicular traffic. In addition to recreational paths in the city's parks, designated off-street trails line the Lakefront, North Shore Channel, North Branch Trail along the Chicago River, Burnham Greenway, and Major Taylor Trail.

## Lakefront Trail

Chicago has one of the prettiest and most accessible shorelines of any city in the US—this is the 500-pound gorilla of recreational paths in Chicago. Use one of Lake Shore Drive's over/underpasses (generally available every half mile or so) and you'll discover 15 miles of bathing beaches and over 20 miles of bike paths—just don't anticipate being able to train for the Tour de France during summer weekends, when the sheer number of people makes it impossible to bike along the path at faster than a snail's pace. But thanks to Burnham and Bennett's 1909 "Plan for Chicago," at least we can count on the shoreline remaining non-commercial, with great cycling, jogging, blading, skating, and swimming opportunities for all.

## Major Taylor Trail

If you've ever wanted to take in a slice of Chicago's southwestern-most corner (and let's face it, who hasn't?), try the six-mile bike route that begins at Dawes Park at 81st and Hamilton Streets near Western Avenue. The route incorporates an abandoned railroad right-of-way and runs to the southeast through Beverly and Morgan Park, ending up at the Cook County Forest Preserve near 130th and Halsted Streets. The trail was named in honor of cycling legend Marshall "Major" Taylor, one of the first African-American cyclists, who lived out the final years of his life in a YMCA in Chicago.

## North Branch Trail

To access the northern end of the trail, take Lake Cook Road to the Chicago Botanic Garden, located east of I-94. You can also start from any of the forest preserves as the path winds southward. To access the southern end of the trail in Chicago, take Milwaukee Avenue to Devon Avenue and head a short way east to the Caldwell Woods Preserve. The North Branch winds along the Chicago River and the Skokie Lagoons, but unlike most of the other trails, this one crosses streets, so be careful and look out for cars as you approach. Still, it represents a great way to get out of the city—and if you make it all the way to the Botanic Garden, admission is free as you won't have to pay for parking!

## Burnham Greenway

The 11-mile stretch of the Burnham Greenway, which extends from 104th Street on the city's south side all the way down to Lansing in the south suburbs, has undergone major work over the past few years. The trail has a bit of a checkered past (the former railroad right-of-way was once cited for major pollution), but current paving projects make it a good bet for biking, skating, and pedestrians. Expect to find all of northern Illinois' major ecosystems, from wetlands to prairies to a Ford Motor plant in close proximity to one another.

## North Shore Channel Trail

This trail follows the North Shore Channel of the Chicago River from Lawrence Avenue through Lincolnwood, Skokie (where you'll find a bizarre sculpture park lining the trail), and Evanston to Green Bay Road at McCormick Boulevard. Not all of the seven miles of the trail are paved bike paths and you'll have to switch back and forth between path and street. Skokie recently paved the trail segment between Oakton and Howard Streets, but there are still many missing links in the route, much to the chagrin of Friends of the Chicago River (FOCR), who are trying to extend and improve the Channel Trail. The Green Bay Trail branches off to the north from the North Shore Channel Trail and will take you past multi-million dollar houses, cute suburban downtowns, and the Ravinia Festival.

## Chicago Park District

Many of the parks under the jurisdiction of the Chicago Park District have paths dedicated to cycling, jogging, walking, rollerblading, and skating. The Chicago Area Runner's Association is so committed to lobbying for runners' rights that it successfully petitioned to have the Lincoln Park running paths plowed and salted through the winter so they could continue their running activities (though prepare to find water fountains that are shut off and bathrooms that are locked). This calls into question the sanity of such masochistic dedication, but we can only assume that the entire year is needed to prepare for the Chicago Marathon, held annually in October. Check out the chart on the facing page to determine Chicago Parks that designate jogging/walking and cycling/skating paths.

# Sports • **Recreational Paths**

| Park District—North Region | Address | Phone | Jog/Walk | Bike/Skate | Map |
|---|---|---|---|---|---|
| Brooks Park | 7100 N Harlem Ave | 773-631-4401 | ■ | | 45 |
| Emmerson Park | 1820 W Granville Ave | 773-761-0433 | ■ | | 36 |
| Eugene Field Park | 5100 N Ridgeway Ave | 773-478-9744 | | ■ | 48 |
| Oz Park | 2021 N Burling St | 312-742-7898 | ■ | | 30 |
| Peterson Park | 5801 N Pulaski Rd | 312-742-7584 | ■ | | 46 |
| Portage Park | 4100 N Long Ave | 773-685-7235 | ■ | | 48 |
| River Park | 5100 N Francisco Ave | 312-742-7516 | | ■ | 38 |
| Shabbona Park | 6935 W Addison St | 773-685-6205 | ■ | | 47 |
| Warren Park | 6601 N Western Ave | 773-262-6314 | ■ | ■ | 33 |
| Frank J Wilson Park | 4630 N Milwaukee Ave | 773-685-6454 | ■ | | 48 |
| Winnemac Park | 5100 N Leavitt St | 312-742-5101 | ■ | | 39 |

| Park District—Central Region | Address | Phone | Jog/Walk | Bike/Skate | Map |
|---|---|---|---|---|---|
| Columbus Park | 500 S Central Ave | 773-287-7641 | ■ | ■ | 49 |
| Douglas Park | 1401 S Sacramento Ave | 773-762-2842 | ■ | | 50 |
| Dvorak Park | 1119 W Cullerton St | 312-746-5083 | ■ | | 26 |
| Humboldt Park | 1400 N Sacramento Ave | 312-742-7549 | ■ | ■ | 50 |
| Riis Park | 6100 W Fullerton Ave | 312-746-5363 | ■ | ■ | 47 |
| Rutherford Sayre Park | 6871 W Belden Ave | 312-746-5368 | ■ | | 47 |
| Union Park | 1501 W Randolph St | 312-746-5494 | ■ | | 24 |

| Park District—Southwest Region | Address | Phone | Jog/Walk | Bike/Skate | Map |
|---|---|---|---|---|---|
| Bogan Park | 3939 W 79th St | 773-284-6456 | ■ | | 53 |
| Cornell Square Park | 1809 W 50th St | 312-747-6097 | ■ | | 54 |
| Hayes Park | 2936 W 85th St | 312-747-6177 | ■ | | 54 |
| LeClaire Courts/Hearst Community | 5120 W 44th St | 312-747-6438 | ■ | | 53 |
| Mt Greenwood Park | 3724 W 111th St | 312-747-6564 | ■ | | 55 |
| Rainey Park | 4350 W 79th St | 773-284-0696 | ■ | | 53 |
| Senka Park | 5656 S St Louis Ave | 312-747-7632 | ■ | | 54 |
| Sherman Park | 1301 W 52nd St | 312-747-6672 | ■ | | 54 |
| Avalon Park | 1215 E 83rd St | 312-747-6015 | ■ | | 57 |
| Bradley Park | 9729 S Yates Ave | 312-747-6022 | ■ | | 60 |
| Gately Park | 810 E 103rd St | 312-747-6155 | ■ | | 59 |
| Hamilton Park | 513 W 72nd St | 312-747-6174 | ■ | | 57 |
| Lake Meadows Park | 3117 S Rhodes Ave | 312-747-6287 | ■ | ■ | 14 |
| Meyering Playground Park | 7140 S Martin Luther King Dr | 312-747-6545 | ■ | | 57 |
| Palmer Park | 201 E 111th St | 312-747-6576 | ■ | | 59 |
| Rosenblum Park | 8050 S Chappel Ave | 312-747-6649 | ■ | | 60 |
| Washington Park | 5531 S Martin Luther King Dr | 773-256-1248 | ■ | ■ | 57 |

| Park District—Lakefront Region | Address | Phone | Jog/Walk | Bike/Skate | Map |
|---|---|---|---|---|---|
| Calumet Park | 9801 S Ave G | 312-747-6039 | ■ | | 60 |
| Jackson Park | 6401 S Stony Island Ave | 773-256-0903 | ■ | ■ | 58 |
| Lincoln Park | 2045 Lincoln Park West | 312-742-7726 | ■ | ■ | 30 |
| Loyola Park | 1230 W Greenleaf Ave | 773-262-8605 | ■ | ■ | 34 |
| Rainbow Park & Beach | 3111 E 77th St | 312-745-1479 | | ■ | 58 |

# General Information

Chicago Park District:  312-742-PLAY (7529);
www.chicagoparkdistrict.com

# Overview

Due to the temperature extremes that Chicago experiences, its residents can enjoy both ice skating and inline skating at various times of the year. Ice skating can be a fun, free, winter activity if you have your own skates, and if you don't, many rinks rent them. Skateboarding is also a popular pastime and a number of parks throughout the city are equipped with skating facilities.

# Inline Skating

As rollerblading continues to re-rise in popularity, especially amongst Chicago's gay community, paths and streets fill up in the summertime with these one-row rollers. Similar to bike riding, inline skating in Chicago serves dual purposes. If you plan on strapping on the blades to get from A to B, be super-careful navigating the streets. As it is, Chicago drivers tend to have difficulty seeing cyclers, and chances are they won't notice you until you've slammed into their open car door. Wear protective gear whenever possible, especially a helmet, and learn to shout loudly so that people can anticipate your approach. If recreational skating is more your speed, check out the Recreational Paths page for cool places to skate. If you'd like to join the hundreds of summer skaters out there, and you don't have your own gear, the following places offer skate rental: Londo Mondo, 1100 N Dearborn St at W Maple St, 312-751-2794; Bike Chicago at Navy Pier, 312-755-0488. Hourly rates range from $7 to $10, while daily rates are from $20 to $35.

# Roller Derby

If watching skating seems far more interesting than actually lacing up, then head over to the UIC pavilion to catch the Windy City Rollers, Chicago's premiere all-female roller derby league (when in season). Featuring tattooed beauties beating the crap out of each other while skating the circular track, the WCR is unlike any other Chicago sporting event out there. Plenty of beer is served, and the atmosphere is fun and loose, while still retaining the competitive spirit that makes the Derby the Derby.

**UIC Pavilion** · 525 S. Racine Ave, 312-413-5740

# Skate Parks

If you're more interested in adrenaline than exercise, grab your blades or board and a couple of buddies and head down to the magnificent Burnham Skate Park (east of Lake Shore Drive at 31st St, 312-747-2200). With amazing grinding walls and rails, vert walls, and banks, Burnham Park presents hours of fun and falls. Less intense but equally fun are the two skate parks with ramps, quarter pipes, and grind rails. One can be found at West Lawn Park (4233 W 65th St, 773-284-2803) the other at Oriole Park (5430 N Olcott Ave, 773-631-6197).

# Ice Skating

The Park District's nine outdoor rinks offer free admission and reasonably priced skate rentals, making ice skating an excellent way to turn bitterly frozen winter lemons into recreational lemon ice. The Millennium Park ice rink (55 N Michigan Ave) is the most visible and well known downtown. Rentals run $10. Parking is available for $14–$34 depending on length of time at the Grant Park North Garage. (Enter from the Michigan Avenue median at Washington or Madison Streets.)

The Olympic-sized skating rink and warming-house complex at Midway Plaisance offer a South Side venue for dropping precise one-footed salchows on an unsuspecting public. Located at 59th and Woodlawn, the rink has free admission and $5 rental skates. During the summer, the facility is used for rollerskating and other entertainment (312-745-2470).

If you, like the rest of Chicago, have recently caught hockey fever, try your hand at one of the many adult and child leagues run year round at Johnny's Ice House, 1350 W. Madison St. Close to downtown, Johnny's offers times and skill levels for any aspiring puckster. An interior bar guarantees a good time, regardless of game results.

Other ice skating rinks are located seasonally at:

**McFetridge Sports Complex** (year-round) · 3843 N California Ave, 773-478-2609 (admission is $4 for kids under 12 years, $5 for adults + $3 skate rental)

**Johnny's Ice House** · 1350 W. Madison St, 312-226-5555 (Rates vary)

**Mt. Greenwood Park** · 3721 W 111th St, 312-747-6564 (free admission + $5 rental)

**Navy Pier Ice Rink** · 600 E Grand Ave, 312-595-5100 ($12 admission + rental)

**Riis Park** · 6100 W Fullerton Ave, 312-746-5735 (free admission + $5 rental)

**The Rink** (roller skating) · 1122 E 87th St, 773-221-2600 ($1)

**The Rink at Wrigley** · 1060 W Addison St, 312-617-7017 ($6 admission children, $10 adults +rental)

**Rowan Park** · 11546 S Avenue L, 773-646-1967 (free admission + $5 rental)

**Warren Park** · 6601 N Western Ave, 773-761-8663 ($4 admission + $5 rental)

**West Lawn Park** · 4233 W 65th St, 773-284-2803 (free admission + $5 rental)

# Gear

If you're after skateboard gear, check out Air Time Skate Boards at 3317 N Clark St, 773-472-6868 and Uprise Skateboard Shop at 1820 N Milwaukee Ave, 773-342-7763.

For skating equipment, Air Time; (above) also does inline skates, as does Londo Mondo which has two locations: 1100 N Dearborn Street at W Maple St, 312-751-2794; and 2148 N Halsted St, 773-327-2218.

For all your ice skating needs, try the Skater's Edge store in the McFetridge Sports Complex (3843 N California Ave, 773-463-1505). They deal in hockey skates and other equipment as well as inline skates and accessories such as sequined dresses!

## General Information

General Park Info: 312-742-PLAY
Department of Beaches and Pools: 312-742-5121

The Chicago Park District offers several indoor and outdoor pools, ten of which are equipped with ramps or lifts for disability access. At the top of our list is the 500-person-capacity outdoor wonderment at **Washington Park (Map 18)**, a 50-meter pool that's connected to a large, oval, side pool where fountains spray into a zero-depth entrance. Even better—it's got a 36-foot, theme-park-style water slide. It's overrun with pool rats during open swim periods, but grown folks like the designated lap times, water aerobics classes, and adult swims.

We also like the 30-meter outdoor pool at **River Park (Map 38)**, an Albany Park spot that boasts a diving well, a spacious deck with lounge chairs and umbrella tables, and an interactive kids' water playground. And when the weather gets cold, there's great lap swimming at the Ida Crown Natatorium at **Eckhart Park (Map 24)**. What's a natatorium? It's a pool inside its own building, and this one looks like it might have been designed by Eero Saarinen, but it wasn't.

All outdoor pools are free for the summer (Memorial Day-Labor Day). During the year, all lap swim fees for indoor pools are for 10-week sessions ($20 before 9 am; $10 after 9 am), and recreational and family swims are free. Get a complete list of facilities and register for aquatic exercise, diving, lifeguard, underwater hockey, and water polo classes at http://chicagoparkdistrict.com.

## Outdoor Pools

| | Address | Phone | Map |
|---|---|---|---|
| Wentworth Gardens Park | 3770 S Wentworth Ave | 312-747-6996 | 13 |
| Taylor Park | 41 W 47th St | 312-747-6728 | 15 |
| Washington Park | 5531 S MLK Dr | 773-256-1248 | 18 |
| Pulaski Park | 1419 W Blackhawk St | 312-742-7559 | 22 |
| Union Park | 1501 W Randolph St | 312-746-5494 | 24 |
| Dvorak Park | 1119 W Cullerton St | 312-746-5083 | 26 |
| Holstein Park | 2200 N Oakley Ave | 312-742-7554 | 28 |
| Wrightwood Park | 2534 N Greenview Ave | 312-742-7816 | 29 |
| River Park | 5100 N Francisco Ave | 312-742-7516 | 38 |
| Chase Park | 4701 N Ashland Ave | 312-742-7518 | 40 |
| McFetridge Sports Center (California Park) | 3843 N California Ave | 773-478-2609 | 41 |
| Hamlin Park | 3035 N Hoyne Ave | 312-742-7785 | 42 |

## Indoor Pools

| | Address | Phone | Map |
|---|---|---|---|
| McGuane Park | 2901 S Poplar Ave | 312-747-6497 | 12 |
| Clemente Park | 2334 W Division St | 312-742-7466 | 21 |
| Eckhart Park/Ida Crown Natatorium | 1330 W Chicago Ave | 312-746-5490 | 24 |
| Harrison Park | 1824 S Wood St | 312-746-5491 | 25 |
| Kelly Park | 2725 W. 41st St. | 312-747-6197 | |
| Sheridan Park | 910 S Aberdeen St | 312-746-5369 | 26 |
| Stanton Park | 618 W Scott St | 312-742-9553 | 31 |
| Mather Park | 5941 N Richmond St | 312-742-7501 | 35 |
| Welles Park | 2333 W Sunnyside Ave | 312-742-7511 | 39 |
| Winnemac Park | 5001 N. Leavitt St. | 312-742-5101 | |
| Gill Park | 833 W Sheridan Rd | 312-742-5807 | 43 |

While we admit we're suckers for any sport that includes the word "love" in its scoring system, we try not to think of the significance that it means "zero" in tennis talk. Find love and more at these Chicago tennis courts.

All tennis courts except Daley Bicentennial Plaza in Grant Park, Diversey Park, Chase Park, California Park, and Waveland Park are free and open to the public on a first-come-first-served basis. Courts are open daily—check each park for individual hours. 312-742-7529 (general info); 773-256-0949 (Lake Front Region Office).

## Tennis Courts

| | Address | Phone | Fees | Map |
|---|---|---|---|---|
| Daley Bicentennial Plaza | 337 E Randolph St | 312-742-7648 | $7/hr; reservations required | 6 |
| Grant Park | 331 E Randolph St | 312-742-7648 | | 6 |
| Roosevelt Park | 62 W Roosevelt Rd | 312-742-7648 | | 8 |
| Mandrake Park | 900 E Pershing Rd | 312-747-7661 | | 12 |
| McGuane Park | 2901 S Poplar Ave | 312-747-6497 | | 12 |
| Armour Square Park | 3309 S Shields Ave | 312-747-6012 | | 13 |
| Ellis Park | 707 E 37th St | 312-746-5962 | | 14 |
| Fuller Park | 331 W 45th St | 312-747-6144 | | 15 |
| Metcalfe Park | 4134 S State St | 312-747-6728 | | 16 |
| Kenwood Community Park | 1330 E 50th St | 312-747-6286 | | 17 |
| Washington Park | 5531 S Dr Martin Luther King Jr Dr | 773-256-1248 | | 18 |
| Clemente Park | 2334 W Division St | 312-742-7466 | | 21 |
| Union Park | 1501 W Randolph St | 312-746-5494 | | 24 |
| Harrison Park | 1824 S Wood St | 312-746-5491 | | 25 |
| Sheridan Park | 910 S Aberdeen St | 312-746-5369 | | 26 |
| Jonquil Park | 1023 W Wrightwood Ave | N/A | | 29 |
| Oz Park | 2021 N Burling St | 312-742-7898 | | 30 |
| Lerner Park | 7000 N Sacramento Ave | N/A | | 33 |
| Rogers Park | 7345 N Washtenaw Ave | 773-262-1482 | | 33 |
| Indian Boundary Park | 2500 W Lunt Ave | 773-742-7887 | | 33 |
| Warren Park | 6601 N Western Ave | 773-262-6314 | | 33 |
| Loyola Park | 1230 W Greenleaf Ave | 773-262-8605 | | 34 |
| Pottawattomie Park | 7340 N Rogers Ave | 773-262-5835 | | 34 |
| Touhy Park | 7348 N Paulina St | 773-262-6737 | | 34 |
| Legion Park at the Chicago River | W Bryn Mawr Ave & N Virginia Ave | N/A | | 35 |
| Green Briar Park | 2650 W Peterson Ave | 773-761-0582 | | 35 |
| Mather Park | 5941 N Richmond St | 312-742-7501 | | 35 |
| Emmerson Playground Park | 1820 W Granville Ave | 773-761-0433 | | 36 |
| Horner Park | 2741 W Montrose Ave | 773-478-3499 | | 38 |
| River Park | 5100 N Francisco Ave | N/A | | 38 |
| Welles Park | 2333 W Sunnyside Ave | 312-742-7511 | | 39 |
| Chase Park | 4701 N Ashland Ave | 312-742-7518 | $5/hr | 40 |
| Revere Park | 2509 W Irving Park Rd | 773-478-1220 | | 41 |
| Brands Park | 3259 N Elston Ave | 773-478-2414 | | 41 |
| McFetridge Sports Center (California Park) | 3843 N California Ave | 773-478-2609 | $16-$24/hr | 41 |
| Hamlin Park | 3035 N Hoyne Ave | 312-742-7785 | | 42 |
| Lincoln Park-Waveland Tennis Center | W Waveland Ave & N Lake Shore Dr | 312-742-7674 | $7/hr; reservations required | 44 |
| Lincoln Park-Diversey Tennis Center | 2800 N Lake Shore Dr | 312-742-7821 | $16/hr; reservations must be made in person | 44 |

## Volleyball Courts

**Lincoln Park/North Avenue Beach** • 312-742-7529 (reservations and price information)
101 courts—12 are always open to the public. Much league play and reserved courts.
Office hours: Mon–Fri: 1 pm–9 pm; Weekends: 8 am–5 pm.
**Lincoln Park/Montrose Beach** • 312-742-5121
50 courts allotted on a first-come-first-served basis. League play in the evening.
**Lincoln Park/Oak Street Beach** •
Nine free courts.
**Jackson Park/63rd Street Beach** • 312-742-4847
Four free courts — first-come-first-served.

## General Information

NFT Map: 11
Address: 1410 S Museum Campus Dr
Chicago, IL 60605
Phone: 312-235-7000
Lost & Found: 312-235-7202
Website: www.soldierfield.net
Box Office: 847-615-BEAR (2327)
Bears Website: www.chicagobears.com
Ticketmaster: 312-559-1212;
www.ticketmaster.com

## Overview

Like many Bears fans, the "new" Soldier Field is big, burly, and visually abrasive, especially the pre-game tailgaters in the parking lots. Plans began for its building in 1919 as a memorial to American soldiers who died in the wars. It officially opened on October 9th, 1924 (the 53rd anniversary of the Chicago Fire) as Municipal Grant Park Stadium. Renamed and dedicated in 1925, Soldier Field eventually became a key installment in the multi-million dollar Lakefront Improvement Plan for the Chicago shoreline between Navy Pier and McCormick Place. An estimated $365 million went towards the renovation of the 63,000-seat stadium, which opened in time for the 2003-2004 NFL Season and debuted on ABC's *Monday Night Football*. Improved Soldier Field amenities include 60% more seating on the sidelines, three times as many concessions stands (400), several cozy meeting nooks throughout the stadium, two 82 x 23-foot video screens, a 100,000-square-foot lounge/entertainment facility, and twice as many bathrooms (although you'd never know it judging by the lines). Once again, the Bears will take to silvery, shiny Soldier Field this year hoping to return to the playoffs before their last Super Bowl appearance fades to a too-distant memory. (Voters Decide: Toilet Bowl Wins in a Landslide!) With a spate of injuries dashing the high hopes of last season, the Bears will take to silvery, shiny Soldier Field this year hoping to return to the playoffs before their last Super Bowl appearance fades to a too-distant memory. Regardless of what you think it looks like.

## How to Get Tickets

Contact Ticketmaster to purchase individual game tickets. Season tickets are nearly impossible to come by within the next ten years as a recent bid by a staff member has him 2,876th in line. The best way to get great seats (other than by having them left to you in a will) is to work with a licensed ticket broker. Fans marked their territory early in 2004 by purchasing a one-time Permanent Seat License (PSL), and in exchange for paying big premiums to help cover construction expenses, PSL holders are promised first choice of ticket seating each year. Of the stadium's 63,000 seats, 27,500 are PSL zones, and the remaining 33,500 are non-licensed seats in the stadium's higher altitudes. A $100 per-seat, non-refundable deposit is required to get on a season ticket waiting list. The deposit will be applied to the first year of non-PSL season tickets, and you can find an application on the Bears website.

## How to Get There

**By Car:** From the north or south, take Lake Shore Drive; follow the signs to Soldier Field. For parking lots, exit at E McFetridge, E Waldron, E 14th Boulevard, and E 18th Drive. From the west, take I-55 E to Lake Shore Drive, turn north, and follow the signs. Travel east on I-290, then south on I-90/94 to I-55; get on I-55 E to Lake Shore Drive. Parking lots surrounding Soldier Field cost between $11 and $19 on non-game days, depending on when you arrive. You can reserve a spot online before you arrive. Rates rise significantly on game days. Call the Standard Parking Customer Service Hotline with questions (312-235-7724). Two parking and game-day tailgating lots are located south of Waldron Drive. There are also lots on the Museum Campus off McFetridge Drive and near McCormick Place off 31st Street and E 18th Street.

**By Train:** On game days, CTA Soldier Field Express bus 128 runs non-stop between the Ogilvie Transportation Center and Union Station to Soldier Field. Service starts two hours before the game, runs up to 45 minutes before kickoff, and up to 45 minutes post-game.

**By L:** Take the Red, Orange, or Green Lines to the Roosevelt station stop. Either board eastbound CTA bus 12 or the free Green Trolley to the Museum Campus, and then walk south to Soldier Field. Walking from Roosevelt station would take approximately 15 minutes...an alternate to waiting for the bus.

**By Bus:** CTA buses 12, 127, and 146 stop on McFetridge Drive near Soldier Field. Contact the RTA Information Center for routes and schedules at 312-836-7000 or online at www. rtachicago.com.

**By Trolley:** The Green Trolley travels along Michigan Avenue, Washington Street, Canal Street, and Adams Street to the Museum Campus. The ride takes around 30 minutes. From there, you can walk south to the field. For routes and schedules, visit www.cityofchicago.org/transportation.

## General Information

NFT Map:      13
Address:      333 W 35th St
              Chicago, IL 60616
General Info: 312-674-1000
Ticket Sales: 866-SOX-GAME
Website:      www.whitesox.com

## Overview

Both of Chicago's major league ballparks are named for corporations (one famous for gum, the other famous for cell phones) but the similarities end there. Any White Sox fan will tell you: tourists pay big bucks to watch ivy grow in the little place on the North Side, real baseball fans head to see the White Sox play at US Cellular Field.

Straddled by the Bridgeport and Bronzeville neighborhoods on Chicago's south side, US Cellular Field opened in 1991 to replace the old Comiskey Park. The new park was built for $167 million—a relative bargain even in 1991. Cost-cutting meant altering the original design, though, and not for the better. What the park lacks in beauty, it makes up for with its friendly staff, terrific sightlines (although the park itself faces the wrong way) and fabulous food—perennially rated among the best in Major League Baseball. Meat-eaters: follow your nose to the grilled onions and say "Polish with." Better yet, say "Polish witt." You'll get a sublimely good Polish sausage smothered in caramelized onions. And for the vegetarian, as long as you keep your voice down, you can snag a very tasty veggie dog at several of the Sox's many concession stands.

Look around and you'll notice that most Sox fans do enjoy their food at the ballpark—not many anorexics or bulimics in this crowd. And if you're hoping to hear about fashion, or business deals, or coffee shops, this ain't the place. Fans here talk about baseball. They love the game, and they love the team that FINALLY brought a World Series trophy to Chicago in 2005.

Roger Bossard—an obsessive-compulsive turf guru who consults to sports franchises around the world—maintains one of the most beautiful, truest playing real-grass surfaces in all of sports. Bill Veeck's scoreboard explodes with fireworks at each home run, and street musicians serenade fans as they head to the red line or the parking lot after games. It's all just about perfect.

## How to Get Tickets

Purchase tickets through the team's website (www.whitesox.com) or at the US Cellular Field Box Office (weekdays: 10 am–6 pm, weekends: 10 am–4 pm).

Children shorter than the park's turnstile arm (approximately 36 inches) are admitted free, but must share your seat. Best Ballpark bargain: Half-Price tickets available for all regular seats (except Premium Lower Box) on Monday home games. Check the website for Value Days schedules.

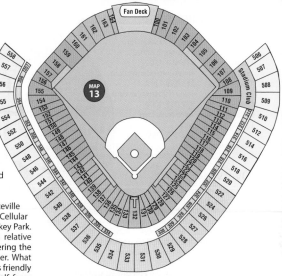

## How to Get There

**By Car:** US Cellular Field is located at the 35th Street exit off the Dan Ryan Expressway. Take I-90/94, stay in the local lanes, and exit at 35th Street. If you possess a prepaid green parking coupon or plan on paying cash for parking ($23), exit at 35th Street. Follow signs to "Sox Parking" at lots E, F, and L on the stadium's south side. Fans with red, prepaid season parking coupons exit at 31st Street, and follow signs for "Red Coupons" to lots A, B, and C just north of the stadium. If the 35th Street exit is closed due to heavy traffic, which is often the case on game days, proceed to the 39th Street exit; turn right for "Sox Parking" and left for "Red Coupons." The handicapped parking and stadium drop-off area is in Lot D, west of the field and accessible via 37th Street. If you're planning to tailgate, the lots open two hours before the game and close one hour after it's over.

**By Bus:** CTA buses 24 and 35 stop closest to the park. Others stopping in the vicinity are the 29, 44, and 39. Armies of cops surround the venue on game days because the neighborhood is rough, especially at night.

**By L:** Ride the Red Line to the Sox-35th Street stop just west of the ballpark. Another good option, especially heading north after the game, is the Green Line. The 35th-Bronzeville-IIT (Illinois Institute of Technology) Station is a little longer walk that the Sox 35th Street stop, but always less crowded.

# Sports • United Center

## General Information

NFT Map: 23
Address: 1901 W Madison St
Chicago, IL 60612
Phone: 312-455-4500
Website: www.unitedcenter.com
Ticketmaster: 312-559-1212;
www.ticketmaster.com
Chicago Bulls: 312-455-4000
Bulls Website: www.bulls.com
Chicago Blackhawks:
312-455-7000
Blackhawks Website:
www.chicagoblackhawks.com

## Overview

The commanding crown of Chicago's developing West Town District, the United Center is home to both the NHL's Blackhawks and the NBA's Bulls. This ultra-high-tech stadium is also a theater, convention hall, and premier concert arena. Opened in 1994, the $175 million stadium was privately funded by deep-pocketed Blackhawks owner William Wirtz and penny-pinching Bulls majority owner Jerry Reinsdorf (a privately funded and owned stadium—what a concept!) and built to replace the beloved but aging Chicago Stadium. The reinvigorated Bulls and Blackhawks franchises have pumped new energy in to the building, and the level of theatrics and delicious way-above average food, make a night at the United Center unlike anything else in the city. And just in case you forget whose "house" this is, the impressive statue of Michael Jordan located in front of the main entrance to the United Center is there to remind you.

A recent infusion of youth in both resident squads has brought a level of excitement to Chicago winter-time sports that has not been seen in years. Chicago native Derek Rose is the Bulls' cherished ingénue, sporting the blossom of youth on his cheek and the promise of future overachievements in his game. Following the recent passing of Blackhawk' owner and resident Chicago villain Bill Wirtz, the 'Hawks have seen a resurgence in talent, ticket sales, and overall interest. After the Blackhawks' Stanley Cup championship in 2010, Chicago hockey fans have looked forward to the beginning of each hockey season with the hopes that they'll have another reason to riot.

## How to Get Tickets

Book tickets over the phone or online with Ticketmaster, by United Center mail order, or visit the United Center box office at Gate 4. Box office hours are Monday to Saturday, 11 am to 6 pm. For Bulls and Blackhawks season tickets and group bookings call the phone numbers above.

## How to Get There

**By Car:** From the Loop, drive west on Madison Street to United Center. From the north, take I-90/94 and exit at Madison Street; head west to the stadium. From the southwest, take I-55 N to the Damen/Ashland exit; head north to Madison Street. From the west, take I-290 E to the Damen Avenue exit; go north to Madison Street.

Parking lots surround United Center, as do countless cops. General public parking in Lots A, E, J, D and F is $20 - $37. Lot H on Wood Street is closest to the stadium and is reserved for VIPs. Disabled parking is in Lots G on Damen Avenue.

**By L:** Take the Forest Park Branch of the Blue Line to the Medical Center-Damen Avenue Station. Walk two blocks north to United Center.

**By Bus:** CTA bus 19 United Center Express is the most intelligent and safest choice. In service only on event and game days, this express bus travels from Chicago Avenue south down Michigan Avenue, then west along Madison Street to the United Center. Michigan Avenue stops are at Chicago Avenue, Illinois Street, and Randolph Street. On Madison Street, stops are at State Street, Wells Street, and Clinton Street ($1.75 one-way). Service starts two hours before events and continues for 45 minutes after events. CTA bus 20 also travels Madison Street beginning at Wabash Avenue and has "owl service."

## General Information

| | |
|---|---|
| NFT Map: | 43 |
| Address: | 1060 W Addison St |
| | Chicago, IL 60613 |
| Cubs Box Office Phone: | 773-404-2827 |
| Tickets.com: | 800-THE-CUBS (843-2827) |
| Lost & Found: | 773-404-4185 |
| Website: | www.cubs.com |

## Overview

In 2014, Wrigley Field will play host to the Chicago Cubs for the 98th year. Unfortunately, it has been even longer since the team has claimed a title. Built in 1914 and originally known as Weeghman Park, the stadium was renamed Wrigley Field in 1926 to honor chewing gum mogul and former Cub owner William Wrigley, Jr. It is the second-oldest ball park in Major League Baseball (Boston's Fenway Park—1912) and is a refreshing throwback to simpler times. Wrigley at it's heart, is a living, breathing, baseball museum. Ivy-strewn walls, a Merion Bluegrass and clover field, and a manual scoreboard transcend both time and technology during this age of artificial playing surfaces and high-tech But get while the getting's good, a recent team sale, and the constant threat of a name change promise that Wrigley Field probably won't be Wrigley Field much longer. The glow from night game lights warms the hearts of most North Chicago locals who aren't game attendees. On the other side of the fence, Wrigleyville activists have lobbied to limit the amount of time the lights are burning, in an attempt to limit their neighborhood's party reputation, to stop drunks peeing in alleyways, and to protect their over-inflated property values. But since the park has been there much, much longer than any of them, they really don't have much of a sober, party-pooping foot to stand on.

Wrigley Field has been the site of some of baseball's most historic moments: Ernie Banks' 500th career home run in 1970, Kerry Wood's twenty strikeouts in 1998, and Sammy Sosa's sixty home runs in 1998, 1999, and 2001. The Cubs haven't won a World Series title since their back-to-back wins over Detroit in 1907 and 1908, and haven't appeared in the Fall Classic since 1945, yet this loveable losing team has one of the most impressive attendance records in Major League Baseball. Of course, most patrons pay no attention to the game as an outing to Wrigley has become an opportunity to drink beer and "be seen." And if you're going to sit in the bleachers, you better be ready to party, because boobs of all type abound. Every year, faithful fans claim this is their year…but 2012 looks to be no better. Yet optimism remains, regardless of record, bad trades, overpaid underperforming players, and airport-style beer pricing. A day at Wrigley is like no other experience in the world, and a must-see for any self-respecting Chicagoan/baseball fan. The recent addition of the Capt. Morgan Club to the front of the park only adds to the good-time atmosphere, and there is nothing, nothing like singing "Take Me Out to The Ballpark" during the seventh inning stretch inside the friendly confines. Because no matter the score, no matter the curse, we will "root, root, root for the Cubbies.

## How to Get Tickets

Individual game tickets can be purchased from the Cubs' website, by calling 800-843-2827, or in person at some Chicagoland Tickets.com outlets (if you're hanging out in Indiana or Wisconsin). You can also buy tickets at the Wrigley Field Box Office, open weekdays from 8 am to 6 pm and weekends from 9 am to 4 pm. You can usually score discount tickets to afternoon games Monday through Thursday in April, May, and September, or by waiting around the ballpark until the game starts. Especially when they are in the typical six-game losing skid. Children aged two and up require tickets.

## How to Get There

**By Car:** If you must… Remember the old days when Wrigleyville hillbillies used to let you park on their front lawns for five bucks? Well, today traffic on game days is horrendous, and parking prices are sky-high. Post-game spill-out from local bars and dozens of mindless cab drivers freeze traffic as police do their best to prevent drunken revelers from stumbling into the streets. From the Loop or south, take Lake Shore Drive north; exit at Irving Park Road, and head west to Clark Street; turn south on Clark Street to Wrigley Field. From the north, take Lake Shore Drive to Irving Park Road; head west to Clark Street, and turn south. From Chicago's West Side, take I-290 E or I-55 N to Lake Shore Drive, then follow directions above. From the northwest, take I-90 E and exit at Addison Street; travel east three miles. From the southwest side, take I-55 N to I-90/94 N. Exit at Addison Street; head east to the park.

Street parking around Wrigley Field is heavily restricted, nearly impossible and insanely expensive. The Cubs operate a garage at 1126 W Grace Street. Purchase parking passes through the mail or at the Wrigley Field Box Office. On game nights, tow trucks cruise Wrigleyville's streets nabbing cars without a resident permit sticker. Park smart at the DeVry Institute, and catch CTA bus 154/Wrigley Express to and from the park. ($6 covers parking and roundtrip shuttle per carload.)

**By L:** Riding the Howard/Dan Ryan Red Line used to be the fastest and easiest way to get to Wrigley Field ($2.00 one-way). It is still easy but recent CTA overhauls, due to mismanagement, embezzlement and general misbehavior have greatly reduced service and increased wait time. Get off at the Addison Street stop one block east of the field.

**By Bus:** CTA buses 22, 8, and 152 stop closest to Wrigley Field ($2.00 one-way). For routes and schedules, visit www.rtachicago.com.

Even with the city constantly ranking amongst the fattest in the country, Chicagoans have had a renewed focus on physical fitness, which is saying something in the land of deep dish pizza and Italian beef. This free publication is available online at www.chicagoaa.com and is on hand at many of the downtown athletic clubs. Leagues aren't just limited to stalwarts like basketball and home grown 16-inch softball; dodgeball and kickball leagues abound, and if you can organize the squad and raise the money necessary to participate, you won't even notice you're working out as you pelt some unsuspecting lame-o in the face with an inflated rubber ball.

## General Tips

If you're interested in finding a specific league or group for a particular sport, a good place to start is *Chicago Athlete* magazine. This free publication is available online at www.chicagoaa.com and is on hand at many of the downtown athletic clubs and the Chicago Department of Tourism. You can look at the site to see which places carry it.

If you're a beginner, before you go spending a ton of money on your sport of choice, check out the Chicago Park District's website to see if they offer something near you on the cheap. They offer loads of clubs, training groups, and classes on a wide range of sports from archery to weightlifting to yoga. Their handy online program guide lets you search by age group, parks, program type, or zip code. The latter is particularly handy if you don't know where to find your local park district building. Check out their site for an excellent starting point for many sports teams and clubs.

## Multiple Sports Leagues and Clubs

Chicago Sport and Social Club (www.chicagosportandsocialclub.com) is the mother of all of the Windy City leagues. Offering volleyball, basketball, football, floor hockey, soccer, dodge ball, dance, bowling, running, kickball, yoga, softball, rock climbing, kayaking, tennis, boot camp and boxing fitness, and even bar games (such as euchre, darts, and pool), this league has it all. Even if you're not interested in joining, you can watch the league's be-thonged hardbodies spike the ball around every summer at Oak Street Beach or North Avenue Beach or vicariously take in an aerobics class while you burn your hide to a crisp.

If you're interested in something a little more (how do we put this?) *queer* in your sports experience, then join the Chicago Metropolitan Sports Association (www.chicagomsa.com). This non-profit is the largest gay and lesbian sports organization in the Midwest. Offering badminton, bowling, flag football, soccer, co-ed and women's softball, tennis, and volleyball, this league is the best place to meet other queer jocks for pick-ups (games and otherwise) and fun in the sun. Again, if you're not interested in playing, it's fun to watch. The games take place along the lakefront. Check their website for more information and game times.

## Running

By far, most of the area sports groups and clubs are focused on running. We're not sure why but, if you're training for a running event, say, the Chicago Marathon or your first 5K, Chicago Area Runner's Association (www.cararuns.org) has you covered. This organization is for all levels of runners—from the seasoned marathoner to the amateur looking to begin running for the first time. With group runs, clinics, training programs, and a monthly newsletter, this organization has it all for anyone wanting to feel the gravel beneath their New Balances, the wind in their hair, and the lakefront gnats in their teeth.

## Triathlon

Want to "tri" something a little more involved? How about a triathlon? The city offers tons of opportunities to get involved with this swim-bike-run race. These clubs run the gamut from volunteer-driven organizations to professional training for a fee. Check out Chicago Endurance Sports (www.chicagoendurancesports.com) Chicago Tri Club (www.chicagotriclub.com), Lakeview YMCA Triathlon Club (www.lakeviewymca.org/proTriathlon.html), or Together We Tri (www.togetherwetri.com). With any of these groups, you can expect to join a group that will tailor your workouts to your needs, find a supportive team environment, attend clinics on transitions and the individual sports, and get a training schedule that you can use on your non-group workout days.

## Rugby

If rugby's your game, then Chicago has opportunities to join in the fun and violence. Two women's teams dominate the Chicago scene—North Shore Women's Rugby (www.northshorerugby.com) and Chicago Women's Rugby (www.cwrfc.com). For the men, Chicago offers more opportunities: Chicago Griffins Rugby Club (www.chicagogriffins.com), Chicago Lions Rugby Football Club (www.chicagolions.com), Lincoln Park Rugby Football Club (www.lprfc.com), and the South Side Irish Rugby (www.southsideirishrugby.com).

## Miscellaneous

If you're interested in swimming, the Central Masters Swimming Association website has everything you're looking for. Check them out at www.chicagomasters.com. If soccer is more your thing, see the Chicago Area Soccer Association at the League Republic's website (www.leaguerepublic.com/soccer.jsp). While their site is less than user-friendly, you can click on "league search" in the upper right-hand corner of the page and type "Chicago" into the search engine. From there, you can find all of the teams you might want to join. Want to rollerblade? Get Inline... Chicagoland is the club for you! Check 'em out at www.getinlinechicagoland.com.

Whether you're an amateur or a seasoned veteran, Chicago offers many opportunities to get out there and become a jock! Check out these options, and have some fun while getting healthier.

## General Information

| | |
|---|---|
| Address: | 10000 W O'Hare |
| | Chicago, IL 60666 |
| Phone: | 773-686-2200 / 800-832-6352 |
| Website: | www.ohare.com |
| Ground Transportation: | 773-686-8040 |
| Lost & Found: | 773-894-8760 |
| Parking: | 773-686-7530 |
| Traveler's Aid: | 773-894-2427 |
| Police: | 773-686-2385 |
| Customs Information: | 773-894-2900 |

## Overview

O'Delay might be a more fitting name for O'Hare, although Beck might take exception to such a name change. What else can we say about one of the world's busiest airports? Still, when you think about it, it's an airport. In a major city. A major city that is sometimes covered in snow. Don't let worries of delays and frozen runways keep you grounded. While the airport is located just 17 miles northwest of the Loop, allow plenty of time to get to the airport, but don't stress too hard about security lines unless you're going to Europe. Or if it's Christmas. Or if you're going to Europe on Christmas. In the event that you do get to your gate early, there's Wi-Fi available for purchase by the hour, day, or month through Boingo. Also, keep in mind if you're taking a red-eye flight that most eateries and shops are closed at night and early morning, so bring snacks and a novel. Or maybe this book.

Expansion spells relief, and the O'Hare modernization and expansion plan begun under former Mayor Daley is currently entering its final phases under Mayor Rahm Emanuel. When the program is complete, O'Hare's capacity should be doubled, with an additional runway and overhauls of the existing seven, among other improvements to help secure its "busiest" title for the rest of the 21st century.

Psst. We'll tell you a secret that will make picking up guests at the airport a lot more pleasant. Sign up online for the airline to notify you of flight information and changes via your cellphone, then park your car, and head to the Hilton bar (located in the airport) to wait out the arrival. Better yet, avoid the stress of driving by taking the train in, then waiting at the Hilton bar for Aunt Sally, and load her and yourself into a cab. You probably shouldn't be driving at this point, anyway.

## How to Get There

**By Car:** Strongly consider taking public transit to O'Hare, peek a few inches forward for information on the L. But if you absolutely must drive, pay close attention here. To be on the safe side, allow over an hour just for the drive (more during rush hours). From the Loop to O'Hare, take I-90 W. From the north suburbs, take I-294 S. From the south suburbs, take I-294 N. From the west suburbs, take I-88 E to I-294 N. Get off all of the above highways at I-190, which leads you directly to the airport. All of the major routes have clear signage, easily legible when you're moving at a snail's pace.

**Parking:** O'Hare Airport's parking garage reflects its hometown's passion for sports. All levels of the Main Parking Garage are "helpfully" labeled with Chicago sports teams' colors and larger-than-life logos (Wolves, Bulls, Blackhawks, White Sox, Bears, and Cubs). Annoying elevator muzak whines each team's fight song.

If this isn't enough to guide you to your car, we can't help you, because the garage's numbering-alphabetical system is more aggravating than the tinny elevator tunes.

If you're parking for less than three hours, go to Level 1. Parking costs $4 for the first 3 hours, $10 for up to 4 hours, and a deterring $51 per day.

## How to Get There—continued

Overnight parking close to Terminals 1, 2, and 3 on Levels 2 through 6 of the garage or in outside lots B and C costs $31 a day. For flyers with cash to burn, valet parking is available on Level 1 of the garage for $10 for the first hour, or $46 per day (8-24 hours). Parking in the International Terminal 5's designated Lot D costs $3 per hour for the first two hours and $2 per hour thereafter; the daily rate is $30; $50 for five days. Incoming international passengers always disembark in Terminal 5 (even if the airline departs from another terminal) because passengers must clear customs.

Long-term parking lots are Economy Lots E ($16), F ($9), and G ($13). From Lot E, walk or take the free shuttle to the free Airport Transit System (ATS) train station servicing all terminals. From Lot G, the shuttle will take you to the ATS stop in Lot E. Budget-conscious frequent flyers may want to purchase a prepaid Lot E "ExpressLane Parking" windshield tag for hassle-free, speedy departure from the airport.

**By Bus:** CTA buses 250 and 330 stop at the airport. he Wisconsin North Central Line departs Union Station for Antioch, with stops at the O'Hare Transfer station five times a day (weekday afternoons only); fares from Union Station are $4.75 one-way. The CTA also offers a special door-to-door service to and from the airport for Chicago-area residents and out-of-towners needing extra assistance. Call 312-663-4357 for additional information.

**By Train:** The odds of the Metra's schedule conveniently coinciding with your flight time are only slightly better than those of the Bulls winning the championship this year. The Wisconsin North Central Line departs Union Station for Antioch with a stop at the O'Hare Transfer station five times a day, starting in the afternoons on weekdays only ($3.30 one-way). Travel time is 30 minutes.

**By L:** We recommend the Blue Line as the best transportation method. The train runs between downtown Chicago and O'Hare 24 hours a day every 8 to 10 minutes ($2.25 one-way or $2 with Chicago Card/Ventra Card). Travel time from the Loop is 45 minutes. The train station is on the lowest level of the airport's main parking garage. Walk through the underground pedestrian tunnels to Terminals 1, 2, and 3. If you're headed for the International Terminal 5, walk to Terminal 3 and board the free Airport Transit System (ATS) train. In 2013, the CTA made price changes meant to hit out-of-towners riding the Blue Line from O'Hare. Unless you have a Chicago Card or a Ventra Card, the ride from O'Hare will cost you $5.

**By Cab:** Join the cab queue at the lower level curb-front of all terminals. There are no flat rates, as all of the cabs run on meters, but you probably won't have to spend more than $40. Beware if you're traveling to certain suburbs, though. Fare rules allow cabbies to raise your fare for these routes by 50%! Ask what the fare will be when you enter the cab. Some cab companies servicing O'Hare include American United, 773-262-8633; Flash Cab, 773-878-8500; Jiffy Cab, 773-487-9000; Yellow Cab, 312-808-9130; and Dispatch, 312-829-4222.

**By Kiss & Fly:** The Kiss & Fly is a convenient drop-off and pick-up point for "chauffeurs" who want to avoid the inevitable chaos at the terminal curb-side. Flyers should leave enough time for the ATS transfer to their terminals. The Kiss & Fly zone is off Bessie Coleman Drive. Take I-190 to the International Terminal exit to Bessie Coleman Drive. Turn left at the light and follow Bessie Coleman Drive north to the Kiss & Fly entrance and ATS stop.

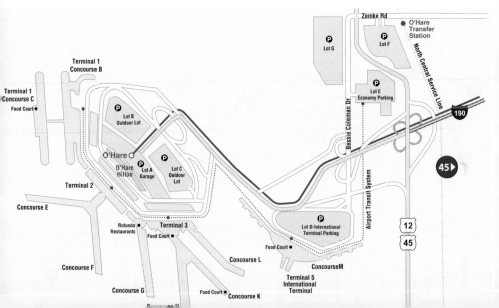

**By Shuttle:** Go Airport Express provides shared ride, door-to-door shuttle service between O'Hare and downtown hotels/attractions daily from 4 am until 11:30 pm. Shuttles depart every 10 - 15 minutes outside the lower level baggage claim area of both domestic and international terminals. Fares range from $23-$28, with group rates available for 2 or more passengers. Visit www.airportexpress.com for details.

Omega Airport Shuttle offers hourly service between O'Hare and Midway beginning around 7 am each day 'til about 11:45 pm and between Hyde Park and O'Hare from 5 am to 11:45 pm. The shuttle leaves from the International Terminal's outside curb by Door 5E and from the airport's Bus Shuttle Center in front of the O'Hare Hilton Hotel by Door 4. Allow at least an hour for travel time between the airports and expect to pay $17 for a one-way fare. Omega also has over 20 pickup and drop-off locations on the South Side serving O'Hare and Midway Airports. (773-734-6688; www.omegashuttle.com).

**By Limousine:** Sounds pricey, but depending on where you're going and how many people you are traveling with, it may be cheaper to travel by limo than by cab or shuttle. Advance reservations recommended. Limo services include O'Hare-Midway Limousine Service, 312-558-1111 (or 800-468-8989 for airport pick-up), www.ohare-midway.com; and My Chauffeur/American Limo, 847-376-6100, www.mychauffeurchicago.com.

## Airlines

| Airline | Terminal | Phone | Airline | Terminal | Phone |
|---|---|---|---|---|---|
| Aer Lingus | 5 | 800-474-7424 | JetBlue | 3 | 800-538-2583 |
| Aero Mexico | 5 | 800-237-6639 | KLM Royal Dutch Airlines | 5 | 800-221-1212 |
| Air Canada | 2 | 888-247-2262 | Korean Air | 5 | 800-438-5000 |
| Air Canada Jazz | 2 | 888-247-2262 | LOT Polish Airlines | 5 | 212-789-0970 |
| Air Choice One | 3 | 866-435-9847 | Lufthansa | 1 dep/5 arr | 800-645-3880 |
| Air France | 5 | 800-237-2747 | Mexicana Airlines | 5 | 800-531-7921 |
| Air India | 5 | 800-621-8231 | Royal Jordanian | 5 | 800-223-0470 |
| Alaska Airlines | 3 | 800-252-7522 | Scandinavian Airlines (SAS) | 5 | 800-221-2350 |
| Alitalia | 5 | 800-223-5730 | Skywest Airlines | 1 | 800-221-6903 |
| Al Nippon | 1,5 | 800-235-9262 | Spirit Airlines | 3 | 800-772-7117 |
| American Airlines: | | 800-443-7300 | Swiss International Airlines | 5 | 877-359-7947 |
| Domestic | 3 | | TACA Airlines | 5 | 800-400-8222 |
| International | 3 dep/5 arr | | Turkish Airlines | 5 | 800-874-8875 |
| American Eagle | 3 | 800-433-7300 | United Airlines: | | 800-241-6522 |
| Asiana Airlines | 5 | 800-227-4262 | Domestic/International dep | 1, 2 | |
| British Airways | 5 | 800-247-9297 | International arr | 5 | |
| Cathay Pacific Airways | 5 | 800-233-2742 | United Express | 1, 2 | 800-241-6522 |
| Cayman Airways | 5 | 800-422-9626 | US Airways | 2 | 800-428-4322 |
| Delta and Delta Shuttle | 2 | 800-221-1212 | USA 3000 | 5 | 877-872-3000 |
| Etihad Airways | 5 | +971-2-511-0000 | Virgin Atlantic | 5 | 800-821-5438 |
| Iberia Airlines | 3 dep/5 arr | 800-772-4642 | Virgin America | 3 | 877-359-8474 |
| Japan Airlines JAL | 3 dep/5 arr | 800-525-3663 | Westjet | 3 | 855-547-2451 |

## Car Rental

Alamo • 560 Bessie Coleman Dr, 800-327-9633/773-694-4646
Avis • 10000 Bessie Coleman Dr, 800-331-1212/773-825-4600
Budget • 580 Bessie Coleman Dr, 800-527-0700/773-894-1900
Dollar • O'Hare Intl Arpt, 800-800-4000/866-434-2226

Enterprise • 4025 Mannheim Rd, 800-867-4595/847-928-3320
Hertz • 10000 Bessie Coleman Dr, 800-654-3131/773-686-7272
National • 560 Bessie Coleman Dr, 800-227-7368/773-694-4646
Thrifty • 3901 N Mannheim Rd, 847-928-2000

## Hotels

All shuttles to airport hotels depart from the Bus Shuttle Center in front of the O'Hare Hilton Hotel in the center of the airport.

Best Western • 10300 W Higgins Rd, 847-296-4471
Clarion • 5615 N Cumberland Ave, 773-693-5800
Courtyard • 2950 S River Rd, 847-824-7000
Crown Plaza • 5440 N River Rd, 847-671-6350
Days Inn • 1920 E Higgins Rd, 847-437-1650
Comfort Inn • 2175 E Touhy Ave, 847-635-1300
DoubleTree • 5460 N River Rd, 847-292-9100
Embassy Suites • 5500 N River Rd, 847-678-4000
Four Points Sheraton • 10249 W Irving Park Rd, 847-671-6000
Hampton Inn • 3939 N Mannheim Rd, 847-671-1700
Hawthorn Suites • 1251 American Ln, 847-706-9007
Hilton • O'Hare Intl Arprt, 773-686-8000
Holiday Inn • 10233 W Higgins Rd, 847-954-8600
Hotel Sofitel • 5550 N River Rd, 847-678-4488

Hyatt Regency • 9300 W Bryn Mawr Ave, 847-696-1234
Hyatt Rosemont • 6350 N River Rd, 847-518-1234
La Quinta Inn • 1900 E Oakton St, 847-439-6767
Marriott Suites • 6155 N River Rd, 847-696-4400
Marriott Hotel • 8535 W Higgins Rd, 773-693-4444
Ramada Plaza • 5615 N Mannheim Rd, 773-693-5800
Residence Inn • 7101 Chestnut St, 847-375-9000
Sheraton Suites • 6501 N Mannheim Rd, 847-699-6300
InTown Suites • 2411 Landmeier Rd, 847-228-5500
Super 8 • 2951 Touhy Ave, 847-827-3133
Travelodge • 3003 Mannheim Rd, 847-296-5541
Westin • 6100 N River Rd, 847-698-6000
Wyndham • 6810 N Mannheim Rd, 847-297-1234

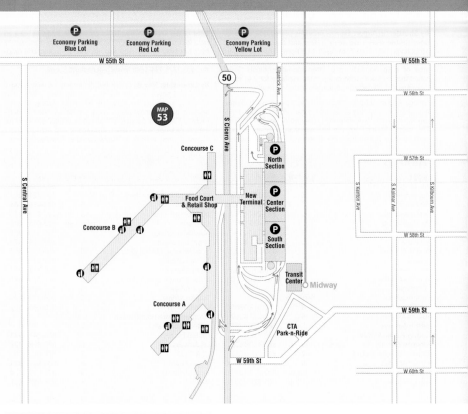

## General Information

| | |
|---|---|
| Address: | 5757 S Cicero Ave<br>Chicago, IL 60638 |
| Phone: | 773-838-0600 |
| Website: | www.midwayairport.org |
| Police: | 773-838-3003 |
| Parking: | 773-838-0756 |
| Customs: | 773-948-6330 |

## Overview

Located just ten miles southwest of downtown Chicago is Midway—one of the fastest-growing airports in the country serving 47,000 passengers daily. Considered the city's outlet mall of airports, Midway primarily provides service from budget carriers like Southwest Airlines and Porter. On the positive side, it is an easy alternative to the bigger, badder O'Hare. Plus the bars for pre-flight entertainment aren't as crowded.

The completion of a recent $739 million terminal development project has given Midway a swank new terminal building, new concourses, additional parking spaces and facilities, a food court, retail corridor, and customs facility to accommodate international flights.

Superstitious travelers beware of fl ying December 8th. On this date in 1972, a Boeing 737 crashed into a residential area during landing. In 2005, exactly 33 years later another Boeing slid off the runway in a landing attempt on December 8. Spooky.

## How to Get There

**By Car:** From downtown, take I-55 S. From the northern suburbs, take I-290 S to I-55 N. From the southern suburbs, take I-294 N to I-55 N. From the western suburbs, take I-88 E to I-294 S to I-55 N. Whether you're traveling north or south along I-55, look for the Cicero Avenue/South/Midway Airport exit.

**By Bus:** CTA buses 55, 59, and 63 all run from points east to the airport. Take the Green Line or the Red Line to the Garfield Station and transfer to bus 55 heading west ($1.75 one-way including transfer). If you're coming from the south on the Red Line, get off at the 63rd Street stop and take bus 63 westbound ($1.80 one-way). Other buses that terminate at the airport include 54B, 379, 382, 383, 384, 385, 386, 831, and 63W.

**By L:** The most convenient and cost-effective method of travel between Midway Airport and the Loop is a 20-30 minute train ride on the CTA Orange Line ($2.25, $2 with Chicago Card/Ventra Card). The first Orange Line train departs Midway, its terminus, at 4 am on weekdays, and 4:30 am on Saturdays and Sundays. The first train of the day from the Loop leaves the Clark/Lake station at 4:29 am and arrives at Midway by 4:56 am (approximately half an hour later on Saturdays and Sundays), well in advance of the airport's first early bird flights. Every night, the last Orange Line train departs Midway at 1:02 am, arrives in the Loop (Clark/Lake) at 1:31 am, and arrives back at Midway around 1:58 am. Trains run every five to seven minutes during weekday rush hours, ten minutes most other times, and fifteen minutes in late evenings. We recommend that wee-hours travelers stay alert at all times. The Orange Line conveniently drops you off inside Midway Airport (a huge plus in winter time!) – allow about 15 minutes to cart yourself and all your accouterments to the security checkpoint.

**By Cab:** Cabs depart from the lower level of the main terminal and are available on a first-come-first-served basis. There are no flat rates (all cabs run on meters), but you can plan on paying around $25 to get to the Loop. Some cab companies servicing Midway include American United, 773-262-8633; Flash Cab, 773-878-8500; Flash Dispatch, 773-561-1444; Jiffy Cab, 773-487-9000; and Yellow Cab, 312-808-9130.

**By Shuttle:** Go Airport Express provides shared ride, door-to-door shuttle service between Midway and downtown hotels/attractions daily from 4 am until 11:30 pm. Shuttles depart every 10 - 15 minutes outside the lower level baggage claim area by door LL3. Fares range from $23-$28, with group rates available for 2 or more passengers. Visit www.airportexpress.com for a fare calculator and to book a shuttle.

Omega Airport Shuttle (773-483-6634; www.omegashuttle.com) offers service leaving every 45 minutes or so between Midway and O'Hare beginning around 7 am each day with the final shuttle departing around 10 pm. Allow at least an hour for travel time between the airports and expect to pay $16 one-way. Contact Omega for information on more than 20 pickup locations on the South Side, to confirm schedules, to make reservations, and to prearrange home pickups.

**By Limousine:** Sounds pricey, but depending on where you're going and how many people you are traveling with, it may be cheaper to travel by limo than by cab or shuttle. Advance reservations recommended. Limo services include O'Hare-Midway Limousine Service, 312-558-1111 (or 800-468-8989 for airport pick-up), www.ohare-midway.com; and My Chauffeur/American Limo, 847-376-6100, www.americanlimousine.com.

## Parking

Short-term, hourly parking is located on Level 1 of the parking garage, with convenient access to the Terminal building. Parking is free for the first 10 minutes, then $2 for 10-30 minutes, and $5 for 30 minutes to 1 hour. The rates increase incrementally with each additional hour, up to $53 for 24 hours ($51 on Saturday/Sunday). Daily parking is available on levels 4, 5 and 6; rates are the same as short-term parking up to 4 hours, after which the fee levels off to $31 per day ($29 for Saturday/Sunday). If you plan on parking for a while, the best option is probably an economy lot or garage for $14 a day – just be sure to budget extra time to get to the Terminal. 24-hour complimentary shuttle service is available 7 days a week between the Terminal building and the economy lots, which are just east of Cicero Avenue and a quarter mile west of Cicero on 55th Street, and the economy garage at 55th and Laramie.

## Airlines

**Concourse A**

| | |
|---|---|
| Air Tran | 800-825-8538 |
| ComAir | 800-927-0927 |
| Delta | 800-221-1212 |
| Frontier | 800-432-1359 |
| Porter Airlines | 888-619-8622 |
| Public Charters/Jet Purple Airways | 877-359-7595 |
| Southwest | 800-435-9792 |
| Volaris Airlines | 866-988-3527 |

**Concourse B**

| | |
|---|---|
| Southwest | 800-435-9792 |

## Car Rental

| | | | |
|---|---|---|---|
| Alamo | 800-327-9633 | Enterprise | 800-566-9249 |
| Avis | 800-331-1212 | Hertz | 800-654-3131 |
| Budget | 800-527-7000 | National | 800-227-7368 |
| Dollar | 800-800-4000 | Thrifty | 800-527-7075 |

## Hotels

Best Western • 8220 S Cicero Ave, 708-497-3000
Fairfield Inn • 6630 S Cicero Ave, 708-594-0090
Hampton Inn • 6540 S Cicero Ave, 708-496-1900
Hilton • 9333 S Cicero Ave, 708-425-7800
Holiday Inn Express • 6500 S Cicero Ave, 708-458-0202
Marriott Midway • 6520 S Cicero Ave, 708-594-5500
Courtyard Midway • 6610 S Cicero Ave, 708-563-0200
Sleep Inn • 6650 S Cicero Ave, 708-594-0001

## General Information

Mailing address:
Chicago Transit Authority
567 W Lake St.
Chicago, IL 60661

Phone: 312-664-7200
CTA information: 888-YOUR CTA (968-7282)
Website: www.transitchicago.com

## Overview

We may never find a system of public transit free from flaws, but if you need a quick, socially responsible way to get from A to Wrigley, CTA's your guy. Once you figure out its complicated card system, CTA service will get you relatively close to where you need to go (most of the time), and sometimes the city's trains and buses are even on schedule!

For location-to-location CTA directions and schedules, we honestly and without irony, recommend the useful CTA trip planner at tripsweb.rtachicago.com. It allows you to plan your course by either estimated departure times or desired arrival times.

## Fares and Fare Cards

The city's tiered, pain-in-the-ass approach to fare payment makes it more expensive to pay with cash and easier to pay with cards. They don't call Chicago the city that works your nerves for nothing.

While buses accept cash and coin, you must use a card to ride the L. Full cash fares are $2.25. Fare card fares are $2.00 per bus ride, and $2.25 per L ride. On both bus and L, your first transfer will cost you 25 cents, and each transfer thereafter is free.

In 2013, the CTA introduced both new fare structures and a new fare card plan that both proved quite controversial. The change in fare structure is mostly to hit tourists as the prices for 1,3,7, and 30-day visitor passes were raised significantly. In addition, if you don't have a visitor pass or a Chicago Card or Ventra Card (we'll get to the Ventra Card, just wait…), a one-way trip from O'Hare on the Blue Line will cost you $5.

Still for visitors who plan to use public transit, the easiest and most worry-free way to use CTA is with a pass.
• 1-Day Visitor Pass for $10
• 3-Day Visitor Pass for $20
• 7-Day Visitor Pass for $28
• 30-Day Visitor Pass for $100
Visitor passes give you unlimited rides on all CTA buses, L trains and PACE (suburban) buses, but CTA Visitor Passes are not valid on Metra (commuter railroad) trains. Your visitor pass activates the first time you use it—it's good for the number of consecutive days shown on the front of the card. Example: a 3-day pass is valid for 72 hours from the first time you insert it into the card reader on L turnstiles or inside the bus. At that point the expiration date and time will be printed on the back of the card.

Here's a breakdown on the benefits, limitations, and rules for fare methods…

**Ventra Card**: The Ventra Card is one of the biggest CTA changes in recent history—a full overhaul of the fare card system. The Ventra Card began into rotation as an acceptable fare card in summer 2013, with the intent to phase out all other fare cards in 2014. The date of this has not been determined, but expect it to come sooner than later in 2014. For this reason, we'll fully explain the Ventra Card, but still give you information on the existing fare card structure. It is just important to note that at a certain point in 2014 (and again we stress that the plan is to begin in early 2014) the Ventra in various forms will be the one and only fare card in use. That means it will function as visitor passes, one-time fare cards and 30-day passes.

Confused yet? Well, lets play a little question and answer game…

**Um, what?**
We know, we know. Ventra is a payment system that will allow customers to use a single fare card for regional transit through the Chicago area. This means it can be used on CTA and Pace.

There are three ways to use the Ventra system:
Ventra Card: Any amount of money can be loaded on to a Ventra Card with cash or online
Ventra Ticket: Think what the current basic fare card looks like, a disposable, paper card. The ticket is for single ride use and day pass unlimited-ride tickets.
Personal bank issued credit cards: Link your personal credit or debit card to your Ventra account and you add value or purchase passes so you can use your own card.

**Am I going to have to pay for this thing?**
Ventra Cards will have a one-time cost fee of $5 that is refunded as transit value if registered and used within 90 days. But use it! If you don't use your card for 18 months, you'll get slapped with a monthly fee. But hey, no worries, you're friends at the CTA will notify you before this happens.

**Hey, but I like my Chicago Card! Can't I use that still?**
Sorry, Charlie, no more Chicago Card. Registered Chicago Card and Chicago Card Plus users will be mailed a Ventra Card to begin using instead and will not be charged the $5 fee.

**My Aunt Martha and Uncle Henry are visiting for the day from the 'burbs. They love to take a ride around the Loop on the L each time they visit. Can they get a single ride card still?**
Why, yes! No need for Aunt Martha and Uncle Henry to worry. They can get a disposable, single ride Ventra ticket. Oh, but bad news, they're going to get penalized for buying that single ride ticket. It will cost them $3, which includes the $2.25 fare, a $.25 transfer and a $.50 limited use ticket fee.

**Transfer?!? But they're not transferring! Limited use ticket fee?!**
Yep. You pay for a transfer whether you take one or not, and you're getting penalized for a single ticket with that $.50. So the best bet is to just get the $5 Ventra Card. Annoying, but true.

**Well, can I still use cash on the bus and will that also cost me $3 for a one-way ride?**
Yes, you can still use cash, and no, it will not cost $3 like a single ride on the L, it will cost the standard $2.25.

**You mentioned I can use my own debit or credit card?**
Yes, you can link it if it is a contactless card. Your card is contactless if it has this symbol: . That means your own card now acts as its own fare card. You link it to your Ventra Card at no charge and you can load money on to it, load it as a day pass of any length or as a monthly pass.

**What is this I hear about using my Ventra Card as a debit card?**
You heard right and this is where all the controversy comes in. Let us stress that this is an option and not a requirement. Here's how it works: If you activate your optional Money Network® MasterCard® Prepaid Debit Account and load funds, you can use your dual-purpose Ventra Card wherever Debit MasterCard® is accepted. In addition to making purchases, you can load funds via direct deposit, make online bill payments, get cash at ATMs and much more. However, these come with a myriad of fees, so don't tell us you haven't been severely warned.

**I'm still confused.**
Right, well so are we. For full answers to all your questions and to learn all about the Ventra system, visit www.ventrachicago.com.

## Page 252, L Map

The current map as listed is outdated. There are two new stations that opened in 2012 that are not on the map as is: the Morgan stop on the Green/Pink Line and the Oakton-Skokie stop on the Yellow Line. In addition, the inset shows the Washington stop for the Red Line, and it has been closed for several years. The Washington stop is still open on the Blue Line, but because there is no longer a Red Line Washington stop, you can't transfer so the transfer needs to be eliminated as well.

For the most current map: http://www.transitchicago.com/assets/1/maps/P19_2012_CTA_Rail_Map.pdf

**Fare Card:** You can purchase the standard paper fare card at any L station from the big blue fare card machines. Fare cards can be purchased in any amount (fare minimum is $2.25) and used on the bus or L. Fares are $2.25, plus 25 cents to transfer. Purchasing a fare card is easy—insert the amount of money you want on your card into the money-eater (whether it will actually accept your crinkly or faded dollar bills or spit them back out at you is entirely another matter), and push the "vend" button. Your card will pop out of the slot (at roughly waist level) below the money eater. Lost or stolen fare cards are not replaceable. Money can be added at any fare card machine. To use a fare card, insert it into the card reader on CTA turnstiles or inside the bus (next to the bus money-eater). No change is given from CTA fare card machines.

**Chicago Card:** The Chicago Card can be purchased online (allow about a week for delivery) or at participating Jewel and Dominick's grocery store locations and some currency exchanges (go to their website for addresses of participating vendors). Chicago cards can be purchased for predetermined amounts ($10, $20) or for specific amounts. Balances can be checked, and Chicago Cards can be reloaded at CTA fare card machines. Touch the card to the Chicago Card sensor, enter your reload amount into the money eater, and retouch your card to the sensor until the readout says, "Thank you." Do not forget to retouch your card to the sensor after adding money, or the money will not be added to your card. To use the Chicago Card, simply press it against the sensor at the turnstile or on the bus. Lost or stolen Chicago Cards can be replaced, with their remaining value, for $5 if you chose the option to register the card (optional card registration is free, so why not?).

**Chicago Card Plus:** The Chicago Card Plus is like the Chicago Card except for a few key differences. Registration of the Chicago Card Plus is mandatory. Card balances can only be checked and/or have money added (credit only) online or by calling CTA customer service. With the Chicago Card Plus, you have the option of choosing pay-as-you-go or purchasing a monthly pass. You must have an e-mail address to use a Chicago Card Plus. Like the regular Chicago Card, there is a $5 fee to replace your Chicago Card Plus if it is lost or stolen.

**Pass Back Option:** At any time, you can share your CTA card with up to six other people traveling with you by passing the card back over the turnstile. The full fare for each rider will be deducted from your card.

**Reduced Fares:** Reduced fares are available for qualified passengers—people with disabilities, senior citizens, and children under 12. Regular cash fare for kids ages 7–11 is $1. Children under age 7 ride free.

Go to the CTA website for more information about reduced fare applicability at www.transitchicago.com.

## CTA Buses

CTA's buses cart about one million sweaty, crabby passengers around Chicago and its surrounding suburbs everyday; the fleet is the second-largest public transportation system in the US. CTA's more than 140 bus routes mirror Chicago's efficient grid system. The majority of CTA routes run north-south or east-west, and in areas where the streets are numbered, the bus route is usually the same as the street.

Recently, the entire CTA bus fleet has been overhauled to comply with ADA accessibility standards. The result is that now all buses kneel, that is, they tilt to make the first step less steep. All buses are equipped with wheelchair lifts and secure wheelchair seating. Additionally, as a boon to the visually impaired and those too busy gawking at Chicago's skyscrapers to read the signs on the front of each bus, all buses clearly and loudly announce the bus number and direction at every stop.

The newest and arguably most helpful addition to the CTA transit system is the Bus Tracker, an online resource for discovering "exactly" when your bus will arrive at its stop. Accessible via www.ctabustracker.com, the Bus Tracker gives a damn good estimate of arrival times, cutting down your wait by a significant margin. You'll be grateful in December. And January. And February. And March…

**Bus Stops:** CTA stops are clearly marked with blue and white signs displaying the name and number of the route, as well as the final destination. Most routes operate from the early morning until 10:30 pm. Night routes, called "Night Owls," are identified on bus stop signage by an owl picture. Owl service runs approximately every half-hour through the night. All bus stop signs are now conveniently labeled with a 'Stop ID number' that you can use to get arrival times by text message. Simply text ctabus [stopID] to 41411 on your cell phone and the bus tracker will text you back with estimated arrival times for all buses at that stop.

**Fares:** Buses accept exact fare only for individual rides. A regular one-way cash fare is $2.25. Transfers are not available with cash fares. Bus fares can also be paid with CTA fare cards or Chicago and Chicago Plus cards. In this case, the fare is $2, plus 25 cents for your first transfer, with each transfer after that free, for up to two hours.. The transfer fee will be charged at the next leg of your journey. You must always insert your fare card into the card machine, or press your Chicago Card on the sensor—even for the free transfer. No money will be deducted for the third leg of a journey after a transfer has been purchased (within the two hour limit).

**Bicycles Onboard:** Designated CTA buses are equipped with bike racks mounted on front grills to carry up to two bikes. Generally speaking, CTA bike buses are those that travel to lakefront beaches, like the 63rd Street, the #72 North Avenue buses, #77 Belmont, or the #92 Foster Avenue bus. Additional buses with bike racks are often added during summer months or for special events.

Loading your bike onto a CTA bus:
- If your bike is the first to be loaded, lower the rack and place it in position with the front wheel facing the curb.
- If there is already a bike on the rack, place your bike's rear wheel toward the curb.
- If two bikes are already loaded and the rack is full; wait for the next bus.

# Transit · The L

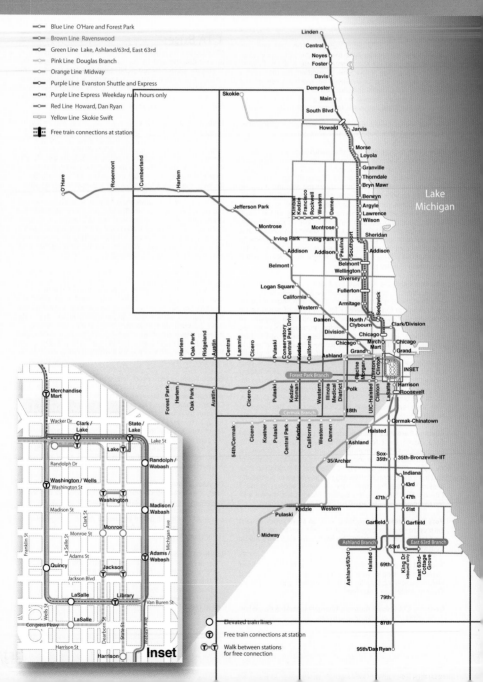

Blue Line  O'Hare and Forest Park
Brown Line  Ravenswood
Green Line  Lake, Ashland/63rd, East 63rd
Pink Line  Douglas Branch
Orange Line  Midway
Purple Line  Evanston Shuttle and Express
Purple Line Express  Weekday rush hours only
Red Line  Howard, Dan Ryan
Yellow Line  Skokie Swift
Free train connections at station

Lake
Michigan

## Inset

Elevated train lines
Free train connections at station
Walk between stations
for free connection

## Overview

Whether traveling underground, on street level, or above the sidewalk, Chicagoans refer to their elevated rapid transit system as the "L." (Though some prefer to call it the "Smell.") No matter which one you choose, either name says Chicago as loud and clear as the high-pitched whine, guttural grumble, and steely grind of the train itself. L tracks lasso Chicago's heart, creating The Loop, where five of the seven L lines ride side-by-side above the pulsating business and financial district.

L trains make 2,145 trips each day and serve 145 stations in the Chicago Metropolitan Area. The two newest stations opened in 2012: the Morgan stop on the Green and Pink Lines and the Oakton-Skokie Station on the Yellow Line. The numerous track delays and stalls in service are a burden to thousands of daily commuters. Nonetheless, due to the general directness of the L routes, easy station-to-station transfers, and the difficulties of parking (especially near popular destinations such as Grant Park and Wrigley Field), the benefits of L transportation usually outweigh the discomforts and inconveniences.

## Fares

The standard full fare on CTA trains is $2.25 with or without a Chicago Card. A 25¢ transfer allows two additional rides within two hours of issuance. Transfer rates are automatically deducted from your fare card when reused within the time limit. Transferring within the rail network is free at determined, connected transfer stations.

To ride the L, you need a farecard. Read the CTA Overview for a thorough discussion on the merits of each fare card option, or go to the CTA website at www.transitchicago.com.

## Frequency of Service

CTA publishes schedules that say trains run every 3 to 12 minutes during weekday rush hours and every 6 to 20 minutes all other times. Nice idea, but the truth is service can be irregular, especially during non-rush hours, after-hours, and in bad weather. While the system is relatively safe late at night, stick to stations in populated areas as much as possible. Buses with Owl Service may be better options in the wee hours.

## L Lines

**Blue Line:** Its 24-hour O'Hare and Forest Park branches service the West and Northwest sides, including getting travelers to and from O'Hare Airport in a jiffy.

**Pink Line:** Chicago's newest elevated rail line took over the Blue Line's former Cermak/Douglas route with service to the near Southwest Side. The first trains leave the 54th/Cermak terminus at 4:05 am, and the last train from the Loop leaves at 1:25 am daily.

**Red Line:** Runs north-south from the Howard Street station down to the 95th Street/Dan Ryan station; operates 24-hours

**Brown Line:** Starts from the Kimball Street station and heads south with service to the Loop and sometimes just to Belmont Avenue, where you can connect with the 24-hour Red Line. On weekdays and Saturdays, the first Loop-bound train leaves Kimball at 4 am; the last Kimball-bound train leaves the Loop at 1 am. Truncated service to and from Belmont continues to run until 2 am on weekdays and Saturdays, with the last Kimball-bound train departing Belmont at 2:25 am. Sunday morning Brown Line service begins at 5 am but only to Belmont; Loop-bound trains don't start running until 6:45 am on Sundays, and go until 12:15 am; after that, you can catch the northbound Brown Line at Belmont until 12:55 am.

**Orange Line:** Service from Midway Airport and Chicago's Southwest Side to and from the Loop. Trains depart Midway at 4 am on weekdays, and 4:30 am on Saturdays and Sundays. The last train leaves the Loop for Midway at 1:20 am on weekdays, and 1:25 am on Sundays.

**Green Line:** Covers portions of west and south Chicago. The Harlem/Lake Street branch travels straight west to suburban Oak Park, while the Ashland/63rd Street and Cottage Grove branches go south and split east and west. Daily service begins around 4 am, depending on the branch, and run until about 1 am. Weekend schedules vary.

**Purple Line:** Shuttles north/south between Linden Place in suburban Wilmette and Chicago's northernmost L station at Howard Street. Service runs at 4:50 am – 1:45 am on weekdays, 4:50 am – 2:15 am on Fridays, 5:30 am – 2:15 am on Saturdays, and 6:30 am – 1:45 am on Sundays/holidays. An express service runs from Linden to the Loop, with no stops between Howard and Belmont, during weekday rush hours. Purple Line Express trains leave Linden between 5:20 am – 9:30 am, and 2:30 pm – 6:30 pm each weekday. The last northbound Purple Line Express train leaves the Loop at 10:15 am during morning rush and 7:10 pm in the evenings.

**Yellow Line:** Also known as the 'Skokie Swift,' the Yellow Line runs between the north suburban Skokie Station and Chicago's Howard Street station, with one intermediate stop at Oakton Street. Weekday service runs 5 am – 11:15 pm, and 6:30 am – 11:15 pm on Saturdays and Sundays.

## Bicycles

Bicycles ride free and are permitted onboard at all times except weekdays from 7 am to 9 am and 4 pm to 6 pm. Only two bikes are allowed per car, so survey the platform for other bikes and check out the cars as they pull into the station for two-wheelers already onboard. When entering a station, either use the turnstile, or ask an attendant to open the gate. Don't try to take your bike through the tall steel gates—it WILL get stuck!

## PACE Suburban – Chicago Buses

Pace buses serve over 35 million passengers in the Chicago suburbs and some parts of the city. With nearly 200 routes covering 3,446 square miles, Pace provides a vital transportation service to commuters traveling between suburbs, within suburbs, to Metra train stations, and into the city. Buses usually run every 20–30 minutes, and service stops by mid-evening. Special express service is offered to Chicago-area entertainment and cultural venues. Contact Pace for specific bus route and schedule information (847-364-PACE; www.pacebus.com).

**Park-n-Ride Stations:** Pace has 12 Park-n-Ride stations located throughout Pace's six-county coverage area (check the Pace website for locations).

**Fares:** Pace fares cost $1.75 for both regular and local or feeder service. Transfers are $.25 for regular service. The one-way fare on express routes 355, 426, 835, and 855 costs $4. CTA Transit Cards may be used on Pace buses. Pass options include the Pace 30-Day Commuter Club Cards (CCC), which allow unlimited Pace rides for $60. A combined CTA/Pace 30-day unlimited ride pass costs $86 and can be used on all Pace buses and CTA trains and buses. A combined Pace/CTA 30-day unlimited pass costs $75 and can be used on all Pace buses and CTA trains and buses. The PlusBus Sticker (sold by Metra with a Metra Monthly Train Pass) costs $30 and allows unlimited Pace bus use.

## Greyhound Buses

Greyhound is the rock-bottom traveler's best friend. The bus line offers dirt-cheap fares, the flexibility drifters prefer, basic station amenities (i.e. dirty toilets and vending machines that steal your money), and the gritty, butt-busting experience of traveling America's scenic blue-line highways and rural byways with some colorful characters.

Tips on riding "the Dog" out of town:
• Pack your own toilet paper and Wet Ones.
• Air freshener, deodorant, a pillow, and earplugs make being bused more bearable.
• Pack a cooler. Then padlock it.
• Charge your iPod. Seriously.
• Bring a cushion.
• Get your shots.

**Stations:** Greyhound's main train station is south of Union Station at 630 W Harrison St in West Loop (312-408-5800). CTA buses 60, 125, 156, and 157 make stops near the terminal. The closest L stop is on the Blue Line's Forest Park Branch at the Clinton Street Station on Congress Parkway. Additional Chicago-area Greyhound stations are located within L train stations: 14 W 95th St in the Red Line's 95th Street/Dan Ryan Station (312-408-5999), and 5800 N Cumberland Ave on the Blue Line's O'Hare Branch in the Cumberland Station (773-693-2474). The general aura of the Chicago Greyhound Station is one of seediness and squalor. Keep your belongings with you at all times.

**Shipping Services:** Greyhound Package Xpress offers commercial and personal shipping services and is available at all three Chicago bus stations. Packages are held at the station for pick-up. The main terminal in th South Loop also houses a UPS shipping office that provides door-to-door package delivery.

**Fares:** Tickets can be purchased on the phone or online with a credit card, or at a station with cash, travelers' checks, credit cards, or a voucher from the local plasma donor center (we kid!).

Regular fare pricing applies for both individual advance ticket sales and minutes-before-departure sales. Tickets can be used for travel to the designated destination on any day or at any departure time. Because Greyhound does not reserve seats, boarding occurs on a first-come-first-served basis, so get in line at the boarding zone for a choice seat. However, Greyhound's bark is bigger than its bite— if a significant number of passengers turn out for the same bus, Greyhound rolls another bus, or two, or three out on the spot. Good dog.

Children under 12 receive 40% discounts off of regular fares, seniors 62 and older receive 5% discounts, military members receive 10% discounts, and patients of Veteran's Administration Hospitals receive a 25% discount. Other discounts are available online. The cost for an individual return ticket is always deeply discounted if it is purchased at the same time as a departure ticket.

Tickets purchased three days in advance earn a half-price companion ticket (no age restrictions). Passengers accompanying someone with a disability always ride at a reduced rate.

## Megabus.com

Roll over Greyhound, there's a new dog in town, and a cheaper one at that! Megabus.com is the Midwest's answer to the East Coast Chinatown buses. An import from the UK, these buses travel between most major Midwest cities, including Minneapolis, Detroit, Milwaukee, St. Louis, Cleveland, Indianapolis, and Pittsburgh! That's not a comprehensive list, and they are always adding more cities as demand increases, so check back.

**Fares:** And that brings us to the best part about Megabus, which is that the ticket prices are determined by how far in advance you buy your tickets, how popular the route is, and what day of the week you travel on. If your Fairy Godmother is on your side, it is possible that you could take a round-trip bus to, say, Kansas City, for TWO DOLLARS. That's right, these bus fares go as low as $1 each way. Of course, as the service becomes more popular, the fares go up. And if you're like us, you don't buy your fares months ahead of time, which adds to the cost. But even so, most fares don't go too much higher than $20 each way. Still a sweet deal, even by Greyhound standards.

**Stations:** Megabus doesn't have stations, per se. But you'll see the line snaking outside Union Station as you approach. Union Station in downtown Chicago is the arrival and departure stop for all buses out of Chicago. Park yourself at the east side of South Canal Street, between Jackson Blvd and Adams Street, and try to get there early. It's first come, first serve seating.

Megabus doesn't run as frequently as Greyhound, but for lapses in service, you can always check in on its umbrella company, Van Galder, which is in turned owned by the corporate bus superpower Coach USA (www.coachusa.com/vangalder) or call 800-747-0994 toll free or 608-752-5407). Van Galder is a touch more expensive, but its routes are more frequent and more comprehensive.

Other important logistics: You can order your Megabus ticket online (www.megabus.com/us) or call for a reservation (877-GO-2-MEGA) up to 45 days in advance. You can only bring one piece of luggage (up to 50 pounds) to stow under the bus and one small carry-on. No bikes allowed. Megabus is more or less wheelchair accessible, just make sure you call and let them know, and they can accommodate you.

**Zone**

A
B
C
D
E
F
G
H
I
J
K
M

| | | |
|---|---|---|
| **UP-N** | **Metra/Union Pacific North Line** | Chicago (OTC) to Kenosha, WI |
| **UP-NW** | **Metra/Union Pacific Northwest Line** | Chicago (OTC) to Harvard & McHenry |
| **UP-W** | **Metra/Union Pacific West Line** | Chicago (OTC) to Geneva |
| **MD-N** | **Metra/Milwaukee District North Line** | Chicago (Union Station) to Fox Lake |
| **MD-W** | **Metra/Milwauvkee District West Line** | Chicago (Union Station) to Elgin/Big Timber |
| **NCS** | **Metra/North Central Service** | Chicago (Union Station) to Anitioch |
| **BNSF** | **Metra/Burlington Northern Santa Fe** | Chicago (Union Station) to Aurora |
| **ME** | **Metra Electric** | Chicago (Randolph St Station) to University Park |
| **HC** | **Metra/Heritage Corridor** | Chicago (Union Station) to Joliet |
| **SWS** | **Metra/South West Service** | Chicago (Union Station) to Orland Park |
| **RI** | **Metra/Rock Island District** | Chicago (La$alle St Station) to Joliet |
| **SS** | **Metra/South Shore** | Chicago (Randolph St Station) to South Bend,IN |

## General Information

| | |
|---|---|
| Metra Address: | Metra Passenger Services |
| | 547 W Jackson Blvd |
| | Chicago, IL 60661 |
| Phone: | 312-322-6777 |
| Website: | www.metrarail.com |
| Metra Passenger Service: | 312-322-6777 |
| South Shore Metra Lines: | 800-356-2079 |
| RTA Information Center: | 312-836-7000; |
| | www.rtachicago.com |

## Overview

With a dozen lines and roughly 495 miles of track overseen by the RTA, Metra does its best to service Cook, DuPage, Lake, Will, McHenry, and Kane counties with 230 stations scattered throughout the city and 'burbs. The rails, emanating from four major downtown stations, are lifelines for commuters traveling to and from the Loop.

The good news for Metra is that ridership is strong; the sheer multitude of folks who live in the suburbs but work in the city (and hate to deal with rush hour a-holes) means that Metra will always have a job. The bad news for riders is that parking at popular stations is difficult, if not impossible, and most people don't live close enough to Metra stations to walk. In an attempt to resolve its parking issues, Metra is purchasing land surrounding many suburban stations and constructing new parking facilities. Check out the website, www. metrarail.com, for updates on development plans.

## Loop Stations

There are four major Metra train stations in the Loop from which 11 train lines emanate. Here's a chart to help clear up any possible confusion:

| Station | Line |
|---|---|
| Ogilvie Transportation Center | Union Pacific Lines |
| Union Station | Milwaukee District Lines |
| | North Central Service |
| | Southwest Service |
| | Burlington Northern |
| | Heritage Corridor |
| | Amtrak |
| LaSalle Street Station | Rock Island Line |
| Randolph Street Station (Millennium Station) | South Shore Railroad |
| | Metra Electric—Branches: |
| | Main Line, South Chicago, |
| | Blue Island |

## Fares

Depending on the number of Metra zones you traverse, one-way, full-fare tickets cost between $2.75 and $9.25. To calculate a base one-way fare, visit www.metrarail. com. Tickets may be purchased through a ticket agent or vending machine at select stations, or onboard the train (with a $3 surcharge if the station at which you boarded the train had a ticket agent or ticket vending machine). There is no reserved seating.

Metra offers a number of reasonably priced ticket packages, including a Ten-Ride Ticket (which saves riders 15% off of one-way fares) and a Monthly Unlimited Ride Ticket (the most economical choice for commuters who use Metra service daily). If your commute includes CTA and/or Pace bus services, consider purchasing a Link-Up Sticker ($45) for unlimited connecting travel on CTA and Pace. Metra's Weekend Pass costs $7 and includes unlimited rides on Saturday and Sunday, with the exception of the South Shore route. You can buy all the aforementioned tickets in person, through the mail, or online at www.metrarail.com.

Children under age seven ride free. Children ages 7–11 ride for half-price on weekdays and for free on the weekends. Children ages 12–17 ride for half-price on weekends. Full-time grade school or high school students are eligibile to receive 50% off the cost of regular one-way fares. Senior citizens/disability fares are approximately half of the regular fare. US Military personnel in uniform ride Metra at a discounted rate. Anyone wearing capri pants after Labor Day will be charged double.

## Water Taxi

Spring through fall, commuters can enjoy a convenient and uniquely scenic way of getting about via Wendella's Chicago Water Taxi, which links Ogilvie Transportation Center to North Michigan Avenue and Chinatown. Chicago Water Taxis operate 7 days a week and tickets may be purchased on board the boat, at the Wendella ticket office at 400 N Michigan Ave, or at dockside kiosks where available. Fares start at $2 one-way, with options for one-day and multiple ride passes available as well. Visit www.chicagowatertaxi.com for more details and schedules. From Union Station, commuters can hop aboard a Shoreline Water Taxi, which makes stops at North Michigan Avenue, Navy Pier, and the Museum Campus, and offers a rush hour commuter service between Union Station and North Michigan Avenue. Fares start at between $2-$3 and may be purchased from dockside kiosks. Visit www.shorelinewatertaxi.com for dock locations and schedules.

## Baggage & Pets

While Metra may be "the way to really fly," Metra's restrictions on baggage are more stringent than those of most airlines, though they now allow bicycles on weekday off-peak hours and on weekends (details on the "Bikes on Trains" program are divulged at www. metrarail.com). Skis, golf clubs, non-folding carts, water buffaloes, and other large luggage items can never be transported on trains. Pets, with the exception of service animals, are also prohibited aboard trains.

## General Information

Loop Station Address: Millennium Station at
Randolph Street
151 E Randolph St
Underground at N Michigan
Ave & E Randolph St
Chicago, IL 60601
Phone: 312-782-0676
Lost & Found: 219-874-4221 x205
Website: www.nictd.com

## Overview

Although the historic South Shore train lines were built in 1903, they still get you from the Loop to Indiana's South Bend Airport in just 2.5 hours. The Northern Indiana Commuter Transportation District (NICTD) oversees the line and its modern electric trains, which serve as a vital transportation link for many northwest Indiana residents working in the Loop.

The South Shore's commuter service reflects its Indiana ridership. Outbound heading from the Loop, there are limited stops before the Hegewisch station, close to the Indiana state line. When traveling by train to Chicago's South Side, you're better off on an outbound Metra Electric Line train departing from the Randolph Street Station (see Metra page). Taking a trip on the South Shore is a rather cheap form of post-industrial voyeurism, as a complete round-trip from the Loop all the way to South Bend can be had for around $20. Along the way you will pass by dozens of antiquated factories, one of the longest stretches of sand-dunes in the Great Lakes region, and, of course, oh-so charming Gary, Indiana.

## Fares

Regular one-way fares can be purchased at the stations (with cash or personal check), onboard trains (cash only), or online (Visa and Mastercards accepted). Ticket prices vary with distance traveled. Tickets purchased onboard the train cost $1 more if the station's ticket windows were open at the time of departure.

Special South Shore fares and packages include commuter favorites: 10-Ride and 25-Ride tickets and the Monthly Pass which is good for unlimited travel. These can be purchased in person at stations staffed with ticket agents, station vending machines, and via the mail. Senior citizens/disability fares offer savings for persons aged 65 and older with valid identification and for disabled passengers. Students with school identification qualify for student fares, including reduced one-way tickets and discounted 25-Ride Tickets good for travel during weekdays. Youth fares include free passage for infants under two years (who must sit in a paying passenger's lap) and half off a regular fare for children aged two to 13 years. Family fares are available on weekends and holidays as well as off-peak times on weekdays. Each fare-paying adult (minimum age 21) may take up to two children (age 13 and under) with them free of charge. Additional children will be charged the reduced youth fare. Active duty military personnel in uniform may request reduced fares with their Common Access Cards (CAC).

## Baggage & Pets

Any accompanying baggage must be placed in the overhead racks. No bicycles are permitted onboard. Apart from small animals in carry-on cages, the only pets allowed onboard are service dogs accompanied by handlers or passengers with disabilities. Animals must not occupy seats.

## General Information

| | |
|---|---|
| Amtrak Reservations: | 800-USA-RAIL (872-7245) |
| Website: | www.amtrak.com |
| Union Station: | 225 S Canal St |
| | Chicago, IL 60606 |
| Phone: | 312-322-6900 |

## Overview

The best city in America for riding the rails, Chicago hubs Amtrak's 500-station national railroad network, which covers every state but Alaska, Hawaii, South Dakota, and Wyoming. Departing from Union Station, Amtrak trains head west to Los Angeles, San Francisco, Portland and Seattle; east to Washington, D.C., New York City and Boston; north to Milwaukee and Minneapolis; and south to New Orleans and San Antonio, Texas.

## Fares

Amtrak offers affordable fares for regional travel, with travel times comparable to flying when you factor in today's early airport check-ins. Their prices can't compete with airfares on longer hauls, but just as airlines offer deeply discounted fares, so does Amtrak. Ask sales agents about special fares and search Amtrak's website for the best deals. (Booking in advance does present some savings.) We recommend the website, as callers risk being on hold longer than it takes to ride a train from Chicago to Los Angeles.

Amtrak offers special fares year-round for seniors, veterans, students, children under 16, and groups of two or more traveling together. The "Hot Deals" page on Amtrak's website lists sale fares. Amtrak has also hooked its cars up with plenty of travel partners to create interesting "Amtrak Vacations" packages, including air-rail deals, whereby you rail it one way and fly back the other—attractive for long-distance travel.

The prices listed below are approximate, likely to change and don't include upgrades like sleeper cars. Check with Amtrak for updates.

## Service

Someday, high-speed rail may come to the Midwest. Meanwhile, only a lucky few can claim to have arrived on time when traveling the longer routes on Amtrak, so tell whoever is picking you up you'll call them on your cell phone when you get close.

Pack food for your ride, as dining-car fare is mediocre and pricey. On the upside, Amtrak's seats are comfortable and roomy; some have electric sockets for computer hookups; bathrooms are in every car; and the train is almost always clean.

And you don't have to travel light. Your ticket lets you carry on two bags and check three, each weighing up to 50 pounds. Check an additional three bags and items such as bicycles, golf bags, baby strollers, musical instruments, and skis with handling fees of $5 to $10 each. Amtrak's default liability for checked baggage tops out at $500, so if your designer duds are worth more than that you'll want to ante up for extra coverage. Weapons; large, sharp objects; corrosive or dangerous chemicals; and the like are all prohibited, just like on planes; check for current regs before you pack.

**Within Illinois and to Missouri:** Amtrak's Illinois Service trains travel to 28 downstate cities from Chicago daily: "The Illinois Zephyr" and "The Carl Sandburg" travel to Quincy (on the Mississippi); "Illini Service" and "The Saluki" roll between Chicago and Carbondale; "The Lincoln Service" goes through corn and soybean country to St. Louis; and "The Ann Rutledge" heads to Kansas City. Also running daily, "The Southwest Chief" stops in Kansas City five hours into its trip to Albuquerque and Los Angeles; the fare runs about $85 one way. "The City of New Orleans" makes a number of downstate stops, too.

**To Milwaukee and Minneapolis:** Frequent enough for commuters, "Hiawatha Service" runs seven trains daily to Sturtevant, Wisconsin (near Racine); Milwaukee's Mitchell Airport; and downtown Milwaukee, leaving Chicago about every two hours and stopping en route in suburban Glenview. The 90-minute trip costs $21 each way (a good alternative to driving on busy weekends and rush hours). "Hiawatha Service" accepts RTA Transit Checks. En route to the Northwest, "The Empire Builder" also stops in Milwaukee, as well as Minneapolis; it takes some eight and a half hours to reach the Twin Cities, with one-way fare about $92.

**To Michigan:** Skip scary driving through the "Snow Belt" by taking the train. Three lines offer daily service to the Winter Water Wonderland: "The Pere Marquette" heads to Grand Rapids; "The Blue Water" takes passengers to Port Huron; and "The Wolverine" goes to Ann Arbor and Detroit, among other places. The ride to the Motor City takes about six hours and costs $27 to $48 one way.

**To the East Coast:** "The Capitol Limited" runs daily through Cleveland and Pittsburgh to Washington, D.C., an 18-hour trip, while "The Cardinal" takes 28 hours to get to New York via Indianapolis, Cincinnati, Philadelphia, and Washington three days a week. The "Lake Shore Limited" passes through Albany, N.Y., and goes to New York City (21 hours) and Boston (24 hours). One-way tickets to the Eastern Seaboard cost between $80 and $150.

**To Seattle or Portland:** The "Empire Builder" takes passengers to Seattle and Portland and everywhere in between. With the journey to Seattle taking around 44 hours, we definitely recommend dropping some additional dollars on a sleeper car. One-way fare costs between $140 and $250.

**To San Francisco:** You'll spend two solid days and then some riding the rails during the 52-hour journey on the "California Zephyr" to San Francisco (Emeryville). The fare costs roughly $175 to $230 one-way. The "Zephyr" passes through Denver, Salt Lake City, and Sacramento, and makes a host of small-town America stops along the way.

**To Los Angeles:** You'll have plenty of time to study your map to the Hollywood stars on the "Southwest Chief," which departs for L.A. daily via Albuquerque, takes almost 42 hours, and costs $200 to $250 one-way.

**To San Antonio:** The mighty "Texas Eagle" doesn't exactly glide to the Alamo. It stops at 40 cities on its way from the Midwest to the Southwest. The 32-hour trip will cost around $117.

**To New Orleans:** The train Chicago's Steve Goodman made famous, "The City of New Orleans," runs from Chicago via Memphis to The Big Easy in roughly 20 hours. The fare runs about $100 to $180 one-way. Good morning, America, how are you?

## Union Station

*210 S Canal St at E Adams St and E Jackson Blvd •*
*312-655-2385 • www.chicagounionstation.com*

An innovation for both design and travel, Chicago's Union Station is the "Grand Dame" of rail service in a city once considered to be the undisputed rail center of the United States. Designed by the architects Graham, Anderson, Probst, and White and built between 1913 and 1925, Union Station is a terminus for six Metra lines and a major hub for Amtrak's long-distance services. In its peak (1940s), this local transportation treasure handled as many as 300 trains and 100,000 passengers on a daily basis. While today's volume is just half that, this monumental station stands as the last remaining grand station still in use in the City of Chicago and was given landmark status in 2002. Most commuters don't take the time to gaze skyward when rushing through the Great Hall of Union Station (who really has the time to stop and assess their surroundings beyond that of their intended use?), but by not doing so, they are missing something special. Take the time to look up at the magnificent light-swathed ceiling and maybe then it will become clear why Union Station's ornate Great Hall is considered one of the United States' great interior public spaces. Union Station is also a premiere location for formal functions as it annually plays host to a multitude of private affairs and black-tie gatherings.

Both Metra's and Amtrak's train services are on the Concourse Level (ground floor) of the station. This level is then further divided into the North Concourse and South Concourse. Although not always adequately staffed, there is an information desk located between the concourses on this level. And while there is signage throughout Union Station, the many escalators, stairways, and multiple entrances/exits can make navigating the block-long building somewhat of a challenge.

**Ticket Windows:** The easiest way to get to Metra ticket agents is to enter Union Station at the Clinton Street entrance near East Jackson Boulevard and go down into and through the Grand Hall. Metra's ticket agents will be on your left in the North Concourse. Metra's ticket office is open daily 6 am – 11 pm. Metra Lines that terminate at Union Station are Milwaukee District East and West Lines, North Central Service, Burlington Northern Santa Fe, Heritage Corridor, and South West Service.

To get to the Amtrak action, enter Union Station off Canal Street, take the escalator down into the Grand Hall, and turn left. Amtrak's attractive, vintage ticket agent desk straddles the two concourses and is open daily 6 am–10 pm. Amtrak's attractive, vintage ticket agent desk straddles the two concourses and is open daily 6 am – 9:20 pm. For more detail on Amtrak service, call 800-872-7245 or visit www.amtrak.com.

**Services:** On the Mezzanine/Street Level, there is a plethora of convenience stores, newsstands, and eateries. ATMs are located in both concourses on this level. One particular stop of note for contrarian travelers should be the in-house bar appropriately called, "The Snuggery". It's a pretty snug fit, and one can find errant Amtrak employees here, along with a revolving cast of grey-flannel suit types.

**Public Transportation:** The closest L stop to Union Station is Clinton Street on the Blue Line, which stops two blocks south of the station. The Orange, Brown, and Purple lines stop three blocks east of the station at the Quincy stop on Wells Street. CTA buses 1, 151, 157, and 125 all stop at Union Station. Most commuters heading to work in the Loop enter and exit the station from the Madison Street, Adams Street, and Jackson Boulevard doorways where cabs line up.

## Richard B. Ogilvie Transportation Center

*500 W Madison St at S Canal St • 312-496-4777*

Built in 1911 and known locally as the North Western or Madison Street Station, the Metra's Union Pacific Lines originate from the Richard B. Ogilvie Transportation Center. Where Union Station is about form and function, Ogilvie focuses solely on function. Overtly stark and sterile, the tall, smoky-glass-and-green-steel-girder building replaced what was once a classic grand train station similar to the ornate, Beaux Arts-inspired Union Station. Though most of the historic fixtures have been removed, some of the original clocks remain and serve as a reminder of earlier days. Even though promised renovations of the unused historic sub-level areas have yet to come to fruition (it is hoped that the empty space under the tracks can be turned into 120,000 square feet of shops and restaurants), this highly trafficked station remains quite active. Roughly 40,000 passengers pass through the Richard B. Ogilvie Transportation Center on a daily basis.

**Ticket Windows:** Metra's ticket office is on the Upper Level, across from the entrance to the train platform and is open 5:30 am–12:40 am Monday–Saturday, and 7 am–12:40 am Sundays. ATMs can be found on the Upper Level at Citibank and next to the currency exchange. Public phones are also by the currency exchange in the southeast corner of the Upper Level.

**Services:** Loads of junk food options are available on the Street Level food court, which also serves as a make-shift waiting room for commuters. If you want healthier fare, try the Rice Market and Boudin Sourdough Bakery on the east side of the building. There is available shopping about if you're killing time or wanting to pick up a last-minute gift. An interesting and annoying amenity footnote: the only restrooms in the station are on the Street Level, which is a LONG escalator ride from the train platform. There are no plans for this to change until the proposed renovations are completed, so it's best to "go before you go."

**Public Transportation:** The closest L station is the Green Line's Clinton Street stop at Lake Street, several blocks north of the station. CTA buses 20, 56, and 157 board at Washington and Canal Streets and travel to North Michigan Avenue and the Loop. Coming from the Loop, take the same bus lines west across Madison Street. If you're after a cab, you'll find other like-minded commuters lining up in front of the main entrance on Madison Street between Canal and Clinton Streets.

## Millennium Station

*151 E Randolph St at N Michigan Ave • 312-322-7819*

Millennium Station offers a few amenities, including an outpost of a certain very, very large coffee chain, ATMs, a florist, gift shops, and an ever-rotating offering of fast-food joints. The underground station, centrally located in the Loop, services up to 100,000 commuters daily. This is also the station where the South Shore Line to South Bend, Indiana originates. Schedules for all are somewhat sporadic except during weekday rush hour commutes. The Van Buren Street Station also serves both the Metra Electric and South Shore lines and is located at East Jackson Boulevard and Van Buren Street (312-322-6777). When planning train travel from the Randolph Street and Van Buren Street stations, it's best to verify schedules and stops with the RTA Information Center (312-836-7000; www.rtachicago.com) before committing to a travel plan.

**Ticket Windows:** Enter the Millennium Station at East Randolph Street and North Michigan Avenue. The ticket office is immediately visible upon descending the steps off Michigan Avenue or entering via the Pedway, which tunnels around the Loop and east under Michigan Avenue, ending at the station. Ticket office hours are 6 am–10:20 pm daily. The waiting room is open 5 am–12:50 am daily.

**Services:** Recently a few shops finally opened in this station, including an outpost of a certain very, very large coffee chain and a couple of regrettably bland retail offerings. On an upbeat note, the bathrooms are rather clean, which is a most welcome find in the Loop.

**Public Transportation:** Millennium Station is served by over a half dozen CTA bus routes, including the 3, 4, 56, 145, 147, 151, and 157. One block west of the train station is the CTA's Randolph/Wabash elevated station, which is serviced by the Orange, Green, Purple, Pink, and Brown Lines.

## LaSalle Street Station

*414 S La Salle St at E Congress Pkwy • 312-322-8957*

The La Salle Street Station, located underneath the Chicago Stock Exchange, serves the Metra Rock Island District Line's passengers. This former behemoth of a station has been greatly reduced in both size and stature, handling roughly 15,000 commuters daily. The service has 11 main line stops and 10 south suburban stops on its way to Joliet.

**Ticket Windows:** Enter the station off LaSalle Street, take the escalator one floor up, and walk through the slim corridor to an open-air area where the tracks are. To your right you'll see the ticket office. Agents are on duty 7 am–8 pm weekdays, 10:30 am–6:30 pm on Saturday, and closed on Sunday.

**Services:** There are no shops to speak of at the LaSalle Street Station, but there is a waiting room is open 6 am–12 am daily.

**Public Transportation:** The Blue Line's La Salle Street stop at Congress Parkway and the Orange, Purple, and Brown lines' La Salle Street stop at Van Buren Street drop L riders right in front of the train station. CTA buses 6 and 146 stop near the station, as well.

## General Information

**City of Chicago Department of Transportation (DOT)**
Non-Emergency/
24-Hour Road Conditions Phone: 311
Street Closings Hotline: 312-787-3387
Website: www.cityofchicago.org

**Illinois Department of Transportation (IDOT)**
Phone: 217-782-7820
IDOT Traffic Hotline: 312-368-4636
Website: www.dot.state.il.us/news.html
Chicago Skyway Bridge: 312-747-8383
Road Conditions: 800-452-4368
WBBM-AM 780: Traffic updates every eight minutes

## Orientation

Anyone who says baldness is hereditary has never found him/herself in a Chicago traffic jam, pulling out his/her hair to pass the time and calm the nerves. We highly recommend taking public transportation whenever possible, especially since Chicago has such strong bus and rail systems. But if you must drive in the city, Chicago's grid system makes it relatively easy to navigate.

The intersection of State and Madison Streets in the Loop serves as the base line for both Chicago's street and house numbering system. Running north and south is State Street—the city's east/west dividing line. Madison Street runs east and west and divides the city into north and south. Street and building numbers begin at "1" at the State and Madison Streets intersection and numerically increase going north, south, east, and west to the city limits. Street signs will let you know in what direction you're heading. The city is divided into one-mile sections, or eight square blocks, each with a consecutively higher series of "100" numbers. For example, Western Ave, sitting at 2400 W, is further west than Ashland Ave, located at 1600 W. In addition, Chicagoans numerically refer to street locations such as Irving Park Road as "40 hundred north" rather than "four thousand north." An interesting historical tidbit about the city's three primary diagonal streets: Milwaukee, Elston, and Lincoln Avenues all used to be Native American trails.

Buildings with even number addresses are on the north and west sides of streets; odd numbers sit on the south and east sides. Chicago's diagonal streets also follow the grid numbering system, most of which receive north or south addresses. East-west streets north of Madison are named, as in Fullerton or Belmont; south of Madison they are generally numbered, as in 31st or 79th, with several major streets being named. Once you get out of the city limits, good luck. Often times you will find that our suburban friends like to refer to the same road by two different names. Roads will also magically turn into something different for no apparent reason. And sometimes they don't bother putting up street signs at all.

## Bridge Lift Season

While bridges spanning the Chicago River contribute to the city's architectural fame, they also serve as a major source of traffic congestion. Boating season demands that bridges lower and rise, so as to allow Chicago's elite access to Lake Michigan in their sailboats. Chicago's bridge lift season runs from early April until June. Each month has designated lift days. Lifts generally begin at 9:30 am and affect the entire downtown area between 11:30 am and 1 pm. During May, more lifts are scheduled on Saturdays between 2 pm and 4 pm. The schedule intensifies on holiday weekends to include evening rush hours. Check out the DOT's website for detailed schedules.

## Snow Routes

Failure to efficiently handle city snow removal seals the re-election fate of Chicago's mayors. The Department of Streets and Sanitation manages the ice and snow removal on Chicago's streets. Over 280 salt spreaders/plows cruise 607 miles of arterial streets divided into 245 designated snow routes. Parking is automatically restricted on these routes when snow is piled at least two inches on the pavement. Unfortunately, the two-inch snow routes are a crap-shoot. Tow trucks will enforce these restrictions by their own rules, it seems. On a snow route, you will either find your car gone or buried by a passing plow. Safety dictates you keep your car off of these routes even if only an inch and a half are predicted. Priority arteries also restrict parking daily from 3 am until 7 am between December 1 and April 1, whether or not snow is present.

## Major Expressways and Tollways

While the city's grid system is logical, the interstate highway system feeding into the city is confusing for those who don't travel it often. Chicago has free expressways and tollways which require paying a fee. The expressways are generally referred to by their names, such as "The Kennedy" or "The Eisenhower." When venturing to Indiana, one can experience the Chicago Skyway, a stretch of elevated road that connects I-94 and the Indiana Toll Road that soars 120 feet above the Calumet River. When using the tollways, which includes the Skyway, I-PASS speeds up the process and can be purchased through the Illinois State Toll Highway Authority by calling 800-824-7277.

## DMVs

The Illinois Department of Motor Vehicles (DMV) is one of life's unavoidable hassles. But you'd be pleasantly surprised to see how many of your car-related responsibilities (like renewing your driver's license, getting vehicle registrations, etc.) can be completed online (www.cyberdriveillinois.com). Unless you're British and enjoy standing in line for hours. Visit the website, or call 312-793-1010 for more information.

| Chicago DMVs | Map | Hours |
|---|---|---|
| 100 W Randolph St | 5 | Mon–Fri: 8 am–5 pm |
| 69 W Washington St, Concourse Level | 5 | Mon–Fri: 8 am–5 pm |
| 17 N State St, Ste 1000 | 5 | Mon–Fri: 8 am–5 pm |
| 5401 N Elston Ave | 46 | Mon – Fri, 8:30 am – 5 pm |
| 9901 S Martin Luther King Dr | 59 | Mon – Fri, 8:30 am – 5 pm |
| 5301 W Lexington Ave | 49 | Tues – Fri, 8 am – 5:30 pm; Sat, 7:30 am – 12 pm |
| 4642 W Diversey St | 48 | Tues – Fri, 8 am – 5:30 pm; Sat, 7:30 am – 12 pm |

## Zip Cars and I-Go

Eco-friendly car sharing has come to the Windy City. Two companies: Zip Car and I-Go, offer a fleet of eco-friendly vehicles (Zip Car's fleet includes Mini Coopers—cute!), at subscribers disposal for short errands or all-day rental. The cars are parked at convenient locations throughout the city. Just scan your card over the code and voila! You're in! Cars can be reserved by phone or online. For more information, including rates and vehicle locations, check out their websites.

I-Go www.igocars.org
Zip Cars www.zipcar.com

## Overview

In 2009, former Mayor Daley added to the problem by leasing all of Chicago's parking meters to a private firm (a 75 year lease!), causing fares to increase each year. Between neighborhood permit-only parking zones, snow routes, and a contant rotation of street fairs, street cleaning, street construction, and on and on, figuring out where and how to park in the city requires an advanced degree in clusterf*ck. Some areas, like Lincoln Park, Lakeview, and Wicker Park, would test the nerves and the patience of the Dalai Lama. These areas are all easily accessible by public transit, and taxi cabs are plentiful, so don't be a jag-off and add to the problem. Just. Don't. Do. It.

## General Information

**Office of the City Clerk—Parking Permits**

| | |
|---|---|
| Mailing Address: | City Hall |
| | 121 N La Salle St, Rm 107 |
| | Chicago, IL 60602 |
| Phone: | 312-744-6861 |
| Hours: | Weekdays, 8 am–5 pm |
| Website: | www.chicityclerk.com |

**Department of Revenue (DOR)—Parking Ticket Payments**

| | |
|---|---|
| Mailing Address: | PO Box 88298 |
| | Chicago, IL 60680-1298 |
| Phone: | 312-747-4747 |
| Website: | www.cityofchicago.org/ revenue |
| Parking Ticket Assistance & "Boot" Inquiries: | 312-744-PARK (7275) |
| Auto Pound Headquarters: (for towed vehicles) | 312-744-4444 |
| City Non-Emergency Phone: | 311 |

## City Stickers

Residents of Chicago who own motor vehicles (see "sadomasochist" at www.wikipedia.org) must have an annually renewed city sticker for their cars, which can be purchased from the Office of the City Clerk through the mail (by returning the renewal application you've received in the mail), in person at one of their offices, or online. Stickers may also be purchased at local currency exchanges, but you might get charged extra there. New residents are required to purchase their sticker in person with a proof of residency at one of the offices within 30 days of their move-in date. A four-passenger vehicle sticker is $85. Senior citizens are also eligible for discounts, but they check IDs, so don't pretend you're over 50; they'll find out you're lying. After March 1st of each year, half-year stickers are available at half-price for new city residents or current residents who've recently purchased a car. For more information on office locations and pricing, call 312-742-9200 or visit the City Clerk's website.

## Residential Zone Permit Parking

If you're lucky enough to find a parking spot, you still need to put a permit on your car. Chicago's Residential Parking Permit program reserves street parking during peak parking hours for neighborhood residents and those who provide a service to the residents. Cars in violation of this ordinance will be ticketed. Take that, suckers. Permits cost $25 annually and are available through the Office of the City Clerk via mail, online, and in person. Applicants must have a valid Chicago City Sticker and an Illinois State license plate. One-day guest passes may also be purchased and distributed by qualified residents. Fifteen 24-hour passes cost $5 per pack at a two-pack limit, so choose your guests wisely and frugally. Check out the City Clerk website or call 312-744-5346 for more information.

## Parking Tickets

The Department of Revenue (DOR) handles the payment of parking tickets. You can pay parking tickets by mail, online, or in person; scribbling curse words on it, ripping it up, and throwing it at the mailbox does not count as "paying" it, according to the stingy DOR. For the addresses and hours of payment processing and hearing facilities, see the DOR website.

Three or more unpaid tickets guarantees a metal, yellow surprise fitted to your car tire; yep, say hello to the boot. Ten or more tickets and the entire car is encased in molybdenum steel. If violations aren't paid within 24 hours of booting, your vehicle will be towed…maybe. In addition to the boot fee, towing, and storage fees must be paid to retrieve your car from a City Auto Pound. If your car is towed due to a boot, contact the City of Chicago's Ticket Help Line (312-744-7275). All payments for outstanding parking ticket debt must be made to a DOR Payment Center, not at the pound. The city has two payment plans available for motorists with large ticket fines. The General Payment Plan requires either a deposit of $500 or 25% of your parking debt (whichever is greater) in addition to all outstanding boot, tow, and storage fees. If you qualify for the Hardship Parking Payment Plan, you can make a deposit of $250 or 25% of your debt, whichever is lower. If either of these cases applies to you, we also suggest you stop parking in Chicago and find another means of travel, since you apparently can't handle the responsibility. Visit the DOR website for further requirements.

## Auto Pounds

To locate your towed vehicle, contact the City of Chicago Auto Pound Headquarters (312-744-4444). There are six auto pounds in addition to the O'Hare Auto Pound (10000 W O'Hare at Remote Lot E, 773-694-0990).

For a standard vehicle, the towing fee is a hefty $150 plus a $10 per day storage fee for the first five days, $35 per day thereafter. Fees can be paid at the pound; they accept cash, cashier's checks, VISA, MasterCard, Discover, American Express, and first-born children. No arms or legs, please.

Failure to claim vehicles or request a hearing within 21 days of notification can result in your convenient mode of transportation being sold or destroyed and, even then, you still owe the city for the outstanding fines. In that case, see the rest of the Transit section for alternate ways of navigating your way through Chicago.

Important note: "Minor" street repairs and construction are common occurrences on Chicago streets, during which signs should be posted on nearby trees or parking meters stating that parking is temporarily prohibited. If you park there, you will be towed. If you parked there on purpose despite seeing the signs, well, you deserve it. If you parked there on accident, we feel for you, so read on for our tips on how to not look like a panicky idiot while trying to find your car. First of all, don't bother contacting the city pound. They will have no idea what you're talking about! Save yourself the embarrassment of reporting your car stolen, and call the number posted on the sign where your car was parked. Chances are it was kindly moved to another location so as to allow workers to continue with important road improvements, but it may not have officially been moved by the city of Chicago. Operators should be able to track it down using your license plate number since city code mandates that the kindly moving of a car must be reported within a few hours, whether it be by the city or the other parking powers that be. Otherwise, you can always walk around your neighborhood aimlessly searching for your car, but we don't recommend it. We've only been successful doing that once or twice, and, anyway, it just turned out that we forgot where we parked after a night of heavy drinking.

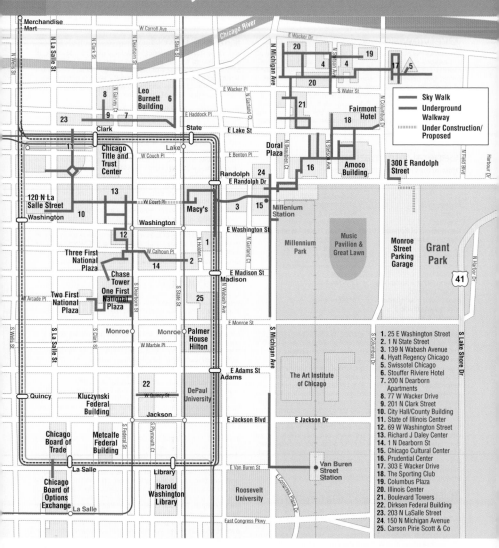

While a number of cold-weather cities are known for their above-ground walkways, Chicago is known for its Pedway, a 40-block network of tunnels and overhead bridges that connects important public, government, and private sector buildings with retail stores, major hotels, rapid transit stations, and commuter rail stations. A subterranean city with shops, restaurants, services, and public art works, the Pedway is a welcome alternative to navigating trafficked intersections on foot and walking outdoors in Chicago's frigid winters. The underground walkway system is open 24 hours; however, access

to a number of the buildings is limited after standard business hours. The first Pedway links were built in 1951 to connect the State Street and Dearborn Street subways at Washington Street and Jackson Boulevard. Today, Chicago's Pedway continues to grow as city government and the private sector cooperate to expand it. Those planning on making a subterranean trip to experience the Pedway in its glory would do well to click on over to www.spiegl.org/pedway/pedway.html for a map of the whole lair.

## Useful Phone Numbers

| | |
|---|---|
| City Board of Elections | 312-269-7900 |
| State Board of Elections | 217-782-4141 |
| ComEd | 800-334-7661 |
| People's Gas Customer Service | 866-556-6001 |
| Peoples Gas Emergencies | 866-556-6002 |
| Drivers Licensing Facilities | 312-793-1010 |
| Office of Mayor Rahm Emanuel | 312-744-5000 |
| Governor's Office | 312-814-2121 |
| General Aldermanic Information | 312-744-3081 |

## Helpful Websites and Local Blogs

**Angie's List** • www.angieslist.com
Membership-driven list rating local contractors and other services.
**Beechwood Reporter** • www.beechwoodreporter.com
Analysis of local and national politics.
**Centerstage Chicago** • www.centerstagechicago.com
Chicago's original online guide.
**The Chicagoist** • www.chicagoist.com
Local news/events blog.
**The Chicago Blog** • http://pressblog.uchicago.edu
Publicity news from the University of Chicago Press, including book reviews, press releases, and "intelligent commentary."
**Chicago City Clerk** • www.chicityclerk.com
Renew your city sticker online!
**Chicago Crime** • www.chicagocrime.org
Chicago criminal activity and statistics.
**Chicago Every Block** • www.chicago.everyblock.com
Crime, news, culture & real estate block-by-block, neighborhood-by-neighborhood.
**Chicago Gangs** • www.chicagogangs.org
Breakdowns on Chicago gang activity, history & culture.
**Chicago Hauntings** • www.chicagohauntings.com
Is the price for that run-down old mansion too good to be true?
**Chicago Recycling** • www.chicagorecycling.org
Where to recycle anything and everything in Chicago.
**Choose Chicago** • www.choosechicago.com
Chicago tourism information about attractions, festivals, events, restaurants, and hotels.
**City of Chicago** • www.cityofchicago.org
Helpful all-purpose guide to city services.
**Cook County Assessor** • www.cookcountyassessor.com
Research properties and tax assessments.
**Cook County Tresurer** • www.cookcountytreasurer.com
Pay your property tax online and download forms
**Daily Candy** • www.dailycandy.com/chicago
Daily dose of shopping, eating and culture.
**DNAinfo** • www.dnainfo.com/chicago
Local local breaking news.
**Eater Chicago** • http://chicago.eater.com
Go-to site for restaurant/bar openings.
**Flavor Pill** • www.chi.flavorpill.net
Lists happenings for hipsters.
**Forgotten Chicago** • forgottenchicago.com
Side streets and byways of the city.
**Gaper's Block** • www.gapersblock.com
A popular Chicago web-publication detailing local news, fun events, and cool places in the city.
**Gas Prices** • www.chicagogasprices.com
The scoop on the highest and lowest gas prices in the city.
**Metromix** • www.metromix.com
City guide put out by the Trib.
**Not For Tourists** • www.notfortourists.com
Duh.
**PadMapper** • www.padmapper.com
Search all apartment and sublet listings on a big Google map.
**Pitchfork Media** • www.pitchforkmedia.com
Cool indie music site and sponsors of the grooviest music fest ever.
**Spacefinder** • www.chireader.com/spacefinder
The source for apartment rentals.
**Taxi Magic** • www.taximagic.com
Book a taxi online, from your home or smartphone.
**Time Out Chicago** • www.timeoutchicago.com
The latest and greatest happenings around town: new restaurants, music listings, you name it.
**Yo Chicago** • www.yochicago.com
Real estate and development news.

## Taxi Cabs

| | |
|---|---|
| Checker | 312-243-2537 |
| American United | 773-248-7600 |
| Flash Cab | 773-561-4444 |
| Yellow Cab | 312-829-4222 |

## We're Number One!!!

World's Busiest Airport: O'Hare International
World's Largest Public Library: Harold Washington Library
World's Largest Aquarium: Shedd Aquarium
World's Largest Free Public Zoo: Lincoln Park Zoo
World's Largest Modern Art Museum:
Museum of Contemporary Art
Worlds Largest Commercial Office Building:
Merchandise Mart, 222 Merchandise Mart Plaza
World's Longest Street: Western Avenue
World's Busiest Roadway: The Dan Ryan Expressway
World's Largest Food Festival: Taste of Chicago

## Chicago Timeline

1779: Jean-Baptiste Point du Sable establishes Chicago's first permanent settlement.
1803: U.S. Army constructs Fort Dearborn, which is later destroyed by Native American forces allied with British during War of 1812, and rebuilt in 1816.
1818: Illinois is admitted into the union.
1833: Chicago incorporates as a town of 350 people, bordered by Kinzie, Des Plaines, Madison, and the lakefront.
1837: Chicago incorporates as a city. The population is 4,170. Ogden becomes the city's first mayor.
1851: Northwestern University is founded.
1856: Fort Dearborn is demolished.
1860: Republican Party nominates Abraham Lincoln for president at Chicago's first political convention.
1865: Merry Christmas! Union Stockyards open on Christmas Day.
1869: Water tower is completed.
1871: Great Chicago Fire!
1885: World's first "skyscraper," the 9-story Home Insurance building, goes up on La Salle Street.
1886: Haymarket Riots. Eight Chicago policemen are killed.
1889: Jane Addams opens Hull House.
1892: World's first elevated trains begin operation.
1893: Columbia Exposition celebrates 400th anniversary of Columbus's discovery of America.
1907: Physicist Abraham Michelson is first American to win Nobel
1910: Original Comiskey Park opens.
1914: Wrigley Field opens.
1927: $750,000 donated to honor Clarence Buckingham fountain.
1929: John G. Shedd presents Shedd Aquarium as gift to city.
1930: Adler Planetarium opens through a gift from Max Adler.
1930: Merchandise Mart built by Marshall Field.
1931: Jane Addams becomes first female to win Nobel Peace Prize.
1931: Al Capone sent to prison for 11 years for evading taxes.
1934: John Dillinger shot by FBI outside Biograph Theater.
1955: O'Hare International Airport opens.
1958: End of the line: Last streetcar in Chicago stops operating.
1968: Democratic National Convention riots.
1971: Chicago Union Stock Yards are closed.
1974: Sears Tower is completed.
1983: Harold Washington elected first black mayor.
1995: A heat wave contributed to the death of over 700 Chicagoans.
1997: City Council absolves Mrs. O'Leary's cow of blame for Great Chicago Fire.
1998: Six-peat! Bulls win sixth championship in eight years.
2003: Four-peat! Richard M. Daley re-elected for historic fourth term!
2005: White Sox win World Series; Cubs fans weep.
2007: Chicago pitched as US bid for 2016 Olympics.
2008: Gov. Rod Blagojevich arrested on corruption charges.
2011: Mayor Emanuel's election signals the end of the Daley era.

## Essential Chicago Movies

Northside 777 (1948)
Man with the Golden Arm (1955)
Raisin in the Sun (1961)
Medium Cool (1969)
The Sting (1973)
Blues Brothers (1980)
Risky Business (1983)
Ferris Bueller's Day Off (1986)
Henry: Portrait of a Serial Killer (1986)
Adventures in Babysitting (1987)
Planes, Trains and Automobiles (1987)
The Untouchables (1987)
When Harry Met Sally (1989)
Backdraft (1991)
Candyman (1992)
Wayne's World (1992)
The Fugitive (1993)
Hoop Dreams (1994)

Mission: Impossible (1996)
My Best Friend's Wedding (1997)
High Fidelity (2000)
Save the Last Dance (2001)
What Women Want (2000)
Barbershop (2002)
Chicago (2002)
Road to Perdition (2002)
The Company (2003)
I Am Trying to Break Your Heart (2003)
Batman Begins (2005)
The Weatherman (2005)
The Lake House (2006)
The Break-Up (2006)
Stranger than Fiction (2006)
The Dark Knight (2008)
Public Enemies (2009
Transformers 3 (2011))

## Overview

**WGN** is the classic Chicago TV station. Its radio affiliate at 720 AM *is* Chicago talk radio. WGN isn't a bad place to find intelligent conversation, particularly through the long-running "Extension 720" program hosted by Milt Rosenberg. **WXRT** is the city's independent rock station—one of the few remaining stations still free from the smothering embrace of Clear Channel Communications. Their Sunday morning Beatles Brunch with host Terri Hemmert (a Chicago institution in her own right) is heaven for fans of the Fab Four. In general the station is a little heavy on the white-boy blues (think Clapton and Stevie Ray Vaughan) and crunchy rock ala Dave Matthews and Hootie—if that's your thing. In terms of print media, we'll put it this way: the *Tribune* appeals to Cubs fans, while the *Sun-Times* is favored by White Sox fans. Chicago indie-media standard bearer (and first stop for slacker job seekers) *The Chicago Reader* has been weathering the effects of a media paradigm shift away from newsprint – after being bought out by Atlanta-based *Creative Loafing* and then *Sun-Times* parent Wrapports LLC, ongoing staff cuts have left the paper with a skeleton crew of hardworking editors. As a result, the copy has gotten increasingly fluffy, although they still manage to print hard-hitting civic stories, such as an insightful look into the Daley-orchestrated Chicago legislative swindle that led to the privatization of city parking meters.

## Television

| | | | | | | |
|---|---|---|---|---|---|---|
| 2 | WBBM | (CBS) | | 32 | WFLD | (Fox) |
| 5 | WMAQ | (NBC) | | 38 | WCPX | ION Television |
| 7 | WLS | (ABC) | | 44 | WSNS | (Telemundo) |
| 9 | WGN | (CW) | | 23 | WFBT | (Brokered—ethnic) |
| 11 | WTTW | (PBS) | | 50 | WPWR | (My 50) |
| 20 | WYCC | (PBS) | | 31 | CLTV | (Cable) |
| 23 | WWME | (Me TV) | | 60 | WXFT-TV | (Telefutura) |
| 26 | WCIU | (the U) | | 66 | WGBO | (Univision) |

## Print

| | | | |
|---|---|---|---|
| *Chicago Defender* | 200 S Michigan Ave, Suite 1700 | 312-225-2400 | Black community newspaper. |
| *Chicago Innerview Magazine* | 1849 S. Blue Island Avenue | 312-850-3635 | Free monthly music mag previewing bands coming to concert in town. |
| *Chicago Magazine* | 435 N. Michigan Ave., Suite 1100 | 312-222-8999 | Upscale glossy mag. |
| *Chicago Reader* | 11 E Illinois St | 312-828-0350 | Free weekly with listings. |
| *Chicago Reporter* | 332 S Michigan Ave | 312-427-4830 | Investigative reporting on issues of race, poverty, and social justice. |
| *Chicago Sun-Times* | 350 N. Orleans St, 10th Fl | 312-321-3000 | One of the big dailies. |
| *Chicago Tribune* | 435 N Michigan Ave | 312-222-3232 | The other big daily. |
| *Crain's Chicago Business* | 360 N Michigan Ave | 312-649-5411 | Business news. |
| *CS* | 200 W Hubbard | 312-274-2500 | Free monthly upscale Chicago lifestyle mag. |
| *Daily Herald* | 155 E Algonquin Rd, Arlington Hts | 847-427-4300 | Suburban news. |
| *Daily Southtown* | 6901 W 159th St, Tinley Pk | 708-633-6700 | News for southsiders. |
| *Ebony* | 820 S Michigan Ave | 312-322-9200 | National glossy about African Americans. |
| *Hoy Chicago* | 435 N Michigan Ave # 22 | 312-527-8400 | Daily Spanish-language newspaper |
| *Hyde Park Herald* | 1435 E. Hyde Park Boulevard | 773-643-8533 | Local for Hyde Parkers. |
| *Korea Times* | 3720 W Devon Ave | 847-626-0388 | Daily Korean-language newspaper. |
| *La Raza* | 6001 N Clark St | 773-273-2900 | Hispanic community paper. |
| *Lerner-Booster-Skyline* | 7331 N Lincoln Ave, Lincolnwood | 847-329-2000 | Conglomeration of neighborhood papers. |
| *N'Digo* | 19 N Sangamon | 312-822-0202 | Black community weekly. |
| *Newcity* | 770 N Halsted Ave | 312-243-8786 | Alternative free weekly. |
| *The Onion* | 47 W Division St | 312-751-0503 | Local listings in AV Club insert. |
| *Red Eye* | 435 N Michigan Ave | 312-222-4970 | Commuter-targeted offshoot of the *Trib* for 20- and 30-somethings. |
| *Today's Chicago Woman* | 150 East Huron | 312-951-7600 | Weekly for working women. |
| *UR Chicago* | 4043 N Ravenswood | 773-404-1497 | Free monthly local entertainment mag. |
| *Venuszine* | 2000 N. Racine, suite 3400 | 773-327-9790 | Subscription based mag on both local and national culture and music. |
| *Windy City Times* | 5443 N. Broadway | 773-871-7610 | Gay-targeted news weekly. |

## Public Radio

| AM | | | FM | | | | | |
|------|------|------|------|------|------|------|------|------|
| 560 | WIND | Talk | 88.1 | WCRX | Columbia College | 98.7 | WFMT | Classical |
| 620 | WTMJ | News/Talk | 88.5 | WHPK | U of Chicago | 99.5 | WUSN | Country |
| 670 | WSCR | Sports | 88.7 | WLUW | Loyola U | 100.3 | WILV | Oldies |
| 720 | WGN | Talk | 89.3 | WNUR | Northwestern | 101.1 | WIQI | Adult Contemporary |
| 780 | WBBM | Talk | 90.1 | WMBI | Christian | 101.9 | WTMX | Adult Contemporary |
| 820 | WCPT | Talk (Progressive) | 90.9 | WDCB | Jazz | 102.7 | WVAZ | Urban Contemporary |
| 850 | WAIT | Religious | 91.5 | WBEZ | NPR | 103.1 | WVIV | Spanish |
| 890 | WLS | News/Talk | 93.1 | WXRT | Rock | 103.5 | WKSC | Top 40 |
| 1000 | WMVP | Sports | 93.9 | WLIT | Adult Contemporary | 103.9 | WXRD | Classic Rock |
| 1110 | WMBI | Religious | 94.7 | WZZN | Oldies | 104.3 | WJMK | Jack FM |
| 1280 | WBIG | Talk | 95.1 | WIIL | Rock | 105.1 | WOJO | Spanish |
| 1390 | WGRB | Gospel | 95.5 | WNUA | Spanish | 105.9 | WCFS | News |
| 1450 | WCEV | Talk (Ethnic) | 95.9 | WREV | Oldies | 106.7 | WPPN | Spanish |
| 1490 | WPNA | Polish | 96.3 | WBBM | Dance | 107.5 | WGCI | Urban Contemporary |
| 1510 | WWHN | Gospel | 97.1 | WDRV | Classic rock | | | |
| 1570 | WBGX | Gospel | 97.9 | WLUP | Rock | | | |

## Essential Chicago Books

*Native Son*, by Richard Wright.
Gripping novel about a young black man on the South Side in the '30s.

*Neon Wilderness*, by Nelson Algren.
Short story collection set in Ukrainian Village and Wicker Park.

*One More Time*, by Mike Royko.
Collection of Royko's *Tribune* columns.

*The Boss: Richard M. Daley*, by Mike Royko.
Biography of the former Mayor.

*The Jungle*, by Upton Sinclair.
Gritty look at life in the meat-packing plants.

*Adventures of Augie March*, by Saul Bellow.
More Chicago in the '30s.

*V.I. Warshawsky*, by Sara Paretsky.
Mystery series firmly rooted in Chicago landscape.

*50 Years at Hull House*, by Jane Addams.
Story of the Near West Side.

*Secret Chicago*, by Sam Weller.
Off-the-beaten path guidebook.

*Ethnic Chicago*, by Melvin Holli & Peter D'A. Jones.
Insider's guide to Chicago's ethnic neighborhoods.

*House on Mango Street*, by Sandra Cisneros.
Short story collection about a Latina childhood in Chicago.

*Our America: Life and Death on the South Side of Chicago*, by Lealan Jones, et al.
Life in the Chicago Projects as told by two schoolchildren.

*The Coast of Chicago*, by Stuart Dybek.
Short stories of Chicago denizens.

*Hairstyles of the Damned*, by Joe Meno.
Teen angst and punk rock in '80s Chicago.

*Never a City So Real: A Walk in Chicago*, by Alex Kotlowitz.
Modern reflection on the city of big shoulders.

*American Pharaoh: Mayor Richard J. Daley*,
by Adam Cohen and Elizabeth Taylor.
Recent work that explores the life and works of Hizzoner the First.

*Studs Lonigan*, by James T. Farrell.
Growing up gritty and Irish in Washington Park, circa the early 20th century.

*Chicago: The Second City*, by A. J. Liebling.
Legendary *New Yorker* columnist and curmudgeon comes to the Windy City, gives it a new sobriquet, and tells all.

*A Guide to Chicago's Murals*, by Mary Lackritz Gray.
Murals, murals, and more murals.

*The Pig and the Skyscraper*, by Marco D'Eramo.
Wandering Italian sociologist comes to Chicago and explores the wide world of capitalism through Chicago's radical history, skyscrapers, and meat-processing plants.

*The Devil in The White City* by Erik Larson
Account of Chicago serial killer H.H. Holmes and the 1893 Chicago World's Fair.

*Chicago Then and Now (Then & Now Thunder Bay)*
by Elizabeth McNulty
Explores Chicago's transformation and progression as a city.

*The Lazarus Project* by Alexander Hemon
A Bosnian writer investigates a historical Chicago crime.

*Sin in the Second City* by Karen Abbott
The colorful history of a Chicago bordello circa the 1900s.

*Memory Mambo* by Achy Obejas
Coming of age as a Cuban lesbian in Chicago.

*The Time Traveler's Wife* by Audrey Niffenegger
Break-out bestseller about time traveling love affair.

From May to September, every corner of the city is hopping with all manner of block parties, church carnivals, neighborhood festivals, and all-out hootenanny. Contact the Mayor's Office of Special Events for a complete list of the city's 100+ festivals.

| Event | When & Where | Description |
|---|---|---|
| Chinese New Year | Sunday after the Chinese New Year (late-January or mid-February), Chinatown | 2014 is the year of the Horse. Celebrate! |
| Chicago Auto Show | Early February, McCormick Place | The nation's largest auto show, over 100 years old. |
| The Black Women's Expo | First weekend of April" | This faith-based event, started in 1993, is undergoing an "evolution." www.theblackwomensexpo.com |
| St Patrick's Day Parade | Saturday prior to St Paddy's, Columbus Ave, Balbo to Randolph | The Chicago River turns green. On purpose. |
| Chicago Flower Show | Mid-March, Navy Pier | Escape from winter. |
| Chicago Latino Film Festival | Early April, various venues | 20+-year-old festival screens the best in local and international Latino film. www.latinoculturalcenter.org/Filmfest |
| Chicago Improv Fest | End of April, Athenaeum Theater | Nation's best improv comedy acts descend on Chicago, the genre's birthplace. www.chicagoimprovfestival.org |
| Bike Chicago | May-September, various venues | More than 100 events including "Bike the Drive" and the midnight LATE Ride. |
| Tulips on the Magnificent Mile | Month of May, Magnificent Mile | Hundreds o thousands of blooming tulips signal arrival of Spring |
| Navy Pier Fireworks | end of May through August, Navy Pier | Fireworks light up the night sky every Wednesday and Saturday www.navypier.com |
| Do-Division Street Fest | First weekend in June, Division St & Leavitt Ave | Annual event kicks off Chicago's summer street fest season www.do-divisionstreetfest.com |
| Ribfest Chicago | Second weekend in June, Lincoln Ave & Irving Park Rd. | Great music, people-watching, and oh…50,000 pounds of finger-lickin' good ribs |
| Printers Row Book Fair | Second weekend in June, Dearborn St, b/w Harrison St & Balbo Dr | Watch for Booksellers Gone Wild, coming soon to pay-per-view. |
| Andersonville Midsommarfest | Second weekend in June, Clark St, b/w Foster & Balmoral Aves | Ain't it Swede? |
| Taste of Chicago | A four-day festival in mid-July, Grant Park | Why go to a restaurant when you can eat standing up in the hot sun in a crowd? |
| Gay Pride Parade | Last Sunday in June, Broadway/Halsted Sts b/w Montrose and Belmont | 400,000 of the city's gay community and their fans take it to the streets. www.chicagopridecalendar.org |
| Chicago Pride Fest | Friday and Saturday before Pride Parade, Halsted and Addison Sts | Boystown comes to life with plenty of festivities to usher in Gay Pride Parade |
| Juneteenth Celebration | Third Saturday in June, 79th & Stony Island | African-American Pride celebration includes parade, music, and lots of barbecue at Rainbow Beach. |
| 57th Street Art Fair | First week in June, 57th & Kimbark | Oldest juried art fair in the Midwest. www.57thstreetartfair.org |
| Chicago Blues Festival | Second weekend in June, Grant Park | As much about the soul food as the music. |
| Old Town Art Fair | Mid-June, 1800 N Orleans St, Menominee St, Lincoln Ave | Arts and crafts. |
| Grant Park Music Festival | mid-June through August, Millennium Park | Free classical music concerts outdoors in Millennium Park |
| Gospel Music Festival | late June in Millennium Park and Bronzeville | Bring the kids for daily Wiggleworms performances, storytelling and more. |
| Gold Coast Art Fair | late June in Grant Park | Fancy arts fest moves to new location downtown. |

| Event | When & Where | Description |
|---|---|---|
| Family Fun Festival | early July through August, Millennium Park | Bring the kids for daily Wiggleworms performances, torytelling and more. |
| Independence Day Fireworks | July 4, Navy Pier | See the night sky above the lakefront lit in a spectacular light show. |
| International Festival of Life | July 4th weekend, Washington Park | Celebrate the food, music, and arts of the African Diaspora on the South Side |
| Chicago Hip-Hop Heritage Month | July 1-31, various venues | Where "New Beat" culture celebrates its past, present, and future. www.chihiphop.org. |
| Rock Around the Block | Second weekend in July | Lots of street-festival-quality live music. Expect Bumpus and Underwater People. |
| Eye on India | mid-July, various venues | Experience the best of Indian culture and arts. |
| Jeff Park Arts & Music Fest | Late July Jefferson Park | Neighborhood festival of guys named Jeff. Okay, just kidding. It's Jefferson Park—get it?" www.jefffest.org |
| Taste of River North | end of July, Ward Park | Food, music, and shopping along the Chicago River's North Branch. |
| Fiesta Del Sol | Last weekend in July, Cermak Rd, b/w Throop & Morgan Sts | One of the most festive of the fests. |
| Bud Billiken Parade | Second Saturday in August, King Dr | World's biggest African-American parade. www.budbillikenparade.com |
| Northalsted Market Days | Second weekend in August, Halsted St b/w Belmont Ave & Addison St | See Gay Pride Parade. Add beer and live music. http://www.northalsted.com/daze.htm |
| Ginza Holiday | Second weekend in August, Old Town | Annual festival celebrates the richness of Japanese culture. |
| Air and Water Show | Third weekend in August, lakefront | The Stealth Bombers never fail to thrill. |
| Taste of Polonia | Last weekend in August, 5200 W Lawrence Ave | Polka and kielbasa! Heaven! Pierogies! Paradise! |
| Chicago Dancing Festival | Fourth week in August, various venues | Last and biggest major afrocentric expo of the year. www.africainternationalhouse.org. |
| SummerDance | mid-July to mid-September, Grant Park | Chicago's and the nation's acclaimed dance troupes strut their stuff. www.chicagodancingfestival.com |
| African Festival of the Arts | Friday to Sunday, Labor Day weekend, Washington Park, 5531 S King Dr | Last and biggest major afrocentric expo of the year. www.africainternationalhouse.org. |
| German-American Fest | Early September, Lincoln & Leland | Oktoberfest in Lincoln Square. Bring your own leiderhosen. |
| World Music Festival | Late September, Grant Park | Music acts from around the world, plus beer. |
| 57th St Children's Book Fair | Late September, b/w Kimbark & Dorchester Aves | Lots of kids. Lots of books. |
| Open House Chicago | Mid-October, various venues | Get a free, behind-the-scenes look at over 150 historical and architectural landmarks |
| Chicago International Film Festival | October, various locations | Worthy display of the best in international cinema. www.chicagofilmfestival.org |
| Chicagoween | Mid to Late October, Daley Plaza | Daley Plaza becomes Pumpkin Plaza with trick-or-treating, pumpkin carving, and storytellers. |
| Halloween Parade | Halloween, Halsted b/w Belmont & Addison | Flamboyant Boystown costume extravaganza. |

*All dates subject to change. For more up-to-date information and a schedule of neighborhood festivals, contact the Department of Cultural Affairs and Special Events, www.cityofchicago.org/dcase.

## Police

While crime in general seems to be continuing a downward trend, in 2009, the murder level of school-aged children in Chicago was the highest in the nation, making national news headlines. The mayor says we're no worse than any other major city—it's just that our juvenile murders get properly classified. Now, doesn't that make you feel better?

| Departments | Address | Phone | Map |
|---|---|---|---|
| 1st District (Central) | 1718 S State St | 312-745-4290 | 11 |
| 9th District (Deering) | 3501 S Lowe Ave | 312-747-8227 | 13 |
| 2nd District (Wentworth) | 5101 S Wentworth Ave | 312-747-8366 | 15 |
| 12th District (Monroe) | 100 S Racine Ave | 312-746-8396 | 24 |
| 14th District (Shakespeare) | 2150 N California Ave | 312-744-8290 | 27 |
| 18th District (Near North) | 1160 N Larrabee St | 312-742-5870 | 31 |
| 24th District (Rogers Park) | 6464 N Clark St | 312-744-5907 | 34 |
| 20th District (Foster) | 5400 N Lincoln Ave | 312-742-8714 | 35 |
| 19th District (Town Hall) | 850 W Addison St | 312-744-8320 | 42 |

Chicago hospitals are as varied and interesting as the citizens they serve. Although you don't have to go far to find medical facilities in this city, finding quality medical care is another story.

The Illinois Medical District on the near southwest side is one of the largest healthcare centers in the world. Here you will find the brand-new **Stroger (Map 25)** hospital (basically the infamous Cook County Hospital with a facelift), home to the nation's first and oldest trauma unit. It is by far the busiest hospital in the area and serves a large and mostly indigent population. Unless you are in danger of certain demise, avoid Stroger's emergency department since waits of up to 12 hours for a non-life-threatening reason may bore you to death. The medical campus is also home to the **University of Illinois at Chicago (Map 25)**, **Rush University Medical Center (Map 25)**, and several smaller hospitals.

On the north side, your best bet is to go to **Advocate Illinois Masonic Medical Center (Map 43)** for anything serious or **St. Joseph's Hospital** (**Map 44**) where you might get a room with a view of Lake Michigan. **Northwestern Memorial Hospital (Map 3)** is also a good choice if you are closer to downtown and/or if you have really good insurance. They also house several hospitals in the same campus, and if you break your neck craning to look up at all the pretty skyscrapers in the Streeterville 'hood, they have a first-rate spinal cord unit.

On the south side, the **University of Chicago (Map 19)** hospitals are second to none. A large and imposing set of buildings set in a somewhat dubious neighborhood, the hospital has a first-rate children's emergency department, world-renowned staff, and an excellent reputation. Park on the street at your own risk—the garage may be expensive, but so is replacing your car stereo.

| Emergency Rooms | Address | Phone | Map |
|---|---|---|---|
| Northwestern Memorial | 251 E Huron St | 312-926-2000 | 3 |
| Mercy | 2525 S Michigan Ave | 312-567-2000 | 11 |
| Provident | 500 E 51st St | 312-572-2000 | 16 |
| University of Chicago | 5841 S Maryland Ave | 773-702-1000 | 19 |
| University of Chicago Children's | 5721 S Maryland Ave | 773-702-1000 | 19 |
| Saints Mary and Elizabeth Medical Center | 1431 N Claremont Ave | 773-278-2000 | 21 |
| Saints Mary and Elizabeth Medical Center | 2233 W Division St | 312-770-2000 | 21 |
| John H Stroger Jr | 1900 W Polk St | 312-864-7203 | 25 |
| Rush University Medical Center | 1650 W Harrison St | 312-942-5000 | 25 |
| St Anthony's | 2875 W 19th St | 773-484-1000 | 25 |
| University of Illinois Medical Center | 1740 W Taylor St | 312-355-4000 | 25 |
| Jesse Brown VA Medical Center | 820 S Damen Ave | 312-569-8387 | 25 |
| Lurie Children's Hospital of Chicago | 225 E Chicago Ave | 312.227.4000 | 30 |
| Swedish Covenant | 5145 N California Ave | 773-878-8200 | 38 |
| Methodist Hospital of Chicago | 5025 N Paulina St | 773-271-9040 | 39 |
| Vanguard Weiss Memorial | 4646 N Marine Dr | 773-878-8700 | 40 |
| Thorek | 850 W Irving Park Rd | 773-525-6780 | 40 |
| Advocate Illinois Masonic Medical Center | 836 W Wellington Ave | 773-975-1600 | 43 |
| St Joseph | 2900 N Lake Shore Dr | 773-665-3000 | 44 |

| Other Hospitals | Address | Phone | Map |
|---|---|---|---|
| Rehabilitation Institute of Chicago | 345 E Superior St | 312-238-1000 | 3 |
| Kindred Chicago-Lakeshore | 6130 N Sheridan Rd | 773-381-1222 | 37 |
| Kindred | 2544 W Montrose Ave | 773-267-2622 | 38 |
| Chicago Lakeshore | 4840 N Marine Dr | 773-878-9700 | 40 |

# General Information • **Post Offices**

| Post Offices | Address | Phone | Map |
|---|---|---|---|
| US Post Office | 222 Merchandise Mart Plz | 312-321-0233 | 2 |
| US Post Office | 540 N Dearborn St | 312-644-3919 | 2 |
| US Post Office | 168 N Clinton St | 312-906-8557 | 4 |
| US Post Office | 100 W Randolph St | 312-263-2686 | 5 |
| US Post Office | 211 S Clark St | 312-427-0016 | 5 |
| US Post Office | 233 S Wacker Dr | 312-876-1024 | 5 |
| US Post Office | 5 S Wabash Ave | 312-427-0016 | 5 |
| US Post Office | 200 E Randolph St | 312-861-0473 | 6 |
| US Post Office | 433 W Harrison St | 312-983-7610 | 7 |
| US Post Office | 2345 S Wentworth Ave | 312-326-6440 | 10 |
| US Post Office | 2035 S State St | 312-225-0218 | 11 |
| US Post Office | 4101 S Halsted St | 773-247-0731 | 15 |
| US Post Office | 4601 S Cottage Grove Ave | 773-924-6658 | 16 |
| US Post Office | 700 E 61st St | 773-493-4047 | 18 |
| US Post Office | 1526 E 55th St | 773-324-0896 | 19 |
| US Post Office | 956 E 58th St | 773-497-4047 | 19 |
| US Post Office | 116 S Western Ave | 312-243-2560 | 23 |
| US Post Office | 1859 S Ashland Ave | 312-733-4750 | 26 |
| US Post Office | 2339 N California Ave | 773-489-2855 | 27 |
| US Post Office | 2405 N Sheffield Ave | 773-929-7041 | 29 |
| US Post Office | 2500 N Clark St | 773-477-9372 | 30 |
| US Post Office | 875 N Michigan Ave | 312-644-0485 | 32 |
| US Post Office | 1723 W Devon Ave | 773-743-2650 | 34 |
| US Post Office | 7617 N Paulina St | 773-743-2830 | 34 |
| US Post Office | 2522 W Lawrence Ave | 773-561-3330 | 38 |
| US Post Office | 2011 W Montrose Ave | 773-472-1314 | 39 |
| US Post Office | 1343 W Irving Park Rd | 773-327-0345 | 40 |
| US Post Office | 4850 N Broadway St | 773-561-1720 | 40 |
| US Post Office | 3750 N Kedzie Ave | 773-539-6210 | 41 |
| US Post Office | 3170 N Sheridan Rd | 773-244-0444 | 44 |

The Chicago Public Library System has 79 branches serving Chicago citizens. Much to the delight of many Windy City book-borrowers, the city has recently constructed several new branches and renovated over 55 existing neighborhood branches with the help of a huge capital improvement program.

With the **Harold Washington Library (Map 5)** as their anchor, two regional libraries, **Sulzer Regional Library (Map 39)** in Lincoln Square and the Southwest side's **Woodson Library (Map 59)**, serve as backup reference and research collections. It is worth noting that Harold Washington Library has a few stand-out exhibits, including one of the history of the blues in the city and, of course, one on the man himself, Chicago's first African-American mayor. Neighborhood branches are geared towards the communities they serve: **Chinatown (Map 10)** has an impressive collection of Asian studies material and literature, and the **Rogers Park (Map 34)** branch features a significant Russian-language selection, and Boystown's **John Merlo (Map 44)** collection houses a considerable offering of gay literature and studies. Many of the smaller branches have a decent selection of juvenile materials as well as career guidance and adult popular literature (and Internet access). Architecturally, some of the more interesting branches include the **Chicago Bee (Map 14)** branch, the former newspaper headquarters that serves as a neighborhood landmark for Bronzeville, and the historic Pullman (Parks & Places) branch, specializing in the history of the Pullman district. Chicago's first library branch, the neo-classical **Blackstone (Map 17)** library, is named after the Stockyards magnate. Families and schools should take advantage of the Chicago Public Library

System's "Great Kids Museum Passports" available only to adult Chicago residents with a valid library card. You can check out any of their free passports using your library card just like you would any other item, and the loan is good for one week. The pass entitles entry for up to 8 people to any one of the eleven participating cultural institutions in the city. If you don't have access to a library card, you can still partake in a bit of book-love by checking out one of the many free lectures or readings that take place at the Harold Washington Library and the galaxy of branch outposts throughout the year. Before visiting Chicago, visitors can also peruse some of the nice digital exhibits the Library has created at www.chipublib. org/digital/digital.html. Here they will find tributes to the late, great Mayor Harold Washington and some interesting exhibits on the history of the city's sewer system (well, interesting for us, at least). For more information, call your local library or visit the general website at www.chipublib.org.

Chicago also has many excellent research libraries and university libraries, one of which is the independent **Newberry Library (Map 32)**, established in 1887. It shelves rare books, manuscripts, and maps, and hosts the raucous annual Bughouse Square debates in late July. Another unique institution, the Pritzker Military Library (104 S Michigan Ave), tells the story of the Citizen Soldier through an extensive book collection, and exhibits of photographs, medals, uniforms and other artifacts. Chicago's universities and colleges generally welcome the public to their libraries during specified hours, but it's best to call first and check.

| Library | Address | Phone | Map |
| --- | --- | --- | --- |
| Albany Park Public Library | 5150 N Kimball Ave | 312-744-1933 | 38 |
| Asher Library-Spertus Institute | 610 S Michigan Ave | 312-322-1712 | 9 |
| Bezazian Public Library | 1226 W Ainslie St | 312-744-0019 | 40 |
| Blackstone Public Library | 4904 S Lake Park Ave | 312-747-0511 | 17 |
| Bucktown–Wicker Park Public Library | 1701 N Milwaukee Ave | 312-744-6022 | 28 |
| Budlong Woods Public Library | 5630 N Lincoln Ave | 312-742-9590 | 35 |
| Canaryville Public Library | 642 W 43rd St | 312-747-0644 | 15 |
| Carter G. Woodson Regional Public Library | 9525 S Halstead St | 312-747-6900 | 49 |
| Chicago Bee Public Library | 3647 S State St | 312-747-6872 | 14 |
| Chinatown Public Library | 2353 S Wentworth Ave | 312-747-8013 | 10 |
| Coleman Public Library | 731 E 63rd St | 312-747-7760 | 18 |
| Hall Public Library | 4801 S Michigan Ave | 312-747-2541 | 16 |
| Harold Washington Public Library | 400 S State St | 312-747-4300 | 5 |
| John Merlo Public Library | 644 W Belmont Ave | 312-744-1139 | 44 |
| King Public Library | 3436 S Dr Martin Luther King Jr Dr | 312-747-7543 | 14 |
| Library of Columbia College | 624 S Michigan Ave | 312-336-7900 | 9 |
| Lincoln Park Public Library | 1150 W Fullerton Ave | 312-744-1926 | 29 |
| Lincoln-Belmont Public Library | 1659 W Melrose St | 312-744-0166 | 42 |
| Logan Square Public Library | 3030 W Fullerton Ave | 312-744-5295 | 27 |
| Lozano Public Library | 1805 S Loomis St | 312-746-4329 | 26 |
| Mabel Manning Public Library | 6 S Hoyne Ave | 312-746-6800 | 23 |
| Malcolm X College Library | 1900 W Van Buren St | 312-850-7000 | 23 |
| Near North Public Library | 310 W Division St | 312-744-0991 | 31 |
| The Newberry Library | 60 W Walton St | 312-943-9090 | 32 |
| Northtown Public Library | 6435 N California Ave | 312-744-2292 | 33 |
| Poetry Foundation | 61 W Superior St | 312-787-7070 | 2 |
| Richard J. Daley Public Library | 3400 S Halsted St | 312-747-8990 | 13 |
| Rogers Park Public Library | 6907 N Clark St | 312-744-0156 | 34 |
| Roosevelt Public Library | 1101 W Taylor St | 312-746-5656 | 26 |
| Sulzer Public Library | 4455 N Lincoln Ave | 312-744-7616 | 39 |
| The Swedenborg Library | 77 W Washington St, Rm 1700 | 312-346-7003 | 5 |
| University of Chicago Harper Memorial Library | 1116 E 59th St | 773-702-6271 | 19 |
| University of Illinois at Chicago Library | 801 S Morgan St | 312-996-2726 | 26 |
| Uptown Public Library | 929 W Buena Ave | 312-744-8400 | 40 |

Serving the nation's busiest convention center, most Chicago hotels are designed for business travelers, complete with expense-account prices. Even a modest downtown room can be outrageously steep.

**Livin' Large:** For a special urban splurge, book a suite at one of Chicago's palace hotels, such as the **Ritz-Carlton (Map 32)**, **Four Seasons (Map 32)**, **Peninsula (Map 2)**, or **Waldorf Astoria (Map 32)**.

**Livin' Classic: The Drake (Map 32)** is the classic Chicago hotel, and a landmark for drivers heading downtown from the northside via Lake Shore Drive. **The Allerton Hotel (Map 3)** is an architecturally significant Chicago landmark circa 1934. After years of decline, it has recently been restored to its former glory. In the Loop, the **Palmer House Hilton's (Map 5)** lobby is all divans and chandeliers. More notoriously historic, the **Chicago Hilton & Towers (Map 9)** was the site of the 1969 Democratic National Convention.

**Livin' Modern:** Hip travelers will want to stay at one of downtown's two **W (Maps 3, 5)** Hotels, the **Sofitel (Map 32)**, **Hotel 71 (Map 2)**, or the **Hard Rock Hotel (Map 6)**, located in the vintage Union Carbide building on Michigan Avenue. **The House of Blues Hotel (Map 2)**, located next to the corn cob Marina Towers, boasts folk-art decorated rooms and a Sunday gospel brunch.

**Livin' Boutique:** Located in a historic landmark, the **Hotel Burnham (Map 5)** is a lovely boutique hotel near the heart of Chicago's theater district. Burnham and its Kimpton Hotel Group sisters, **Hotel Allegro (Map 5)** and **Hotel Monaco (Map 5)**, also in the theater district, feature free wine receptions every evening for hotel guests. **Hotel Blake (Map 8)** on Printer's Row offers boutique-type amenities with handsome rooms, although the views can leave a bit to the imagination.

**Livin' Cheap:** Steer budget-conscious out-of-town guests toward the **Travelodge Downtown (Map 8)**. It's not eye candy, but the location (just off Michigan Avenue, between Millennium Park and the Museum Campus) makes it quite a deal. Around the corner at the **Congress Plaza Hotel (Map 9)**, picketers have been toting their placards for years. The Hotel Workers Union is on strike pending serious concessions from the management, and their dispute does not seem to be cooling. The strike has hurt business, which has cut prices—let your conscience be your travel agent, and brace yourself for heckling should you book here (and remember that Upton Sinclair would not approve).

Good values can also be had away from downtown. **City Suites (Map 43)**, and its "Neighborhood Inns of Chicago" partners, **The Majestic (Map 44)**, and **Willows (Map 44)**, in Chicago's Lakeview and Lincoln Park neighborhoods, offer small hotel charm at reasonable rates. If those are still above your station, **Heart o' Chicago Motel (Map 37)** is skipping distance from the Edgewater White Castle and a short walk from the

vivacious Andersonville strip. **Sheffield House (Map 43)**, once a transient hotel, offers spare, cheap rooms, appealing to backpacking European travelers and frugal Cubs fans—it's a pop fly's distance from Wrigley Field.

**B&Bs:** Compared to cities of similar expanse, Chicago doesn't offer much by way of B&B's. **The Wheeler Mansion (Map 11)**, near McCormick Place, is luxurious and antique-filled, with fireplaces, custom baths and bedding, and ridiculously high ceilings. The more modest **Wicker Park B&B (Map 21)** dishes up a good breakfast—the owners also own the nearby Alliance bakery, where morning sweets are baked fresh daily. **The Flemish House B&B (Map 32)** is on a quiet, tree-lined lane, a calm refuge from the Rush Street and Oak Street Beach hullabaloo. **The Old Town Bed and Breakfast (Map 4)**, run by the friendly and eccentric Serritella family, features stylish bedrooms and a common area with a grand piano, formal dining room, and deluxe gourmet kitchen available for guests to use—it's where a John Cheever character would bunk. On the Southside, the luxe **Bronzeville B&B (Map 14)** is located in the landmark Goldblatt's mansion. Nearby, the quaint **Benedictine Bed & Breakfast (Map 12)** is run by monks from the adjacent Monastery of the Holy Cross.

**Livin' Real Cheap:** There are also three youth hostels in Chicago open to the public with rates as low as $15 a night for card-carrying International Youth Hostel members. For deals, Hot Rooms is a Chicago-based reservation service offering low-rates on undersold rooms: www.hotrooms.com.

**Livin' Flop House:** Before the construction of I-90/94, Lincoln Avenue was the main access point to the city from all points north. In the 20s-40s, a bunch of motels sprouted up on north Lincoln to serve truckers and other travelers entering the city. For a while these vintage motels were popular cheap spots for touring indie bands on a budget; eventually most of them become too seedy for even traveling indie bands on a budget. Many of the motels have fallen prey to the wrecking ball; a few, including the local landmark, **The Diplomat (Map 35)** and the **Apache Motel (Map 35)** remain, frequented, we assume, by people having affairs.

As a general rule, if a Chicago hotel price seems too good to be true, it is. Chicago is chock-a-block with run-down SROs providing semi-temporary housing to the down-on-their-luck, and extremely short-term housing to the occasional unwitting and unfortunate foreign traveler, cheapskate, or hapless student.

Chicago is a kid's kind of town. From sandy beaches and leafy parks to diverse downtown museums, concerts, and suburban attractions, Chicago's options for family fun are non-stop—just like your kids.

## The Best of the Best

The best part about Chicago family-style is that lots of stuff is *free*...or practically free. Great entertainment and educational venues keep cash in parents' pockets for school supplies, groceries, gas, and an occasional adult night out.

- **Top Park:** Lincoln Park (Lake Shore Dr & North Ave, 312-742-2000; www.lpzoo.com). From an expansive sandy beach, baseball diamonds, basketball courts, and bike paths to grassy meadows, fishing lagoons, museums, and the nation's oldest free zoo, Lincoln Park promises a full day of outdoor activity.

- **Spellbinding Story Time:** Lincoln Park Zoo (2200 N Cannon Dr, 312-742-2000; www.lpzoo.com). Donning safari khakis and pith helmet, Mr. Singer spins adventurous tales and sings for preschoolers at the *Farm-in-the-Zoo*. Wildly popular, this story hour is the toughest ticket in town. Arrive early to secure admission (donation suggested).

- **Slickest Sledding Hill:** Soldier Field Lakefront Park (312-742-7529; www.chicagoparkdistrict.com). The best part of the Soldier Field's pretty 17-acre park is the free, giant sledding hill with frozen lake views. BYO ride and bundle up for frigid lakefront winds. In warmer months, check out the Children's Garden.

- **Coolest Ice Rink:** McCormick Tribune Ice Rink in Millennium Park (Michigan Ave and Washington St, 312-742-1168, www.millenniumpark.org). Skate hand-in-hand in the shadow of architectural landmark buildings lining the Mag Mile. Open daily, admission is free to the 16,000-square-foot rink; skate rental available and warming room on-site.

- **Best-Kept Secret:** Chicago Public Library's "Kraft Great Kids Museum Passport" (Main Branch at 400 S State St, 312-747-4300 and branches city-wide; www.chipublib.org). Families can't afford not to know about the passports—on loan for one week at a time, they provide family members with free admission to over a dozen of Chicago's premier (read: pricey) cultural institutions, including the biggies at the Museum Campus plus the Art Institute, Peggy Notebaert Museum, and Chicago History Museum (formerly the Chicago Historical Society). Available only to Chicago Public Library card-carrying adult Chicago residents. See website for participating institutions and details.

- **Railroad Shop That Rocks:** Berwyn's Toy Trains & Models (7025 Ogden Ave, Berwyn, 708-484-4384). A roundhouse of activity where engineers of all ages can play at the many display train tables and enjoy a charming, 7-by-14-foot tooting layout in the back. Keep with the transportation theme and stop by Berwyn's *Spindle*, a massive sculpture just two miles south on Cermak and Harlem—it's an enormous desk organizer, skewering eight de-commissioned cars. For real.

- **WOW Waterparks:** (312-742-7529; www.chicagopark district.com). The Chicago Park District operates over 20 free waterparks with arching jets, umbrella sprays, pipe falls, and bubble jets in Chicago's neighborhood parks and beaches. All facilities open daily in summer 11 am to 8 pm.

- **Best Beach:** North Avenue Beach (1600 North Ave, 312-742-7529; www.chicagoparkdistrict.com). From swimming, spiking volleyballs, and kickboxing to sunbathing and sipping sun-downers, this expansive beach on Lake Michigan rivals any on the California coast. The tug-boat shaped beach house has locker facilities and rents volleyball equipment, roller blades, and bikes. On the upper deck is Castaways restaurant and ice cream parlor. There's also a full outdoor fitness center with weights and spin cycles plus a roller blade rink for pick up hockey under the summer sun.

- **Sensational Soda Fountain:** Margie's Candies (1960 N Western Ave, 773-384-1035). Celebrating 85 years of scoop, this old-fashioned ice cream parlor serves yummy frozen treats like soda fountains of yesteryear. Kids who flash report cards with an A get a free ice cream cone.

- **A Child's Choice Bakery:** Sweet Mandy B's (1208 W Webster Ave, 773-244-1174). Trendy and tasty, this cheery bakery's kid confections include awesome cupcakes, chunky whoopee pies, and whimsical cut-out frosted cookies. Signature sweet: "Dirt Cups"—a cake, crushed Oreo cookie, and whipped cream combo crawling with psychedelic gummy worms.

- **Coolest Family Concerts:** Joe Segal's Jazz Showcase (59 W Grand Ave, 312-670-2473; www.jazzshowcase.com). Hipster kids and jiving parents and grandparents hang out at this swank, serious jazz club's Sunday 4 pm matinee performances where top musicians jam. Non-alcoholic beverages and snacks served. Discount adult admission; children under 12 free. All Ages Blue Chicago Show (536 N Clark St, 312-661-0100; www.bluechicago.com) on Saturday nights from 8 pm to 3 am where families rock to the Gloria Shannon Blues Band in the basement of the Blue Chicago store. Adult admission $8; kids under age 11 free. No alcohol or smoking allowed. Jammin' at the Zoo (Lincoln Park Zoo, Lake Shore Dr & North Ave, 312-742-2000; www.lpzoo.com) once a month during the summer, shows starting at 7 pm. Serving the needs of cross-generational rock aficionados, previous concerts have featured They Might Be Giants, Collective Soul and The Gin Blossoms. Adult admission $23; kids pay $12.

- **Flying High:** Chicago Kids and Kites Festival (Lakefront, 312-744-3316; www.explorechicago.org). Every spring and fall, the Windy City lives up to its blow-hard reputation, lifting kids' spirits and kites to new heights along the lakefront. Kite flying professionals and instructors help enthusiasts of all ages construct kites and fl y them for free. Complimentary kite kits provided or bring your own. Free family entertainment, crafts, and storytelling on-site.

- **Not So Little League:** Chicago White Sox FUN damentals Field (U.S. Cellular Field, 333 W 35th St, 312-674-1000; www.whitesox.com). Little sluggers age three and up play ball in a 15,000-square-foot field of their own within the White Sox's home park. While junior trains, parents spy the pro game going on below from the new, kid-friendly interactive baseball diamond and skills area perched above the left-field concourse. Budding all-stars hone their pitching, batting, and base-running techniques under the sharp eyes of college and pro coach-instructors from the year-round Chicago White Sox Training Academy in Lisle. Better yet, it's all free with ball-park admission.

- **Masterpiece Portraits:** Classic Kids (917 W Armitage Ave, 773-296-2607; 566 Chestnut St, Winnetka, 847-446-2064). Pricey but priceless photos from this studio capture your kid at his or her model best. Pay a $300 sitting fee plus cost for handcrafted prints and treasure your tyke forever.

- **Weirdest City Sight:** Chicago River runs green (Chicago River downtown along Wacker Dr). No, it's not algae or bile, but bio-degradable green dye. Every St. Patrick's Day, the city turns the Chicago River emerald green like the Incredible Hulk.

- **Parents' Parking Dream:** Little Parkers Program, Standard Parking Garages (888-700-7275; www.standardparking.com). Select garages downtown specially equip families for road trips home with puzzles, crayons, and coloring books. Family-friendly garage amenities include spacious bathrooms with diaper-changing stations. Some rent family videos to monthly parkers. Participating garages: Grant Park North Garage, 25 N Michigan Ave; East Monroe Garage, 350 E Monroe St; Chicago Historical Society Garage, 1730 N Stockton Dr; Huron-St. Claire Self Park near Northwestern Memorial Hospital; Erie-Ontario Self Park in Streeterville neighborhood; and 680 N Lake Shore Dr Self Park.

- **Kudos Kids' Theatre:** Marriott Theatre for Young Audiences (Marriott Lincolnshire Resort, 10 Marriott Dr, Lincolnshire, 847-634-0200; www.marriotttheatre.com). Not a bad seat in the house at this intimate arena theater where actors welcome pint-sized audience participation and roam the aisles interacting with kids. Post-performance, the actors conduct Q&A answering kids' theatrical questions. Family productions run year-round. Tickets $12 per person; free parking.

- **Oscar Performances:** Children's International Film Festival (city-wide, 773-281-9075; www.cicff.org). For over two weeks each fall, Chicago's theater venues feature hundreds of witty, ingenious long- and short-form children's movies from around the world, some created by kids. Filmmakers, directors, and animators teach seminars for movie-lovers of all ages.

- **Free Family Fun:** Millennium Park's Family Fun Festival (201 E Randolph St, 312-742-1168; www.millenniumpark.org) is the place to be for kids of all ages every summer. From 10 am – 3 pm, youngsters will enjoy daily performances and storytelling, including sing-alongs and games with Wiggleworms instructors from the Old Town School of Folk Music, and hands-on craft and gardening activities led by local museums and cultural institutions. Best of all, admission is free!

- **Hippest Halloween Happening:** Chicago Symphony Orchestra's Hallowed Haunts Concert (220 S Michigan Ave, 312-294-3000; www.cso.org). Skeletons rattle and ghosts boogie to classical morbid music at the Chicago Symphony Orchestra's creepy family concert featuring hair-raising Romantic-Era pieces and medieval chants. Come in costume to the concert and ghoulish pre-performance party. Tickets: $7–$45.

- **Perfect Pumpkin Patch:** Sonny Acres Farm (29 W 310 North Ave, West Chicago, 630-231-9515; www.sonnyacres.com). During October, the Feltes family homestead has it all for fall: jack-o-lanterns for carving, homemade pies, decorative Thanksgiving and Halloween displays, and a killer costume shop. Kids love the mountains of pumpkins, crunchy caramel apples, scary hay rides, youngster carnival rides, and haunted barns (one for tiny tikes and another for blood-thirsty teens). Free farm admission and parking; purchase tickets for attractions.

- **Fields of Dreams:** Of course Wrigley Field, but a family outing at the venerable ballpark amounts to a month's down payment on a mini van. For $10 or less per ticket, take the family to the 'burbs' farm league games at pristine ballparks complete with entertainment, eats, and fireworks: Kane County Cougars (34W002 Cherry Ln, Geneva, 630-232-8811; www.kccougars.com) and Shaumburg Flyers (1999 S Springinsguth Rd, Schaumburg, 847-891-2255; www.flyersbaseball.com).

- **No-Flab Family Workout:** Tri-Star Gymnastics' Family Fun Night (1401 Circle Ave, Forest Park, 708-771-7827; www.tri-stargym.org). Families bounce on trampolines, swing on bars, tumble across mats, and climb ropes together at Tri-Star's warehouse-sized gymnastic training facility. Held from 4:30 pm to 5:30 pm on Saturday nights during the school year, admission is $5 per child and parents get in free. Parental supervision (no more than two kids per adult) and signed waiver required.

- **Musical Encounter:** The Chicago Symphony Orchestra (220 S Michigan Ave, 312-294-3333, www.cso.org) presents year-round family concert performances with their Kraft Matinee Series.

- **Horse'n Around:** Arlington Park Race Track's Family Day (2200 W Euclid Ave, Arlington Heights, 847-385-7500; www.arlingtonpark.com). From mid-May through mid-September it's a sure bet you'll win big with the kids on a Sunday afternoon at the horse races. Wild West, luau, and circus-themed family activities surround the seriously fun thoroughbred racing action at this swank, clean track. Pony rides, face painters, and petting zoo on-site. From noon to 4 pm, attend the free Junior Jockey Club events (847-870-6614) including educational equine care talks and behind-the-scenes track tours (children 12 and under).

- **Brightest Christmas Lights:** Cuneo Museum and Gardens' Winter Wonderland Holiday Light Festival (1350 N Milwaukee Ave, Vernon Hills, 847-362-3042; www.cuneomuseum.org). The largest drive-through Christmas display in Northern Illinois twinkles with millions of lights creating dazzling holiday scenes. Superhero and storybook light sculptures dance in the woods. Festival runs first Friday after Thanksgiving through New Year's weekend from 6 pm to 10 pm. Admission per car is $10 on weekends, $5 weekdays.

- **Winter Blahs Buster:** Fantasy Kingdom (1422 N Kingsbury St at Evergreen St, 312-642-5437; www.fantasykingdom.org). When Chicago's plunging temps prevent playground play, take tykes to this warehouse-turned-play-space magic kingdom to blow off steam. Kids clamor through a giant castle fitted with slides and tunnels (socks required) while donning Camelot costumes for dress-up fun. $12 per child.

- **Shadiest Theme Park:** Pirate's Cove (901 Leicester Rd, Elk Grove Village, 847-439-2683; www.elkgroveparks.org). On the other hand, when Chicago's soaring temps make playing outdoors as appealing as a trip down the Styx, hit this blessedly small-scale, low-tech theme park. Your (10-and-under) mateys will scramble up the Smugglers Cove, ride a rope-and-pulley griffin, and paddle around a wee lagoon, all while you actually keep cool in this heavily-shaded treasure. Great low-cost birthday party site. $6 for residents, $8 for nonresidents.

## Rainy Day Activities

**Art Institute of Chicago**, 111 S Michigan Ave, 312-443-3600; www.artic.edu. While kids find the doll house–sized Thorne Miniature Rooms and shiny medieval armor very cool, they also discover artistic expression from around the world at the Kraft Education Center. Interactive exhibitions introduce children to art from other cultures, time periods, and world-wide geographic regions. "Edutaining" art books and masterpiece puzzles in the children's library reinforce visual learning. Free kids' programs and drawing workshops are also held throughout museum galleries. Free children's artmaking events and gallery walks take place every weekend in the Ryan Education Center of the museum's new Modern Wing.

**Cernan Earth and Space Center,** Triton College Campus, 2000 Fifth Ave, River Grove, 708-456-0300, ext. 3372; www.triton.edu/cernan. Named after Apollo astronaut Eugene Cernan, a native Chicagoan and the last man on the moon, this cozy planetarium's intimate dome theater features kids' star programs ($5), earth and sky shows, and laser light shows. Monthly sky watch and lectures hosted. Mini space-related museum (free admission) and great celestial gift shop.

**Chicago's Museum Campus**, 1200–1400 S Lake Shore Dr. The closest you'll come to an educational amusement park. Dinosaurs, live sharks, giant mechanical insects, ancient mummies, and exploding stars are just a handful of adventures your kids will encounter on the lakefront's brainy peninsula home to the Field Museum (312-922-9410; www.fieldmuseum.org), Adler Planetarium & Astronomy Museum (312-922-7827; www.adlerplanetarium.org), and John G. Shedd Aquarium (312-939-2438; www.shedd.org). Check with each institution for its free admission days and special family programs.

**Diversey River Bowl,** 2211 W Diversey Pkwy, 773-227-5800; www.drbowl.com. Families, couples, and serious bowlers mix it up at this upbeat city alley. Decent grilled food served and full bar on-site. Wednesday through Sunday nights at 8 pm, glow-in-the-dark bowling known as Rock 'n Bowl goes well past the little one's bedtime but is fun for teens with chaperones.

**DuPage Children's Museum,** 301 N Washington St, Naperville, 630-637-8000; www.dupagechildrensmuseum.org. The 45,000-square-foot museum loaded with hands-on, action-packed exhibits keeps pre-schoolers with nano-second attention spans exploring until exhaustion.

**Exploritorium,** 4701 Oakton St, Skokie, 847-674-1500, x2700; www.skokieparkdistrict.org. From finger paints and water games to costumes and a multi-storied jungle gym, this facility tuckers tykes out. The climbing gym outfitted with twisting ropes, tubes, and tunnels even brings out the Tarzan in parents. Miniscule admission fee; free for Skokie adult residents and kids under 3.

**Federal Reserve Bank of Chicago Visitors' Center**, 230 S LaSalle St, 312-322-5322; www.chicagofed.org. The buck stops here where kids learn the power of pocket change through hands-on and computerized exhibits explaining the Fed's role in managing the nation's money. Kids love the rotating, million-dollar cube of cash and $50,800 coin pit. Sneak a peak into the vault stocked with $9 million, trace our country's currency history, and learn how to identify fake bills. Free admission. Open weekdays 9 am–4 pm; free guided tours on Mondays at 1 pm.

**Garfield Park Conservatory,** 300 N Central Park Ave, 312-746-5100; www.garfield-conservatory.org. Kids really dig Plants Alive!, the free, landmark Conservatory's 5,000-square-foot greenhouse blooming with child-friendly vegetation. Kids climb a two-story twisting daisy stem that doubles as a slide and come nose-to-stinger with a Jurassic-sized bumble bee. Attend story-telling, plant seeds, and dig in the soil pool.

**Kohl Children's Museum of Greater Chicago,** 2100 Patriot Blvd, Glenview, 847-832-6600; www.kohlchildrensmuseum.org. Kids climb the rigging of a pirate ship, "ride" an L train, meander through mazes, and push mini carts through a fully stocked grocery store.

**Mitchell Museum of the American Indian,** 2600 Central Park Ave on Kendall College Campus, Evanston, 847-475-1030; www.mitchellmuseum.org. From real teepees and dug-out canoes to bow-and-arrows and tom-toms, this compact sensory museum's engaging hands-on exhibits and craft sessions teach kids about the rich Native American life and culture. During the school year, sessions are offered semi-monthly on Saturdays, and on Tuesdays, Wednesdays, and Thursdays in summer. All programs held from 10:30 am to noon.

**Museum of Science and Industry**, 57th St at S Lake Shore Dr, 773-684-1414; www.msichicago.org. The ultimate hands-on learning experience for families, this massive museum is a tsunami of scientific exploration. Favorite kid exhibits are the 3,500 square-foot The Great Train Story model railroad, the United Airlines jet, a walk-through human heart, a working Coal Mine, and the Idea Factory workshop packed with gears, cranks, and water toys. OMNIMAX Theater on-site. Call for free day schedule.

**Navy Pier**, 600 E Grand Ave, 312-595-7437; www.navypier.com. A mega-sized free entertainment emporium jutting into Lake Michigan, Navy Pier has an IMAX Theater and tons of carnival-like attractions. The renowned Shakespeare Theater performs kid-friendly shorts of Willy's works. The 57,000-square-foot Chicago Children's Museum has 15 permanent engaging exhibits for toddlers to pre-teens (312-527-1000; www.chichildrensmuseum.org). Museum admission free on Thursday nights from 5 pm to 8 pm.

**Oak Brook Family Aquatic Center,** 1450 Forest Gate Rd, Oak Brook, 630-990-4233; www.obparks.org. Wet, wild fun for the whole family at this splashy indoor aquatic facility. They've got a zero-depth pool and slide for tadpoles as well as an Olympic-sized pool for bigger fish. Special swim events include watery holiday-themed parties, arts and crafts, water sports days, and dive-in movie nights where you can watch a family flick from your inflatable raft.

**Peggy Notebaert Nature Museum,** 2430 N Cannon Dr, 773-755-5100; www.naturemuseum.org. Kids delight in Butterfly Haven, a soaring tropical greenhouse habitat, home to hundreds of exotic winged beauties from around the world. The Children's Gallery replicates prairie and wetland habitats. Hands-on, free scientific activities and animal feedings always scheduled. Chicago residents enjoy a $1 discount on admission fee. On Thursdays, admission is free to Illinois residents.

**Pelican Harbor Indoor/Outdoor Aquatic Park,** 200 S Lindsay Ln, Bolingbrook, 630-739-1700; www.bolingbrookparks.org. Chicago area's only indoor/outdoor waterpark open year-round. Kids zip down six thrilling water slides (one 75-foot tall), float on inner tubes, and plunge into the diving well. There is a large zero-depth pool for little swimmers, lap pool, sand volleyball, whirlpool, and concessions.

**Shops at Northbridge,** 520 N Michigan Ave, 312-327-2300; www.westfield.com/northbridge. The entire third floor is not only lined with child apparel, toy, and accessory stores, but has The LEGO Store with play stations and a spacious LEGO building zone. Best part is parents don't have to clean up those blasted colored blocks!

**Wonder Works,** 6445 W North Ave, Oak Park, 708-383-4815; www.wonder-works.org. About half a mile west of Chicago's city limits, this modest children's museum is far more accessible for many city families than the Chicago Children's Museum at Navy Pier and boasts the triple advantages of being low-cost ($5 admission + free street parking), low-key, and packed with friendly volunteers. Usually closed on Mondays and Tuesdays, Wonder Works often makes an exception for school holidays (call to confirm, though).

## Outdoor and Educational

Fresh air family fun venues that work your kids' muscles and minds pack the city and suburbs. Here are some of the best:

**Brookfield Zoo,** First Ave & 31st St, Brookfield, 708-485-0263; www.brookfieldzoo.org. Chicago's largest zoo, spanning 216 wooded acres, is home to over 2,500 animal residents from around the world. Hamill Family Play Zoo and the Children's Zoo offer interactive programs on animal antics and opportunities to pet kid-friendly creatures babysat by helpful docents. Several dolphin shows daily. Family and child educational classes offered, plus summer camps and special holiday events. Explore the woodsy Indian Lake district where a life-sized dinosaur "lives." Open daily. Admission is free October through March on Tuesdays and Thursdays and January through February on Saturdays and Sundays.

**Cantigny Park,** 1 S 151 Winfield Rd, Wheaton, 630-668-5161; www.cantignypark.com. The 15-acre complex named after a World War I battle is home to the First Division Museum showcasing the history of the famed U.S. Army's 1st Infantry Division and *Chicago Tribune* founder's Robert R. McCormick Mansion Museum. After clamoring over the cannons, kids can stop to smell the flowers blooming in the manicured gardens. Family programs and concerts scheduled year-round. Park opens Tuesday through Sunday 9 am to sunset; museum is open 9 am–4 pm. Park and museum admission free; car parking fee, $7 Monday to Friday, and $8 on the weekends. Nearby is the top-rated, public Cantigny Golf Course (630-668-3323) offering junior golf instruction and a 9-hole Youth Links Course.

**Chicago Botanic Garden,** 1000 Lake Cook Rd, Glencoe, 847-835-5440; www.chicagobotanic.org. Open daily, admission is free to this 385-acre living preserve with more than 1.2 million plants rooted in 23 gardens, three tropical greenhouses, three natural habitats, eight lagoons, and bike paths. Kids love the winding, willow-branch tunnel in the Children's Garden where they can dig for worms and plant seeds. On Monday nights in summer, picnickers listen to the resonating chimes of carillon bell concerts on Evening Island. Late May through October, come for the Jr. Railroad where model trains puff through a garden of America's best loved landmarks (exhibit admission charged); in early December, make sure to check out the Reindog Parade (think bassets with antlers), with or without a Fido of your own.

**Cuneo Museum and Gardens,** 1350 Milwaukee Ave, Vernon Hills, 847-362-3042; www.cuneomuseum.org. Kids romp through the 75-acre wooded estate's formal gardens, animal sanctuaries, and deer park surrounding a palatial Italianate mansion. Open Tuesday–Sunday 10 am–5 pm; $5 grounds admission fee; mansion tours cost $12 for adults, $7 for children.

**Fermi National Accelerator Laboratory,** Kirk Rd & Pine St, Batavia, 630-840-3351; www.fnal.gov. Release energy outdoors biking, hiking, and rollerblading the nature trails at the nuclear plant's 680-acre campus. Rare species of butterflies, plants, birds, and baby buffalos live on the rural grounds. Guided prairie tours offered in summer. Picnickers welcome and lake fishing available. Open daily; admission free. Kids power up their nuclear knowledge at the Leon M. Lederman Science Education Center learning about nature's secrets and how the universe began. Admission free; open weekdays. Fermilab physicists conduct behind-the-scenes lab tours and Q&A with guests the first weekend of every month.

**Graceland Cemetery,** Clark St & Irving Park Blvd, 312-922-3432. Eerie and educational, the famous 119-acre necropolis built in 1860 is a national architectural landmark fi lled with palatial mausoleums, haunting headstones, and reportedly disappearing angelic statues marking the graves of Chicago's rich, famous, and infamous. The Chicago Architecture Foundation's (www.architecture.org) spine-chilling cemetery tour is a drop-dead Halloween family favorite.

**Grosse Point Lighthouse,** Sheridan Rd & Central St, Evanston, 847-328-6961; www.grossepointlighthouse.net. The pretty grounds surrounding the charming, white, tapering lighthouse built in 1873 and fairy-tale stone cottage are open year-round. Tours of both structures are offered weekends June through September for children aged 8 and up. A wooded trail twists down a grassy slope to the isolated Lighthouse Landing Beach.

**Tempel Lipizzans Farm**, Wadsworth Rd & Hunt Club Rd, Wadsworth, 847-623-7272; www.tempelfarms.com. Trained in the centuries-old tradition of the Spanish Riding School in Vienna, dancing, white Lipizzaner stallions fl y through the air performing fancy four-footed feats. Performances are Wednesdays and Sundays, June through August. Tours of the historic stables offered year-round.

**Lambs Farm,** 14245 W Rockland Rd, Libertyville, 847-362-4636; www.lambsfarm.org. Over 40 years old, this is Chicagoland's favorite farmyard, a non-profit residential farm for persons with developmental disabilities. Animal petting zoo, mini-golf, and vintage carousel open in season. Year-round feel-good family events include an old-fashioned Breakfast with Santa, Easter Brunch, fall festival, and more. Shops and kid-friendly country restaurant open Tuesday through Sunday.

**Lincoln Park Zoo,** 2200 N Cannon Dr, 312-742-2000; www.lpzoo.com. The nation's oldest free zoo hasn't rested on its laurels—come see the up-to-date Ape House, Regenstein African Journey habitat, and North American animal exhibit at the Pritzker Family Children's Zoo. Kids love the graceful giraffes, lumbering elephants, and giant hissing Madagascar cockroaches. Additional family favorites are the Farm-in-the-Zoo, lion house, sea lion pool, and old-fashioned carousel (summer). Call for information on family programs including the ever popular Night Watch where families sleep over at the zoo!

**Morton Arboretum,** 4100 Illinois Rte 53, Lisle, 630-968-0074; www.mortonarb.org. Forests, meadows, gardens, and wetlands cover 1,700 acres of this outdoor tree and plant museum with paved roads and 14 miles of trails for hiking and biking. Kids particularly dig the Children's Adventure Garden and Maze. Overall, a great place to tromp around and picnic. Food service on-site. Guided tours and kid/family nature classes offered year-round. Favorite family fall activities include leaf collecting and the "Scarecrow Trail." Open daily. Discounted admission on Wednesdays.

**Naper Settlement,** 523 S Webster St, Naperville, 630-420-6010; www.napersettlement.org. Kids experience life on the Midwestern prairie of the past at this re-creation of a 19th-century agrarian community. Working blacksmith shop, post office, and school house manned by costumed interpreters. The living history village's seasonal programs cater to kids with games, pony rides, and entertainment.

**North Park Village Nature Center,** 5801 N Pulaski Rd, 312-744-5472; www.cityofchicago.org/environment. You'll think you're a hundred miles west of the city at this 46-acre rolling woods and wetlands where deer roam and owls screech. Nature paths throughout. Admission free; open year-round. Popular week-long EcoExplorers summer camps for kids aged five to 14 years also offered.

**Willis Tower (Sears Tower) Skydeck,** 233 S Wacker Dr, 312-875-9696; www.theskydeck.com. OK, so only a pane of glass separates your baby from the sky blue. But the Knee-High Chicago kids' exhibit is worth the parental panic. Interactive displays tell tales of Chicago from a bird's eye view. A touch-and-talk computer explains city landmarks.

## Classes

Many of the city's fine cultural institutions have stellar, kid-focused curricula and host popular summer camps. Chicago and suburban park districts offer solid sports instruction, dance, and crafts classes. But private specialty schools also instruct many pint-sized prodigies. Here are some of the most popular and pedigreed organizations:

**Academy of Movement and Music**, 605 Lake St, Oak Park, 708-848-2329. This 34-year-old school offers popular dance and movement classes. The cool, creative Boys Production class for guys ages five to nine focuses on high-energy body movement practically applied to mini-manly visual arts projects, including mazes, puzzles, murals, sculptures, and machinery.

**After School Matters**, 66 E Randolph St, 312-744-8925; www.afterschoolmatters.org. Spearheaded by the late Maggie Daley, wife of former Mayor Richard Daley, After School Matters' creative curriculum provides 14- to 21-year-old Chicago residents with educational on-the-job training in the visual, literary, media, culinary, and performing arts. Under the direction of professional artists, apprentices are paid while creating art projects throughout the city such as bench-painting, sculpture, play-writing, and multicultural dance. Eight-week summer program and limited programming during school year. Applications required.

**Alliance Francaise**, 810 N Dearborn St, 312-337-1070; www.afchicago.com. Cultivating everything French in Chicagoans of all ages since 1897, this institution breeds petite Francophiles through intense language classes, camps, and cultural programs.

**Bubbles Academy**, 1504 N Fremont St, 312-944-7677; www.bubblesacademy.com. Yoga for youngsters taught with a creative twist in an open, airy studio.

**Dennehy School of Irish Dance**, 2555 W 111th St, 773-881-3990; www.dennehydancers.com. A South Side Irish institution, Dennehy has churned out high-stepping Irish dancers for over forty years. Its most-famous pupil so far is egomaniac, foot-pounding Michael Flatley of stage hits *Riverdance* and *Lord of the Dance*.

**Flavour Cooking School**, 7401 W Madison St, Forest Park, 708-488-0808; www.flavourcookingschool.com. Kids learn to really stir it up from scrambled eggs and lasagna to stir-fry and California cuisine at this cozy cooking school and culinary cookware shop. Class content determined by chefs' ages: Kitchen Helpers (age 4–6); Young Chefs (age 7–11); Sous Chefs (age 12+). Kids' summer cooking camps are also offered.

**Illinois Rhythmic Gymnastics Center**, 636 Ridge Rd, Highland Park, 847-831-9888; www.ilrhythmicgymnastics.com. This top flexible factory turns out more national and Olympic gymnastic team members than any other in the country.

**Language Stars**, locations city-wide, 866-557-8277; www.languagestars.com. Children aged one through 10 are instructed in foreign language through play-based immersion.

**Lou Conte Dance Studio**, 1147 W Jackson Blvd, 312-850-9766; www.hubbardstreetdance.org. The dance studio of esteemed Hubbard Street Dance Chicago offers killer classes for teens (aged 11 to 14) in hip-hop, tap, jazz, ballet, African, modern, and more. Also teaches children and teen dance classes through the new, thriving Beverly Arts Center (2407 W 111th St, 773-445-3838; www.beverlyartcenter.org).

**Merit School of Music**, 38 S Peoria St, 312-786-9428; www.meritmusic.org. This tuition-free conservatory provides economically disadvantaged youth with excellent instruction in playing classical and jazz instruments. An answer to the public school system's sad arts education cuts.

**Music Institute of Chicago**, 1490 Chicago Ave, Evanston, 847-905-1500; www.musicinst.com. Students of all ages flock to this esteemed school specializing in the Suzuki Method for many instruments. Group and private instruction in string, wind, brass, and percussion instruments offered.

**Old Town School of Folk Music**, 4544 N Lincoln Ave & 909 W Armitage Ave, 773-728-6000; www.oldtownschool.org. Opened in 1957, this is Chicago's premier all-American music center specializing in lessons on twangy instruments. The school is best known for its Wiggleworms music movement program catering to the under-five folk. Engaging teen curriculum in music, theater, dance, and art is also offered. Kids' concerts— actually, all concerts—rock.

**Ruth Page Center for the Arts**, 1016 N Dearborn St, 312-337-6543; www.ruthpage.com. Prima ballerina classes for beginners to advanced students offered at this fine school whose graduates dance for the American Ballet Theatre, the New York City Ballet, and professional companies world-wide.

**Second City Training Center**, 1616 N Wells St, 312-664-3959; www.secondcity.com. Sign up your bucket of laughs for famed Second City's improvisational classes. Hilarious kids ages 4–12 attend hour-long sessions on Saturdays. Teen improv program is also offered.

**Sherwood Conservatory of Music**, 1312 S Michigan Ave, 312-427-6267; www.sherwoodmusic.org. Over-a-century-old Sherwood Conservatory specializes in the Suzuki Method for children ages three to 12 in cello, violin, viola, fl ute, piano, harp, and guitar. Also teaches classes at the South Side's Beverly Arts Center (2407 W 111th St, 773-445-3838; www.beverlyartcenter. org).

**The Chopping Block**, 4747 N Lincoln Ave, 773-472-6700; www.thechoppingblock.net. The Lincoln Square neighborhood store and kitchen complex of this sophisticated culinary store hosts cooking classes for kids ages 7–12 two times a week. Four-day cooking camp for two hours a day held in summers.

**Tri-Star Gymnastics**, 1401 Circle Ave, Forest Park, 708-771-7827; www.tri-stargym.org. This women-run gym pumps out gymnastic champs ages 18 months through teens. Flexing its muscle since 1987, the not-for-profit center offers caring instruction for boys and girls in gymnastics, tumbling, and trampoline. The center is home to a GIJO Team (Junior Olympics) and USGA Teams.

## Shopping Essentials

Designer duds, high-style child furniture, imaginative toys, and kids' tunes—Chicago stores have it all for newborns to teens. Here's just a sampling of the top shops:

- **Alamo Shoes** • 5321 N Clark St • 773-334-6100
  6548 W Cermak Rd, Berwyn • 708-795-818
  Experienced staff for toddler shoe fittings.
- **American Girl Place** • 835 N Michigan Ave •
  877-247-5223• Dolls and books.
- **Bearly Used** • 401 Linden Ave, Wilmette
  847-256-8700 • Fab deals on duds and furniture.
- **Building Blocks Toy Store** • 3306 N Lincoln Ave
  773-525-6200 • Old-fashioned, brain-building toys.
- **Carrara Children's Shoes** • 2506 ½ N Clark St
  773-529-9955 • Tot soles from Italy.
- **Children in Paradise** • 909 N Rush St • 312-951-5437
  Personable kids' bookseller.
- **Cut Rate Toys** • 5409 W Devon Ave • 773-763-5740
  Discounted favorites.
- **Disney Store** • 108 N State St • 888-447-8148
  Princess paraphernalia and Mouse gear.
- **Fly Bird** • 719 Lake St, Oak Park • 708-383-3330
  Off-beat furnishings, fashion and toys from baby to adult
- **Forest Bootery** • 492 Central Ave, Highland Park
  847-433-1911; 284 E Market Sq, Lake Forest
  847-234-0201 • Great but pricey shoe store.
- **Galt Toys + Galt Baby** • 900 N Michigan Ave
  312-440-9550; 2012 Northbrook Court, Northbrook
  847-498-4660 • High-end toy store and baby supplies.
- **Gymboree** • 835 N Michigan Ave • 312-649-9074
  Designer preemie and kids' clothes.
- **Kozy's Bike Shop** • 601 S LaSalle St • 312-360-0020
  Everything for biking families.
- **LMNOP** • 2570 N Lincoln Ave • 773-975-4055

Hip, fun kids' clothes.
- **Land of Nod** • 900 W North Ave • 312-475-9903
  (stores also in Oak Brook Center and Northbrook Court) • Cute kids' furniture.
- **Lazar's Juvenile Furniture** • 6557 N Lincoln Ave,
  Lincolnwood • 847-679-6146
  Tried-and-true children's furniture store.
- **Little Strummer** • 909 W Armitage Ave
  773-751-3410 • Kids' tunes.
- **Madison and Friends** • 940 N Rush St • 312-642-6403
  Designer clothes.
- **Magic Tree Bookstore** • 141 N Oak Park Ave, Oak Park
  708-848-0770 • Friendly and expert independent booksellers.
- **Mini Me** • 900 N Michigan Ave • 312-988-4011
  European designer clothes.
- **Oilily** • 520 N Michigan Ave • 312-527-5747
  Colorful patterned kids' clothes.
- **Pottery Barn Kids** • 2111 N Clybourn Ave
  773-525-8349 (stores also in Oak Brook Center, Old Orchard Center, and Deer Park Town Center) Furnishings for the completely coordinated kid's boudoir.
- **Psycho Baby** • 1630 N Damen Ave • 773-772-2815
  Funky kids' clothes.
- **Pumpkin Moon** • 1028 North Blvd, Oak Park
  708-524-8144 • Funky, vintage toys.
- **Red Balloon Company** • 2060 Damen Ave
  773-489-9800 • Toys, clothes, furniture.
- **The Right Start** • 2121 N Clybourn Ave
  773-296-4420 • Baby equipment galore.
- **Shops at Northbridge** • 520 N Michigan Ave
  312-327-2300 • Entire third floor is kids' clothing, toys, and accessories, including Nordstrom.
- **The Second Child** • 954 W Armitage Ave
  773-883-0880 • Gently used designer clothes.
- **Timeless Toys** • 4749 N Lincoln Ave • 773-334-4445
  Old-fashioned, hand-crafted toys.
- **Toyscape** • 2911 N Broadway St • 773-665-7400
  Toys galore.
- **Uncle Fun** • 1338 W Belmont Ave • 773-477-8223
  Hilarious novelties and vintage tin wind-up toys.
- **U.S. Toy–Constructive Playthings** • 5314 W Lincoln
  Ave, Skokie • 847-675-5900 • Educational toys favored by teachers.

## Where to go for more information

*Chicago Parent Magazine*
   www.chicagoparent.com

*Oaklee's Guide for Chicagoland Kids*
   www.oakleesguide.com

*Time Out Chicago Kids*
   www.timeoutchicagokids.com/

# Dog Parks, Runs, and Beaches

Make no bones about it, Chicago is a dog's kind of town. More than 750,000 canines live and play in the Windy City. Dogs socialize and exercise their owners daily at designated Dog-Friendly Areas (DFAs), shady parks, and sprawling beaches.

## Dog-Friendly Areas

DFAs are off-leash areas reserved just for canines. Amenities vary by park but often include: doggie drinking fountains; agility equipment; wood chips, pea pebble, and asphalt surfaces; "time out" fenced-in areas for shy or overexcited dogs; trash receptacles and doggie bags for, well, not take-out; and bulletin boards and information kiosks to post animal lovers' announcements.

DFAs are managed jointly by the neighborhoods' dog owners' councils and the Chicago Park District. These spaces are essential to the happiness of Chicago dogs and their owners, as police are notorious for dealing out hefty fines and even arresting dog owners who fail to clean up after or leash their dogs. But at the DFA, canines run free and poop where they please. Just remember to clean up after your pooch, ensure that your dog is fully immunized, de-wormed, licensed, and wearing ID tags. There are limits on how many pups one person can bring at once and please no puppies under four months, dogs in heat, dogs with the name "Killer," or children under 12.

- **Challenger Park**, 1100 W Irving Park Rd (Map 40)
  Nestled next to a cemetery and under the EL tracks, this relatively new DFA has plenty of amenities and neighborhood action. Avoid at all costs during Cubs games.

- **Churchill Field Park**, 1825 N Damen Ave (Map 28)
  This triangular space next to the train tracks is covered with pea gravel and asphalt and many abandoned tennis balls (Golden Retrievers can't get enough).

- **Coliseum Park**, 1466 S Wabash Ave (Map 11)
  Long, narrow, and fenced-in park where dogs race the overhead trains. Nothing to write home about, but, hey, it's legal.

- **Hamlin Park**, 3035 N Hoyne Ave at Wellington Ave (Map 42)
  Located in the shady southwest corner, this active L-shaped park appeals to tennis-ball chasers and fetching owners.

- **Margate Park**, 4921 N Marine Dr (Map 40)
  Called "Puptown" by the Uptown canine-loving community, this beloved DFA is usually packed with doggone fun. Locals are diligent about keeping the pea gravel picked up.

- **Noethling (Grace) Park**, 2645 N Sheffield Ave (Map 29)
  Dogs and owners from the Lincoln Park area love to hang out at the "Wiggley Field" dog run—Chicago's pilot pooch park. Wiggley's got a doggy obstacle course, an asphalt surface, drinking fountain, "time out" area, and info kiosk.

- **Ohio Place Park**, N Orleans St and W Ohio St (Map 2)
  Next to the I-90/94 exit ramp, this fenced-in strip of concrete flanked by bushes isn't pretty, but a dog can play fetch here without a leash. Careful: As the lot is not a Chicago Park District facility, it is not double-gated.

- **River Park**, 5100 N Francisco Ave (Map 38)
  The city's newest DFA.

- **Walsh Playground Park**, 1722 N Ashland Ave (Map 29)
  A 4,500-square-foot park with a small off-leash area for fetching with pea gravel and shade.

- **Wicker Park**, 1425 N Damen Ave (Map 21)
  Popular pooch as well as dog owner pick-up park. Often packed with dog-walkers wrangling fleets of frisky canines.

Creating a DFA takes a serious grass-roots effort spearheaded by the neighborhood's dog owners. They must organize themselves to get the community to bow to their desires through site surveys and three community meetings and raise one-half of the funds needed to build the DFA. Most importantly, they must unleash the support of their alderman, police precinct, and park district. For information on DFAs, call the Park District at 312-742-7529. Chicago's Dog Advisory Work Group, DAWG, (312-409-2169) also assists neighborhood groups in establishing DFAs

## Top Dog Parks and Beaches

Leashed dogs and well-behaved owners are welcome in most of Chicago's parks and on its beaches, except during the height of swimming season when the sands are off-limits. Here are some local canines' top picks.

- **Calumet Park and Beach (9800 South)**
  A 200-acre beach and park getaway in the city with tennis courts, baseball fields, basketball courts, water fun, and plenty of parking.

- **Dog Beach (3200 N Lake Shore Dr)**
  This crescent of sand at the north corner of Belmont Harbor is separated from the bike path by a fence, making it an unofficial dog sand box. But the water is dirty, and the police do ticket, so it's not the most ideal dog-frolicking area.

- **Horner Park (2741 W Montrose Ave)**
  Dog heaven with lots of trees, grass, squirrels to chase, and other pups to meet, particularly after work.

- **Lincoln Park (2045 Lincoln Park W)**
  Paws down, the best dog park in town for romping, fetch, and Frisbee. Unofficial "Bark Park" where pet lovers congregate is a grassy area between Lake Shore Dr and Marine Dr.

- **Montrose/Wilson Avenue Beach (MonDog) (4400 North)**
  The city's only legal off-leash beach, MonDog is perfect for pooches to practice dogpaddling. Lake water is shallow and the beachfront is wide.

- **Ohio Street Beach and Olive Park (400 N Lake Shore Dr)**
  The perfect combo for cross-training canines: Olive Park's fenced-in grassy areas for running and neighboring Ohio Street Beach's calm waters for swimming.

- **Promontory Point (5491 South Shore Dr)**
  Radical run for daring, buff dogs that dive off the scenic picnic area's rocks into the deep water below.

- **Sherman Park (1301 W 52nd St)**
  The best place in the city for a Victorian-style stroll over picturesque bridges and through lagoons.

## More Doggie Information

Chicago's canine community keeps up to snuff on doggie doings through *Chicagoland Tails Magazine*, www.chicagolandtails.com and the Chicago Canine website, www.chicagocanine.com. The definitive local resource for all things dog is Margaret Littman's book *The Dog Lover's Companion to Chicago* (Avalon Travel Publishing).

## Internet

| | | Phone | Map |
|---|---|---|---|
| Panera Bread | 501 S State St | 312-922-1566 | 8 |
| Windy City Cyber Café | 2246 W North Ave | 773-384-6470 | 21 |
| Efebos Internet Café | 1640 S Blue Island Ave | 312-633-9212 | 26 |
| Panera Bread | 2070 N Clybourn Ave | 773-325-9035 | 29 |
| Office Mart | 2801 W Touhy Ave | 773-262-3924 | 33 |
| Panera Bread | 6059 N Lincoln Ave | 773-442-8210 | 35 |
| Screenz | 5212 N Clark St | 773-334-8600 | 37 |
| Ignite Center | 3171 N Clybourn Ave | 773-404-7033 | 42 |
| Panera Bread | 616 W Diversey Pkwy | 773-528-4556 | 44 |
| Panera Bread | 6059 N Lincoln Ave | 773-442-8210 | NW |

## Wi-Fi

| | | Phone | Map |
|---|---|---|---|
| Caribou Coffee | 600 N Kingsbury St | 312-335-0576 | 1 |
| Cosi | 55 E Grand Ave | 312-321-1990 | 2 |
| Caribou Coffee | 500 W Madison St | 312-463-1130 | 4 |
| Bean Addiction | 555 W Madison St | 312-474-9140 | 4 |
| Caribou Coffee | 10 S La Salle St | 312-609-5108 | 5 |
| Argo Tea | 16 W Randolph St | 312-553-1551 | 5 |
| Chicago Cultural Center | 77 E Randolph St | | 5 |
| Lavazza | 27 W Washington St | 312-977-9971 | 5 |
| Cosi | 28 E Jackson Blvd | 312-939-2674 | 5 |
| Cosi | 33 N Dearborn St | 312-727-0290 | 5 |
| Intelligentsia Coffee & Tea | 53 W Jackson Blvd | 312-253-0594 | 5 |
| Caribou Coffee | 55 W Monroe St | 312-214-0852 | 5 |
| Lavazza | 134 N La Salle St | 312-977-9701 | 5 |
| Argo Tea | 140 S Dearborn St | 312-553-1551 | 5 |
| Caribou Coffee | 200 N La Salle St | 312-223-1606 | 5 |
| Cosi | 203 N La Salle St | 312-368-4400 | 5 |
| Cosi | 230 W Monroe St | 312-782-4755 | 5 |
| Cosi | 230 W Washington St | 312-422-1002 | 5 |
| Daley Plaza | 50 W Washington St | | 5 |
| Caribou Coffee | 311 W Monroe St | 312-920-9746 | 5 |
| Cosi | 116 S Michigan Ave | 312-223-1061 | 6 |
| The Coffee Beanery | 150 N Michigan Ave | 312-781-9970 | 6 |
| Caribou Coffee | 41 E 8th St | 312-786-9205 | 8 |
| Panera Bread | 501 S State St | 312-922-1566 | 8 |
| Caribou Coffee | 800 S Wabash Ave | 312-786-9205 | 8 |
| Café Au Lait | 1900 S State St | 312-225-3940 | 11 |
| Bridgeport Coffeehouse | 3101 S Morgan St | 773-247-9950 | 12 |
| Hidden Pearl Café | 1060 E 47th St | 773-285-1211 | 17 |
| Third World Café | 1301 E 53rd St | 773-288-3882 | 19 |
| Istria Café | 1520 E 57th St | 773-955-2556 | 19 |
| Einstein Bros Bagels | 5706 S University Ave | 773-834-1018 | 19 |
| Argo Tea | 5758 S Maryland Ave | 773-834-0366 | 19 |
| Barista Café | 852 N Damen Ave | 773-489-2010 | 21 |
| Café Ballou | 939 N Western Ave | 773-342-2909 | 21 |
| Filter | 1585 N Milwaukee Ave | 773-227-4850 | 21 |
| Alliance Bakery | 1736 W Division St | 773-278-0366 | 21 |
| Letizia's Natural Bakery | 2144 W Division St | 773-342-1011 | 21 |
| Windy City Cyber Café | 2246 W North Ave | 773-384-6470 | 21 |
| Coffee on Milwaukee | 1046 N Milwaukee Ave | 773-276-3200 | 22 |
| Atomix | 1957 W Chicago Ave | 312-666-2649 | 23 |
| Muse Café | 817 N Milwaukee Ave | 312-850-2233 | 24 |
| West Gate Coffeehouse | 924 W Madison St | 312-829-9378 | 24 |
| Sip Coffee House | 1223 W Grand Ave | 312-563-1123 | 24 |
| Bialy's Café | 1421 W Chicago Ave | 312-733-7165 | 24 |
| Swim Café | 1357 W Chicago Ave | 312-492-8600 | 24 |
| Café Jumping Bean | 1439 W 18th St | 312-455-0019 | 26 |
| Mi Cafetal | 1519 W 18th St | 312-738-2883 | 26 |
| Efebos Internet Café | 1640 S Blue Island Ave | 312-633-9212 | 26 |
| Kristoffer's Café & Bakery | 1733 S Halsted St | 312-829-4150 | 26 |
| Coffee Beanery | 2158 N Damen Ave | 773-278-4200 | 28 |
| Panera Bread | 2 N Michigan Ave | 312-332-6895 | 29 |
| Apple Stores at | 679 N Michigan Ave | 312-529-9500 | 29 |
| | 801 W North Ave | 312-777-4200 | 44 |
| Bean Café | 2235 N Sheffield Ave | 773-325-4577 | 29 |
| Savor the Flavor | 2545 N Sheffield Ave | 773-883-5287 | 29 |
| Ambrosia Café | 1963 N Sheffield Ave | 773-404-4450 | 29 |
| Bourgeois Pig Café | 738 W Fullerton Ave | 773-883-5282 | 30 |
| Cosi | 2200 N Clark St | 773-472-2674 | 30 |
| Caribou Coffee | 2453 N Clark St | 773-327-9923 | 30 |
| Argo Tea | 2485 N Clark St | 773-733-4231 | 30 |
| Argo Tea | 819 N Rush St | 312-951-5302 | 32 |
| Ennui Café | 6981 N Sheridan Rd | 773-973-2233 | 34 |
| Café Utjeha | 5350 N Lincoln Ave | 773-907-8853 | 35 |
| Metropolis Coffee | 1039 W Granville Ave | 773-764-0400 | 37 |
| Pause | 1107 W Berwyn Ave | 773-334-3686 | 37 |
| Trivoli Café | 1147 W Granville Ave | 773-338-4840 | 37 |
| Screenz | 5212 N Clark St | 773-334-8600 | 37 |
| Coffee Chicago | 5256 N Broadway St | 773-784-1305 | 37 |
| Red Eye Café | 4164 N Lincoln Ave | 773-327-9478 | 39 |
| Perfect Cup | 4700 N Damen Ave | 773-989-4177 | 39 |
| Café Marrakech Expresso | 4747 N Damen Ave | 773-271-4541 | 39 |
| So Addicted | 4805 N Damen Ave | 773-561-3210 | 39 |
| Urban Tea Lounge | 838 W Montrose Ave | 773-907-8726 | 40 |
| Corona's Coffee Shop | 909 W Irving Park Rd | 773-529-1886 | 40 |
| Nick's on Wilson | 1140 W Wilson Ave | 773-271-1155 | 40 |
| Dollop Coffee | 4181 N Clarendon Ave | 773-755-1955 | 40 |
| MoJoe's Hot House | 2849 W Belmont Ave | 773-596-5637 | 41 |
| MoJoe's Café Lounge | 2256 W Roscoe St | 773-388-1236 | 42 |
| Ignite Center | 3171 N Clybourn Ave | 773-404-7033 | 42 |
| Cosi | 1023 W Belmont Ave | 773-868-1227 | 43 |
| My Place for Tea | 3210 N Sheffield Ave | 773-525-8320 | 43 |
| Caribou Coffee | 3240 N Ashland Ave | 773-281-3362 | 43 |
| Mellow Grounds Coffee Lounge | 3807 N Ashland Ave | 773-528-2877 | 43 |
| House of Hookah | 607 W Belmont Ave | 773-348-1550 | 44 |
| Panera Bread | 616 W Diversey Pkwy | 773-528-4556 | 44 |
| Caribou Coffee | 3025 N Clark St | 773-529-6366 | 44 |
| Intelligentsia Coffee Roasters | 3123 N Broadway St | 773-348-8058 | 44 |
| Argo Tea | 3135 N Broadway St | 773-248-3061 | 44 |
| Café Latakia | 3204 N Broadway St | 773-929-6667 | 44 |
| Caribou Coffee | 3300 N Broadway St | 773-477-3695 | 44 |
| Caribou Coffee | 3500 N Halsted St | 773-248-0799 | 44 |
| Panera Bread | 6059 N Lincoln Ave | 773-442-8210 | NW |
| Open Hearth | 5207 N Kimball Ave | 773-279-9686 | NW |
| J Bean Coffee & Café | 7221 W Forest Preserve Ave | 708-583-2245 | NW |
| Euro Café | 3435 N Harlem Ave | 773-286-8544 | NW |
| Caffe' Italia | 2625 N Harlem Ave | 773-889-0455 | NW |
| Humboldt Pie | 1001 N California Ave | 773-342-4743 | W |
| Café Luna | 1742 W 99th St | 773-239-8990 | SW |
| Spoon's Coffee Boutique | 712 E 75th St | 773-874-3847 | S |
| Café Mozart | 600 Davis St | 847-492-8056 | Evanston |

## Overview

Chicago is widely regarded as a world-class food destination, and rightly so, we say. It's a goldmine for anyone searching for fl avors, romantic dining or simply a place to clog arteries. Whether you're looking for a $2 hot dog at one of the city's hot dog stands, a $200 20-course marathon at one the city's foodie destinations or a meal at one of the myriad mom-and-pop neighborhood spots where you can't understand the costs because you don't speak the owner's language, you'll find it here.

In the past decade, Chicago's adventuresome appetite has come to life with a whole new school of Chicago restaurants coming to the fore. Once fueled by students of the masters: Bayless, Trotter, Gordon Sinclair, and so on, the Chicago dining renaissance is already in its second or third generation, and now the students of the students, those who honed their skills at places like Trio and Tru, are taking the reins as they charge into Chicago's culinary future.

What follows is a breakdown of some of our favorite spots, old and new. Of course, with every new restaurant opening, there is likely another one closing. Therefore, we recommend pulling out your smartphone and downloading the latest app that answers your appetite's every question. Or you could just call.

## Chicago Staples

Some restaurants are more than just places to eat and drink; they're defining institutions of the city where politicians scheme and drunk baseball fans pass out. The original **Billy Goat Tavern (Maps 3, 5, 24)** is known to baby boomers as the birthplace of John Belushi's "cheezeboiga" skit, but Chicagoans appreciate it as the dank watering hole where reporters from the Tribune and Sun-Times would once gather after work to talk shop. Today, it's mostly frequented by wide-eyed tourists who play at slumming it. "The original Chicago-style pizza" is a title claimed by nearly every pizza shack in town. Of the lot, **Pizzeria Uno's (Map 2)** claim seems the most legit--their cheese-filled recipe dates back to 1943. Other Chicago pizza institutions include **Lou Malnati's (Map 2)** and **Gino's East (Maps 2, 43)**. Equally important is the Chicago Dog--that is, a hot dog on a steamed bun "dragged through the garden" with a virtual salad on top--onions, relish, tomatoes, pickle spears, sport peppers, mustard (no ketchup, thank you very much), and a dash of celery salt. Post-pub dogs at **Wiener's Circle (Map 30)** are a Lincoln Park rite-of-passage--the servers are infamous for their saucy attitudes. Chicago is more than hot dogs, though. It's hamburgers and heavy metal at **Kuma's Corner (Map 41)** where tatted servers dish up patties named after Pantera, Slayer and other bands with guitar gods. While there are plenty of Chicago institutions that put the city on the international culinary radar, Rick Bayless' **Frontera Grill (Map 2)** stands out from the rest of the pack with creative and upscale Mexican fare in a festive environment.

## The New Kids on the Block

Although Lincoln Park legend Charlie Trotter closed down his namesake restaurant in 2012 to enroll in a Master's program in philosophy (!) at the University of Chicago, the cast of Chicago's eateries continues to evolve. For diners searching to spend lots of dollars, the menu at West Town's **Next (Map 24)** changes every few months to offer a taste of a different region of the world, but the price generally stays the same: very high. On the lower end of the price spectrum, River North's **Farmhouse (Map 2)** features a rotating menu based on what's available at local Midwestern farms. Downtown diners who love intestinal casings will find a new take on the Chicago classic at **Westminster Hot Dog (Map 5).** In Lincoln Park, bring your own booze and create your own patty masterpiece at **Butcher & the Burger (Map 29)**. Logan Square continues to give residents more reasons to move west and eat more with the addition of wine-bar-food-art-mecca **Telegraph (Map 27)**.

## Chicago's Best Dining Bets

*For the Diner with Dollars to Burn*

So you have a lot of money? Well, congratulations. There's no better way to get rid of your cash than to go on a dining tour of Chicago's high-end dining destinations. Here are some of Chicago's spendiest special-occasion options. Newcomer **Girl and the Goat (Map 24)** arrived on the scene and wasted no time taking money from hungry guests. **Alinea (Map 30)** welcomes you with scientific culinary creations and sends you home with a bill that will leave your wallet limping toward the door. Other classic spends include **Everest (Map 5)**, **Nomi (Map 3)**, and **Les Nomades (Map 3)**. **Tru (Map 3)** is renowned for its caviar staircase; **Spiaggia (Map 32)** for it's gorgeous lake view. For something even, um, more expensive, **Next (Map 24)** is another newbie where diners can shell out an insane amount of cash before they even eat. You must buy tickets in advance for this restaurant's coveted tour of different regions of the world. If you're looking for a massive hunk of meat, head to other Chicago steakhouse classics like **Morton's (Map 32)**, David Burke's **Primehouse (Map 2)**, or **Gene & Georgetti (Map 2)**.

## For the Diner Holding a Sign Begging for Dollars

So you're broke? Perhaps you fell victim to a Ponzi scheme or you're just like the rest of America and don't have much money. Do not fret, dear friend. Cheap taquerias, hot dog stands, and corner grills abound. For a romantic dinner without the added weight of a bar tab, try **Los Nopales (Map 39)**. This super delicious and BYOB Mexican spot offers authentic south-of-the-border flavors with south-of-the-border prices. Basically, order anything and go swimming in the Mole sauce. Save room for dessert, and order the tres leches cake. For a cheap date with French flair, **La Creperie (Map 44)** is loaded with low-price charm. This 40-year-old French classic has the shabby look of Parisian authenticity, a gorgeous outdoor patio, and free live French music on Thursday evenings. If your taste buds are in an American mood, head to new BYOB **Jam 'n Honey (Map 29)** where you'll find a menu of omelets, pancakes, burgers, sandwiches and well, any item that satisfies an all-day appetite.

## Pizza Pizza Pizza

Crust, cheese and more cheese. Chicago is a pizza city, and classic spots such as **Pizzeria Uno (Map 2)**, **Lou Malnati's (Map 2)** and **Gino's East (Map 2)** attract tourists and suburbanites in droves. Meanwhile, **Candlelite (Map 33)** in Roger's Park has been serving fresh, hot pies to the local community for decades. **Art of Pizza (Map 43)** has won numerous awards and acclaim for its scrumptious deep disher. If you're not into three inches of mozzarella, you're in luck: this city offers thin crust zza, too. **Piece (Map 21)** serves up New Haven-style pies with a selection of microbrews crafted in-house. Farther north, **Spacca Napoli (Map 39)** gives the wood-fired pizza a Neapolitan twist.

## Chicago for Herbivores

Yes, people love gulping down a succulent steak here, but many Windy City restaurants are introducing more veggie items than the token pasta or risotto. Additionally, more vegetarian-only restaurants been appearing on our beefy shores to let Midwestern cattle breath a sigh of relief. **Chicago Diner (Map 44)** and **Heartland Café (Map 34)** (which does serve some meat) are the crunchy, old-school standard bearers. Raw foodies flock to **Karyn's (Map 30)** in Lincoln Park, which attracted such a following for its raw food menu that Karyn opened **Karyn's Cooked (Map 2)** in River North. If you're heading further north, **Mysore Woodlands (Map 33)** serves vegetarian food from southern India on Devon, while **Arya Bhavan (Map 33)** specializes in Indian vegetarian food from the north and south. **Amitabul (Northwest Chicago)** does Vegan Thai on the Northwest side, and Soul Vegetarian East (South Chicago) in the Southside Chatham neighborhood. For upscale vegetarian, try the **Green Zebra (Map 24)**, or **Mana (Map 21)** in Wicker Park. In Logan Square, down-to-earth scenester spot **Lula (Map 27)** is known for being particularly vegetarian friendly, and the redesigned interior makes this great for casual dates.

For a very special and seriously spendy night, choose the fixed-price vegetarian tasting menus at **Arun's (Map 38)**. Finally, vegetarians and non-vegetarians alike line up for breakfasts served by followers of Sri Chimnoy at Roscoe Village's popular **Victory's Banner (Map 42)**. Call here first: the followers close twice each year for a spiritual retreat.

## Poor Man's Steak and Other Meaty Matters

In the past few years, **Kuma's Corner (Map 41)** has emerged as the popular and critical favorite for best burger in the city, although northside loyalists still swear by **Moody's (Map 37)**, and southsiders hanker for Top Notch Beefburger (Southwest). Even the fast food burger has stepped up their game. In the South Loop, **Epic Burger (Map 8)** delivers sustainable grilled ground beef on a bun. If, on the other hand, you like your meat served on the bone with tangy sauce, head to the **Gale Street Inn (Northwest)** in Jefferson Park, street-festival mainstay **Robinson's (Maps 4, 30)**, hot links king **Uncle John's Barbecue (South)** and **Honey 1 (Map 28)**. **Smoque (Northwest)** attracts droolers from all over the city for, arguably, Chicago's best 'cue. As for encased meats, Chicago has no lack of options--just follow the Vienna Beef signs. For something different, try encased exotic meats such as ostrich or alligator at **Hot Doug's (Map 41)**, a destination stop for top chefs from around the world. On weekends, they feature french fries cooked in duck fat (and lines out the door).

## Soul Food and Southern Cooking

We say soul food is the most American of American cuisines. **Valois (Map 19)** serves no frills, cafeteria-style soul food. **Miss Lee's Good Food (Map 18)** offers gut-busting Southern food for carry-out only. For Cajun food, try Chicago breakfast staple **Wishbone (Map 24)** or Jimmy Banno's famous **Heaven on Seven (Maps 3, 5)**.

## Drink More, Spend Less

Nothing says romance like a bottle (or box) of wine, and Chicago's restaurant scene makes it easy to keep your beverage total low with an array of BYOB spots. If you're looking to savor South American flavors while sipping your own bottle of red, head to **Tango Sur (Map 43)** for massive cuts of Argentinian steak. Forget travel restrictions and bar tabs when you head to **90 Miles Cuban Cafe (Map 42)** where you'll find a more casual dining experience and more meat. Sushi also tastes better when you're not paying for cocktails, so head to **Coast (Map 28)** for slow service that lets you drink more. For non-seaweed options, **Cozy Noodles 'N Rice (Map 43)** serves up noodle dishes close to the endless line of bars in Wrigleyville. Further south, West Town's **Butterfly Sushi (Map 24)** offers sushi and noodles to satisfy any Asian craving. East Lakeview's **Chilam Balam (Map 44)** serves up small plate Mexican with a side of whatever you bring to drink (note: limit one bottle of wine per 2 people).

## Passport to Good Eating

Culinarily, you can travel the world and never leave Chicago. While some of Chicago's dining emporiums fly high on the local radar, we have a soft spot for the ramshackle storefronts where the home cooking's happening. You don't have to live in Chicago a long time to discover that Devon Street is the place to go if you crave Indian food. We love **Hema's Kitchen (Map 33)**, and the Pakistani fare at Rogers Park's **Ghareeb Nawaz (Map 34)**. Pilsen is the destination neighborhood for Mexican muy authentico. **Nuevo Leon (Map 26) has been serving revelatory Mexican home cooking for ages**, and Birreria Reyes de **Ocatlan (Map 26)** is a favorite of celebrity chef Rick Bayless. Off the Pilsen path, **Birrierra Zaragoza (West)** serves a traditional goat stew that really shouldn't be missed. The city's best Vietnamese can be found in the New Saigon section of Argyle Street, right under the L stop, and Albany Park is the place to go for Middle Eastern and Korean fare. Of the former, we think the classic falafel sandwiches at **Dawali (Map 38)** really are something special, stuffed with potatoes and cauliflower as well as the formed garbanzo balls. The greater northwest side is bountiful with Eastern European restaurants and supper clubs. You'll find plenty of great African and Caribbean food behind no-frills storefronts in Rogers Park. As for **Good to Go Jamaican Jerk and Juice Bar (Map 34)**, the name says it all. We shouldn't have to tell you to head to Chinatown for dim sum or Greek Town for flaming cheese or Little Italy for a sampling of Sicily. Perhaps one of the most surreal ethnic dining experiences in Chicago is the Thursday night-only all-you-can-eat Korean vegan buffet at **Dragon Lady Lounge (Map 41)**, the ultimate dive bar.

## Breakfast

There is one crucial ingredient for the morning after an extended evening of exploring Chicago's magnificent miles of bars: breakfast. Well, more like brunch. From egg scramble creations at **John's Place (Map 29)** to syrupy-soaked goodness at **Waffles (Map 9)** to a brick of a breakfast burrito at **Kitsch'n (Map 42)**, you and your hangover can travel anywhere in the city and find some solace with a fork, a plate and perhaps a Bloody Mary.

## Diners

Sometimes you just want a cup of joe and a patty melt, and other times you just want a five-egg omelet, which you'll find at **Pauline's (Map 36)**. If that cholesterol-raising recipe isn't up your alley, Chicago has plenty of other greasy spoon options, including **Salt and Pepper Diner (Map 43)**, **Nookie's (Map 30)**, **Salonica Grill (Map 19)**, **Lou Mitchell's (Map 4)**, **Hollywood Grill (Map 22)**, **The Golden Apple (Map 43)** and **The Golden Angel (Map 39)**. Yes, diners really are golden.

## Flavors on the Go

A rapidly developing food trend in Chicago is unfortunately one that we can't place on a map: the food truck craze. From macaroni and cheese to falafel to cupcakes, Chicagoans have fallen in love with flavors served from the back of a truck. The location of these mobile businesses varies from day to day, and many residents follow their favorite four-wheeled chefs on social media to be the first in line at whatever corner they're calling home for the day. For news on where to be when for what meal, count on **Food Truck Freak** for daily updates.

## Foodies on the Web

Need a recommendation?

Both professional food critics and the vox populi weigh in on the popular restaurant sites of the **Chicago Reader** (www.chicagoreader.com) and the Chicago Tribune's Metromix (chicago.metromix.com). Both offer search categories, so you can find places by location, price, type of cuisine, etc. If you're going somewhere off-the-beaten path, however, be sure to phone first-- **Metromix**, in particular, often seems to be out-of-date.

Professional chefs and passionate eaters chat about both the latest hot spots and hidden neighborhood gems on the **LTH Forum** (www.lthforum.com). The foodie debates, all in the spirit of fun, can get raucous, and sometimes even local celebrity chefs enter the fore to throw down. A warning: Regular posting on the LTH Forum is a tell-tale sign of your descent down the slippery slope of food geekdom.

## Get it Delivered

Finally, if the sun scares you from leaving the comfort of your home, **Grub Hub** and **Seamless** are your hook-ups for delivery that isn't pizza. Well, there's pizza, too, but you can also choose from a massive array of culinary hotspots where you might not be able to get a table.

Chicago is a city of neighborhoods, and as such, we are a city of great little neighborhood taverns. These are the places where the beer you drink is on tap, the bartender throws a basket of pretzels in front of you when you grab your stool, and you can find the men and women who fill the pages of Studs Terkel's beloved Working, stealing precious time between the bossman and the kids. And then there's the jukebox. The best ones feature all your favorite bar songs, from Hank Williams to The Cars, Blondie to Sly and the Family Stone, and "My Way" sung in Polish or Korean just for the hell of it.

Although you'll find a low-key feel at many bars, Chicago has built a strong reputation as a nightlife capital. With bass-pumping dance clubs, warm weather rooftop bars and VIP lounges, the city keeps the rapt attention of every club crazy scenester.

No matter your interest, there's always something going on in the city. To help you keep on top of it all, check out listings in The Reader, Time Out Chicago, and New City. Websites like **Gapers Block** (www.gapersblock.com) list events and specials.

## Dive Bars

Rub shoulders with the characters from a Nelson Algren story at any of the following joints: In Old Town, the **Old Town Ale House (Map 31)** was once voted best dive bar in the country by someone-mumblemumble-we-forget-who. In Edgewater, **Ollie's Lounge (Map 37)** has long drawn a friendly crowd of boozy locals. Other dives such as **Ola's Liquor (Map 21)** can be identified by the mere presence of the "Old Style" bar sign out front.

## Arty Crowd

Young urban arty types have carved out their kitsch-embracing niches at Ukrainian Village and Wicker Park spots such as **Club Foot (Map 21)**, **The Gold Star Bar (Map 21)**, **The Inner Town Pub (Map 21)**, **Rainbo Club (Map 21)**, and **Small Bar (Map 21)**, while their Pilsen and River West brethren drink their PBR at **Skylark (Map 26)** and **The Matchbox (Map 24)**, respectively. On the west side, **The California Clipper (West Chicago)** appeals to today's rat pack wannabes, and on the north side, get drunk with happy hipsters and local punters at **The Village Tap (Map 42)**, **The Long Room (Map 40)**, and **The Edgewater Lounge (Map 37)**.

## Live Music

Some of Chicago's best live music venues are also neighborhood spots. The legendary **Checkerboard Lounge (Map 19)** is making a comeback in Hyde Park. **Katerina's (Map 39)**, on an unassuming stretch of Irving Park in North Center, features regular live gypsy music along with local acts. In the West Village, the **Empty Bottle (Map 21)** is the place to catch touring indie bands. Further west, **Rosa's Lounge (Northwest Chicago)** is a friendly venue for live blues. Catch live jazz any night of the week at Uptown's **Green Mill Lounge (Map 40)**. On the northwest side, **The Abbey Pub (Northwest)** features everything from alternative rock acts like The Breeders and Peaches, to singer-songwriter showcases and burlesque. If you want to put some twang in your thang, alt-country acts from the Bloodshot Records label regularly perform at Bucktown's **Hideout (Map 29)**.

## Shake a Tailfeather

In Chicago, even the best place to get your groove on is often the one right around the corner. Despite the concentration of huge, dazzling and super expensive high-concept nightclubs in River North and River West, (which are typically the domains of tourists and suburbanites), many local folk prefer smaller, friendlier, and cheaper local options to catch Saturday (or Monday, or Thursday) night fever. In Lincoln Park, **Neo (Map 30)** attracts children of the Eighties and their wannabes with retro dance tunes ranging from goth to new wave. Legendary gay bar **Berlin (Map 43)**, in Lakeview, draws a pansexual crowd for their ever-rotating array of theme nights. **Smart Bar (Map 43)**, in the basement of the rock club **Metro (Map 43)**, spins dance music with an edge. **Funky Buddha (Map 1)** draws a diverse crowd united by a desire to get funky.

## What's Your Poison?

Whether you are a wino, a beer swiller, a whiskey sipper or a tequila shooter, have we got a bar for you. If you're a brewhead, then you surely know that Chicago's home to some of the best beer bars in the country, including microbrew aficionados **The Map Room (Map 28)**, **Sheffield's (Map 43)**, **Risque Café (Map 43)**. At all of those locations, be prepared to read before you order because they have full-on booklets listing all their brews. At **Quenchers (Map 28)** you can drink your way around the world. If it's Belgians you crave, try getting a seat at Andersonville's **Hopleaf (Map 40)**. If it's something stronger that you crave, **Delilah's (Map 29)** serves a world-class collection of whiskey to an amiable crowd of aging hipsters and once-were punks. **Marty's (Map 37)** and **Martini Ranch (Map 2)** are fine places to be shaken and not stirred. Viticultural trill-seekers need look no further than **The Tasting Room** where the wine selection is as fine as the view.

In the last couple of years, the cocktail has become king in Chicago, with many noted mixologists shaking up fresh ingredients to make some of the best stuff you've ever tasted. Celebrity chef Grant Achatz's **The Aviary (Map 24)** has upped the game in the cocktail scene the way his Alinea redefined the culinary world. **The Drawing Room (Map 32)** features modern mixology and takes on classic cocktails. **The Violet Hour (Map 21)** is designed as a speakeasy (look for the yellow light outside) with some of the best mixes in the city. You can also find the speakeasy theme at 1914 at the back of **Red Ivy (Map 43)**. For those who appreciate a good cocktail but are on a budget, check out **The Whistler (Map 27)**, whose short list of classic cocktails won't sap your wallet.

## Irish Pubs

Yes, Chicago is full of Irish—and "Irish"—pubs. Some are pretty damn authentic though, so if you're on the north side and it's a good Shepherd's Pie or football match you're craving along with your pint, seek out **The Irish Oak (Map 43)**, **Chief O'Neill's (Map 41)**, or **The Globe Pub (Map 39)**. On the South Side, well, you can't even contemplate Irish drinking culture in the city without a tip o' the hat to the strip of Western Avenue in Beverly that is home to the annual South Side St. Patrick's Day Parade. **Keegan's Pub (Southwest)**, **Cork & Kerry (Southwest)**, and **Mrs. O'Leary's Dubliner (Southwest)** are all loaded with craic. Every Friday and Saturday Night, the **Irish-American Heritage Center (Northwest)** hosts the **Fifth Province Pub (Northwest)**, an authentic Irish Pub, featuring Irish beer, Irish food, and Irish entertainment.

## Smoker-Friendly

Since the smoking ban hit, it's harder than ever to enjoy two vices at once. However, some places are more enjoyable than others, including the stoop at **Club Foot (Map 21)**, the beer garden at **Happy Village (Map 21)**, the back porch at **Simon's (Map 37)**, and **Fizz Bar & Grill (Map 43)** that's tented during the winter.

## Mag Mile and Oak Street: Bring Your Bars of Gold

The Mag Mile has long replaced State Street as downtown Chicago's premier (and tourist-friendly) shopping strip. This stretch of prime real estate, spanning from the Chicago River to Oak Street features Chicago outposts of many destination shopping spots, including **Niketown (Map 3)**, **The Apple Store (Map 3)**, Needless-Markup (a.k.a. **Neiman-Marcus**) **(Map 3)**, **American Girl Place (Map 32)**, and the high-end boutiques and department stores, (think **Tiffany (Map 3)**, **Gucci (Map 32)**, and **Hermes (Map 32)** connected to **Water Tower Place (Map 32)** and the **900 North Michigan Mall (Map 32)**.

Around the corner on Oak Street lay tonier boutiques. While Mag Mall attracts goggle-eyed Midwestern families, who'll likely stop for lunch at the Cheesecake Factory or Bubba Gump, Oak Street appeals more to the Gold Coast and North Shore set: **Prada (Map 32)**, **Barney's (Maps 32)** and **BCBG MAXAZRIA (Map 32)** are all located on this tiny strip.

Not far away on Rush Street, **Ikram (Map 32)** is a favorite of First Lady Michelle Obama.

## Boutique Shopping

You don't have to go down to Oak Street to find funky designer boutiques selling everything from original fashions by local designers to housewares and hostess gifts. Lincoln Park and Wicker Park in particular are heavy on cool women's fashion boutiques. In Lincoln Park, check out Armitage, Clark, and Halsted for shops such as **Lori's Designer Shoes (Map 30)** and **Kaveri (Map 29)**. In Wicker Park, the highest concentration of cool little shops, like the fashion boutique **Penelope (Map 21)**, line Division street, but if you love to shop, you'll want to work the whole Bermuda triangle of Division, Milwaukee, and North Avenue. Southport Avenue in Wrigleyville boasts a string of women's boutiques, including **Krista K (Map 43)** and **Leahey & LaDue Consignment (Map 43)**.

## Home Design and Decor

Forget River North, Clark Street in Andersonville has emerged as a mini designer's row. Shops like **Scout (Map 37)** and **Cassona (Map 37)** have designers flocking from all over the city. **Architectural Artifacts (Map 39)** and **Restoration Hardware (Map 22)** are treasure islands for vintage rehabbers. **Community Home Supply (Map 42)** is one of the city's best (and priciest) kitchen and bath boutiques.

## Best of the 'Hoods

In many cases, Chicago's neighborhood shopping destinations say something unique about the character of the 'hood. Funky little punk-rock indie shops in Logan Square for example, or gay-friendly places like **GayMart (Map 44)**, **Unabridged Bookstore (Map 44)**, and He **Who Eats Mud (Map 44)** in Boystown. Lincoln Square caters to the NPR-lovin', micro-brew swillers that call that 'hood home, and Andersonville has something for everyone: feminist books (**Women & Children First (Map 37)**), chic home furnishings, men's and women's fashions, Swedish souvenirs, and, count them, two clean, friendly, and non-oogly-feeling sex-toy stores (**Early to Bed (Map 37)** and **Tulip (Maps 37, 44)**).

Ethnic enclaves also make for great shopping. Try gifts and cookware in Chinatown, gorgeous saris and Bollywood flicks on West Devon, hookahs and Moroccan teas sets on north Kedzie in Albany Park, and Irish arts and crafts in Beverly.

## One Man's Trash...

Is another man's treasure. Whether you wants are driven by the desire to save the planet or just to save a buck, Chicago offers a plentitude of places to buy other people's old crap. Vintage wear boutiques thrive in arty 'hoods like Wicker Park, East Lakeview, and Roscoe Village. Some faves: **Una Mae's Freak Boutique (Map 21)**, **Silver Moon (Map 21)**, and the **Hollywood Mirror (Map 44)**. **Ragstock (Maps 43, 21)**, a used-and-off-sale clothing chain, has two Chicago outposts: one near Clark and Belmont, the other on Milwaukee Avenue.

For one-stop antique shopping, check out one of Chicago's many antique malls--huge enclosed spaces that lease space to small dealers. Not to be missed are the **Broadway Antique Market (Map 37)**, the **Edgewater Antique Mall (Map 37)**, and the **Lincoln Antique Mall (Map 38)**.

In terms of thrift stores, there's either a **Salvation Army (Maps 40, NW)**, a **Unique Thrift (Maps 12, 40, W, NW)** or a **Village Discount (Maps 27, 38, 40, NW, W, SW)** in nearly every neighborhood in the city. Meanwhile, **The Brown Elephant (Maps 37, 44)** thrift stores benefit Howard Brown Health Center's HIV research.

## Audiophilia

Although two huge chain record stores (Tower Records and the Virgin Superstore) have folded in the past five years, Chicago loves our independent record stores. Among our faves, **Reckless Records (Maps 5, 21, 44)** serves the indie rock crowd and **Borderline (Map 44)** spins Euro dance hits. **Gramaphone (Map 44)** is where Chicago's DJs pick-up the hottest wax. **Hyde Park Records (Map 19)** supplies Hyde Parkers with all its old-school vinyl needs, while **Dusty Groove (Map 22)**, which specializes in old R&B and soul, provides the same service to West Towners. **Laurie's Planet of Sound (Map 39)**, in Lincoln Square, offers an eclectic array of mostly-indie music without the attitude that is often associated with indie record store clerks.

For stereo equipment and electronics, DJs shop at **Midwest Pro Sound (Map 43)**. **DeciBel (Map 21)** serves the Wicker Park and Bucktown crew. **Saturday Audio Exchange (Map 43)**, only open on Thursdays, Saturdays, and Sundays, sells high-end stereo brands for cheap, (well, relatively cheap, anyways) as well as used and refurbished woofers, tweeters, receivers, and all that other audio-geek stuff.

## Get Foodie

The gourmet and specialty food trade has exploded in the past few years, as have the high-end houseware stores that are supplying upscale home cooks with their Le Creuset pans and Wüstof knives. Today, if you find yourself hard-up for locally-produced caviar, lavender extract, stinky artisinal cheese, curry leaves, or whatever other weird ingredient they don't stock at the Jewel, all you have to do is follow your nose. Of Chicago's many, many gourmet or specialty food shops, there are a few that are particularly dear to our hearts. **Pastoral Artisan (Maps 5, 44)**, a specialty cheese and wine shop, is a great stop on your way to a dinner party to pick up cheese, wine, olives, or other tasty treats. We also love **Goddess and the Grocer (Maps 28, 32)**, **Provenance Food and Wine (Maps 27, 39)**, and, perhaps, the best-smelling shop in town, Old Town's **The Spice House (Map 31)**. In Logan Square, **The Dill Pickle Food Co-op (Map 27)** is the place to pick up locally sourced and organic food goodness. Ethnic markets are great places to track down hard-to-find ingredients. **Middle East Bakery (Map 37)** in Andersonville sells amazing homemade hummus and falafel, as well as olive oil, pine nuts, and dried fruit at prices significantly lower than Whole Paycheck. **Joong Boo Market (NW)** is one-stop shopping for Korean culinary adventures, and they have a decent cafe in the back if you just can't wait to have your bibimbap.

Oh, and that local caviar? Look no further than **The FishGuy Market (NW)**.

## Mall Rats

Normally we'd scoff, but look, it's Chicago, and it gets damn cold. So, if occasionally you want to do your shopping without having to venture too far into the great outdoors, we're not going to point any fingers.

**Block 37 (Map 5)** is an entire city block of mall greatest hits, and it's in the Loop. On the Mag Mile, **Water Tower Place (Map 32)** offers pretty typical mall fare--there's a Sephora, Godiva, and Victoria's Secret--but their food court has more in common with a Las Vegas buffet than anywhere you'd be able to grab an Orange Julius or a Mrs. Fields cookie. A block north, the shops at **900 N Michigan (Map 32)**, offer higher-end fare, (no surprise, as it's attached to the super-luxe Four Seasons hotel). Shops here include Coach, Diesel, MaxMara, and Williams-Sonoma. In East Lakeview, the **Century Shopping Centre (Map 44)** is kept in business by its fine art house cinema and Bally's outpost, certainly not by the mundane shops contained within (Limited, Express, or Bath & Body Works, anyone?). Housed in a building where bombers were built during WWII, today the huge **Ford City Mall (SW)** is a popular hang-out for local kids without much else to do, but otherwise boasts nothing very exceptional--a few low-end department stores, a movie theater, and all of the shops and fast food joints you'd expect to find in a mall. Anchored by a Target and a Kohl's, **Harlem Irving Plaza (NW)**, like the Ford City Mall, is a popular stomping ground for high school students but offers little beyond the same old shops despite that location-specific nom de mall.

## Oddities

Some of our favorite Chicago shops defy easy definition. Among them, **American Science and Surplus (NW)** offers one-stop shopping for professional-quality laboratory beakers, school supplies, crime-scene tape, pirate flags, and life-sized anatomy models. At **Uncle Fun (Map 43)** you can find all the coolest vintage and wind-up toys, as well as oodles of strange and playful things for under $5, making it the gag gift headquarters of Chi-town. Recent acquisitions: a bacon-scented air-freshener, a week's worth of fake moustaches, and a "Mr. T in Your Pocket" keychain.

To cast a curse or to break one, stop by **Athenian Candle Company (Map 4)**, where, in addition to 12-foot, gold-detailed, church-quality candles, you can also pick up a bottle of "Law Be Gone" floor wash or "Love Come Back" air spray. Prefer high-end designer beach wear with your candles? Stop by **Calypso Christiane Cello (Map 32)** for sunny beaded tunics and sweet-smelling French candles.

## State Street: Student Mecca

The student population in the Loop has soared, thanks to new student housing for Columbia and School of the Art Institute Students. State Street has made a comeback by filling up with cheap, hip, chic shops catering to this crowd. **H&M, (Map 32)**, **Urban Outfitters (Maps 5, 30, 32)**, **Blick Art Materials (Maps 5, 22)**, and **Central Camera (Map 5)** cater to the art student within all of us.

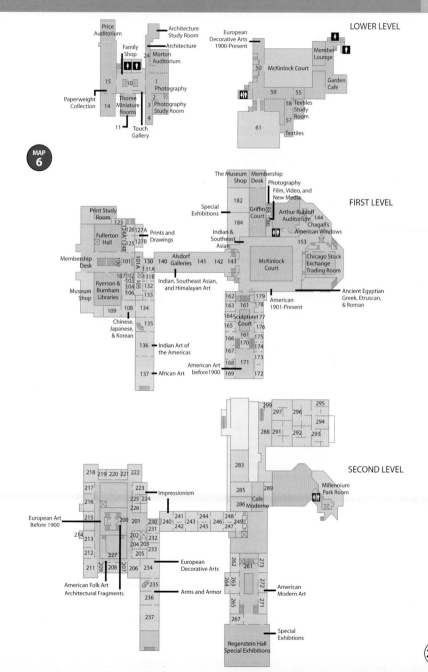

LOWER LEVEL

Price Auditorium

Architecture Study Room

Architecture

European Decorative Arts 1900-Present

Member Lounge

Family Shop

24 Morton Auditorium

50 McKinlock Court

Garden Cafe

15 10

1 Photography

59 55

Paperweight Collection

14

2

58 Textiles Study Room

Thorne Miniature Rooms

3 Photography Study Room

57

11 Touch Gallery

4

61 Textiles

MAP 6

FIRST LEVEL

The Museum Shop | Membership Desk

Photography Film, Video, and New Media

182

Special Exhibitions

Griffin Court

183 186

Arthur Rubloff Auditorium 144

Print Study Room

123

184

Chagall's American Windows

126 127A
124A 124B
125 127B

Prints and Drawings

Indian & Southeast Asian

153

Fullerton Hall

Chicago Stock Exchange Trading Room

Membership Desk

100 101 101A

130 131A 131B

140 Alsdorf Galleries 141 142 143

McKinlock Court

Museum Shop

107 102
103
104 105 132
106

109 108 133

134

162 179
163 161 178
164 Sculpture 177
165 Court 176
166 161 175
167 170 174
168 171 173
169 172

Ancient Egyptian Greek, Etruscan, & Roman

Ryerson & Burnham Libraries

Indian, Southeast Asian, and Himalayan Art

American 1901-Present

Chinese, Japanese, & Korean

135

136 Indian Art of the Americas

137 African Art

American Art before 1900

SECOND LEVEL

299 295
297 296 294
288 291 292 293

283

Millennium Park Room

218 219 220 221 222

285 289

223 Impressionism

286 Cafe Moderno

217

216

225 224
226

215 European Art Before 1900

200 201 230 240 241 243 244 248 249
242 245 246 247

214 213

202 231
204 203 232
205 233

262 273
261
263 272
264
265 271
267

American Modern Art

212

227

211 209 208 207 206 234

American Folk Art Architectural Fragments

235 Arms and Armor

European Decorative Arts

236

237

Regenstein Hall Special Exhibitions

Special Exhibitions

(293)

## General Information

| | |
|---|---|
| NFT Map: | 6 |
| Address: | 111 S Michigan Ave |
| | Chicago, IL 60603 |
| Phone: | 312–443–3600 |
| Website: | www.artic.edu |
| Hours: | Daily 10:30 am–5 pm; Thursday until 8 pm; Thanksgiving, Christmas, & New Year's Days: closed |
| Admission: | $23 for adults ($20 for Illinois residents, $18 for Chicago residents), $17 for students/ seniors ($14 for Illinois studentes/seniors, $12 for Chicago students/seniors), free for children aged 14 and under, free for Illinois residents on Thursday evenings 5– 8 pm |

## Overview

Built in 1892 as part of the 1893 Columbian Exposition, the Classical Revival-style Allerton Wing of the Art Institute of Chicago began life as the World's Congress Auxiliary Building for the World's Fair. (The lions were added two years later.) Today the Art Institute is one of the preeminent art museums in the country, housing the largest collection of 19th–Century French art outside of Paris (and its modern art collection isn't anything to sneeze at, either). Walking up the grand staircase in the main entrance, visitors are presented with an eclectic collection of architectural fragments wrenched from Chicago buildings that were standing in the way of, well, you know: "progress." There are also impressive exhibitions such as the Japanese wood block prints, the Touch Gallery designed specifically for the visually impaired, as well as really, really old vases and things, but who are we kidding? Everyone comes here for an up–close and personal look at such celebrated paintings as Caillebotte's *Paris Street; Rainy Day*, Seurat's *Grand Jatte*, Grant Wood's *American Gothic,* and Hopper's *Nighthawks*, along with their impressive collection of Monets, Manets, Van Goghs, and Picassos.

The completion of Renzo Piano's Modern Wing in 2009 makes the Art Institute the nation's second largest art museum (we're gaining on you, Metropolitan Museum of Art!). The $300 million addition, which makes great use of filtered natural light thanks to Piano's "magic carpet" floating roof, includes a first floor gallery of film and electronic media, and an impressive exhibition of the museum's Surrealist collection, with many pieces new, reframed, or on display for the first time. A pedestrian bridge connects the new wing's third floor to Millennium Park, across the street.

## Restaurants and Services

The Museum Café, on the lower–level of the Rubloff Building, offers self–service dining with burgers, pizza, and deli sandwiches at reasonable prices 11 am–3 pm daily. For a more elegant lunch, dine next door at the McKinlock Court Restaurant. Open during warm weather from 11:30 am to 2:30 pm daily (Thursday evenings 5-7:30 pm), the restaurant features patio dining with seasonal cuisine.

Chef Tony Mantuano's Terzo Piano on the third level of the Modern Wing (free entrance from Monroe Street) brings a fine dining experience to the museum, featuring authentic and elegant Italian dishes. Terzo Piano also supplies less expensive options at Caffè Moderno overlooking the Modern Wing's Griffin Court and outdoors at Piano Terra amid the museum's North Garden on Michigan Avenue.

While postcards, books, and magnets may be purchased at kiosks throughout the museum, the Museum Shop, just off the main lobby, offers an extensive collection of art–oriented gifts and souvenirs, while the Modern Wing Shop at the Modern Wing's Monroe Street entrance sells similar items focusing on modern art (and you don't have to pay admission to shop at either!).

## School of the Art Institute of Chicago

Boasting such illustrious alumni as Georgia O'Keefe, Claes Oldenburg, Laurie Anderson, and David Sedaris, the School of the Art Institute of Chicago (SAIC) offers a fine art higher education for tomorrow's budding Renoirs.

## Gene Siskel Film Center

*160 N State St, 312–846–2600; www.siskelfilmcenter.org*

The film branch of the Art Institute offers art house, foreign films, and revivals, with frequent lectures by academics and industry professionals. Highlights include an Annual European Union Film Festival, and Oscar Night America, Chicago's only Academy-sanctioned party.

## How to Get There

**By Car:** The Art Institute is located on Michigan Avenue between Monroe and Jackson. From I–90/94 N (the Dan Ryan), exit to Congress East (Loop exit). From I–90/94 S (Kennedy Expressway), exit Monroe Steet East. Affordable parking is located underground at Millennium Park garages (enter at Columbus and Monroe) and Grant Park garages (enter on Michigan, either between Madison and Randolph or between Van Buren and Adams).

**By Metra:** Nearest stops are the Randolph and Van Buren stations served by the Metra Electric and South Shore Lines. For other Metra lines, transfer to the 151 Sheridan Avenue bus at Union Station.

**By Bus:** Numerous lines serve this strip of Michigan Avenue. Important buses include (from the south) the 3 King Drive, the 4 Collage Grove, and the 6 Jackson Park Express, (from the west) the 126 Jackson and 20 Madison, and (from the north) the 151 Sheridan, the 145 Wilson–Michigan Express, and the 146 Inner Drive/Michigan Express.

**By L:** From the Red and Blue lines, exit at Monroe. Brown, Orange, Purple, Pink and Green exit at Adams and Wabash.

Chicago has always been a bookish city and even so seems to be experiencing a literary renaissance of sorts. Great local authors, plentiful reading series, and the emergence of some notable small presses such as Featherproof Books and OV Books are all evidence of a thriving literary culture, augmented by the existence of several outstanding indie bookshops and a healthy smattering of big box stores.

## Independent Bookstores

**Printer's Row (Map 8)**, a section of Dearborn Street in the South Loop, was once the epicenter of Chicago's print and publishing trade. While most of that industry has shuttered or moved on, the remaining stalwart indie bookstores **Sandemeyer's (Map 8)** is worth a visit for bibliophiles.

For general, all–purpose bookshops, **Barbara's (Map 3, 5)** is a Chicago Institution, as is **Unabridged Books (Map 44)** with its specialties in literary fi ction, kids' books, travel, cookbooks, and gay and lesbian titles. Down by the University of Chicago campus, **57th Street Books (Map 19)** and **Seminary Co-op Bookstore (Map 19)** both appeal to the brainiac set. Up north **Book Cellar (Map 39)** is a super-friendly Lincoln Square indie with a cute wine bar. Get lit while getting lit.

## Specialty Bookstores

Specialty stores abound in the city. We think **Women & Children First (Map 37)** may have the largest selection of feminist and woman–focused books in the country, and their children's section is also top-notch. **The Occult Bookstore (Map 21)** on Milwaukee Avenue offers everything a budding witch or warlock could desire. And you can overthrow your repressed bookshelf with works by Marx and Mao from **Revolution Books (Map 22)** on Ashland. **Quimby's (Map 21)**, in Wicker Park, specializes in esoteric small–press books and 'zines with a marked counter–culture feel. You'll fi nd your John Fante, Kathy Acker, and Georges Bataille here.

## Used Bookstores

Shuffle through the used stacks at **Bookworks (Map 43)** on North Clark or **Myopic (Map 21)** in Wicker Park. **Selected Works (Map 6)** on Michigan sells used books and sheet music. **Ravenswood Used Books (Map 39)** is as chaotically crammed with books as a used bookshop should be.

## Comics

**Chicago Comics (Map 43)** is such a pleasant store that it's easy to forget about any comic-nerd stigma (don't fool yourself—you're still a dweeb). **Dark Tower (Map 39)** and **Variety Comic Book Store (Map 39)** serves Lincoln Square fanboys. In Wicker Park they head to **Brainstorm (Map 21)**, in Lincoln Park, **Graham Crackers Comics (Map 30)** is full of Marvels…

## Reading Series and Literary Happenings

Several Chicago bookstores are known for their active reading series. Most of **Barbara's Bookstore's (Map 3, 5)** regularly scheduled event stake place in their UIC and Oak Park stores. Catering to the University of Chicago community, Hyde Park's **Seminary Co-op Bookstore (Map 19)** features theorists, philosophers, and literary authors, **Women & Children First's (Map 37)** active schedule favors top name women writers and feminists, as well as lots of local talent, **Quimby's (Map 21)** attracts the indie-press and alt-lit crowd, and **Book Cellar (Map 39)** hosts a monthly popular local authors night, and **Myopic (Map 21)** has a renowned poetry series.

**The Harold Washington Library (Map 5)** is another great place to catch free author readings and literary events. Furthermore, Chicago is host to a plethora of fun and dynamic literary series that occur on a regular basis at bars and cafes all around town. Of them, the Sunday night Uptown Poetry Slam at the **Green Mill (Map 40)** is one of the most enduring. The raucous RUI (Reading Under the Influence), which takes place the first Wednesday of the week at **Sheffield's (Map 43)** celebrates the connection between writers and booze. The first-rate, first-person stories of Second Story, which takes place at **Webster's Wine Bar (Map 29)** and other venues throughout the city, are scored with a live deejay, or occasionally, a live band. The Danny's Reading Series, at **Danny's Tavern (Map 28)**, has justly earned a devoted audience of fans; the Windy City Story Slam and the Literary Death Match add a competitive edge to the shenanigans, and for the GLBT community, Homolatte (twice a month at **Big Chicks (Map 40)**) features queer voices. Sappho's Salon, which occurs the third Saturday of each month at **Women & Children First Bookstore (Map 39)**, celebrates lesbian creative expression. The Guild Literary Complex (www.GuildComplex.org) hosts literary readings, series and events.

In late July, the Newberry Library Bookfair is a used book lover and value hunters dream, featuring thousands of used books at rock bottom prices. The Printers Row Lit Fest, which occurs in early June, showcases hundreds of vendors along with an active reading series featuring local and internationally known talent, as well as several topical panels on topics ranging from self-promotion to the future of the book.

## Map 2 · Near North / River North

| | | | |
|---|---|---|---|
| Abraham Lincoln Book Shop | 357 W Chicago Ave | 312-944-3085 | History and military specialty store. |
| After-Words | 23 E Illinois St | 312-464-1110 | New and used. |
| Beck's Book Store | 50 E Chicago Ave | 312-944-7685 | Where there's a Beck's, there's a campus. |

## Map 3 · Streeterville / Mag Mile

| | | | |
|---|---|---|---|
| Barbara's | 201 E Huron St | 312-926-2665 | Branch of local chain. |
| Northwestern University Bookstore | 710 N Lake Shore Dr | 312-503-8486 | Textbooks. |
| University of Chicago Graduate School of Business | 450 N Cityfront Plz Dr | 312-464-8650 | Textbooks. |

## Map 5 · The Loop

| | | | |
|---|---|---|---|
| Barbara's | 111 N State St | 312-781-3033 | Branch of local chain. |
| Barbara's | 233 S Wacker Dr | 312-466-0223 | Branch of local chain. |
| Beck's Book Store | 60 E Lake St | 312-630-9113 | Where there's a Beck's, there's a campus. |
| Beck's Book Store | 315 S Plymouth Ct | 312-913-0650 | Where there's a Beck's, there's a campus. |
| Books-a-Million | 144 S Clark St | 312-857-0613 | Chain. |
| Graham Crackers Comics | 77 E Madison St | 312-629-1810 | Comics. |
| Selected Works Bookstore | 410 S Michigan Ave | 312-447-0068 | Quirky, junky used book store. |

## Map 6 · The Loop / Grant Park

| | | | |
|---|---|---|---|
| Art Institute of Chicago | 111 S Michigan Ave | 312-443-3583 | Art books and souvenirs. |
| Chicago Architecture Foundation | 224 S Michigan Ave | 312-922-3432 | Lots of pretty pictures. |

## Map 8 · South Loop / Printers Row / Dearborn Park

| | | | |
|---|---|---|---|
| Books In The City | 545 S State St | 312-291-1111 | Textbooks. |
| Sandmeyer's Book Store | 714 S Dearborn St | 312-922-2104 | General. |

## Map 9 · South Loop / South Michigan Ave

| | | | |
|---|---|---|---|
| Columbia College | 624 S Michigan Ave | 312-427-4860 | Some general books, mostly textbooks. |

## Map 10 · East Pilsen / Chinatown

| | | | |
|---|---|---|---|
| Chinese Champion Book & Gift | 2167 S China Pl | 312-326-3577 | Chinese books. |
| World Journal | 2116 S Archer Ave | 312-842-8005 | A world of Chinese books. |

## Map 11 · South Loop / McCormick Place

| | | | |
|---|---|---|---|
| Paragon Book Gallery | 1507 S Michigan Ave | 312-663-5155 | Asian arts. |

## Map 14 · Prairie Shores / Lake Meadows

| | | | |
|---|---|---|---|
| Matthews Illinois College of Optometry Bookstore | 3241 S Michigan Ave | 312-949-7471 | Textbooks. |

## Map 19 · Hyde Park

| | | | |
|---|---|---|---|
| 57th Street Books | 1301 E 57th St | 773-684-1300 | Frequented by U of C brainiacs. |
| Frontline Books & Crafts & Crystal Power | 5206 S Harper Ave | 773-288-7718 | New age. |
| O'Gara & Wilson | 1448 E 57th St | 773-363-0993 | Used books. |
| Powell's | 1501 E 57th St | 773-955-7780 | Remainders and off-price books. Mostly scholarly. |
| Seminary Co-op Bookstore | 5757 S University Ave | 773-752-4381 | Underground trove of scholarly books for all. |
| University of Chicago Bookstore | 970 E 58th St | 773-702-7712 | Textbooks. |

## Map 21 • Wicker Park / Ukrainian Village

| Brainstorm | 1648 W North Ave | 773-384-8721 | Comic books. |
| Myopic Books | 1564 N Milwaukee Ave | 773-862-4882 | Rare and collectable books. |
| Quimby's Bookstore | 1854 W North Ave | 773-342-0910 | Edgy, counter-culture bookshop. |

## Map 22 • Noble Square / Goose Island

| N Fagin Books | 917 N Ashland Ave | 312-330-5699 | Social sciences. |
| Occult Bookstore | 1164 N Milwaukee Ave | 773-292-0995 | I put a spell on you. |
| Revolution Books | 1103 N Ashland Ave | 773-489-0930 | Radical and revolutionary books. |

## Map 25 • Illinois Medical District

| Tianguis | 2003 S Damen Ave | 312-492-8350 | Books & Tea! |
| UIC Medical Bookstore | 828 S Wolcott Ave | 312-413-5550 | Reading material for when you're laid up. |

## Map 26 • University Village / Little Italy / Pilsen

| Chicago Textbook | 1076 W Taylor St | 312-733-8398 | Textbooks. |
| Libreria Giron | 1443 W 18th St | 312-226-2086 | Spanish. |

## Map 28 • Bucktown

| Libreria Nazareth De Lourves | 1907 N Milwaukee Ave | 773-342-8890 | Spanish books. |

## Map 29 • DePaul / Wrightwood / Sheffield

| Barnes & Noble | 1441 W Webster Ave | 773-871-3610 | Convenient for the run-in-and-grab-something shopper. |

## Map 30 • Lincoln Park

| Graham Crackers Comics | 2562 N Clark St | 773-665-2010 | Where good and evil meet. |

## Map 32 • Gold Coast / Mag Mile

| Barnes & Noble | 1130 N State St | 312-280-8155 | Chain. |
| The Newberry's A.C. McClurg Bookstore | 60 W Walton St | 312-255-3520 | Connected to the cultural library. |
| Rosenblum's World of Judaica | 2906 W Devon Ave | 773-262-1700 | Your source for quality Judaica and Books. |

## Map 33 • Rogers Park / West Ridge

| India Book House & Journals | 2551 W Devon Ave | 773-764-6567 | Spiritual/cultural. |
| Iqra Book Center | 2751 W Devon Ave | 773-274-2665 | Islamic books. |
| Russian American Book Store | 2746 W Devon Ave | 773-761-3233 | Floor to ceiling with musty books, as it should be. |

## Map 34 • East Rogers Park

| Beck's Book Store | 6550 N Sheridan Rd | 773-743-2281 | Where there's a Beck's, there's a campus. |

## Map 35 • Arcadia Terrace / Peterson Park

| Chicago Christian Book Center | 5786 N Lincoln Ave | 773-561-0055 | Thou shalt not buy bibles from Amazon. |
| Korean Books | 5773 N Lincoln Ave | 773-769-1010 | Korean books. |

## Map 37 • Edgewater / Andersonville

| Ginkgo Leaf Books | 1759 W Rosehill Dr | 773-989-2200 | Rare and collectable books. |
| Stern's Psychology Book Store | 1256 W Victoria St | 773-506-0683 | Psychology books. |
| Women & Children First | 5233 N Clark St | 773-769-9299 | Spacious feminist bookshop. |

# Arts & Entertainment • **Bookstores**

## Map 39 • Ravenswood / North Center

| | | | |
|---|---|---|---|
| Book Cellar | 4736 N Lincoln Ave | 773-293-2665 | General books and café. |
| Ravenwood Used Books | 4626 N Lincoln Ave | 773-593-9166 | General used. Classic literature. |
| Variety Comic Book Store | 4602 N Western Ave | 773-334-2550 | Comic books. |

## Map 40 • Uptown

| | | | |
|---|---|---|---|
| Beck's Book Store | 4520 N Broadway St | 773-784-7963 | Where there's a Beck's, there's a campus. |
| Shake Rattle and Read Book Box | 4812 N Broadway St | 773-334-5311 | Weird little store. Mostly used, some new. |

## Map 41 • Avondale / Old Irving

| | | | |
|---|---|---|---|
| Devry University Chicago Bookstore | 3300 N Campbell Ave | 773-477-2600 | Textbooks, etc. |

## Map 42 • North Center / Roscoe Village / West Lakeview

| | | | |
|---|---|---|---|
| Casa de Carina | 2834 N Western Ave | 773-395-2834 | Spanish language self-help and personal growth. |
| Galaxy Comic Zone | 3804 N Western Ave | 773-267-1043 | Comic books. |

## Map 43 • Wrigleyville/ East Lakeview

| | | | |
|---|---|---|---|
| Beasley Books | 1533 W Oakdale Ave, 2nd Fl | 773-472-4528 | Jazz/Blues, Labor History. |
| Bookworks | 3444 N Clark St | 773-871-5318 | Used and rare books. |
| Chicago Comics | 3244 N Clark St | 773-528-1983 | Fun! Not geeky, really. . . |
| The Gallery Bookstore | 923 W Belmont Ave | 773-281-9999 | Used books. |

## Map 44 • East Lakeview

| | | | |
|---|---|---|---|
| Bookleggers Used Books | 2907 N Broadway St | 773-404-8780 | Used books. |
| Unabridged Bookstore | 3251 N Broadway St | 773-883-9119 | Great literary bookshop, best gay selection in town. |

The Grande Dames of Chicago's museum scene, **The Art Institute of Chicago (Map 6)**, the **Museum of Science and Industry (Map 20)**, and the Museum Campus's **Adler Planetarium (Map 11)**, **Field Museum (Map 11)**, and **Shedd Aquarium (Map 9)**, may offer a lifetime of wonder, speculation, and enrichment; but impressive as they are, these cultural epicenters are only the tip of the iceberg when it comes to our city's museum offerings.

## Art Museums

Although the Art Institute's collection *is* undeniably impressive (see p293), Chicago's true art lovers know to look past the lions to some of Chicago's less-celebrated treasures.

Columbia College's **Museum of Contemporary Photography (Map 9)** is one of two accredited photography museums in the nation. Other campus–linked art museums include University of Chicago's **Smart Museum (Map 19)**, where the collection spans some 5,000 years. Catch the Lunch at **Loyola University Museum of Art (Map 34)** series for a quick bite with artists and experts on exhibits. Artwork created by and commemorating veterans of war hangs on the walls of the **National Veterans Art Museum (Map 48)**.

One of the country's largest collections of art post–1945 is housed at the always eye–opening **Museum of Contemporary Art (Map 3)**. The first Friday of the month, hundreds of twenty–something singles converge here for cocktails, live entertainment, and friendly flirtation.

## History

The **Chicago History Museum (Map 32)** (previously the Chicago Historical Society) is a tremendous archive of the city's past and present. African–American history is celebrated at the nation's oldest museum focusing on the black experience, the **DuSable Museum of African–American History (Map 18)**. The **Oriental Institute (Map 19)** specializes in artifacts from the ancient Near–East, including Persia, Mesopotamia, and Egypt. Nobel Prize–winning sociologist **Jane Addams's Hull–House (Map 26)** examines Chicago's history of immigration, ethnic relations, and social work.

## Science and Technology

As if the aforementioned **Adler Planetarium (Map 11)**, **Shedd Aquarium (Map 9)**, and **Field Museum (Map 11)** (all of which get special treatment within the Parks & Places listings under "Museum Campus") and the **Museum of Science and Industry (Map 20)** (listed with "Jackson Park") weren't enough to satisfy your inner nerd, Chicago is also home to a handful of quirky, smaller science museums. The **International Museum of Surgical Science (Map 32)** offers a window to the world of questionable surgical practices of yore. For kids, the **Children's Museum (Navy Pier)** presents a hands–on approach to learning about science and geography. Conservation and the environment are the focus of the **Peggy Notebaert Nature Museum (Map 30)**, which also features a butterfly haven, delighting the child in us all.

## Architecture

The city itself is perhaps one of the best architecture museums in the world. Examine it by embarking on one of the tours offered by the **Chicago Architecture Foundation (Map 6)**. Frank Lloyd Wright's influence on Chicago architecture can be examined at the **Robie House (Map 19)** in Hyde Park and the Frank Lloyd Wright Home and Studio in Oak Park. Chicago's Prairie Avenue District offers an architectural glimpse at Chicago's Victorian Golden Age. Joint tours of the oldest house in Chicago, the **Clarke House (Map 11)** (c. 1836), and the neighboring **Glessner House (Map 11)** offer the curious an interesting inside peek.

## Ethnic Museums

Immigration made Chicago into the "City of Neighborhoods." The **Swedish American Museum Center (Map 37)**, the **Chinese American Museum of Chicago (Map 10)**, the **Balzekas Museum of Lithuanian Culture (Map 53)**, and the **Polish Museum of America (Map 22)** all explore the impact of immigration on Chicago. The impressive new home of the **National Hellenic Museum (Map 6)** is a celebration of all things Greek. The **National Museum of Mexican Art (Map 25)** is the largest such museum in the country, and examines the Mexican experience through art and culture. The **Spertus Institute of Jewish Studies (Map 9)** specializes in Jewish history and heritage through events, lectures and an evolving exhibit on the Jewish experience in Chicago.

## Miscellaneous

Housed in the former home of the legendary, influential blues label, Chess Records, Willie Dixon's **Blues Heaven Foundation (Map 11)** offers tours of where Chuck Berry, Muddy Waters, and even the Rolling Stones once recorded. (The site is memorialized in the Stones' song "2120 South Michigan.")

For the darker side of sightseeing, the **Leather Archives and Museum (Map 34)** exhibits eight galleries of fetish, bondage, and S&M artifacts including photographs, clothing, toys, and more. The **Antiques Fabricare Museum (Map 48)** offers a seemingly "cleaner" afternoon out with the chance to view antique irons, washing machines, and decades–old washing powders.

The **Museum of Broadcast Communications (Map 2)**, one of only three broadcast museums and home to the only Radio Hall of Fame in the nation, recently moved from the Chicago Cultural Center to its own space on State Street.

| Museum | Address | Phone | Map |
|---|---|---|---|
| A Philip Randolph Pullman Porter Museum | 10406 S Maryland Ave | 773-928-3935 | South |
| Adler Planetarium & Astronomy Museum | 1300 S Lake Shore Dr | 312-922-7827 | 11 |
| Antiques Fabricare Museum | 4213 W Irving Park Rd | 773-282-6216 | South |
| Art Institute of Chicago | 111 S Michigan Ave | 312-443-3600 | 6 |
| Balzekas Museum of Lithuanian Culture | 6500 S Pulaski Rd | 773-582-6500 | SW |
| Bronzeville Children's Museum | 9600 S Western Ave | 708-636-9504 | SW |
| Charnley-Persky House | 1365 N Astor St | 312-915-0105 | 32 |
| Chicago Architecture Foundation | 224 S Michigan Ave | 312-922-3432 | 6 |
| Chicago Blues Museum | 3636 S Iron St | 773-828-8118 | 12 |
| Chicago Children's Museum | 700 E Grand Ave, Navy Pier | 312-527-1000 | p209 |
| Chicago History Museum | 1601 N Clark St | 312-642-4600 | 32 |
| Chicago Maritime Society | 310 S Racine Ave | 312-421-9096 | 24 |
| Chinese Historical Society of America | 238 W 23rd St | 312-949-1000 | 10 |
| Clarke House Museum | 1827 S Indiana Ave | 312-745-0040 | 11 |
| Columbia College Center for Book & Paper Arts | 1104 S Wabash Ave | 312-344-6630 | 8 |
| DePaul University Art Museum | 2350 N Kenmore Ave | 773-325-7506 | 29 |
| DL Moody Museum | 820 N La Salle Dr | 312-329-4000 | 32 |
| DuSable Museum of African-American History | 740 E 56th Pl | 773-947-0600 | 18 |
| The Field Museum | 1400 S Lake Shore Dr | 312-922-9410 | 11 |
| Frank Lloyd Wright Home and Studio | 951 Chicago Ave, Oak Park | 708-848-1976 | p211 |
| Glessner House Museum | 1800 S Prairie Ave | 312-326-1480 | 11 |
| Hellenic Museum and Cultural Center | 801 W Adams St | 312-655-1234 | 6 |
| Holocaust Memorial Foundation of Illinois | 4255 Main St, Skokie | 847-677-4640 | p215 |
| Hyde Park Historical Society | 5529 S Lake Park Ave | 773-493-1893 | 19 |
| International Museum of Surgical Science | 1524 N Lake Shore Dr | 312-642-6502 | 32 |
| Intuit: Center for Intuitive and Outsider Art | 756 N Milwaukee Ave | 312-243-9088 | 24 |
| Irish-American Heritage Center | 4642 N Knox Ave | 773-282-7035 | NW |
| Jane Addams Hull-House Museum | 800 S Halsted St | 312-413-5353 | 26 |
| Jazz Institute of Chicago | 410 S Michigan Ave | 312-427-1676 | 6 |
| Leather Archives & Museum | 6418 N Greenview Ave | 773-761-9200 | 34 |
| Loyola University Museum of Art | 820 N Michigan Ave | 312-915-7600 | 32 |
| Mexican Fine Arts Center | 1852 W 19th St | 312-738-1503 | 25 |
| Museum of Contemporary Art | 220 E Chicago Ave | 312-280-2660 | 3 |
| Museum of Contemporary Photography | 600 S Michigan Ave - Columbia College | 312-663-5554 | 9 |
| Museum of Science and Industry | 5700 S Lake Shore Dr | 773-684-1414 | 20 |
| National Vietnam Veterans Art Museum | 1801 S Indiana Ave | 312-326-0270 | 11 |
| The Newberry Library | 60 W Walton St | 312-943-9090 | 32 |
| Oriental Institute Museum | 1155 E 58th St | 773-702-9514 | 19 |
| Peggy Notebaert Nature Museum | 2430 N Cannon Dr | 773-755-5100 | 30 |
| Polish Museum of America | 984 N Milwaukee Ave | 773-384-3352 | 22 |
| Ridge Historical Society | 10621 S Seeley Ave | 773-881-1675 | SW |
| Robie House | 5757 S Woodlawn Ave | 773-834-1847 | 19 |
| Rogers Park/West Ridge Historical Society | 7344 N Western Ave | 773-764-4078 | 33 |
| Shedd Aquarium, John G | 1200 S Lake Shore Dr | 312-939-2438 | 9 |
| Skokie Heritage Museum | 8031 Floral Ave, Skokie | 847-677-6672 | p215 |
| Smart Museum of Art | 5550 S Greenwood Ave | 773-702-0200 | 19 |
| Smith Museum of Stained Glass | 700 E Grand Ave, Navy Pier | 312-595-5024 | p209 |
| Spertus Museum | 610 S Michigan Ave | 312-322-1700 | 9 |
| Swedish American Museum | 5211 N Clark St | 773-728-8111 | 37 |
| Ukrainian Institute of Modern Art | 2320 W Chicago Ave | 773-227-5522 | 23 |
| Ukrainian National Museum | 2249 W Superior St | 312-421-8020 | 23 |
| Willie Dixon's Blues Heaven Foundation | 2120 S Michigan Ave | 312-808-1286 | 11 |

The impeccably restored **Music Box Theatre (Map 43)**, built in 1929, features fantastic Moorish architecture, fl oating clouds on the ceilings, and live organ music at many weekend screenings. Specialties include the latest art house and international releases, as well as restored classics and weekend matinee double–features that follow monthly themes. Holiday season sing–alongs of White Christmas are huge hits that sell out in advance. The Music Box is also the major screening ground for International Film Festival and Gay and Lesbian Film Festival releases.

Other worthy art–house screening rooms include the **Landmark Century Centre Cinema (Map 44)** at the Century Mall. For even more  refined or esoteric options, pick up  schedules for the **Gene Siskel Film Center (Map 5)** of the Art Institute, **Facets Multimedia (Map 29)** in the DePaul neighborhood, **Chicago Filmmakers (Map 37)** in Andersonville.

The latest action features should be seen at **Loews (Map 29)** at Webster Place, **ICE Chatham (South)** off of 87th & the Dan Ryan, and Streeterville's **AMC River East (Map 3)**, which offer ample theaters and show times. Cheap seats on relatively new releases can be had at Lincoln Square's **Davis Cinema (Map 39)** and Rogers Park's **New 400 Theater (Map 32)**, while second-run films can be found at a discount price in the newly renovated (thank god) **Logan Theatre (Map 27)** in Logan Square. The legendary **University of Chicago Doc Films (Map 19)** in Hyde Park has the perfect balance of historical, contemporary and international fi lms. This student-run film society boasts cheap shows and seduces the intellectual crowd.

One of Chicago's most notorious places to catch a flick is **The Vic's "Brew and View," (Map 43)** where the drunken frat boy audiences are almost as annoying as the movies that they show.

| Movie Theaters | Address | Phone | Map | |
|---|---|---|---|---|
| The Alliance Francaise | 810 N Dearborn St | 312-337-1070 | 32 | Sparse, almost free French films. |
| AMC Ford City 14 | 7601 S Cicero Ave | 773-582-1839 | SW | Mainly teeny-boppers & families coming from the mall. |
| AMC Loews 600 | 600 N Michigan Ave | 312-255-9347 | 3 | Good concession options, limited times, expensive parking. |
| AMC Loews Gardens 1/6 | 175 Old Orchard Ctr, Skokie | 847-674-0072 | p215 | Standard Megaplex. |
| AMC Loews Norridge 10 | 4520 N Harlem Ave | 708-452-6677 | NW | Megaplex suburbanite hell, unless you're a suburbanite. |
| AMC River East | 322 E Illinois St | 312-596-0333 | 3 | Blockbuster flicks, billiards, bar & bowling. |
| Brew & View | 3145 N Sheffield Ave | 312-618-8439 | 43 | For the lush who likes old movies. |
| Chicago Cultural Center | 78 E Washington St | 312-744-6630 | 5 | Free, cultural films and docs. |
| Chicago Filmmakers | 5243 N Clark St | 773-293-1447 | 37 | Classes and films, no mainstream mess & no pretense. |
| Davis Theater | 4614 N Lincoln Ave | 773-784-0893 | 39 | Four screens. Old, cute, cash-only, homie. |
| Facets Multimedia | 1517 W Fullerton Ave | 773-281-4114 | 29 | Obscure independent films anyone? |
| Gene Siskel Film Center | 164 N State St | 312-846-2800 | 5 | Tasty smorgasbord of international films. |
| Henry Crown MSI Omnimax | 5700 S Lake Shore Dr | 773-684-1414 | 20 | Bring kids, 3-D glasses, and loot, cuz it ain't cheap. |
| ICE Chatham 14 | 210 87th St | 773-783-8711 | South | Mega-theater with comfy seats and fab parking. |
| Kerasotes Chicago City North 14 | 2600 N Western Ave | 773-394-1600 | 28 | Multiple spacious theaters, diverse crowd, plenty of parking. |
| Kerasotes Chicago Webster | 1471 W Webster Ave | 773-327-1314 | 29 | Huge crowds, common date spot, latest movies. |
| Landmark Century Centre Cinema | 2828 N Clark St | 773-248-7759 | 44 | Get stimulated by international films, then go shopping at mall. |
| Logan Theater | 2646 N Milwaukee Ave | 773-252-0628 | 27 | Charming neighborhood spot, second-run, $3 flicks. |
| Museum of Contemporary Art Movie Theater | 220 E Chicago Ave | 312-397-4010 | 3 | Few films, more live performance art. |
| Music Box Theatre | 3733 N Southport Ave | 773-871-6604 | 43 | Antiquated theater with character, bad seats & great films. |
| Navy Pier IMAX Theatre | 600 E Grand Ave, Navy Pier | 312-595-5629 | p209 | Expensive, but cute spot for families with youngens. |
| ShowPlace ICON at Roosevelt Collection | 1011 S Delano Court E | 312-386-7440, | 8 | Dine-in theater equipped with bar/lounge. |
| University of Chicago Doc Films | 1212 E 59th St | 773-702-8575 | 19 | Student-run film society, kickass variety of films, dirt cheap. |
| Village Art Theater | 1548 N Clark St | 312-642-2403 | 32 | Small and dank, but cheap price for slightly old flicks. |

# Street Index

Some of the townships and communities immediately adjoining Chicago proper thought it would be a fun joke to restart street numbering at their borders—or name a street exactly the same name as an entirely unrelated Chicago street. These cases are designated with an asterisk.*

| Street / Range | Page | Grid |
|---|---|---|
| N 1st Ave | 47 | A1/B1/C1 |
| 3rd St | 45 | B1 |
| S 5th St | 49 | C2 |
| E 8th St | 8 | B2 |
| 9th Ave | 47 | C1 |
| E 9th St | 8 | B2 |
| W 9th St | 8 | B1/B2 |
| W 13th Pl | | |
| (2630–2699) | 50 | C3 |
| (3400–3599) | 49 | C2 |
| E 13th St | 11 | A1 |
| W 13th St | | |
| (29–49) | 10 | A2 |
| (600–1725) | 26 | B1/B2 |
| (1726–2399) | 25 | B1/B2 |
| (2600–3264) | 50 | C3 |
| (3265–5925) | 49 | C1/C2 |
| E 14th Pl | 11 | A1 |
| W 14th Pl | | |
| (500–662) | 10 | A1 |
| (663–1724) | 26 | B1/B2 |
| (1725–1799) | 25 | B2 |
| (2600–2631) | 50 | C3 |
| E 14th St | 11 | A1/A2 |
| W 14th St | | |
| (1–535) | 10 | A1/A2 |
| (600–1726) | 26 | B1/B2 |
| (1727–2499) | 25 | B1/B2 |
| (2700–2799) | 50 | C3 |
| (3730–5923) | 49 | C1/C2 |
| E 15th Pl | 11 | B1 |
| W 15th Pl | | |
| (700–1559) | 26 | B1/B2 |
| (2400–2559) | 25 | B1 |
| (2600–3199) | 50 | C3 |
| (4600–5599) | 49 | C1/C2 |
| W 15th St | | |
| (1–699) | 10 | A1/A2 |
| (700–1723) | 26 | B1/B2 |
| (1724–2559) | 25 | B1/B2 |
| (2560–3265) | 50 | C3 |
| (3266–5923) | 49 | C1/C2 |
| E 16th St | 11 | B1 |
| W 16th St | | |
| (1–649) | 10 | B1/B2 |
| (650–1748) | 26 | C1/C2 |
| (1700–2549) | 25 | C1/C2 |
| (2550–3264) | 50 | C3 |
| (3265–5923) | 49 | C1/C2 |
| W 17th Pl | 26 | C2 |
| W 17th St | | |
| (38–499) | 10 | B1/B2 |
| (700–1705) | 26 | C1/C2 |
| (1706–2458) | 25 | C1/C2 |
| (2600–2699) | 50 | C3 |
| (4200–4399) | 49 | C2 |
| W 18th Dr | 50 | C3 |
| W 18th Pl | | |
| (900–1705) | 26 | C1/C2 |
| (1706–2399) | 25 | C1/C2 |
| (4300–4399) | 49 | C2 |
| E 18th St | 11 | B1 |
| W 18th St | | |
| (1–649) | 10 | B1/B2 |
| (700–1705) | 26 | C1/C2 |
| (1706–2549) | 25 | C1/C2 |
| (2550–2859) | 50 | C3 |
| (3400–5923) | 49 | C1/C2 |
| W 19th Pl | 26 | C1/C2 |
| W 19th St | | |
| (39–749) | 10 | B2 |
| (734–1714) | 26 | C1/C2 |
| (1715–2499) | 25 | C1/C2 |
| (2500–3264) | 50 | C3 |
| (3265–5923) | 49 | C1/C2 |
| W 20th Pl | | |
| (534–599) | 10 | B1 |
| (900–1199) | 26 | C1/C2 |
| W 20th St | 51 | A2 |
| W 21st Pl | | |
| (700–1749) | 26 | C1/C2 |
| (1750–2499) | 25 | C1/C2 |
| (2600–3099) | 50 | C3 |
| (4000–5599) | 49 | C1/C2 |
| E 21st St | 11 | B1 |
| W 21st St | | |
| (120–699) | 10 | B1/B2 |
| (700–1749) | 26 | C1/C2 |
| (1750–2499) | 25 | C1/C2 |
| (2550–3264) | 50 | C3 |
| (3265–5923) | 51 | A1/A2 |
| W 22nd Pl | | |
| (200–299) | 10 | C2 |
| (800–899) | 26 | C2 |
| (1800–2899) | 52 | A3/A4 |
| (4800–5799) | 49 | A1/C1 |
| W 23rd Pl | | |
| (200–499) | 10 | C1/C2 |
| (2100–4850) | 52 | A3 |
| (4851–5799) | 49 | A1 |
| E 23rd St | 11 | C1/C2 |
| W 23rd St | | |
| (1–499) | 10 | A2/C1/C2 |
| (800–3314) | 52 | A3/A4 |
| (3315–5925) | 51 | A1/A2 |
| W 24th Blvd | 52 | A3 |
| E 24th Pl | 11 | C1 |
| W 24th Pl | | |
| (200–599) | 10 | C1/C2 |
| (2300–2799) | 52 | A3 |
| (4000–4849) | 51 | A2 |
| (4850–5599) | 49 | A1 |
| E 24th St | 11 | C1/C2 |
| W 24th St | | |
| (1–499) | 10 | C1/C2 |
| (2100–3314) | 52 | A3 |
| (3315–5925) | 51 | A1/A2 |
| W 25th Pl | | |
| (500–729) | 10 | C1 |
| (730–783) | 13 | A1 |
| (2600–2999) | 52 | A3 |
| (4000–4812) | 51 | A2 |
| (4813–5599) | 49 | A1 |
| E 25th St | 11 | C1/C2 |
| W 25th St | | |
| (1–498) | 10 | C1/C2 |
| (700–3314) | 52 | A3/A4 |
| (3315–5925) | 51 | A1/A2 |
| W 26th Pl | | |
| (30–99) | 13 | A2 |
| (2801–2835) | 52 | A3 |
| E 26th St | 14 | A1 |
| W 26th St | | |
| (1–25) | 14 | A2 |
| (26–799) | 13 | A1/A2 |
| (829–852) | 12 | A2 |
| (2400–3315) | 52 | A3 |
| (3316–5927) | 51 | A1/A2 |
| W 27th St | | |
| (1–15) | 14 | A1 |
| (16–815) | 13 | A1/A2 |
| (816–940) | 12 | A2 |
| (2200–3314) | 52 | A3 |
| (3315–5999) | 51 | A1/A2 |
| E 28th St | 14 | A1 |
| W 28th Pl | | |
| (200–599) | 13 | A1/A2 |
| (4900–4999) | 49 | A1 |
| E 28th St | 14 | A1 |
| W 28th St | | |
| (400–799) | 13 | A1/A2 |
| (2200–3314) | 52 | A3 |
| W 28 St | 52 | A3 |
| (3315–5999) | 51 | A1/A2 |
| E 29th Pl | | |
| (330–399) | 13 | A2 |
| (4900–5299) | 49 | A1 |
| E 29th St | 14 | A1/A2 |
| W 29th St | | |
| (30–860) | 13 | A1/A2 |
| (861–4815) | 12 | A2 |
| (4816–5199) | 51 | A1 |
| W 30th Pl | | |
| (330–399) | 13 | A2 |
| (2743–2761) | 52 | A3 |
| (4900–5499) | 49 | A1 |
| E 30th St | 14 | A1 |
| W 30th St | | |
| (1–28) | 14 | A1 |
| (29–799) | 13 | A1/A2 |
| (3100–3314) | 52 | A3 |
| (3315–5499) | 51 | A1/A2 |
| W 31st Blvd | 52 | A3 |
| E 31st Pl | 14 | B1/B2 |
| W 31st Pl | | |
| (903–1403) | 12 | B1/B2 |
| (1728–2099) | 52 | A3/A4 |
| (4900–5199) | 49 | A1 |
| E 31st St | 14 | B1/B2 |
| W 31st St | | |
| (1–23) | 14 | A3 |
| (24–813) | 13 | B1/B2 |
| (814–1499) | 12 | B1/B2 |
| (1600–3298) | 52 | A3/A4 |
| (3295–5999) | 51 | A1/A2 |
| E 32nd Pl | 14 | B2 |
| W 32nd Pl | | |
| (900–1649) | 12 | B1/B2 |
| (1650–5199) | 49 | A1 |
| E 32nd St | 14 | B1/B2 |
| W 32nd St | | |
| (200–816) | 13 | B1/B2 |
| (817–1699) | 12 | B1/B2 |
| (1800–3101) | 52 | A3 |
| (3600–5599) | 51 | A1/A2 |
| E 33rd Pl | 14 | B1/B2 |
| W 33rd Pl | | |
| (800–849) | 13 | B1 |
| (850–1649) | 12 | B2 |
| (1650–1899) | 52 | A4 |
| E 33rd St | 14 | B1/B2 |
| W 33rd St | | |
| (1–44) | 14 | B1 |
| (45–811) | 13 | B1/B2 |
| (812–1649) | 12 | B1/B2 |
| (1650–2399) | 52 | A3/A4 |
| (2700–5499) | 51 | A1/A2 |
| W 34th Pl | | |
| (800–849) | 13 | B1 |
| (850–1849) | 12 | B2 |
| (1850–2499) | 52 | B3 |
| E 34th St | 14 | B1 |
| W 34th St | | |
| (40–54) | 14 | B1 |
| (55–849) | 13 | B1/B2 |
| (850–1624) | 12 | B1/B2 |
| (1625–2499) | 52 | B3/B4 |
| (3700–5999) | 51 | B1/B2 |
| W 35th Pl | | |
| (800–849) | 13 | C1 |
| (850–999) | 12 | C2 |
| (2200–2799) | 52 | B3 |
| (4000–4499) | 51 | B2 |
| E 35th St | 14 | B1/B2 |
| W 35th St | | |
| (1–40) | 14 | B1 |
| (41–849) | 13 | B1/B2 |
| (850–1614) | 12 | B2/C1 |
| (1615–3407) | 52 | B3/B4 |
| (3408–5999) | 51 | B1/B2 |
| E 36th Pl | 14 | C1/C2 |
| W 36th Pl | | |
| (1200–1299) | 12 | C2 |
| (2600–3299) | 52 | B3 |
| E 36th St | 14 | C1/C2 |
| W 36th St | | |
| (500–849) | 13 | C1 |
| (850–1614) | 12 | C2 |
| (1615–3333) | 52 | B3/B4 |
| (4000–5999) | 51 | B1/B2 |
| E 37th Pl | 14 | C1/C2 |

# Street Index

| Street / Range | Page | Grid |
|---|---|---|
| **W 37th Pl** | | |
| (200–899) | 13 | C1/C2 |
| (900–1649) | 12 | C1/C2 |
| (1650–3349) | 52 | B3 |
| (3350–3399) | 49 | B2 |
| (3400–3499) | 51 | B2 |
| **E 37th St** | 14 | C1/C2 |
| **W 37th St** | | |
| (200–849) | 13 | C1/C2 |
| (850–1624) | 12 | C1/C2 |
| (1625–3299) | 52 | B3/B4 |
| (3300–5999) | 51 | B1/B2 |
| **E 38th Pl** | 14 | C2 |
| **W 38th Pl** | | |
| (200–849) | 13 | C1/C2 |
| (850–1649) | 12 | C2 |
| (1650–3349) | 52 | B3 |
| (3350–3399) | 49 | B2 |
| (3400–3599) | 51 | B2 |
| **E 38th St** | 14 | C1/C2 |
| **W 38th St** | | |
| (1–849) | 13 | C1/C2 |
| (850–1649) | 12 | C1/C2 |
| (1650–3349) | 52 | B3/B4 |
| (3350–5999) | 51 | B1/B2 |
| **W 39th Pl** | 52 | B3 |
| **W 39th St** | 51 | B1 |
| **W 40th Pl** | | |
| (300–599) | 15 | A1/A2 |
| (2600–3199) | 52 | B3 |
| **E 40th St** | | |
| (1–862) | 16 | A1/A2 |
| (863–999) | 17 | A1 |
| **W 40th St** | | |
| (1–825) | 15 | A2 |
| (826–3199) | 52 | B3/B4 |
| (4000–4299) | 51 | B2 |
| **E 41st Pl** | 17 | A1 |
| **W 41st Pl** | 52 | B3 |
| **E 41st St** | | |
| (38–949) | 16 | A1/A2 |
| (950–1099) | 17 | A1 |
| **W 41st St** | | |
| (433–799) | 15 | A1 |
| (1300–3199) | 52 | B3/B4 |
| (3800–4399) | 51 | B2 |
| **W 41th St** | 52 | B4 |
| **W 42nd Ct** | 51 | B2 |
| **E 42nd Pl** | | |
| (400–874) | 16 | A1/A2 |
| (875–1199) | 17 | A1 |
| **W 42nd Pl** | | |
| (300–599) | 15 | A1/A2 |
| (1200–3199) | 52 | B3/B4 |
| (4000–4299) | 51 | B2 |
| **E 42nd St** | | |
| (38–899) | 16 | A1/A2 |
| (1100–1198) | 17 | A1 |
| **W 42nd St** | | |
| (300–799) | 15 | A1/A2 |
| (1200–3199) | 52 | B3/B4 |
| (3800–3999) | 51 | B2 |
| **W 43rd Pl** | | |
| (200–799) | 15 | B1/B2 |
| (1200–1329) | 52 | B4 |
| **E 43rd St** | | |
| (1–884) | 16 | B1/B2 |
| (885–1199) | 17 | B1 |
| **W 43rd St** | | |
| (1–799) | 15 | A1/A2 |
| (1000–3309) | 52 | B3/B4 |
| (3310–4999) | 51 | B1/B2 |
| **S 44th Ct** | 55 | C2 |
| **E 44th Pl** | | |
| (500–599) | 16 | B2 |
| (1200–1231) | 17 | B1 |
| **S 44th Pl** | 55 | B2/C2 |
| **W 44th Pl** | | |
| (200–799) | 15 | B1/B2 |
| (1200–1330) | 52 | B4 |
| (4300–4999) | 51 | B2/C1 |
| **E 44th St** | | |
| (1–899) | 16 | B1/B2 |
| (900–1199) | 17 | B1 |
| **W 44th St** | | |
| (100–699) | 15 | B1/B2 |
| (1200–3314) | 52 | B3/B4 |
| (3315–5199) | 51 | B1/B2 |
| **S 45th Ave** | 55 | C2 |
| **E 45th Pl** | 16 | B1 |
| **W 45th Pl** | | |
| (100–599) | 15 | B1/B2 |
| (2300–2599) | 52 | C3 |
| (3800–3829) | 51 | C2 |
| **E 45th St** | | |
| (0–899) | 16 | B1/B2 |
| (900–1199) | 17 | B1 |
| **W 45th St** | | |
| (100–849) | 15 | B1/B2 |
| (850–3299) | 52 | B4/C3/C4 |
| (3400–5199) | 51 | C1/C2 |
| **S 46th Ct** | 49 | C2 |
| **E 46th Pl** | 16 | B1/B2 |
| **W 46th Pl** | | |
| (101–717) | 15 | B1/B2 |
| (2400–2599) | 52 | C3 |
| (3800–3831) | 51 | C2 |
| **E 46th St** | | |
| (0–899) | 16 | B1/B2 |
| (900–1299) | 17 | B1 |
| **W 46th St** | | |
| (200–799) | 15 | B1/B2 |
| (1200–3315) | 52 | C3/C4 |
| (3316–5199) | 51 | C1/C2 |
| **S 47th Ave** | 49 | C2 |
| **S 47th Ct** | 49 | C2 |
| **W 47th Ct** | 49 | C2 |
| **E 47th Pl** | | |
| (800–839) | 16 | B2 |
| (1346–1399) | 17 | B2 |
| **W 47th Pl** | | |
| (600–849) | 15 | C1 |
| (850–3264) | 50 | C3/C4 |
| (1000–2859) | 52 | C3/C4 |
| (3265–3329) | 49 | C2 |
| (3330–3544) | 51 | C2 |
| **E 47th St** | | |
| (0–899) | 16 | B1/B2 |
| (900–1420) | 17 | B1/B2 |
| **W 47th St** | | |
| (1–62) | 16 | B1 |
| (63–849) | 15 | B1/B2 |
| (850–899) | 50 | C4 |
| (900–3314) | 52 | C3/C4 |
| (3315–5599) | 51 | C1/C2 |
| **S 48th Ct** | | |
| (1200–3299) | 49 | A1/C2 |
| (8900–9299) | 55 | A2 |
| **E 48th Pl** | 16 | C1 |
| **W 48th Pl** | | |
| (230–799) | 15 | C1/C2 |
| (2300–3331) | 52 | C3 |
| (3332–3350) | 50 | C3 |
| (3351–3369) | 49 | C2 |
| (3370–3599) | 51 | C2 |
| **E 48th St** | | |
| (1–899) | 16 | C1/C2 |
| (900–1450) | 17 | C1/C2 |
| **W 48th St** | | |
| (600–799) | 15 | C1 |
| (1000–2798) | 52 | C3/C4 |
| (3800–5599) | 51 | C1/C2 |
| **S 49th Ave** | | |
| (1200–3299) | 49 | A1/C2 |
| (8900–9899) | 55 | A2 |
| **S 49th Ct** | | |
| (1200–2199) | 49 | C2 |
| (8700–8849) | 53 | C2 |
| (8850–9399) | 55 | A2 |
| **W 49th Pl** | | |
| (700–849) | 15 | C1 |
| (850–899) | 50 | C4 |
| (900–2199) | 52 | C3/C4 |
| **E 49th St** | | |
| (1–899) | 16 | C1/C2 |
| (900–1699) | 17 | C1/C2 |
| **W 49th St** | | |
| (698–799) | 15 | C1 |
| (1134–2399) | 52 | C3/C4 |
| (3700–5599) | 51 | C1/C2 |
| **S 50th Ave** | | |
| (1200–5099) | 49 | A1/C1 |
| (8700–8849) | 53 | C2 |
| (8850–9499) | 55 | A2 |
| **S 50th Ct** | | |
| (1200–3299) | 49 | A1/C1 |
| (9500–9899) | 55 | A2 |
| **E 50th Pl** | | |
| (432–799) | 16 | C1/C2 |
| (1600–1625) | 17 | C2 |
| **W 50th Pl** | | |
| (700–849) | 15 | C1 |
| (850–899) | 50 | C4 |
| (900–2399) | 52 | C3/C4 |
| (3728–3799) | 51 | C2 |
| **E 50th St** | | |
| (41–886) | 16 | C1/C2 |
| (887–1699) | 17 | C1/C2 |
| **W 50th St** | | |
| (200–849) | 15 | C1/C2 |
| (850–899) | 50 | C4 |
| (900–2799) | 52 | C3/C4 |
| (3700–5599) | 51 | C1/C2 |
| **S 51st Ave** | | |
| (1200–3299) | 49 | A1/C1 |
| (8700–8849) | 53 | C2 |
| (8850–9899) | 55 | A2 |
| **S 51st Ct** | | |
| (1200–2199) | 49 | C1 |
| (10300–10499) | 55 | B2 |
| **W 51st Pl** | | |
| (300–849) | 57 | A1 |
| (850–2399) | 54 | A3/A4 |
| (7000–7198) | 53 | A1 |
| **E 51st St** | | |
| (39–885) | 16 | C1/C2 |
| (874–1128) | 17 | C1 |
| **W 51st St** | | |
| (1–66) | 16 | C1 |
| (67–899) | 15 | C1/C2 |
| (900–999) | 52 | A4 |
| (1000–3924) | 54 | A3/A4 |
| (3925–6933) | 53 | A1/A2 |
| **S 52nd Ave** | | |
| (8700–8809) | 53 | C2 |
| (8810–10299) | 55 | A2/B2 |
| **S 52nd Ct** | | |
| (3100–3799) | 49 | A1/B1 |
| (9100–9199) | 55 | A2 |
| **E 52nd Pl** | 19 | A2 |
| **W 52nd Pl** | | |
| (300–2030) | 57 | A1 |
| (2031–2199) | 54 | A3 |
| **E 52nd St** | | |
| (0–199) | 18 | A1/A2 |
| (800–1539) | 19 | A1/A2 |
| **W 52nd St** | | |
| (232–819) | 57 | A1 |
| (820–3919) | 54 | A3/A4 |
| (3920–7199) | 53 | A1/A2 |
| **S 53rd Ave** | | |
| (2200–3899) | 49 | A1/B1/C1 |
| (8700–8814) | 53 | C2 |
| (8815–10199) | 55 | A2 |
| **S 53rd Ct** | | |
| (2900–3799) | 49 | A1/B1 |
| (9100–9499) | 55 | A2 |
| **W 53rd Pl** | | |
| (800–3499) | 54 | A3/A4 |
| (5200–5299) | 53 | A2 |
| **E 53rd St** | | |
| (38–369) | 18 | A1 |
| (370–1545) | 19 | A1/A2 |
| (1546–1799) | 20 | A1 |
| **W 53rd St** | | |
| (100–817) | 57 | A1 |
| (818–3914) | 54 | A3/A4 |
| (3915–7299) | 53 | A1/A2 |
| **S 54th Ave** | | |
| (1200–3799) | 49 | A1/B1/C1 |
| (9100–9999) | 55 | A2 |
| **S 54th Ct** | | |
| (3100–3699) | 49 | A1/B1 |
| (9100–9499) | 55 | A2 |
| **E 54th Pl** | | |
| (340–1539) | 19 | A1/A2 |
| (1600–1625) | 20 | A1 |

W 54th Pl
(330–849) 57 A1
(850–3499) 54 A3/A4
(5800–5899) 53 A1
E 54th St
(200–369) 18 A1
(370–1539) 19 A1/A2
(1624–1799) 20 A1
W 54th St
(1–63) 18 A1
(64–849) 57 A1
(850–3965) 54 A3/A4
(3966–7199) 53 A1/A2
S 55th Ave
(1600–3699) 49 A1/B1/C1
(8700–8805) 53 C2
(8806–9899) 55 A2
S 55th Ct
(1200–3699) 49 A1/B1/C1
(8700–8764) 53 C2
(8765–9499) 55 A2
E 55th Pl
(200–399) 18 B1
(1342–1499) 19 A2/B2
W 55th Pl
(3600–3949) 54 A3
(3950–4649) 53 A2
E 55th St
(0–1605) 19 A1/A2/B1
(1606–1899) 20 B1
W 55th St
(2400–3963) 54 A3
(3964–6498) 53 A1/A2
S 56th Ct 49 A1/B1/C1
E 56th Pl 18 B2
W 56th Pl
(332–599) 57 A1
(3600–3949) 54 A3
(3950–4199) 53 A2
E 56th St
(1–370) 18 B1
(371–1573) 19 B1/B2
(1574–1849) 20 B1
W 56th St
(400–814) 57 A1
(815–3949) 54 A3/A4
(3950–7219) 53 A1/A2
S 57th Ave 49 A1/B1/C1
S 57th Ct 49 A1/B1/C1
E 57th Dr 20 B1
W 57th Pl
(1–63) 18 B1
(64–599) 57 A1
(3500–3949) 54 A3
(3950–7299) 53 A1/A2
E 57th St
20 B1
(1–799) 18 B1/B2
(800–1523) 19 B1/B2
W 57th St
(1–63) 18 B1
(64–814) 57 A1
(815–3949) 54 A3/A4
(3950–7219) 53 A1/A2
S 58th Ave 49 A1/B1/C1
S 58th Ct 49 A1/B1/C1
W 58th Pl
(3500–3949) 54 A3
(3950–7299) 53 A1/A2
E 58th St
(1–370) 18 B1
(371–1435) 19 B1/B2
W 58th St
(230–814) 57 A1
(815–3949) 54 A3/A4
(3950–7299) 53 A1/A2
S 59th Ave 49 A1/B1/C1
S 59th Ct 49 A1/B1/C1
W 59th Pl
(238–399) 57 A1
(3300–3999) 54 B3
E 59th St
(1–368) 18 B1
(369–1631) 19 B1/B2
W 59th St
(1–70) 18 B1
(71–814) 57 A1
(815–3949) 54 A3/A4
(3950–7299) 53 A1/A2/B1
N 5th Ave 47 C1
W 5th Ave
(2800–3249) 50 B3
(3250–4799) 49 B2/C2
W 60th Pl
(240–799) 57 A1
(3300–3949) 54 B3
(3950–7299) 53 B1
E 60th St
(1–750) 18 C1/C2
(751–1599) 19 C1/C2
W 60th St
(1–69) 18 C1
(70–864) 57 A1
(865–3949) 54 B3/B4
(3950–7299) 53 B1/B2
E 61st Pl 19 C1/C2
W 61st Pl
(240–799) 57 A1
(3200–3949) 54 B3
(3950–7299) 53 B1
E 61st St
(1–764) 18 C1/C2
(765–1567) 19 C1/C2
W 61st St
(1–98) 18 C1
(81–864) 57 A1
(865–3949) 54 B3/B4
(3950–7299) 53 B1/B2
E 62nd Pl 19 C2
W 62nd Pl
(3200–3949) 54 B3
(3950–7299) 53 B1
E 62nd St
(400–764) 18 C2
(765–1599) 19 C1/C2
W 62nd St
(130–705) 57 A1
(900–3949) 54 B3/B4
(3950–7299) 53 B1/B2
E 63rd Pl 57 A2
W 63rd Pl
(600–2498) 57 A1
(3200–3949) 54 B3
(3950–7299) 53 B1/B2
E 63rd St
(1–764) 18 C1/C2
(765–1599) 19 C1/C2
W 63rd St
(1–99) 18 C1
(100–864) 57 A1
(865–3949) 54 B3/B4
(3950–7231) 53 B1/B2
E 64th Pl 57 A2
W 64th Pl
(3200–3949) 54 B3
(3950–7299) 53 B1/B2
E 64th St 57 A1/A2
W 64th St
(1–864) 57 A1
(865–3949) 54 B3/B4
(3950–7199) 53 B1/B2
E 65th Pl 57 A2
W 65th Pl
(400–547) 57 A1
(3200–3949) 54 B3
(3950–4599) 53 B2
E 65th St 57 A1/A2
W 65th St
(1–864) 57 A1
(865–3949) 54 B3/B4
(3950–7229) 53 B1/B2
E 66th Pl 57 A1/A2
W 66th Pl
(400–799) 57 A1
(3200–3949) 54 B3
(3950–7099) 53 B1/B2
E 66th St 57 A1
W 66th St
(41–864) 57 A1
(865–3949) 54 B3/B4
(3950–7399) 53 B1/B2
E 67th Pl 57 A2
W 67th Pl 54 B3
E 67th St
(500–1866) 57 A1/A2
(1867–2399) 58 A3
W 67th St 53 B2
S 68th Ave 55 C1
S 68th Ct 55 A1/C1
W 68th Pl 54 B3
E 68th St
(1–1864) 57 B1/B2
(1865–2399) 58 B3
W 68th St
(39–864) 57 B1
(865–3949) 54 B3/B4
(3950–6899) 53 B1/B2
S 69th Ave 55 A1/C1
S 69th Ct 55 A1/C1
E 69th Pl 57 B1/B2
W 69th Pl
(2000–3949) 54 B3
(3950–4199) 53 B2
E 69th St
(1–1864) 57 B1/B2
(1865–2399) 58 B3
W 69th St
(1–864) 57 B1
(865–3949) 54 B3/B4
(3950–7199) 53 B1/B2
S 70th Ave 55 C1
S 70th Ct 55 C1
E 70th Pl
(332–609) 57 B1
(2200–2399) 58 B3
W 70th Pl
(300–2049) 57 B1
(2050–3949) 54 B3
(3950–5599) 53 B2
E 70th St
(1–1864) 57 B1/B2
(1865–2399) 58 B3
W 70th St
(39–864) 57 B1
(865–3949) 54 B3/B4
(3950–4153) 53 B2
S 71st Ave 55 C1
S 71st Ct 55 B1/C1
E 71st Pl
(1200–1819) 57 B2
(1900–2199) 58 B3
W 71st Pl
(1200–3599) 54 B3/B4
(7000–7199) 53 B1
E 71st St
(1–1873) 57 B1/B2
(1874–2601) 58 B3
W 71st St
(1–864) 57 B1
(865–3965) 54 B3/B4
(3966–7299) 53 B1/B2
N 72nd Ct 47 B2/C2
S 72nd Ct 55 C1
E 72nd Pl
(1200–1899) 57 B2
(1930–2599) 58 B3
W 72nd Pl
(1200–3599) 54 B3/B4
(4200–7199) 53 B2/C1
E 72nd St
(1–1858) 57 B1/B2
(1859–2599) 58 B3
W 72nd St
(42–864) 57 B1
(865–3999) 54 B3/B4
(4300–7299) 53 B1/B2
N 73rd Ave 47 B2/C2
S 73rd Ave 55 B1/C1
N 73rd Ct 47 B2/C2
S 73rd Ct 55 B1/C1
E 73rd Pl
(1500–1799) 57 B2
(1928–2741) 58 B3
W 73rd Pl
(1200–3599) 54 C3/C4
(7000–7199) 53 C1
E 73rd St
(1–1858) 57 B1/B2
(1859–2672) 58 B3

W 73rd St
(42–864) 57 B1
(865–3829) 54 B3/B4
(4800–7299) 53 C1/C2
N 74th Ave 47 B1/C1
S 74th Ave 55 C1
N 74th Ct 47 B1/C1
E 74th Pl
(1500–1699) 57 B2
(2438–2642) 58 B3
W 74th Pl
(1200–1789) 54 C4
(5300–7299) 53 C1/C2
E 74th St
(1–1834) 57 B1/B2
(1835–2799) 58 B3
W 74th St
(42–864) 57 B1
(865–4029) 54 C3/C4
(4030–7299) 53 C1
N 75th Ave 47 B1/C1
N 75th Ct 47 B1/C1
E 75th Pl
(1030–1599) 57 B2
(2700–2740) 58 B3
W 75th St
(1600–3999) 54 C3/C4
(5200–5999) 53 C1/C2
E 75th St
(1–1861) 57 B1/B2
(1846–2898) 58 B3
W 75th St
(17–864) 57 B1
(865–3557) 54 C3/C4
(5200–7299) 53 C1/C2
N 76th Ave 47 B1/C1
N 76th Ct 47 B1/C1
E 76th Pl
(1100–1599) 57 B2
(2700–2843) 58 B3
W 76th Pl
(2130–3949) 54 C3/C4
(5200–5899) 53 C1/C2
E 76th St
(1–1864) 57 B1/B2
(1865–2899) 58 B3
W 76th St
(22–864) 57 B1
(865–4149) 54 C3/C4
(4150–7299) 53 C1/C2
N 77th Ave 47 B1/C1
N 77th Ct 47 B1/C1
E 77th Pl 58 B3
W 77th Pl
(1–99) 57 B1
(2130–3899) 54 C3/C4
(4000–5399) 53 C2
E 77th St
(1–1864) 57 B1/B2
(1865–2999) 58 B3
W 77th St
(1–864) 57 B1
(865–3937) 54 C3/C4
(4800–7299) 53 C1/C2
N 78th Ave 47 B1/C1
N 78th Ct 47 B1/C1

E 78th Pl 58 B3
W 78th Pl
(1–347) 57 B1
(1200–3899) 54 C3/C4
(4100–5399) 53 C2
E 78th St
(1–1861) 57 B1/B2
(1862–3099) 58 B3
W 78th St
(1–864) 57 B1
(865–3999) 54 C3/C4
(4100–7298) 53 C1/C2
N 79th Ave 47 B1/C1
N 79th Ct 47 C1
E 79th Pl
(1129–1199) 57 B2
(3000–3099) 58 B3
W 79th Pl
(400–499) 57 B1
(2000–3899) 54 C3/C4
(4100–6199) 53 C1/C2
E 79th St
(1–1863) 57 B1/B2
(1864–3313) 58 B3
W 79th St
(2–863) 57 B1
(864–4029) 54 C3/C4
(4030–7299) 53 C1/C2
N 80th Ave 47 B1/C1
E 80th Pl 58 B3
W 80th Pl
(600–699) 57 B1
(2000–4021) 54 C3/C4
(4022–6199) 53 C1/C2
E 80th St
(1–1870) 57 B1/B2
(1871–3199) 58 B3
W 80th St
(31–864) 57 B1
(865–3899) 54 C3/C4
(4024–7295) 53 C1/C2
E 81st Pl
(1100–1199) 57 C2
(2928–2999) 58 C3
W 81st Pl
(500–727) 57 C1
(2200–4063) 54 C3
(4064–7198) 53 C1/C2
E 81st St
(1–1850) 57 B2/C1/C2
(1851–3199) 58 B3
W 81st St
(30–864) 57 C1
(865–4106) 54 C3/C4
(4107–7328) 53 C1/C2
E 82nd Pl
(1100–1199) 57 C2
(2900–2999) 58 C3
W 82nd Pl
(325–599) 57 C1
(2000–4066) 54 C3/C4
(4067–7199) 53 C1/C2
E 82nd St
(1–1743) 57 C1/C2
(1900–3199) 58 C3

E 78th Pl 58 B3
W 82nd St
(28–864) 57 C1
(865–3999) 54 C3/C4
(4100–7313) 53 C1/C2
E 83rd Pl
(600–1799) 57 C1/C2
(2950–3199) 58 C3
W 83rd Pl
(500–599) 57 C1
(2600–3999) 54 C3
(4500–6599) 53 C1/C2
E 83rd St
(1–1849) 57 C1/C2
(1850–3399) 58 C3
W 83rd St
(1–899) 57 C1
(900–4014) 54 C3/C4
(4015–7399) 53 C1/C2
E 84th Pl 57 C2
W 84th Pl
(2600–3999) 54 C3
(4500–7199) 53 C1/C2
E 84th St
(1–1864) 57 C1/C2
(1865–3399) 58 C3
W 84th St
(31–899) 57 C1
(900–4014) 54 C3/C4
(4015–7399) 53 C1/C2
E 85th Pl 57 C2
W 85th St
(2600–3999) 54 C3
(4800–7199) 53 C1/C2
E 85th St
(0–1864) 57 C1/C2
(1865–3399) 58 C3
W 85th St
(530–899) 57 C1
(900–4014) 54 C3/C4
(4015–7305) 53 C1/C2
E 86th Pl 57 C1/C2
W 86th Pl
(820–875) 57 C1
(876–3928) 54 C3
(4800–6299) 53 C1/C2
E 86th St
(1–1864) 57 C1/C2
(1865–3399) 58 C3
W 86th St
(531–898) 57 C1
(891–4014) 54 C3/C4
(4015–7399) 53 C1/C2
E 87th Pl 57 C1/C2
W 87th Pl 53 C1/C2
E 87th St
(1–1864) 57 C1/C2
(1865–3329) 58 C3
W 87th St
(1–904) 57 C1
(905–4021) 54 C3/C4
(4001–7399) 53 C1/C2
E 88th Pl 57 C1/C2
W 88th Pl 55 A1/A2
E 88th St
(1–1815) 57 C1/C2
(1816–3329) 58 C3

W 88th St
(200–914) 57 C1
(915–3199) 54 C3/C4
(4501–6799) 55 A1/A2
E 89th Ct 55 A2
E 89th Pl 57 C1/C2
W 89th Pl
(1800–2799) 56 A3/A4
(4000–6799) 55 A1/A2
E 89th St
(1–1815) 57 C1/C2
(1816–3499) 58 C3
W 89th St
(200–899) 57 C1
(901–3199) 56 A2/A3/A4
(4500–6299) 55 A1/A2
E 90th Pl 57 C1/C2
W 90th Pl
(200–399) 57 C1
(1700–4018) 56 A3/A4
(4019–7299) 55 A1/A2
E 90th St
(1–1815) 57 C1/C2
(1816–3499) 58 C3
W 90th St
(400–865) 57 C1
(866–3199) 56 A3/A4
(4030–7351) 55 A1/A2
E 91st Pl 57 C1/C2
W 91st Pl
(100–399) 57 C1
(1700–4012) 56 A4
(4013–6799) 55 A1/A2
E 91st St
(1–1815) 57 C1/C2
(1816–3399) 58 C3
W 91st St
(1–829) 57 C1
(932–3999) 56 A3/A4
(4500–7369) 55 A1/A2
E 92nd Pl
(500–1799) 57 C1/C2
(2229–2399) 58 C3
W 92nd Pl
(1020–2399) 56 A3/A4
(6200–6399) 55 A1
E 92nd St
(1–1814) 57 C1/C2
(1815–3399) 58 C3
W 92nd St
(50–904) 57 C1
(905–3999) 56 A1/A3/A4
(4600–7353) 55 A1/A2
E 93rd Ct 58 C3
E 93rd Pl 57 C2
W 93rd Pl
(200–251) 57 C1
(1600–4014) 56 A3/A4
(4015–7199) 55 A1/A2
E 93rd St
(1–1814) 57 C1/C2
(1815–3299) 58 C3
W 93rd St
(30–914) 57 C1
(915–4012) 56 A3/A4
(4013–7333) 55 A1/A2

# Street Index

| Street | Range | Page | Grid |
|---|---|---|---|
| E 94th Pl | | 58 | C3 |
| W 94th Pl | (300–399) | 57 | C1 |
| | (2600–2799) | 56 | A3 |
| | (6400–6599) | 55 | A1 |
| E 94th St | (1–1799) | 57 | C1/C2 |
| | (2000–3599) | 58 | C3 |
| W 94th St | (50–914) | 57 | C1 |
| | (915–3999) | 56 | A3/A4 |
| | (4500–7199) | 55 | A1/A2 |
| E 95th Pl | (1230–1299) | 59 | A2 |
| | (2024–2528) | 60 | A3 |
| W 95th Pl | (400–499) | 59 | A1 |
| | (1100–3599) | 56 | A3/A4 |
| | (6800–7099) | 55 | A1 |
| 95th St | | 55 | A1 |
| E 95th St | (1–1399) | 59 | A1/A2 |
| | (3530–3699) | 58 | C3 |
| | (3630–4099) | 60 | A3/A4 |
| W 95th St | (1–899) | 59 | A1 |
| | (922–4042) | 56 | A3/A4 |
| | (1515–1831) | 57 | C2 |
| | (1920–3599) | 58 | C3 |
| | (4043–7399) | 55 | A1/A2 |
| E 96th Pl | (1230–1299) | 59 | A2 |
| | (2100–2799) | 60 | A3 |
| W 96th Pl | (400–499) | 59 | A1 |
| | (2600–3199) | 56 | A3 |
| | (4600–7099) | 55 | A1/A2 |
| E 96th St | (100–1599) | 59 | A1/A2 |
| | (1832–3630) | 60 | A3 |
| W 96th St | (34–899) | 59 | A1 |
| | (900–4013) | 56 | A3/A4 |
| | (4014–7199) | 55 | A1/A2 |
| E 97th Pl | (1230–1599) | 59 | A2 |
| | (2100–2599) | 60 | A3 |
| W 97th Pl | (400–499) | 59 | A1 |
| | (1027–3330) | 56 | A3/A4 |
| | (4101–6999) | 55 | A1/A2 |
| E 97th St | (100–1599) | 59 | A1/A2 |
| | (1900–3798) | 60 | A3 |
| W 97th St | (100–899) | 59 | A1 |
| | (900–4061) | 56 | A3/A4 |
| | (4062–6999) | 55 | A1/A2 |
| E 98th Pl | (1–841) | 59 | A1/A2 |
| | (2100–2199) | 60 | A3 |
| W 98th Pl | (200–898) | 59 | A1 |
| | (893–3599) | 56 | A3/A4 |
| | (4600–5699) | 55 | A2 |
| E 98th St | (1–1599) | 59 | A1/A2 |
| | (2000–4098) | 60 | A3/A4 |
| W 98th St | (200–899) | 59 | A1 |
| | (900–3999) | 56 | A3/A4 |
| | (4100–7199) | 55 | A1/A2 |
| E 99th Pl | | 59 | A1/A2 |
| W 99th Pl | (300–499) | 59 | A1 |
| | (2600–4099) | 56 | A3 |
| | (4100–6998) | 55 | A1/A2 |
| E 99th St | (100–1301) | 59 | A1/A2 |
| | (2000–3799) | 60 | A3 |
| W 99th St | (1–899) | 59 | A1 |
| | (876–3999) | 56 | A3/A4 |
| | (4000–7199) | 55 | A1/A2 |
| E 100th Dr | | 58 | C3 |
| E 100th Pl | | 59 | A2 |
| W 100th Pl | (1–499) | 59 | A1 |
| | (1300–3199) | 56 | A3/A4 |
| | (4400–7399) | 55 | A1/A2 |
| E 100th St | (1–1359) | 59 | A1/A2 |
| | (2040–3799) | 60 | A3 |
| W 100th St | (1–899) | 59 | A1 |
| | (900–4066) | 56 | A3/A4 |
| | (4067–7099) | 55 | A1/A2 |
| E 101st Pl | | 59 | A2 |
| W 101st Pl | (1–499) | 59 | A1 |
| | (1226–3999) | 56 | A3/A4 |
| | (4500–5799) | 55 | A1/A2 |
| E 101st St | (1–1199) | 59 | A1/A2 |
| | (2188–3699) | 60 | A3 |
| W 101st St | (1–899) | 59 | A1 |
| | (900–4065) | 56 | A3/A4 |
| | (4066–6399) | 55 | A1/A2 |
| E 102nd Pl | | 59 | A1/A2 |
| W 102nd Pl | (300–499) | 59 | A1 |
| | (1172–3999) | 56 | A4/B3/B4 |
| | (4500–6617) | 55 | B1/B2 |
| E 102nd St | (1–699) | 59 | A1/A2 |
| | (2200–4041) | 60 | A3/A4 |
| W 102nd St | (1–899) | 59 | A1 |
| | (900–4099) | 56 | — |
| | | 55 | B1/B2 |
| E 103rd Pl | | 59 | A1/A2 |
| W 103rd Pl | (1–599) | 59 | A1 |
| | (1000–2651) | 56 | B3/B4 |
| | (5300–5599) | 55 | B2 |
| E 103rd St | (1–1799) | 59 | A1/A2 |
| | (1789–3867) | 60 | A3/A4 |
| W 103rd St | (1–899) | 59 | A1 |
| | (900–4023) | 56 | B3/B4 |
| | (4024–7399) | 55 | B1/B2 |
| W 104 St | | 55 | B2 |
| E 104th Pl | (1–100) | 55 | A1 |
| | (101–199) | 57 | A2 |
| | (500–799) | 59 | A2 |
| W 104th Pl | (13–399) | 59 | A1 |
| | (1000–4049) | 56 | B3/B4 |
| | (4050–6799) | 55 | B1/B2 |
| E 104th St | (1–999) | 59 | A1/A2 |
| | (2331–3899) | 60 | A3/A4 |
| W 104th St | (2–899) | 59 | A1 |
| | (900–4099) | 56 | B3/B4 |
| | (4700–6699) | 55 | B1/B2 |
| E 105th Pl | | 59 | A2 |
| W 105th Pl | (200–399) | 59 | B1 |
| | (1400–4049) | 56 | B3/B4 |
| | (4050–6999) | 55 | B1/B2 |
| E 105th St | (1–899) | 59 | A1/A2 |
| | (2400–3999) | 60 | A3/A4 |
| W 105th St | (1–899) | 59 | A1 |
| | (900–4059) | 56 | B3/B4 |
| | (4060–7419) | 55 | B1/B2 |
| W 106th Pl | (1–399) | 59 | B1 |
| | (1700–4049) | 56 | B3/B4 |
| | (4050–6999) | 55 | B1/B2 |
| E 106th St | (200–899) | 59 | A3/A4 |
| | (1932–3629) | 60 | A3/B3 |
| W 106th St | (200–914) | 59 | B1 |
| | (915–3999) | 56 | B3/B4 |
| | (4000–6799) | 55 | B1/B2 |
| W 107th Pl | (200–399) | 59 | B1 |
| | (1000–3912) | 56 | B3/B4 |
| | (4300–6999) | 55 | B1/B2 |
| E 107th St | (1–999) | 59 | B1/B2 |
| | (2400–4099) | 60 | B3/B4 |
| W 107th St | (1–905) | 59 | B1 |
| | (906–4075) | 56 | B3/B4 |
| | (4076–7399) | 55 | B1/B2 |
| 107th Court Way | | 55 | B1 |
| W 108th Pl | (1–399) | 59 | B1 |
| | (1000–3915) | 56 | B3/B4 |
| | (4200–7399) | 55 | B1/B2 |
| E 108th St | (1–699) | 59 | B1/B2 |
| | (2500–4099) | 60 | B3/B4 |
| W 108th St | (1–899) | 59 | B1 |
| | (930–3899) | 56 | B3/B4 |
| | (4200–7399) | 55 | B1/B2 |
| W 109th Pl | (1–399) | 59 | B1 |
| | (930–3899) | 56 | B3/B4 |
| | (5800–7399) | 55 | B1 |
| E 109th St | (16–599) | 59 | B1/B2 |
| | (2500–4099) | 60 | B3/B4 |
| W 109th St | (1–929) | 59 | B1 |
| | (1000–4075) | 56 | B3/B4 |
| | (4076–7399) | 55 | B1/B2 |
| E 110th Pl | | 59 | B1/B2 |
| W 110th Pl | (1–499) | 59 | B1 |
| | (1000–3899) | 56 | B3/B4 |
| | (4500–7399) | 55 | B1/B2 |
| E 110th St | (1–799) | 59 | B1/B2 |
| | (2501–4065) | 60 | B3/B4 |
| W 110th St | (13–899) | 59 | B1 |
| | (1000–4099) | 56 | B3/B4 |
| | (4600–7399) | 55 | B1/B2 |
| E 111th Pl | | 59 | B1/B2 |
| W 111th Pl | (1–399) | 59 | B1 |
| | (1028–2399) | 56 | B3/B4 |
| | (6500–7399) | 55 | B1 |
| E 111th St | (1–1099) | 59 | B1/B2 |
| | (3233–4099) | 60 | B3/B4 |
| W 111th St | (1–924) | 59 | B1 |
| | (925–4099) | 56 | B3/B4 |
| | (4100–7399) | 55 | B1/B2 |
| E 112th Pl | | 59 | B1 |
| W 112th Pl | (1–359) | 59 | B1 |
| | (1000–3799) | 56 | B3/B4 |
| | (4900–7399) | 55 | B1/B2 |
| E 112th St | (1–999) | 59 | B1 |
| | (3234–4099) | 60 | B3/B4 |
| W 112th St | (2–929) | 59 | B1 |
| | (1000–3199) | 56 | B3/B4 |
| | (6400–7399) | 55 | B1 |
| E 112th St Cir | | 59 | B2 |
| W 113th Ct | | 55 | B2 |
| E 113th Pl | | 59 | B1 |
| W 113th Pl | (14–399) | 59 | B1 |
| | (1000–3670) | 56 | B3/B4 |
| | (5100–7399) | 55 | B1/B2 |
| E 113th St | (1–1035) | 59 | B1/B2 |
| | (3234–3799) | 60 | B3 |
| W 113th St | (1–2267) | 59 | B1 |
| | (2268–3799) | 56 | B3 |
| | (4900–7399) | 55 | B1/B2 |
| E 114th Pl | | 59 | B1/B2 |
| W 114th Pl | (1–72) | 59 | B1 |
| | (929–3799) | 56 | B3/B4 |
| | (5100–7399) | 55 | B1/B2 |

| Street (range) | Page | Grid |
|---|---|---|
| E 114th St | | |
| (1–899) | 59 | B1/B2 |
| (1900–3830) | 60 | B3 |
| W 114th St | | |
| (1–829) | 59 | B1 |
| (2300–3759) | 56 | B3 |
| (5100–7399) | 55 | B1/B2 |
| W 115th Pl | | |
| (924–3999) | 56 | B3/B4 |
| (4400–7199) | 55 | B2/C1 |
| E 115th St | | |
| (1–948) | 59 | B1/B2 |
| (3600–3839) | 60 | B3 |
| W 115th St | | |
| (1–958) | 59 | B1 |
| (959–4078) | 56 | B3/B4 |
| (4079–7499) | 55 | B1/B2/C1 |
| W 115th St Cir | 56 | B4 |
| W 116th Pl | | |
| (600–948) | 59 | B1 |
| (933–3999) | 56 | C3/C4 |
| (4400–4699) | 55 | C2 |
| E 116th St | | |
| (1–399) | 59 | B1/B2 |
| (1900–3699) | 60 | B3 |
| W 116th St | | |
| (1–964) | 59 | B1 |
| (965–4059) | 56 | — |
| (4060–7199) | 55 | C1/C2 |
| E 117th Pl | 59 | B1 |
| W 117th Pl | | |
| (600–799) | 59 | B1 |
| (1800–2599) | 56 | C3/C4 |
| (5800–5899) | 55 | C1 |
| E 117th St | | |
| (1–399) | 59 | B1/B2 |
| (1900–3899) | 60 | B3 |
| W 117th St | | |
| (100–964) | 59 | B1 |
| (965–4064) | 56 | C3/C4 |
| (4065–5199) | 55 | C2 |
| E 118th Pl | 59 | B1 |
| W 118th Pl | | |
| (730–799) | 59 | B1 |
| (2524–2599) | 56 | C3 |
| (4100–4399) | 55 | C2 |
| E 118th St | | |
| (1–399) | 59 | B1/B2 |
| (1900–3715) | 60 | B3 |
| W 118th St | | |
| (1–964) | 59 | B1 |
| (965–4099) | 56 | C3/C4 |
| (4300–5999) | 55 | C1/C2 |
| E 119st St | 60 | B3 |
| E 119th Pl | 59 | B1/B2 |
| W 119th Pl | | |
| (2000–2399) | 56 | C3/C4 |
| (4200–7399) | 55 | C1/C2 |
| E 119th St | | |
| (1–799) | 59 | B1/B2 |
| (2130–2625) | 60 | B3 |
| W 119th St | | |
| (1–950) | 59 | B1 |
| (950–4064) | 56 | C3/C4 |
| (4065–5199) | 55 | C2 |
| E 11th St | 8 | C2 |
| E 120th Pl | | |
| (1–399) | 59 | B1/B2 |
| (2134–2231) | 60 | B3 |
| W 120th Pl | | |
| (2000–3857) | 56 | C3/C4 |
| (5000–5299) | 55 | C2 |
| E 120th St | | |
| (1–901) | 59 | B1/B2 |
| (2130–2625) | 60 | B3 |
| W 120th St | | |
| (1–974) | 59 | B1 |
| (975–4064) | 56 | C3/C4 |
| (4065–7433) | 55 | C1/C2 |
| E 121st Pl | | |
| (1–299) | 59 | B1/B2 |
| (2200–2243) | 60 | B3 |
| W 121st Pl | | |
| (2100–3852) | 56 | C3/C4 |
| (4800–5299) | 55 | C2 |
| E 121st St | | |
| (1–399) | 59 | B1/B2 |
| (2200–2625) | 60 | B3 |
| W 121st St | | |
| (1–199) | 59 | B1 |
| (1400–3799) | 56 | C3/C4 |
| (4899–7433) | 55 | C1/C2 |
| E 122nd Pl | 59 | C1 |
| W 122nd Pl | 56 | C3 |
| E 122nd St | | |
| (1–166) | 59 | C1 |
| (167–3299) | 60 | B3/C3 |
| W 122nd St | | |
| (1–966) | 59 | C1 |
| (967–3999) | 56 | C3/C4 |
| (4400–7433) | 55 | C1/C2 |
| E 123rd Pl | | |
| (2200–3827) | 56 | C3/C4 |
| (4400–5399) | 55 | C2 |
| E 123rd St | | |
| (1–199) | 59 | C1 |
| (200–1983) | 60 | C3 |
| W 123rd St | | |
| (1–963) | 59 | C1 |
| (964–4108) | 56 | C3/C4 |
| (4109–7433) | 55 | C1/C2 |
| E 124th Pl | 59 | C1 |
| W 124th Pl | | |
| (3400–3999) | 56 | C3 |
| (4101–6399) | 55 | C1/C2 |
| E 124th St | | |
| (1–199) | 59 | C1 |
| (200–1981) | 60 | C3 |
| W 124th St | | |
| (1–918) | 59 | C1 |
| (919–3999) | 56 | C3/C4 |
| (4400–7433) | 55 | C1/C2 |
| E 125th Pl | 59 | C1 |
| W 125th Pl | | |
| (1–599) | 59 | C1 |
| (5100–6198) | 55 | C1/C2 |
| W 125th St | | |
| (1–799) | 59 | C1 |
| (1000–3699) | 56 | C3/C4 |
| (4400–7433) | 55 | C1/C2 |
| E 126th Pl | 59 | C1 |
| W 126th Pl | | |
| (1–559) | 59 | C1 |
| (4800–6525) | 55 | C1/C2 |
| E 126th St | | |
| (1–99) | 59 | C1 |
| (2638–3030) | 60 | C3 |
| W 126th St | | |
| (200–799) | 59 | C1 |
| (1200–3399) | 56 | C3/C4 |
| (4000–7433) | 55 | C1/C2 |
| W 127th Pl | | |
| (500–599) | 59 | C1 |
| (1139–1123) | 56 | C4 |
| (4400–6399) | 55 | C1/C2 |
| E 127th St | | |
| (1–154) | 59 | C1 |
| (155–2929) | 60 | C3 |
| W 127th St | | |
| (1–799) | 59 | C1 |
| (1000–4099) | 56 | C3/C4 |
| (4100–7433) | 55 | C1/C2 |
| W 128th Pl | 59 | C1 |
| E 128th St | 60 | C3 |
| W 128th St | | |
| (500–599) | 59 | C1 |
| (1230–1729) | 56 | C4 |
| W 129th Pl | 59 | C1 |
| E 129th St | 60 | C3 |
| W 12th Pl | | |
| (569–646) | 10 | A1 |
| (700–799) | 26 | B2 |
| (2600–2899) | 50 | C3 |
| (3400–4799) | 49 | C2 |
| E 130th Pl | 59 | C2 |
| E 130th St | | |
| (1–1666) | 59 | C2/C3 |
| (1667–3599) | 60 | C3 |
| E 131st Pl | 59 | C2 |
| E 131st St | | |
| (400–1199) | 59 | C2 |
| (2650–3599) | 60 | C3 |
| 132nd Ct | 59 | C2 |
| E 132nd Pl | 59 | C2 |
| E 132nd St | | |
| (200–1299) | 59 | C2 |
| (2831–3599) | 60 | C3 |
| E 133rd Pl | 59 | C2 |
| E 133rd St | | |
| (100–1199) | 59 | C2 |
| (2900–4030) | 60 | C3/C4 |
| E 134th Pl | 59 | C2 |
| E 134th St | | |
| (100–1858) | 59 | C1/C2 |
| (1859–4059) | 60 | C3/C4 |
| W 134th St | 59 | C1 |
| E 135th St | 60 | C3 |

## A

| Street (range) | Page | Grid |
|---|---|---|
| S Abbott Ave | 57 | C1 |
| N Aberdeen St | 24 | A2/B2 |
| S Aberdeen St | | |
| (1–499) | 24 | C2 |
| (500–1599) | 26 | A2/B2 |
| (3100–3499) | 12 | B2 |
| (4700–4999) | 52 | C4 |
| (5000–5049) | 50 | C4 |
| (5050–8932) | 54 | A4/B4/C4 |
| (8933–12849) | 56 | A4/B4/C4 |
| Academy Pl | 4 | B1 |
| Achsah Bond Dr | 11 | A2 |
| W Acme Ave | 59 | C1 |
| Acme Dr | 59 | C1 |
| Ada Ln | 55 | C1 |
| N Ada St | | |
| (1–799) | 24 | A1/B1 |
| (1236–1624) | 22 | B1 |
| (1625–1699) | 29 | C1 |
| S Ada St | | |
| (619–1799) | 26 | A1/C1 |
| (4700–5049) | 52 | C4 |
| (5050–8956) | 54 | A4/B4/C4 |
| (8901–12849) | 56 | A4/B4/C4 |
| W Adams Blvd | 49 | B1 |
| E Adams St | 5 | B2 |
| W Adams St | | |
| (1–367) | 5 | B1/B2 |
| (368–864) | 4 | B1/B2 |
| (865–1647) | 24 | C1/C2 |
| (1648–2549) | 23 | C1/C2 |
| (2550–3249) | 50 | B3 |
| (3250–5999) | 49 | B1/B2 |
| W Addison St | | |
| (500–814) | 44 | A1/B1 |
| (815–1614) | 43 | A1/A2 |
| (1615–2473) | 42 | A2/B1/B2 |
| (2466–3599) | 41 | A1/A2/B1 |
| (3600–5849) | 48 | B3/B4 |
| (5850–8399) | 47 | B1/B2 |
| Adeline Dr | 55 | B2 |
| E Administration Dr | 18 | B2 |
| W Agatite Ave | | |
| (800–1199) | 40 | B1/B2 |
| (2101–2199) | 39 | B1 |
| (2600–2799) | 38 | B2 |
| (3640–5599) | 48 | A3/A4 |
| (7000–8699) | 47 | A1/A2 |
| W Ainslie St | | |
| (800–1649) | 40 | A1/A2 |
| (1650–2420) | 39 | A1/A2 |
| (2421–3599) | 38 | A1/A2 |
| (3600–5750) | 48 | A3/A4 |
| (5751–8699) | 47 | A1/A2 |
| W Airport Dr | 53 | A2 |
| N Albany Ave | | |
| (1–899) | 50 | A3/B3 |
| (1100–2749) | 27 | A1/B1/C1 |
| (2750–3949) | 41 | A1/B1/C1 |
| (3950–5999) | 38 | A1/B1/C1 |
| (6000–6349) | 35 | A1 |
| (6350–7531) | 33 | A1/C1 |
| S Albany Ave | | |
| (1–2249) | 50 | B3/C3 |
| (2250–4699) | 52 | A3/B3/C3 |
| (5100–8849) | 54 | A3/B3/C3 |
| (8850–11299) | 56 | A3/B3 |

| Street | Page | Grid |
|---|---|---|
| W Albion Ave | | |
| (1000–2055) | 34 | B2/C1/C2 |
| (2056–3199) | 33 | C1/C2 |
| (3300–5099) | 46 | B3/B4 |
| (6501–7227) | 45 | B2/C2 |
| W Albion Ave * | | |
| (1–1474) | 45 | B1/B2 |
| W Aldine Ave | | |
| (400–824) | 44 | B1 |
| (825–899) | 43 | B2 |
| Alexander Pl | 55 | A2 |
| W Alexander St | 10 | C2 |
| N Algonquin Ave | 46 | B3 |
| Alice Ct | 55 | A2 |
| N Allen Ave | 48 | B4 |
| S Allport St | 26 | C1 |
| Almansa Ln | | |
| (4000–4036) | 56 | A3 |
| (4037–4099) | 55 | A2 |
| S Alpine Dr | 55 | C2 |
| N Alta Vista Ter | 43 | A2 |
| W Altgeld St | | |
| (800–1681) | 29 | A1/A2 |
| (1682–2464) | 28 | A1/A2 |
| (2465–3599) | 27 | A1/A2 |
| (3600–5815) | 48 | C3/C4 |
| (5816–7999) | 47 | C1/C2 |
| W Amelia Dr | 45 | A1 |
| W Ancona St | | |
| (800–863) | 1 | A1 |
| (864–1399) | 24 | A1/A2 |
| Andersen Ave | 55 | A1/B1 |
| Ann St | 56 | C3 |
| W Anson Pl | 23 | B1 |
| N Anthon Ave | 47 | A1 |
| S Anthony Ave | | |
| (6800–8249) | 57 | B1/B2/C2 |
| (8250–9422) | 58 | C3 |
| S Arbor Dr | 56 | C3 |
| W Arbor Pl | 24 | B1 |
| S Arbor Trl | 55 | C1 |
| W Arcade Pl | | |
| (100–399) | 5 | B1 |
| (500–741) | 4 | B1/B2 |
| (1000–1399) | 24 | C1/C2 |
| (1733–1799) | 23 | C2 |
| S Arch St | 12 | A1 |
| S Archer Ave | | |
| (1900–2427) | 10 | B2/C1/C2 |
| (2428–4499) | 52 | — |
| (2531–3143) | 12 | A1/A2/B1 |
| (4484–5074) | 51 | C2 |
| (5075–6399) | 53 | A1/A2 |
| S Archer Ave W | 53 | A2 |
| W Archer Ave | 53 | A1 |
| W Ardmore Ave | | |
| (900–2415) | 37 | B1/B2 |
| (2416–3210) | 35 | B1/B2 |
| (3211–5599) | 46 | C3/C4 |
| (5800–7835) | 45 | C1/C2 |
| W Argyle St | | |
| (821–1499) | 40 | A1/A2 |
| (1800–2398) | 39 | A1/A2 |
| (2501–3599) | 38 | A1/A2 |
| (3600–5399) | 48 | A3/A4 |
| (6000–8699) | 47 | A1/A2 |
| W Arlington Pl | 30 | A1 |
| W Armitage Ave | | |
| (300–864) | 30 | B1/B2 |
| (865–1659) | 29 | B1/B2 |
| (1657–2440) | 28 | B1/B2 |
| (2441–3599) | 27 | B1/B2 |
| (3600–4599) | 48 | C3/C4 |
| (6200–7799) | 47 | C1/C2 |
| N Armour St | 24 | A1/B1 |
| W Armstrong Ave | 46 | C3 |
| Arnold Pl | 56 | B3 |
| Arnold St | 47 | C1 |
| N Artesian Ave | | |
| (200–599) | 23 | A1/B1 |
| (1200–1649) | 21 | A1/B1 |
| (1650–2699) | 28 | A1/C1 |
| (2700–3741) | 42 | A1/C1 |
| (4400–4749) | 38 | B2 |
| (4750–6349) | 35 | A2/B2/C2 |
| (6350–7499) | 33 | A2/C2 |
| S Artesian Ave | | |
| (300–399) | 23 | C1 |
| (2500–5049) | 52 | A3/B3/C3 |
| (5050–8299) | 54 | A3/B3/C3 |
| (9800–12699) | 56 | A3/B3/C3 |
| S Artesion Ave | 54 | C3 |
| W Arthington St | | |
| (500–517) | 7 | B1 |
| (518–1399) | 26 | A1/A2 |
| (2400–2549) | 25 | A1 |
| (2550–3249) | 50 | C3 |
| (3250–5933) | 49 | C1/C2 |
| W Arthur Ave | | |
| (1200–2064) | 34 | C1/C2 |
| (2065–3199) | 33 | C1/C2 |
| (3300–4799) | 46 | B3/B4 |
| (7100–7199) | 45 | B2 |
| Arthur St | 45 | B1 |
| Asbury Ave | 33 | A2 |
| N Ashland Ave | | |
| (400–814) | 24 | A1/B1 |
| (815–1649) | 22 | A1/B1/C1 |
| (1650–2699) | 29 | A1/B1/C1 |
| (2700–3949) | 43 | A1/B1/C1 |
| (3950–5165) | 40 | A1/B1/C1 |
| (5166–5729) | 37 | B1/C1 |
| (6400–7699) | 34 | A1/B1/C1 |
| N Ashland Ave * | | |
| (200–599) | 45 | B1/B2 |
| S Ashland Ave | | |
| (1–424) | 24 | C1 |
| (425–2399) | 26 | A1/B1/C1 |
| (1300–2099) | 45 | C1 |
| (2400–3973) | 12 | A1/B1/C1 |
| (3974–5049) | 52 | B4/C4 |
| (5050–8899) | 54 | A4/B4/C4 |
| (8900–12899) | 56 | A4/B4/C4 |
| N Ashland Blvd | 24 | B1 |
| N Astor St | | |
| (1200–1549) | 32 | A1/B1 |
| (1550–1599) | 31 | C2 |
| W Attrill St | 27 | B2 |
| S Auburn Ave | 55 | C1 |
| W Augusta Blvd | | |
| (1042–1664) | 22 | B1/B2 |
| (1665–2449) | 21 | B1/B2 |
| (2450–3249) | 50 | A3 |
| (3250–5899) | 49 | A1/A2 |
| N Austin Ave | | |
| (1600–5346) | 47 | A2/B2/C2 |
| (5401–8799) | 45 | A1/A2/C2 |
| S Austin Ave | | |
| (4800–8764) | 53 | A1/B1/C1 |
| (8800–14031) | 55 | A1/B1/C1 |
| Austin Ave | 45 | A1 |
| Auxplaines Ave | 47 | C1 |
| S Avalon Ave | | |
| (7528–9399) | 57 | B2/C2 |
| (9500–9899) | 59 | A2 |
| S Avenue B | 60 | A4/B4 |
| S Avenue C | 60 | A4/B4 |
| S Avenue D | 60 | A4/B4 |
| S Avenue E | | |
| (10400–11199) | 60 | A4/B4 |
| (10600–10649) | 60 | A4 |
| S Avenue F | 60 | A4/B4/C3 |
| S Avenue G | 60 | A3/B3/B4 |
| Avenue G | 58 | A3 |
| S Avenue H | 60 | A3/B3 |
| S Avenue J | 60 | A3/B3 |
| S Avenue K | 60 | A3/C3 |
| S Avenue L | 60 | A3/B3/C3 |
| S Avenue M | 60 | A3/B3/C3 |
| S Avenue N | | |
| (9500–13399) | 60 | A3/B3/C3 |
| (10600–13499) | 60 | A3/C3 |
| S Avenue O | | |
| (8900–9099) | 58 | C3 |
| (10200–13399) | 60 | A3/B3/C3 |
| (10600–13499) | 60 | A3/C3 |
| N Avers Ave | | |
| (300–1649) | 49 | A2/B2 |
| (1650–5199) | 48 | A4/B4/C4 |
| (6100–8799) | 46 | A4/B4/C4 |
| S Avers Ave | | |
| (1200–2249) | 49 | C2 |
| (2250–4919) | 51 | A2/C2 |
| (5100–7299) | 54 | A3/B3 |
| (9100–12299) | 56 | A3/B3/C3 |
| Avery Pl | 53 | C2 |
| S Avon Ave | 55 | B2 |
| W Avon Ave | 55 | A1 |
| N Avondale Ave | | |
| (1800–2399) | 28 | A1/B1/B2 |
| (2600–2870) | 27 | A2 |
| (2871–3128) | 41 | C1 |
| (3200–5124) | 48 | A3/B4 |
| (5125–5328) | 47 | A2 |
| (5600–6799) | 45 | — |
| Avondale Ave | 45 | B1 |

## B

| Street | Page | Grid |
|---|---|---|
| Babb Ave | 46 | A3 |
| S Baker Ave | 58 | C3 |
| E Balbo Ave | | |
| (1–99) | 8 | B2 |
| (100–399) | 9 | B1 |
| S Baldwin Ave | 58 | B3 |
| W Balmoral Ave | | |
| (1000–1749) | 37 | C1/C2 |
| (1750–2414) | 36 | C1/C2 |
| (2415–3214) | 35 | C1/C2 |
| (3215–5599) | 46 | C3/C4 |
| (6037–8399) | 47 | A1/A2 |
| S Baltimore Ave | | |
| (8300–9524) | 58 | C3 |
| (9525–13499) | 60 | A3/C3 |
| E Banks St | 32 | B1 |
| W Barber St | 26 | B2 |
| Barnard Dr | 55 | B1 |
| W Barry Ave | | |
| (300–833) | 44 | C1/C2 |
| (834–1649) | 43 | C1/C2 |
| (1650–2455) | 42 | C1/C2 |
| (2456–3599) | 41 | C1/C2 |
| (3600–5815) | 48 | B3/B4 |
| (5816–7999) | 47 | B1/B2 |
| Barton Ave | 33 | A2 |
| N Bauwans St | 22 | B1 |
| W Beach Ave | | |
| (1600–3249) | 21 | A2 |
| (3250–3599) | 49 | A2 |
| N Beacon St | 40 | B1 |
| Beau Dr | 45 | A1 |
| N Beaubien Ct | 6 | A1 |
| S Beck Pl | | |
| (8700–8799) | 53 | C2 |
| (8800–9099) | 55 | A2 |
| W Belden Ave | | |
| (300–815) | 30 | B1 |
| (816–1499) | 29 | B1/B2 |
| (2200–2449) | 28 | B1 |
| (2450–3599) | 27 | B1/B2 |
| (3600–5865) | 48 | C3/C4 |
| (5866–7799) | 47 | C1/C2 |
| Belden Ave | 47 | C1 |
| N Bell Ave | | |
| (300–399) | 23 | B1 |
| (1200–1649) | 21 | A1/B1 |
| (1650–2199) | 28 | B1 |
| (3300–3949) | 42 | A1/B1 |
| (3950–4999) | 39 | A1/C1 |
| (5300–6364) | 36 | A1/C1 |
| (6365–7599) | 33 | A2/B2/C2 |
| S Bell Ave | | |
| (100–299) | 23 | C1 |
| (500–2249) | 25 | A1/B1 |
| (2250–3533) | 52 | A3/B3 |
| (5700–7349) | 54 | A3/B3 |
| (7350–11899) | 56 | — |
| W Belle Plaine Ave | | |
| (800–1649) | 40 | C1/C2 |
| (1650–2449) | 39 | C1/C2 |
| (2450–3599) | 38 | C1/C2 |
| (3600–5814) | 48 | A3/A4 |
| (5815–8399) | 47 | A1/A2 |
| Belle Plaine Ave | 45 | B1 |
| Bellefort Pl | 45 | A2 |
| Belleforte Ave | 45 | A2 |
| E Bellevue Pl | 32 | B1 |

| | | |
|---|---|---|
| W Belmont Ave | | |
| (300–809) | 44 | B1/B2 |
| (810–1649) | 43 | B1/B2 |
| (1650–2476) | 42 | B1/B2 |
| (2477–3599) | 41 | B1/B2 |
| (3600–5857) | 48 | B3/B4 |
| (5833–8698) | 47 | B1/B2 |
| N Belmont Harbor Dr | | |
| | 44 | A1/B2 |
| S Belt Circle Dr | 53 | B1 |
| S Benck Dr | 56 | C3 |
| W Benck Dr | 56 | C3 |
| S Bennett Ave | | |
| (6700–9499) | 58 | A3/B3/C3 |
| (9500–9599) | 60 | A3 |
| S Bensley Ave | 60 | A3/B3 |
| S Benson St | 12 | B1 |
| E Benton Pl | 5 | A2 |
| W Berenice Ave | | |
| (1800–2449) | 42 | A2 |
| (2450–5849) | 48 | B3 |
| (5850–6637) | 47 | B2 |
| S Berkeley Ave | 17 | A1/B1 |
| N Bernard St | | |
| (2400–5249) | 48 | A4/B4/C4 |
| (5250–6299) | 46 | C4 |
| Berry Pky | 45 | B1 |
| W Berteau Ave | | |
| (1400–1649) | 40 | C1 |
| (1650–2449) | 39 | C1/C2 |
| (2450–3599) | 38 | B1/C1/C2 |
| (3600–5765) | 48 | A3/A4 |
| (5766–8399) | 47 | A1/A2 |
| W Berwyn Ave | | |
| (921–1749) | 37 | C1/C2 |
| (1750–2399) | 36 | C1/C2 |
| (2400–3214) | 35 | C1/C2 |
| (3215–5599) | 46 | C3/C4 |
| (5900–8799) | 47 | A1/A2 |
| N Besly Ct | 29 | C1 |
| E Best Dr | 18 | B2/C2 |
| W Betty Ter | 45 | A1 |
| S Beverly Ave | | |
| (8700–8862) | 54 | C4 |
| (8863–11029) | 56 | A4/B4 |
| W Beverly Glen Pky | 56 | A4 |
| N Bingham St | 27 | B2 |
| Birch Ave | 45 | A2 |
| Birch St | 55 | A1 |
| W Birchdale Ave | 47 | C1 |
| W Birchwood Ave | | |
| (1300–2065) | 34 | A1/A2 |
| (2066–3299) | 33 | A1/A2 |
| (3800–5399) | 46 | B3/B4 |
| (6900–7749) | 45 | B1/B2 |
| Birdsall St | 56 | C3 |
| S Birkhoff Ave | 57 | C1 |
| Birmingham St | 55 | B1 |
| N Bishop St | | |
| (1–810) | 24 | A1/B1 |
| (806–899) | 22 | C1 |
| S Bishop St | | |
| (800–1899) | 26 | A1/C1 |
| (4600–5049) | 52 | C4 |
| (5050–8899) | 54 | A4/B4/C4 |
| (8900–12899) | 56 | A4/B4/C4 |
| N Bissell St | 29 | B2/C2 |
| W Bittersweet Pl | | |
| (434–799) | 40 | C2 |
| (6500–6599) | 47 | A2 |
| Black Dr | 54 | B4 |
| W Blackhawk St | | |
| (400–864) | 31 | A1/A2 |
| (865–1664) | 22 | A2/B1/B2 |
| (1665–1699) | 21 | B2 |
| S Blackstone Ave | | |
| (4900–5149) | 17 | C2 |
| (5150–6314) | 19 | A2/B2/C2 |
| (6315–9299) | 57 | A2/B2/C2 |
| S Blake St | 52 | B3 |
| W Bliss St | 22 | B2 |
| W Bloomingdale Ave | | |
| (1401–1664) | 29 | C1 |
| (1665–2464) | 28 | C1/C2 |
| (2465–3599) | 27 | C1/C2 |
| (3800–5864) | 48 | C3/C4 |
| (5865–7999) | 47 | C1/C2 |
| S Blue Island Ave | | |
| (1200–2224) | 26 | B1/B2/C1 |
| (2225–2599) | 52 | A3/A4 |
| Bobolink Ter | 46 | A3/A4 |
| S Bonaparte St | 12 | A1 |
| S Bond Ave | 58 | C3 |
| S Bonfield St | 12 | A1/A2 |
| Bonita Dr | 45 | C1 |
| Bonnie Ave | 45 | C1 |
| N Bosworth Ave | | |
| (1200–1649) | 22 | A1/B1 |
| (1650–2774) | 29 | A1/B1 |
| (2775–3799) | 43 | A1/B1 |
| (6400–7699) | 34 | A2/B2/C2 |
| S Boulevard Way | 52 | A3 |
| E Bowen Ave | 16 | A1/A2 |
| E Bowen Dr | 19 | A1 |
| W Bowler St | 25 | A1 |
| N Bowmanville Ave | 36 | C1 |
| Boyle Ter | 47 | B1 |
| W Bradley Pl | | |
| (800–849) | 44 | A1 |
| (850–2199) | 42 | A1/A2 |
| (2500–2699) | 41 | A2 |
| S Brainard Ave | 60 | C3 |
| S Brandon Ave | | |
| (7900–9498) | 58 | B3/C3 |
| (13000–13499) | 60 | C3 |
| Brandt Ave | 55 | A2 |
| W Brayton St | 59 | C1 |
| W Breen St | 45 | A2 |
| S Brennan Ave | 60 | A3 |
| W Briar Pl | 44 | C1/C2 |
| Briartree Ln | 53 | C2 |
| S Brickton Pl | 45 | C1 |
| S Brighton Pl | 52 | B3 |
| S Broad St | 12 | A1 |
| N Broadway St | | |
| (2800–3936) | 44 | A1/B1/C1 |
| (3937–5163) | 40 | — |
| (5164–6349) | 37 | A2/B2/C2 |
| (6350–6399) | 34 | C2 |
| W Brodman Ave | 47 | A1 |
| W Brompton Ave | 44 | A1/B1 |
| Bronx Ave | 46 | A3 |
| Brookline Ln | 45 | A1 |
| Brooks Ln | 55 | B1 |
| Brophy Ave | 45 | C1 |
| W Bross Ave | 52 | A3 |
| Brown St | 46 | A3 |
| E Browning Ave | 14 | C2 |
| W Bruce Dr | 45 | A1 |
| Brummel St | 46 | A3/A4 |
| W Bryn Mawr Ave | | |
| (900–1749) | 37 | B1/B2 |
| (1750–2415) | 36 | B2 |
| (2416–3224) | 35 | B1/B2 |
| (3225–5715) | 46 | C3/C4 |
| (5716–8799) | 45 | C1/C2 |
| W Buckingham Pl | 44 | B1 |
| Buckley Ave | 55 | A2 |
| N Budd St | 47 | C1 |
| Buell Ave | 55 | A2/B2 |
| W Buena Ave | 40 | C2 |
| S Buffalo Ave | | |
| (8200–10649) | 58 | C3 |
| (10650–13499) | 60 | B3/C3 |
| Burkhardt Dr | 50 | C3 |
| S Burley Ave | | |
| (8200–9299) | 58 | C3 |
| (10700–13499) | 60 | B3/C3 |
| N Burling St | | |
| (1200–1608) | 31 | A1/B1 |
| (1609–2699) | 30 | A1/B1/C1 |
| (2800–2999) | 44 | C1 |
| S Burnham Ave | 58 | B3/C3 |
| S Burnside Ave | 57 | C1/C2 |
| Burr Oak Ave | 56 | C3/C4 |
| Burr Oak St | | |
| (800–965) | 59 | C1 |
| (966–1018) | 56 | C4 |
| Burris Ct | 55 | C1 |
| E Burton Pl | 32 | A1 |
| W Burton Pl | | |
| (1–99) | 32 | A1 |
| (140–199) | 31 | A2 |
| N Busse Ave | 47 | A2 |
| Busse Hwy | 45 | A1/B1/B2 |
| S Butler Dr | | |
| (12600–12755) | 59 | C2 |
| (12756–12899) | 60 | C3 |
| Butler Pl | 45 | B1 |
| W Byron St | | |
| (1000–1615) | 43 | A1/A2 |
| (1616–2499) | 42 | A1/A2 |
| (2800–3499) | 41 | A1 |
| (3600–5849) | 48 | B3/B4 |
| (5850–8399) | 47 | B1/B2 |

**C**

| | | |
|---|---|---|
| W Cabrini St | | |
| (500–699) | 7 | B1 |
| (1054–1299) | 26 | A1/A2 |
| W Cahill Ter | 47 | B1 |
| N Caldwell Ave | | |
| (5700–6599) | 46 | B3/C3 |
| (6601–8525) | 45 | A2/B2 |
| S Calhoun Ave | 60 | A3/B3/C3 |
| W Calhoun Pl | 5 | B1/B2 |
| N California Ave | | |
| (1–1549) | 50 | A3/B3 |
| (1550–2724) | 27 | A2/B2/C2 |
| (2725–3949) | 41 | A2/B2/C2 |
| (3950–5150) | 38 | A2/B2/C2 |
| (5151–6349) | 35 | A2/B2/C2 |
| (6350–7599) | 33 | A1/B1/C1 |
| S California Ave | | |
| (1–2215) | 50 | B3/C3 |
| (2216–5009) | 52 | A3/B3/C3 |
| (5050–8849) | 54 | A3/B3/C3 |
| (8850–12849) | 56 | A3/B3/C3 |
| S California Blvd | 52 | A3 |
| W California Ter | 44 | C1 |
| Callan Ave | 34 | A1 |
| Callie Ave | 45 | A2 |
| S Calumet Ave | | |
| (1800–2509) | 11 | B1/C1 |
| (2510–3950) | 14 | A1/B1/C1 |
| (3951–5200) | 16 | A1/B1/C1 |
| (5201–6326) | 18 | A1/B1/C1 |
| (6327–9449) | 57 | A1/B1/C1 |
| (9450–13399) | 59 | A2/B2/C2 |
| S Calumet River St | 60 | A3 |
| Calumet Sag Rd | 55 | C1/C2 |
| N Cambridge Ave | | |
| (800–1199) | 31 | B1/C1 |
| (2300–2399) | 30 | B1 |
| (2800–3199) | 44 | B1/C1 |
| Cambridge St | 55 | A1 |
| N Campbell Ave | | |
| (1–622) | 23 | A1/B1 |
| (623–1549) | 50 | A3/B3 |
| (1550–2749) | 27 | A2/B2/C2 |
| (2750–3966) | 41 | A2/B2/C2 |
| (3967–4749) | 38 | B2/C2 |
| (4750–6349) | 35 | A2/B2/C2 |
| (6350–7499) | 33 | A2/B2/C2 |
| S Campbell Ave | | |
| (1–399) | 23 | C1 |
| (500–1299) | 25 | A1/B1 |
| (3248–5049) | 52 | A3/B3/C3 |
| (5050–8299) | 54 | A3/B3/C3 |
| (9400–11899) | 56 | A3/B3/C3 |
| W Campbell Park Dr | 25 | A1 |
| N Canal St | | |
| (1–249) | 4 | A2/B2 |
| (250–499) | 1 | B2/C2 |
| S Canal St | | |
| (1–499) | 4 | B2/C2 |
| (600–1333) | 7 | A2/B2/C2 |
| (1330–2549) | 10 | A1/B1/C1 |
| (2550–3999) | 13 | A1/B1/C1 |
| (4300–4399) | 15 | A1/B1 |
| Canal Bank Dr | 53 | A1 |
| S Canalport Ave | | |
| (1744–1963) | 10 | B1 |
| (2000–2199) | 26 | C2 |
| N Canfield Ave | | |
| (4400–5469) | 47 | A1 |
| (5470–6399) | 45 | B1/C1 |
| N Canfield Ave * | | |
| (1236–3817) | 45 | C1 |
| N Canfield Rd | 45 | B1 |
| N Cannon Dr | 30 | A2/B2/C2 |
| Capitol St | 46 | A4 |

| Street | Range | Page | Grid |
|---|---|---|---|
| Capulina Ave | | | |
| (5700–5849) | 46 | A3 | |
| (5850–6374) | 45 | A2 | |
| Carey Ave | 47 | C1 | |
| Carl Cassata Sr Ln | 47 | A2 | |
| Carmel Ln | 53 | C1 | |
| W Carmen Ave | | | |
| (830–1699) | 40 | A1/A2 | |
| (1700–2449) | 39 | A1 | |
| (2450–3599) | 38 | A1/A2 | |
| (3600–5714) | 48 | A3/A4 | |
| (5715–8799) | 47 | A1/A2 | |
| W Carol Ave | | | |
| (3600–5849) | 46 | A3/A4 | |
| (5850–7099) | 45 | A2 | |
| Carol Ct | 45 | A2 | |
| W Carol Ln | 55 | C1 | |
| W Carol St | | | |
| (4800–5499) | 46 | A3 | |
| (7300–8599) | 45 | A1/A2 | |
| W Carol St * | | | |
| (1200–1499) | 45 | A1 | |
| S Carolyn Ln | 55 | C2 | |
| S Carondolet Ave | 60 | B3/C3 | |
| Carpenter Rd | 46 | B3 | |
| N Carpenter St | | | |
| (1–828) | 24 | A2/B2/C2 | |
| (829–899) | 22 | C2 | |
| S Carpenter St | | | |
| (400–449) | 24 | C2 | |
| (450–2199) | 26 | A2/C2 | |
| (3221–5049) | 12 | B2 | |
| (5050–8935) | 54 | A4/B4/C4 | |
| (8934–12999) | 56 | A4/B4/C4 | |
| Carriage Ln | 55 | C2 | |
| W Carroll Ave | | | |
| (36–199) | 2 | C1/C2 | |
| (800–863) | 1 | C1 | |
| (864–1649) | 24 | B1/B2 | |
| (1650–2199) | 23 | B1/B2 | |
| (2900–3299) | 50 | B3 | |
| (3300–4799) | 49 | B2 | |
| E Carver Plz | 14 | C1 | |
| Cass St | 55 | A2 | |
| Castle Dr | 45 | C1 | |
| W Castle Island Ave | 47 | A1 | |
| W Castlewood Ter | 40 | A2 | |
| W Catalpa Ave | | | |
| (1000–1799) | 37 | C1/C2 | |
| (2400–2429) | 36 | C1 | |
| (2428–3214) | 35 | C1/C2 | |
| (3215–5715) | 46 | C3/C4 | |
| (5709–8799) | 45 | C1/C2 | |
| W Catherine Ave | 47 | A1 | |
| W Caton St | 28 | C1 | |
| Cedar Ln | 45 | A1 | |
| Cedar St | 45 | B1/B2 | |
| E Cedar St | 32 | B1 | |
| Cedar Creek Ct | 55 | C1 | |
| Center Ave | 47 | C1 | |
| N Central Ave | | | |
| (1–1649) | 49 | A1/B1 | |
| (1650–5217) | 48 | A3/B3/C3 | |
| (5215–8810) | 46 | A3/B3/C3 | |

| Street | Range | Page | Grid |
|---|---|---|---|
| S Central Ave | | | |
| (1–4299) | 49 | A1/B1/C1 | |
| (4500–5049) | 51 | C1 | |
| (5050–8816) | 53 | A2/B2/C2 | |
| (8817–12799) | 55 | A2/B2/C2 | |
| N Central Park Ave | | | |
| (1–1562) | 49 | A2/B2 | |
| (1563–5145) | 48 | A4/B4/C4 | |
| (5601–8849) | 46 | A4/B4/C4 | |
| S Central Park Ave | | | |
| (8850–12699) | 56 | A3/B3/C3 | |
| (600–2259) | 49 | B2/C2 | |
| (2260–3699) | 51 | A2/B2 | |
| (5700–8699) | 54 | A3/B3/C3 | |
| S Central Park Blvd | 49 | B2 | |
| E Cermak Rd | 11 | B1 | |
| W Cermak Rd | | | |
| (1–44) | 11 | B1 | |
| (45–655) | 10 | B1/C2 | |
| (624–1749) | 26 | C1/C2 | |
| (1750–2549) | 25 | C1/C2 | |
| (2524–3314) | 50 | C3 | |
| (3315–5999) | 49 | C1/C2 | |
| W Chalmars Pl | 29 | B2 | |
| N Chalmers St | 29 | B2 | |
| S Champlain Ave | | | |
| (4200–5099) | 16 | A2/B2/C2 | |
| (6000–6349) | 18 | C2 | |
| (6350–9499) | 57 | A1/B1/C1 | |
| (10500–13099) | 59 | A2/B2/C2 | |
| W Chanay St | 27 | B2 | |
| Channel Rd | | | |
| 33 | | A1 | |
| (7200–7599) | 46 | B4 | |
| S Chappel Ave | | | |
| (6700–9423) | 58 | A3/B3/C3 | |
| (9526–11399) | 60 | A3/B3 | |
| S Charles St | 56 | A4/B4 | |
| W Charleston St | | | |
| (2000–2524) | 28 | B1 | |
| (2525–2549) | 27 | B2 | |
| W Charmaine Rd | 47 | A1 | |
| W Chase Ave | | | |
| (1200–2049) | 34 | A1/A2 | |
| (2050–3199) | 33 | A1/A2 | |
| (3600–5199) | 46 | B3/B4 | |
| (7100–7733) | 45 | B1/B2 | |
| W Chelsea Pl | 56 | B4 | |
| E Cheltenham Pl | 58 | B3 | |
| N Cherry Ave | 22 | A2/B2 | |
| W Cherry Ave | 45 | B2 | |
| Cherry Ln | 46 | B4 | |
| Cherry St | 45 | B1/B2 | |
| N Chester Ave | | | |
| (4400–5509) | 47 | A1 | |
| (5465–8899) | 45 | A1/C1 | |
| N Chester Ave * | | | |
| (1–299) | 45 | B1 | |
| S Chester Ave | 45 | B1/C1 | |
| Chestnut St | 45 | A2 | |
| E Chestnut St | 32 | C1/C2 | |
| W Chestnut St | | | |
| (1–118) | 32 | C1 | |
| (119–537) | 31 | C1/C2 | |
| (900–1599) | 22 | C1/C2 | |
| S Cheyenne Dr | 55 | C1 | |

| Street | Range | Page | Grid |
|---|---|---|---|
| E Chicago Ave | | | |
| (1–126) | 2 | A2 | |
| (127–499) | 3 | A1 | |
| S Chicago Ave | 57 | B2 | |
| W Chicago Ave | | | |
| (1–367) | 2 | A1/A2 | |
| (368–841) | 1 | A1/A2 | |
| (842–1664) | 24 | A1/A2 | |
| (1665–2449) | 23 | A1/A2 | |
| (2450–3264) | 50 | A3 | |
| (3265–5999) | 49 | B1/B2 | |
| S Chicago Skwy | 57 | B1 | |
| S Chicago Beach Dr | 17 | C2 | |
| Chicago Ridge Mall | 55 | A1 | |
| E Chicago River Dr | 6 | A2 | |
| N Chicora Ave | 46 | B3 | |
| N Childrens Plz | 30 | B1 | |
| S China Pl | 10 | B2 | |
| S Chippewa Ave | 60 | B3 | |
| Chippewa Dr | 55 | C1 | |
| N Christiana Ave | 48 | A4/B4 | |
| (600–1199) | 49 | A2/B2 | |
| (2800–3949) | 41 | A1/B1/C1 | |
| (3950–5249) | 38 | A1/B1/C1 | |
| (5250–8599) | 46 | A4/B4/C4 | |
| S Christiana Ave | | | |
| (300–2249) | 49 | B2/C2 | |
| (2250–4782) | 51 | A2/B2/C2 | |
| (4783–4999) | 50 | C3 | |
| (4820–4879) | 52 | C3 | |
| (5000–8599) | 54 | A3/B3/C3 | |
| (10300–11231) | 56 | B3 | |
| S Church St | 56 | B4/C4 | |
| W Churchill St | 28 | C1 | |
| N Cicero Ave | | | |
| (1–1599) | 49 | A2/B2 | |
| (1600–5199) | 48 | A3/B3/C3 | |
| (5200–7399) | 46 | B3/C3 | |
| S Cicero Ave | | | |
| (1–2299) | 49 | B2/C2 | |
| (2300–6099) | 51 | A2/B2/C2 | |
| (5100–8814) | 53 | A2/B2/C2 | |
| (8700–12765) | 55 | A2/B2/C2 | |
| NE Circle Ave | 45 | C2 | |
| NW Circle Ave | 45 | C2 | |
| Circle Ct | 55 | A1 | |
| W Circle Dr | 55 | B1 | |
| N Cityfront Plaza Dr | 3 | B1 | |
| Civic Center Dr | 45 | A2 | |
| W Clara Ct | 45 | A1 | |
| W Clara Dr | 45 | A1 | |
| N Claremont Ave | | | |
| (239–599) | 23 | A1/B1 | |
| (1300–1649) | 21 | A1/B1 | |
| (1650–2199) | 28 | B1 | |
| (3300–3949) | 42 | A1/B1 | |
| (3950–5129) | 39 | A1/B1/C1 | |
| (5130–6349) | 36 | A1/C1 | |
| (6350–7599) | 33 | A2/C2 | |
| S Claremont Ave | | | |
| (500–1399) | 25 | A1/B1 | |
| (2500–3645) | 52 | A3/B3 | |
| (5400–8199) | 54 | A3/B3/C3 | |
| (8900–10699) | 56 | A3/B3 | |
| W Clarence Ave | 45 | C1/C2 | |
| N Clarendon Ave | 40 | B2/C2 | |

| Street | Range | Page | Grid |
|---|---|---|---|
| W Clark Dr | 56 | A3 | |
| N Clark St | | | |
| (1–261) | 5 | A2/B2 | |
| (262–821) | 2 | A2/B2/C2 | |
| (822–1649) | 32 | A1/B1/C1 | |
| (1650–2749) | 30 | — | |
| (2750–3173) | 44 | C1 | |
| (3174–3963) | 43 | A1/A2/B2 | |
| (3964–5164) | 40 | A1/B1/C1 | |
| (5165–6363) | 37 | A1/B1/C1 | |
| (6364–7599) | 34 | A1/B1/C1 | |
| S Clark St | | | |
| (1–449) | 5 | B2/C2 | |
| (450–1343) | 8 | A1/B1/C1 | |
| (1344–2199) | 10 | A2/B2 | |
| Clarmont Ave | 23 | A1 | |
| N Cleaver St | 22 | A1/B1 | |
| Cleveland Ave | 45 | B1 | |
| N Cleveland Ave | | | |
| (800–1649) | 31 | A1/B1/C1 | |
| (1650–2399) | 30 | B1/C1 | |
| W Cleveland St | | | |
| (3300–5760) | 46 | A3/A4 | |
| (5761–7599) | 45 | A1/A2 | |
| N Clifford Ave | 46 | C3 | |
| Clifford Ter | 46 | A4 | |
| N Clifton Ave | | | |
| (1916–2399) | 29 | B2/C2 | |
| (3000–3899) | 43 | A2/B2/C2 | |
| (4333–4799) | 40 | B1 | |
| (8100–8599) | 45 | A1 | |
| N Clifton Ave * | | | |
| (1–1199) | 45 | A1/B1 | |
| S Clifton Ave | 45 | B1/C1 | |
| N Clifton St | 47 | A1 | |
| S Clifton Park Ave | 56 | A3 | |
| Clinton Ave | 56 | C3 | |
| N Clinton St | | | |
| (1–249) | 4 | A2/B2 | |
| (100–199) | 45 | B1 | |
| (250–599) | 1 | B2/C2 | |
| (2400–2799) | 47 | C1 | |
| S Clinton St | | | |
| (1–420) | 4 | B2/C2 | |
| (421–1214) | 7 | A1/B1/C1 | |
| (1215–1899) | 10 | A1/B1 | |
| N Clover St | 48 | A3 | |
| N Clybourn Ave | | | |
| (1200–1649) | 31 | A1/B1 | |
| (1650–2407) | 29 | B1/C2 | |
| (2408–2737) | 28 | A2 | |
| (2716–3199) | 42 | B1/C1/C2 | |
| S Clyde Ave | | | |
| (6700–9514) | 58 | A3/B3/C3 | |
| (9515–11959) | 60 | A3/B3 | |
| Coast Guard Dr | 58 | A3 | |
| Cochran St | 56 | C3 | |
| S Coles Ave | 58 | B3/C3 | |
| S Colfax Ave | | | |
| (7400–9524) | 58 | B3/C3 | |
| (9525–9699) | 60 | A3 | |
| S Colhoun Ave | 60 | B3 | |
| College Dr | 55 | C1 | |
| Collins St | 56 | C3/C4 | |
| Columbia Ave | 45 | B1 | |

**W Columbia Ave**
| | | |
|---|---|---|
| (1018–2032) | 34 | C1/C2 |
| (3300–4599) | 46 | B3/B4 |
| (6700–7762) | 45 | B1 |

| | | |
|---|---|---|
| Columbia Dr | 20 | B1 |
| Columbia Malt Dr | 60 | A3/A4 |

**W Columbus Ave**
| | | |
|---|---|---|
| (2400–4037) | 54 | C3 |
| (11000–11299) | 55 | B1 |

| | | |
|---|---|---|
| Columbus Dr | 55 | A2 |

**N Columbus Dr**
| | | |
|---|---|---|
| (0–299) | 6 | A1/B1 |
| (400–499) | 3 | B1/C1 |

**S Columbus Dr**
| | | |
|---|---|---|
| (100–499) | 6 | B1/C1 |
| (502–1199) | 9 | A1/B1 |
| (1200–2479) | 11 | A1/B2/C2 |

**S Commercial Ave**
| | | |
|---|---|---|
| (7900–9549) | 58 | B3/C3 |
| (9550–13399) | 60 | A3/C3 |

**S Commodove Whalen Dr**
| | | |
|---|---|---|
| | 58 | A3 |

| | | |
|---|---|---|
| N Commons Dr | 47 | A1 |

**N Commonwealth Ave**
| | | |
|---|---|---|
| (2300–2399) | 30 | B1 |
| (2800–2941) | 44 | C2 |

**N Concord Ln**
| | | |
|---|---|---|
| (4400–4599) | 46 | A3 |
| (6784–6999) | 45 | B2 |

| | | |
|---|---|---|
| W Concord Ln | 30 | C2 |

**W Concord Pl**
| | | |
|---|---|---|
| (300–799) | 30 | C1 |
| (900–2017) | 29 | C1/C2 |
| (2018–2199) | 28 | C1 |
| (3700–5199) | 48 | C3/C4 |

**E Congress Pky**
| | | |
|---|---|---|
| (1–71) | 8 | A2 |
| (72–129) | 9 | A1 |

**W Congress Pky**
| | | |
|---|---|---|
| (2–199) | 8 | A1/A2 |
| (530–699) | 7 | A1 |
| (1000–1665) | 26 | A1/A2 |
| (1666–2501) | 25 | A1/A2 |
| (2502–3249) | 50 | B3 |
| (3250–5599) | 49 | B1/B2 |

**E Congress Plaza Dr**
| | | |
|---|---|---|
| (407–453) | 9 | A1 |
| (454–499) | 6 | C1 |

**Conrad St**
| | | |
|---|---|---|
| (4800–5499) | 46 | A3 |
| (7200–7399) | 45 | A2 |

| | | |
|---|---|---|
| N Conservatory Dr | 49 | B2 |

**S Constance Ave**
| | | |
|---|---|---|
| (6700–8749) | 57 | A2/B2/C2 |
| (8750–9599) | 58 | C2/C3 |

| | | |
|---|---|---|
| Conti Pky | 47 | C1 |
| Cook Ave | 55 | A2/B2 |
| Coral Dr | 47 | A1 |

**S Corbett St**
| | | |
|---|---|---|
| (2400–2489) | 52 | A4 |
| (2490–2499) | 12 | A2 |

| | | |
|---|---|---|
| W Corcoran Pl | 49 | B1 |

**S Corcoran Rd**
| | | |
|---|---|---|
| (8700–8799) | 53 | C2 |
| (8800–9099) | 55 | A2 |

| | | |
|---|---|---|
| S Corliss Ave | 59 | A2/B2/C2 |

**W Cornelia Ave**
| | | |
|---|---|---|
| (500–814) | 44 | B1 |
| (815–1617) | 43 | B1/B2 |
| (1618–2399) | 42 | B1/B2 |
| (3000–3099) | 41 | B1 |
| (3600–5849) | 48 | B3/B4 |
| (5850–8399) | 47 | B1/B2 |

**S Cornell Ave**
| | | |
|---|---|---|
| (4900–5199) | 17 | C2 |
| (5200–6399) | 20 | A1/B1/C1 |
| (6400–9399) | 57 | A2/B2/C2 |

| | | |
|---|---|---|
| Cornell Dr | 17 | B2/C2 |
| W Cortez Dr | 50 | A3 |
| N Cortez St | 22 | B1 |

**W Cortez St**
| | | |
|---|---|---|
| (1200–1664) | 22 | B1 |
| (1665–2449) | 21 | B1/B2 |
| (2450–3249) | 50 | A3 |
| (3250–5599) | 49 | A1/A2 |

| | | |
|---|---|---|
| Cortland Ct | 47 | C1 |
| W Cortland Pky | 47 | C1 |

**W Cortland St**
| | | |
|---|---|---|
| (1200–1649) | 29 | C1 |
| (1650–2449) | 28 | C1/C2 |
| (2450–3599) | 27 | C1/C2 |
| (3600–5849) | 48 | C3/C4 |
| (5850–7930) | 47 | C1/C2 |

| | | |
|---|---|---|
| W Cottage Pl | 24 | C1 |

**S Cottage Grove Ave**
| | | |
|---|---|---|
| (2200–2499) | 11 | B1/C1 |
| (2901–3902) | 14 | A2/B2/C2 |
| (3903–5120) | 16 | A2/B2/C2 |
| (5121–6349) | 19 | A1/B1/C1 |
| (6350–9499) | 57 | A2/B2/C2 |
| (9675–12945) | 59 | A2/B2/C2 |

**W Couch Pl**
| | | |
|---|---|---|
| (1–299) | 5 | A1/A2 |
| (600–799) | 4 | A1 |

| | | |
|---|---|---|
| Coulter St | 52 | A3 |
| Country Club Dr | 56 | A3 |
| W Country Club Ln | 47 | C1 |

**W Court Pl**
| | | |
|---|---|---|
| (1–339) | 5 | A1/A2 |
| (634–799) | 4 | A1 |

**Courtland Ave**
| | | |
|---|---|---|
| (5000–8199) | 45 | A1 |

**Courtland Ave ***
| | | |
|---|---|---|
| (100–1999) | 45 | B1/C1 |

**W Coyle Ave**
| | | |
|---|---|---|
| (2400–2999) | 33 | B1/B2 |
| (4800–5399) | 46 | B3 |
| (7200–7399) | 45 | B2 |

**Crain St**
| | | |
|---|---|---|
| (1405–5849) | 46 | A3/A4 |
| (5850–8599) | 45 | A1/A2 |

**Crain St ***
| | | |
|---|---|---|
| (1200–1404) | 45 | A1 |

| | | |
|---|---|---|
| Cranbrook Ln | 53 | C1 |
| W Crandall Ave | 55 | B1 |

**S Crandon Ave**
| | | |
|---|---|---|
| (6700–9499) | 58 | A3/B3/C3 |
| (9600–12159) | 60 | A3/B3 |

| | | |
|---|---|---|
| Crawford Ave | 46 | A4/B4 |
| Crecy Ln | 55 | A2 |
| Creek Dr | 56 | C3 |
| S Cregier Ave | 57 | A2/B2/C2 |

**N Crescent Ave**
| | | |
|---|---|---|
| (4800–4999) | 47 | A1 |
| (5600–5699) | 45 | C1 |

| | | |
|---|---|---|
| S Crescent Ave | 45 | B1/B2/C1 |
| W Crescent Ave | 45 | B1/B2 |
| Crescent Ct | 55 | A1 |
| W Cressett Dr | 47 | C1 |
| W Crestline Ave | 53 | C2 |
| N Crilly Ct | 30 | C2 |
| S Crilly Dr | 60 | A3/A4 |
| N Croname Rd | 45 | A2 |
| N Crosby St | 31 | B1 |
| S Crowell St | 12 | A1/A2 |
| Crystal Ln | 55 | C1 |

**W Crystal St**
| | | |
|---|---|---|
| (1251–1399) | 22 | B1 |
| (1723–2199) | 21 | B1/B2 |
| (2600–3249) | 50 | A3 |
| (3250–5599) | 49 | A1/A2 |

| | | |
|---|---|---|
| E Cullerton St | 11 | B1 |

**W Cullerton St**
| | | |
|---|---|---|
| (1–599) | 10 | B1/B2 |
| (800–1731) | 26 | C1/C2 |
| (1712–2499) | 25 | C1/C2 |
| (2500–3099) | 50 | C3 |
| (4000–4399) | 49 | C2 |

**W Cullom Ave**
| | | |
|---|---|---|
| (900–1649) | 40 | C1/C2 |
| (1650–2450) | 39 | C1/C2 |
| (2451–3599) | 38 | C1/C2 |
| (3600–5749) | 48 | A3/A4 |
| (5750–7799) | 47 | A1/A2 |

**Cumberland Ave**
| | | |
|---|---|---|
| (5001–5483) | 47 | A1 |
| (5210–5227) | 47 | A1 |
| (5420–5899) | 45 | C1 |

| | | |
|---|---|---|
| N Cumberland Ave | 45 | A1/B1 |
| S Cumberland Ave | 45 | B1/C1 |
| Cusic Ct | 49 | B2 |
| Custer Ave | 34 | A1 |
| E Cuttriss St | 45 | A1 |
| W Cuttriss St | 45 | A1 |

**W Cuyler Ave**
| | | |
|---|---|---|
| (800–1499) | 40 | C1/C2 |
| (1800–2449) | 39 | C1/C2 |
| (2450–3399) | 38 | C1/C2 |
| (4619–5399) | 48 | A3/A4 |
| (6200–6399) | 47 | A2 |

| | | |
|---|---|---|
| Cynthia Ave | 45 | A1 |
| S Cyril Ave | 58 | B3 |

## D

| | | |
|---|---|---|
| Dahlin Dr | 45 | A2 |

**W Dakin St**
| | | |
|---|---|---|
| (800–849) | 40 | C2 |
| (850–2449) | 43 | A2 |
| (2450–2499) | 41 | A2 |
| (3900–5849) | 48 | B3/B4 |
| (5850–6799) | 47 | B2 |

**N Damen Ave**
| | | |
|---|---|---|
| (1–824) | 23 | A2/B2 |
| (825–1620) | 21 | A2/B2/C2 |
| (1621–2685) | 28 | A2/B2/C2 |
| (2686–3949) | 42 | A2/B2/C2 |
| (3950–5158) | 39 | A2/B2/C2 |
| (5159–6199) | 36 | A2/B2/C2 |
| (6400–7599) | 34 | A1/B1/C1 |

**S Damen Ave**
| | | |
|---|---|---|
| (1–449) | 23 | C2 |
| (450–2214) | 25 | A2/B2/C2 |
| (2215–4999) | 52 | A3/B3/C3 |
| (5000–5049) | 50 | C3 |
| (5050–8685) | 54 | A4/B4/C4 |
| (9000–10099) | 56 | A4 |

| | | |
|---|---|---|
| S Daniel Dr | 59 | C2 |
| S Dante Ave | 57 | A2/B2/C2 |

**S Dauphin Ave**
| | | |
|---|---|---|
| (8700–9359) | 57 | C2 |
| (10000–10899) | 59 | A2/B2 |

| | | |
|---|---|---|
| David Ct | 55 | A1 |
| Davis St | 56 | C4 |
| N Davisson St | 47 | C1 |
| N Davlin Ct | 48 | B4 |
| S Davol St | 56 | B4 |
| N Dawson Ave | 48 | B4 |
| N Days Ter | 45 | B2 |

**N Dayton St**
| | | |
|---|---|---|
| (1400–1632) | 31 | A1/B1 |
| (1633–2149) | 30 | B1/C1 |
| (2150–2749) | 29 | A2/B2 |
| (2750–3299) | 43 | B2/C2 |
| (4300–4399) | 40 | B2 |

| | | |
|---|---|---|
| W de Koven St | 7 | C1 |
| W de Saible St | 13 | C2 |
| Dean Dr | 56 | B3 |
| N Dean St | 21 | A2 |

**N Dearborn St**
| | | |
|---|---|---|
| (1–250) | 5 | A2/B2 |
| (251–821) | 2 | A2/B2/C2 |
| (822–1599) | 32 | A1/B1/C1 |

**S Dearborn St**
| | | |
|---|---|---|
| (1–449) | 5 | B2/C2 |
| (450–699) | 8 | A2 |
| (700–2499) | 10 | A2/B2/C2 |
| (2500–3949) | 13 | A2/B2/C2 |
| (3950–4125) | 15 | A2 |
| (4639–4699) | 16 | B1 |
| (5100–5499) | 18 | A1 |

| | | |
|---|---|---|
| Deblin Ln | 55 | B2 |
| S Deer Park Dr | 56 | C3 |
| W Deer Park Dr | 56 | C3 |
| E Delaware Pl | 32 | C1/C2 |

**W Delaware Pl**
| | | |
|---|---|---|
| (1–116) | 32 | C1 |
| (117–537) | 31 | C1 |

**N Delphia Ave**
| | | |
|---|---|---|
| (4500–5449) | 47 | A1 |
| (5450–5599) | 45 | C1 |

**N Delphia Ave ***
| | | |
|---|---|---|
| (1–1199) | 45 | A1/B1 |

| | | |
|---|---|---|
| S Delphia Ave | 45 | B1/B2/C1 |

**W Deming Pl**
| | | |
|---|---|---|
| (400–4449) | 30 | A1 |
| (4450–5399) | 48 | C3 |

| Street | Range | Page | Grid |
|---|---|---|---|
| W Dempster St | | | |
| | (2550–5812) | 46 | A3/A4 |
| | (5813–8816) | 45 | A1/A2 |
| N Denal St | | 47 | A1 |
| S Denvir Ave | | 50 | B3 |
| Depot St | | 55 | B1/C1 |
| N Des Plaines St | | | |
| | (1–224) | 4 | A1/B1 |
| | (218–599) | 1 | B1/C1 |
| S Des Plaines St | | | |
| | (1–499) | 4 | B1/C1 |
| | (600–1199) | 7 | A1/B1/C1 |
| | (1600–2099) | 10 | B1 |
| Des Plaines River Rd | | 47 | C1 |
| W Devon Ave | | | |
| | (1200–2064) | 34 | C1/C2 |
| | (2065–3199) | 33 | C1/C2 |
| | (3200–5807) | 46 | B3/B4 |
| | (5808–7799) | 45 | B1/B2 |
| W Devon Ave * | | | |
| | (1–1499) | 45 | B2/C1 |
| Dewey Ave | | 33 | A1 |
| N Dewitt Pl | | 32 | B2/C2 |
| W Dickens Ave | | | |
| | (308–864) | 30 | B1/B2 |
| | (865–1499) | 29 | B1/B2 |
| | (1800–2815) | 28 | B1/B2 |
| | (2816–3599) | 27 | B1 |
| | (3600–5864) | 48 | C3/C4 |
| | (5865–7799) | 47 | C1/C2 |
| N Dickinson Ave | | 48 | A3 |
| Ditka Dr | | 47 | C1 |
| W Diversey Ave | | | |
| | (4000–5816) | 48 | C3/C4 |
| | (5817–7999) | 47 | C1/C2 |
| W Diversey Pky | | | |
| | (100–814) | 44 | C1/C2 |
| | (815–1665) | 43 | C1/C2 |
| | (1666–2465) | 42 | C1/C2 |
| | (2466–3599) | 41 | C1/C2 |
| | (3600–3999) | 48 | B4/C4 |
| W Diversey School Ct | | 43 | C2 |
| Division St | | 56 | C4 |
| E Division St | | 32 | B1 |
| W Division St | | | |
| | (1–130) | 32 | B1 |
| | (131–847) | 31 | B1/B2 |
| | (848–1665) | 22 | B1/B2 |
| | (1664–2463) | 21 | B1/B2 |
| | (2464–3249) | 50 | A3 |
| | (3250–5899) | 49 | A1/A2 |
| Dixie Dr | | 55 | B2 |
| S Dobson Ave | | | |
| | (7100–9249) | 57 | B2/C2 |
| | (9500–13399) | 59 | A2/C2 |
| Dobson St | | | |
| | (3800–5299) | 46 | A3/A4 |
| | (6800–7220) | 45 | A2 |
| Dodge Ave | | 33 | A1 |
| S Dogwood Ln | | 55 | C1 |
| N Dominick St | | 29 | B1 |
| Doral Dr | | 53 | C1 |
| S Dorchester Ave | | | |
| | (445–5149) | 17 | B2/C2 |
| | (5150–6349) | 19 | A2/B2/C2 |
| | (6350–8965) | 57 | A2/B2/C2 |
| | (9500–10029) | 59 | A2 |
| S Doty Ave | | 59 | B2/C2 |
| W Doty Ave S | | 59 | C2 |
| Douglas Ave | | 53 | A1 |
| W Douglas Blvd | | | |
| | (3100–3299) | 50 | C3 |
| | (3300–3799) | 49 | C2 |
| N Dover St | | 40 | B1 |
| W Dover St | | 55 | A1 |
| N Dowagiac Ave | | 46 | B3 |
| S Dr Martin Luther King Jr Dr | | | |
| | (9450–13398) | 59 | C2/A2/B2 |
| | (2100–2549) | 11 | B1/C1/C2 |
| | (2550–3920) | 14 | B1/C1/A1 |
| | (3900–5199) | 16 | A1/B1/C1 |
| N Drake Ave | | | |
| | (400–1199) | 49 | A2/B2 |
| | (1600–5199) | 48 | A4/B4/C4 |
| | (5600–8799) | 46 | A4/B4/C4 |
| S Drake Ave | | | |
| | (1400–2257) | 49 | C2 |
| | (2258–4699) | 51 | A2/B2/C2 |
| | (8532–8559) | 54 | C3 |
| | (10300–11471) | 56 | B3 |
| W Draper St | | 29 | A1 |
| S Drew St | | 56 | B4 |
| S Drexel Ave | | | |
| | (3900–6328) | 19 | — |
| | (6329–9399) | 57 | A2/B2/C2 |
| | (9700–13099) | 59 | A2/C2 |
| S Drexel Blvd | | | |
| | (3900–4099) | 16 | A2 |
| | (4100–5099) | 17 | A1/B1/C1 |
| E Drexel Sq | | 19 | A1 |
| W Drummond Pl | | | |
| | (526–699) | 30 | A1 |
| | (1100–1199) | 29 | A2 |
| | (3400–3499) | 27 | A1 |
| | (4200–5599) | 48 | C3/C4 |
| Drury Ln | | 56 | A3 |
| | (5400–5499) | 55 | A2 |
| S Duffy Ave | | | |
| | (8700–8749) | 53 | C2 |
| | (8750–8899) | 55 | A2 |
| Dumke Dr | | 55 | A2 |
| S Dunbar Ave | | 57 | C1 |

## E

| Street | Range | Page | Grid |
|---|---|---|---|
| W Early Ave | | 37 | B1/B2 |
| East Ave | | 45 | A1/B1 |
| N East Brook Rd | | 47 | C1 |
| S East End Ave | | | |
| | (4900–6749) | 17 | C2 |
| | (6750–9399) | 57 | B2/C2 |
| East Frontage Rd | | 46 | A3/B3 |
| N East Prairie Rd | | 46 | A4/B4 |
| N East River Rd | | 47 | A1 |
| East Shore Dr | | 55 | A2 |
| S East View Park | | 20 | A1 |
| N Eastlake Ter | | 34 | A2 |
| W Eastman St | | | |
| | (800–850) | 31 | B1 |
| | (851–1129) | 22 | B2 |
| W Eastwood Ave | | | |
| | (800–2049) | 40 | B2 |
| | (2050–2449) | 39 | B1 |
| | (2450–3399) | 38 | B1/B2 |
| | (3716–5749) | 48 | A3/A4 |
| | (5750–8299) | 47 | A1/A2 |
| S Eberhart Ave | | | |
| | (3130–3149) | 14 | B2 |
| | (6000–6349) | 18 | C2 |
| | (6350–9449) | 57 | A1/B1/C1 |
| | (9450–13399) | 59 | A2/B2/C2 |
| W Ebinger Dr | | 45 | B2 |
| S Edbrooke Ave | | | |
| | (10500–10599) | 55 | A1 |
| | (10600–13399) | 59 | B1/C1/C2 |
| S Edbrooke Ct | | 59 | C2 |
| W Eddy St | | | |
| | (1001–1399) | 43 | B1/B2 |
| | (1800–1999) | 42 | B2 |
| | (3100–3599) | 41 | B1 |
| | (3600–5849) | 48 | B3/B4 |
| | (5850–6399) | 47 | B2 |
| N Edens Pky | | 46 | C3 |
| Edge Lake Dr | | 55 | B1 |
| N Edgebrook Ter | | 45 | B2 |
| Edgemont Ln | | 45 | A1 |
| W Edgewater Ave | | 37 | B1 |
| Edison Ave | | | |
| | (3300–3399) | 56 | C3 |
| | (5330–5599) | 55 | A2 |
| Edison St | | 56 | C3 |
| W Edmaire St | | 56 | B4 |
| W Edmunds St | | 48 | A3 |
| N Edward Ct | | 30 | B1 |
| Edward Barron Dr | | 60 | A4 |
| S Eggleston Ave | | | |
| | (5900–9461) | 57 | A1/B1/C1 |
| | (9462–12999) | 59 | A1/B1/C1 |
| N Elaine Pl | | 44 | B1 |
| N Elbridge Ave | | 48 | B4 |
| Elder Ct | | 55 | A1 |
| S Eleanor St | | 12 | A1 |
| S Elias Ct | | 12 | A2 |
| W Elizabeth Ave | | 45 | A1 |
| N Elizabeth St | | | |
| | (1–799) | 24 | A1/B1 |
| | (900–999) | 22 | C1 |
| S Elizabeth St | | | |
| | (4700–5049) | 52 | C4 |
| | (5050–8899) | 54 | A4/B4/C4 |
| | (8900–12899) | 56 | A4/B4/C4 |
| N Elk Grove Ave | | 21 | A2 |
| W Ellen St | | 21 | B2 |
| S Elliott Ave | | 57 | C2 |
| S Ellis Ave | | | |
| | (2600–3961) | 14 | A2/B2/C2 |
| | (3962–5149) | 17 | A1/B1/C1 |
| | (5150–6399) | 19 | A1/B1/C1 |
| | (6400–9299) | 57 | A2/B2/C2 |
| | (9700–13299) | 59 | A2/B2/C2 |
| Elm Ave | | 55 | B1 |
| Elm Cir | | 55 | A2 |
| Elm Dr | | | |
| | (7900–8099) | 47 | A1 |
| | (12000–12099) | 56 | C3 |
| Elm Ln | | 45 | A2 |
| Elm St | | | |
| | (4800–5199) | 46 | A3 |
| | (6300–6499) | 45 | A2 |
| | (12500–12899) | 56 | C3 |
| Elm St * | | | |
| | (1–1499) | 45 | B1/B2 |
| E Elm St | | 32 | B1 |
| W Elm St | | | |
| | (1–117) | 32 | B1 |
| | (118–699) | 31 | B1/B2 |
| Elm Ter | | 46 | A3 |
| W Elmdale Ave | | 37 | A1/A2 |
| W Elmgrove Dr | | 47 | B1/C1 |
| Elmore St | | 45 | A1/B1 |
| Elmwood Ave | | 33 | A2 |
| Elmwood St | | 46 | A3 |
| S Elsdon Ave | | 54 | A3 |
| N Elston Ave | | | |
| | (800–1629) | 22 | — |
| | (1630–2072) | 29 | B1/C1 |
| | (2073–2733) | 28 | A1/B2 |
| | (2734–2905) | 42 | C1 |
| | (2906–3755) | 41 | — |
| | (3756–5279) | 48 | A3/A4/B4 |
| | (5226–5815) | 46 | C3 |
| | (5816–6199) | 45 | C2 |
| S Elsworth Dr | | | |
| | (5030–5099) | 16 | C1 |
| | (5100–5150) | 18 | A2 |
| S Emerald Ave | | | |
| | (2400–2499) | 52 | A4 |
| | (2500–3499) | 13 | A1/B1/C1 |
| | (3950–5149) | 15 | A1/B1 |
| | (5150–9449) | 57 | A1/B1/C1 |
| | (9450–12999) | 59 | A1/B1/C1 |
| S Emerald Dr | | 57 | A1 |
| W Emerald Way | | 55 | C2 |
| N Emmett St | | 27 | A1 |
| W End Ave | | 49 | B2 |
| Enfield Ave | | 46 | A3 |
| W Enger Ln | | 47 | B1 |
| W Engle Rd | | 55 | C2 |
| W Englewood Ave | | 57 | A1 |
| W Eric St | | 24 | A2 |
| E Erie St | | | |
| | (1–114) | 2 | A2 |
| | (115–499) | 3 | B1/B2 |
| N Erie St | | 47 | C1 |
| W Erie St | | | |
| | (1–375) | 2 | A1/A2 |
| | (376–864) | 1 | A1/A2/B1 |
| | (865–1649) | 24 | A1/A2 |
| | (1650–2449) | 23 | A1/A2 |
| | (2450–5999) | 49 | B1/B2 |
| N Ernst Ct | | 32 | B1/C1 |
| S Escanaba Ave | | | |
| | (7800–9549) | 58 | B3/C3 |
| | (9550–13299) | 60 | A3/C3 |
| S Esmond St | | 56 | B4 |
| S Essex Ave | | 58 | B3/C3 |

# Street Index

| Street | Range | Page | Grid |
|---|---|---|---|
| W Estes Ave | | | |
| | (1300–2029) | 34 | B1/B2 |
| | (2030–3598) | 33 | B1/B2 |
| | (3800–5199) | 46 | B3/B4 |
| | (5824–7599) | 45 | B1/B2 |
| Euclid Ave | | 45 | B1 |
| S Euclid Ave | | | |
| | (6700–9549) | 58 | A3/B3/C3 |
| | (9550–9699) | 60 | A3 |
| W Eugenie St | | 30 | C1/C2 |
| S Evans Ave | | | |
| | (4300–5099) | 16 | B2/C2 |
| | (6100–6349) | 18 | C2 |
| | (6350–9399) | 57 | — |
| | (13000–13499) | 59 | C2 |
| E Evans Ct | | 2 | A2 |
| W Evelyn Ln | | 47 | A1 |
| W Everell Ave | | 45 | C1/C2 |
| S Everett Ave | | 20 | A1/B1 |
| W Evergreen Ave | | | |
| | (200–839) | 31 | B1/B2 |
| | (840–1663) | 22 | B1/B2 |
| | (1664–2199) | 21 | A2/B1/B2 |
| | (2600–3249) | 50 | A3 |
| | (3250–3599) | 49 | A2 |
| | (6800–6899) | 55 | C1 |
| Ewing Ave | | 46 | A4 |
| S Ewing Ave | | | |
| | (9200–9499) | 58 | C3 |
| | (10600–12099) | 60 | B3 |
| S Exchange Ave | | | |
| | (7100–9549) | 58 | B3/C3 |
| | (9550–13299) | 60 | A3/C3 |
| W Exchange Ave | | | |
| | (788–849) | 15 | A1 |
| | (850–1199) | 52 | B4 |
| Executive Ct | | 47 | A1 |

**F**

| Street | Range | Page | Grid |
|---|---|---|---|
| W Fair Pl | | 31 | B1 |
| N Fairbanks Ct | | 3 | A1/B1 |
| Fairfax St | | 55 | B2 |
| N Fairfield Ave | | | |
| | (200–1549) | 50 | A3/B3 |
| | (1550–2799) | 27 | A2/B2/C2 |
| | (2900–2999) | 41 | C2 |
| | (4800–4999) | 38 | A2 |
| | (5600–6349) | 35 | A2/B2 |
| | (6350–7499) | 33 | A1/C1 |
| S Fairfield Ave | | | |
| | (900–2199) | 50 | C3 |
| | (4146–5049) | 52 | B3/C3 |
| | (5050–8849) | 54 | A3/B3/C3 |
| | (8850–11500) | 56 | A3/B3 |
| Fairlane Dr | | 55 | A1 |
| Fairview Ave | | | |
| | (5500–5699) | 45 | C1 |
| | (12400–12699) | 56 | C3 |
| S Fairview Ave | | 45 | A1/B1/C1 |
| Fairview Ln | | 46 | B3 |
| Fairway Cir | | 56 | C3 |
| W Fargo Ave | | | |
| | (1300–2065) | 34 | A1/A2 |
| | (2066–3199) | 33 | A1/A2 |
| | (3800–5499) | 46 | B3/B4 |
| | (6900–7750) | 45 | B1/B2 |

| Street | Range | Page | Grid |
|---|---|---|---|
| Farnsworth Dr | | 45 | A1 |
| W Farragut Ave | | | |
| | (1400–1749) | 37 | C1 |
| | (1750–2449) | 36 | B3/B4 |
| | (2450–2999) | 35 | C1/C2 |
| | (5500–5599) | 46 | C3 |
| | (6900–8399) | 47 | A1/A2 |
| S Farragut Dr | | 58 | B3 |
| S Farrar Dr | | 50 | C3 |
| S Farrell St | | 12 | A2 |
| W Farwell Ave | | | |
| | (1100–2024) | 34 | B1/B2 |
| | (2025–2999) | 33 | B1/B2 |
| | (4700–5299) | 46 | B3 |
| | (7200–7399) | 45 | B2 |
| Father Burns Dr | | 55 | B2 |
| S Federal St | | | |
| | (300–449) | 5 | C2 |
| | (450–1259) | 8 | A1/C1 |
| | (1260–2549) | 10 | A2/B2/C2 |
| | (2550–3987) | 13 | A2/B2/C2 |
| | (3988–5168) | 15 | A2/B2/C2 |
| | (5169–5499) | 57 | A1 |
| Feldner Ct | | 55 | C1 |
| N Felton Ct | | 31 | B2 |
| W Ferdinand St | | | |
| | (1600–2398) | 23 | A1/A2 |
| | (3630–5499) | 49 | B1/B2 |
| N Fern Ct | | 30 | C1 |
| Fernald Ave | | 45 | A2 |
| Ferris Ave | | 45 | A2 |
| W Fey Ln | | 55 | C2 |
| N Field Blvd | | 6 | A2/B2 |
| Field Dr | | 45 | A1 |
| Field Plaza Dr | | 9 | C2 |
| S Fielding Ave | | 57 | B1 |
| W Fillmore St | | | |
| | (1300–1599) | 26 | A1 |
| | (1800–2549) | 25 | A1/A2 |
| | (2550–3249) | 50 | C3 |
| | (3250–5933) | 49 | C1/C2 |
| S Financial Pl | | | |
| | (300–499) | 5 | C1 |
| | (600–999) | 8 | A1/B1 |
| Fireside Dr | | 55 | B1 |
| W Fitch Ave | | | |
| | (2400–2999) | 33 | B1/B2 |
| | (3800–5199) | 46 | B3/B4 |
| | (5900–7346) | 45 | B2 |
| Fitzjames Walk | | | |
| | (4000–4019) | 56 | A3 |
| | (4020–4099) | 55 | A2 |
| S Flambeau Dr | | 55 | C1 |
| W Fletcher Ave | | | |
| | (700–819) | 44 | C1 |
| | (820–999) | 43 | B2 |
| W Fletcher St | | | |
| | (1200–1649) | 43 | B1 |
| | (1650–2449) | 42 | C1/C2 |
| | (2450–3099) | 41 | B1/B2 |
| | (4100–5399) | 48 | B3/B4 |
| | (6000–7999) | 47 | B1/B2 |
| Floral Ave | | 46 | A3 |
| Florence Ave | | 33 | A2 |
| W Florence St | | 56 | C4 |

| Street | Range | Page | Grid |
|---|---|---|---|
| W Flournoy St | | | |
| | (1205–1669) | 26 | A1 |
| | (1670–2538) | 25 | A1/A2 |
| | (2539–3249) | 50 | B3 |
| | (3250–5599) | 49 | C1/C2 |
| S Ford Ave | | 26 | C2 |
| W Ford City Dr | | | |
| | (4000–4045) | 54 | C3 |
| | (4046–4799) | 53 | C2 |
| E Foreman Dr | | 60 | A3 |
| Forest Ave | | 47 | C1 |
| S Forest Ave | | | |
| | (9100–9449) | 57 | C1 |
| | (9450–13499) | 59 | A2/B2/C2 |
| Forest Ln | | 55 | B1 |
| N Forest Glen Ave | | 46 | C3 |
| W Forest Preserve Dr | | 47 | A2/B1/B2 |
| Forest View Ave | | 59 | C1 |
| | (2400–2699) | 47 | C1 |
| W Forest View Ln | | 45 | B2 |
| N Forestview Ave | | 47 | A1 |
| Forestview Rd | | 46 | A4 |
| S Forrestville Ave | | | |
| | (4300–5099) | 16 | B2/C2 |
| | (11100–13434) | 59 | B2/C2 |
| W Foster | | 47 | A1 |
| W Foster Ave | | | |
| | (800–1749) | 37 | C1/C2 |
| | (1750–2499) | 36 | C1/C2 |
| | (2500–3215) | 35 | C1/C2 |
| | (3216–3599) | 38 | A1 |
| | (3601–5720) | 48 | A3/A4 |
| | (5721–8799) | 47 | A1/A2 |
| W Foster Dr | | 37 | C2 |
| W Foster Pl | | 47 | A2 |
| Foxfire Dr | | 53 | C1 |
| Foxwoods Ct | | 55 | B2 |
| Foxwoods Dr | | 55 | B2 |
| Frances Pky | | 45 | C1 |
| W Francis Pl | | 27 | B2 |
| N Francisco Ave | | | |
| | (1–1199) | 50 | A3/B3 |
| | (1600–2749) | 27 | A1/B1/C1 |
| | (2750–3949) | 41 | A1/B1/C1 |
| | (3950–5163) | 38 | A1/B1/C1 |
| | (5164–6349) | 35 | A1/B1/C1 |
| | (6350–7599) | 33 | A1/B1/C1 |
| S Francisco Ave | | | |
| | (1–1199) | 50 | B3/C3 |
| | (2400–4699) | 52 | A3/B3/C3 |
| | (5100–8849) | 54 | A3/B3/C3 |
| | (8850–12898) | 56 | A3/B3/C3 |
| Frank Pky | | 47 | A1 |
| Franklin Ave | | 55 | A2 |
| W Franklin Blvd | | | |
| | (3000–3257) | 50 | B3 |
| | (3231–3628) | 49 | B2 |
| N Franklin St | | | |
| | (1–248) | 5 | A1/B1 |
| | (219–815) | 2 | A1/B1/C1 |
| | (816–1125) | 31 | B2/C2 |
| S Franklin St | | | |
| | (1–399) | 5 | B1/C1 |
| | (400–599) | 7 | A2 |
| N Franks Ave | | 45 | B2 |

| Street | Range | Page | Grid |
|---|---|---|---|
| N Fremont St | | | |
| | (1500–1599) | 22 | A2 |
| | (1700–3549) | 29 | B2/C2 |
| | (3550–3964) | 43 | A2 |
| | (3965–3999) | 40 | C2 |
| S Front Ave | | 59 | B2 |
| Frontage Rd | | 46 | A3/B3 |
| E Frontage Rd | | 46 | A3 |
| N Frontage Rd | | 46 | B3 |
| W Frontage Rd | | 46 | A3 |
| S Frontenac Ave | | 57 | A1 |
| N Frontier Ave | | | |
| | (1500–1599) | 31 | A1 |
| | (3900–3999) | 40 | C2 |
| W Fry St | | 22 | C1/C2 |
| W Fuller St | | 12 | A1 |
| W Fullerton Ave | | | |
| | (1–823) | 30 | A2/B1/B2 |
| | (824–1676) | 29 | B1/B2 |
| | (1677–2499) | 28 | B1/B2 |
| | (2477–3599) | 27 | B1/B2 |
| | (3600–5865) | 48 | C3/C4 |
| | (5866–8299) | 47 | C1/C2 |
| W Fulton Blvd | | 49 | B2 |
| W Fulton St | | | |
| | (500–864) | 1 | C1/C2 |
| | (865–1649) | 24 | B1/B2 |
| | (1650–2524) | 23 | B1/B2 |
| | (2525–3199) | 50 | B3 |
| | (3800–5933) | 49 | B1/B2 |

**G**

| Street | Range | Page | Grid |
|---|---|---|---|
| W Gale St | | 48 | A3 |
| Galitz St | | 46 | A3 |
| Garden St | | 45 | B1 |
| E Garfield Blvd | | 18 | A2/B1/B2 |
| W Garfield Blvd | | | |
| | (1–99) | 18 | A1/B1 |
| | (100–799) | 57 | A1 |
| | (801–4655) | 54 | A3/A4 |
| Garfield Sq | | 49 | B2 |
| N Garland Ct | | | |
| | (1–261) | 5 | A2/B2 |
| | (262–299) | 2 | C2 |
| N Garvey Ct | | | |
| | (200–260) | 5 | A2 |
| | (261–299) | 2 | C2 |
| W Gaslight Square Dr | | 56 | C3 |
| N Geneva Ter | | 30 | A1/B1 |
| S Genoa Ave | | | |
| | (8700–8999) | 57 | C1 |
| | (9200–9999) | 56 | A4 |
| W George St | | | |
| | (800–849) | 44 | C1 |
| | (850–1599) | 43 | C1/C2 |
| | (1900–2449) | 42 | C1/C2 |
| | (2450–3399) | 41 | C1/C2 |
| | (3600–5815) | 48 | B3/B4/C4 |
| | (5816–7799) | 47 | B1/B2 |
| Georgia Ave | | 55 | B2 |
| Georgia Dr | | | |
| | (6900–7099) | 45 | A2 |
| | (10700–10899) | 55 | B2 |
| Georgiana Ave | | 45 | A2 |

| Street | Page | Grid |
|---|---|---|
| W Germania Pl | 32 | A1 |
| W Gettysburg St | 48 | A3 |
| W Giddings St | | |
| (2000–2399) | 39 | B1 |
| (2700–2940) | 38 | B1/B2 |
| (3700–5749) | 48 | A3/A4 |
| (5750–8299) | 47 | A1/A2 |
| S Gilbert Ct | 57 | C1 |
| S Giles Ave | 14 | B1/C1 |
| Gillick St | 45 | B1 |
| S Givins Ct | 57 | C1 |
| W Gladys Ave | | |
| (700–799) | 4 | C1 |
| (1000–1240) | 24 | C2 |
| (1241–2433) | 23 | C1 |
| (2600–2799) | 50 | B3 |
| (3300–5599) | 49 | B1/B2 |
| Glen Dr | 56 | C3 |
| Glenlake Ave | 45 | C1 |
| W Glenlake Ave | | |
| (900–1799) | 37 | A1/A2 |
| (2300–2414) | 36 | A1 |
| (2415–2960) | 35 | A1/A2 |
| (3300–4799) | 46 | C3/C4 |
| (7727–7820) | 45 | C1 |
| S Glenroy Ave | 56 | B4 |
| N Glenwood Ave | | |
| (4900–5165) | 40 | A1 |
| (5166–6363) | 37 | A1/B1/C1 |
| (6364–7199) | 34 | B2/C2 |
| E Goethe St | 32 | B1 |
| W Goethe St | | |
| (1–116) | 32 | B1 |
| (117–799) | 31 | B1/B2 |
| S Golf Dr | 49 | B1 |
| W Goodman St | 48 | A3 |
| W Gordon Ter | 40 | C2 |
| W Governors Pky | 49 | B2 |
| N Grace Ave | 45 | A1/B1 |
| S Grace Ave | 45 | C1 |
| W Grace St | | |
| (600–849) | 44 | A1 |
| (850–1614) | 43 | A1/A2 |
| (1615–2499) | 42 | A1/A2 |
| (2800–3599) | 41 | A1/B1 |
| (3600–5849) | 48 | B3/B4 |
| (5850–8399) | 47 | B1/B2 |
| S Grady Ct | 12 | A1 |
| E Grand Ave | | |
| (1–114) | 2 | B2 |
| (115–1001) | 3 | B1/B2 |
| W Grand Ave | | |
| (1–385) | 2 | B1/B2 |
| (386–865) | 1 | B1/B2 |
| (866–1664) | 24 | A1/A2 |
| (1665–2465) | 23 | A1/A2 |
| (2466–3237) | 50 | A3/B3 |
| (3238–4449) | 49 | A2 |
| (4450–5864) | 48 | C3 |
| (5865–8699) | 47 | C1/C2 |
| Grand Blvd | 45 | B1 |
| Grand Ct | 45 | A1 |
| N Grand St | 45 | A1 |
| Grant Pl | 45 | B1 |
| W Grant Pl | 30 | B1 |
| Grant St | 56 | B3 |
| Granville Ave | 45 | C1 |
| W Granville Ave | | |
| (900–1767) | 37 | A1/A2 |
| (1768–2415) | 36 | A1/A2 |
| (2416–3199) | 35 | A1/A2 |
| (3400–4399) | 46 | C3/C4 |
| S Gratten Ave | 12 | A2 |
| N Green St | | |
| (1–249) | 4 | A1/B1 |
| (250–831) | 1 | A1/B1/C1 |
| S Green St | | |
| (1–499) | 4 | B1/C1 |
| (2401–2529) | 52 | A4 |
| (2600–3299) | 12 | A2/B2 |
| (5200–5949) | 54 | A4 |
| (5950–9449) | 57 | A1/B1/C1 |
| (9450–12999) | 59 | A1/B1/C1 |
| S Green Bay Ave | | |
| (8300–9199) | 58 | C3 |
| (10300–13499) | 60 | A3/B3/C3 |
| Greendale Ave | 45 | A1 |
| W Greenleaf Ave | | |
| (1200–2024) | 34 | B1/B2 |
| (2025–2999) | 33 | B1/B2 |
| (3300–4899) | 46 | A4/B3/B4 |
| (5800–8699) | 45 | A2/B2 |
| Greenleaf St | | |
| (4800–5499) | 46 | A3 |
| (7200–7899) | 45 | A1/A2 |
| N Greenview Ave | | |
| (800–1599) | 22 | A1/B1/C1 |
| (2230–2773) | 29 | A1/B1 |
| (2774–3950) | 43 | A1/B1/C1 |
| (3951–5964) | 40 | B1/C1 |
| (5965–6364) | 37 | A1 |
| (6365–7499) | 34 | A2/B2/C2 |
| Greenview Passage | 29 | A1 |
| N Greenwood Ave | | |
| (4800–4999) | 47 | A1 |
| (8200–8906) | 45 | A1 |
| S Greenwood Ave | | |
| (1–4249) | 45 | A1/B1/C1 |
| (4250–5149) | 17 | B1/C1 |
| (5150–6319) | 19 | A1/B1/C1 |
| (6320–9399) | 57 | A2/B2/C2 |
| (9500–12827) | 56 | A4/C3 |
| (13000–13399) | 59 | C1 |
| Greenwood Ter | 47 | C1 |
| Gregory St | 56 | C3 |
| W Gregory St | | |
| (1400–1749) | 37 | B1 |
| (1750–3099) | 35 | B1/B2 |
| (4827–4869) | 46 | C3 |
| (6229–9858) | 45 | C1/C2 |
| W Grennan Pl | 45 | A1/A2 |
| W Grenshaw Ave | 49 | C2 |
| W Grenshaw St | | |
| (536–599) | 7 | C1 |
| (1300–1399) | 26 | B1 |
| (1800–2499) | 25 | A1/B1/B2 |
| (3300–4599) | 49 | C2 |
| N Gresham Ave | 48 | B4 |
| Grey Ave | 33 | A1 |
| Griffith Ct | 55 | C1 |
| W Gross Point Rd | | |
| (6000–7724) | 45 | A2/B2 |
| (7725–8872) | 46 | A3 |
| Grove Ave | 45 | C1 |
| S Grove Ave | 10 | B1/C1 |
| Grove Ct | 45 | A2 |
| Grove St | 47 | C1 |
| S Grove St | 12 | A1/A2 |
| E Groveland Park | 14 | B2 |
| W Grover St | 48 | A3 |
| Gruenwald St | 56 | C3 |
| S Gullikson Rd | 53 | B1 |
| W Gunnison St | | |
| (754–1231) | 40 | A1/A2 |
| (2400–2499) | 39 | A1 |
| (2500–3099) | 38 | A1/A2 |
| (4430–5749) | 48 | A3 |
| (5750–8399) | 47 | A1/A2 |

## H

| Street | Page | Grid |
|---|---|---|
| E Haddock Pl | 5 | A2 |
| W Haddock Pl | 5 | A1/A2 |
| W Haddon Ave | | |
| (1500–1664) | 22 | B1 |
| (1665–2449) | 21 | B1/B2 |
| (2450–3309) | 50 | A3 |
| (3310–5599) | 49 | A1/A2 |
| W Haft St | 45 | C2 |
| W Haines St | 31 | B1 |
| S Hale Ave | 56 | B4/C4 |
| Hallberg Ln | 45 | A1 |
| S Halsted Pky | | |
| (900–999) | 54 | B4 |
| (6198–6499) | 57 | A1 |
| N Halsted St | | |
| (1–258) | 4 | A1/B1 |
| (259–844) | 1 | A1/B1/C1 |
| (845–1632) | 31 | A1/B1/C1 |
| (1629–2749) | 30 | A1/B1/C1 |
| (2750–3799) | 44 | A1/B1/C1 |
| S Halsted St | | |
| (1–447) | 4 | B1/C1 |
| (448–2249) | 26 | A2/B2/C2 |
| (2230–2568) | 52 | A4 |
| (2558–3924) | 13 | A1/B1/C1 |
| (3925–5124) | 15 | A1/B1/C1 |
| (5125–9449) | 57 | A1/B1/C1 |
| (9450–13599) | 59 | A1/B1/C1 |
| N Hamilton Ave | | |
| (2200–2398) | 28 | B1 |
| (3000–3949) | 42 | A1/B1/C1 |
| (3950–4999) | 39 | A1/B1 |
| (6100–6199) | 36 | A1 |
| (6400–7399) | 33 | A2/B2/C2 |
| S Hamilton Ave | | |
| (200–299) | 23 | C1 |
| (1000–1799) | 25 | A1/C1 |
| (3200–3947) | 52 | A3/B3 |
| (5300–8860) | 54 | A3/B3/C3 |
| (8861–10699) | 56 | A4/B4 |
| Hamilton Dr | | |
| (6951–7099) | 45 | A3 |
| (8500–8563) | 46 | A3 |
| S Hamlet Ave | 56 | B4 |
| N Hamlin Ave | | |
| (300–1549) | 49 | A2/B2 |
| (1550–5115) | 48 | A4/B4/C4 |
| (6100–8814) | 46 | A4/B4/C4 |
| S Hamlin Ave | | |
| (8815–12299) | 56 | A3/B3/C3 |
| (1400–2249) | 49 | C2 |
| (2250–4899) | 51 | A3/B3/C3 |
| (5100–8699) | 54 | A3/B3/C3 |
| S Hamlin Blvd | 49 | B2 |
| N Hamlin Blvd | 49 | B2 |
| S Hamlin Ct | 56 | C3 |
| N Hampden Ct | | |
| (2600–2749) | 30 | A1 |
| (2750–2799) | 44 | C1 |
| Hanover St | | |
| (7100–7199) | 55 | A1 |
| (7200–7217) | 53 | A1 |
| Hansen Pl | 45 | B1 |
| S Harbor Ave | 58 | C3 |
| N Harbor Dr | 6 | A2 |
| S Harbor Dr | 6 | B2 |
| N Harbour Dr | 6 | B2 |
| N Harding Ave | | |
| (236–1649) | 49 | A2/B2 |
| (1650–5099) | 48 | A4/B4/C4 |
| (6000–8799) | 46 | A4/B4/C4 |
| S Harding Ave | | |
| (1200–2199) | 49 | C2 |
| (2324–4899) | 51 | A2/C2 |
| (5100–5349) | 53 | A2 |
| (5350–7221) | 54 | A3/B3 |
| (9100–12499) | 56 | A3/B3/C3 |
| N Harlem Ave | | |
| (1700–5410) | 47 | A2/B2/C2 |
| (5401–8899) | 45 | A2/B2/C2 |
| S Harlem Ave | | |
| (5200–8805) | 53 | A1/B1/C1 |
| (8806–12819) | 55 | A1/B1/C1 |
| S Harlem Dr | 53 | A1 |
| Harms Rd | 46 | A3 |
| Harnew Rd E | 55 | A2 |
| Harnew Rd S | 55 | B2 |
| Harnew Rd W | 55 | A2 |
| S Harper Ave | | |
| (5100–5149) | 17 | C2 |
| (5150–6349) | 19 | A2/B2/C2 |
| (6350–9427) | 57 | A2/B2/C2 |
| (9630–10499) | 59 | A2 |
| Harper Ct | 19 | B2 |
| W Harrington | 46 | C4 |
| S Harrison Ave | 45 | B1 |
| Harrison St | 45 | B1 |
| E Harrison St | 8 | A2 |
| W Harrison St | | |
| (1–249) | 8 | A1/A2 |
| (225–714) | 7 | A1/A2 |
| (715–1664) | 26 | A1/A2 |
| (1665–2511) | 25 | A1/A2 |
| (2512–3249) | 50 | B3 |
| (3250–5599) | 49 | B1/B2 |
| S Harry J Rogowski Dr | 56 | B3/C3 |
| N Hart St | 23 | B2 |
| Hartford St | 55 | A1 |
| N Hartland Ct | 23 | A2 |

| Street | Page | Grid |
|---|---|---|
| Hartrey Ave | 33 | A1 |
| W Harts Rd | 45 | B2 |
| S Hartwell Ave | 57 | A1 |
| S Harvard Ave | | |
| (6300–9472) | 57 | A1/B1/C1 |
| (9473–9499) | 55 | A1 |
| (9500–12699) | 59 | A1/B1/C1 |
| Harvard St | 45 | A2 |
| Harvard Ter | 46 | A3/A4 |
| Harwood St | 47 | A2 |
| Hastings St | 45 | B1 |
| W Hastings St | | |
| (1200–1724) | 26 | B1 |
| (1725–2199) | 25 | B1/B2 |
| N Haussen St | 48 | B4 |
| W Hawthorne Pl | 44 | B1 |
| W Hayes Ave | 45 | B2 |
| E Hayes Dr | 20 | C1/C2 |
| W Hayford St | 54 | C3 |
| Haymond Ave | 47 | C1 |
| S Hayne Ave | | |
| (3900–3931) | 52 | B3 |
| (6100–6199) | 54 | B3 |
| S Haynes Ct | 12 | A1/A2 |
| N Hazel St | 40 | B2/C2 |
| S Heath Ave | 25 | B1 |
| W Henderson St | | |
| (1200–1599) | 43 | B1 |
| (1700–2862) | 42 | B2 |
| (2863–3599) | 41 | B1 |
| (4100–5849) | 48 | B3/B4 |
| (5850–7046) | 47 | B2 |
| Hennings Ct | 45 | A2 |
| W Henry Ct | 27 | B2 |
| W Hermione St | 45 | C2 |
| N Hermitage Ave | | |
| (1–820) | 23 | A2/B2 |
| (821–1649) | 21 | B2/C2 |
| (1650–1949) | 28 | C2 |
| (1950–3949) | 42 | A2/B2 |
| (3950–5032) | 39 | A2/B2/C2 |
| (5600–6368) | 37 | A1/B1 |
| (6369–7599) | 34 | A1/C1 |
| S Hermitage Ave | | |
| (300–399) | 23 | C2 |
| (698–1131) | 25 | A2 |
| (1132–5049) | 52 | B4/C4 |
| (5050–8849) | 54 | A4/B4/C4 |
| (8850–9099) | 56 | A4 |
| S Hermitage St | 52 | B4 |
| S Hermosa Ave | 56 | B4 |
| Herrick Ave | 47 | C1 |
| N Hessing St | 47 | C1 |
| N Hiawatha Ave | | |
| (6000–6765) | 46 | B3/C3 |
| (6764–7129) | 45 | B2 |
| N Hickory Ave | 22 | B2 |
| Higgins Rd | 45 | C1/C2 |
| W Higgins Rd | | |
| (5400–5707) | 48 | A3 |
| (5708–6815) | 47 | A2 |
| (6816–7899) | 45 | C1/C2 |
| N High Bridge Ln | 46 | C4 |
| Highland Ave | 56 | C3 |
| W Highland Ave | | |
| (1400–1766) | 37 | A1 |
| (1767–4363) | 36 | A1 |
| (4364–7288) | 45 | B2/C2 |
| Highland Rd | 55 | B1 |
| W Hill St | 31 | B2 |
| S Hillock Ave | | |
| (2500–2555) | 52 | A4 |
| (2556–2899) | 12 | A1/A2 |
| Hilton Dr | 55 | A2 |
| W Hirsch Dr | 50 | A3 |
| W Hirsch St | | |
| (2200–2464) | 21 | B1 |
| (2465–3249) | 50 | A3 |
| (3250–5899) | 49 | A1/A3 |
| W Hobart Ave | 45 | C2 |
| W Hobbie St | 31 | B1 |
| N Hobson Ave | 28 | B2 |
| S Hoey St | 12 | A2 |
| Hoffman St | 46 | A3 |
| W Holbrook St | 45 | C2 |
| N Holden Ct | 5 | B2 |
| S Holden Ct | 8 | A2/B2/C2 |
| S Holiday Dr | 55 | C2 |
| S Holland Rd | 57 | C1 |
| Hollett Dr | 54 | B3 |
| N Holly Ave | 28 | B2 |
| W Hollywood Ave | | |
| (1000–2415) | 37 | B1/B2 |
| (2416–3258) | 35 | B1/B2 |
| (3259–4499) | 46 | C3/C4 |
| S Holmberg Ct | 55 | C2 |
| W Holmberg Ct | 55 | C2 |
| N Homan Ave | | |
| (1–1565) | 49 | A2/B2 |
| (1566–1599) | 48 | C4 |
| S Homan Ave | | |
| (1–2249) | 49 | B2/C2 |
| (2250–4699) | 51 | A2/B2/C2 |
| (4400–4999) | 52 | B2/C2 |
| (5000–8499) | 54 | A3/B3/C3 |
| (9100–12807) | 56 | A3/B3/C3 |
| Home Ave | 55 | C1 |
| W Homer St | | |
| (1500–2049) | 29 | B1/C1 |
| (2050–2465) | 28 | C1 |
| (2466–3199) | 27 | B2/C1 |
| (4500–5199) | 48 | C3 |
| Homestead Ln | 55 | A1 |
| Hometown Ln | 53 | C2 |
| S Homewood Ave | 56 | B4/C4 |
| N Honore St | | |
| (900–1649) | 21 | A2/B2 |
| (1650–2299) | 28 | B2/C2 |
| (2900–3199) | 42 | B2/C2 |
| (4200–4399) | 39 | B2 |
| (5200–6764) | 36 | C2 |
| (6765–7399) | 34 | A1 |
| S Honore St | | |
| (1–299) | 23 | C2 |
| (500–599) | 25 | A2 |
| (3500–4999) | 52 | B3/B4/C4 |
| (5100–8899) | 54 | A4/B4/C4 |
| (11800–12899) | 56 | C4 |
| W Hood Ave | | |
| (1200–1599) | 37 | A1/A2 |
| (1800–2129) | 36 | A1/A2 |
| (3000–3145) | 35 | A1 |
| (7100–7799) | 45 | C1/C2 |
| N Hooker St | | |
| (1000–1129) | 31 | B1 |
| (1130–1505) | 22 | A2/B2 |
| W Hopkins Pl | 56 | A4 |
| Horner Park | 38 | C2 |
| W Hortense Ave | 45 | C1/C2 |
| S Houston Ave | | |
| (8000–9549) | 58 | B3/C3 |
| (9550–13499) | 60 | A3/C3 |
| W Howard St | | |
| (317–2029) | 34 | A1/A2 |
| (2031–3249) | 33 | A1/A2 |
| (3226–5799) | 46 | A3/A4 |
| (5799–7757) | 45 | A1/A2 |
| W Howdy Ln | 55 | C2 |
| N Howe St | | |
| (1100–1899) | 31 | B1 |
| (1900–2099) | 30 | B1 |
| W Howland Ave | 54 | C4 |
| S Hoxie Ave | 60 | A3/B3/C3 |
| N Hoyne Ave | | |
| (1–814) | 23 | A1/B1 |
| (815–1612) | 21 | A1/B1/C1 |
| (1613–2699) | 28 | B1/C1 |
| (2700–3949) | 42 | A1/B1/C1 |
| (3950–4999) | 39 | A1/B1/C1 |
| (5200–6299) | 36 | A1/C1 |
| (6300–7599) | 33 | A2/C2 |
| S Hoyne Ave | | |
| (0–399) | 23 | B1/C1 |
| (500–2214) | 25 | A1/B1/C1 |
| (2215–5029) | 52 | A3/B3/C3 |
| (5030–5064) | 50 | C3 |
| (5065–8599) | 54 | A3/B3/C4 |
| (8900–12828) | 56 | A4/B4/C4 |
| N Hoyne Av Dr | | |
| (1525–1565) | 50 | A3 |
| (1566–1599) | 27 | C1 |
| S Hoyt Ave | 52 | A3 |
| E Hubbard St | 2 | B2 |
| W Hubbard St | | |
| (1–385) | 2 | B1/B2 |
| (386–853) | 1 | B1 |
| (854–1674) | 24 | B1/B2 |
| (1643–2499) | 23 | A2/B1/B2 |
| (4700–4999) | 49 | B2 |
| N Hudson Ave | | |
| (654–837) | 1 | A2 |
| (838–1649) | 31 | A2/B2/C2 |
| (1650–2199) | 30 | B1/C1 |
| (3130–3199) | 44 | B1 |
| N Huguelet Pl | 32 | B1 |
| Hull St | 46 | A3/A4 |
| N Humboldt Blvd | 27 | B1/C1 |
| N Humboldt Dr | 50 | A3 |
| W Hunt Ave | 56 | A4 |
| W Huntington St | 45 | C2 |
| W Hurlbut St | 45 | C2 |
| E Huron St | | |
| (1–114) | 2 | A2 |
| (115–499) | 3 | B1/B2 |
| W Huron St | | |
| (1–367) | 2 | A1/A2 |
| (368–880) | 1 | A1/A2 |
| (881–1649) | 24 | A1/A2 |
| (1650–2449) | 23 | A1/A2 |
| (2450–3264) | 50 | B3 |
| (3265–5999) | 49 | B1/B2 |
| W Hutchinson St | | |
| (642–2049) | 40 | C1/C2 |
| (2050–2449) | 39 | C1 |
| (2450–3399) | 38 | C1/C2 |
| (4400–5599) | 48 | A3/A4 |
| W Hyacinth St | 45 | C2 |
| E Hyde Park Blvd | | |
| (1125–1699) | 17 | C1/C2 |
| (5300–5699) | 20 | A1 |
| S Hyde Park Blvd | 20 | B1 |
| Hyland Pl | 55 | B1 |

**I**

| Street | Page | Grid |
|---|---|---|
| E IBM Plz | 2 | C2 |
| W Ibsen St | 45 | B1/B2 |
| E Illinois St | | |
| (1–114) | 2 | B2 |
| (115–699) | 3 | B1/B2 |
| W Illinois St | | |
| (1–385) | 2 | B1/B2 |
| (386–498) | 1 | B2 |
| W Imlay Ave | 45 | B2 |
| Imperial St | 45 | B1 |
| S Independence Blvd | 49 | B2/C2 |
| N Indian Rd | | |
| (5700–5999) | 46 | C3 |
| (6100–6399) | 45 | C2 |
| Indian Boundary Rd | 47 | C1 |
| S Indiana Ave | | |
| (1200–1249) | 9 | C1 |
| (1250–2549) | 11 | A1/B1/C1 |
| (2550–3949) | 14 | A1/B1/C1 |
| (3950–5156) | 16 | A1/B1/C1 |
| (5157–6626) | 18 | A1/B1/C1 |
| (6627–9449) | 57 | A1/B1/C1 |
| (9450–13530) | 59 | — |
| Indiana Ct | 59 | C2 |
| S Indianapolis Ave | 58 | A3 |
| (10000–10598) | 60 | A3/A4 |
| S Indianapolis Blvd | 60 | A3/A4 |
| Industrial Dr | 59 | C1 |
| S Ingleside Ave | | |
| (4700–4799) | 17 | B1 |
| (5100–6349) | 19 | A1/B1/C1 |
| (6350–8699) | 57 | A2/B2/C2 |
| (9740–13199) | 59 | A2/C2 |
| W Institute Pl | 31 | C2 |
| N Ionia Ave | | |
| (5699–6843) | 46 | B3/C3 |
| (6844–7199) | 45 | B2 |
| W Iowa St | | |
| (513–537) | 31 | C1 |
| (1800–2449) | 21 | C1/C2 |
| (2450–2799) | 50 | A3 |
| (3330–5999) | 49 | A1/A2 |
| N Irene Ave | 41 | B1 |
| S Iron St | 12 | B1/C1 |

| Street | Page | Grid |
|---|---|---|
| Irving Ave | | |
| (3900–4010) | 52 | B3 |
| (11900–12845) | 56 | C4 |
| W Irving Park Rd | | |
| (500–1627) | 40 | C1/C2 |
| (1628–2449) | 39 | C1/C2 |
| (2450–3599) | 38 | C1/C2 |
| (3600–5764) | 48 | A3/A4/B3 |
| (5765–8399) | 47 | B1/B2 |
| Isabel St | 46 | A4 |
| W Isham St | 45 | B1 |

## J

| Street | Page | Grid |
|---|---|---|
| E Jackson Blvd | 5 | C2 |
| W Jackson Blvd | | |
| (1–371) | 5 | C1/C2 |
| (372–914) | 4 | C1/C2 |
| (915–1649) | 24 | C1/C2 |
| (1650–2511) | 23 | C1/C2 |
| (2512–3239) | 50 | B3 |
| (3240–5998) | 49 | B1/B2 |
| E Jackson Dr | 6 | C1 |
| James Dr | 46 | A3 |
| S James Dr | 55 | C2 |
| James Pl | 55 | A1 |
| W James St | 54 | A3/A4 |
| Janet Ln | 55 | A1 |
| N Janssen Ave | | |
| (2200–2749) | 29 | A1/B1 |
| (2750–3949) | 43 | A1/B1 |
| (3950–4999) | 40 | A1 |
| Jarlath Ave | 46 | B3 |
| W Jarlath St | | |
| (2600–3199) | 33 | A1 |
| (3800–4899) | 46 | B3/B4 |
| (7701–7728) | 45 | B1 |
| W Jarvis Ave | | |
| (1200–2065) | 34 | A1/A2 |
| (2066–3199) | 33 | A1/A2 |
| (3500–5699) | 46 | B3/B4 |
| (5700–7729) | 45 | B1/B2 |
| S Jasper Pl | 12 | C1 |
| N Jean Ave | | |
| (6700–6881) | 45 | B2 |
| (6882–6899) | 46 | B3 |
| W Jean St | 55 | C2 |
| N Jefferson St | | |
| (1–249) | 4 | A1/B1 |
| (250–499) | 1 | B1/C1 |
| S Jefferson St | | |
| (1–426) | 4 | B1/C1 |
| (427–1231) | 7 | A1/B1/C1 |
| (1220–2199) | 10 | A1/B1 |
| S Jeffery Ave | | |
| (6600–6749) | 58 | A3 |
| (6750–13499) | 60 | B3/C3 |
| S Jeffery Blvd | | |
| (6800–9512) | 58 | B3/C3 |
| (9513–9899) | 60 | A3 |
| S Jensen Blvd | 49 | B1 |
| Jerome Ave | 46 | B3/B4 |
| W Jerome St | | |
| (2501–3199) | 33 | A1/A2 |
| (7700–7749) | 45 | B1 |
| N Jersey Ave | | |
| (5600–5724) | 35 | B1 |
| (5725–6157) | 46 | C4 |
| N Jessie Ct | 23 | B1 |
| Joalyce Ct | 55 | C2 |
| S Joalyce Dr | 55 | B2/C2 |
| W Jobev Ln | 55 | C2 |
| Jodan Dr | 55 | B2 |
| W Johanna Dr | 45 | A1 |
| N Jones St | 28 | A1 |
| Jonquil Ter | 45 | A1/A2 |
| S Jourdan Ct | 26 | C2 |
| W Joyce Ln | 47 | A2 |
| Joyce Pl | 45 | A1 |
| W Julia Ct | 27 | B2 |
| W Julian St | 21 | A2 |
| Julian Ter | 47 | C1 |
| W Junior Ter | 40 | C2 |
| N Justine St | 24 | B1 |
| S Justine St | | |
| (3300–3449) | 12 | B1 |
| (3450–3499) | 50 | C4 |
| (4500–5049) | 52 | C2 |
| (5050–8899) | 54 | A4/B4/C4 |
| (8900–12899) | 56 | A4/B4/C4 |

## K

| Street | Page | Grid |
|---|---|---|
| W Kamerling Ave | 49 | A1/A2 |
| Kanst Dr | 54 | B3 |
| N Karlov Ave | | |
| (1–1558) | 49 | A2/B2 |
| (1559–50019) | 48 | A4/B4/C4 |
| (5600–8814) | 46 | A4/B4/C4 |
| S Karlov Ave | | |
| (8815–11999) | 55 | A2/B2/C2 |
| (1–2199) | 49 | B2/C2 |
| (2349–5035) | 51 | A2/B2/C2 |
| (5348–8699) | 53 | A2/B2/C2 |
| N Kasson Ave | 48 | A4 |
| S Kathleen Ct | 56 | C3 |
| E Kathleen Dr | 45 | A1 |
| W Kathleen Dr | 45 | A1 |
| Kathleen Ln | 55 | B2 |
| N Kearsarge Ave | 48 | B4 |
| N Keating Ave | | |
| (1400–1649) | 49 | A2 |
| (1650–5199) | 48 | A3/B3/C3 |
| (5800–8699) | 46 | B3/B4/C3 |
| S Keating Ave | | |
| (4200–4999) | 51 | B2/C2 |
| (4400–5049) | 49 | B2/C2 |
| (5050–8699) | 53 | A2/B2/C2 |
| (8800–11099) | 55 | A2/B2 |
| Keating Ln | 53 | C2 |
| N Kedvale Ave | | |
| (800–1599) | 49 | A2/B2 |
| (1600–5099) | 48 | A4/B4/C4 |
| (5600–8799) | 46 | A4/B4/C4 |
| S Kedvale Ave | | |
| (600–1799) | 49 | B2/C2 |
| (2200–5071) | 51 | A2/B2/C2 |
| (5072–8699) | 53 | A2/B2/C2 |
| (9100–12499) | 55 | A2/B2/C2 |
| N Kedzie Ave | | |
| (1–1564) | 50 | A3/B3 |
| (1565–2749) | 27 | A1/B1/C1 |
| (2750–3949) | 41 | A1/B1/C1 |
| (3950–5160) | 38 | A1/B1/C1 |
| (5161–6431) | 35 | A1/C1 |
| (6432–7599) | 33 | A1/B1/C1 |
| S Kedzie Ave | | |
| (1–2249) | 50 | B3/C3 |
| (2250–5037) | 52 | A3/B3/C3 |
| (5038–8849) | 54 | A3/B3/C3 |
| (8850–12799) | 56 | A3/B3/C3 |
| N Kedzie Blvd | 27 | A1/B1 |
| Kedzie St | 45 | A1/A2 |
| S Keefe Ave | 57 | B1 |
| N Keeler Ave | | |
| (1–1649) | 49 | A2/B2 |
| (1650–5199) | 48 | A4/B4/C4 |
| (6000–8825) | 46 | A4/B4/C4 |
| S Keeler Ave | | |
| (1–2249) | 49 | B2/C2 |
| (2250–5024) | 51 | A2/B2/C2 |
| (5025–8726) | 53 | A2/B2/C2 |
| (8727–12699) | 55 | A2/B2/C2 |
| S Keeley St | 12 | A2 |
| N Keene Ave | 46 | C3 |
| Keeney Ct | 45 | A2 |
| Keeney St | | |
| (3600–5749) | 46 | A3/A4 |
| (5750–7999) | 45 | A1/A2 |
| N Kelso Ave | 48 | A4 |
| W Kemper Pl | 30 | B1 |
| N Kenmore Ave | | |
| (1836–2719) | 29 | B2/C2 |
| (2720–3899) | 43 | A2/B2/C2 |
| (4000–5149) | 40 | A2/B2/C2 |
| (5150–6349) | 37 | A2/B2/C2 |
| (6350–6399) | 34 | C2 |
| N Kenneth Ave | | |
| (200–241) | 49 | B2 |
| (1900–5199) | 48 | A3/B3/C3 |
| (5600–8399) | 46 | A3/B3/C3 |
| S Kenneth Ave | | |
| (700–2258) | 49 | C2 |
| (2259–5049) | 51 | A2/C2 |
| (5050–8799) | 53 | A2/B2/C2 |
| (9500–12899) | 55 | A2/B2/C2 |
| S Kenneth Ct | 53 | C2 |
| Kenneth Ter | 46 | A3 |
| N Kennicott Ave | 48 | A4 |
| N Kennison Ave | 48 | A3 |
| N Kenosha Ave | 48 | B4 |
| E Kensington Ave | 59 | B2 |
| Kent Ave | 45 | C1 |
| N Kenton Ave | | |
| (1–1649) | 49 | B2 |
| (1650–5199) | 48 | A3/B3/C3 |
| (5600–8899) | 46 | A3/B3/C3 |
| S Kenton Ave | | |
| (2–2199) | 49 | B2/C2 |
| (4555–8699) | 53 | A2/C2 |
| (9100–11699) | 55 | A2/B2/C2 |
| S Kenton Ct | 53 | C2 |
| N Kentucky Ave | 48 | A3 |
| S Kenwood Ave | | |
| (4700–5149) | 17 | B1/C1 |
| (5150–6349) | 19 | A2/B2/C2 |
| (6350–9499) | 57 | A2/B2/C2 |
| N Keokuk Ave | 48 | A4 |
| N Keota Ave | 46 | B3 |
| N Kerbs Ave | 46 | C3 |
| N Kercheval Ave | 46 | C3 |
| S Kerfoot Ave | 57 | C1 |
| N Kewanee Ave | 48 | A4 |
| N Keystone Ave | | |
| (100–1649) | 49 | A2/B2 |
| (1650–5099) | 48 | A4/B4/C4 |
| (5600–8799) | 46 | A4/B4/C4 |
| N Kilbourn Ave | | |
| (1–1621) | 49 | A2/B2 |
| (1622–5199) | 48 | A3/B3/C3 |
| (5600–8399) | 46 | A3/B3/C3 |
| S Kilbourn Ave | | |
| (1–2199) | 49 | B2/C2 |
| (2700–5049) | 51 | A2/C2 |
| (5050–8899) | 53 | A2/B2/C2 |
| (9100–11699) | 55 | A2/B2 |
| N Kildare Ave | | |
| (2–1649) | 49 | A2/B2 |
| (1650–5199) | 48 | — |
| (5300–8812) | 46 | A4/B4/C4 |
| S Kildare Ave | | |
| (8813–12099) | 55 | A2/B2/C2 |
| (1–2263) | 49 | B2/C2 |
| (2264–5049) | 51 | A2/B2/C2 |
| (5050–8899) | 53 | A2/B2/C2 |
| N Kilpatrick Ave | | |
| (1–1626) | 49 | A2/B2 |
| (1627–4999) | 48 | A3/B3/C3 |
| (5800–8824) | 46 | A3/B3/C3 |
| S Kilpatrick Ave | | |
| (8825–11099) | 55 | A2/B2 |
| (1–5049) | 49 | B2/C2 |
| (4200–4999) | 51 | B2/C2 |
| (5050–8699) | 53 | A2/B2/C2 |
| Kilpatrick Ln | 53 | C2 |
| N Kimball Ave | 48 | A4/B4/C4 |
| (625–2762) | 27 | A1/B1/C1 |
| (2763–3949) | 41 | A1/B1/C1 |
| (3950–5249) | 38 | A1/B1/C1 |
| (5250–8799) | 46 | A4/B4/C4 |
| Kimball Pl | 55 | A2 |
| S Kimbark Ave | | |
| (4737–5149) | 17 | B1/C1 |
| (5150–6349) | 19 | A2/B2/C2 |
| (6350–9399) | 57 | A2/B2/C2 |
| N Kimberly Ave | 48 | A3 |
| (5200–6349) | 18 | A2/B2/C2 |
| (6350–9449) | 57 | A1/B1/C1 |
| N Kingsbury St | | |
| (390–899) | 1 | A2/B2/C2 |
| (900–1301) | 31 | B1 |
| (1302–1649) | 22 | A2/B2 |
| (1650–2099) | 29 | B1/C1/C2 |
| N Kingsdale Ave | 46 | C3 |
| S Kingston Ave | 58 | B3/C3 |
| E Kinzie St | 2 | B2/C2 |

| Street / Range | Page | Grid |
|---|---|---|
| **W Kinzie St** | | |
| (1–374) | 2 | C1/C2 |
| (375–828) | 1 | — |
| (829–1674) | 24 | B1/B2 |
| (1675–2331) | 23 | B1/B2 |
| (3649–5499) | 49 | B1/B2 |
| **N Kinzua Ave** | 46 | B3 |
| **N Kiona Ave** | 48 | A4 |
| **N Kirby Ave** | 46 | C3 |
| **Kirk Dr** | 45 | A1 |
| **Kirk St** | | |
| (3800–5599) | 46 | A3/A4 |
| (6200–7399) | 45 | A2 |
| **S Kirkland Ave** | | |
| (2200–2276) | 49 | C2 |
| (2277–2431) | 51 | A2 |
| (7913–8099) | 53 | C2 |
| **N Kirkwood Ave** | 46 | B3/C3 |
| **Kitty Ave** | 55 | A1/B1 |
| **Klehm Ct** | 46 | A3 |
| **N Knight Ave** | | |
| (4800–5099) | 47 | A1 |
| (8200–8399) | 45 | A1 |
| **N Knight Ave *** | | |
| (1–1199) | 45 | A1/B1 |
| **S Knight Ave** | 45 | B1/C1 |
| **N Knox Ave** | | |
| (2200–4799) | 48 | A3/B3/C3 |
| (5600–8849) | 46 | A3/B3/C3 |
| **S Knox Ave** | | |
| (8850–11699) | 55 | A2/B2 |
| (4200–4999) | 51 | B2/C2 |
| (4400–5049) | 49 | B2/C2 |
| (5050–11599) | 53 | A2/B2/C2 |
| **S Knox Ct** | | |
| (8346–10149) | 53 | C2 |
| (10150–10199) | 55 | A2 |
| **N Kolin Ave** | 49 | A2/B2 |
| **S Kolin Ave** | | |
| (1200–2269) | 49 | C2 |
| (2270–5049) | 51 | A2/C2 |
| (5050–8799) | 53 | A2/B2/C2 |
| (8800–11899) | 55 | A2/B2/C2 |
| **N Kolmar Ave** | | |
| (200–1649) | 49 | A2/B2 |
| (1650–5199) | 48 | A3/B3/C3 |
| (5600–8899) | 46 | A3/B3/C3 |
| **S Kolmar Ave** | | |
| (300–4499) | 49 | B2/C2 |
| (4500–4699) | 51 | C2 |
| (5000–8699) | 53 | A2/B2/C2 |
| (9100–11699) | 55 | A2/B2 |
| **S Komensky Ave** | | |
| (1200–1899) | 49 | C2 |
| (2600–5099) | 51 | A2/B2/C2 |
| (5400–8823) | 53 | A2/B2/C2 |
| (8824–9649) | 55 | A2 |
| (9650–11999) | 56 | A3/B3/C3 |
| **N Kostner Ave** | | |
| (1–1603) | 49 | A2/B2 |
| (1604–5199) | 48 | A3/B3/C4 |
| (5600–8499) | 46 | A3/B3/C3 |
| **S Kostner Ave** | | |
| (1–2299) | 49 | B2/C2 |
| (2300–5049) | 51 | A2/B2/C2 |
| (5050–8799) | 53 | A2/B2/C2 |
| (8793–12699) | 55 | A2/B2/C2 |
| **Kostner Ter** | 46 | A3 |
| **S Kreiter Ave** | 58 | C3 |
| **S Kroll Dr** | 55 | C2 |
| **Krueger St** | 56 | C3 |
| **N Kruger Ave** | 48 | A3 |
| **L** | | |
| **N La Crosse Ave** | | |
| (144–299) | 49 | B2 |
| (1800–5249) | 48 | A3/B3/C3 |
| (5250–7999) | 46 | A3/B3/C3 |
| **S La Crosse Ave** | | |
| (4400–4442) | 49 | B1 |
| (4443–5049) | 51 | C1 |
| (5050–7899) | 53 | A2/B2/C2 |
| (9500–12841) | 55 | A2/B2/C2 |
| **N La Salle Dr** | | |
| (300–821) | 2 | A1/B1/C1 |
| (818–1649) | 31 | A2/B2/C2 |
| (1650–1799) | 30 | C2 |
| **W La Salle Dr** | 30 | C2 |
| **N La Salle St** | | |
| (1–258) | 5 | A1/B1 |
| (259–299) | 2 | C1 |
| **S La Salle St** | | |
| (1–449) | 5 | B1/C1 |
| (450–999) | 8 | A1/B1 |
| (2000–2599) | 10 | B2/C2 |
| (2601–3924) | 13 | A2/B2/C2 |
| (3925–4299) | 15 | A2 |
| (5200–9449) | 57 | A1/B1/C1 |
| (9450–12599) | 59 | A1/B1/C1 |
| **N Lacey Ave** | 46 | C3 |
| **S Lafayette Ave** | | |
| (5500–6199) | 18 | B1/C1 |
| (6500–9449) | 57 | A1/B1/C1 |
| (9450–12399) | 59 | A1/B1/C1 |
| **S Laflin Cir** | 26 | B1 |
| **S Laflin Pl** | 12 | C1 |
| **N Laflin St** | 24 | B1 |
| **S Laflin St** | | |
| (1–399) | 24 | C1 |
| (600–2401) | 26 | A1/B1/C1 |
| (2402–2599) | 50 | C4 |
| (4500–5049) | 52 | C4 |
| (5050–8899) | 54 | A4/B4/C4 |
| (8900–12899) | 56 | A4/B4/C4 |
| **Lahon St** | 45 | A1 |
| **E Lahon St** | 45 | A1 |
| **Lake Ave** | 45 | B1 |
| **E Lake St** | | |
| (1–85) | 5 | A2 |
| (86–399) | 6 | A1 |
| **W Lake St** | | |
| (1–374) | 5 | A1/A2 |
| (375–863) | 4 | A1/A2 |
| (864–1649) | 24 | B1/B2 |
| (1650–2506) | 23 | B1/B2 |
| (2507–3299) | 50 | B3 |
| (3300–5999) | 49 | B1/B2 |
| **Lake Katherine Dr** | 55 | C1 |
| **S Lake Park Ave** | | |
| (2900–3999) | 14 | A2/B2/C2 |
| (4000–5149) | 17 | — |
| (5150–5549) | 19 | A2 |
| (5550–7899) | 58 | B3 |
| **E Lake Shore Dr** | 32 | B2 |
| **N Lake Shore Dr** | | |
| (100–299) | 6 | A2 |
| (300–828) | 3 | A2/B2/C2 |
| (800–1599) | 32 | — |
| (2000–2443) | 30 | A2/B2 |
| (2622–3998) | 44 | —/C2 |
| (3900–5073) | 40 | A2/B2/C2 |
| (5074–5801) | 37 | B2/C2 |
| **S Lake Shore Dr** | | |
| (100–299) | 6 | B2/C2 |
| (300–1299) | 9 | A2/B2/C2 |
| (1300–2568) | 11 | A1/B2/C2 |
| (2444–4110) | 14 | A2/C2 |
| (4111–5164) | 17 | A1/B1/B2 |
| (5165–6381) | 20 | — |
| **W Lakeside Ave** | 40 | B2 |
| **N Lakeview Ave** | | |
| (2400–2749) | 30 | A1 |
| (2750–2799) | 44 | C2 |
| **N Lakewood Ave** | | |
| (2000–2749) | 29 | A1/B1 |
| (2750–3928) | 43 | A1/B1/C1 |
| (3929–6349) | 37 | A2/B2/C2 |
| (6350–6939) | 34 | B2/C2 |
| **Lamb Dr** | 55 | B2 |
| **S Lambert Ave** | 46 | C3 |
| **N Lamon Ave** | | |
| (1–1613) | 49 | A2/B2 |
| (1614–5249) | 48 | A3/B3/C3 |
| (5250–7999) | 46 | A3/B3/C3 |
| **S Lamon Ave** | | |
| (0–4415) | 49 | B1/C2 |
| (4416–5049) | 51 | C1 |
| (5050–8699) | 53 | A2/B2/C2 |
| (10300–12399) | 55 | B2/C2 |
| **N Landers Ave** | 46 | C3 |
| **S Langley Ave** | | |
| (3800–3915) | 14 | C2 |
| (3916–4999) | 16 | A2/B2/C2 |
| (6000–6349) | 18 | C2 |
| (6350–9499) | 57 | — |
| (10500–13399) | 59 | A2/B2/C2 |
| **N Lansing Ave** | 46 | C3 |
| **N Laporte Ave** | | |
| (141–299) | 49 | B1 |
| (2000–5249) | 48 | A3/C3 |
| (5250–6799) | 46 | B3/C3 |
| **S Laporte Ave** | | |
| (4300–4419) | 49 | B1 |
| (4420–5049) | 51 | C1 |
| (5050–8699) | 53 | A2/B2/C2 |
| (10300–12799) | 55 | B2/C2 |
| **N Laramie Ave** | | |
| (1–1634) | 49 | A1/B1 |
| (1600–5249) | 48 | A3/B3/C3 |
| (5250–8719) | 46 | A3/B3/C3 |
| **S Laramie Ave** | | |
| (1–3999) | 49 | A1/B1/C1 |
| (4500–5049) | 51 | C1 |
| (5050–8699) | 53 | A2/B2/C2 |
| (10300–12699) | 55 | B2/C2 |
| **W Larchmont Ave** | 42 | A2 |
| **N Larned Ave** | 46 | C3 |
| **N Larrabee St** | | |
| (600–799) | 1 | A1 |
| (800–1649) | 31 | A1/B1/C1 |
| (1650–2199) | 30 | B1/C1 |
| **N Las Casas Ave** | 46 | C3 |
| **S Lasalle St** | 57 | C1 |
| **N Latham Ave** | 46 | C3 |
| **N Latrobe Ave** | | |
| (1–1649) | 49 | A1/B1 |
| (1650–5249) | 48 | C3 |
| (5250–8499) | 46 | A3/B3/C3 |
| **S Latrobe Ave** | | |
| (4700–5049) | 51 | C1 |
| (5050–8699) | 53 | A2/B2/C2 |
| (12300–12399) | 55 | C2 |
| **N Lavergne Ave** | | |
| (1–1599) | 49 | A1/B1 |
| (2000–5199) | 48 | A3/B3/C3 |
| (6800–7842) | 46 | A3/B3 |
| **S Lavergne Ave** | | |
| (1–4424) | 49 | B1/C1 |
| (4425–5049) | 51 | C1 |
| (5050–8699) | 53 | A2/B2/C2 |
| (10300–12398) | 55 | B2/C2 |
| **Laverne Ave** | 45 | A1 |
| **N Lawler Ave** | | |
| (400–1599) | 49 | A1/B1 |
| (2000–5249) | 48 | A3/C3 |
| (5250–5498) | 46 | C3 |
| (7300–7474) | 45 | A2 |
| **S Lawler Ave** | | |
| (4400–4449) | 49 | B1 |
| (4450–5049) | 51 | C1 |
| (5050–8699) | 53 | A2/B2/C2 |
| (10300–12049) | 55 | B2/C2 |
| **N Lawndale Ave** | | |
| (400–1549) | 49 | A2/B2 |
| (1501–5104) | 48 | A4/B4/C4 |
| (6000–8699) | 46 | A4/B4/C4 |
| **S Lawndale Ave** | | |
| (600–2269) | 49 | B3/C2 |
| (2270–5049) | 51 | A2/B2/C2 |
| (5050–8699) | 54 | A3/B3/C3 |
| (9200–13399) | 56 | A3/B3/C3 |
| **W Lawrence Ave** | | |
| (0–1649) | 40 | A2/B1/B2 |
| (1650–2399) | 39 | A1/A2/B1 |
| (2400–3599) | 38 | A1/A2/B1 |
| (3600–5749) | 48 | A3/A4 |
| (5750–8799) | 47 | A1/A2 |
| **Lawrence Ct** | 55 | A2 |
| **Lawton Ave** | 55 | A2 |
| **N Le Mai Ave** | 46 | B3 |
| **W Le Moyne St** | | |
| (1200–1649) | 22 | A1 |
| (1650–2464) | 21 | A1/A2 |
| (2465–2799) | 50 | A3 |
| **N Leader Ave** | 46 | C3 |

N Leamington Ave
(100–1599) 49 A1/B1
(1900–5249) 48 A3/C3
(5250–5399) 46 C3
S Leamington Ave
(1–4449) 49 B1/C1
(4450–5049) 51 C1
(5050–8699) 53 A2/B2/C2
(11100–12453) 55 B2/C2
N Leavenworth Ave 46 C3
N Leavitt St
(1–814) 23 A1/B1
(815–1615) 21 A1/B1/C1
(1616–2749) 28 A1/B1/C1
(2750–3949) 42 A1/B1/C1
(3950–5176) 39 A1/B1/C1
(5177–6364) 36 A1/C1
(6365–6517) 33 C2
S Leavitt St
(1–448) 23 C1
(424–2214) 25 A1/B1/C1
(2215–3999) 52 A3/B3
(5400–8865) 54 A3/C3
(8866–10699) 56 A3/B3/B4
N Leclaire Ave
(1–1614) 49 A1/B1
(1615–5230) 48 A3/B3/C3
(5231–8799) 46 A3/B3/C3
S Leclaire Ave
(4400–5049) 51 B2/C1
(5050–8699) 53 A2/B2/C2
(10500–11899) 55 B2/C2
Lee Ct 46 A3
W Lee Pl 23 A1
S Lee Rd 55 B2
Lee St
(3300–5761) 46 A3/A4
(5762–7811) 45 A1/A2
N Legett Ave 46 B3/C3
N Lehigh Ave
(6330–6974) 46 B3/C3
(6975–8899) 45 A2/B2
N Lehmann Ct
(2600–2749) 30 A1
(2750–2799) 44 C1
W Leland Ave
(720–1649) 40 B1/B2
(1650–2414) 39 B1/B2
(2415–3599) 38 B1/B2
(3600–5749) 48 A3/A4
(5750–8752) 47 A1/A2
N Lemai Ave 46 B3/C3
S Lemington Ave 53 B2
N Lemont Ave 46 B3/C3
Lemoyne Dr 50 A3
W Lemoyne St
(3201–3250) 50 A3
(3251–5899) 49 A1/A2
N Lenox Ave 46 B3/C3
N Leona Ave 46 B3/C3
N Leonard Ave
(5500–5849) 46 C3
(5850–5946) 45 C2
Leonard Dr 47 A1
Leonard St 45 B1
W Leonora Ln 47 C1

N Leoti Ave
(6150–6660) 46 B3/C3
(6661–7051) 45 B2
N Leroy Ave 46 B3/C3
Leslie Ln 55 B1
N Lessing St
(800–825) 24 A2
(826–899) 22 C2
N Lester Ave 48 A3
S Levee St 12 A1
Lewis St 56 C3
N Lexington Ln 45 B2
W Lexington St
(536–599) 7 B1
(1200–1499) 26 A1
(2100–2518) 25 A1
(2519–3249) 50 C3
(3250–5649) 49 C1/C2
Leyden Ave 47 C1
N Liano Ave 46 C3
W Liberty St 26 B2
N Lieb Ave
(5200–5229) 48 A3
(5230–5499) 46 C3
N Lightfoot Ave 45 B2
W Lill Ave 29 A1/A2
W Lill Ct 45 A1/A2
Lillibet Ter 46 A3
Lincoln Ave
(5762–8799) 45 A2
N Lincoln Ave
(1800–2429) 30 B1/C1/C2
(2430–2699) 29 A2
(2700–3266) 43 B1/C1/C2
(3267–3932) 42 A2/B2
(3933–4883) 39 —
(4884–5163) 38 A2
(5164–8320) 46 —
(5200–6039) 35 —
(5230–5299) 35 C2
N Lincoln Ave *
(1–1699) 45 A1/B1
S Lincoln Ave 45 B1/B2/C1
N Lincoln Ln 45 A1
N Lincoln Plz 30 C2
S Lincoln St 56 C4
N Lincoln Park West 30 B2/C2
Lincolnwood Dr 46 A4/B3
N Lind Ave 46 C3
Linden Ave 45 C1
N Linden Pl 27 A1
N Linder Ave
(1400–1649) 49 A1
(1650–4899) 48 A3/B3/C3
(5300–8449) 46 A3/B3/C3
S Linder Ave
(4700–5049) 51 C1
(5050–8699) 53 A2/B2/C2
(10300–10807) 55 B2
S Linder Ct 46 A3
W Linecrest Dr 55 B2
S Linn White Dr 11 A2
Linus Ln 55 B2
N Lipps Ave 48 A3
N Lister Ave 28 B2

W Lithuanian Plaza Ct
54 B3
S Lituanica Ave 12 B2/C2
N Livermore Ave 46 C3
S Lloyd Ave 12 A1
W Lloyd Dr 55 B1
S Lock St 12 A1
N Lockwood Ave
(1–1649) 49 A1/B1
(1650–5299) 48 A3/B3/C3
(5300–8827) 46 A3/B3/C3
S Lockwood Ave
(8828–12199) 55 B2/C2
(1–899) 49 B1/C1
(4700–5049) 51 C1
(5050–8699) 53 A2/B2/C2
Lockwood Ct 55 B2/C2
W Locust St 31 C1/C2
W Lode Dr 55 B1
W Logan Blvd
(2200–2399) 28 A1
(2420–3198) 27 A1/A2
Lois Ave 45 C1
Lois Ct 45 C1
N Loleta Ave
(6600–6749) 45 B2
(6750–6899) 46 B3
W Lomax Pl 7 A2
Lombard Ave 55 B1/C2
S Lombard Ln 55 C2
N London Ave 48 A3
N Long Ave
(1–1649) 49 A1/B1
(1650–5258) 48 A3/B3/C3
(5259–8799) 46 A3/B3/C3
S Long Ave 49 C1
(4700–5049) 51 C1
(5050–8699) 53 A2/B2/C2
(10300–10899) 55 B2
N Longmeadow Ave 46 B3
S Longwood Dr
(8700–8899) 54 C4
(9054–12299) 56 A4/B4/C4
Longwood Ln 56 B3
S Loomis Blvd
(1399–8699) 54 A4/B4/C4
(4600–5049) 52 C4
S Loomis Pl 12 C1
N Loomis St 24 B1
S Loomis St
(1–407) 24 C1
(408–2499) 26 A1/B1/C1
(2500–3099) 12 A1/A2
(3900–4199) 52 B4
(8700–8931) 54 C4
(8932–12899) 56 A4/B4/C4
S Loop Dr 18 B2
N Lorel Ave
(1–1649) 49 A1/B1
(1650–2499) 48 C3
(6800–8199) 46 A3/B3
S Lorel Ave
(4700–5049) 51 C1
(5050–8699) 53 A2/B2/C2
(10500–10899) 55 B2
N Loring Ave 46 C3

N Loron Ave
(6600–6849) 45 B2
(6850–6898) 46 B3
S Lothair Ave 56 B4
W Lothair St 56 B3
N Lotus Ave
(1–1649) 49 A1/B1
(1650–5199) 48 A3/B3/C3
(5300–8551) 46 A3/C3
S Lotus Ave
(1–649) 49 B1
(650–5049) 51 C1
(5050–8627) 53 A2/C2
S Lotus Dr 46 A3
N Louise Ave 46 A4/C3
Louise St 46 A3
N Lovejoy Ave
(5100–5299) 48 A3
(5300–5499) 46 C3
S Loveland St 55 C2
S Lowe Ave
(2400–2564) 52 A4
(2565–3949) 13 A1/B1/C1
(3950–5149) 15 A1/B1
(5150–9449) 57 A1/B1/C1
(9450–12999) 59 A1/B1/C1
N Lowell Ave
(1600–5199) 48 A4/B4/C4
(5300–8399) 46 —
Lowell Ter 46 A4
N Lower Orleans St 2 C1
E Lower South Water
6 A1
Lower Stetson Ave 6 A1
E Lower Wacker Dr
(108–58) 2 C2
(108–499) 6 A2
Loyola Ave 46 B4
W Loyola Ave 34 C1/C2
N Lucerne Ave 46 C3
N Ludlam Ave 46 C3
S Luella Ave
(7100–9425) 58 B3/C3
(9600–16059) 60 A3/B3
Luis Munoz Marin Dr 50 A3
S Lumber St
(1200–1399) 7 C2
(1400–2279) 10 A2/B1/B2
W Lumber St 52 A4
N Luna Ave
(1400–1649) 49 A1
(1650–4799) 48 A3/B3/C3
(5268–7999) 46 A3/C3
S Luna Ave
(4700–5049) 51 C1
(5050–8699) 53 A2/C2
N Lundy Ave 46 C3
W Lunt Ave
(1100–2056) 34 B1/B2
(2057–2999) 33 B1/B2
(3300–5599) 46 B3/B4
(7200–7799) 45 B1/B2
W Luther St 52 A3
W Lutz Pl 31 A1
Lyman Ave 55 B1
S Lyman St 12 A1/A2

| Street | Page | Grid |
|---|---|---|
| N Lynch Ave | 46 | C3 |
| W Lyndale St | | |
| (2030–2517) | 28 | B1 |
| (2518–3599) | 27 | B1/B2 |
| (3700–4599) | 48 | C3/C4 |
| (8600–8799) | 47 | C1 |
| Lynwood Dr | 55 | A1 |
| Lynwood Manor Dr | 55 | A1 |
| S Lyon Ave | 57 | C2 |
| S Lytle St | 26 | A1 |

## M

| Street | Page | Grid |
|---|---|---|
| N Macchesneyer Dr | 2 | C2 |
| S Mackinaw Ave | | |
| (8200–10649) | 58 | C3 |
| (10650–13499) | 60 | B3/C3 |
| Madison Ct | 45 | A1/A2 |
| W Madison Dr | 45 | A1 |
| E Madison St | 5 | B2 |
| W Madison St | | |
| (1–371) | 5 | B1/B2 |
| (372–898) | 4 | B1/B2 |
| (830–1649) | 24 | C1/C2 |
| (1650–2599) | 23 | C1/C2 |
| (2601–3275) | 50 | B3 |
| (3276–5898) | 49 | B1/B2 |
| (3300–5761) | 46 | A3/A4 |
| (5762–7699) | 45 | A1/A2 |
| E Madison Park | 17 | C1 |
| N Magnet Ave | | |
| (5300–5399) | 46 | C3 |
| (5400–5531) | 45 | C2 |
| N Magnolia Ave | | |
| (1400–1610) | 22 | A1 |
| (1900–2749) | 29 | A1/B1 |
| (2750–3799) | 43 | A1 |
| (4400–4999) | 40 | A1/B1 |
| (5200–6349) | 37 | A2/B2/C2 |
| (6350–6499) | 34 | C2 |
| S Magnolia Ln | 55 | B2 |
| Main St | | |
| (3200–5812) | 46 | A3/A4 |
| (5813–7999) | 45 | A1/A2 |
| Main St * | | |
| (2–198) | 45 | B1 |
| S Main St | | |
| (8800–8829) | 54 | C3 |
| (8826–8963) | 53 | C2 |
| (8964–9099) | 55 | A2 |
| N Major Ave | | |
| (1600–5151) | 48 | A3/B3/C3 |
| (5500–5829) | 46 | A3/C3 |
| S Major Ave | | |
| (4900–4999) | 51 | C1 |
| (5000–8799) | 53 | — |
| (8830–12699) | 55 | A1/B1/C1 |
| N Malden St | 40 | B1 |
| S Malta St | 56 | A4/B4 |
| N Mandell Ave | 46 | C3 |
| N Mango Ave | | |
| (1600–4499) | 48 | A3/B3/C3 |
| (4900–5144) | 47 | A2 |
| (5500–5799) | 45 | C2/C3 |
| (8000–8899) | 46 | A3 |

| Street | Page | Grid |
|---|---|---|
| N Manila Ave | | |
| (5300–5367) | 47 | A2 |
| (5368–5399) | 46 | C3 |
| S Manistee Ave | | |
| (7900–9549) | 58 | B3/C3 |
| (9550–13199) | 60 | A3/C3 |
| N Mankato Ave | 45 | B2 |
| Mann Dr | 54 | B3 |
| N Manor Ave | 38 | A1/B1/B2 |
| Manor Ln | 45 | C1 |
| Mansfield Ave | 45 | A2 |
| S Mansfield Ave | | |
| (7500–8849) | 53 | C1 |
| (8850–12699) | 55 | A1/B1/C1 |
| N Manton Ave | | |
| (5700–5849) | 46 | C3 |
| (5850–5999) | 45 | C2 |
| Maple Ave | | |
| (8100–8399) | 47 | A1 |
| (9900–10149) | 55 | A2 |
| (10150–12827) | 56 | C3 |
| Maple Ln | 55 | C1 |
| Maple St | 47 | C1 |
| W Maple St | | |
| (1–117) | 32 | B1 |
| (118–199) | 31 | B2 |
| (3300–3499) | 56 | A3 |
| N Maplewood Ave | | |
| (200–1549) | 50 | A3/B3 |
| (1550–2749) | 27 | A2/B2/C2 |
| (2750–2921) | 41 | C2 |
| (4000–4749) | 38 | B2/C2 |
| (4750–6349) | 35 | A2/B2 |
| (6350–7599) | 33 | A2/C2 |
| S Maplewood Ave | | |
| (130–799) | 50 | B3/C3 |
| (3500–5049) | 52 | B3/C3 |
| (5050–8299) | 54 | A3/B3/C3 |
| (9500–11899) | 56 | A3/B3/C3 |
| W Marble Pl | | |
| (1–199) | 5 | B1/B2 |
| (700–741) | 4 | B1 |
| N Marcey St | 29 | C1/C2 |
| W Margate Ter | 40 | A2 |
| N Maria Ct | 47 | A1 |
| N Marine Dr | | |
| (3800–3899) | 44 | A1 |
| (4024–5149) | 40 | A2/B2/C2 |
| (5150–5199) | 37 | C2 |
| Marion Ave | 55 | A1 |
| N Marion Ct | 21 | B2 |
| N Markham Ave | 45 | C2 |
| N Marmora Ave | | |
| (2100–5461) | 47 | A2/B2/C2 |
| (5462–8899) | 45 | A2/C2 |
| S Marquette Ave | | |
| (7600–9630) | 58 | B3/C3 |
| (9631–13099) | 60 | A3/C3 |
| E Marquette Dr | | |
| (1600–1857) | 57 | A2 |
| (1858–2399) | 58 | A3 |
| E Marquette Rd | 57 | A1/A2 |
| W Marquette Rd | | |
| (1–864) | 57 | A1 |
| (865–3949) | 54 | B3/B4 |
| (3950–4799) | 53 | B2 |

| Street | Page | Grid |
|---|---|---|
| Marshall Ave | 55 | B1 |
| S Marshall Blvd | | |
| (201–2218) | 50 | C3 |
| (2219–2420) | 52 | A3 |
| N Marshfield Ave | | |
| (400–820) | 24 | A1/B1 |
| (821–1649) | 22 | B1/C1 |
| (1650–2699) | 29 | A1/C1 |
| (2700–3949) | 42 | A2/B2 |
| (3950–7698) | 34 | A1 |
| S Marshfield Ave | | |
| (300–1849) | 26 | A1/C1 |
| (3400–5049) | 52 | B4/C4 |
| (5050–8899) | 54 | A4/B4/C4 |
| (8900–12899) | 56 | A4/B4/C4 |
| Martin Ln | 55 | A1 |
| W Marwood Ave | 47 | C1 |
| Marwood St | 47 | C1 |
| S Mary St | 12 | A2 |
| S Maryland Ave | | |
| (4900–4949) | 16 | C2 |
| (5300–6324) | 19 | A1/B1 |
| (6325–8699) | 57 | A2/B2/C2 |
| (9700–13499) | 59 | A2/C2 |
| N Mason Ave | | |
| (1600–5340) | 47 | A2/B2/C2 |
| (5448–8849) | 45 | A2/B2/C2 |
| S Mason Ave | | |
| (8850–12899) | 55 | A1/B1/C1 |
| (4800–4949) | 51 | C1 |
| (4950–8299) | 53 | A1/B1/C1 |
| N Massasoit Ave | 49 | A1 |
| S Massasoit Ave | | |
| (5100–8699) | 53 | A1/B1/C1 |
| (9100–12699) | 55 | A1/B1/C1 |
| Mather Ave | 55 | A1/B2 |
| W Matson Ave | 45 | C2 |
| N Maud Ave | 29 | B2/C2 |
| N Mautene Ct | 22 | B1 |
| W Maxwell St | | |
| (536–599) | 10 | A1 |
| (600–1130) | 26 | B2 |
| N May St | | |
| (1–818) | 24 | A2/B2 |
| (819–929) | 22 | C2 |
| S May St | | |
| (700–2199) | 26 | A2/B2/C2 |
| (3100–3799) | 12 | B2/C2 |
| (4800–5049) | 52 | C4 |
| (5050–8899) | 54 | A4/B4/C4 |
| (8900–12899) | 56 | A4/B4/C4 |
| N Mayfield Ave | | |
| (1–999) | 49 | A1/B1 |
| (1600–1899) | 47 | C2 |
| S Mayfield Ave | | |
| (1–1199) | 49 | B1/C1 |
| (5100–8764) | 53 | A1/B1/C1 |
| (8765–11799) | 55 | A1/B1/C1 |
| Mayfield Ct | 55 | C1 |
| W Maypole Ave | | |
| (1600–2554) | 23 | B1/B2 |
| (2555–3299) | 50 | B3 |
| (3300–5817) | 49 | B2/B2 |
| N McAlpin Ave | 45 | B2 |
| N McClellan Ave | 46 | C3 |
| N McClurg Ct | 3 | B2/C2 |

| Street | Page | Grid |
|---|---|---|
| N McCook Ave | 45 | C2 |
| McCormick Blvd | 46 | A4/B4 |
| N McCormick Rd | 46 | B4 |
| N McCrea Dr | 49 | B2 |
| S McDaniel St | 55 | C2 |
| S McDowell Ave | 52 | C4 |
| E McFretridge Dr | 11 | A1 |
| W McLean Ave | | |
| (1400–1499) | 29 | B1 |
| (2000–2499) | 28 | B1/B2 |
| (2800–3599) | 27 | B1 |
| (3600–4799) | 48 | C3/C4 |
| (6400–6499) | 47 | C2 |
| N McLeod Ave | 45 | C2 |
| McNichols Dr | 55 | A2 |
| N McVicker Ave | | |
| (1600–5403) | 47 | A2/B2/C2 |
| (5400–8499) | 45 | A2/B2/C2 |
| S McVicker Ave | | |
| (5100–8799) | 53 | A1/B1/C1 |
| (8800–9099) | 55 | A1 |
| S McVickers Ave | 55 | B1/C1 |
| Meacham Ave | 45 | A1/B1 |
| N Meacham Ct | 45 | A1 |
| N Meade Ave | | |
| (1600–5417) | 47 | A2/B2/C2 |
| (5418–7399) | 45 | B2/C2 |
| S Meade Ave | | |
| (5000–8899) | 53 | A1/B1/C1 |
| (8900–12699) | 55 | A1/C1 |
| Meadow Ln | 56 | C3 |
| S Meadow Lane Dr | 56 | B3 |
| W Meadow Lane Dr | 56 | B3 |
| N Medford Ave | 45 | B2 |
| W Medill Ave | | |
| (1200–1299) | 29 | B1 |
| (1600–2449) | 28 | B1/B2 |
| (2450–3599) | 27 | B1/B2 |
| (4800–5199) | 48 | C3/C4 |
| (6700–7199) | 47 | C2 |
| N Medina Ave | 45 | C2 |
| Melody Ln | 55 | C1 |
| W Melrose St | | |
| (400–1222) | 44 | B1 |
| (1223–1649) | 43 | B1 |
| (1650–2399) | 42 | B1/B2 |
| (2500–3542) | 41 | B2/B1 |
| (4000–5849) | 48 | B3/B4 |
| (5850–7046) | 47 | B2 |
| N Melvina Ave | | |
| (1600–5416) | 47 | A2/B2/C2 |
| (5417–7499) | 45 | B2/C2 |
| S Melvina Ave | | |
| (5100–8799) | 53 | A1/B1/C1 |
| (8800–12799) | 55 | A1/C1 |
| W Memory Ln | 47 | A1 |
| N Menard Ave | | |
| (1–1649) | 49 | A1/B1 |
| (1650–4199) | 48 | A3/B3/C3 |
| (4200–5427) | 47 | A2 |
| (5428–8500) | 45 | A2/C2 |
| (8501–8799) | 46 | A3 |
| S Menard Ave | | |
| (1–4999) | 49 | B1/C1 |
| (5000–8764) | 53 | A1/B1/C1 |
| (8800–12779) | 55 | A1/B1/C1 |

| Street | Range | Page | Grid |
|---|---|---|---|
| Menard Dr | | 49 | B1 |
| N Mendell St | | 29 | B1 |
| N Mendota Ave | | 45 | B2 |
| Menominee Pky | | 55 | C1 |
| W Menomonee St | | 30 | C1/C2 |
| W Merchandise Mart Plz | | 2 | C1 |
| N Meredith Ave | | 46 | C3 |
| S Merrill Ave | | | |
| | (6700–9425) | 58 | A3/B3/C3 |
| | (9600–16059) | 60 | A3/B3 |
| N Merrill St | | 45 | A1/B1 |
| S Merrill St | | 45 | B1 |
| N Merrimac Ave | | | |
| | (1600–5136) | 47 | A2/B2/C2 |
| | (5637–7899) | 45 | A2/B2/C2 |
| S Merrimac Ave | | | |
| | (4900–8799) | 53 | A1/B1/C1 |
| | (8800–10099) | 55 | A1 |
| S Merrion Ave | | | |
| | (9500–9599) | 58 | A3 |
| | (9600–9899) | 60 | A3 |
| S Merrion Ln | | 53 | C2 |
| W Merrion Ln | | 56 | C3 |
| Merry Ln | | 55 | C1 |
| Merton Ave | | 55 | A1 |
| Metron Dr | | 59 | C2 |
| W Metropole St | | 47 | B1 |
| N Meyer Ct | | 30 | C1 |
| W Miami Ave | | 45 | C2 |
| Michael John Dr | | 45 | A1 |
| N Michigan Ave | | | |
| | (1–375) | 6 | A1/B1 |
| | (376–813) | 3 | A1/B1/C1 |
| | (814–999) | 32 | B2/C2 |
| S Michigan Ave | | | |
| | (1–449) | 6 | B1/C1 |
| | (450–1199) | 9 | A1/B1 |
| | (1200–2549) | 11 | A1/B1/C1 |
| | (2550–3949) | 14 | A1/B1/C1 |
| | (3950–5156) | 16 | A1/B1/C1 |
| | (5157–6361) | 18 | A1/B1/C1 |
| | (6362–9449) | 57 | A1/B1/C1 |
| | (9450–13399) | 59 | A1/B1/C1 |
| W Midway Park | | 49 | B1 |
| Midway Plaisance | | 18 | B2 |
| | | 19 | — |
| | | 20 | B1 |
| Mies Van der Rohe Way | | 32 | C2 |
| N Mildred Ave | | | |
| | (2600–2749) | 29 | A2 |
| | (2750–2999) | 43 | C2 |
| S Millard Ave | | | |
| | (527–2264) | 49 | B2/C2 |
| | (2265–3299) | 51 | A2 |
| | (5100–7299) | 54 | A3/B3 |
| | (9100–12299) | 56 | A3/B3/C3 |
| S Miller St | | 26 | A2/B2/C2 |
| N Miltmore Ave | | | |
| | (5600–5982) | 45 | C2 |
| | (5983–5999) | 46 | C3 |
| N Milwaukee Ave | | | |
| | (200–640) | 1 | B1/C1/C2 |
| | (641–821) | 24 | A2 |
| | (822–1284) | 22 | B1/C1/C2 |
| | (1255–1627) | 21 | A2/B2 |
| | (1628–2061) | 28 | B1/C1 |
| | (2062–2769) | 27 | A1/B1/B2 |
| | (2770–2799) | 41 | C1 |
| | (2800–5270) | 48 | — |
| | (5271–5434) | 46 | C3 |
| | (5435–8899) | 45 | — |
| S Minerva Ave | | 57 | A2 |
| N Minnehaha Ave | | 46 | B3 |
| Minnesota Ave | | 56 | C3 |
| S Minnesota Dr | | 53 | B1 |
| N Minnetonka Ave | | 46 | B3 |
| Minnick Ave | | 55 | A2/B2 |
| N Minntonka Ave | | 46 | B3 |
| Mint Julip Dr | | 55 | B2 |
| Mission Dr | | 47 | A1 |
| N Mobile Ave | | | |
| | (1600–5424) | 47 | A2/B2/C2 |
| | (5425–7199) | 45 | B2/C2 |
| S Mobile Ave | | | |
| | (5100–8799) | 53 | A1/B1/C1 |
| | (8800–12799) | 55 | A1/C1 |
| Moffat St | | 48 | C3 |
| W Moffat St | | | |
| | (2000–2449) | 28 | C1 |
| | (2450–3199) | 27 | C1/C2 |
| N Mohawk St | | | |
| | (800–1649) | 31 | A1/B1/C1 |
| | (1650–2099) | 30 | B1/C1 |
| N Monitor Ave | | | |
| | (1000–1649) | 49 | A1 |
| | (1650–2449) | 48 | C3 |
| | (2450–5449) | 47 | A2/B2/C2 |
| | (5450–6099) | 45 | C2 |
| S Monitor Ave | | | |
| | (900–4949) | 49 | C1 |
| | (4950–7899) | 53 | A1/B1/C1 |
| | (9100–12899) | 55 | A1/B1/C1 |
| N Monon Ave | | 45 | B2 |
| W Monroe Ct | | 45 | A2 |
| E Monroe St | | | |
| | (1–71) | 5 | B2 |
| | (72–410) | 6 | B1/B2 |
| W Monroe St | | | |
| | (1–352) | 5 | B1/B2 |
| | (353–864) | 4 | B1/B2 |
| | (865–1662) | 24 | C1/C2 |
| | (1663–2549) | 23 | C1/C2 |
| | (2550–3249) | 50 | B3 |
| | (3250–5599) | 49 | B1/B2 |
| | (5200–5599) | 46 | A3 |
| | (5800–8399) | 45 | A1/A2 |
| N Mont Clare Ave | | | |
| | (4800–5449) | 47 | A2 |
| | (5450–5532) | 45 | C2 |
| W Montana St | | | |
| | (900–1599) | 29 | A1/A2 |
| | (2300–4449) | 28 | A1 |
| | (4450–5299) | 48 | C3 |
| N Montclare Ave | | 47 | B2/C2 |
| N Monterey Ave | | 47 | A1 |
| W Monterey Ave | | 56 | B4 |
| S Montgomery Ave | | 52 | B3 |
| W Montgomery Ave | | 52 | B3 |
| N Monticello Ave | | | |
| | (400–1549) | 49 | A2/B2 |
| | (1550–5144) | 48 | A4/B4/C4 |
| | (6000–8899) | 46 | A4/B4/C4 |
| W Montrose Ave | | | |
| | (600–1650) | 40 | B1/B2 |
| | (1651–2414) | 39 | B1/B2 |
| | (2415–3599) | 38 | B1/B2 |
| | (3600–5764) | 48 | A3/A4 |
| | (5765–8699) | 47 | A1/A2 |
| W Montrose Dr | | 40 | B2/C2 |
| W Montvale Ave | | 56 | B4 |
| N Moody Ave | | | |
| | (1600–5432) | 47 | A2/B2/C2 |
| | (5433–7199) | 45 | B2/C2 |
| S Moody Ave | | | |
| | (5100–8899) | 53 | A1/B1/C1 |
| | (8900–12699) | 55 | A1/B1/C1 |
| N Moorman St | | 21 | B2 |
| N Moreland Ave | | 47 | A1 |
| Morgan Dr | | 18 | B2 |
| N Morgan St | | 24 | A2/B2 |
| S Morgan St | | | |
| | (1–424) | 24 | C2 |
| | (410–2299) | 26 | A2/B2/C2 |
| | (2300–3911) | 12 | B2/C2 |
| | (3912–5064) | 52 | B4/C4 |
| | (5065–8949) | 54 | A4/B4/C4 |
| | (8934–12999) | 56 | A4/B4/C4 |
| Morris St | | 45 | B1 |
| W Morse Ave | | | |
| | (1100–2060) | 34 | B1/B2 |
| | (2061–2999) | 33 | B1/B2 |
| | (3700–5476) | 46 | B3/B4 |
| Morton Ave | | 45 | A2 |
| N Moselle Ave | | 45 | B2 |
| Mozart St | | | |
| | (1–1199) | 50 | B3/C3 |
| | (12700–12830) | 56 | C3 |
| N Mozart St | | | |
| | (100–1299) | 50 | A3/B3 |
| | (1600–2699) | 27 | A1/B1/C1 |
| | (2700–3949) | 41 | A1/C1 |
| | (3950–5099) | 38 | A1/B1/C1 |
| | (5600–6349) | 35 | A1/B1 |
| | (6350–6799) | 33 | B1/C1 |
| S Mozart St | | | |
| | (3500–4699) | 52 | B3/C3 |
| | (5100–8849) | 54 | A3/B3/C3 |
| | (8850–9699) | 56 | A3 |
| Mulberry Ave | | 55 | A2 |
| W Mulford St | | | |
| | (3900–5599) | 46 | A3/A4 |
| | (6000–7599) | 45 | A1/A2 |
| N Mulligan Ave | | | |
| | (1800–5449) | 47 | A2/B2/C2 |
| | (5450–5999) | 45 | C2 |
| S Mulligan Ave | | 53 | A1/B1/C1 |
| Mulligan St | | 55 | A1 |
| E Museum Dr | | 20 | B1 |
| Music Ct Cir | | 49 | B2 |
| S Muskegon Ave | | | |
| | (7726–9549) | 58 | B3/C3 |
| | (9550–13299) | 60 | A3/C3 |
| W Myrick St | | 54 | C3 |
| W Myrtle Ave | | 45 | C1/C2 |

# N

| Street | Range | Page | Grid |
|---|---|---|---|
| N Nagle Ave | | | |
| | (1600–5449) | 47 | A2/B2/C2 |
| | (5450–7999) | 45 | A2/B2/C2 |
| S Nagle Ave | | | |
| | (5000–8699) | 53 | A1/B1/C1 |
| | (10700–12499) | 55 | B1/C1 |
| N Naper Ave | | 45 | C2 |
| N Naples Ave | | 45 | C2 |
| Naples Dr | | 47 | C1 |
| N Napoleon Ave | | 45 | C2 |
| N Narragansett Ave | | | |
| | (1600–4799) | 47 | A2/B2/C2 |
| | (8700–8799) | 45 | A2 |
| S Narragansett Ave | | 53 | A1/B1/C1 |
| N Nashotah Ave | | 45 | C2 |
| N Nashville Ave | | | |
| | (1600–5449) | 47 | A2/B2/C2 |
| | (5450–6599) | 45 | B2/C2 |
| S Nashville Ave | | | |
| | (5100–8765) | 53 | A1/B1/C1 |
| | (8766–12599) | 55 | A1/B1/C1 |
| N Nassau Ave | | 45 | C2 |
| N Natchez Ave | | | |
| | (1600–5449) | 47 | A2/B2/C2 |
| | (5450–7999) | 45 | A2/C2 |
| S Natchez Ave | | | |
| | (5100–8699) | 53 | A1/B1/C1 |
| | (9300–12562) | 55 | A1/B1/C1 |
| N National Ave | | 45 | A2 |
| N Natoma Ave | | | |
| | (1600–5408) | 47 | A2/B2/C2 |
| | (5409–6599) | 45 | B2/C2 |
| S Natoma Ave | | | |
| | (5100–8769) | 53 | A1/B1/C1 |
| | (8770–12699) | 55 | A1/B1/C1 |
| N Navajo Ave | | 46 | B3/C3 |
| S Navajo Ct E | | 55 | C1 |
| S Navajo Ct W | | 55 | C1 |
| E Navajo Dr | | 55 | C1 |
| S Navajo Dr | | 55 | C1 |
| W Navajo Dr | | 55 | C1 |
| N Navarre Ave | | 45 | C2 |
| N Neenah Ave | | | |
| | (2800–5449) | 47 | A2/B2 |
| | (5450–6399) | 45 | B2/C2 |
| S Neenah Ave | | | |
| | (5100–8599) | 53 | A1/B1/C1 |
| | (10700–11699) | 55 | B1/C1 |
| W Nelson St | | | |
| | (800–1649) | 43 | C1/C2 |
| | (1650–2399) | 42 | C1/C2 |
| | (2600–2999) | 41 | C1/C2 |
| | (4000–5399) | 48 | B3/B4 |
| | (6000–6999) | 47 | B2 |
| Nelson Walk | | | |
| | (4023–4030) | 55 | A2 |
| | (4029–4033) | 56 | A3 |
| N Neola Ave | | 45 | C2 |
| N Nettleton Ave | | 45 | C2 |
| Neva Ave | | | |
| | (1600–5449) | 47 | A2/B2/C2 |
| | (5450–8312) | 45 | A2/B2/C2 |

S Neva Ave
(5200–8099) 53 A1/C1
(9300–9499) 55 A1
N New St 3 B2
N New England Ave
(1600–5411) 47 A2/B2/C2
(5412–8999) 45 A2/B2/C2
S New England Ave
(5100–8799) 53 A1/B1/C1
(9500–11599) 55 A1/B1/C1
New Gross Point Rd 45 A2
N New Hampshire Ave 45 C2
N Newark Ave 45 B2/C2
S Newberry Ave 26 B2/C2
N Newburg Ave 45 C2
N Newcastle Ave
(1600–5424) 47 A2/B2/C2
(5425–8299) 45 A2/B2/C2
S Newcastle Ave 53 A1/B1/C1
N Newgard Ave 34 B2/C2
N Newland Ave
(1600–5414) 47 A2/B2/C2
(5415–8399) 45 A2/B2/C2
S Newland Ave 53 A1/B1/C1
W Newport Ave
(800–845) 44 B1
(846–1399) 43 B1/B2
(1700–1999) 42 B2
(3300–3399) 41 B1
(4000–5849) 48 B3/B4
(5850–7046) 47 B2
Newton Ave 45 C1
N Niagara Ave 45 C2
N Nickerson Ave 45 C2
N Nicolet Ave 45 C2
Niles Ave
(7100–7199) 45 A2
(7700–8199) 46 A3
W Niles Ter 45 B2
Niles Center Rd 46 A3/B3
N Nina Ave 45 C2
N Nixon Ave 45 B2
N Noble St
(400–849) 24 A1/B1
(850–2531) 22 A1/B1/C1
N Nokomis Ave 46 B3/C3
Nora Ave 55 A1
N Nora Ave
(2900–3999) 47 B2
(7214–8099) 45 A2/B2
N Nordica Ave
(1600–5413) 47 A2/B2/C2
(5414–7999) 45 A2/B2/C2
S Nordica Ave
(5100–8699) 53 A1/C1
(9300–10899) 55 A1/B1
Norfolk Ln 55 B1
S Normal Ave
(1600–2549) 10 B1/C1
(2550–3949) 13 A1/B1/C1
(3950–4757) 15 A1/B1/C1
(5200–9449) 57 A1/B1/C1
(9450–12999) 59 A1/B1/C1
W Normal Ave 45 A1
S Normal Blvd 57 A1
W Normal Ct 45 A1
S Normal Pky 57 B1
W Normal Pky 57 B1
N Normandy Ave
(1600–5387) 47 A2/B2/C2
(5388–6699) 45 B2/C2
S Normandy Ave
(5100–8775) 53 A1/B1/C1
(8776–11699) 55 A1/B1/C1
Norridge St 47 A1
E North Ave 32 A1
W North Ave
(1–141) 32 A1
(142–884) 31 A1/A2
(885–1664) 22 A1/A2
(1665–2464) 21 A1/A2
(2465–3599) 27 C1/C2
(3600–3814) 48 C4
(3815–5898) 49 A1/A2
North St 52 B3
W North Ter 45 A1
N North Branch St
(900–949) 31 B1
(950–1399) 22 B2
North Capitol Dr 46 B4
N North Park Ave
(1330–1598) 31 A2/B2
(1600–1798) 30 B2/C2
North Riverside Plz 1 C2
W North Shore Ave
(1016–1799) 34 C1/C2
(2400–3098) 33 C1/C2
(3300–5199) 46 B3/B4
(6700–7799) 45 B1/B2
E North Water St 3 C1/C2
N Northcott Ave 45 C2
N Northwest Hwy
(5314–5445) 47 A2
(5446–6999) 45 B1/B2/C2
S Northwest Hwy 45 A1/B1/B2
(729–5313) 48 A3
Norwood Ct 47 A2
W Norwood St
(1200–1599) 37 A1
(1800–2199) 36 A1/A2
(4300–4399) 46 C3
(6200–7799) 45 C1/C2
N Nottingham Ave
(3000–5422) 47 A2/B2
(5423–7707) 45 A2/B2/C2
S Nottingham Ave
(5121–8699) 53 A1/B1/C1
(9400–9999) 55 A1
N Nursery St 29 B1


## O


W O'Brien St 26 B2
O'Connell Dr 55 A1
O'Connor Dr 47 B1
Oak Ave 55 B1
W Oak Ln 45 A1
Oak St
(300–399) 45 B1
(1800–2599) 56 C3/C4
(5201–5329) 55 A2
E Oak St 32 B1
N Oak St 47 A1/C1
W Oak St
(1–99) 32 B1
(100–1002) 31 B1/B2
Oak Center Dr 55 A2/B2
N Oak Park Ave
(1600–5419) 47 A2/B2/C2
(5420–7599) 45 A2/B2/C2
S Oak Park Ave
(5100–8858) 53 A1/B1/C1
(8748–11599) 55 A1/B1/C1
Oak Tree Dr 55 B1
W Oakdale Ave
(300–849) 44 C1/C2
(850–1599) 43 C1/C2
(1800–2299) 42 C1/C2
(3600–5399) 48 B3/B4
(6900–6999) 47 B2
Oakdale Dr 55 B2
S Oakenwald Ave 17 A1/B1
S Oakland Cir 17 A1
W Oakleaf Ave 47 C1
N Oakley Ave
(1600–2413) 28 B1/C1
(2414–3949) 42 A1/B1/C1
(3950–5164) 39 A1/B1/C1
(5165–6349) 36 A1/C1
(6350–7599) 33 A2/B2/C2
S Oakley Ave
(1200–2214) 25 B1/C1
(2215–5029) 52 A3/B3/C3
(5030–5064) 50 C3
(5065–8199) 54 A3/B3/C3
(8900–11899) 56 A3/B3/C3
N Oakley Blvd
(1–814) 23 A1/B1
(815–1599) 21 A1/B1/C1
S Oakley Blvd
(1–449) 23 C1
(438–1199) 25 A1/B1
Oakton Ct 45 A2
Oakton St 45 A1
W Oakton St
(3200–5775) 46 A3/A4
(5750–8398) 45 A1/A2
N Oakview Ave 45 C1
N Oakview St 47 A1
E Oakwood Blvd
(400–824) 16 A2
(825–1199) 14 C2
E Oakwood St 16 A1
N Oconto Ave
(3000–5460) 47 A2/B2
(5461–8399) 45 A2/B2/C2
S Oconto Ave 53 C1
Oconto Ct 55 B1
N Octavia Ave
(3000–5465) 47 A2/B2
(5466–8399) 45 A2/B2/C2
S Octavia Ave
(8000–8499) 53 C1
(8900–11499) 55 A1/B1/C1
N Odell Ave
(3000–5549) 47 —
(5550–8399) 45 A2/B2/C2
Odell Ct 55 B1
N Ogallah Ave 45 B1/B2
N Ogden Ave
(1–818) 24 A1/A2/B1
(819–1011) 22 B2/C2
(1012–1599) 31 A1/B1
(1900–1999) 30 B2/C1
W Ogden Ave
(1500–1663) 24 C1
(1664–1831) 23 C2
(1832–2299) 25 A1/A2/B1
(2601–3265) 50 C3
(3266–4070) 49 C2
(4071–5999) 51 A1/A2
S Oglesby Ave
(6700–9549) 58 A3/B3/C3
(9550–12399) 60 A3/B3/C3
E Ohio St
(1–114) 2 B2
(115–1011) 3 B1/B2
W Ohio St
(1–417) 2 B1/B2
(418–863) 1 B1/B2
(864–1666) 24 A1/A2
(1667–2499) 23 A1/A2
(2700–3264) 50 B3
(3265–5999) 49 B1/B2
N Oketo Ave
(3000–5499) 47 A1/B1
(5500–8850) 45 A2/B1/C2
S Oketo Ave 55 B1
N Olcott Ave
(3000–5572) 47 A1/B1
(5500–8899) 45 A1/B1/C1
Old Harlem 53 B1
N Oleander Ave
(3000–5341) 47 A1/A2/B1
(5700–8899) 45 A1/B1/C1
N Oliphant Ave 45 B1
W Olive Ave
(1400–1799) 37 B1
(3200–3299) 35 B1
(7200–7843) 45 C1/C2
Olive St 56 C3
N Olmsted Ave 45 B1/B2
N Olympia Ave
(5000–5137) 47 A1
(6000–6799) 45 B1/B2/C1
Olympic Dr 55 A1
N Onarga Ave 45 B1/B2
N Oneida Ave
(5000–5199) 47 A1
(6400–6499) 45 B1
W Onekema Dr 55 C1
E Ontario St
(1–98) 2 B2
(100–499) 3 B1/B2
W Ontario St
(1–339) 2 B1/B2
(336–499) 1 B2
(1600–1699) 23 A2
(3930–3999) 49 B2
N Opal Ave 47 A1/B1
N Orange Ave
(3200–4999) 47 A1/B1
(5700–5799) 45 C1

| Street | Page | Grid |
|---|---|---|
| Orchard Dr | 55 | C1 |
| Orchard Ln | 55 | A1/B1 |
| N Orchard St | | |
| (1500–1613) | 31 | A1 |
| (1608–2749) | 30 | A1/B1/C1 |
| (2750–3199) | 44 | B1/C1 |
| S Orchard St | 55 | C2 |
| W Orchard St | 56 | C3/C4 |
| N Oriole Ave | | |
| (3001–5466) | 47 | A1/B1 |
| (5467–8899) | 45 | A1/B1/C1 |
| N Orleans St | | |
| (300–812) | 2 | A1/B1/C1 |
| (813–1599) | 31 | A2/B2/C2 |
| (1700–2099) | 30 | B1/C1 |
| N Osage Ave | | |
| (3200–4699) | 47 | A1/B1 |
| (5600–5799) | 45 | C1 |
| N Osceola Ave | | |
| (3000–5399) | 47 | A1/A2/B1 |
| (5500–8899) | 45 | — |
| N Oshkosh Ave | 45 | B1 |
| N Oswego Ave | 45 | A1 |
| N Oswego St | 24 | B1 |
| N Otsego Ave | 45 | B1 |
| Ottawa Ave | 45 | A1 |
| N Ottawa Ave | | |
| (3200–5137) | 47 | A1/B1 |
| (5600–8849) | 45 | A1/B1/C1 |
| Otto Ln | 55 | C1 |
| Otto Pl | 55 | A2 |
| N Outer Lake Shore Dr | 44 | — |
| Overhill Ave | 45 | A1 |
| N Overhill Ave | | |
| (3200–5464) | 47 | A1/B1 |
| (5465–8599) | 45 | A1/B1/C1 |
| N Owen Ave | 45 | B1 |
| N Oxford Ave | 45 | B1 |
| S Oxford Ave | 55 | B1 |
| Oxford St | 55 | A1 |
| N Ozanam Ave | | |
| (3200–5464) | 47 | A1/B1 |
| (5465–8999) | 45 | A1/B1/C1 |
| N Ozanam Ave * | | |
| (498–1666) | 45 | B1 |
| N Ozark Ave | | |
| (3200–5199) | 47 | A1/B1 |
| (5600–8899) | 45 | A1/B1/C1 |

## P

| Street | Page | Grid |
|---|---|---|
| N Pacific Ave | 47 | A1/B1 |
| S Pacific Ave | 55 | A1 |
| Pacific Pl | 55 | B1 |
| S Packers Ave | 52 | B4/C4 |
| N Page Ave | 47 | B1 |
| S Page St | 55 | C4 |
| W Palatine Ave | 45 | C1/C2 |
| Palisade Dr | 56 | C3 |
| W Palmer Sq | 27 | B1 |
| W Palmer St | | |
| (2200–2499) | 28 | B1 |
| (2500–3599) | 27 | B1/B2 |
| (3600–5729) | 48 | C3/C4 |
| (6100–8999) | 47 | C1/C2 |
| S Palos Ave | 55 | C1 |
| W Palos Ave | 55 | C1 |
| Pamela Ln | 55 | B1 |
| N Panama Ave | | |
| (3200–5482) | 47 | A1/B1 |
| (5483–5599) | 45 | C1 |
| N Paris Ave | | |
| (3000–5499) | 47 | A1/B1 |
| (5500–5599) | 45 | C1 |
| Park Ave | 46 | A3 |
| S Park Ave | | |
| (5600–5799) | 46 | A3 |
| (5800–6399) | 45 | A2 |
| W Park Ave | 49 | A1/B1 |
| N Park Dr | 3 | B1/C1 |
| W Park Ln | 45 | A1 |
| Park Pl | 55 | C1 |
| E Park Pl | 19 | B2 |
| S Park Ter | 8 | B1/C1 |
| W Park Lane Dr | | |
| (3100–3199) | 56 | C3 |
| (4300–4399) | 55 | C2 |
| Park Ridge Blvd | 45 | C1 |
| E Park Shore East Ct | 19 | C2 |
| S Park Shore East Ct | 19 | C2 |
| Parke Ave | 55 | A2 |
| W Parker Ave | | |
| (3400–3499) | 27 | B1 |
| (4000–5599) | 48 | C3/C4 |
| N Parkside Ave | | |
| (1–1649) | 49 | A1/B1 |
| (1650–5224) | 48 | A3/B3/C3 |
| (5225–8399) | 46 | A3/C3 |
| S Parkside Ave | | |
| (1–199) | 49 | B1 |
| (5100–8849) | 53 | — |
| (8850–12699) | 55 | — |
| N Parkview Ter | 48 | B4 |
| S Parnell Ave | | |
| (2900–4318) | 13 | A1/B1/C1 |
| (4319–4399) | 15 | B1 |
| (5900–9449) | 57 | A1/B1/C1 |
| (9450–12999) | 59 | A1/B1/C1 |
| W Patterson Ave | | |
| (600–699) | 44 | A1 |
| (1100–1999) | 43 | A2 |
| (1800–1999) | 42 | A2 |
| (4000–5849) | 48 | B3/B4 |
| (5850–7499) | 47 | B1/B2 |
| N Patton Ave | 47 | A1 |
| Paulina Dr | 55 | B1 |
| N Paulina St | | |
| (1–820) | 23 | A2/B2 |
| (821–1649) | 21 | A2/B2/C2 |
| (1650–2770) | 28 | A2/C2 |
| (2771–3949) | 42 | A2/B2/C2 |
| (3950–5164) | 39 | A2/B2/C2 |
| (5165–6369) | 37 | A1/B1/C1 |
| (6370–7699) | 34 | A1/B1/C1 |
| S Paulina St | | |
| (1–424) | 23 | C2 |
| (425–1099) | 25 | A2 |
| (1100–2249) | 26 | B1/C1 |
| (2250–5049) | 52 | A4/B4/C4 |
| (5050–8899) | 54 | A4/B4/C4 |
| (8900–12899) | 56 | A4/C4 |
| S Paxton Ave | | |
| (6700–9549) | 58 | A3/B3/C3 |
| (9550–16059) | 60 | A3/B3 |
| Paxton Rd | 55 | A2 |
| Payne Dr | 18 | A2/B2 |
| S Peach Tree Ln | 55 | B2 |
| Peale Ave | 45 | B1 |
| E Pearson St | 32 | C1/C2 |
| W Pearson St | | |
| (1–37) | 32 | C1 |
| (501–539) | 31 | C1 |
| (1500–1664) | 22 | C1 |
| (1665–1799) | 21 | C2 |
| Pembroke Ln | 55 | A1 |
| Penn St | 50 | C3 |
| W Pensacola Ave | | |
| (900–2049) | 40 | B2/C1 |
| (2050–2449) | 39 | B1 |
| (2450–3399) | 38 | B1/B2 |
| (4700–5799) | 48 | A3/A4 |
| (7000–7399) | 47 | A2 |
| S Peoria Dr | | |
| (6300–6358) | 54 | B4 |
| (6359–6399) | 57 | A1 |
| N Peoria St | | |
| (1–819) | 24 | A2/B2 |
| (820–933) | 22 | C2 |
| S Peoria St | | |
| (1–499) | 24 | C2 |
| (500–2199) | 26 | A2/B2/C2 |
| (2600–2698) | 12 | A2 |
| (4000–5099) | 52 | B4/C4 |
| (5100–5114) | 50 | C4 |
| (5115–8299) | 54 | A4/B4/C4 |
| (8300–9449) | 57 | C1 |
| (9450–12998) | 59 | A1/B1/C1 |
| S Peoria Cul de Sac | 59 | B1 |
| S Perry Ave | | |
| (5500–9499) | 57 | A1/B1/C1 |
| (9500–13479) | 59 | A1/B1/C1 |
| W Pershing Pl | 52 | B3 |
| E Pershing Rd | 14 | C1/C2 |
| W Pershing Rd | | |
| (1–17) | 14 | B1 |
| (18–899) | 13 | C1/C2 |
| (900–1649) | 12 | C1/C2 |
| (1650–3349) | 52 | B3/B4 |
| (3350–5599) | 51 | B1/B2 |
| N Peshtigo St | 3 | B2 |
| W Peter Ter | 45 | A1 |
| W Peterson Ave | | |
| (1600–1757) | 37 | A1 |
| (1758–2424) | 36 | B1/B2 |
| (2425–3214) | 35 | A1/A2 |
| (3215–5738) | 46 | C3/C4 |
| (5739–7799) | 45 | C1/C2 |
| W Peterson Ave * | | |
| (200–1499) | 45 | C1 |
| S Phillips Ave | 58 | B3/C3 |
| W Pierce Ave | | |
| (1600–3250) | 21 | A1/A2 |
| (3251–4129) | 49 | A2 |
| N Pine Ave | 49 | A1/B1 |
| Pine Pl | 55 | C1 |
| N Pine Grove Ave | | |
| (2700–3949) | 44 | A1/B1/C1 |
| (3950–3999) | 40 | C2 |
| Pinehurst Ct | 53 | C1 |
| N Pioneer Ave | | |
| (3200–5499) | 47 | A1/B1 |
| (5500–5599) | 45 | C1 |
| W Pippin St | 54 | C3 |
| S Pitney Ct | 12 | A1 |
| N Pittsburgh Ave | | |
| (3200–5488) | 47 | A1/B1 |
| (5489–5599) | 45 | C1 |
| S Plahm Ct | 55 | B1 |
| N Plainfield Ave | 47 | A1/B1 |
| W Plattner Dr | 55 | C2 |
| E Playfield Dr | 55 | C2 |
| W Playfield Dr | 55 | C2 |
| S Pleasant Ave | | |
| (8800–8858) | 54 | C4 |
| (8859–9499) | 56 | A4 |
| Pleasant Blvd | 55 | B1/B2 |
| S Plymouth Ct | | |
| (300–449) | 5 | C2 |
| (450–1250) | 8 | A2/B2/C2 |
| (1251–1451) | 10 | A2 |
| N Poe St | 29 | C2 |
| N Point St | 27 | B2 |
| W Polk St | | |
| (1–199) | 8 | B1/B2 |
| (300–717) | 7 | B1/B2 |
| (718–1674) | 26 | A1/A2 |
| (1675–2524) | 25 | A1/A2 |
| (2525–3249) | 50 | C3 |
| (3250–5299) | 49 | C1/C2 |
| N Ponchartrain Blvd | 46 | B3 |
| N Pontiac Ave | 47 | A1/B1 |
| E Pool Dr | 18 | B2 |
| S Poplar Ave | 12 | A2 |
| Portland Ave | 15 | B2 |
| N Post Pl | | |
| (200–226) | 5 | A1 |
| (227–233) | 2 | C1 |
| N Potawatomie Ave | 47 | A1 |
| N Potawatomie St | 47 | A1 |
| W Potomac Ave | | |
| (1300–1499) | 22 | B1 |
| (1722–2464) | 21 | B1/B2 |
| (2465–3249) | 50 | A3 |
| (3250–5899) | 49 | A1/A2 |
| Prairie Ave | 45 | B1 |
| S Prairie Ave | | |
| (1400–2549) | 11 | A1/B1/C1 |
| (2550–3949) | 14 | A1/B1/C1 |
| (3950–5199) | 16 | A1/B1/C1 |
| (5200–6749) | 18 | A1/B1/C1 |
| (6750–9449) | 57 | B1/C1 |
| (9450–13399) | 59 | A2/B2/C2 |
| Prairie Ct | 59 | C2 |
| S Prairie Dr | 55 | C2 |
| W Prairie Dr | 55 | C2 |
| Prairie St | 56 | C3/C4 |
| W Pratt Ave | | |
| (3300–5399) | 46 | B3/B4 |
| (7200–7599) | 45 | B1/B2 |

# Street Index

| Street | Page | Grid |
|---|---|---|
| **W Pratt Blvd** | | |
| (1000–2079) | 34 | B1/B2 |
| (2032–3199) | 33 | B1/B2 |
| S Preller Ave | 55 | B1 |
| N Prescott Ave | 46 | C3 |
| Princess Ave | 55 | B1 |
| **S Princeton Ave** | | |
| (2198–2549) | 10 | B2/C2 |
| (2550–3949) | 13 | A2/B2/C2 |
| (3950–5124) | 15 | A2/B2/C2 |
| (5125–9399) | 57 | A1/B1/C1 |
| (9500–12699) | 59 | A1/B1/C1 |
| W Prindiville St | 27 | B2 |
| W Proesel Ave | 46 | B4 |
| S Promontory Dr | 58 | A3 |
| **N Prospect Ave** | | |
| (4800–4999) | 47 | A1 |
| (5500–8899) | 45 | A1/C1 |
| **N Prospect Ave *** | | |
| (1–999) | 45 | A1/B1 |
| **S Prospect Ave** | | |
| (9500–11099) | 56 | A4/B4 |
| **S Prospect Ave *** | | |
| (1–1999) | 45 | B1/C1 |
| W Prospect Ct | 45 | A1 |
| S Prospect St | 56 | A4 |
| W Pryor Ave | 56 | B4 |
| Public Way | 41 | B2 |
| E Public Way | 19 | C2 |
| **N Pulaski Rd** | | |
| (1–1649) | 49 | A2/B2 |
| (1650–5324) | 48 | A4/B4/C4 |
| (5325–6399) | 46 | B4/C4 |
| **S Pulaski Rd** | | |
| (1–2273) | 49 | B2/C2 |
| (2274–5049) | 51 | A2/B2/C2 |
| (5050–7149) | 53 | A2/B2 |
| (7133–8888) | 54 | B3/C3 |
| (8889–12799) | 56 | A3/B3/C3 |

## Q

| Street | Page | Grid |
|---|---|---|
| **W Quincy St** | | |
| (1–568) | 5 | C1/C2 |
| (569–799) | 4 | C1 |
| (1000–1249) | 24 | C2 |
| (1250–4899) | 23 | C2 |
| (4900–5599) | 49 | B1 |
| S Quinn Dr | 56 | C3 |
| S Quinn St | 12 | A2 |

## R

| Street | Page | Grid |
|---|---|---|
| **W Race Ave** | | |
| (1200–1599) | 24 | A1 |
| (1800–2299) | 23 | A1/A2 |
| (4600–5099) | 49 | B1/B2 |
| **N Racine Ave** | | |
| (1–824) | 24 | A2/B2 |
| (825–1956) | 22 | B2/C2 |
| (1957–2749) | 29 | A2/B2 |
| (2750–3899) | 43 | A2/B2/C2 |
| (4226–4799) | 40 | B1 |

| Street | Page | Grid |
|---|---|---|
| **S Racine Ave** | | |
| (1–424) | 24 | C2 |
| (421–2299) | 26 | A1/B1/C1 |
| (2300–3924) | 12 | B2/C2 |
| (3925–5049) | 52 | B4/C4 |
| (5050–8899) | 54 | A4/B4/C4 |
| (8900–12899) | 56 | A4/B4/C4 |
| W Railroad Ave | 49 | C1 |
| W Railroad Pl | 25 | C1 |
| Rainey Dr | 18 | B2 |
| N Ramona St | 46 | B3 |
| Rance Ter | 46 | B4 |
| **E Randolph St** | | |
| (1–84) | 5 | A2 |
| (85–599) | 6 | B1/B2 |
| **W Randolph St** | | |
| (1–371) | 5 | A1/A2 |
| (372–864) | 4 | A1/A2 |
| (865–2034) | 24 | B1/B2 |
| (2035–2164) | 23 | B1 |
| (3100–3199) | 50 | B3 |
| **W Rascher Ave** | | |
| (1400–1799) | 37 | C1 |
| (2000–2099) | 36 | C1 |
| (2526–2999) | 35 | C1/C2 |
| (6200–6799) | 45 | C2 |
| (7200–8599) | 47 | A1/A2 |
| W Raven St | 45 | C2 |
| **N Ravenswood Ave** | | |
| (3001–3899) | 42 | A2/B2/C2 |
| (3901–5129) | 39 | A2/B2/C2 |
| (5131–6349) | 36 | A2/B2/C2 |
| (6351–7099) | 34 | B1/C1 |
| Raymond Ave | 55 | A2 |
| Reba Ct | 45 | A2 |
| **Reba St** | | |
| (5400–5749) | 46 | A3 |
| (5750–5999) | 45 | A2 |
| N Recreation Dr | 40 | C2 |
| Redfield Dr | 54 | B3 |
| **Redwood Dr** | | |
| (4400–5421) | 47 | A1 |
| (5422–5705) | 45 | C1 |
| S Reilly Ave | 54 | C3 |
| Rene Ct | 45 | A1 |
| N Reserve Ave | 47 | A1 |
| N Reta Ave | 43 | A2 |
| S Rexford St | 55 | C2 |
| **S Rhodes Ave** | | |
| (3100–3899) | 14 | B2/C2 |
| (6000–6349) | 18 | C2 |
| (6350–9449) | 57 | A1/B1/C1 |
| (9450–13299) | 59 | A2/B2/C2 |
| **W Rice St** | | |
| (1800–2449) | 21 | C1/C2 |
| (2450–2699) | 50 | A3 |
| (3330–5999) | 49 | A1/A2/B1 |
| Richard Rd | 55 | A1 |
| Richard St | 47 | C1 |
| **S Richards Dr** | | |
| (6300–6349) | 20 | C1 |
| (6350–6599) | 58 | A3 |

| Street | Page | Grid |
|---|---|---|
| **N Richmond St** | | |
| (800–1199) | 50 | A3 |
| (1600–2749) | 27 | A1/B1/C1 |
| (2750–3949) | 41 | A1/B1/C1 |
| (3950–4599) | 38 | B1/C1 |
| (5600–6349) | 35 | A1/B1 |
| (6350–6799) | 33 | B1/C1 |
| **S Richmond St** | | |
| (300–1199) | 50 | B3/C3 |
| (3500–4824) | 52 | B3/C3 |
| (5100–8849) | 54 | A3/B3/C3 |
| (8850–9699) | 56 | A3 |
| **N Ridge Ave** | | |
| (5600–6063) | 37 | A1/B1/B2 |
| (6052–6330) | 36 | A2 |
| (6331–7021) | 34 | B1/C1 |
| (7022–7599) | 33 | A2/B2 |
| N Ridge Blvd | 34 | B1 |
| Ridge Dr | 55 | B1 |
| Ridge St | 47 | C1 |
| Ridge Ter | 45 | B1 |
| Ridge Cove Dr | 55 | B1 |
| **S Ridgeland Ave** | | |
| (6700–9399) | 57 | A2/B2/C2 |
| (8700–12834) | 55 | A1/B1/C1 |
| Ridgemont Ln | 55 | B1 |
| **N Ridgeway Ave** | | |
| (400–1549) | 49 | A2/B2 |
| (1550–5113) | 48 | A4/B4/C4 |
| (6200–6748) | 46 | A4/B4/C4 |
| **S Ridgeway Ave** | | |
| (1400–2249) | 49 | C2 |
| (2250–5066) | 51 | A2/B2/C2 |
| (5066–7899) | 54 | A3/B3/C3 |
| (9100–12829) | 56 | A3/B3/C3 |
| Ridgewood Ave | 47 | A1 |
| S Ridgewood Ct | 19 | A2 |
| N Ritchie Ct | 32 | B1 |
| River Dr | 45 | A2 |
| E River Dr | 3 | C2 |
| W River Grove Ave | 47 | C1 |
| S Riverdale Ave | 59 | C2 |
| N Riveredge Ter | 46 | C4 |
| N Riverside Dr | 45 | B2 |
| N Riverside Plz | 4 | A2/B2 |
| S Riverside Plz | 4 | B2/C2 |
| N Riverview Dr | 45 | B2 |
| Robertson Ave | 55 | A2 |
| **S Robinson St** | | |
| (2697–3146) | 52 | A4 |
| (3147–3199) | 12 | B1 |
| E Rochdale Pl | 19 | A2 |
| **N Rockwell St** | | |
| (358–1549) | 50 | A3/B3 |
| (1550–2749) | 27 | A2/B2/C2 |
| (2750–3950) | 41 | A2/B2/C2 |
| (3951–5164) | 38 | A2/B2/C2 |
| (5165–6349) | 35 | A2/B2/C2 |
| (6350–7599) | 33 | A2/B2/C2 |
| **S Rockwell St** | | |
| (1–2217) | 50 | B3/C3 |
| (2218–5049) | 52 | A3/B3/C3 |
| (5050–8849) | 54 | A3/B3/C3 |
| (8850–11499) | 56 | A3/B3 |

| Street | Page | Grid |
|---|---|---|
| **N Rogers Ave** | | |
| (5232–7249) | 46 | C3/C4 |
| (7250–7651) | 34 | A1/A2 |
| Ronald St | 47 | A2 |
| E Roosevelt Dr | 9 | C1/C2 |
| Roosevelt Ln | 47 | C1 |
| **E Roosevelt Rd** | | |
| (1–48) | 8 | C2 |
| (100–148) | 9 | C1 |
| **W Roosevelt Rd** | | |
| (1–315) | 8 | C1/C2 |
| (300–650) | 7 | C1/C2 |
| (651–1706) | 26 | B1/B2 |
| (1707–2449) | 25 | B1/B2 |
| (2480–3264) | 50 | C3 |
| (3265–5928) | 49 | C1/C2 |
| N Root Ct | 45 | A1 |
| Root St | 45 | B1 |
| N Root St | 45 | A1 |
| W Root St | 15 | A1/A2 |
| **W Roscoe St** | | |
| (400–873) | 44 | B1 |
| (874–1614) | 43 | B1/B2 |
| (1615–2449) | 42 | B1/B2 |
| (2450–3199) | 41 | B1/B2 |
| (3600–5849) | 48 | B3/B4 |
| (5850–8199) | 47 | B1/B2 |
| **W Rosedale Ave** | | |
| (1200–1317) | 37 | B2 |
| (1318–5599) | 46 | C3 |
| (6100–7899) | 45 | C1/C2 |
| W Rosehill Dr | 37 | B1 |
| N Rosemary Ave | 45 | B2 |
| N Rosemary Ln | 45 | B2 |
| S Rosemary Ln | 55 | C2 |
| **W Rosemont Ave** | | |
| (400–899) | 45 | C1 |
| (900–1599) | 37 | A1/A2 |
| (2100–2415) | 36 | A1 |
| (2416–3199) | 35 | A1/A2 |
| (3428–4825) | 46 | C3/C4 |
| W Roseview Dr | 45 | A1 |
| W Roslyn Pl | 30 | A1 |
| S Ross Ave | 57 | A1 |
| Roth Ter | 46 | A4 |
| **S Ruble St** | | |
| (1382–1399) | 26 | B1/B2 |
| (1600–2099) | 10 | B1 |
| Ruby St | 55 | A2 |
| **W Rumsey Ave** | | |
| (3700–3999) | 54 | C3 |
| (4500–4599) | 55 | A2 |
| W Rundell Pl | 24 | C2 |
| **N Rush St** | | |
| (400–813) | 2 | A2/B2 |
| (814–1131) | 32 | B1/C1 |
| Russell Dr | 18 | B2 |
| N Rutherford Ave | 47 | A2/B2/C2 |
| **S Rutherford Ave** | | |
| (5100–8899) | 53 | A1/B1/C1 |
| (9400–11099) | 55 | A1/B1 |
| S Ryan Rd | 55 | A2 |

## S

N Sacramento Ave
(1000–1199) 50 A3
(2200–2750) 27 A1/B1
(2751–3949) 41 A1/B1/C1
(3950–4899) 38 A1/B1/C1
(5600–6349) 35 A1/B1
(6350–7599) 33 A1/B1/C1
S Sacramento Ave
(2200–2249) 50 C3
(2250–4699) 52 A3/B3/C3
(5100–8849) 54 A3/B3/C3
(8850–12820) 56 A3/B3/C3
N Sacramento Blvd 50 A3/B3
S Sacramento Blvd 50 B3/C3
W Sacramento Blvd 50 B3
S Sacramento Dr
(1200–1899) 50 C3
(11501–11799) 56 B3/C3
S Saginaw Ave
(7500–9499) 58 B3/C3
(12600–13099) 60 C3
S Saint Johns Ct 46 C4
W Saint Joseph Ave 47 A1
S Saint Louis Ave 56 A3
N Sandburg Ter 32 A1/B1
N Sangamon St
(1–818) 24 A2/B2
(819–930) 22 C2
S Sangamon St
(1–449) 24 C2
(409–3517) 26 A2/B2/C2
(3518–3835) 12 C2
(5200–8899) 54 A4/B4/C4
(8921–9499) 56 A4
(9500–12999) 59 A1/B1/C1
S Sangamon Cul de Sac
56 B4
Saratoga Dr 55 A1
N Sauganash Ave 46 B3/C3/C4
N Sauganash Ln 46 C4
Sawgrass Dr 53 C1
N Sawyer Ave 48 A4/B4/C4
(418–999) 50 A3/B3
(1600–2767) 27 A1/B1/C1
(2768–3949) 41 A1/B1/C1
(3950–5249) 38 A1/B1/C1
(5250–5999) 46 C4
S Sawyer Ave
(1200–2249) 50 C3
(2250–4699) 52 A3/B3/C3
(5100–8599) 54 A3/B3/C3
(9100–11469) 56 A3/B3
N Sayre Ave
(1600–5420) 47 A2/B2/C2
(5421–8899) 45 A2/B2/C2
S Sayre Ave
(5100–8799) 53 A1/B1/C1
(9300–10199) 55 A1
N Schick Pl 31 B1
E Schiller St 32 A1/B1
W Schiller St
(1–118) 32 A1/B1
(119–768) 31 B1/B2
(1900–2199) 21 B1/B2

N School St 45 A2/B2
W School St
(900–1614) 43 B1/B2
(1615–2399) 42 B1/B2
(2925–3545) 41 B1
(3600–5849) 48 B3/B4
(5850–8330) 47 B1/B2
W Schorsch St 47 B2
N Schrader Dr 49 B2
W Schreiber Ave
(1500–1799) 34 C1/C2
(6600–7199) 45 B2
W Schubert Ave
(600–799) 30 A1
(830–1399) 29 A1/A2
(2300–2464) 28 A1
(2465–3599) 27 A1/A2
(3600–5815) 48 C3/C4
(5816–7899) 47 C1/C2
W Scott Dr 56 C3
Scott Ln 55 A2
E Scott St 32 B1
W Scott St 31 B1/B2
S Scottsdale Ave 53 C2
Searle Pky 46 A3
N Sedgwick St
(644–829) 1 A2
(809–1624) 31 A2/B2/C2
(1625–2299) 30 B1/C1
N Seeley Ave
(126–419) 23 B1/B2
(2200–2399) 28 B1
(2822–3949) 42 A1/B1/C1
(3950–4998) 39 A1/B1
(6100–6349) 36 A2
(6350–7599) 34 A1/B1/C1
S Seeley Ave
(1–399) 23 C1
(1000–1099) 25 A1
(2300–4999) 52 A3/B3/C3
(5000–5049) 50 C3
(5050–8599) 54 A3/B4/C4
(9500–10799) 56 A4/B4
W Seipp St 54 C3
N Seminary Ave
(1900–2791) 29 A2/B2
(2792–3965) 43 A2/B2/C2
(3966–3999) 40 C2
W Seminole St
(5600–5716) 46 C3
(5717–8801) 45 C1/C2
N Seneca St 32 B2/C2
W Senior Pl 47 A2
S Senour Ave 12 A2
Serbian Rd 45 C1
Seward St 45 A2
Shady Ln 55 C1
W Shakespeare Ave
(1400–2049) 29 B1
(2050–2399) 28 B1
(2500–3599) 27 B1/B2
(3600–4899) 48 C3/C4
(6800–6931) 47 C2

N Sheffield Ave
(1542–1649) 22 A2
(1650–2786) 29 A2/B2/C2
(2787–3899) 43 A2/B2/C2
S Shelby Ct 26 C2
N Sheridan Rd
(2800–3798) 44 —
(3900–3944) 43 A2
(3934–5149) 40 A2/B2/C2
(5150–6349) 37 A2/B2/C2
(6350–7637) 34 A2/B2/C2
W Sheridan Rd
(600–849) 44 A1
(850–999) 43 A2
(968–1199) 34 C2
Sherman Dr 54 A4
N Shermer Rd 45 A2
W Sherwin Ave
(1190–1699) 34 A1/A2
(2400–3199) 33 A1/A2
(3800–5399) 46 B3/B4
(6000–7734) 45 B1/B2
W Shiawassie Dr 55 C1
S Shields Ave
(2600–3799) 13 A2/B2/C2
(4134–5099) 15 A2/B2/C2
(5300–5899) 57 A1
S Shirley Ln 56 C3
W Shirley Ln 55 C2
S Shore Dr 17 B2/C2
S Short St 12 A1
W Sibley St 45 A1/B1
N Simonds Dr
(4700–5100) 40 A2
(5100–5199) 37 C2
N Sioux Ave
(6600–6799) 46 B3
(7000–7157) 45 B2
Skokie Blvd 46 A3/B3
Smith Ln 47 B1
Smithwood Dr 45 A2
Solidarity Dr 11 A2
Sorrento Dr 55 C1
South St 52 B3
S South Chicago Ave
(6700–8186) 57 B1/B2/C2
(8173–9499) 58 C3
S South Shore Dr
(5401–5598) 20 A1/B1
(6700–8499) 58 A3/B3/C3
W South Water Market
26 B1/B2
Southfield Dr 55 A1
N Southport Ave
(1900–2749) 29 A1/B1
(2750–3949) 43 A1/B1/C1
(3950–4199) 40 C1
Southwest Hwy 55 A1/A2/B1
N Spaulding Ave 48 A4/B4/C4
(401–1565) 49 A2/B2
(1566–2764) 27 A1/B1/C1
(2765–3949) 41 A1/B1/C1
(3950–5249) 38 A1/B1/C1
(5250–6799) 46 B4/C4

S Spaulding Ave
(1–2116) 49 B2/C2
(2117–2249) 50 C3
(2250–5049) 52 A3/B3/C3
(5050–8499) 54 A3/B3/C3
(9100–11499) 56 A3/B3
W Spencer Ln 55 C2
S Spencer St 55 C2
N Spokane Ave 46 B3
Spring Rd 55 A2
Spring St 45 B1
N Springfield Ave
(400–1649) 49 A2/B2
(1650–5999) 48 A4/B4/C4
(6100–8815) 46 A4/B4/C4
S Springfield Ave
(8816–12699) 56 A3/B3/C3
(1–2259) 49 B2/C2
(2260–4899) 51 A2/C2
(5100–8699) 54 A3/B3/C3
Sproat Ave
(8700–8849) 53 C2
(8850–9499) 55 A2
S Spruce St 55 C1
N St Clair St 3 A1/B1
N St Claire St 3 B1/C1
W St George Ct 27 B2
W St Helen St 27 B2
St James Ct 55 B1
St James Pl 45 B1
W St James Pl 30 A1
S St Lawrence Ave
(4100–5099) 16 A2/B2/C2
(5900–6349) 18 B2/C2
(6350–9449) 57 A1/B1/C1
(9450–13499) 59 A2/B2/C2
N St Louis Ave
(200–1564) 49 A2/B2
(1565–5249) 48 A4/B4/C4
(5250–8799) 46 A4/B4/C4
S St Louis Ave
(1–2249) 49 B2/C2
(2250–4899) 51 A2/B2/C2
(5100–8499) 54 A3/B3/C3
(9100–11699) 56 A3/B3/C3
N St Mary St 27 B2
N St Michaels Ct 30 C1
W St Paul Ave
(200–2049) 30 C2
(2050–2399) 28 C1
(4800–5199) 48 C3
S Stanford Dr 55 A1
Stanley Ave 45 B1
S Stark St 12 A2
N State Pky 32 A1/B1
State Rd
(5101–8699) 53 C1/C2
(5400–7560) 53 C2
N State St
(1–258) 5 A2/B2
(259–813) 2 A2/B2/C2
(814–1199) 32 B1/C1

# Street Index

**S State St**
| | | |
|---|---|---|
| (1–449) | 5 | B2/C2 |
| (450–1269) | 8 | A2/B2/C2 |
| (1270–2557) | 11 | A1/B1/C1 |
| (2558–3899) | 14 | A1/B1/C1 |
| (3900–5099) | 16 | A1/B1/C1 |
| (5101–6308) | 18 | A1/B1/C1 |
| (6309–9449) | 57 | A1/B1/C1 |
| (9450–12699) | 59 | A1/B1/C1 |

| | | |
|---|---|---|
| State Line Ave | 60 | A4/B4 |
| S State Line Rd | 60 | B4 |
| N Stave St | 27 | B2 |
| Staycoff Ln | 53 | C2 |
| Stephen Dr | 55 | B1 |
| N Stetson Ave | 6 | A1 |
| W Steuben St | 56 | B4 |
| N Stevens Ave | 46 | C4 |
| Stevens Dr | 53 | C2 |
| Stewart Ave | 45 | B1 |

**S Stewart Ave**
| | | |
|---|---|---|
| (1600–2540) | 10 | B1/C1 |
| (2541–3459) | 13 | A2/B2 |
| (4000–4699) | 15 | A2/B2 |
| (5500–9399) | 57 | A1/B1/C1 |
| (11100–12699) | 59 | B1/C1 |

| | | |
|---|---|---|
| Stillwell Pl | 56 | B3 |

**N Stockton Dr**
| | | |
|---|---|---|
| (1700–2399) | 30 | B2/C2 |
| (2401–2799) | 44 | C2 |

| | | |
|---|---|---|
| W Stolting Rd | 45 | A1 |
| N Stone St | 32 | B1 |
| Stone Circle Dr | 55 | A2 |
| Stony Creek Dr | 55 | B2 |

**S Stony Island Ave**
| | | |
|---|---|---|
| (5600–6353) | 20 | B1/C1 |
| (6354–9524) | 57 | A2/B2/C2 |
| (9525–12699) | 59 | A2/B2/C2 |

| | | |
|---|---|---|
| W Stratford Pl | 44 | B1 |
| N Streeter Dr | 3 | B2 |

**W Strong St**
| | | |
|---|---|---|
| (3900–5299) | 48 | A3/A4 |
| (5800–8299) | 47 | A1/A2 |

| | | |
|---|---|---|
| Struckman Ave | 47 | C1 |
| Sub Lower Wacker Dr | 6 | A1/A2 |
| W Sullivan St | 31 | B1 |

**W Summerdale Ave**
| | | |
|---|---|---|
| (1400–1749) | 37 | C1 |
| (1750–2199) | 36 | C1/C2 |
| (2523–2999) | 35 | C1/C2 |
| (4300–4369) | 46 | C4 |
| (6900–8799) | 47 | A1/A2 |

| | | |
|---|---|---|
| W Summerset Ave | 45 | C2 |
| N Summit Ave | 45 | B1 |
| S Summit Ave | 57 | C1 |
| Sunny Ln | 55 | C1 |

**W Sunnyside Ave**
| | | |
|---|---|---|
| (800–1649) | 40 | B1/B2 |
| (1650–2414) | 39 | B1/B2 |
| (2415–3599) | 38 | B1/B2 |
| (3600–5765) | 48 | A3/A4 |
| (5766–8699) | 47 | A1/A2 |

| | | |
|---|---|---|
| Sunrise Ln | 47 | A1 |
| W Sunset Dr | 47 | B1/C1 |
| W Sunset Rd | 45 | A1 |

**E Superior St**
| | | |
|---|---|---|
| (1–114) | 2 | A2 |
| (115–499) | 3 | A1 |

**W Superior St**
| | | |
|---|---|---|
| (1–367) | 2 | A1/A2 |
| (368–852) | 1 | A1/A2 |
| (853–1649) | 24 | A1/A2 |
| (1650–2449) | 23 | A1/A2 |
| (2450–2799) | 50 | B3 |
| (4600–5999) | 49 | B1/B2 |

| | | |
|---|---|---|
| W Surf St | 44 | C1/C2 |
| N Surrey Ct | 29 | A1 |
| N Susan Ct | 45 | A1 |
| N Sutton Pl | 32 | B1 |
| W Swann St | 15 | B2 |
| Sycamore Dr | 55 | B1 |

## T

**N Tahoma Ave**
| | | |
|---|---|---|
| (6400–6599) | 46 | B3 |
| (6900–7098) | 45 | B2 |

| | | |
|---|---|---|
| W Talcott Ave | 45 | C1/C2 |
| Talcott Pl | 45 | C1 |
| W Talcott Rd | 45 | B1/C1 |

**N Talman Ave**
| | | |
|---|---|---|
| (1–1549) | 50 | A3/B3 |
| (1550–2699) | 27 | A2/B2/C2 |
| (2800–4749) | 41 | A2/C2 |
| (4750–4999) | 38 | A2 |
| (5600–6349) | 35 | A2/B2 |
| (6350–7429) | 33 | A2/C1 |

**S Talman Ave**
| | | |
|---|---|---|
| (1200–1499) | 50 | C3 |
| (3928–5049) | 52 | B3/C3 |
| (5050–8899) | 54 | A3/B3/C3 |
| (9900–11499) | 56 | A3/B3 |

| | | |
|---|---|---|
| S Tan Ct | 10 | B1/B2 |
| Tarpey Ln | 47 | C1 |
| Taylor Ave | 55 | B1 |

**W Taylor St**
| | | |
|---|---|---|
| (1–199) | 8 | B1/B2 |
| (300–718) | 7 | B1/B2 |
| (667–1652) | 26 | A1/A2 |
| (1653–2549) | 25 | A1/A2 |
| (2550–3199) | 50 | C3 |
| (3600–5699) | 49 | C1/C2 |

| | | |
|---|---|---|
| Terminal Ave | 46 | A3 |
| W Termunde Dr | 55 | C2 |
| W Terra Cotta Pl | 28 | A2 |
| Terrace Ln | 55 | C2 |
| N Thatcher Ave | 47 | A1/B1/C1 |
| N Thatcher Rd | 47 | A1 |

**Theobald Rd**
| | | |
|---|---|---|
| (5500–5810) | 46 | A3 |
| (5811–5899) | 45 | A2 |

**W Thomas St**
| | | |
|---|---|---|
| (1300–1599) | 22 | B1 |
| (1800–2449) | 21 | B1/B2 |
| (2450–3249) | 50 | A3 |
| (3250–5899) | 49 | A1/A2 |

**W Thome Ave**
| | | |
|---|---|---|
| (1400–1767) | 37 | A1 |
| (1768–2231) | 36 | A1/A2 |
| (4400–4429) | 46 | C3 |

| | | |
|---|---|---|
| Thompson Dr | 50 | C3 |

| | | |
|---|---|---|
| Thorndale Ave | 45 | C1 |

**W Thorndale Ave**
| | | |
|---|---|---|
| (900–1799) | 37 | B1/B2 |
| (2400–2431) | 36 | B1 |
| (2432–3099) | 35 | B1/B2 |
| (3200–4621) | 46 | C3/C4 |
| (5900–7829) | 45 | C1/C2 |

**N Throop St**
| | | |
|---|---|---|
| (1–799) | 24 | A1/B1 |
| (1026–1626) | 22 | A1/B1 |
| (1627–1799) | 29 | C1 |

**S Throop St**
| | | |
|---|---|---|
| (1–399) | 24 | C1 |
| (1000–2417) | 26 | A1/B1/C1 |
| (2428–3299) | 12 | A2/B1 |
| (4700–5049) | 52 | C4 |
| (5050–8964) | 54 | A4/B4/C4 |
| (8909–12901) | 56 | A4/B4/C4 |

**S Tilden St**
| | | |
|---|---|---|
| (1000–1062) | 26 | A2 |
| (1063–1199) | 24 | C2 |

**W Tilden St**
| | | |
|---|---|---|
| (500–629) | 7 | A1 |
| (800–831) | 4 | C1 |

| | | |
|---|---|---|
| Tomcin Trl | 55 | B2 |
| N Tonty Ave | 45 | B2 |
| W Tooker Pl | 32 | C1 |
| S Torrence Ave | 60 | A3/B3/C3 |

**W Touhy Ave**
| | | |
|---|---|---|
| (1200–2029) | 34 | B1/B2 |
| (2030–3199) | 33 | B1/B2 |
| (3200–5678) | 46 | B3/B4 |
| (5679–7769) | 45 | B1/B2 |

**W Touhy Ave ***
| | | |
|---|---|---|
| (1–499) | 45 | B1 |

| | | |
|---|---|---|
| Tower Ct | 46 | B3 |
| E Tower Ct | 32 | C1 |
| N Tower Circle Dr | 46 | B3 |
| Trafalgar Ln | 56 | A3 |
| W Transit Ave | 52 | B4 |
| W Tremont St | 57 | A1 |

**N Tripp Ave**
| | | |
|---|---|---|
| (500–1649) | 49 | A2/B2 |
| (1650–5199) | 48 | A4/B4/C4 |
| (5600–8399) | 46 | A4/B4/C4 |

**S Tripp Ave**
| | | |
|---|---|---|
| (600–1599) | 49 | B2/C2 |
| (2600–5026) | 51 | A2/C2 |
| (5027–8699) | 53 | A2/B2/C2 |
| (9100–12699) | 55 | A2/B2/C2 |

| | | |
|---|---|---|
| Tripp Ct | 55 | B2 |
| W Trowbridge Pl | 54 | A3 |

**S Troy Ave**
| | | |
|---|---|---|
| (8700–8849) | 54 | C3 |
| (8850–9899) | 56 | A3 |

| | | |
|---|---|---|
| Troy Dr | 56 | B3/C3 |

**N Troy St**
| | | |
|---|---|---|
| (400–899) | 50 | A3/B3 |
| (1600–2749) | 27 | A1/C1 |
| (2750–3949) | 41 | A1/B1/C1 |
| (3950–5165) | 38 | A1/B1/C1 |
| (5166–6349) | 35 | A1 |
| (6350–6599) | 33 | C1 |

**S Troy St**
| | | |
|---|---|---|
| (137–2249) | 50 | B3/C3 |
| (2250–4699) | 52 | A3/B3/C3 |
| (5100–8299) | 54 | A3/B3/C3 |
| (10300–11499) | 56 | B3 |

**N Trumbull Ave**
| | | |
|---|---|---|
| (399–1110) | 49 | A2/B2 |
| (2200–8799) | 46 | A4/B4 |

**S Trumbull Ave**
| | | |
|---|---|---|
| (318–2249) | 49 | B2/C2 |
| (2250–4699) | 51 | A2/B2/C2 |
| (5100–8099) | 54 | A3/C3 |
| (9100–12599) | 56 | A3/B3/C3 |

**Tulley Ave**
| | | |
|---|---|---|
| (8700–8810) | 53 | C2 |
| (8811–9899) | 55 | A2 |

| | | |
|---|---|---|
| S Turner Ave | 56 | A3 |

## U

| | | |
|---|---|---|
| W Ulth St | 10 | B1 |
| N Union Ave | 1 | B1/C1 |

**S Union Ave**
| | | |
|---|---|---|
| (0–2194) | 26 | A2/B2/C2 |
| (2201–2399) | 52 | A4 |
| (2600–3949) | 13 | A1/B1/C1 |
| (3950–5149) | 15 | A1/B1/C1 |
| (5150–9449) | 57 | A1/B1/C1 |
| (9450–12999) | 59 | A1/B1/C1 |

**S University Ave**
| | | |
|---|---|---|
| (4400–5149) | 17 | B1 |
| (5150–6319) | 19 | A1/B1/C1 |
| (6320–9399) | 57 | A2/B2/C2 |
| (9500–9899) | 59 | A2 |

| | | |
|---|---|---|
| Upper Randolph Dr | 6 | B1 |
| S Urban Ave | 57 | C1 |

**S Utica Ave**
| | | |
|---|---|---|
| (8700–8849) | 54 | C3 |
| (8850–10299) | 56 | A3 |

## V

| | | |
|---|---|---|
| S Van Beveren Dr | 55 | C2 |

**E Van Buren St**
| | | |
|---|---|---|
| (1–71) | 5 | C2 |
| (72–132) | 6 | C1 |

**W Van Buren St**
| | | |
|---|---|---|
| (1–412) | 5 | C1/C2 |
| (413–903) | 4 | C1/C2 |
| (871–1659) | 24 | C1/C2 |
| (1660–2511) | 23 | C1/C2 |
| (2512–3249) | 50 | B3 |
| (3250–5599) | 49 | B1/B2 |

| | | |
|---|---|---|
| S Van Vlissingen Rd | 60 | A3 |
| S Vanderpoel Ave | 56 | A4 |

**W Vermont Ave**
| | | |
|---|---|---|
| (600–965) | 59 | C1 |
| (966–1099) | 56 | C4 |

**S Vernon Ave**
| | | |
|---|---|---|
| (2700–3899) | 14 | A1/B1/C1 |
| (3964–4330) | 16 | A2/B2 |
| (6000–6349) | 18 | C2 |
| (6350–9449) | 57 | A1/B1/C1 |
| (9450–13499) | 59 | A2/B2/C2 |

| | | |
|---|---|---|
| Vernon St | 56 | C3 |

| Street (Range) | Page | Grid |
|---|---|---|
| W Vernon Park Pl (534–599) | 7 | B1 |
| (716–1199) | 26 | A1/A2 |
| W Veterans Pl | 48 | A3 |
| W Victoria St (1200–1599) | 37 | B1/B2 |
| (3212–4235) | 46 | C4 |
| (7632–7899) | 45 | C1 |
| S Villa Ct | 55 | B2 |
| S Vincennes Ave (3545–3916) | 14 | C2 |
| (3917–5099) | 16 | A2/B2/C2 |
| (6924–8899) | 57 | B1/C1 |
| (8998–12699) | 56 | — |
| Vine Ave (4800–4899) | 47 | A1 |
| (5544–5699) | 45 | C1 |
| Vine Ave * (100–2099) | 45 | B1/B2/C1 |
| N Vine St | 30 | C1 |
| S Vintage Ave | 12 | A1 |
| N Virginia Ave (4500–4767) | 38 | B2 |
| (4768–5999) | 35 | A1/B1/C1 |

## W

| Street (Range) | Page | Grid |
|---|---|---|
| W Wabansia Ave (1300–1665) | 29 | C1 |
| (1666–2464) | 28 | C1/C2 |
| (2465–3599) | 27 | C1/C2 |
| (3600–5899) | 48 | C3/C4 |
| (5900–7799) | 47 | C1/C2 |
| Wabash Ave (10300–10599) | 59 | A1 |
| S Wabash Ave (10600–12499) | 59 | B1/C1 |
| N Wabash Ave (1–257) | 5 | A2/B2 |
| (258–812) | 2 | A2/B2/C2 |
| (813–928) | 32 | C1 |
| (1–449) | 5 | B2/C2 |
| (450–1250) | 8 | A2/B2/C2 |
| (1251–2549) | 11 | A1/B1/C1 |
| (2550–3949) | 14 | A1/B1/C1 |
| (3950–5199) | 16 | A1/B1/C1 |
| (5200–6299) | 18 | A1/B1/C1 |
| (5200–9499) | 55 | A1/A2 |
| (6600–9449) | 57 | A1/B1/C1 |
| S Wabash St | 59 | A1 |
| E Wacker Dr (1–87) | 2 | C2 |
| (88–599) | 6 | A1/A2 |
| N Wacker Dr | 5 | A1/B1 |
| S Wacker Dr (1–411) | 5 | B1/C1 |
| (412–599) | 7 | A2 |
| W Wacker Dr | 2 | C1/C2 |
| E Wacker Pl (4–84) | 2 | C2 |
| (85–123) | 6 | A1 |
| Wahl St | 56 | C3 |
| Wainwright Pl | 56 | B3 |
| S Walden Pky | 56 | A4/B4 |
| E Waldron Dr | 11 | B1/B2 |
| S Wallace St (2400–2549) | 10 | C1 |
| (2550–3949) | 13 | A1/B1/C1 |
| (3950–4849) | 15 | A1/B1/C1 |
| (5300–9449) | 57 | A1/B1/C1 |
| (9450–12999) | 59 | A1/B1/C1 |
| W Wallen Ave (1600–1799) | 34 | C1 |
| (3700–3999) | 46 | B4 |
| N Waller Ave | 49 | A1/B1 |
| S Waller Ave | 49 | B1/C1 |
| W Walnut St (636–699) | 1 | C1 |
| (700–1649) | 4 | A1 |
| (1650–2399) | 23 | B1/B2 |
| (2800–3299) | 50 | B3 |
| (3300–4799) | 49 | B2 |
| W Walsh Ln | 47 | B1 |
| W Walter Ln | 56 | C3 |
| S Walton Dr | 58 | A4 |
|  | 60 | A4 |
| E Walton St | 32 | B1/B2 |
| W Walton St (1–99) | 32 | B1/C1 |
| (140–537) | 31 | B1/B2 |
| (1300–1664) | 22 | C1 |
| (1665–2449) | 21 | C1/C2 |
| (2450–3199) | 50 | A3 |
| (4200–5999) | 49 | A1/A2 |
| W Warner Ave (1400–1499) | 40 | C1 |
| (1800–2199) | 39 | C1/C2 |
| (2400–3399) | 38 | B1/C1/C2 |
| (4800–5399) | 48 | A3/A4 |
| (6432–6523) | 47 | C2 |
| Warren Ave | 55 | A2 |
| W Warren Ave | 4 | B1 |
| W Warren Blvd (1500–1649) | 24 | B1 |
| (1650–2549) | 23 | B1/B2 |
| (2550–3349) | 50 | B3 |
| (3350–3499) | 49 | B2 |
| Warren Ct | 45 | A2 |
| Warren St (3800–5749) | 46 | A3/A4 |
| (5750–5999) | 45 | A2 |
| W Warwick Ave (4000–5849) | 48 | B3/B4 |
| (5850–6399) | 47 | B2 |
| W Waseca Pl | 56 | B4 |
| W Washburne Ave (1200–1724) | 26 | B1 |
| (1725–2499) | 25 | B1/B2 |
| Washington Ave (5244–5321) | 47 | A1 |
| (9700–10499) | 55 | A2/B2 |
| (11900–12299) | 56 | C4 |
| N Washington Ave | 45 | A1/B1/B2 |
| S Washington Ave | 45 | B1/B2/C1 |
| W Washington Blvd (400–865) | 4 | B1/B2 |
| (866–1649) | 24 | B1/B2 |
| (1650–2549) | 23 | B1/B2 |
| (2550–3299) | 50 | B3 |
| (3300–5932) | 49 | B2 |
| Washington Pl | 45 | C1 |
| Washington St | 55 | B1/B2 |
| E Washington St | 5 | B2 |
| N Washington St (5322–5477) | 47 | A1 |
| (5478–8885) | 45 | A1/C1 |
| W Washington St (1–371) | 5 | B1/B2 |
| (372–5599) | 46 | A3 |
| S Washington Pk Ct | 16 | C2 |
| N Washtenaw Ave (1–1549) | 50 | A3/B3 |
| (1550–2799) | 27 | A2/B2/C2 |
| (2800–3399) | 41 | B2/C2 |
| (4700–5125) | 38 | A2/B2 |
| (5200–6349) | 35 | A2/B2/C2 |
| (6350–7599) | 33 | A1/B1/C1 |
| S Washtenaw Ave (1–2214) | 50 | B3/C3 |
| (2215–5049) | 52 | A3/B3/C3 |
| (5050–8849) | 54 | A3/B3/C3 |
| (8850–11499) | 56 | A3/B3 |
| S Water St | 6 | A1 |
| N Waterloo Ct | 44 | C1 |
| E Waterway St | 59 | C2 |
| S Watkins Ave | 56 | B4/C4 |
| N Waukegan Rd | 45 | A2/B2 |
| N Waukesha Ave | 46 | B3 |
| N Waveland Ave | 48 | B3 |
| W Waveland Ave (600–849) | 44 | A1 |
| (850–1614) | 43 | A1/A2 |
| (1615–2499) | 42 | A1/A2 |
| (2800–3599) | 41 | A1 |
| (3600–5849) | 48 | B3/B4 |
| (5850–8399) | 47 | B1/B2 |
| W Wayman St (600–864) | 1 | C1 |
| (865–931) | 24 | B2 |
| (4600–4799) | 49 | B2 |
| N Wayne Ave (2100–2749) | 29 | A1/B1 |
| (2750–3949) | 43 | A1 |
| (3950–6349) | 37 | A2/B2/C2 |
| (6350–6939) | 34 | B2/C2 |
| W Webster Ave (300–814) | 30 | B1/B2 |
| (815–1625) | 29 | B1/B2 |
| (1626–2199) | 28 | B1/B2 |
| N Webster St | 47 | C1 |
| W Weed St (613–829) | 31 | A1 |
| (900–1099) | 22 | A2 |
| W Wellington Ave (300–824) | 44 | C1/C2 |
| (822–1649) | 43 | C1/C2 |
| (1650–2299) | 42 | C1/C2 |
| (2500–3399) | 41 | C1/C2 |
| (3800–5815) | 48 | B3/B4 |
| (5816–7999) | 47 | B1/B2 |
| N Wells St (1–258) | 5 | A1/B1 |
| (259–813) | 2 | A1/B1/C1 |
| (814–1616) | 31 | A2/B2/C2 |
| (1617–1826) | 30 | C2 |
| S Wells St (1–449) | 5 | B1/C1 |
| (450–999) | 8 | A1/B1 |
| (2600–3949) | 13 | A2/B2/C2 |
| (3950–5148) | 15 | A2/B2/C2 |
| (5100–6459) | 57 | A1 |
| W Wendell St | 31 | B2 |
| S Wentworth Ave (1600–2567) | 10 | B2/C2 |
| (2568–3978) | 13 | A2/B2/C2 |
| (3900–5099) | 15 | A2/B2/C2 |
| (5201–9499) | 57 | A1/B1/C1 |
| (9453–13499) | 59 | A1/B1/C1 |
| N West Brook Rd | 47 | C1 |
| W West End Ave | 49 | B1/B2 |
| West Shore Dr | 55 | A2 |
| N Western Ave (1–814) | 23 | A1/B1 |
| (815–1649) | 21 | A1/B1/C1 |
| (1633–2749) | 28 | A1/B1/C1 |
| (2750–3965) | 42 | A1/B1/C1 |
| (3966–5162) | 39 | A1/B1/C1 |
| (5163–6349) | 36 | A1/B1/C1 |
| (6350–7999) | 33 | A2/B2/C2 |
| S Western Ave (1–449) | 23 | C1 |
| (450–2224) | 25 | A1/B1/C1 |
| (1604–1698) | 45 | C1 |
| (2225–5049) | 52 | A3/B3/C3 |
| (5050–8811) | 54 | A3/B3/C3 |
| (8812–12830) | 56 | A3/B3/C3 |
| S Western Blvd (3251–5066) | 52 | A3/B3/C3 |
| (5035–5499) | 54 | A3 |
| S Westgate Ave | 55 | C1 |
| W Westgate Ter | 26 | A1 |
| Westwood Dr | 47 | C1 |
| Whipple Dr | 56 | B3 |
| N Whipple St (300–440) | 50 | B3 |
| (1600–2749) | 27 | A1/B1/C1 |
| (2750–3949) | 41 | A1/B1/C1 |
| (3950–4999) | 38 | A1/B1/C1 |
| (5800–6349) | 35 | A1/B1 |
| (6350–6899) | 33 | B1/C1 |
| S Whipple St (1–2249) | 50 | B3/C3 |
| (2250–5065) | 52 | A3/B3/C3 |
| (5066–8999) | 54 | A3/B3/C3 |
| (10226–11499) | 56 | B3 |
| Wick Dr | 55 | A2/B2 |
| N Wicker Park Ave | 21 | A2/B2 |
| N Wieland St | 31 | A2 |
| W Wilcox St (2300–2524) | 23 | C1 |
| (2525–2999) | 50 | B3 |
| (3800–4599) | 49 | B2 |
| Wilder St | 46 | A4 |
| N Wildwood Ave (6700–6949) | 45 | B2 |
| (6950–6999) | 46 | B3 |
| N Willard Ct (100–949) | 24 | A1/B2 |
| (950–1051) | 22 | B1 |
| N Willetts Ct | 27 | A1 |
| William Pl | 55 | A2 |

# Street Index

| | | |
|---|---|---|
| S Williams Ave | 57 | C1 |
| Willow Ln | 55 | A1 |
| W Willow St | | |
| (200–864) | 30 | C1/C2 |
| (865–1499) | 29 | C1/C2 |
| (2000–2099) | 28 | C1 |
| Willow Wood Dr | 55 | C1 |
| Wilma Pl | 45 | A1 |
| N Wilmot Ave | 28 | B1/C1 |
| W Wilson Ave | | |
| (700–1649) | 40 | B1/B2 |
| (1650–2414) | 39 | B1/B2 |
| (2415–3599) | 38 | B1/B2 |
| (3600–5749) | 48 | A3/A4 |
| (5750–8754) | 47 | A1/A2 |
| W Wilson Dr Ct | 40 | B2 |
| N Wilton Ave | | |
| (2600–2784) | 29 | A2 |
| (2785–3899) | 43 | A2/B2/C2 |
| N Winchester Ave | | |
| (400–431) | 23 | B2 |
| (800–1649) | 21 | B2/C2 |
| (1650–2399) | 28 | B2/C2 |
| (4200–5149) | 39 | A2/B2/C2 |
| (5150–6299) | 36 | A2/C2 |
| (6400–7599) | 34 | A1/C1 |
| S Winchester Ave | | |
| (1–299) | 23 | C2 |
| (600–799) | 25 | A2 |
| (2300–5049) | 52 | A3/B3/C3 |
| (5050–8884) | 54 | A4/B4/C4 |
| (8865–12899) | 56 | A4/C4 |

| | | |
|---|---|---|
| W Windsor Ave | | |
| (800–999) | 40 | B2 |
| (2140–2199) | 39 | B1 |
| (2600–2799) | 38 | B2 |
| (3700–5749) | 48 | A3/A4 |
| (5750–8505) | 47 | A1/A2 |
| Windsor Ln | 55 | A1 |
| N Winnebago Ave | 28 | C1 |
| W Winneconna Pky | 57 | B1 |
| W Winnemac Ave | | |
| (1200–1649) | 40 | A1 |
| (1650–2449) | 39 | A1/A2 |
| (2450–2799) | 38 | A2 |
| (4800–5399) | 48 | A3 |
| (6700–8599) | 47 | A1/A2 |
| W Winona St | | |
| (840–1649) | 40 | A1/A2 |
| (1650–2449) | 39 | A1/A2 |
| (2450–3145) | 38 | A1/A2 |
| (4900–5399) | 48 | A3 |
| (7400–8599) | 47 | A1 |
| S Winston Ave | 56 | A4 |
| N Winthrop Ave | | |
| (4600–5149) | 40 | A1/B1 |
| (5150–6349) | 37 | A2/B2/C2 |
| (6350–6599) | 34 | C2 |
| Wireton Rd | 56 | C3 |
| W Wisconsin St | | |
| (200–864) | 30 | C1/C2 |
| (865–1199) | 29 | C2 |
| N Wisner Ave | 48 | B4 |
| N Wisner St | 45 | A1/B1 |

| | | |
|---|---|---|
| N Wolcott Ave | | |
| (1–817) | 23 | A2/B2 |
| (818–1399) | 21 | A2/B2/C2 |
| (1600–2758) | 28 | A2/B2/C2 |
| (2759–3965) | 42 | A2/B2/C2 |
| (3966–5149) | 39 | A2/B2/C2 |
| (5150–6764) | 36 | A2/B2/C2 |
| (6765–7599) | 34 | A1/B1 |
| S Wolcott Ave | | |
| (1–299) | 23 | C2 |
| (600–2212) | 25 | A2/B2/C2 |
| (2213–4999) | 52 | A3/B3/C3 |
| (5000–5049) | 50 | C3 |
| (5050–8699) | 54 | A4/B4/C4 |
| (11800–11899) | 56 | C4 |
| S Wolf Lake Blvd | 60 | B3/C3 |
| Wolfe Dr | 55 | B2 |
| W Wolfram St | | |
| (800–849) | 44 | C1 |
| (850–1649) | 43 | C1/C2 |
| (1650–2399) | 42 | C1/C2 |
| (3500–3599) | 41 | B1 |
| (3600–5399) | 48 | B3/B4 |
| (6900–7099) | 47 | C2 |
| Wood Ave | 55 | C1 |
| N Wood St | | |
| (1–815) | 23 | A2/B2 |
| (816–1649) | 21 | A2/B2/C2 |
| (1650–2399) | 28 | B2/C2 |
| (2400–2699) | 47 | C1 |
| S Wood St | | |
| (1–399) | 23 | C2 |
| (600–2211) | 25 | A2/B2/C2 |
| (2212–4999) | 52 | A4/B4/C4 |
| (5000–5049) | 50 | C4 |
| (5050–8849) | 54 | A4/B4/C4 |
| (8850–12899) | 56 | A4/B4/C4 |

| | | |
|---|---|---|
| N Woodard St | 48 | B4 |
| E Woodland Park Ave | | |
| | 14 | B2 |
| S Woodlawn Ave | | |
| (4427–5149) | 17 | B1/C1 |
| (5150–6318) | 19 | A2/B2/C2 |
| (6319–9481) | 57 | A2/B2/C2 |
| (9482–10301) | 59 | A2 |
| W Woodriver Dr | 45 | A2 |
| Woodward Dr | 49 | B2 |
| S Worth Ave | 55 | B1/C1 |
| W Wright Ter | | |
| (3740–5399) | 46 | A3/A4 |
| (6951–7199) | 45 | A2 |
| W Wrightwood Ave | | |
| (400–817) | 30 | A1 |
| (818–1663) | 29 | A1/A2 |
| (1664–3234) | 28 | A2 |
| (3235–3599) | 27 | A1 |
| (3600–5815) | 48 | C3/C4 |
| (5816–8799) | 47 | C1/C2 |
| W Wyandot Dr | 55 | C1 |

## Y

| | | |
|---|---|---|
| S Yale Ave | | |
| (6300–9499) | 57 | A1/B1/C1 |
| (9500–12699) | 59 | A1/B1/C1 |
| S Yates Ave | 60 | A3/B3/C3 |
| S Yates Blvd | | |
| (7100–9549) | 58 | B3/C3 |
| (9550–10299) | 60 | A3 |
| Yost Ave | 45 | C1 |

## General

| | |
|---|---|
| All emergencies | **911** |
| AIDS Hotline | 800-342-AIDS |
| Animal Anti-Cruelty Society | 312-644-8338 |
| Chicago Dental Referral Service | 312-836-7305 |
| Chicago Department of Housing | 773-285-5800 |
| City of Chicago Board of Elections | 312-269-7900 |
| Dog License (City Clerk) | 312-744-6875 |
| Driver's Licenses | 312-793-1010 |
| Emergency Services | 312-747-7247 |
| Employment Discrimination | 312-744-7584 |
| Gas Leaks | 312-240-7000 |
| Income Tax (Illinois) | 800-732-8866 |
| Income Tax (Federal) | 800-829-3676 |
| Legal Assistance | 312-332-1624 |
| Mayor's Office | 312-744-4000 |
| Parking (City Stickers) | 312-742-9200 |
| Parking Ticket Inquiries | 312-744-7275 |
| Report Crime in Your Neighborhood | 312-372-0101 |
| Passports | 312-341-6020 |
| Police Assistance (non-emergency) | 311 |
| Social Security | 773-890-2492 |
| Streets and Sanitation | 312-744-5000 |
| Telephone Repair Service | 888-611-4466 |
| Voter Information | 312-269-7900 |
| Water Main Leaks | 312-744-7038 |

## Helplines

| | |
|---|---|
| Alcoholics Anonymous | 312-346-1475 |
| Alcohol, Drug and Abuse Helpline | 800-234-0420 |
| Alcoholism and Substance Abuse | 312-988-7900 |
| Domestic Violence Hotline | 800-799-7233 |
| Drug Care, St. Elizabeth's | 773-278-5015 |
| Gamblers Anonymous | 312-346-1588 |
| Illinois Child Abuse Hotline | 800-252-2873 |
| Narcotics Anonymous | 708-848-4884 |
| Parental Stress Services | 312-372-7368 |
| Runaway Switchboard | 800-621-4000 |
| Sexual Assault Hotline | 888-293-2080 |
| United Way Community Information and Referral | 312-876-0010 |
| Violence – Anti-Violence Project | 773-871-CARE |

## Complaints

| | |
|---|---|
| Better Business Bureau of Chicago | 312-832-0500 |
| Consumer Fraud Division (Attorney General's Office) | 312-814-3000 |
| Chicago Department of Consumer Services | 312-744-9400 |
| Citizen's Utility Board | 800-669-5556 |
| Department of Housing Inspection Complaints | 312-747-9000 |
| Mayor's Office | 312-744-4000 |
| Postal Service Complaints | 312-983-8400 |

# NOT FOR TOURISTS™ Custom Books

## Customize your NFT.

We can put **your organization's logo or message** on NFT using custom foil stamps of your (or our) design. Not For Tourists Guidebooks make **great gifts** for employees, clients, and promotional events.

For more information, call us at 212-965-8650, or visit www.notfortourists.com/corporatesales.aspx

 **Not For Tourists™**
**www.notfortourists.com**
Boston · Brooklyn · Chicago · London · Los Angeles · New York City · San Francisco · Washington DC

# NOT FOR TOURISTS™ Custom Mapping

# We'll map your world.

### Need a custom map?

NFT will work with you to design a custom map that promotes your company or event. NFT's team will come up with something new or put a fresh face on something you already have. We provide custom map-making and information design services to fit your needs—whether simply showing where your organization is located on one of our existing maps, or creating a completely new visual context for the information you wish to convey. NFT will help you—and your audience—make the most of the place you're in, while you're in it.

For more information, call us at 212-965-8650 or visit
www.notfortourists.com/custommapping.aspx

**Not For Tourists™**
www.notfortourists.com
Boston · Brooklyn · Chicago · London · Los Angeles · New York City · San Francisco · Washington DC

# NOT FOR TOURISTS™ Guidebooks

## Departures

NFT–NEW YORK CITY
NFT–BROOKLYN
NFT–LONDON
NFT–CHICAGO
NFT–LOS ANGELES
NFT–BOSTON
NFT–SAN FRANCISCO
NFT–WASHINGTON DC

# Tired of your own city?

You buy the ticket, we'll be the guide.

**Not For Tourists™**
www.notfortourists.com
Boston · Brooklyn · Chicago · London · Los Angeles · New York City · San Francisco · Washington DC